D0105664

A LIBRARY OF LITERARY CRITICISM

LEONARD S. KLEIN

General Editor

A Library
of Literary Criticism

VOLUME IV

SUPPLEMENT

 Frederick Ungar Publishing Co., New York

MODERN BRITISH LITERATURE

Compiled and edited by

MARTIN TUCKER

Professor of English
Long Island University

RITA STEIN, Ph.D.

Second Printing, 1976

Library of Congress Cataloging in Publication Data
Temple, Ruth Zabriskie, comp.
    Modern British literature.

    (A Library of literary criticism)
    Volume 4: Supplement, compiled and edited by
M. Tucker and R. Stein.
    Includes bibliographies and index.
    1. English literature—20th century—History
and criticism—Addresses, essays, lectures.
I. Tucker, Martin, joint ed.   II. Stein, Rita,
joint ed.   III. Title.
PR473.T4   820'.9'0091   65–16618
ISBN 0–8044–3275–9

INTRODUCTION TO THE SUPPLEMENT

This supplement to the three-volume Library of Literary Criticism: *Modern British Literature*, published in 1966, follows the same basic principles set forth in the Introduction to Volume I of the work. Our aim in Volume IV is twofold: first, to bring criticism up to date on approximately one-third of the authors included in the original volumes, both long-established writers and those whose reputations were just being made around 1965, some of whom, like Pinter and Burgess, have since become major figures; second, to add other writers who have come to critical attention since 1965. Forty-nine of these "new" writers are included.

The authors in the original three volumes have been selectively updated. Our criterion has been continued or renewed critical interest in them over the last decade, rather than simply, in the case of authors still living, continuing literary production. Hence, some writers who still publish, even voluminously, are not included in this supplement because we felt that they have been sufficiently covered in the original volumes. In addition, from the perspective of 1974, twentieth-century British literature does not seem to be linked to an age of criticism quite as much as it appeared in 1965. Thus, commentary on only the most important critics-as-authors has been updated and only a few critics have been added to our list of authors.

Criticism on the forty-nine new novelists, poets, dramatists, critics, and essayists dates from the beginning of their careers, not just from 1965 onward. Names of the new writers are preceded by a bullet in the list of authors included, in the text, and in the bibliographies. The additions are for the larger part younger writers who have risen to prominence over the last ten years, although in a few cases we have included older authors, some deceased, who were overlooked in the original volumes for one reason or another.

In our choice of sources there has been continuing stress on reviews in periodicals, but these have been balanced by more material from books and scholarly journals. We tried for a greater emphasis on American criticism than there was in the original three volumes.

The bibliographies at the end of the book have been updated for the older authors and are complete through 1974 for the new ones. An explanatory note precedes the bibliographies, which differ slightly in format from those in Volumes I–III.

The editors are grateful to the many copyright holders who have granted permission to reproduce the selections in this book. Only in a very few instances have we been unable to use an excerpt because a copyright holder either denied permission or demanded an unreasonable fee. We also wish to thank the reference librarians at Columbia University, Long Island University, New York University, and the New York Public Library (42nd Street) for their invaluable assistance. And we are especially indebted to Leonard Klein, our Ungar editor, for his patient handling of the many small details and his astute suggestions about the large decisions that went into compiling this book.

M.T.
R.S.

AUTHORS INCLUDED

Authors added in this volume are preceded by a bullet.

Richardson, Dorothy
Rolfe, Frederick
   (pseud., Baron
   Corvo)
Sansom, William
Sassoon, Siegfried
Sayers, Dorothy
● Shaffer, Peter
Shaw, George Bernard
Silkin, Jon
Sillitoe, Alan
● Simpson, N. F.
Sitwell, Edith
Sitwell, Osbert
Sitwell, Sacheverell
Smith, Stevie
Snow, C. P.
Spark, Muriel
Spender, Stephen
● Steiner, George
Stephens, James
● Stoppard, Tom
● Storey, David
Synge, John Millington

Thomas, Dylan
Thomas, Edward
Thomas, R. S.
Tolkien, J. R. R.
Tomlinson, Charles
● Trevor, William
Wain, John
Warner, Sylvia Townsend
● Waterhouse, Keith
Watkins, Vernon
Waugh, Evelyn
Wells, H. G.
Wesker, Arnold
West, Rebecca
   (pseud. of Cicely Isabel
   Fairfield)
● Whiting, John
● Williams, Heathcote
Wilson, Angus
Wilson, Colin
Wodehouse, P. G.
Woolf, Leonard
Woolf, Virginia
Yeats, William Butler

PERIODICALS USED

Listed below are their titles, their abbreviations, if any, and place of publication. If no place is indicated, *London* is to be understood.

Adam	Adam International Review
	Agenda
	America (New York)
AmS	The American Scholar (Washington, D.C.)
AWR	Anglo-Welsh Review (Caerleon, Wales)
	Ariel (Calgary)
	The Bell (Dublin)
BW	Book Week (New York)
BkWd	Book World (Chicago)
CSM	The Christian Science Monitor (Boston)
Cmty	Commentary (New York)
Com	Commonweal (New York)
	Confrontation (Brooklyn)
CL	Contemporary Literature (Madison, Wisc.)
CR	Contemporary Review
CQ	The Critical Quarterly (Manchester)
	Critique (Atlanta)
	The Dalhousie Review (Halifax, N.S.)
DS	Drama Survey (Minneapolis)
ETJ	Educational Theatre Journal (Washington, D.C.)
	Éire-Ireland (Saint Paul, Minn.)
	Encore
Enc	Encounter
G	The Guardian (Manchester)
Harper's	Harper's Magazine (New York)
HC	The Hollins Critic (Hollins College, Va.)
HdR	The Hudson Review (New York)
List	The Listener
L	London Magazine
MalahatR	The Malahat Review (Victoria, B.C.)
MR	The Massachusetts Review (Amherst, Mass.)

MQR	The Michigan Quarterly Review (Ann Arbor, Mich.)
	Midstream (New York)
MD	Modern Drama (Toronto)
ModOc	Modern Occasions (Waltham, Mass.)
	Mosaic (Winnipeg, Manitoba)
Nation	The Nation (New York)
NatR	National Review (New York)
NAR	New American Review (New York)
NL	The New Leader (New York)
NR	The New Republic (Washington, D.C.)
NS	New Statesman
NSN	New Statesman and Nation
NYHT	New York Herald Tribune Book Section (New York)
NYR	The New York Review of Books (New York)
NYT	The New York Times Book Review (New York)
NYTd	The New York Times, daily (New York)
NYTm	The New York Times, Sunday Magazine (New York)
NYTts	The New York Times, Sunday Theater Section (New York)
Obs	The Observer
PR	Partisan Review (New Brunswick, N.J.)
PP	Plays and Players
	Poetry (Chicago)
PoetryR	Poetry Review
	Proceedings of the British Academy
	Prose (New York)
QQ	Queen's Quarterly (Kingston, Ont.)
Ramparts	Ramparts Magazine (Berkeley, Cal.)
REL	A Review of English Literature
RES	Review of English Studies (Oxford)
Sat	Saturday Review (New York)
SwR	The Sewanee Review (Sewanee, Tenn.)
	Shenandoah (Lexington, Va.)
SAQ	South Atlantic Quarterly (Durham, N.C.)
SoR	The Southern Review (Baton Rouge, La.)
Spec	The Spectator
	Stand (Newcastle on Tyne)
Studies	Studies: An Irish Quarterly Review (Dublin)
TSLL	Texas Studies in Literature and Language (Austin, Tex.)
TL	The Times
TLS	The Times Literary Supplement
TDR	Tulane Drama Review (New Orleans, later New York, as The Drama Review)
TSE	Tulane Studies in English (New Orleans)
TCL	Twentieth Century Literature (Los Angeles)

VP	Victorian Poetry (Morgantown, W.Va.)
VV	The Village Voice (New York)
WSCL	Wisconsin Studies in Contemporary Literature (Madison, Wisc.)
YR	The Yale Review (New Haven, Conn.)

NOTE: In citations of books throughout the text, the place of publication is to be understood as London if no other place is indicated.—The abbreviation BC/Longmans means: published for the British Council by Longmans, Green.

● ABSE, DANNIE (1923–   )

We have in English a respectable body of literature that explores the corridors of childhood and adolescence with all their pain and pathos, their comedy and beauty. With *Ash on a Young Man's Sleeve*, Dannie Abse would add to that body. An authoritative note informs us that "This book is not autobiographical, for events and characters have been thoroughly fictionalized." But the dust jacket tells us that Dannie Abse is poet and playwright as well as novelist, that he was born in Cardiff, Wales in 1923, and that he lived there until he was eighteen. The novel begins with a boy "ten years high" telling us what Cardiff was like in the summer of 1933, and it ends when he is eighteen as his father says, "He can't earn a living by poetry." And—oh, yes—the boy's name is Dan.

Dan's experiences are those commonly attributed to that fabled animal, the average boy. He has a schoolmate, Keith, with whom he is alternately friend and enemy; he comes to know the meaning of death through that of Keith's mother and his own pet frog; he learns of family strife and grievances, of the existence of girls, of the large outside world, of Berente, Spain and Dachau. The incidents, presented to us in a roughly chronological order, are related only because they happen to a single person. In E. M. Forster's terms, we have here a story but no plot.

As the events are unfolded we say "and then—and then?" But there is no causal relation between them; we do not ask "why?" The merit of the novel rests, thus, upon the incremental value of the separate incidents, and these, while interesting enough to read about, are seldom affecting or impressive enough to remember. Those that linger are usually the comic or the outrageous. . . .

A constant irritant throughout the book is a confusion attendant upon the identity of the narrator. Is it the child Dan, a mature reflective Dan, or the author? . . .

There is an odd "poetical" quality about much of the writing that enables it to be distinctive without being distinguished. It reads like a pale imitation of Dylan Thomas, or as if the author had waged a losing struggle to find in English the equivalent for a foreign idiom. When Mr. Abse resorts to relatively direct statement, he does much better. There is an excellent description of the ennui and directionless activity that fill the Sundays of many people, and an equally good passage in which Dan penetrates to the mystery of existence and holds it in his hands for an entire afternoon. These pages are so good that one wishes the other pages were on the same level, that the entire novel measured up to them. But they don't, and it doesn't.

James D. Finn. Com. March 18, 1955, p. 638

Four of the poems from this collection [*Poems, Golders Green*] appeared in the Spring number of this magazine and readers will therefore have some idea of the kind of poetry they will find in Dannie Abse's fourth book of poems, which is, justly, a Poetry Book Society Choice. Among the many careful and fastidious voices of contemporary poets Dannie Abse's sounds with distinct and distinctive timbre, human, compassionate and real. Like many poets who began to publish in the forties his early work was often too cluttered up with mythology, was too allegorical, often too clogged with romantic adjectives. Gradually this language has been pared down but not emasculated, and his preoccupations have become more closely concerned with the predicaments, the lonelinesses, longings, hopes and fears of the human animal. I can think of no other poet of the moment who catches so exactly the tone of suburban man's anxieties, love and unrest—Auden perhaps in some early poems but his tone is more clinical, his preoccupations are with the upper rather than the middle class. There is none of the impersonal smoothness of fashionable poets in these poems. They are the poems of and for the man who sees the morning stubble of beard on his face, who suffers the common cold, is worried by the trifles that wear away our lives, but by being human both suffers and is calmed by intimations of the divine. They lay before us the worried agnosticism of twentieth-century man.

As the title perhaps almost belligerently announces, these are the poems of a Jew and I think the Jewishness is sometimes rather overdone; occasionally, too, I find him being tricked into writing from a good idea that is not finally the right one for transmuting into that indefinable object, a true poem. There are also lines . . . which I find curiously lacking in verbal taste. But to compensate for these there are lines in which the freshly discovered images prick the mind into new awareness. In some ways he reminds me of Donne in that the rhythms of his verse at a first reading often seem clumsy and inexpert but on a closer reading are revealed to be weighed precisely for the sense of what is being said; then, as one reads further, the poems reveal subtleties of assonance, interior rhymes, echoes and cadences that give an added purely linguistic satisfaction that is proper to all good poetry. Also, like Donne, his love poems are the love poems of a real human being and not idealistic troubadour confections. His "Three Voices" is marvellously tender.

We talk a lot nowadays about why does the poet not speak to the man in the street and only too often when a poet tries he starts to write ominously bad verse. I don't think Dannie Abse tries; he is a poet writing poetry. But I believe his work, and this latest book, as well as being admired by other poets, has a great deal to offer the ordinary reader, which means all of us.

John Smith. *PoetryR*. Autumn, 1962,
pp. 248–49

Tenants of the House, which contains poems written between 1951 and 1956, is, to my mind, the high plateau of Abse's achievement. The organisation of the contents under five headings, "Metaphysical Ironies," "Social Ironies," "The Identity of Love," "The Identity of Place," and "The Identity of the World," warns one against the attempt to draw any inferences about the chronological order of composition; but it is interesting, if not significant, that the fourth group includes, in "Field" and "Port of Call," two of the weakest and most ineffective poems to come from Dannie Abse's pen at any time. Another poem in the same group, "Postcard from Cornwall," a late, last outburst of Dylanism, is not very much better. But the term "plateau" justifies itself for the remainder. Of some thirty poems there is scarcely one which is not more successful than all but the very best in *Walking under Water*, his volume immediately previous, and perhaps half of the thirty reach for higher ground yet.

But in *Poems, Golders Green* the altitude falls. Not by many feet, perhaps, but, for the climber who has come so far, enough for significance. With the exception of that magnificent poem, "Return to Cardiff," and perhaps "The Water Divine" . . . the first part of the book contains few, if any, pieces which are not in some way flawed. To this extent there is a rough correspondence between Dannie Abse's own feeling about his poetic condition at that time and the contour which I am drawing now. But it was not inspiration he then lacked (inspiration, that is, in the sense of the provision of an idea, an angle, an incident for the poem's forming) so much as the energy and the discernment to cut the secondary material away and carry through the intended theme unobscured to its conclusion. In the second half of the book, however, (and I bear in mind that this again may have no basis in a real chronology of composition) there appears a spinney of poems on high ground which perhaps overtops the little-varying levels of the volume previous. . . . It is at least interesting that he seems latterly to have moved away from the *public* poetry and the hortatory tone formerly so characteristic of him.

Roland Mathias. *AWR*. Winter, 1967, pp. 84–85

Dannie Abse's short, very visual entertainment [*O. Jones, O. Jones*] concerns Ozy, medical student, jaunty, amiable, inventive in repartee and sexual campaigning, less disenchanted than unenchanted with medicine, bouncing between the traditional misadventures of roaring youth. He loses his room for sheltering a Soho bum who steals the land-lady's silver, tries to ride a bus on half-fare, fakes sickness for a night's hospital bed, fakes ownership of a room for an afternoon's love. His season is packed with curious, sometimes agitating insets of the lives, coupling, celebrating, collapsing, lingering beneath London roofs. An old lady's behaviour when she thinks herself alone, bizarre hospital patients and alarming medical details, actors temporarily out of work for twenty-two years, Taffy's modern paintings—good investments, "apart, of course, from being a remedy for the starved senses." Mr. Wells before his mirror, fully dressed, though as a woman, Angela, the unhappy virgin: "It was as though she'd worn that smile forever, for years, as if somehow the photographer had failed to turn up and she had never noticed."

Ozy's adroit good humour is a relief after a surfeit of lengthier, more fashionable and brutal burnt offerings, though occasionally one has a sensation of Dr. Abse, in his first fiction for some years, turning aside from work more serious—poem, play, book on medicine—to relax in a medium easier, even inferior. Duke of York's, Fitzroy, Bricklayers' Arms, Wheatsheaf are now a somewhat tired litany. With his unshakable concern for individuals, his professional skills, medical as well as literary, giving him highly unusual insights into human behaviour, he has outstanding qualifications to write a very substantial, a very modern novel.

Peter Vansittart. *Spec.* Oct. 17, 1970, p. 444

● ALVAREZ, A. (1929–   )

Each time I look on the dust-jacket and see the year 1929 given as the year of Mr. Alvarez's birth, I question whether the book [*Stewards of Excellence*] is really as fine as I think it is. That a man a year younger than myself should have the audacity to be so good! Not that there are no shortcomings. Many of the conclusions partake of the commonplace. The idea that Hart Crane is a lyric poet rather than an epic poet is not likely to shock many readers of modern poetry. But then truth has a way of being commonplace. There are two things that chiefly impress me about this critic. In the first place he accepts the full task of criticism. He not only defines and analyzes, but he also assesses and evaluates. In the second place he impresses me with the acuteness of his sensibilities.

The result of the first point is that you sometimes violently disagree with him. Personally, I find his dismissal of Dylan Thomas as a man whose poetry is impressively poetic on its creator's tongue and so much "verbal preciosity" on the printed page, a good deal this side of the kingdom of truth. But on the other hand I applaud, from my personal opinions, the partial deflation of Pound and Auden, and the balanced appraisals of Stevens, Crane, and Empson. His championship of the work of D. H. Lawrence caused me to reread the poetry, and this is certainly one of the functions of criticism. I do not find myself completely won over by his arguments, but I am more amenable to the poetry than I was formerly.

The book is divided into eight chapters: Eliot and Yeats, Ezra Pound, William Empson, W. H. Auden, The Lyric of Hart Crane, Wallace Stevens, D. H. Lawrence, and a final chapter entitled Art and Isolation in which he investigates "the tentative exploratory independence" of modern poetry from all traditions. There is a thesis in the book: ". . . that 'modernism'—in inverted commas—has been predominantly an American concern, a matter of creating, almost from scratch, their own poetic tradition." This I find interesting, and effectively presented, but the greatest value of the work lies in its individual essays. These are brief, but in each case Mr. Alvarez hits upon a central core of definition that illuminates the entire work of the poet under consideration. Some of these points are well-known, but the critic italicizes them with perceptions and modes of expression that are uniquely his own. . . . Mr. Alvarez seems to me one of the finest of the younger critics.

Paul Petrie. *Poetry.* Nov., 1959, pp. 125–26

At last, a hopeful sign: critical books seem to be getting shorter—this is the fourth I have read in the past six months that does not exceed the limit of two hundred pages. Mr. Alvarez [in *The School of Donne*] also recognizes that the critic has got to *write* for his money and not simply paste together scraps of practical criticism that we can all do for ourselves. His formulations are succinct and memorable. His scholarly information is tucked away in two appendices, surviving, as he nicely puts it, "as a silent background" for the criticism which is the main purpose of his undertaking.

The ground, of course, has been well cleared in the first place by other critics and Mr. Alvarez profits by this fact, his approval of "tough intelligence" leaning a little heavily at times on Eliot's "tough reasonableness beneath the lyric grace," his account of the post-Baconian scene deriving from L. C. Knights' paper on Bacon, which receives scant acknowledgment, and the chapter on Herbert again drawing on Knights' "well-bred ease of manner of the gentleman." This last is legitimately and, I think, beautifully extended to give what must surely be one of the keenest appreciations we have of "Love Bade Me Welcome," Herbert's poetic being summarized as "a realism based on manners rather than dialectic."

The most substantial parts of the book are its beginning and its end. It opens with an extremely cogent account of the real nature of Donne's contribution to metaphysical poetry. One is easier here with the general drift of the piece than with some of the local formulae. Alvarez plugs rather than defines the word "intelligence." "Donne . . . was the first Englishman to write verse in a way that reflected the whole complex activity of intelligence." What of Shakespeare, one asks, and are we to withhold or re-define "intelligence" if we think of Chaucer or Langland or the author of *Sir Gawain*? Their range is, surely, immense. What is impressive about the account of Donne is the sense it gives us of his coterie affiliations and his ability to use the freedom of this coterie of witty, learned, and "unpoetical" men, to branch out away from acknowledged pieties and theory.

The end of the book is concerned with changing attitudes to the imagination, the split of poetry into the separate elements of Judgment and Fancy and the philosophical reasons for this. It is detailed, compact, and penetrating. . . .

Mr. Alvarez's middle chapters are his least sustained and sustaining, but they all contain rewarding suggestions. The most graceful is that on Herbert, the most ingenious that on Crashaw which very plausibly suggests that he was the forbear not of Hopkins but of Poe; that Poe was one of the few poets who handled English rather as though it were French and that Crashaw, in short, anticipated him in so far as he was a Continental poet writing in English, using a rhetoric foreign to our own poets.

In all this one is aware of a liveliness of mind and a persuasiveness of style which argue well for the development of this critic and which, at the same time, provide the teacher with a general guide that he can confidently put into the hands of his students without blunting their appetites.

Charles Tomlinson. *Poetry*. Jan., 1962,
pp. 261–62

Mr. Alvarez is, to my mind, a reviewer rather than a critic. The best things in his book [*Beyond All This Fiddle*] are those that introduced his readers to something which they had not read, whether Robert Lowell's *Life Studies* or Sylvia Plath's last poems. (The worst things are in the section "Classics.") Certainly there are still men whose reviews are so rammed with life that they shall gather strength of life with being. Mr. Alvarez pays tribute to one of them: Edmund Wilson. But Mr. Alvarez does not have what he praises in Edmund Wilson. Instead he has what he praises in Jan Kott: "an exacerbated insight into present troubles, present preoccupations, present styles." So that *Beyond All This Fiddle* is a remarkable demonstration not only of how Mr. Alvarez meets literature, but of how a reviewer meets it. . . .

Mr. Alvarez is a good reviewer for the same reason that he is a good anthologist: he can tell the difference between a good poem and a bad one. He is less good as a critic precisely because he is less skilled at—less interested in—arguing in detail about taste. You can usually trust his choices but not his arguments (but then reviewing has less room for arguments). . . . In the end, a critic too ought to take risks; but in the beginning a reviewer must. If Mr. Alvarez continually exaggerates the virtue of extremism, decisiveness, pushing things to their limits, that is because his sense of literature too much yields to his unspoken—perhaps unrecognised—sense of what it is to be a reviewer.

Christopher Ricks. *List*. Feb. 29, 1968, pp. 275–76

A. Alvarez's *The Savage God* is a wonderfully readable, though frequently irritating, work in which this English poet-critic—himself a failed suicide—tries to approach the subject intimately and directly, as a kind of experience open to dramatic portrayal.

The Savage God breaks into several compartments: personal testimonies, as in the now-famous chapter on Sylvia Plath and the finely restrained account of Alvarez's own attempt; a neat historical summation of the range of attitudes toward and theories about suicide; and a series of case histories of famous writers who have been drawn to undertake or seriously reflect upon suicide.

A major criticism of Alvarez at the outset: he does not distinguish sufficiently between suicide as a literary theme or element in the life of literary men and suicide as a problem affecting humanity as a whole. Like many literary people, he tends to forget that the "evidence" of the extreme instance, while crucial in modernist literature, is by no means convincing for general statements about humanity; what seems pertinent to the work of avant-garde artists may have only a tenuous connection with the daily experience of ordinary people. I am not saying there is no connection between the two, since that would have chilling consequences for those of us who believe in the centrality of literature;

I am only saying that we can't be at all certain as to what the connections are. *The Savage God* is best read not as a general study of suicide but as a statement of why suicide has had so strong an attraction for writers in the modern period—a statement sometimes admirably dispassionate but sometimes verging on the notion that suicide constitutes a cause.

Irving Howe. Harper's. June, 1972, p. 102

AMIS, KINGSLEY (1922–   )

The Amis protagonist does not suffer fools gladly. In fact, a good deal of his energy goes into wishing violence on them. He wants to kick them, smash them, push buildings over on them. But what he does instead is to fantasize, and Amis' unique creative powers are nowhere more impressive than in these fantasies. In Jim Dixon's sanity-saving array of faces there is enough inventive genius to sustain a dozen comic novels. (The more extroverted characters, too, blaze on the inside; even Roger Micheldene [in *One Fat Englishman*] lives an inner life of fury unsuspected by those who see only his surface nastiness.)

While the Amis hero is likely to be anti-intellectual, he is always cerebral. Unlike the Romantic hero who feels when everyone else is busy thinking and knowing, he sees when everyone else is busy feeling and pretending to think. It is what he sees that drives him to rage. But the rage is itself a function of his insight. Instead of being blinded by rage, Amis' characters are able to see clearly by its light. Anger is an instrument of revelation. And of self-revelation.

The enraged perceptions in Amis' fiction are universally valid, which is why the critical class labels have so little to do with what his novels really communicate. . . . For the phoney is what Kingsley Amis is attacking, although that term so dear to American writers does not often appear in his books.

Ralph Caplan. In Charles Shapiro, ed.,
Contemporary British Novelists (Carbondale,
Southern Illinois Univ. Pr., 1965), pp. 9–10

Kingsley Amis's *I Want It Now* [is] a satire on the British and American Establishments, the rich, the television industry, and varieties of human—and sub-humankind. . . .

The title is replete with innuendos. What the hero, Ronnie Appleyard, wants is "fame and money with a giant's helping of sex thrown in," preferably accompanied by sensitivity, appreciation and understanding, peace of mind, altruism and humanity. In short—and in view of the name Appleyard wafting faint scents of symbolism—paradise now. . . .

That Ronnie gives over his ambitions and learns that "when you fall back into the ranks of the failed shits you start taking on responsibility for other people" is ambiguous even in terms of the fairy-tale finale. Like Lucky Jim he can remain an endearing fraud sniping at repugnant frauds, and like the rest of us unluckies awaits the deus ex machina to rescue him from the bores that plague, the media that stultify, the institutions that manipulate. But it may take more than a leap of faith to believe that Ronnie, beginning as a kind of Satan in the modern Eden of Success, can wind up like Adam, shuffling "arms about shoulders" with Eve toward a paradise regained. If the happy ending seems possible it is because pompousness, sham and self-aggrandizement are never pushed to the point of danger.

Robert K. Morris. Nation. April 28, 1969,
p. 546

In Amis's England, it is the unruliness of sexual desire, coupled with the brisk feasibility of promiscuity, that so complicates the conflict between the generations. Now that the conflict is well nigh primal, there is more than one obstacle to the injunction, *"Hommes de la trentaine, de la quarantaine*, assert yourselves." For the men of thirty and forty confronted by Girl, 20, there is a fatal clash between the desire to assert themselves and the desire to insert themselves. Sir Roy [in *Girl, 20*] recalls "some other chap, in some book by a French man I seem to remember, who said he couldn't read 'Girl, 20,' in a small-ad column without getting the horn." Sir Roy's girls are "getting younger at something like half the rate he gets older"; for him the generation gap will soon be legally unpluggable.

Amis's narrator, Douglas Yandell, is in his thirties; he wants to assert himself against the girl (seventeen, actually) who's taking Sir Roy away from his wife (forty-six or forty-seven). But though Douglas finds it nothing but easy to detest that particular girl (some venom coursing finely here), he can't help enjoying Sir Roy's daughter (twenty-three). By the time Douglas comes really to like her as well as her person, she's one of the doomed youth—this part of the book seems a submerged pun on "heroine." . . .

There are those who think that when Malcolm Muggeridge excoriates present-day England, he seems oblivious of the fact that he played some part in the making of present-day England; did not the rot set in when he became editor of *Punch*? Likewise there are those who think that the England of today owes a good deal of its tone, style, manners, and preoccupations to those novelists who not so long ago were Angry Young Men and who now are angry with young men. But Amis has always thrived as a writer on "It-ill-becomes-someone-who . . ." situations. The irony and the quandary are such as to elicit from him here much that is shrewd, fretful, and lugubriously funny, founded upon self-scrutiny and not self-regard.

Christopher Ricks. *NYR*. March 9, 1972,
pp. 24–25

The turns in Mr. Amis's work can be understood most easily in relation to the changes in his attitude to life and society. The author of his recent work is still a bit of a joker, like the author of *Lucky Jim*, and even a bit of a private joker. . . .

But although the author both of *Lucky Jim* and of the recent *Girl, 20* sees the behaviour of people as comic, there is a great difference in tone and attitude between the two books. The basic difference is that the thirty-year-old poet and lecturer at Swansea who wrote *Lucky Jim* and its successor *That Uncertain Feeling* enjoyed nothing more than cocking a snook at authority in general, and bumbling provincial bureaucracy in particular. Twenty years later he is not exactly in favour of authoritarianism, but is looking for a philosophy of life "pitched between ancestral verities and the next Conservative Party policy statement." . . .

In a positive way, it is hardly possible to say much more than that a novelist should learn what his talents are, and then work within them. And perhaps a writer in his fifties shouldn't make too many jokes, Catonic or otherwise. To the extent that *The Riverside Villas Murder* is a joke or an evasion, it can only be regretted, but there is no recipe for the production of a novel like *Girl, 20*. Kingsley Amis's gifts are unique in his generation of British novelists. What sort of books are produced through them in the future depends on his own ability to order his talent.

TLS. April 6, 1973, pp. 393–94

● **ARDEN, JOHN (1930–   )**

Behind Arden's work there seems to be brooding one basic principle: not exactly the obvious one that today there are no causes—that would be altogether too facile, and in any case just not true—but that there are too many. There are as many causes as there are people (more, since many are quite capable of espousing two or more mutually exclusive causes at the same time), and only the naïve can suppose that any two people who are, say, pacifists (to choose a nice, convenient label) will believe the same things for the same reasons. In other words, in all Arden's plays the characters we meet are first and foremost just people: not concepts cast into a vaguely human mould, with built-in labels saying "good" or "bad," "hero" or "villain," to help us into the right grooves. (Arden himself in an interview has expressed "grave objections to being presented with a character on the stage whom you know to be the author's mouthpiece" and said that he "cannot see why a social play should not be so designed that we may find ourselves understanding the person's problems, but not necessarily approving his reactions to them.")

It follows, therefore, that the behaviour of any one person or group does not imply any general judgment. *The Waters of Babylon* is not a play in favour of prostitution and tenant-exploitation (or for that matter the reverse); *Live Like Pigs* tells us nothing about "The Welfare State"; *Serjeant Musgrave's Dance* is not for or against pacifism *per se*; *The Happy Haven* offers no solution to the problem of old age: they are just plays about individual people affected one way or another by these issues. Hence, perhaps—until one gets used to Arden's way of seeing things at least—the confusions and irritation of his audiences: when "parity of esteem" for all the characters is pushed so far, identification and taking sides become difficult if not impossible, and though undeniably the characters conflict—they are conflicting all the time— for many theatregoers a conflict in which they are not asked themselves to participate is in effect no conflict at all; left rudderless and all at sea, they end up lost and bored. . . .

One thing seems certain, though: difficult though Arden's vision may be to accept on first acquaintance, and puzzling his way of expressing it, familiarity makes the approach much easier and breeds nothing but respect and admiration. John Arden is one of our few complete originals, and for the occasional faults in his plays—a desire to force a gallon into a pint pot, a tendency perhaps to overdo the gusty, gutsy side of things just a little from time to time—there are numerous and irreplaceable merits. Sooner or later his definitive success with a wider public is assured.

John Russell Taylor. The Angry Theatre
(N.Y., Hill and Wang, 1962), pp. 73, 86

The hope of nourishing a sense of evolution is very openly John Arden's reason for choosing to set several of his plays in the past.

These aren't history plays in the same flattened sense as, say, Drinkwater's; for Arden the past is a dimensional device, a way of refocusing upon the present. *Serjeant Musgrave's Dance* contains a line of perspective to Cyprus. *Left-Handed Liberty* manages to ask some modern questions about the motives for Magna Carta. His new play at Chichester, *Armstrong's Last Goodnight*, is set in sixteenth-century Scotland but connects directly to the Katanga crisis in the Congo.

By a design that is probably instinctive, the two chief characters in the play are themselves separated from each other temperamentally by what seems like centuries; with this sort of time-tug existing between them, the ripple passes along the rope to the present very strongly. . . .

Arden's work throws up visual images vividly. There is a clump-footed reel that looks like Brueghel, an almost cinematic shot of a girl lugging the corpse of her untrue lover into the woods, a hanged body that turns like a salmon on a hook, a ring of soldiers with jagged black hair sitting in a Japanese-looking squat with one knee up and one on the ground. They are the sort of pictures that a child retains from narrative poetry read aloud, part of the world of ballad, like most of the other good things in the play: sweet love scenes and swift treacheries, a sense of tragedy that is cool and rather chaste, and an amazing fluency in using a language that often sounds like the clashing of broadswords that are almost too heavy to lift.

But if the powers belong to ballad, so do the frailties. The passions are sturdy enough but the characterisation is a wretched invalid. Stage people often don't seem to prosper on the forced march of epic narrative, and the lack of focus that there is about arena staging makes things worse. No wonder the political positions are hard to distinguish and retain. Arden's work sometimes has a bewildering effect of seeming primal and academic at the same time; I think it is because he overcharges the deliberately brutal outlines of his characters with rather unclear and attributed ideas.

Penelope Gilliatt. *Obs.* July 11, 1965, p. 21

In case you can't see how a work [that is, *Serjeant Musgrave's Dance*] might be both pre-eminent in its generation and imperfect in itself, let me remind you of Thomas Hardy. The more I think about Arden, the more their cases seem parallel. Both started life as architects, in their writing, both opt for fabrication rather than confession. Both were provincials born who, submitting superficially to official metropolitan culture, became highly literary, slightly old-fashioned stylists, handling words self-consciously but, sometimes, with a knotty lyricism better than grace. At their worst, there's something neo-Gothic and Gilbert Scottish about both of them: I can imagine Hardy relishing the unperformed scene of medieval peasant high-jinks by the Wise Men of Gotham in the published version of *Left-Handed Liberty*, as I can imagine Arden, some incautious year, turning his hand to another *Dynasts*.

Yet they share a massiveness which makes most of their contemporaries seem light-weight. Beneath their acquired literariness, they put down roots to a primitive strength which forces you to compare them with the classics: Hardy with Aeschylus, Arden (as Irving Wardle recently urged) with Aristophanes. Despite his failure to produce one unflawed major work, to bear comparison with Hardy is no small thing. Beneath the somewhat glacial, invented language, Arden fishes as Hardy did ponds like the one Ted Hughes's pike haunted, deep as England.

Ronald Bryden. *NS*. Dec. 17, 1965, p. 979

That Arden is in some sense a thoroughly political playwright has never been at issue; every one of his works is steeped in politics and is the product of an imagination for which non-political reality—private myth, insular fortune, the discrete ego—would seem to have no independent standing as material for drama. No, what is at issue is the fate of political subject matter in his plays, the unpolitical uses to which he puts it, the transformations it undergoes under the action of his half-lyrical, half-civic and polemical sensibility, the sensibility, one might call it, of a passionate citizen, a brooding burgher.

What is the nature of political reality and how does the rest of the life of man . . . relate to it, or rather how does man's life come to know itself in the crucible of power, rule, and social governance? What are the prices that political necessity exacts from the moral self and the psyche? How does one celebrate life in the midst of abstractions? Such are the chief energizing questions of Arden's plays. They are what make him something extraordinarily different from a traditionally "political" or "sociological" playwright, by which, if definitions and terminology have not already descended into chaos, we mean someone for whom the immediate data of political or social organization are paramount, for whom, too, the choices involved in public existence are more or less co-terminous with the choices involved in all existence, and for whom, finally, a play is an exemplification, subtle or gross, of the virtue of making the right choices or of the cost of failing to make them.

For Arden, however, there are no clear choices—which is what pitches him above ideology; although there is a clear necessity to act publicly—which is what keeps his plays anchored in a perception of social actuality. Again and again, in one form or another, he questions, or rather raises to the dignity and ambiguous sincerity of a question, something we might call the humanness of politics, its role and function as the process and measure of our life in common. That public life *has* to be organized, and that power *has* to be exerted, are the assumptions, with their roots in a tragic awareness, of all his plays; that the private self rebels against this inexorability, in the name of its spontaneous, wayward life, of all distinct values and of the simplicities of what it considers its natural choices, is the agency which generates the "drama" of his dramas.

Richard Gilman. *TDR*. Winter, 1966,
pp. 55–56

Arden's pessimism . . . isn't by itself enough to connect him significantly with the playwrights of the Absurd. What distinguishes them is not just pessimism but the way they express their pessimism through farce. In a religious play like *The Business of Good Government*, such farce would be quite inappropriate, but there is plenty of it in Arden's more typical plays—in the medical inspection scene of *The Happy Haven,* for instance, or in *The Workhouse Donkey*, where Alderman Butterthwaite, so used to taking the initiative in his progress from workhouse to political leadership, resorts to robbing the town hall safe when pressed for gambling debts. And where the action is not farcical, it usually has, at any rate, the grotesqueness of farce, as, for instance, in Serjeant Musgrave's dance beneath the uniformed skeleton of one of his comrades.

But there is an important difference between Arden's farce, even where it is complete farce, and that of the playwrights of the Absurd. The "reality with which the Theatre of the Absurd is concerned," [Martin] Esslin points out, "is a psychological reality expressed in images that are the outward projection of states of mind, fears, dreams, nightmares, and conflicts within the personality of the author." Arden's farce, on the contrary, takes place unambiguously in the external world. The subjectivity of the Absurd playwrights would seem to relate to their preoccupation with man as an individual. Social issues, of course, come into their plays, but are looked at from the individual's point of view. Pozzo and Lucky, for instance, the exploiter and exploited in Beckett's *Waiting for Godot*, stand for the two equally repugnant roles which society has to offer the individual. In Pinter's *The Caretaker*, the struggle of the tramp, Davies, to secure his position in the apartment where he has been allowed temporary shelter, expresses the individual's need to belong somewhere that modern society fails adequately to satisfy. Arden, on the other hand, thinks of human beings collectively. His plays are full of such vigorous individualists as Musgrave, Blomax and the rest, but Musgrave's failure and Blomax's success are both seen as a tragic commentary on the state of society. It is always society and its predicament that we are finally faced with.

J. D. Hainsworth. *REL*. Oct., 1966, pp. 47–48

Arden presents an enigma to critics and public alike; almost anything that may be said of him can be contradicted, generally by Arden himself. You can, for example, claim correctly that he is that most Brechtian of British playwrights, and yet he does not commit himself to any one side. Is *Serjeant Musgrave's Dance* a pacifist play? At first it appears to be so, but in the end other cross-currents intervene, the serjeant outwardly strong is a simple confused man who does not know how to communicate his message or set his plans in action. Arden believes that it is objectivity in the theatre which counts, in both emotion and causes —but who is to decide? "If a character starts off," Arden has written . . . "by being sympathetic and then turns off in a direction that people don't like, that is in fact what often happens with people that one knows in life. I never write a scene so that an audience can identify with any particular characters . . . it's not up to me to make audience's judgments on the various characters in the play." So much for Arden's intentions, but has he the vision to reveal things of which an audience was not previously aware, can he lead them into a new dimension by thinking faster, seeing further than them? Or is his view the average one of confusion, the incomplete crossword puzzle mentality?

Perhaps we are asking too much of him, by reminding ourselves of the standards of great writers, whereas maybe Arden will never be more than a writer in the old "popular tradition," without finding the public he deserves. For here is another anomaly, Arden has set himself against the current towards the metropolis and capital cities, and his reputation was confirmed not by London but the support of the provinces. Arden is in the best sense a regional writer. . . .

Frederick Lumley. *New Trends in 20th Century Drama* (N.Y., Oxford Univ. Pr., 1967), pp. 260–61

The evidence Arden's works offer of a practical, visual approach is confirmed by statements he has made in interviews. In one recorded by the British Council, London, entitled "The Art of the Dramatist" (undated, but probably 1960), the first thing he says is that he chose drama as his medium because, possibly out of vanity, he modestly adds, he likes to see his work being acted on the stage. He says that his ideas take a visual shape, and he usually sees the settings first, combined with a story in outline, with individual scenes presenting themselves to his mind's eye. He feels himself that his architectural training is significant in providing him with definite ideas on settings, décor and costumes, and that he often thinks in these terms when writing. An example of this is that *Serjeant Musgrave's Dance* came to be set in the nineteenth century because the scarlet uniforms of the period would be theatrically attractive, he felt.

Because of his concern with these practical matters, Arden likes to be in consultation with the director and designer at an early stage of production. He enlarges on this in the preface to *Soldier, Soldier*: "When a piece involves anything new in terms of style of writing, or staging, only the author knows exactly what is wanted, and at times not even the author. The director must learn it from him, and it is often impossible for either of them to find the exact solution to various problems until rehearsals have already commenced. Therefore it is essential that an author should always be asked to rehearsals and to early discussions with the director—even if the play appears a pretty simple one on the surface."

Arden emerges, then, as a conscious and imaginative exploiter of visual effects and stage resources. His knowledge of stage history and his trained eye add dimensions to his work that are often absent from that of more "literary" writers. These are aspects that must not be ignored when his contribution to the drama is considered, and it is through them that he is likely to make a lasting contribution to the theatre too, in helping to break down theatre conventions and in striving towards a richer and more active relationship between actors and audience.

Joan Tindale Blindheim. *MD*. Dec., 1968,
p. 316

Closely identified though John Arden has become with the other young British playwrights who began writing in the late 1950s, his dramatic career has taken an entirely individual and in some ways disturbing direction. The controlled originality of his technique was the more remarkable at a time when John Osborne and Arnold Wesker, for all their uncompromising innovations in subject-matter, were still writing within conventional formal molds: and the unequivocal left-wing commitment of such writers contrasted strongly with the scrupulous balance of argumentative power in Arden's early plays. Yet in recent years Arden's professionalism has been diluted, in effect if not inten- tion, by an almost exclusive involvement with community and fringe theatre groups—and this has itself reflected a shift in the political emphasis of his plays. Bolder and often cruder in outline, they have become more and more directly propagandist, yet at the same time simply less accessible (in any sense) to a wide playgoing public. . . .

In attempting to sum up Arden's qualities, one still occasionally senses that a virtue may be mistaken for a vice if it goes unexplained—for each characteristic tends to throw off some unexpected and even opposite implication. It is in part because of this that one needs to have seen the complex of the plays several times before they begin fully to reveal their riches; indeed, Arden himself once admitted, a little unhappily, that "a lot of my plays are more easily understood after a second visit." Yet it is only in an age of instant eulogy and casual condemnation that this could be regarded as a serious fault, especially since Arden's narrative skill is so sinuously strong that on a first acquaintance his plays will satisfy simply in their story-lines, a deeper understanding developing once one already *knows what happens*. Of course, a prior acquaintance with the story is implicit in the nature of chronicle plays, and Arden's acceptance and utilization of this fact may help to explain why he is the one modern playwright apart from Brecht who has been able to dramatize history into more than hopefully intellectual costume dramas. And history also lends that degree of *distance* from an action that Arden, again like Brecht, prefers to maintain—though in Arden's case this distance serves not so much Brecht's purpose of making the familiar strange as of making the strange familiar, often by suggesting a parallel that tangentially illuminates the present.

Simon Trussler. John Arden (N.Y., Columbia
Univ. Pr., 1973), pp. 3, 45

AUDEN, W. H. (1907–1973)

Auden has been particularly acute in anticipating his reader's response and then gauging the most effective final disposition of poetic raw material. His alertness to his audience is manifested in his periodic revisions of poems and titles and his use of editorial devices to modify the context in which a poem is presented to the reader. He is remarkable among poets in the extent to which he is actively concerned with the reader's perspective on what he writes. Outside his own poems, his catholic taste and acuity of insight as a reader assure him a high place in the long line of distinguished poet-critics in English.

Whatever the final impact of Auden's poetry, he has established an admirable model for literature in at least one respect. Despite the difficulties inherent in our amorphous culture, he has insisted on the necessity of reestablishing contact with the world outside one's own subjectivity. His success in bringing his private vision into contact with the public world has demonstrated that poetry need not abandon even such a world as we live in.

In his poem on Yeats, Auden speaks of the relation between the poet and his language in a most significant manner. He describes the poet not as one who lives by language, but as one by whom language lives. Just so, it is Auden's ability to give life to language that will assure his being read. If, years hence, the vision expressed in Auden's poetry fails to move the readers of the future, the virtuosity and versatility of his power with language may lead him to be treated as a poet's poet, as Spenser frequently has been. For the present his vision at its best achieves the rare virtue of illuminating profoundly our condition as individual human beings and as a civilization.

John G. Blair. *The Poetic Art of W. H. Auden*
(Princeton, N.J., Princeton Univ. Pr., 1965),
pp. 193–94

Though at different times certain formulations of the distinction between ego and self are more applicable to an understanding of Auden than others, all imply a constant view of the human condition. Conceive the opposition as narrowly as that, say, between "will" and "desire," or so broadly as to encompass conscious mind with all its cultural predispositions on the one hand and, on the other, vital energy, the Id, or the Unconscious; the unvarying problem is that the ego stands isolated in its experience of freedom, a prey to the anxiety of relating the individual to the world and of seeking for this purpose a viable knowledge of and relationship with the self. Whatever the indebtedness of Auden's thought, whether to the psychology of Homer Lane or D. H. Lawrence, or to Marx, or to the Christian existentialism of Kierkegaard or Reinhold Niebuhr, what he is primarily doing is seeking an answer to the fundamental question of how ego and self shall inter-relate; his debt to these authors is a response to the analysis they offer of this problem; his underlying interest is in the principle envisioned as guiding this relationship towards the end of individual fulfillment.

The pursuit of such a principle is evident in a Quest for what he has variously referred to as the Necessary, the Unconditional, or the Logos. Stephen Spender is right, however, when he suggests that the direction of Auden's poetry has been "towards the defining of the concept of love," for the two processes are identical. If Auden has consistently addressed himself to the question "How shall we live?" his conviction that love is the basic energy of life has provided that the question mean, essentially, "How shall we love?" And love has always implied for him what the title of a well-known poem, "Law Like Love," suggests: namely "law," in the sense of "natural law," but also in the broader sense of "that which is required of us."

Herbert Greenberg. Quest for the Necessary:
W. H. Auden and the Dilemma of Divided
Consciousness (Cambridge, Mass., Harvard
Univ. Pr., 1968), pp. 6–7

The most important fact about the poetry of the "new" Auden, which one encounters for the first time in *Nones*, is the lack of tension between the poet and his experience. Both man and world simply are; no more, no less. The only problem, a nonmetaphysical one, is recognizing, accepting, and praising the existence of both. The "new" Auden seems to be telling us that all the agonies or hopes of the thirties were mere nonsense, just a kind of joke, the by-product of a frivolous and spent youth. Now that we have all grown up, we can, and should, realize that there simply is no such thing as progress and that the knowledge we were told to search for so diligently is valuable only as amusement; that poetry, like psychology or sociology, is silly business, mere froth and fun, an employment for idle hands and heads.

Experience no longer bothers Auden the poet; in fact, Auden the man no longer bothers Auden the poet. He has made a separate peace and now is able to turn and smile benignly at the rest of us. I think it is this smile that so irritated Jarrell, among others; no radical could stand to watch Lenin take off his coat and be revealed as an Anglican bishop. But what we think is smugness in the smile is only surety— Auden finally knows he is right; it is as simple as that. As a result, he no longer will permit our questions; we may either accept or reject his stand and his work, but we may no longer hope for "a change of heart."

Gerald Nelson. Changes of Heart: A Study of
the Poetry of W. H. Auden (Berkeley, Univ.
of California Pr., 1969), p. 145

The most impressive aspect of the poetry in *About the House* is its capacity to express Auden's awareness of his faults and limitations as a human being. Pride, in Auden's view of it, is the only sin which manifests itself in the same way in all human beings. The others are perversions of "something in our nature which in itself is innocent [and] necessary to our existence and good." In Auden's later poetry he has achieved an appropriate mode for the embodiment of human and religious truths, and for the expression of his Christian humility. . . .

Auden's extension of the possibilities of the long poem has had little influence on poetry in English, in spite of his generally pervasive effect on the language of younger poets. This gap may reflect the difficulties a long poem presents for the writer who has neither the complexity of thought nor the fully developed craft which Auden possesses. Auden's abandonment of this form in the fifties, although it has been regarded by some critics as an admission of failure, may well be the result of a feeling on the part of Auden that he had accomplished all he could in that realm. Whatever the reason for the shift, nevertheless, it is clear that Auden learned a great deal from his work with long poems. The expanded form of the lyric in "The Shield of Achilles," "In Praise of Limestone," "Homage to Clio," and other poems, reflects the discipline and scope present in the longer poems; the composition of three sequences, "Bucolics," the "Horae Canonicae," and "Thanksgiving for a Habitat" may well have been made possible by Auden's work in the forties. In the best of the shorter poems of the fifties and sixties Auden developed and unified extensive and diverse materials, accommodating them to a voice the range of which is astonishing.

George W. Bahlke. *The Later Auden* (New Brunswick, N.J., Rutgers Univ. Pr., 1970), pp. 181–82

Auden is very much a partisan of humanity, one who believes that in our age the mere act of making and the maintenance of a personal voice are intensely, perhaps subversively, political acts. "Thanksgiving for a Habitat" is Auden's fullest expression of this point of view; once we accept the idea that by "intimate," in tone and dwelling, Auden means what "public" signifies in its classic use, the series makes a substantial political statement. The series is microcosmic and parabolic in a special way: it describes in miniature the "proper" relations among man's various activities, including his participation as an "actor" in larger groups; it locates the public realm, in its true, rather than its popular sense, as the sphere in which man may disclose his humanity; and it instances a variety of actions of this sort. Its miniaturization is not, however, simply that of microcosm and parable; it is also a mimetic representation of the public realm in the modern world.

Auden attempts to represent the historical shift of the public realm into what was once considered the private, to represent the shrinkage of the sphere of significant action. Although he seems to espouse a kind of privatism and dissociation from the larger world, he is being primarily descriptive and analytical, not prescriptive; there is indeed a strain of sadness in the description. Nonetheless, granted the shrinkage of the public realm and the movement into the household of the activities once possible in polis and forum, the prescriptive and positive bent of the

poem—recommending the creation of spheres of action wherever possible—remains dominant.

Auden's deepest concern is with the means of achieving humanity: not the place of the house in the large world but the occurrences
within the house. The argument of the series puts its own language, its
own architecture, in a special focus. If speech viewed as personal disclosure and not simply as communication is one of the definitional
human acts, and if making, of which poetry is a prime example, is the
precondition of significant human action, then the language of the
poems has special exemplary functions: it instances human fabrication
and disclosure. Auden takes the view that making language into speech
and transforming words into verbal architecture are distinctive and
estimable activities, and the language and craft of the poems become
part of the definitional and celebratory purposes of the sequence.
Poetry is analogous to other forms of disclosure and acts of making, to
any other form of activity by which man expresses or achieves humanity; but it does not claim singularity. The poems are about themselves:
this is a truism about modern poetry, but it has a special sense here.
They are about themselves in that they build the architectural and
philosophical space in which their language exists as significant speech;
they make a true architecture of humanism.

> Richard Johnson. *Man's Place: An Essay on
> Auden* (Ithaca, N.Y., Cornell Univ. Pr.,
> 1973), pp. 240–42

"For Valéry," W. H. Auden has remarked, "a poem ought to be a
festival of the intellect, that is, a game, but a solemn, ordered, and
significant game, and a poet is someone to whom arbitrary difficulties
suggest ideas." For Valéry, and now for Mr. Auden, especially in
About the House, City without Walls, and *Epistle to a Godson,* books
written according to the principle that, whatever life is, poetry is a
carnival. The poet begins with language, delighting in the exercise of its
possibilities, and he stops short of Mardi gras only by requiring his
language to recognize the existence of the primary world in which we
live.

The poem makes a secondary world, according to prescriptions as
congenial as they are ingenious. In *Epistle to a Godson* the primary
world contains for the most part certain grand maladies of the quo-
tidian: age, loss, grief, loneliness, violence, nuances of damage, bloody-
minded monsters at large. The secondary world is still managed with
the most charming intention, and a prosody of good humor, good taste,
good luck. The dominant tone implies that the quest is now too perilous
to be undertaken directly, better wait till morning and the possibility of

"cleansed occasions." Meanwhile the poet writes short, brisk poems, a few smacks administered to the world's bottom, for its good. There is a lot of grousing, but no harm is meant, the poet is merely telling young people to mind their manners, speak decent English, and wash occasionally.

Denis Donoghue. *NYR*. July 19, 1973, p. 17

BARKER, GEORGE (1913–　　　)

Mr. George Barker is a poet of an extraordinary consistency of style: it is both his strength and his weakness. From the moment when he appeared on the general scene, with his volume of *Poems* from Messrs. Faber & Faber, over thirty years ago, he dazzled us in the armour of his romantic, rhetorical, high-flown manner; and he still wears it. Fashions have changed since then; but Mr. Barker hardly at all. He has in his time written some poems which, in their reckless, anything-goes unevenness, a brilliant and original passage followed by a crash of bathos, are surely among the worst produced by his generation. He has also written others which, for my money, are among the most memorable of the last three decades. No one else could have written "Letters to a Young Poet": I have read it dozens of times, and am still as grateful for it as I was the first time.

He has an ungovernable addiction to Blakean visions, punning conceits and paradoxes and personified abstractions. I have sometimes tried to imagine Mr. Barker sitting on the top of a bus, his head filled, not with the everyday preoccupations of the rest of us, but with these coruscating metaphysical images flung hither and thither as the lava of one of his poems erupts within his imagination. It is a rather terrifying thought: but it inspires compassion as well as awe. For it seems to me that he is in reality the prisoner of his style, and would dearly like to escape now and then. Even when he is attempting something more down-to-earth, as in his long autobiographical work, facetious paradoxes continue to form themselves as if they were out of control, eating up the development of the poem like a malignant cancer.

It was with these thoughts in mind that I turned eagerly to his new collection, *Dreams of a Summer Night*, and to the series of linked elegiac reflections of the title poem first of all. It is a moving poem, full, it seems to me, of a desperate sadness and nostalgia; but Mr. Barker is still encased in his armour, with its florid baroque devices gaudily embossed upon it, often to lamentably grotesque effect. . . .

John Lehmann. PoetryR. Summer, 1966,
p. 105

George Barker resembles Lawrence in certain thematic preoccupations —most notably love, sex, friendship, the body, modern commercial civilization, and death—and in the fact that he too has produced hundreds of poems, most of which I have found eminently forgettable. His *Collected Poems: 1930–1965* gathers up again the work of half a lifetime, together with several pieces never before published (it does not incorporate his book-length poem, *The True Confession of George Barker*, which is separately available and which was no intolerable omission in any case); and it would be gratifying to be able to praise so thick a volume, representing so many years of consecration and sweat and merciless language-torturing. One would like to agree with the *London Sunday Times*, that limbo of easy-to-please judgments about contemporary poetry, when it singles out Mr. Barker as "a poet whose visions and eloquence would be remarkable in any age, let alone in this." Mr. Barker, after all, has *tried*. He writes and writes. He gives himself to his poetry with that pyrotechnic, slam-bang energy and industry which have enabled him to keep on keeping on, in spite of everything, decade after decade. More importantly, a few of his poems are by no means eminently forgettable.

He is capable, on occasion, of catching you up with a whole poem that comes close to showing you what poetry is. . . . The point, however, is that Mr. Barker's most profitable poems are in every case his least characteristic. I know of no instruments by which to get an exact assay, but my estimate would be that something like ninety per cent of the work throughout these *Collected Poems* is botched and disfigured by a forced, self-indulgent poeticizing in which poems become so many set-pieces, so many contrived exercises in the welding of junk sculptures and the busy pasting up of rhetoric. . . . In the final analysis, I suppose, any poet is fortunate if a tithe of his poems prove worth saving, worth preserving for the semi-perpetuity of a "collected" edition. George Barker, therefore, cannot quite be dismissed. But so far as I am concerned his *Collected Poems* can be appreciated only in a very mixed and limited fashion, with the rueful feeling that their 273 pages should have been smelted down into a rigorous selection that would leave perhaps one poem in ten.

Robert L. Stilwell. *SwR*. Summer, 1968,
pp. 524–26

Barker's best work, like all great poetry, engages and repays us, as anything of value does, with repeated contact; and yet the initial reading often dazzles us with its music and dramatic vitality. If we prefer delicacy and detachment, we may not give a Barker poem the attention it requires. We may dismiss Barker as a poseur, overlook his seriousness, and consequently miss the rewards of his verse. . . . When he is most successful, we are first stirred by his response to events in the moral history of man. A true Romantic, he is rarely concerned with ideas apart from feeling. Reading him can be an exercise in tolerance, a study of romantic and religious reaction to an age of secularism and reason, an education of the sensibility, and an exciting esthetic experience.

In 1959 Stephen Spender likened the modern critic to a giant who throws a great rock at a little fly: he either smashes or misses his prey. Because so many writers have crushed, missed, or only clipped Barker's wings—or, worse, have tried to scotch him with pebbles—Barker remains a controversial figure. Unlike many of his contemporaries, he hasn't gained the poetic notoriety that critical attention can create in an age of criticism. Any reader who is not intimidated by giants, or taken in by literary biases, will find a poetry remarkable for its power. If he does not reject Barker's moral intensity, he will find poems, moving and musical, ranging from impassioned lyricism to symphonic grandeur to colloquial directness. A significant number combine compulsive rhetoric and fundamental brainwork to convey with courage and audacity Barker's *Sturm und Drang* Romanticism. At their best, they are a tonic for apathy and dilettantism, pedestrian rationalism and cool disaffiliation—a tonic for the times.

Martha Fodaski. *George Barker*
(N.Y., Twayne, 1969), pp. 172–73

● **BARSTOW, STAN (1928–   )**

[Barstow's] hero, Victor Brown [in *A Kind of Loving*], is a coalminer's son who dreams of having a romantic affair with one Ingrid in the typists' pool. When she actually sinks to the grass of the park in his arms, his bliss reaches its peak. At which point Mr. Barstow springs his second surprise. Victor rises from the grass totally uninterested in Ingrid, but Ingrid rises totally enamoured of Victor. Most novelists would spend chapters describing such an absolute exchange in the feelings of their characters. But Mr. Barstow does the job in one paragraph —and does it so sharply that his novel, which has not been particularly interesting up to this point, suddenly begins to show quality as well as quantity. It continues to do so until the end, one surprise following another. Not content with boring Victor to death, Ingrid becomes pregnant too, so Victor must do the decent thing and marry her.

What does it add to in the end? Again the author has a fine surprise. Vic, bound for life to a woman in whom he is quite uninterested, is simply going to have to stay that way. If he is good-natured and sensible enough—which he is—married life will teach him "a kind of loving." It won't be the glamorous loving he has dreamed of—in fact, it will be more a kind of living than loving. Possibly it won't be too bad —and certainly it will never be unreal. It may even turn out to be something almost likable.

Mr. Barstow is not being cynical when he reaches this conclusion. He is just being hard-headed and practical—which is what Yorkshire-men were sent into the world to be. His attitude commands respect, particularly as his humor is always there to lighten his remarkable austerity. He and his characters have never heard of words like "neurosis" and "maladjustment." They just get into trouble, as if trouble were part of the business of living. This point of view is almost too surprising in a modern novelist.

Nigel Dennis. NYT. Jan. 22, 1961, p. 32

A Kind of Loving was Stan Barstow's affirmation of the power of goodness. His hero, Victor Brown, was at heart a good lad, so much so that he accepted the convention of marrying a girl he didn't love after getting her in trouble. Joby Weston [in *Joby*], quite obviously, will do the same. He is Victor Brown at the age of eleven, possessing the same background, the same intelligence, the same education in morality. *Joby* is the story of the boy's summer holiday, spent in comparative freedom while his mother is in hospital, and while waiting to go to the grammar school. His time is spent wandering the streets and countryside of Yorkshire, learning bad ways from bad boys, about sex from precocious girls; gradually growing out of childishness. Mr. Barstow has caught the boy's eye view of those long days when comics and "spend" meant Saturday, when talk of Eyeties and Fashists merely inspired a new game. He has recorded exactly the childish conversations, half boastful, half groping, by which Joby and his pals communicate. Joby's father's mild but touching affair with cousin Mona is imparted as Joby saw it: from behind the kitchen door.

Mr. Barstow writes with compassion and control, bringing back clearly those long days of a pre-war childhood. If there is sometimes a hint of sermonizing in his tone, it is because he believes in goodness, and would have us learn, like Joby, to be kind to old ladies and not to steal from shops. Admirable; but this novel gave me the feeling that all Joby could look forward to was a life of compromise and *A Kind of Loving*.

Maggie Ross. List. Feb. 13, 1964, p. 285

Stan Barstow, author of a number of novels since 1960 and notably *A Kind of Loving*, has recently written an excellent exercise in realism, *The Hidden Part*. Through his protagonist Tom Simpkins, Barstow projects his chief theme, the inevitable consequences which stem from any specific act: "There was no end except the grave and until then you went on through life's endless ramifications, watching not so much things coming home to roost (a phrase for him too laden with guilt and remorse, and finally, as a philosophy, life-destroying) but the limitless unprophesiable patterns of cause and effect, actions and consequences." The affair between Simpkins and Norma Moffat allows her a sensual satisfaction that her husband Sid, drained of his energies by the First War, could not give her. When after Sid's death the Moffat children (Nicholas is Sid's child and Shirley, Tom's) learn the facts, the results are painful, almost disastrous. Yet Norma's denial of Tom would have entailed its own frustrations and a tragic withering of her vitality and sympathies. Norma's balancing of adultery and fidelity may not have been the most forthright solution for her problem but it may have been the only possible one.

Both action and inaction have their fateful consequences. In the newer generation, Andrea Warner cannot look forward even to an illicit relationship with Philip Hart, the teacher with whom she falls in love. He loves her passionately but cannot leave his wife whom he loves in another way and his children to whom he is devoted. In effect, Philip has to choose between differing kinds of fulfillment. His decision may be the only feasible one, but still "the hidden part" of his act will be the inevitable bitterness enveloping all these people. There is something to be said for Andrea's and Philip's "decent" behavior, but not too much.

Barstow's novel is moving and finally powerful, though it is somewhat conventional in presentation. In the first third the affair between Tom and Norma is trite and predictable. Thereafter, the novel achieves pace and intensity when the relationship between Andrea and Philip brings the one between Tom and Norma more clearly into focus and when the children come to register the effects on them of their mother's past. The novel then opens out to suggest more of the involutions in a perplexing moral situation than we might have at first felt possible. Barstow registers, too, his full sense of life in a Yorkshire town. . . . Barstow's is a good and absorbing novel, but finally not venturesome enough in conception to approach the highest distinction.

Frederick P. W. McDowell. *CL.*
Autumn, 1970, pp. 546–47

BECKETT, SAMUEL (1906–   )

The convention of total illusion, and of man's inability to communicate, seems . . . merely the most recent and most bourgeois of platitudes. But when this is so, we are in danger of missing those few works which go beyond the formulas and create the experience in depth.

The most remarkable example, in this kind, is Beckett's *Waiting for Godot*. . . . It presents a total condition of man, and this belongs within the familiar structure of feeling. . . . Yet the dramatic method is in fact unlike that of Chekhov and Pirandello, where the movement is normally a single action showing how the characters fit in with each other, sharing comparable illusions. The method of *Waiting for Godot* is older. The play is built around an unusually explicit set of contrasts: between the tramps, Vladimir and Estragon, and the travellers, Pozzo and Lucky; and the further contrasts within each pair.

This polar opposition of characters was used in early expressionism to present the conflicts of a single mind. But now the method has been developed to present the conflicts within a total human condition. It is an almost wholly static world, with very narrow limits set to any significant human action. Yet the struggles for significance, of each of the pairs, are sharply contrasted. The movement of the play is the action of waiting. . . .

The compassion which was always present in Chekhov had virtually disappeared by the time of Pirandello and his successors. Their exposure of illusion (as indeed in Beckett's own other work) carried a mocking harshness which could not go beyond itself. The world and life had been "seen through," and that was that. In the Pozzo-Lucky sequences, Beckett continues this tone, but he combines it with what had seemed to be lost: the possibility of human recognition, and of love, within a total condition still meaningless. Strangely, this answering life, at a point beyond the recognition of stalemate, is convincing and moving.

Raymond Williams. *Modern Tragedy*
(Stanford, Cal., Stanford Univ. Pr., 1966),
pp. 153–55

Beckett is frequently arraigned on two charges: that he is a perverse "messenger of gloom" and that he writes only of the extraordinary in terms of unnecessary complexity. It is not entirely irrelevant to ask why

Beckett should be easy, cheerful and reassuring or even, as he did himself in the essay on Joyce, why art should be without difficulty. . . . The purpose of his art, as he understood it in *Proust*, is not to explain but to contemplate; the will, he stated, is not a condition of the artistic experience. This art does not suppose to solve and make plain but to discover and perhaps to comprehend—by perception and intuition, not by the intelligence. And if the subject of his contemplation withholds a meaning then the duty of this art is not to impose one but to remain in doubt. A resolution is comparable to believing that all is well with the world—which it obviously isn't. Thus the boy in *Endgame* may or may not be a sign of resurrection, Beckett's point is precisely this, he doesn't know and will not presume. . . . In Beckett one remains with an ignorance that does not pretend to be otherwise and it is this, easily mistaken for obscurity, that discomforts the reader.

Furthermore, his art cannot be judged irresponsible or idiosyncratic because it does not apparently concern itself with the social or political circumstance of its time. It is precisely because the destructive forces of the twentieth century have given the lie to progress, reason, stability, perfectability and simplicity that Beckett subscribes to none of them and his writing is as it is. Beckett does not write of the hydrogen bomb or of Dachau but he does portray in a unique poetry, and with an even more unique truthfulness the cruelty, suffering and helplessness which is the human climate of a world in which the bomb exists and such events take place. . . .

The one fundamental behind all of Beckett's work is the ancient tragic knowledge which has been revived by the absurd, of man's solitude, imprisonment and pain in an intolerable universe that is indifferent to his suffering. Beckett is, if in these conditions the word retains a meaning, a pessimist, which is to say he writes what he considers to be true and not what he knows is diverting. This is not a criticism of a right or wrong approach: only a test of where one places the value in life. The world in which Beckett begins to write is without unity, clarity, rationality or hope, and where man, absurdly conscious that he is conscious and bound to die, feels himself alone and a stranger in a place which itself will one day cease to exist. From this confrontation between the unreasonable silence of the universe and the human need to be and to be known, there arises that futile revolt against existence; the anguished rebellion of the spirit against Apollinaris's three necessities, the abject necessity of being born, the hard necessity of living and the sharp necessity of dying, which is constant throughout his work.

Michael Robinson. *The Long Sonata of the Dead: A Study of Samuel Beckett* (Hart-Davis, 1969), pp. 299–300

We seem . . . to possess in the fiction of Samuel Beckett an example of thorough-going consistency in a progressive evolution. This rigour has been achieved not only because the author has always taken the next logical step forward, but also because he has remained faithful to certain basic themes, his literary "obsessions," which he has developed with undeviating honesty and intrepidity. He has not shirked any of the conclusions his pen has led him into, however nonsensical, cruel or obscene they may seem. His prose is sometimes physically hard to read, his thought difficult to follow, his remarks unpalatable and his subject-matter unsavoury: *Beckett grince*, admits Mayoux, an admirer, for there is no denying the shock and pain that this author inflicts on our sensibilities. But this is the price to be paid, by writer and reader alike, for the acquisition of a body of work that goes in everything to the limit, without shame or fear. . . .

[His] consistency of development does not, however, mean that Beckett's novels are repetitive or at all similar; the *œuvre* grows from skilful, clever but somewhat sterile beginnings to a full and rich maturity. The first novel was written by a sensitive intellectual made disdainful by circumstance, who, feeling incapable of penning a popularly acceptable book, clothed his pain in recondite confabulation spiced with esoteric wit. The later works, while still conceding nothing to current taste, offer for the delight of all who are prepared to make an effort to penetrate them, extraordinarily invigorating and intense fictions that invite an exploration of a world which, on the face of it, seems so unpromising to literary activity, but which on examination shows itself to be one of interest and significance.

Beckett's world is both relevant and irrelevant to that of our day-to-day experience. We do not, of course, expect to learn anything from this author about Proust's Faubourg St. Germain, Forster's India or Faulkner's South; we do not read him to gain an insight into the psychology of human beings in love, as we read Mme. de La Fayette and her numberless followers; we do not believe that he will strive, like D. H. Lawrence, to change our attitude to anything, nor that he will seek, like Mauriac, to translate a religious vision into art. He is unlike other novelists, and indeed seems even deliberately to exclude from his works much of what constitutes the staple of other fiction. But although he is not interested in what attracts his colleagues' attention, he has adopted one small section of the population as his own field of study by predilection: the group that embraces the tramp, the homeless outcast and the poverty-stricken old man. "My characters have nothing," he has said, but they manage to survive nonetheless. Their means are however totally reduced; Beckett shows what it feels like to have not even the bare necessities, and how one must therefore set about acquiring a bottle of milk and a hole to sleep in.

John Fletcher. *The Novels of Samuel Beckett* (Chatto and Windus, 1970), pp. 224–25

The fundamental feature of Beckett's characters is that they are schizophrenic, in the accepted clinical sense of the word, or at the least are definitely schizoidal types. And the important fact about his presentation of these characters is that, unlike the traditional novelist, he does not merely report their behaviour from the point of view of an outside observer, but imaginatively describes their subjective experience of psychosis as it appears to their disturbed minds. . . .

Beckett's characters . . . are acutely aware of the hostility of the outer world from which they seek to protect themselves by bodily flight from people and by mental flight into phantasy. But they are always searching for that immanent central self which they posit as the basis of those "homeless mes and untenanted hims" that are the manifestations of their fragmented personalities. This central self goes under many names: In the twelfth *Text for Nothing* the tramp, realizing the inadequacy of a human witness (since his reality too is equally in question), postulates the need for a god, an "unwitnessed witness of witnesses," who would be this central self, unmanifest but aware of the manifesting person. Murphy called it a "matrix of surds"; Watt knew it as Mr. Knott; Malone spoke of it as "the other," and in *The Unnamable* M. calls it "the silence." In the first play it is the unseen, unknown Mr. Godot for whom the tramps wait interminably—differing here from the heroes of the novels in that they do not search for this central self within themselves because they mistakenly conceive it as an outside power, at first as an important official who could help them but finally as a Jehovah who will probably punish them. Later, in *Play*, this central self is presented as an impersonal light, and in *Cascando* it is the Opener which switches off and on arbitrarily to animate the human puppet.

All Beckett's main themes converge round this concept of a central self being the only ultimate reality: life as mere "play," a filling-up of time with futile actions performed by an unreal pseudo-self; birth as the original sin; the necessity for a witness to one's existence; the search for the real "me," and the conviction that when found it will prove to be a void, a nothing which is the source of everything.

G. C. Barnard. *Samuel Beckett: A New Approach* (N.Y., Dodd, Mead, 1970), pp. 132–33

Samuel Beckett's fictional world, especially *Watt*, contains a quasi-Rabelaisian parody of all the rhetorical and logical devices that have permitted Western man, like Beckett's Ubu-esque creation, the "man-pot" Mahood, to hold a "partially waterproof tarpaulin" over his skull. Describing, reasoning, discussing, examining—Beckett's characters never tire of these activities, though no two of them proceed in exactly the same way. They share our "deplorable mania" not only for "when something happens wanting to know what" but furthermore for wanting, like Watt, to know why. Beckett is thus something of a contemporary Faust who, through the agency of his characters, indiscriminately, and with ferocious humor, undermines all our past and present attempts to give reality a: intelligible structure, to "think out" our human situation.

We can thus readily understand that Beckett should find philosophy unintelligible—as regards its proposed aims, not its intellectual procedures. These he tirelessly ridicules. Not without reason did he invent Macmann, that character Malone talks to himself about, who, while believing that "he had done as any man of good will would have done in his place and with very much the same results, in spite of his lack of experience," nonetheless acknowledges that, in gardening, he is "incapable of weeding a bed of pansies or marigolds and [of] leaving one standing." Beckett's verbal clowning produces a similar devastation, as do certain Jarry-like inventions which allow him to reduce our relations with the physical world to the status of a simple diagram: two pots for r•urishment and evacuation; a bag of canned foods; a pebble or, in prosperous times, sixteen pebbles to suck, and so forth.

Like Joyce, perhaps still more than Joyce, Beckett seems marked by the scholasticism of his philosophy classes at Trinity College. We can find many traces of it in his imaginary world. Descartes and Geulincx are perhaps given an important role in his early novels because they broke with the great intellectual tradition which from Plato to Thomas Aquinas, via Aristotle, conceived creation as a moving hierarchy of creatures oriented toward a perfect and definitive form, a final cause, God. Descartes thus unintentionally prepared the way for Beckett's "great articulates"—creatures whose special articulation, in body, thought or speech, even though sadly defective, makes them forget that they are really "frightened vagabonds," willy-nilly dragging aimlessly along, dying by degrees, while words and images spin round and round inside their bony white skulls. Skulls, jars, rooms, or other habitations, and the monotonous surrounding "country" form two inseparable and rhythmically alternating settings for the adventures of Beckett's great articulates: beings who travel, or rather wander, toward some illusory "home" or "refuge," telling each other their adventures, while their dual disarticulation proceeds insidiously, "by direct route."

Germaine Brée. In Melvin J. Friedman, ed.,
Samuel Beckett Now (Chicago, Univ. of
Chicago Pr., 1970), pp. 74–75

Beckett's poetry turned out to be less "self-contained" than is some poetry. It has its aesthetic dimension and its antiaesthetic dimension. It points both to itself as art and to its maker as man, existing in the outer world of time and space and the inner world of the "Nothing, than which . . . naught is more real." The poems are difficult, if not hermetic, primarily because they are filled with allusions to worlds beyond the world of poetry—to literature and philosophy, to Ireland and France and especially the Dublin and Paris that Beckett knew as a young man, to events in the life of the poet. . . . This complex was the habitat of the young Beckett, the universe of his loves and antipathies. Perhaps there is something more deeply human than idle curiosity that leads us to look beyond even privileged works of art to the human realities from which they spring. In any case, there is no easy breaking point between the best of Beckett's poems and their existential ground. . . .

As we move through the collected poetry an evolution becomes apparent, an evolution in thought, attitude, and style that transcends the poetry. The last two poems Beckett wrote, published in the Addenda to *Watt*, are at once the clearest expression of the reality he reached at the terminus of his poetic evolution and the manifesto of the prose and drama to come, which he envisioned as explorations and *approfondissements* of this essential reality. These two little poems form, as it were, the ideal bridge between the early Beckett and the mature artist possessed of and by his vision and fully in command of his artistic means. . . .

His later prose and dramatic writing are densely poetic in the sense that narration and dialogue expand at every moment beyond storytelling and communication to produce the distance of aesthetic contemplation through images that in the context become emblematic of man's condition and destiny. When he writes in a reflexive mode—as critic and theorist—about the novel, drama, poetry, painting, and criticism and theory themselves, we become aware that the practitioner of poetry was not long in developing a consistent view of art as making that can apply not only to poetry, not only to the various literary genres, but to all the arts.

Lawrence E. Harvey. *Samuel Beckett: Poet &
Critic* (Princeton, N.J., Princeton Univ. Pr.,
1970), pp. ix–xi

In *Play* the form is co-existent with the content, for although the light acts as the interrogator of the three protagonists, bidding them speak or be silent by its shining or not shining on each of their faces, it is also the condition of their existence for themselves and for the audience. The metaphor on the stage is the failure of a three-cornered relationship, the staple content of a thousand boulevard comedies (*Play*'s French title is, of course, *Comédie*), but the light in which it is seen, the darkness in which it is not seen are also the author's opening and shutting eye, the actors' prompters and the audience's only means of participation. The "inner" impotence and ignorance of the metaphor now blend with the "outer" impotence and ignorance of the means, as the "inner" and "outer" waiting blended in *Waiting for Godot*. The two radio plays, *Words and Music* and *Cascando*, written at about the same time as *Play*, use variations of this discovery, adapted to the special circumstances of radio.

Beckett's most recent work in the theatre has not yet gone beyond *Play*, except in paring down the content. In the same way his most recent fiction, the four short pieces, *Imagination Dead Imagine, Enough, Ping* and *Lessness* (French title: *Sans*), have been parings down of *How It Is*, but it is worth remarking that in these works the pictorial element and the prose-poetry in which it is conveyed are growing still more prominent and concentrated, that Beckett has always in the past used his fiction as the spearhead of changes in his work, and that every new technical impetus in his development has been brought about by the conflict between an apparently pulverized content and Beckett's inexorable "obligation" to invent a form capable of pulverizing it still further. He has brought his theatre to the threshold of abstraction, but not yet beyond. His dustbins are still self-evidently dustbins and can still give rise to "sermons in stones," to moral, social and philosophical dissertations, however distasteful he may find them. Whether or not he himself ever makes the final step over the threshold into abstract theatre, whether or not it is possible for the theatrical experience to be genuinely abstract, he has—after the wicked fashion of all outstanding artists—apparently closed every other door in the faces of his successors, just as Joyce must once have seemed to close every door but impotence in his.

John Fletcher and John Spurling. *Beckett: A Study of His Plays* (N.Y., Hill and Wang, 1972), pp. 45–46

Beckett has not yet abandoned his work in planetary engineering. Very recently he published approximately fifty pages entitled *Le Dépeupleur* [*The Lost Ones*]. Like *How It Is* and *Imagination Dead Imagine* it is a

Dantean epic in miniature, ringed and self-contained. Its design is of consummate mathematical exactitude: a cylinder, fifty meters in circumference by sixteen in height, resting on the earth, capped at the top. Within, the cylinder is lit throughout by vibrating yellow light. The temperature ranges from five to twenty-five degrees, oscillating from high to low to high again over eight-second intervals. All variations of light and temperature cease at rare intervals for about ten seconds. The cylinder is populated by one body per square meter or in round figures two hundred bodies. The bodies are divided into four categories, of which three are seekers . . . and the fourth are "nonchercheurs" or better "ex-chercheurs" who sit for the most part against the wall (in the attitude, the author notes, which evoked from Dante one of his rare smiles).

There are also ladders, about fifteen, resting at various points against the wall of the cylinder, used for two purposes: simply to get off the ground or to climb up into caves that riddle the upper part of the wall. Some of these caves are connected by tunnels. The behavior of the seekers is governed by certain laws pertaining to time allowed in the caves, access to the ladders, investigation of bodies, and other matters. These and numerous other details and refinements are carefully blueprinted in fifteen paragraphs, each paragraph devoted to an aspect of the world, the last dealing with the time just preceding *"l'impensable fin si cette notion est maintenue."*

It would appear that Beckett has pushed his indulgence in planetary design to an extreme. There are no memories to haunt this creator. Like the creator of *Imagination Dead Imagine*, he stands outside his creation. There is no need to destroy it, to say that it is "all balls." No need even to leave it in search of better worlds. It is a kind of game now. Yet, as in the games of Malone, ages ago, the escape to another planet is a return to our own. . . .

H. Porter Abbott. *The Fiction of Samuel Beckett* (Berkeley, Univ. of California Pr., 1973), pp. 149–50

In Beckett's first extant publication, he wrote that literary criticism is not book-keeping. One technique of such book-keeping is reduction of an oeuvre to a few major themes. But what have we grasped of Shakespeare when we reduce him to appearance-reality? And what of Beckett when we reduce him to life-death, self-other, silence-words, being-nothing, though these tensions are present in his work? The unaccountable wealth of his oeuvre is not reducible to themes, and the whole oeuvre is greater than the sum of its parts. But we know the whole only through the parts, and the consistency in the parts is astonishing: the "assumption" of Beckett's first published story is sustained through *Lessness*; the "ping" of his first unpublished novel sounds through one of his last lyrics of fiction; "Cascando" is a poem in 1935, a drama in 1963; Belacqua appears from the 1932 *Dream* sporadically through the 1966 *Dépeupleur*. But consistency of focus is not necessarily a virtue unless the vision thereby acquires penetrative power. And it is deepening penetration that distinguishes work after Beckett work, accumulating into an oeuvre that moves through a residue of wide range into depth.

Beckett himself occasionally speaks of his oeuvre as though it has taken place in his absence; or as though he were a resonator for works that speak through rather than from him. He feels that the root of each of his works lies in a previous work, and he is sometimes puzzled by the order in which the works come to him—as in the case of the *nouvelles* or the *Têtes-Mortes*. What he sketches is a variant of the artist as seer. And yet, it is not into his works but into himself that Beckett sinks in order to write—a self that cannot be divested of its experience, nor of words that, willy-nilly, recall experience.

Ruby Cohn. Back to Beckett (Princeton, N.J., Princeton Univ. Pr., 1973), pp. 270–71

BEERBOHM, MAX (1872–1956)

By flaunting the triviality of his subject matter, Max dared the public to call his work second-rate. We cannot call it that, though our criticism lacks the tools to tell us why we cannot. One reason may be that Max achieves perfection within his prescribed limits. Another better reason, I think, is that his work is steeped in literary culture; so that we recognize in our response to it those faculties of cultural memory and association that we use in responding to great literature. It is usually literary ideas, styles, and postures that are parodied in Max's work. To chuckle over his story, "Enoch Soames," you have to know about *Faust*, Baudelaire, the poetry of the nineties, histories of literature and the controversy over phonetic spelling. Max's airy confections are for those who have already digested very many heavy books, or at least live in an ambience where such books have been so thoroughly assimilated as to have passed into the conversational idiom.

Like Milton, Max wrote for "fit audience . . . though few." What money he earned came mainly from his drawings, which were not only published but were also exhibited and sold in the original at a London art gallery. I rather fear for the future of his audience in this country at least. For his work is only for readers who love literature, and American readers of that sort are these days too much on the make culturally to be willing to spend time on anything less than Great Books. (The English err in the opposite direction; they are all too ready to settle for littleness.) Another difficulty is that Max's literary allusions are becoming increasingly historical; so that his work may be in the end the special reward reserved for literary scholars, who will guarantee him the sentence or two in literary history that Enoch Soames wanted so badly and was not to have.

Robert Langbaum. *VP*. Spring, 1966, p. 122

Careful writer that he was, Beerbohm strove always to preserve the illusion of spontaneity and to appear the skillful amateur even when he had professional craft. In short essays, even on literary subjects, he succeeded admirably. He must have doubted his capacity to sustain his style and manner in longer, more systematic works. He refused, in a word, to turn from youthful brilliance to mature competence in full-scale projects.

So far as this hypothesis is true, and there is surely something in it, there is a suggestion that perhaps Beerbohm's work has been over-valued because he was so young when he did it. What valid ideas did he have, and how relevant are they today? Why could he not make the transition to the postwar world? . . .

Beerbohm was no thinker. He himself would heartily agree. It was not for systematic ideas that he was valued in his own day, and his fame will endure for other reasons. So long as the late nineteenth century continues to be of interest, Beerbohm's drawings, his writings, and his early career will be indispensable comments on the age. So long as drama entertains and enlightens us, Beerbohm's dramatic criticism will speak for the discriminating and articulate playgoer. For knowing readers, his style will preserve his prejudices as well as his wisdom, and sorting the prejudices from the wisdom will be part of the fun. . . .

Bruce R. McElderry, Jr. *Max Beerbohm*
(N.Y., Twayne, 1972), pp. 158–59

BEHAN, BRENDAN (1923–1964)

Everybody says Brendan Behan loved life. If he did he did not dominate it; it dominated him. He loved it so much that it slew him. He gave himself no time to tame it or to write it. He did not write his last book [*Confessions of an Irish Rebel*]; it was recorded on tape, transcribed and edited by Rae Jeffs, a proper English lady whom he enchanted into nonconformity; "once-proper" is her own word today. I am not sure that it is right even to call this record a book, if that word conveys at least a beginning, middle and end—temporalities that no more existed in Brendan's being than they do in eternity.

Who recorded it anyway? Brendan, or Life pouring over him and out of him in song, verse, drink, passion, guff, rude jokes and flat statements (such as that Lord Carson's real name was Carsoni, or that London is named after a Celtic god), blasphemy (he says he always liked it and most Catholics do—who else *can* blaspheme?), cursing, praise of the Lord, lots of F-words, S-words, and other such explosives, but all too rarely that priceless stuff that ends up as unforgettable print. How lamentably the good Lord distributes talent! I could name offhand 10 Irish writers with 10 times Brendan's talents who would give their eyeteeth for a hundredth part of his amazing vitality and combustibility, and a thousandth part of his experience.

What a man! And then one pauses, and asks the chilling question: What kind of a writer? Did he really and truly ever want to be a writer at all? Or did he belong to that type of writer, something on the order of Thomas Wolfe, who acts as if he believes that if you live hard enough, and emotionally enough, literature will follow as a matter of course—the eye in a fine frenzy rolling? I do not know if Brendan ever read Thomas Mann's "Tonio Kröger," with its dismaying if salutary description of how an artist really works, moving from primal, hot excitement into coldly deliberate creation. It could hardly have been Brendan's cup of tea, or glass of malt.

Rae Jeffs, in her highly percipient Foreword, sees the fundamental truth about him: childlike in his frankness and candor, full of innocence, tenderness and sensitivity behind all his outward ferocity, the prisoner and victim of a fatal persona or role, a man who did not want to die, only to stop living the self-destructive life that he had concocted for himself. All this is made perfectly clear in these *Confessions*, where his reactions to life are sometimes deep but mostly very simple, and utterly spontaneous—always provided one agrees that every Irishman is conditioned from birth by the immemorial and inescapable Irish myth and tradition.

Sean O'Faolain. *NYT*. June 26, 1966, p. 7

Behan can not be ranked among the great writers, for he did not produce a sufficient volume of work, and even what he did produce is not without flaw. . . . Nevertheless, Behan was much more than a gifted leprechaun. He was a conscious artist, and the charge that his work is slapdash is not altogether justified. He took the same liberties with traditional notions of language, plot construction, and character development as have many other contemporary writers. He realized, with such writers as Beckett, Ionesco, Osborne, and Pinter, that nineteenth-century standards would not serve twentieth-century artists. Unfortunately, a good many critics who admire the unorthodox structure of the plays of Beckett or those of Pinter decry the same structure in Behan's plays. . . .

Behan possessed a marvelous comic talent. That he wasted a good deal of it cannot diminish his solid achievements. He wrote two of the best plays of the contemporary theater, and one of the best auto-biographies of this century. He wrote with an exuberance and a humanity which will remain unexcelled. To a confused and self-destructive world, Behan gave a simple and cogent reminder: human existence, though painful, is worthwhile. Or, as Behan stated it in *The Quare Fellow*, life is "a bloody sight better than death any day of the week."

Ted E. Boyle. *Brendan Behan* (N.Y., Twayne, 1969), p. 134

Brendan, at his eloquent best, was the equivalent of a one-man show —except that he had no script and the run was unlimited. Unlike a stage act when his performance is over, Brendan's obligation to his art did not cease when he stopped talking. It was then he should have settled down to serious writing. But in his public performance he had syphoned off so much energy that he was often too exhausted to lift a pen. This was to be his great dilemma. If he indulged the extrovert side of his character, he lessened his chances of doing the only thing in life that really mattered to him—writing. . . .

After Christmas in 1960 Brendan began the first of the books that he was to produce by tape recorder. He had been commissioned by Hutchinson some time before, to do a book on Ireland with drawings by Paul Hogarth, the English artist. Hogarth had gone to Ireland and finished his part of the job, and was understandably anxious to see his illustrations in print, and accompanied by a text. . . .

Brendan Behan's Island was to receive wide acclaim two years later when it appeared. "One immediately likes Behan," writes Cyril Connolly in the *Sunday Times* in October, 1962, referring to the book. "He has more than charm, he has instinctive kindness and charity. A verbal grace, an unforced assertion of his strong personality that may even have a touch of greatness, a demonic energy that notoriety has not entirely dimmed." . . .

Compared with *Borstal Boy* or *The Quare Fellow*, Brendan's "talk" books are not of great value, but they do preserve a record of the range and variety of his conversation. On one page the reader can be taken through history, poetry, politics, or sport, all told in the special form of anecdote and humorous comment which was the keystone of his conversational technique. . . .

Brendan was a popular writer in the sense that no literary personality of his time had been. Thousands who had never read his book felt they knew him intimately from his appearances on television and the reports of his escapades in the newspapers.

With his death, the legend grew. He was to become a symbol for many too young even to have known his name when he was alive.

He has remained in the public mind as an iconoclast who defied convention, a precursor of the permissive society. Of those who manned the barricades in Paris, who sat-in at Berkeley or loved-in in Central Park, there are not a few to whom Brendan has been a father-figure.

Had he chosen it, his role might have been a different one. At the back of his mind lurked the image of the eighteenth-century Gaelic poet who had beguiled his boyhood; mocking, picaresque figures who brought high culture to the hearth, indifferent how they used their bodies in drink, lust, or rage if they caught for a moment in verse, the fine frenzy that overflowed their imagination.

Ulick O'Connor. Brendan Behan (Hamish
Hamilton, 1970), pp. 225, 235–37, 319

Brendan Behan's *The Hostage* is a popular play just now—popular with producing companies and audiences alike. Its mode and energy are especially appealing to those interested in the new, freer, not-so-literary theatre of the moment. The evolution of the play from the original Gaelic conception, to the English version for Dublin's Abbey, to its fuller development under the direction of Joan Littlewood at her London theatre at Stratford-East is widely known. That the play grew to its present shape out of improvisations by Littlewood's actors, that it still contains open-ended dramatic structures, and has no definitive text demanding respect are features that invite directors to mount original, even eccentric productions for the immediate purposes of particular theatres and audiences. In fact, it is probably impossible to produce *The Hostage* without expanding the scenario to define and clarify certain characters and actions that the text leaves obscure. But this obscurity is only apparent; while Behan leaves the surface data of his dramatic ideas open to invention and improvisation, he is careful enough with his essential drama.

In order to see this drama clearly, we must look past the language, an uncertain element here, and, as though looking through the wrong end of a telescope, watch the action in broadest outline, the diverting detail of its "concatenated events" no longer visible. Paradoxically, the characters, miniaturized by the inverted optics, take on a larger meaning: they now suggest their archetypes and put us on the proper track toward understanding the structure that they represent. *The Hostage* invites us to look for a rhythm and shape built into the spectacle's scenario and residing on the far side of literature where a poetry unique to the theatre lies deeper than the words. This poetry arises from the kind of discoveries that Jerzy Grotowski's actors make as action bombards action, actor confronts character and himself to reveal new elements of myth and emotion in dramatic concert. Ludwik Flaszen writing on Grotowski says, "Theatre starts where the word is not sufficient." Behan's theatre springs from such beginnings, and in *The Hostage* the playwright develops a heroic rhythm not very different from the *tragic rhythm* that Francis Fergusson describes in his *The Idea of a Theater* as the essential of tragic action.

Gordon M. Wickstrom. *ETJ*. Dec., 1970,
p. 406

The success of *The Hostage* in the late fifties was, unarguably, the worst thing that ever happened to Brendan Behan. When it was revived last week by Theatre Workshop at the Theatre Royal, Stratford-atte-Bow, I sat there . . . moping fractiously about this, rather than worrying over the question of how well or ill the fourteen-year-old work fitted the contemporary Irish situation. There is food though for thought on that point in a play that deals—when it is eventually pinned down to deal with anything at all—with the capture of a young Cockney soldier by I.R.A. men who hold him in a Dublin lodging-cum-bawdy house, as hostage for the life of one of their own men condemned to death in Belfast for shooting a policeman. But seeing this play it was Behan's tragedy—or, rather, the macabre comedy in which his life dissolved—and the loss to us of his ebullient talent that haunted the mind; for *The Hostage* was, quite simply, the death of him.

Earlier, in 1956, he had written himself into theatrical history with the exuberant eloquence of *The Quare Fellow:* the Irish, it could be seen from this moving of "wild laughter in the throat of death" (the play is a ribald comedy set in a prison on the eve of an execution), had at last another dramatist to tread in the footsteps of her great men who had enriched "English" dramatic literature from Farquhar, Sheridan and Goldsmith to Synge, Shaw and O'Casey. . . .

I've no idea how he might have revised [*The Hostage*] had he been able to look soberly upon it and the Irish scene of 1972, and it may be a shade pertinent to assume that he would go along with the casual, half-baked up-dating of [Joan] Littlewood's present revival. It might, perhaps, have occurred to him that there is more to that kind of revision than merely dropping a few contemporary names into the dialogue, and that if you're going to have characters airing their memories of the Easter Rising, it would be sensible to have them looking nearer seventy than forty. He might even have thought, as an unconquerably humane man, that his perceptive ironies and jolly jokes about I.R.A. bungling, valid enough in his original context, were not altogether apposite to 1972.

Kenneth Hurren. Spec. June 10, 1972, p. 903

BELLOC, HILAIRE (1870–1953)

[Belloc] was also a poet, a true poet, but one who, if only because of the smallness of his output, could not be claimed as a major poet. In his noble poem—*Heroic Poem in Praise of Wine* he revealed new qualities of strength and dignity in the heroic couplet. Many of his shorter poems will keep their place in the anthologies. It was strange that while he wrote his prose swiftly and in white heat, he lingered over his poetry, which he retouched, polished and corrected. He felt that in his poetry he was working in marble or bronze or hard wood: it has about it the quality of endurance. He himself looked primarily to his verse, which he never called poetry, for his survival as a writer.

His comic verse was chiefly written when he came down from Oxford and was the writing that first made him known. These pieces were written with such precision of metre, such elegance, such wit and point that in their own exclusive genre they are classics. Whatever about his serious verse, this comic verse seems destined to live. It would surely be one of the ironies of literary fortune if those *jeux d'esprit* dashed off by an undergraduate, would outlive the vast output of a lifetime of serious, dedicated activity. Belloc himself would be the first to smile grimly at such a verdict of posterity.

It would be easy to dislike Belloc the man: easier still to reject a lot of the opinions and views he stood for and advocated so vigorously. As an author he will not be forgotten. Time will winnow the vast harvest of his pen and leave a considerable residue of literature that will abide. But there is the man as well as the author. It would be a serious injustice to fail to see that Belloc was not merely a great writer but was one of the great men of his time. His whole life was a struggle on behalf of good things. In his fight he threw in all he had. He risked everything. He could have reached to fame and fortune if he had swum with the current. He breasted it and tried to roll it back. Only a great man could have waged the fight that Belloc waged. Only a man of outstanding personality, of great integrity and courage, of strong granite convictions could have put up such an unequal fight. One can disagree with much of what he said, but in fairness one must recognize the greatness of the man. The widespread interest aroused by his centenary is a sign that his true dimensions are being recognized.

Hugh Kelly. Studies. Winter, 1970, pp. 402–3

Hilaire Belloc was essentially an extrovert, a lover of achievement. We have already noticed the meticulous care with which he analysed the structure of Froude's sentences. His verse was always restrained, classical, and most strict in obedience to its scheme of metre. He admired Ruth Pitter for her regularity and restraint of form. Readers of *The Cruise of the Nona* will know all about his love of the sea and of the boat that sailed on it—the strict rules for arranging the tackle which he laid down, though he confessed that he did not obey them. Some have regretted that he did not impose on his opinions a similar discipline of restraint to that which he imposed on his form. Such criticism, I think, misunderstands the contribution that Belloc had to make to English Catholic thought. It is true that we have now moved into an ecumenical age in which it is the fashion to speak with all courtesy of those who differ from us and in which we can with confidence look for fair-mindedness from them in return. All that is to be welcomed, but, if we feel inclined to criticise Belloc for not writing in that manner, it is necessary to remember what was the confidently Protestant English mentality of Victorian times, what was the language in which it was then the fashion to speak of Catholic beliefs, and we may then understand how it was perhaps necessary to challenge that world with a gesture of bravado in order to break down its self-confidence. If the modern Catholic writers can write to an audience from which they can confidently expect to receive fair play and can address it in moderate terms, it is largely because Belloc in his time breached for them the wall through which they can enter as perfect gentlemen and without a ruffle to the parting of their hair. . . .

He remains, if not considered a very great historian, at the least and beyond challenge a very great artist—great in spite of the fact that, French in so many other ways, he had in him no trace of that French reverence for the writer as the cher maître—an attitude which he always found as ridiculous as it was contemptible.

Christopher Hollis. Foreword to Hilaire
Belloc's Prefaces (Chicago, Loyola Univ. Pr.,
1971), pp. 24–25

BENNETT, ARNOLD (1867–1931)

Arnold Bennett's conventional reputation, his niche in the textbooks of literary history, is that he was "the English Realist." That, growing up in the seventies and eighties of the nineteenth century, he broke with the tradition of English fiction that runs down from Fielding through Dickens and Thackeray and expresses itself in kindliness, sentimentality, profusion of incident, and love of oddities. That he was the first, and remains the only, English novelist to have made a determined effort to cultivate in English soil the Continental, and primarily French, realistic novel with its matter-of-factness, its gray and truthful atmosphere, its disenchanted look at the realities of modern life. That he is the only English writer to have captured anything of the spirit of Balzac, Flaubert, and Zola.

I agree with this view. . . . Bennett's work is sufficiently robust and various to yield interesting crops to any kind of critical husbandry, and in fact one critic, Mr. James G. Hepburn, has devoted an interesting book, *The Art of Arnold Bennett* (1963), to putting forward an interpretation that ignores the "realistic" side and looks instead for symbolism. Mr. Hepburn manages to make this most prosaic of novelists seem very much like a poet, and the result is valuable because it emphasizes that there is no one "correct" approach to literary art, that a body of work imagined with sufficient solidity will look solid from any angle. Nevertheless, it is Bennett the realist who concerns me. Though his early interest in French realism and naturalism faded steadily, so that by 1910 his private touchstone for his own work was not Balzac or Flaubert but Dostoievsky, his mind took its permanent shape under the pressure of the universal drive toward realism which dominated the arts in every Western country.

John Wain. *Arnold Bennett* (N.Y., Columbia
Univ. Pr., 1967), pp. 3–4

"Do you want me to do my best and most serious work," [Bennett] asked a magazine editor, "or do you want me to adopt a popular standard?" He could and did do both, altering the level according to the demand, and to avoid competing with himself. (He was so copious a writer that he had to vary his work so as not to flood the market; in a letter to his agent he described himself aptly as "an engine for the production of fiction.") Bennett's own account of his work done during

1908 gives a fair example of the variety of things that he was able to do, almost simultaneously: *"Buried Alive,* ¾ of *The Old Wives' Tale, What the Public Wants, The Human Machine, Literary Taste: How to Form It*; about half a dozen short stories, including *A Matador in the Five Towns*; over 60 newspaper articles. Total words, 423,500." A popular novel, a serious novel, a play, a book of popular philosophy and one of literary advice, newspaper sketches and a serious story, articles for journals ranging from *T. P.'s Weekly*, a popular penny paper, to the intellectual-socialist *New Age*—all this came from one man, and in one year. And all of it was equally expressive of Bennett's nature: merchant and artist spoke antiphonally, and with equivalent authority.

It is this equivalence that gives Bennett his unique quality, both as a novelist and as a critic. It means that he brought to his work, and to his judgments of other men's work, two kinds of standards: the standards of the craftsman, who respects good work and does his own as well as he can; and the standards of the artist, who aspires to create a permanent and living work of the imagination, and measures all art by that aspiration. As a craftsman, Bennett acknowledged many levels of literary work—he could write sympathetically about Turgenev or about the latest romance with equal facility and careful judgment. He asked only that the work be well done of its kind, and that the writer use his tools well, whatever task he set them to. He deplored the misuse of language wherever he found it, in a novel by Virginia Woolf or an ad for the Piccadilly Hotel, and scolded the misusers in his articles. When a piece of work was well done, he praised it generously, though he was always careful to distinguish the literary artist from the merely popular writer; he never confused his standards.

Bennett's receptiveness to the more popular kinds of writing was more than a matter of commercial interest; he was naturally drawn to the mass audience, those semi-educated members of his own class whose hunger for literature was greater than their taste. "The public," he said, "is a great actuality, like war," and it was that great actuality that he sought to reach. He addressed his "pocket philosophies" to those readers, explaining how to gain mental efficiency, how to develop literary taste, how to live with a wife; he addressed reviews and articles to them through their penny papers; but he also wrote novels for them. He believed, he said, in the democratization of art—that a gifted writer could reach this public, and remain an artist.

Samuel Hynes. Intro. to *The Author's Craft, and Other Critical Writings of Arnold Bennett* (Lincoln, Univ. of Nebraska Pr., 1968), pp. xii–xiii

Why should it matter what Arnold Bennett happened to say about the politics, industry, home life, culture, or religion of his times? For generations writers had been recording the shortcomings of society. What could Bennett present that had not been put wittily by Swift or Fielding, or more recently by Thackeray, or with moral indignation by Dickens, or with sober reflection by George Eliot, Mrs. Gaskell, and innumerable journalists? If one is looking only for generic matters, the answer is "little enough." If one asks whether Bennett studied his predecessors before launching upon his own panoramic depiction, the answer, again, is "Not very much." He knew them, of course; two or three times, for example, he mentions *A Tale of a Tub*, and, despite his professed dislike for Dickens, he is now and then almost Dickensian. But the only author whom he seems to have valued highly for his representation of the social scene was Balzac, and there is a vast difference between Bennett's subjects and those of his French master.

Consequently we find him traversing afresh old pathways without benefiting much from the travelogues of his predecessors. He attacks hypocrisy, cultural sterility, and wrongheadedness as if they had never been assaulted before. Just the same, there is a difference. The ancient ills were still abroad in the 1890's and early 1900's, but their avatars wore new clothing. More important, man's perspectives had changed. In Bennett we find a point of view that is transitional, inclining decidedly toward the very modern. When they treat of the same topics, such as the position of women, he is in accord with Meredith and Thomas Hardy; but even then his women's problems are somewhat altered from those of an Aminta Ormont or a Sue Bridehead.

As for his originality among his contemporaries—here we have to deal mainly with Galsworthy and Wells and with the journals and newspapers of the time. It is impossible to say when Bennett is pioneering and when he is developing a hint which he has come across somewhere. What we can do is ascertain the convictions which he came to hold and often to emphasize. In so doing we get an insight into the life of the times as it appeared to one sensitive contemporary mind.

Walter F. Wright. *Arnold Bennett: Romantic Realist* (Lincoln, Univ. of Nebraska Pr., 1971), pp. 32–33

● **BERGER, JOHN (1926–   )**

John Berger's book [*Permanent Red*] is a selection of his essays and reviews published in the *New Statesman* over the past ten years.

During this period I have been repeatedly maddened by the author because, while he has tried to say something important and has seemed to judge painters from some fixed premises, these assumptions have never been made explicit, neither have they been argued for. While the critic who is a connoisseur, an apologist, an expounder or an explorer of art need not justify his assumptions, clearly a critic who proceeds as Berger does must do this. Therefore, I had looked forward to this book in the hope that, taken together, and with a preface, these occasional pieces would have demonstrated their own logic and assumption; but they hardly do this. The crucial passages are the definitions of realism, content and formalism at the end, the section on drawing and who is an artist near the beginning, and especially pages 15–18 of the Introduction.

He proposes a single criterion for judging a work of art, "Does this work help men to know and claim their social rights?"; but when he comes to interpret this, he does so in terms that could apply to any picture. "A valid work of art promises in some way or another the possibility of an improvement . . . it is not the subject, it is the artist's way of looking at the subject." He defines Realism in such general terms as to include almost any original painter whose work is not completely abstract. In short his criteria are so vague that it would be possible to fit any painter to them from Munnings to Pollock. It is not surprising, therefore, that his application of them appears quite arbitrary. It would be impossible to deduce from these general assumptions which painters he would prefer. It would not be difficult, however, to guess from the feelings which underlie them. He is a kind of humanist (Marx is described on the jacket as the man who put man first!) and rationalist with a proletarian bias but a clearly middle-class turn of mind, so that the little patches of Marxism seem out of place in the generally humanistic trend of the book.

He dislikes painting which deals in things; though a humanist, he attaches no value to the unconscious and sees no meaning in what people do, only what they look like. Most strikingly of all he despises the kind of art that people actually want. . . .

Nevertheless, this is a book well worth reading, mainly for its brilliant descriptions of painting and sculpture; but also because it is good to read strong opinions clearly expressed. It remains literature and its author is, I feel, the Ruskin of our time, rather than a true critic.

Michael Compton. CR. Jan., 1961, pp. 50–51

The poetic novel has always been with us, but generally in the six-penny barrow. So the new wave of as-it-were-poetic novels was careful to keep its poetry decent. Atmosphere was the thing: a thing quite distinct from smell. But nothing happened: or if it did, the author strove to hide the fact. . . .

Novels of this kind aim to enjoy the best of both worlds without paying the admission fee to either. They often have titles which sound symbolic but turn out to be literal. Like *The Foot of Clive*. "Six men lie in their beds in the foot of Clive Ward, in a general hospital." But—while his descriptions are the only effortless thing in this book, and a lot of derivative technique is put to little purpose, and nothing really happens—Mr. Berger is no part of this new wave of contrived vagueness. Convictions break through (I wish they had broken through more often), the smell of humanity disturbs the literary atmospherics and, though the blurb's mention of Mr. Berger's "belief in man's potential for change" has a nice frankness which the novel largely manages to avoid, the book does have some meaning.

We watch Mr. Berger tackling a hard job: trying to be real, not merely documentary, to suggest more than he says, but to steer clear of portentousness. He often goes very wrong. In, for instance, "tableaux" reminiscent of those old German films which send us back to Hollywood with a new appreciation. And in a curious kind of bestiary, which seemed to me the sauce to an entirely different dish. More serious—as it could hardly help but be—is that the literal and the symbolic seem barely to have been introduced to each other. Sometimes the one, sometimes the other, makes away like a very large can with a very small dog tied to its tail. Yet the sort of writing which a novelist ought to be producing keeps turning up: like the old man who "maintains that money is always a temptation. He says this as though he has known all the temptations since they were little children." Mr. Berger knows what the problems are, and clearly he isn't going to be satisfied with any easy option, now or later.

D. J. Enright. NS. March 16, 1962, pp. 382–83

Corker's Freedom is basically a series of suburban interior monologues in which each character is given free rein to voice his innermost thoughts. Corker himself, the elderly proprietor of an employment agency, has decided to leave his bullying sister and set up house on the premises. John Berger charts the momentous day on which the bid for freedom is made. We follow Corker as he interviews clients, chats to Alec his clerk (plotting his own more carnal path to freedom), indulges in reveries, moves furniture, and gives a lantern lecture at the local church hall. This is a fascinating novel, technically tedious with its interminable use of an explanatory thought-stream in which nothing is left unstated. It is, nevertheless, an infinitely more interesting exploration of the imprisoned psyche than Mr. Berger's last novel, *The Foot of Clive*. At least one relationship—Corker and his clerk—is developed with an insight previously lacking. Here is a writer of honesty and power whose ideas tend to proliferate to such an extent that the solidity of the main design becomes obscured. I hope that he will again attempt to fight the battle of inarticulate man in a story richly complex.

Maggie Ross. *List*. March 26, 1964, p. 529

In John Berger's excellent and fascinating new novel *G.*, "a novel on the theme of Don Juan," dedicated to "Anya and her sisters in Women's Liberation," there appears not the sexual coup-counter of the Freudians, but the Don Juan who captured the European imagination for more than 200 years—Tirso de Molina's Don Juan, Molière's Don Juan, Mozart's Don Giovanni, Byron's Don Juan—the symbol of eternal freedom, the eternal rebel against God, against nature, against society, against culture, in the name of a world in which the only complex and authentic elaborations of identity and relation are made sexually. . . .

Part of the power and fascination of *G.* comes from this extraordinary mixture of historical detail and sexual meditation—for at the intersection of *G.* and history is Berger's attitude toward heroism. *G.* is neither the public romantic Garibaldi, who galvanizes an entire people, nor is he a private romantic like his friend Chavez, who in 1910 won a prize for being the first man to fly over the Alps. . . .

G. belongs . . . to the tradition of George Eliot, Tolstoy, D. H. Lawrence and Norman Mailer, the tradition of fallible wisdom, rich, nagging and unfinished. To read *G.* is to find again a rich commitment to the resources and possibilities of the genre—and a writer one demands to know more about. Not to sit at the feet of his aphorisms or unravel the tangles of his allusions, but to explore more fully an intriguing and powerful mind and talent.

Leo Braudy. *NYT*. Sept. 10, 1972, pp. 5, 18

G. seems to me a fascinating work which, for all my admiration, I may well still be underestimating. It is one of the few serious attempts of our time to do for the novel what Brecht did for drama to reshape it in the light of 20th-century experience and theory other than the purely subjective or self-analytical. Since most of us have become more or less incapable of responding to any art which is *not* so based, *G.* isn't an easy book to deal with. To get on to the right track Thomas Mann is no doubt a help, but one might also profitably go back to the early Dos Passos novels.

Dos Passos, like almost all 20th-century American novelists, seems to have been ruined by a demon of sentimentality which I suppose is linked, culturally, with a long standing Anglo-Saxon contempt for any kind of systematized thinking. But in *USA* he was trying to tackle some of the problems Berger is faced with in *G.*, though the latter is an intensely European book. Dos Passos managed to achieve what perhaps Berger doesn't, an immediate impact at once appreciable by an audience reared in a quite different tradition. But he achieved it at the expense of undermining the very aims of objectivity and demystification which one part of him was seeking. Berger is infinitely more conscious of what he is up to and what it implies in terms of art. It is possible, perhaps, to feel that he is *too* self-conscious and that this costs him an element, not so much of human complexity (he gets that all right) as of human warmth. But maybe such a reaction is itself part of the imprecision of feeling he is fighting. Fifteen years ago I'd have suppressed the doubt: now it seems important not to. But, emphatically, within the context of saluting a fine, humane and challenging book.

Arnold Kettle. *NR*. Oct. 7, 1972, p. 31

BETJEMAN, JOHN (1906–   )

In Betjeman's poetry we do find, in the decades since Hardy died, something approaching the rigidity and intricacy of Hardy's metrical procedures. If the particular model in some of Betjeman's poems is Kipling rather than Hardy, this does not alter our sense that in any case the forms are inappropriate to the historical circumstances in which the poet is using them, and indeed that Betjeman is in many instances attracted to them for just this reason; in other words, that there is an air of antiquarianism and connoisseurship which hangs heavily around many of Betjeman's poems which are most expert and intricate as metrical constructions.

Thus, I find Betjeman most successful and most moving when his writing least reminds me of anything one might find in Hardy or Kipling or another poet of their generation. This holds true even when the master that we hear Betjeman's poem allude to is a poet of an earlier generation yet, for instance Tennyson. The effect is more valuable still when Betjeman has asserted his independence of Hardy not just in his verse forms but also in what he chooses to say; for instance, when he is as straightforwardly and unaffectedly Christian as Hardy is atheist. One of Betjeman's most touching and valuable poems is one that qualifies on both these counts, "Sunday Afternoon Service in St. Enodoc's Church, Cornwall."

Donald Davie. Thomas Hardy and British
Poetry (N.Y., Oxford Univ. Pr., 1972), p. 106

Among his fellow poets, [Betjeman] is an enigma and an irrelevance, but he stands so far apart from them that it is almost meaningless to discuss him in terms of the disregarded world of poetic movements, of obscure, tortured essays in self-exploration which pass for poetry in the universities and the Arts Council award committees. He appears to have missed the modernist cul-de-sac almost entirely, and writes in the tradition of Chesterton, Brooke and the World War I poets, having skipped an entire generation—or, in their own self-important reckoning, about three generations—of British poets.

The average term of the 16 Poet Laureates who have preceded him has been slightly over 19 years—poets, unlike other artists, are remarkable for their longevity. Betjeman confesses to being haunted by a terror of death, but he has little to fear on present showing. Already, he has contributed four or five poems to that undefinable and extremely limited anthology which every educated Englishman carries in his memory—more than any of his predecessors since Lord Tennyson. . . .

Every time the laureateship falls vacant, a phony Great Debate starts on whether it is worth continuing at all. On Tennyson's death it was proposed that it should fall into abeyance as a mark of reverence to our greatest national poet since Shakespeare. On the death of Robert Bridges, there were those who suggested that it had outlived its original purpose. On Masefield's death, they pointed out that nobody read the modern poets, and Betjeman was too much disliked by the poetry establishment, dominated then as now by the modern movement, to be acceptable. On Day-Lewis's death, those who feared that they were not going to be appointed criticized the whole idea of comparative excellence among poets, reducing the poetic impulse to some sort of meat-market auction.

Sir John Betjeman is the perfect answer to all these criticisms. A quiet, modest, despairing man, who welcomes the honor as he would have welcomed a cricket cap, he is the only man who keeps poetry alive in England, saving it at the same time from the errors of populist mediocrity and the precious, self-regarding obscurantism of the reigning oligarchs. His inability to produce anything but rubbish to commemorate a rubbishy event is a perfect commentary on the times and a perfect justification for the appointment. Long may he reign.

Auberon Waugh. NYTm. Jan. 6, 1974, p. 26

BLUNDEN, EDMUND (1896–1974)

Mr. Blunden's reputation as a poet is, today, not unlike the reputation of Robert Graves twenty or thirty years ago, when all lovers of poetry bought Mr. Graves's new volumes; reviewers praised them; but the poet seemed not able to attract the writers of learned articles or academic monographs. There is now a sizable Graves industry, and Mr. Francis Warner, who has chosen the poems in this pamphlet [*Eleven Poems*], is at work on a full-length study of Mr. Blunden's poetry. Mr. Blunden may, like Mr. Graves or Robert Frost, in the end prove just as attractive to close critics as such poets as Ezra Pound, say, or T. S. Eliot. Like Mr. Graves, Mr. Blunden obviously finds verse composition pleasant and sometimes, perhaps, dangerously easy. Many of these poems were written after a hard day's work of classes and committees in Hongkong when Mr. Blunden was Professor of English there. They are on the whole slight and occasional. The apparently slight may, in this poet's work, have a memorable quality. . . .

War and its griefs are never far from Mr. Blunden's imagination; they have something to do with the cherishing sadness with which he salutes beauty as in "L.C." or a little poem about the song of the golden oriole or one about "three graces under dark green boughs" in the Woman's Christian College at Tokyo.

TLS. March 31, 1966, p. 264

Blunden sometimes writes in deliberate *pastiche* of a late Augustan or early Romantic diction, but the felicity here comes from a more general sense of being soaked in the older English poetry. Blunden, in an interview, rightly insisted on his *skill* as his main obvious qualification for the Professorship. He has written a number of unsuccessful or only fragmentarily successful poems and, like most English poets, he is more likely to be very successful in fairly short than in fairly long poems; the ruminative tendency, which he inherits from the Romantics, is dangerous in long poems. Still, as Lord Acton suggested, we should judge poets and artists always at their best, just as we should judge men of action always at their worst. A good writer's failures harm nobody but himself.

Blunden's great long poem, though it is written in prose, is *Undertones of War*. The books with which one naturally compares it are Sassoon's *Memoirs of an Infantry Officer* and Graves's *Good-Bye to All That*. Blunden is not a natural story-teller, as Graves is; nor has he, like Sassoon, that compulsive recall of total social situations which makes for the great memoir. He has something of that incuriosity about other people, as distinguished from the impact which they make on him at a particular moment, that separates the poet from the novelist. The "place" of *Undertones of War* is not really Flanders or the trenches, but the poet's mind and that mind shrinks from displaying in detail the whole brutality of war.

G. S. Fraser. L. April, 1966, p. 82

Blunden is distinguished for his quiet, pastoral poetry and for his scholarship in the field of literary criticism. Because the themes of his poems have centered on an idyllic Nature, he has often been linked with the "Georgian group" of poets. Blunden's "retreat" from the ugliness of the modern world into the shade of 18th and 19th century rural grace has occasioned criticism from those who admire his intelligence and sympathy but wish for a stronger commitment to present realities. Thus the scholar-poet found himself attacked by poets of the Left in the 1930s and 1940s. Blunden, however, has never faltered in his celebration of the joys of childhood in an English countryside and man's noble qualities in a difficult world.

Blunden's talent was recognized quickly. Following his early volumes of poetry, his fame was established with the publication of *The Waggoner* (1920) and *The Shepherd* (1922). . . . His greatest popularity was achieved by *Undertones of War* (1928), a reminiscence of World War I that included several of Blunden's war poems. Blunden's later poetry—particularly *Shells by a Stream* (1944) and *After the Bombing* (1949)—convey his faith in the joy of beauty as a means of personal survival. . . .

The romantic period seems Blunden's favorite age; in addition to his work on John Clare, he has written biographies of and commentaries on John Keats, Charles Lamb, and Leigh Hunt. *Shelley—A Life Story* (1946) is one of Blunden's most popular successes.

Martin Tucker. In Encyclopedia of World
Literature in the 20th Century
(N.Y., Ungar, 1967), pp. 146–47

● BOLT, ROBERT (1925–   )

Robert Bolt's *A Man for All Seasons* . . . is one of the finest achievements of the modern theatre, and one of the great dramas of selfhood
of all time. *A Man for All Seasons* is a history play dealing with the life
of the famous sixteenth-century statesman and churchman, Sir Thomas
More. But like all great history plays, it is more about the time *in* which
it is written than the time *about* which it is written.

Bolt sees all too clearly the effects collectivism have had upon the
individual. In his preface he describes how in our time we have lost all
conception of ourselves as individual men, and as a result we have
increasingly come to see ourselves in the third person. As this happens
we are less and less able to deal with life's psychic, social, and spiritual
collisions. Thomas More does not see himself in this way; he is "a man
with an adamantine sense of his own self. He knew where he began and
left off," and the action of the play is best described as a series of collisions between More and a group of powerful and able men who would
have him deny his selfhood to serve the wishes of his king. . . .

Sir Thomas More did not believe the natural end of man was
martyrdom, and as the forces of the opposition began closing in on him,
this end was not temptation for him. . . . The law . . . was his defense.
. . . Bolt has no illusions about the sufficiency of human law, but he
sees it as the only defense man can create to fight against the forces of
evil. . . . Ultimately, because men and their laws are corruptible, More
cannot escape that fatal web that has ensnared him; but he dies knowing that his soul is his own, and "a man's soul is his self." He died, as
he lived, with full consciousness and pure respect for his own selfhood
and the selfhood of all men.

Robert W. Corrigan. Intro. to *The New Theatre
of Europe* (N.Y., Dell, 1962), pp. 27–28, 30

Robert Bolt tries to sermonise in *The Thwarting of Baron Bolligrew*
and, though it's interesting to examine the muddle he gets into, I'm
glad the son I took was too young to be confused: the play's intended
for an older-age group, but in fact it's quite suitable for a four-year-old
boy (little girls don't care for all-male shows). Bolt seems to take the
gentleman myth more seriously than wee, girding Barrie. Sebastian
Shaw, once again a dear old sexless knight, sobs like the Walrus when
he kills baby dragons, spouts pacifism and practises self-defence. He

does it charmingly, but my son wanted "the killing man" to quell him. Not cruel, he knows perfectly well these are just people dressed up. . . .

This is a classy show: the dragon and the fights are off-stage and the sets are like clean Gatt and Abbatt toys. Many children will prefer the scruffy, detailed muddle of *Peter Pan*, with the fine flights, and the swordplay and crocodile they're allowed to see.

D. A. N. Jones. *NS*. Jan. 6, 1967, p. 22

A striking example of the coincidence of opposites has been created by Robert Bolt in his play, *A Man for All Seasons*. The crude stagehand dressed in satanic black and called the "Common Man" is an exact shadow of Thomas More, the saint-protagonist. More and the Common Man, who at first sight seem so irreconcilable, are two sides of an equation which, as far as I know, has not been observed by critics. . . .

The theme of recognition in *A Man for All Seasons* has further implications if we consider Bolt's acknowledged debt to Bertolt Brecht's theatre of alienation. . . . In this genre the audience is reminded by startling contrivance of its distance from the action. It watches from the outside, deprived of involvement with the players. The use of an actor like the Common Man, who addresses the audience and comments on the action, is a typical alienation device. But Bolt says quite plainly in the Preface that the Common man is meant to draw the audience *into* the play by addressing it "in character." What Bolt is preferring to alienation is *recognition*. He challenges the audience with the ancient "know thyself."

Anselm Atkins. *MD*. Sept. 1967, pp. 182, 187

The Flowering Cherry—an ironic title, since Jim's orchard never bloomed, just as he himself never matured in any meaningful sense—is an honest, well-written drama on a significant theme, despite the fact that this theme is approached through a negative character. It suffers most in an inevitable comparison with *Death of a Salesman*, which is an altogether more artistically mature drama. Miller's Willy Loman is a more universal symbol of a dreamer and his inability to make his dream come true. Both Willy and Jim look back on earlier, better times; both long for some contact with nature; both have a knack with clients; both have wives who defend them to children who are unsympathetic while having some of their father's weaknesses; both are liars and dreamers. Willy is the more moving and meaningful character because his condition implies a criticism of the society which helped to cultivate in him the dreams of material success based on dishonesty and immorality. Poor Willy had all the wrong dreams and went about attaining them in the wrong way. There is nothing wrong with Jim

Cherry's dream, nor the way he might have attained it. There is only something wrong with Cherry, and finally he stands for no more than the dreamer he is.

The Tiger and the Horse . . . was produced in London in August, 1960, only a few weeks after the presentation there of *A Man for All Seasons*. In this work, the themes of commitment and selfhood do not remain in the background. They are, in fact, so much insisted on that the drama begins to seem "preachy," perhaps because it is the most personal treatment of a problem Bolt is much concerned with, nuclear disarmament. Thus, his characters are interesting as people, but they are first of all mouthpieces for the dramatist, more so than in any of his other plays. Bolt himself admits that he made the characters "unnaturally articulate and unnaturally aware of what they 'stood for.' " The themes of selfhood and commitment here relate first and specifically to a stand on nuclear disarmament and only secondly to a more universal dilemma of man's search for integrity.

Gene A. Barnett. *The Dalhousie Review*.
Spring, 1968, pp. 17–18

Ten years after *A Man for All Seasons*, Robert Bolt returns to the task of staging Tudor history with a study of Elizabeth and Mary Queen of Scots [*Vivat! Vivat Regina!*]: a theme with obvious attractions and obvious limitations. There is no stretch of the English past with greater popular theatrical appeal, but it is so engrained that it curtails the dramatist's freedom of manoeuvre.

Mr. Bolt is no iconoclast and in general he upholds the legend in orthodox patriotic terms, even changing his original title from *Remarkable Women* to one that focuses the main attention on Elizabeth. History, as he shows it, is not even the "bastardized Brecht" of *A Man for All Seasons*: it is a parade of famous names with the monarchs at the head of the procession. We are to take personal interest in them because they were born to greatness: saints or villains, their lives count for more than that of the common man. Given the two figures in question here, it is still possible to get away with this approach.

The play, in fact, is an immensely skilful piece of cosmetic surgery: adding the common touch and the freeflowing action of epic theatre, while leaving the assumptions of heroic costume drama untouched. You get an idea of the approach from the opening scene showing the French court shivering with cold under their rich formal dress.

Besides its display of splendidly animated history in the courts of France, Scotland and England, the play's purpose is to draw a detailed contrast between the two Queens: the virgin, and (as Knox calls her) the whore. . . . The play is a study of two forms of imprisonment but its treatment of the two Queens leaves no doubt of where Bolt's main interest lies. Where Mary views Elizabeth simply as a political rival, Elizabeth views Mary as an alter ego pursuing the life which she has stifled in herself. "I think," says Cecil, "our Queen sees Mary in the mirror."

Irving Wardle. TL. May 21, 1970, p. 11

● BOND, EDWARD (1934–   )

What the majority has refused to see in this case (the majority of critics, that is—the second-night audience, with whom weeklies were invited, listened intently and applauded vehemently) is that *Saved* is a play about poverty in Britain now. True, it's difficult for most news-papers to recognize such poverty. Haven't they established that the poor are no longer with us, except for the "new poor," ground by taxes to the point where they must skimp to educate their children privately, deprived now even of their expense-account lunches? . . . Mr. Bond is out to rub noses in the fact that the real new poor are the old poor plus television, sinking deeper in a form of poverty we do not yet recognize—poverty of culture. . . .

It is also, of course, the notorious scene in which five tittering South London youths torment Pam's baby to death in its pram. This runs slightly over five minutes out of some 160: it is not the reason for the play; the play is the reason for the scene. "Sooner murder an infant in its cradle," the programme quotes Blake, "than nurse unacted desires." The rest of *Saved* is about all the frustrations which explode in that act of savagery, the slow strangling of lives for which it is an inarticulate revenge. They are strangled literally in a lack of concepts, a lack of words: these people communicate only in blunt, concrete monosyllables. . . .

Ronald Bryden. NS. Nov. 12, 1965, p. 759

At least agreement seems to have been pretty general on *The Cresta Run* [by N. F. Simpson] but *Saved* has revived things a bit by being "controversial"—i.e., about two critics liked it, the rest hated it with quite extraordinary vehemence, and before we knew where we were it had spawned letters to the papers, television controversy, and even a Sunday-night teach-in presided over by Kenneth Tynan. Despite all of which, it is not really as curious, or radical, or alarming, or good, or bad, as everyone says. To capsulate, it is by *Infanticide in the House of*

Fred Ginger out of *Say Nothing*: a pleasant, ordinary young man goes to bed with an apparently pleasant, ordinary young woman, moves into her home as lodger, and rapidly finds that he has walked into a madhouse. . . .

Perhaps what the play needs, in fact, is not less violence but more, some sort of real sadistic kick which might urge us, however shamefacedly, to identify with these characters and share their emotions instead of coolly watching the actors going through the motions of violence. . . . It is in the scenes of gloomily obsessive life that Mr. Bond shows, intermittently as yet, some real quality as a writer, and it would be a pity if all the fuss about the weaker sections of his play were to divert him from the areas where his genuine talent lies.

John Russell Taylor. *PP*. Jan., 1966, pp. 20, 22

[Bond], I take it, is not a collectively-minded Left-Winger . . . but chiefly an anarchistic individualist in a state of almost complete despair about the modern world in all its aspects: politics, education, industrialism, commercial entertainment, etc. . . . In view of this, it is a little surprising that Mr. Bond should have chosen to give aesthetic expression to his concern by "reworking" Shakespeare's *Lear*. . . . The Shakespearian play deals with the eternal evil of human nature in an elemental, relatively primitive society, not corrupted at all by education, industrialism, or commercial entertainment. I heard Mr. Bond being condescending about Shakespeare on television, because, he said, Shakespeare is reconciled to things in the end. This is like Shaw maintaining that Shakespeare "onions the handkerchief." . . . Mr. Bond, I suspect, objects to [Shakespeare] because behind the anarchistic individualist is a half-revolutionary who would like to think that evil is produced by society and could be eliminated from the world by rearrangement. The difference between Shaw and Mr. Bond is that Shaw recoils from evil and will not contemplate it honestly (this is one of the factors that limit him, in spite of his exhilarating intelligence), whereas Mr. Bond is fascinated with evil in some of its forms, and indeed seems to me to have a strong sadistic streak. . . .

If the incidental sadism is removed, Mr. Bond's *Lear* is just a simplistic fable, set in some indefinite modern period. . . . The message is that successive regimes behave mistakenly in similar ways in order to preserve their authority, and that improvement can only come through a change of heart. We have heard this a thousand times in connection with the replacement of dynastic or class autocracies by totalitarian regimes, but the fable is too abstract to have much relevance to our problems in the confused and relatively tolerant world of the Western democracies. We are not bothered much at the moment by Lears,

Bodices and Cordelias, at least in internal policies, but rather by the complexities of industrial society. The horror that Mr. Bond presents us with—mangling, gouging out of eyes, goring of a ghost by pigs, etc.—is not symbolically representative of the evils of our society; it is a projection of individual cruelty, of which Mr. Bond is genuinely conscious. . . . Mr. Bond has a black vision of a humanity of ferocious beasts, far less redeemable than the characters in Shakespeare's *Lear*, and scarcely leavened at all by the presence of one or two decent people.

John Weightman. Enc. Dec., 1971, pp. 30–31

Bond has wanted to change society through his plays, for he is convinced that society today is in no way capable of driving out the animal in man; rather, it cultivates it. He welcomes every effect, however shocking, that will make man come to his senses. In *Early Morning* the regression to primitive life is even more marked [than in *Saved*]. The monster man takes the greatest pleasure in feeding on his own kind. His limbs continue to grow without stopping so that murder and death can go on for all eternity—a horrifying picture. *Narrow Road to the Deep North*, called a comedy by Bond, takes place in an imaginary Japan of the past. As in his previous plays, the main character is caught in a trap; he does not struggle to escape and instead commits suicide. Bond has used almost exclusively the lowest possible form of language in his dialogue. The directness and obscenity of this idiom is part of the shock effect that is his goal. . . .

Bond considers existing society primitive, dangerous, and corrupt. He calls himself an anarchist, because government is anticreative and only oriented toward law and order, and he, as artist, is searching for personal justice. The time has come to stop telling people that the few shall lead the many. Bond considers man's gravest danger the fact that he lives in a social order for which he is not biologically equipped. The human organism, for instance, is not suited for work in factories. This has led to the development of an aggressive society, in which things like hydrogen bombs exist. This situation is aggravated by the educational system. Bond equates schools with prisons: both serve, according to Bond, to create slaves, or at least people who have so adapted themselves to the prevailing forms of society that they will conform to it. He does not object to knowledge itself, only to the force-feeding of knowledge. By nature man is not violent; on the contrary, love is the natural condition in which man is born—the ability to love and be loved. Bond feels that this ability is being beaten out of man so that he can conform more willingly.

Horst W. Drescher. In World Literature since
1945 (N.Y., Ungar, 1973), pp. 117–18

BOWEN, ELIZABETH (1899–1973)

Elizabeth Bowen casts a warm cold eye. Though still alive, she comes down to us with a reputation already frozen: a conservative fallen among avant-gardists, another Jamesian, a British Edith Wharton. Even the honor she gets as a stylist is suspect. It suggests good house-keeping—picking up and arranging the pieces scattered by more headlong predecessors.

In actuality Miss Bowen is one of the few radical explorers in the recent novel. The part of her work that looks conservative really shows her recognition of change. By the time she found herself, in the middle thirties, the revolutionary positions of the previous age were no longer revolutionary. Yet because they still seemed so to many, an elite could adopt them as guides for living—and signs of an intellectual aristocracy. Goals that in writers of the twenties kept fairly separate ways now seemed combinable. Advanced people could think of themselves as valuing deep and complex inner experience, like Proust, Mann, Virginia Woolf, and Joyce, while trying to achieve dramatic intensity, like Hemingway, Huxley, and Fitzgerald. But in practice these ideals were proving less compatible than in imagination. New tensions resulted, and produced their own poets.

Elizabeth Bowen is a born consolidator. She wants no less than a *smooth* mixture of all the best ingredients available. She feels the need not for new alternatives, but for harmonized ones. Virginia Woolf's heroines have soul, but can barely manage a dinner party; Elizabeth Bowen's assume that they have soul, but would not like living in the scatterbrained fashion of Mrs. Ramsay. They value competence and control too. The new novelist thus wants deep feeling to coalesce with style, drama, participation, and, unlike Waugh, will not settle for being half-ashamed of the effort. Ideally, the once revolutionary attitudes would become absorbed experience, enliveners of continuity rather than curious discoveries, domesticated carriers of vigorous hopes. But this intense wish for depth, liveliness, and safety meets within Miss Bowen a clarity about all the obstacles to its fulfilment—and the conflict makes her a novelist.

James Hall. *The Lunatic Giant in the Drawing
Room: The British and American Novel since
1930* (Bloomington, Indiana Univ. Pr.,
1968), pp. 17–18

Perhaps it is wrong to attempt to place authors too carefully—wrong . . . to try to sort them into first, second, third and fourth divisions. But even if wrong it is a natural desire, and I can think of few novelists who more arouse the desire and more successfully frustrate it than Elizabeth Bowen. What, after all, is she up to? Is she merely the highly elegant, dazzlingly intelligent star of the psychological thriller class, or is she a serious contender for a place in the great tradition? And what, anyway, would be the distinctions—of genre, of talent, of purpose?

Her new novel, *Eva Trout*, is certainly a most impressive book. It creates a world so engrossing, so fully imagined in its own terms, that when interrupted while in the middle of reading it I would look up, vaguely, no longer quite sure where I was. This kind of creation is in itself a rare gift: one shared by Iris Murdoch, who also shares some of Miss Bowen's other eccentricities. Their worlds, in fact, are not dissimilar: the background of *Eva Trout* is one of Gothic castles, vicarage gardens, expensive hotels and restaurants, feminine institutions, suicidal homosexual passions. . . .

The theme—corruption, wealth and innocence—is worthy of Henry James, whose name is indeed invoked by the writer herself. . . . As well as the theme, as an additional benefit, there are those marvelous passages of description, for which Elizabeth Bowen is so justly famous: the prose, always elegant even when—or perhaps most when —tortuous, achieves a number of effects that are breathtaking. . . . She is also witty: several of her puns are really most satisfying. . . .

With all these qualities, it would seem grudging to complain. And yet finally one must, because there is something about the book that cheats the very seriousness with which the reader wishes to take it. The ending is symptomatic. It is crude, melodramatic, improbable—despite the careful plotting of the revolver and the constant premonitions of violent death—and it is at once facile and contrived. Worst of all, it makes one look back through the book at things which had seemed solid, and question their substance. . . .

Also, it is a pity that some of the characters should be so insubstantial. . . . Miss Bowen is magnificent when she writes about conspiracy, duplicity and ambiguity, and her achievement—despite her final cutting of the Gordian knot—is extremely impressive. But with the simple, with the world of common sense, she does not cope. Though perhaps in that (for good or for ill, see it as one may) she is merely the closer to Henry James.

Margaret Drabble. *List.* Feb. 13, 1969,
pp. 214, 216

The combination of a wit so accurate and a warmth so pervasive led to mistaken impressions [about Elizabeth Bowen]. It was hard to believe that these usually incompatible forces were held in such arresting suspension. She was wrongly thought of—as recently as two years ago in London—as "a woman's writer," all hearthrob and fuzz. If they'd read her, Congreve would have been shocked at the opinion and so would have Henry James. She belongs to the great tradition of English moral comedy going back to Jane Austen, stopping off at Henry James, with some of the aromas of Proust, a writer she greatly admired. She was incapable of dishonesty, though she may have written too many blurbs for unknown writers. She was more generous than can be imagined and had no sense of the "strategy" of literary careers or the dark scrimmage of "reputations." She had so much intrinsic power that I don't think the idea of acquiring any ever crossed her mind. In all, the matter of semblances never came up, so strikingly positive was her impression, so absolutely steady the aura around her, and so precise what she thought and what she had to say. . . .

I think she was one of the natural masters of English prose. I hope *Collected Impressions* will be reprinted, and in paperback. Anyone interested in writing should have it close by—the essay on Flaubert is worth the price of admission. A *Collected Stories* is long overdue— "Her Table Spread" might be used in every short story class to advantage. It does in 12 pages what a lot of writers never get around to doing at all. An early novel, *Friends and Relations*, since it's practically unknown, should be made available, and I think *To the North*, a small marvel, is still strangely unappreciated. That's true, too, of *A World of Love*, the fifth chapter of which I would recommend to anyone writing a novel. There will be a reassessment, naturally. It's high time.

Howard Moss. NYT. April 8, 1973, pp. 2–3

BRADBURY, MALCOLM (1932–   )

Malcolm Bradbury's first novel *Eating People Is Wrong* had a well-deserved success as a witty examination of the liberal conscience in a middle-aged professor at a provincial university. His new book [*Stepping Westward*], which attacks the same theme from a different angle, is just as entertaining, with some truly hilarious moments, and a lot of very sharp observation. This time the hero, James Walker, is a wilting provincial writer, thirtyish, going to fat . . . with three "promising" novels behind him and a yearning for spiritual revitalisation. Invited to be resident creative writer at Benedict Arnold University in the remote American west, he steels himself to seize the chance of a new vision. Much of the comedy of the book rises out of the hard job America has prodding open this inert, tweed-suited, non-car-driving limey into some semblance of assertion and commitment.

In one sense the attempt fails, since the hero returns home to his wife (whom in a heady moment he had contemplated divorcing) without having completed his year, but in another sense he turns the tables on America by mildly refusing to sign a loyalty oath and becoming the storm-centre of a controversy which delights his American sponsor, Professor Froelich. A fruitful clash of English and American liberalisms is what Froelich had hoped for and what the serious passages in the novel are concerned with: the former seems effete, non-committal, fuzzy-edged, personal, a "faith of unbelief," and the latter vigorous, public, outgoing, articulate and positive—or so his American friends would persuade Walker. Yet Walker's various defeats and insufficiencies as he shambles across the States . . . don't cancel a certain respect he rouses both in Froelich and in the reader. Anti-hero or not, he sometimes reminds us that what America claims to offer him for his rebirth is what Saul Bellow's Henderson had to leave America to find. Apart from the fact that too much time (a third of the novel) is spent getting the hero across the Atlantic, this is a fresh, stimulating, and very amusing book.

Edwin Morgan. NS. Aug. 6, 1965, p. 191

Professor Bradbury's book [The Social Context of Modern English Literature] seems best described as an experimental exploration of the literature-society relationship which tries, on the whole successfully, to render its unwieldy subject-matter manageable by selecting one paradigmatic "moment" within the field in question: the relation between those rapidly altering styles of belief, ideology, and social organization, dating roughly from 1870, which he terms "modernization," and the literary phenomenon known as Modernism. It is a packed, stimulating, and informative book moving with aplomb from provocatively intelligent literary generalization to illuminating local detail; but it is also an essentially empiricist work, in a field where the major problem seems, precisely, that of evolving a sufficiently rigorous method. . . .

There are some excellent insights into the treatment of the city and the machine in modern literature, and some acute analyses of the complex interweaving of the "modernist" trend with more settled and traditional literary forms in the twentieth century. The book ends with a series of analyses of the status of the writer in modern society, the climate and institutions of literary culture, the nature of the media, and of "high" and "mass" culture. All of this has a good deal to offer, but it offers it at the risk of a certain diffuseness, an over-readiness to cram everything in, which tends to displace attention from those aspects of the book's central thesis which remain problematical. . . .

Terry Eagleton. *RES*. May, 1972, pp. 245–46

BRAINE, JOHN (1922–   )

This readable novel [*Stay with Me Till Morning*] about adulteries among executives of the Yorkshire wool trade might, if it had appeared immediately after *Room at the Top*, have been mistaken for an ironic satire on provincial conservative values. The most desirable human condition is presented as "normality," with special reference to sexual behaviour. Oral intercourse is acceptable now, but a woman must not seem "whorish" or "butch," and a man must not seem "camp." These are negative demands. The positive values are property values. . . .

[It is a] drab tale in which the author explicitly condones his characters' mean ways and low standards in a spirit of perverse defensiveness. It is dedicated to Kingsley Amis, and it reads as though Mr. Braine were emulating Mr. Amis's effort in *Take a Girl Like You*—that attempt to stand up for "normal" attitudes, too easily despised and labelled philistine in the literary ambiance. But Mr. Braine's posture seems false, unnatural, as if he had deliberately thought up attitudes which most thoughtful people would consider illiberal, and then forced them upon his characters. It is hard to believe that these ordinary conservative provincials would be so obsessed with their antagonism to equality, cooperation and deviations from their social norm. They seem mere puppets, created to illustrate a defiantly perverse and negative thesis.

TLS. June 25, 1970, p. 679

England is hardly backward sexually, but the literary tradition is so much more firmly built in there that many literary conventions, in verse as well as prose, that have been bludgeoned to death here, are still thriving there. John Braine's new novel [*The View from Tower Hill*] is an instance of the kind of conventionality that has been howled out of New York publishing except in the real slickies—westerns, mysteries, soap operas. If you want to look serious about fiction among the big-city entrepreneurs now, you have to dislike the novel's mannerly past aggressively. . . . *The View from Tower Hill* presents us with a twenty-year saga of old-marrieds, together with the separate affairs the husband and wife are eventually driven to, with a grace and fullness of perception that will surely make many younger readers find it irrelevant.

Also it beats around the bush. The novel of manners tends to conceal, veil, subdue or at least postpone confrontations, franknesses (so, it should be added, does the life of manners). People do *not* always say all they think, but oddly, they are not necessarily turned into empty bourgeois automatons thereby; their comparative reticence may even enrich rather than impoverish them. At least John Braine operates on this assumption. He works to display the tension between the said and the unsaid, and to trace the progress of the unsaid *into* the said. We watch the awareness of marital woe grow in Clive and Robin; we see it finally burst out like the measles overnight; and then we watch the return to a sort of health. . . .

I don't know that I'd call Braine's novel well made in the old sense, but its whole being is certainly conditioned by old-time assumptions: a stable social and familial order, lives with inherited obligations and decorums. These preliminary assumptions are what separate Braine from vogue in the U.S. . . .

So, here is John Braine, who still does have, largely because he is not an American, a complicated and interesting problem in blasted old human relationships on the agenda for his novel. This is where he begins, and for my money where he begins gives him a big advantage over his American competitors.

Reed Whittemore. NR. Feb. 13, 1971, p. 25

John Braine's latest novel [*The Queen of a Distant Country*] has all the virtues of a typical John Braine novel—it is quite readable, it focuses on recognizable human beings, its prose is lucid and generally unpretentious. It is, in short, a craftsmanlike work as well as a sincere and human one. Curiously enough, however, the novel fails to impress the reader. It's the sort of book he can take or leave, for he feels that he has read it all before, long ago.

In a way, Braine reworks a few of the plot elements of his very successful first novel, *Room at the Top*. The narrator, a young man from a working-class background, this time wants to climb the literary ladder rather than the social one (he is, by the way, a much less calculating type than Joe Lampton of *Room*). As in *Room*, he forms an attachment with an older woman, but this time the relationship remains platonic. The woman, Miranda, a formerly important writer, adopts him as her protégé and hopes to guide him to literary success. Again as in *Room,* the young man temporarily forgets the woman to pursue a young, attractive girl, but this time the girl is lower-class, and the narrator is motivated by lust rather than by greed. Miranda and the narrator eventually part, and he goes on to become a professional writer. Later in life, he attempts to return to her, but he cannot bridge the emotional gap that now separates them.

The reader experiences déjà vu not only because the book is vaguely reminiscent of Braine's early novel, but also because the voice and the concerns of the narrator seem somewhat dated, lack urgency and originality. *Room at the Top* and books by Sillitoe, Wain, Amis, and Storey popularized, in the Fifties and early Sixties, the so-called "Angry Young Man," and for a while at least the reading public, the British reading public especially, was taken by this struggling, class-conscious hero. But that fascination passed (perhaps the Angry Young Man suffered from overexposure), and the novelists were forced to explore new territory. For some of them, there was no new territory to explore, and they floundered. Braine hasn't floundered, but he hasn't been able to entirely free himself of the tough, limited, so-I-unbuttoned-her-blouse, Joe Lampton sensibility which, at this point in literature, seems like the product of another age. . . .

In his recent books, Braine hasn't had very much to say. This was the case with *Tower Hill* and *The Crying Game,* and it's also the case with *Queen of a Distant Country.* Aside from its lack of complexity and resonance, and its annoying obligatory sex scenes, the new novel is not quite convincing. . . . One longs for the tightness and intensity that were the hallmarks of his best book, *The Jealous God.*

Ronald De Feo. *NatR.* June 8, 1973,
pp. 643–44

BROOKE, RUPERT (1887–1915)

When Brooke died it was not primarily the poet that his friends mourned. It was rather the sense that an outstanding personality and intellect had been extinguished. His poetic faculties might have increased in power or perhaps they would have waned with the growth of more critical and scholarly perceptions. His creativeness might have taken quite other turns, but we believed he would have left his mark in some unexpected way on the life of England. Nevertheless Brooke's poetry has been so widely and consistently read until the present time that it has reached the status of a national heritage, even though the artificially segregated period of "Georgian poetry" is now out of favour with the critics. It is therefore likely to be for some little time of real interest to a great many present and future readers, who will want to know something of the background of the writer.

Every poet's work can be better understood, apart from purely critical and literary "evaluation," if his circumstances in time and space can be appreciated. There can surely be no more direct way of finding this context than by reading the poet's letters written in a variety of moods to a number of friends, some deliberately and self-consciously posed, others unself-consciously poured out in a state of enthusiasm, excitement, depression, or emotional conflict. All these states of mind will be found in this selection of Brooke's letters, but judgment must be based on general impressions rather than on isolated passages. His love affairs sometimes led to much unhappiness, this being reflected in artless letters, which, by their very artlessness, show how false the "legend" was. Brooke was far from perfect, but the human imperfections, the goodness, the weaknesses and the strength composing the whole man make a more interesting and credible personality than the lay figure created by the myth.

Geoffrey Keynes. Preface to Geoffrey Keynes,
ed., *Letters of Rupert Brooke* (N.Y.,
Harcourt, Brace, 1968), pp. xiii–xiv

For all the enduring popularity of his poems, Rupert Brooke is at most a minor figure in English literature. Yet he has already attracted to himself a formidable body of biographical and critical attention, and a disproportionate amount of his own writing has been published. Why, then, it may be asked, another book of and about him? The short answer is that no writer, major or minor, has been so widely misjudged and misrepresented, not only by his denigrators but by many of those who would call themselves his friends. . . .

Brooke was from the first a deliberate poet. . . . Evidence of the hard work and an indication of his methods of composition may be found in a few surviving notebooks. . . .

It should not be adduced that Brooke depended always on literary stimuli for his poems: far from it. More often, as other notebooks show, they begin by his "collecting a few words, detaching lines from the ambient air." . . .

Above all, the poems are charged with a surrender—at times with a surprising fullness—that "individual and bewildering ghost," his personality. . . . He assumed, indeed, and with a disarming sincerity, that his own fortunes must be nearest his readers' hearts; we cannot read him with detachment. . . .

It is the chief value of Brooke's writing as a whole that it forms a living record of the man. It does not often take the reader beyond the shrines of the Penates. It is not for flights of fancy or for the deeper philosophic insights that we may read him; rather, for his sensitive response to a short but vivid life.

> Timothy Rogers. *Rupert Brooke* (Routledge
> & Kegan Paul, 1971), pp. 1, 180–81, 183, 190

BROOKE-ROSE, CHRISTINE (1923–   )

The jacket tells us that *Such*, Christine Brooke-Rose's new post-James Joycean novel, is about "A physicist turned psychiatrist for a university radio-astronomy unit." Certainly it's useful to know before one starts reading the book, because it's difficult to tell after. Through the stream of scientific "hithering thithering of," one glimpses Miss Brooke-Rose grappling with the theory that our individual natures are particulate —a theory arrived at by inference, I imagine, from the theory (which underlies Joycean writing) that our experience of living is particulate. As the latter theory is not borne out by experiment, it's understandable that she gets into difficulties with the former. However, it's possible that we're supposed to take it that "all is in the writing"—not in the content. On this level her stream of scientific terms used with an engagingly learned air in metaphor that doesn't figure, and simile that can't relate is fun, a sort of nonsense poetry. What seems to me the danger Miss Brooke-Rose may not have foreseen is that it asks to be taken as 110 per cent serious by people who fancy their chance as highbrows. It would be a sad and inappropriate fate for her, a clever and gifted artist, to find herself acclaimed their queen.

> William Cooper. *List*. Oct. 20, 1966, p. 583

Christine Brooke-Rose's *Between* makes an immediate appeal to the reviewer on two counts: its brevity and its remarkably pretty dust-jacket. The novel itself, a contribution to the French *nouveau roman* rather than to any English tradition, is the stream of consciousness of a simultaneous translator; flying hither and thither, seated in her aircraft as though in a church aisle, lying alone (a vicarious relief, I must say) in almost identical hotel bedrooms, attending gibberish conferences anent This and That, speaking, seeing, hearing a multitude of languages, her consciousness is recognisably of our time. You too, surely, have sat and said to yourself: "The label on the bottle says VICHY ETAT—Eau Minerale Naturelle." The point is that if this is not quite the sort of novel we are used to reading, it depicts very imaginatively the kind of life many people are perfectly used to living (not just the thousand simultaneous translators, but travellers of all sorts). It is almost, I suppose, a small bit of soc./psych., but what a difference from the usual: as if your story about the accountant were told by the accountant in the form of a tax-return.

Henry Tube. *Spec.* Nov. 15, 1968, p. 702

Miss Brooke-Rose [in *Go When You See the Green Man Walking*] is concerned with visual details, using the *nouveau roman* technique of repetitive, precise, objective descriptions, lists of contents (a fantasist spinster's trousseau for the girl-baby Messiah she believes she's chosen to bear) and the metronomic beat of incantatory phrases which suggest obsession—one of the most effective stories is "told" by the amputated foot of a model girl who's suffering phantom pain "related to a central excitatory state with emphasis on the internuncial pool of the spinal cord . . . afferent proprioceptive." . . .

Miss Muriel Spark's reputation was launched by a collection of stories: the wit, eccentricity and graceful virtuosity in this collection deserve to do as much to widen public appreciation of Miss Brooke-Rose.

TLS. Nov. 20, 1970, p. 1347

BROPHY, BRIGID (1929–   )

"People (even those who do not mean to be rude) often ask me whether my journalism interferes with my serious writing. As a matter of fact, my journalism *is* serious writing." Thus Brigid Brophy by way of foreword to her new collection of previously printed essays and reviews [*Don't Never Forget*], and I for one will call "Amen." For whatever else may be said of them every one of these pieces, which range from moral homilies of some length down to brief thriller-notices, is scrupulously and seriously written round a point which is of serious import—to Miss Brophy if nobody else. I am sorry that it is necessary to qualify in this fashion; but I have to say at once that, while most of these pages are as full of sweet reason as a honeycomb is full of honey, there are occasional passages (among them some of the most intense in the whole book) of a dottiness almost beyond belief.

There are, it seems, two hands at work here. One, let us say, is that of Brophy, an intelligent writer of clear and masculine prose, sensitive indeed to every shade of meaning and every twist of moral subtlety, but in the sum tough, incisive and direct; while the other hand is that of Brigid, a faddy and finicking prig. . . .

Taking a four-square eighteenth-century stance, Brophy deposes that what distinguishes man from the animals is his ability to adapt nature, that terrifying and incommoding old bore, to his own taste and convenience. Man makes light to banish nature's darkness; he tunnels under, flies over or even lays flat the mountains which nature has set up as barriers; he drains nature's pestiferous marshes, irrigates nature's dreary deserts, and sets up magnificent cities to which nature is admitted only in the form of seemly and disciplined parks. It is therefore ridiculous, Brophy goes on, to praise the "natural" man or to make a song and dance about the "natural" way of life. The triumph of man lies in his civilisation . . . and in his artificiality. . . .

Simon Raven. Spec. Nov. 25, 1966, p. 685

In its encyclopedic knowledge of Firbank's life and its unqualified admiration for his work, Brophy's book [*Prancing Novelist*] will be eagerly devoured by Firbankians. She has investigated every odd nook of his mind and fiction, and no detail of either is too trivial to escape a torrent of exegesis and speculation. But those not already committed to Firbank will hardly be encouraged to sample him by the tendentiousness and irresponsibility of much of this book. Nor will they be persuaded by the self-conscious, at times exasperatingly cute prose. The archness of language and design running throughout *Prancing Novelist* continually intrudes between the reader and Firbank, undermining the cause the book is trying to serve. All too often our attention is focused on Brophy's antics—leaving Firbank, I am afraid, bloated and alone, still obliged to pay his own publication costs.

Michael Rosenthal. NYT. July 22, 1973, p. 4

● BUNTING, BASIL (1900–   )

Mr. Bunting's verse has been inaccessible since the *Active Anthology* (1933) went out of print; after eighteen years there should be a few hundred people to be interested in the present collection [*Poems:*

1950]. What he has to offer that is not in the work of his elders doesn't depend on his having read different books, gone to a different school, and formed a preference for different women, adjectives, and cheeses. Neither Mr. Bunting's interest nor his readers' is focused on Mr. Bunting's insides. The reflection has preceded the poems, has preceded, as it were, the very mapping of the interests they articulate; the poem isn't a transcription of the poet's trying to think, nor a noise attending spiritual indigestion. . . .

It is probably the novelty of encountering verse not held together solely by a sense of the writer's personality that makes Bunting seem, at first, fragmentary. The reader brought up on the presently popular tradition of more or less dramatic introspection may need to be persuaded at some length that a thing is what it is, that anything honestly recorded has the incalculable value of honesty. . . .

Bunting's extreme concentration is not unconnected with an air of contrivance. Not that his verse is the null product of a will to turn out so many lines on a theme; it is the contrivance of a man who knows what it is he means to contrive. Word never suggests word, mood is never prolonged because a groove held it. On the other hand, one has only seldom the sense that—as with Pound or Yeats—the right words are miraculously presenting themselves instant by instant. This is only to say that Mr. Bunting isn't (and doesn't claim to be) a major poet. He has done a few things right; his superiors (whom at his best he isn't inferior to) did more things well, and weren't betrayed into publishing their attempts on subjects a little beyond their skill. Bunting's virtue is that he always knows what he wants to do; he does it so deliberately that one occasionally notices the hand reaching for the next tool. . . .

Mr. Bunting has learned from Pound, but gotten far beyond the early *Personae* at which most Poundlings stick. (His debt is rather to *Cathay* and *Propertius*.) He has learned from W. C. Williams, and been sufficiently original to dissociate the assimilable techniques from the highly personal (and hence, to the imitator, far more tempting) astringencies. He has learned techniques where others have borrowed voices. His defects (occasional strain after a contrast; rhythm bogging while attention pauses on lexicographic concision) depend on virtues. He is alive to much more than the things he has read about, or the commonplaces which assume a spurious uniqueness when they happen at length to *me*.

Of these 54 pages some 5 may or should enter the *corpus poeticum*; a way of saying that Bunting's subjects and treatment have an interest outlasting the area in which they were conceived.

Hugh Kenner. *Poetry*. Sept., 1951, pp. 361–65

Bunting's art . . . "aspires to a condition of music"—"accompanying tones of the words" that "are their own experience"—and in coming to *The Spoils* (1951) one sees time and again how the music achieved there was of the greatest possible transitional importance for the all-over musical structure of *Briggflatts*, published fourteen years later. In *The Spoils*, experience prepares the ground and music plays over against that ground. . . .

The music of *Briggflatts* lies not only in tones, rhyme, the articulation of syntax, but in the use throughout of recurrent motifs. . . . The music Bunting refers to for his imagery (Byrd, Monteverdi, "Schoenberg's maze") suggests voice against voice, line against line—madrigal and canon, not impressionistic sound painting. The achievement of the poem—and here one is reducing to abstraction all that is art and art's particulars—derives from the attempt to bring Then into as close a relation with Now as possible. The aligning of the two comes about by the central device of imitating "the condition of music." Then and Now are brought to bear upon each other as are the different voices in a madrigal. In the poem this cannot be done simultaneously; but, by juxtaposition, Now can be played over against Then as Then—summoned up by motif and left echoing in the mind—stands forth counterpoised rather than counterpointed, against the ensuing motif of Now. . . .

From the measured quantities of *Loquitur* through the more intricate rhyme and line of *The Spoils*, Bunting has come, in his late poetry, to a music that combines strength and delicacy in patternings that to the reader are a constant delight and that to the young poet should prove of intense and liberating technical interest. Not least among the poem's achievements is the way an erotic incident that could have been sentimental or, in the manner of some of the *Loquitur* poems, trivial has been made as real for the reader as for the poet, realised, as it is, with a novelistic specificness. We can completely accept, for the purpose of the poem, this valuation of it, which is a measure of how far Bunting has come since "the teashop girls" of his earlier verses.

Charles Tomlinson. *Agenda.* Autumn, 1966,
pp. 13–17

For years Basil Bunting was known to scholars of the modern movement and to Americans (often the same people) as the most unjustly neglected of Pound's epigoni. Now at last the full text of his poems [*Collected Poems*] is here and it is more welcome than the legend. It's fair to ask if this is the work of a major poet, but, before this, to look at Pound's influence on Bunting and even to try to establish the kind of poet Pound is himself. As Schoenberg forbade anyone to see modern music except as a consequence of his own existence, so Pound shaped twentieth-century poetry in English by his example. However, despite the stream of pilgrims to the silent shrine at Rapallo, Pound is not yet assimilated into the blood of poets writing today. Pound the opinionated, the village-explainer and, above all, the martyr is influential enough but this is not the Pound that counts. His days more than his works are what fire audiences. Bunting, perhaps uniquely, derives from the works. . . .

A great teacher passes on a lot of himself to a star pupil, so Bunting has Pound's eccentric subjective objective antimony. Each of the major poems in this book—"Villon," "The Well of Lycopolis," "The Spoils" and "Briggflatts"—is inhabited by the Bunting persona, a lecturer on history and society who is given to cryptic autobiographical sketches, a prophet who has read a lot but whose shaping principle is the sound of the voice, the organizational powers of the ear. Bunting says poetry, like music, is to be heard. But the two arts are constructed in different ways. The Bunting method of working to cadences leads to considerable obscurity, especially as his poems roam over wide tracts of references. "Briggflatts" is called an autobiography but needs its full quota of help from interviewing journalists if the reader is going to work out the story. It's also, to me, the least instinctive of his poems in its music. The sound is harsh and rushed, the close rhymes crowd the short lines into bristling sentences.

Peter Porter. *L*. June, 1969, pp. 76–77

Just as the modern poet can renew the past for the present by putting it in his poetry, so the works of the past can teach the modern poet techniques and ideas that are new to him in his situation in the modern world. Use of the literary tradition in poetry after the Eliot-Pound-Bunting manner is not just a question of reflecting the past. When Bunting does this by reproducing the tone of a typical Cino love lament, as in "Attis," the result can be clumsy. On the other hand, when another poet is a source of inspiration and a mainspring to thematic material, as in "Villon" or "Chomei at Toyama," the result is fruitful. Bunting learned much from other poets, both living and dead, and not least of these is the one he celebrates directly, Villon. Bunting learned from Villon directness and simplicity of expression. He may also have discovered—by comparing himself with Villon (and others, of course)—the sense of his own artistic inadequacy, a major theme of his poems. Also, Villon helped to show Bunting to be a poet of his own time, a "poète de la vie moderne" in Baudelaire's sense of the term, open to all kinds of experience (not just literature) as material for poetry.

Art that draws on literary sources of the past shows at least a faith in, if not the accomplishment of, a power to overcome time. Bunting's work is a monument to time in the same way as that of Eliot and Pound, but there is an evolution in his treatment of the theme that resembles Eliot rather than Pound. In his early poems, Bunting depends mainly on quotations from or references to literature of the past to express the theme of time and the eternal presence of the things of the past in our lives. It is only rarely that he expresses his theme directly (in the decay-renewal imagery of Part I of "Attis," for example). "Chomei at Toyama" (1932) is different from the other long poems of about the same period; although it refers to time by juxtaposing a literary source with the present, the reference is not obtrusive and obscure as in "Attis" and "The Well of Lycopolis." *The Spoils* of 1951 represents another step; here Bunting deals with time in the form of the poem by juxtaposing three movements—the life of a people in the past, the continuation of their civilization in the present, and the phenomenon of modern warfare. The banality of much of the language in the final section accounts for the failure of this scheme. It is only with the far more subtle juxtapositions of past and present to be found in *Briggflatts* that Bunting succeeds with the form towards which he was groping in *The Spoils*. In *Briggflatts*, the form is not only more subtle but more complex because of the musical nature of the thought patterns which are brought to a peak of perfection hitherto not touched upon in his work.

Anthony Suter. *CL.* Autumn, 1971, pp. 524–25

BURGESS, ANTHONY (1917–   )

Anthony Burgess published his first novel in 1956, his most recent one in the present year, a fact which becomes of interest only when it is added that in the intervening period he published fourteen additional novels. No doubt the figure is already dated for there are no signs of slowing down; in a recent apologetic valedictory to reviewing theater for *The Spectator* he confessed ruefully to not having written a novel in six months or more. One raises an eyebrow at all this plenty, yet only one of the novels marks itself off as a casual, slight creation, nor does the astonishing rate of production signal slapdash composition. . . .

Burgess is a comic writer, a term broad and common enough to cover supposed refinements of it such as satire, grotesque, or farce. None of the labels substantially promotes understanding of his work, nor does the knowledge that he, like all British comic novelists, is "the funniest . . . since Evelyn Waugh." If comparisons are desired, one would begin with the guess that the contemporary novelist Burgess most admires is Nabokov; beyond that one goes to Joyce, to Dickens, ultimately to Shakespeare as the literary examples most insistently behind his work. In *Nothing Like the Sun*, his novel about Shakespeare, the hero sees himself as a "word man," and his author is not likely to quarrel with the term as a description of himself. But then, like Nabokov or Joyce or Dickens or Shakespeare, he is more than just a word man: the brilliant exploration of a verbal surface will lead to the discovery of truths about life, of inward revelation. Or will it, does it in fact lead to such truths in the unfolding of Burgess' best work? The question is an interesting one to entertain, though only after we have first been moved and delighted by the books themselves and the continuing presence of their author. . . .

Burgess, despite the variety of narrators and situations in his fiction, speaks to us as one of us: a fallen man with the usual amount of ambition, irritation, guilt, decency and common sense. Given such ordinary qualities or modest sins, how can things go as wrong as they do for the heroes of these painful books? That they go not just wrong, but marvelously wrong, is the result of the one quality Burgess does not share with the rest of us or with his heroes—the art of the novelist.

William H. Pritchard. MR. Summer, 1966,
pp. 525–26, 539

Tremor of Intent marks the entrance of Anthony Burgess into the field of espionage fiction. Readers familiar with the past achievements of this gifted man will be expecting an exhilarating display of literary craftsmanship, and they should know that Burgess has not let them down: on its simplest level the book is a superb spy thriller. And they should also know that Burgess will not let them get away so easily: the coiling language, the unique insights that illuminate subject matter while commenting upon all of us, and the intelligence—uneasy, uncannily perceptive, moralistic—that haunted the earlier books are all present here, and Burgess has produced a troubling examination of the morality of espionage, and something else.

It is the "something else" that seems to frighten Burgess' critics, and leads them to speed-write such things as "his books are easier to enjoy than to summarize" and flee. But espionage isn't the only business that demands occasional risks, one has to go out on a limb in some of the more sedentary trades, and it seems to me that the book's subtitle—"An Eschatological Spy Novel"—gives us warning, and Burgess has presented us with an adventure yarn, a moral commentary, and an account of a soul's progress from the rejection of belief through doubt and torment to purgation and final religious commitment. . . .

Don Crinklaw. *Com.* Dec. 16, 1966, p. 329

Enderby the English poet [in *Enderby Outside* is] part Brendan Behan, part Dylan Thomas. Mr. Burgess has written about artists before: a book on James Joyce [*ReJoyce*] that shines with all the dazzle of his wild novels and a novel about Shakespeare (*Nothing Like the Sun*]. The super-egregious teen-age punk who narrates *A Clockwork Orange* dons a mask "of Pee Bee Shelley" to rob; and Shelley's early confederate in revolution, Thomas Jefferson Hogg, provides a pseudonym for Enderby when he needs a change of name. The artist as seen by artists is usually a man too much with the world, rather than too much out of it, as critics and the world itself like to think. Burgess' Enderby is a slob, a prey of designing women, a lethal glutton (a jar of pickles, a cup of boiled tea, and spaghetti for breakfast), an inept lover, and accident-prone sonneteer. . . .

It is by now widely known that Anthony Burgess is no ordinary novelist. There are novelists who could have created Enderby; there are fewer novelists who could have written Enderby's poetry for him— poetry that we aren't quite certain isn't parody; there are very few novelists who could have topped this and invented a Muse who reels off top-notch textual criticism of the densest of Enderby's poems (for Enderby, who is never wholly in on what his poems mean, and, of course, for us). Add to this Mr. Burgess' rolling prose rhythms and his canny aptitude for languages (such as the slang of expatriate Englishmen in Morocco), and the category in which we can place Mr. Burgess seems to contain Mr. Burgess alone.

Guy Davenport. *NatR.* June 18, 1968,
pp. 613, 615

The book that made Anthony Burgess' reputation in the United States is *A Clockwork Orange*, which is his own particular vision of horrors yet to come. It is probably not as good a book as *1984*, it is certainly not as chilling as *Brave New World* where the slaves do not even know they are slaves and the miserable have lost the power to recognize or name their misery, but it is quite good enough, and it serves well as an introduction to the Burgess canon. Set in England some time in the future, written only partly in English and partly in a language devised by Burgess for the occasion, it is the story of a young thief-rapist-murderer who is betrayed to the police by one of his comrades, jailed, treated by doctors and cured at once of his criminal tendencies and of all his humanity. The effect of the book is made no less dour by the ending that restores Alex to his old, vicious, music-loving self. He is set loose to kill again, to mug old men for the fun of it, except now he will be sheltered by the government because the matter of his chemical brain washing has become a political *cause célèbre*. We leave him listening to Beethoven, speaking his own curious lingo, thinking his salacious thoughts.

At the other end of Burgess' range is his first written—though not first published—novel, and not one of his strongest, *A Vision of Battlements*. This is a mundane story of a soldier's life in the relatively safe precincts of Gibraltar. The book is, as one might expect, generally and in some way specifically autobiographical. The hero, Richard Ennis, is a composer—as is Burgess—and Burgess tells us in a preface to the American edition that he spent three years of his own army service on Gibraltar, and that the writing of *Battlements* was in part an effort to exorcise the pain and loneliness that he suffered there. The lines along which the narrative develops are of no consequence: there is a little sex, a little violence, a good deal of satirical writing about army life and army types. But the book does display in at least a rudimentary form Burgess' gloomy, tolerant and comic view of the human condition, his love of words and his gift for them, his extravagant sense of image and of plot. Thus, as different as the two books are, in their basic technical achievements and their primary philosophical thrusts, *Battlements* and *Clockwork Orange* fit the same mould. . . .

It is easy to get the feeling, reading his fiction, that prolific as Burgess is, his creative life is a hand to mouth affair. For him, there may really be a Muse, and one can imagine him sitting down to work in the morning having no notion of where he is going, sublimely content to follow in any direction that his mind might lead. Usually, his mind leads well, and even in moments of weak motivation and flawed structure, Burgess can rely on his wit and his extraordinary sense of language to see him through.

Walter Sullivan. HC. April, 1969, pp. 1–3

Burgess's most recent novel, *Enderby*, is a combination of *Inside Mr. Enderby* and *Enderby Outside* which Burgess had published under the pseudonym Joseph Kell. Though not explicitly dialectical in its method or theme, *Enderby* relies heavily on the tension between sin and innocence as it affects artistic creation and the opposing relation between the artist and his world. . . .

Though Burgess is concerned both with the proper balance of experience and imagination as poetic materials and with the artist-castrating tendency of our time, *Enderby* is not written to an intellectual formula, but rather written around a complex character and his escapades. In one way the novel is more satisfying than *The Wanting Seed* because Burgess shifts emphasis; Enderby rivals Denham in complexity. The novel is considerably looser in structure and selection of incident than *A Clockwork Orange*, perhaps indicating a duality in Burgess between the intellectually, politically, or theologically committed novel and the novel of complex characterization.

Burgess's novels have any amount of common subjects, situations, and themes, but the essential and characteristic feature of both theme and technique is opposition. In novel after novel Burgess plays off culture against culture, character against character, value against value for both aesthetic and conceptual ends. The explanation for this choice of technique may lie in literary influence (Burgess greatly admires Joyce, has obviously read Marx), in publishing history (his rate of production may necessitate writing to a handy opposition), or in aesthetic principle (he defines art as the "representation of the Ultimate, under its aspect of unity, formal harmony, Brunoian reconciliation of opposites"). Whatever the explanation, Burgess's dialectic has not yet reached its completion, the total synthesis of value, character, and technique.

Thomas LeClair. Critique. Vol. 12, No. 3,
1971, pp. 92–93

Unlike those empty commodities regularly passed off as examples of prose fiction nowadays, Anthony Burgess's new novel [*MF*] is really something: a book which represents a genuine achievement for author and publisher alike, as elegantly printed and bound as it is fully realized. Intricate and imaginatively daring as it is, the novel is never given to disintegration and it affords all the pleasures of language at work and play.

But the reader should be forewarned that although *MF* is consistently coherent, has a plot and characters, and satisfies many of the hungers fed by realistic fiction, it is not, for all that, an obliging book: ambitiously conceived, it does not yield its meanings easily, and its intellectual aggressiveness and underlying somber power are not likely to make everybody comfortable. Moreover, far from relieving the pressures of contemporary, war-torn reality, it intensifies those pressures and lays bare in familiar headlines the lineaments of ultimate anxiety. In the process the novel succeeds in arousing the reader's prurient metaphysical interest; for, as its title suggests, *MF* is a meditation on incest—incest as idea as well as act. . . .

[The] complexities of the author's intention are reflected in the elements of his technique: for example, although the narrative drive remains unrelenting throughout and the story progresses clearly from point to point, the prose itself establishes its own closed circuit, which joins various times and places into a single here and now. In this respect as well as a number of others (for the most part related to the transformations of language and the fascination with the pun as a kind of shuttle between various realms of experience), the conception of the book is deeply Joycean. The reader interested in pursuing the connection might begin with Burgess's reflections on the "Proteus" episode of *Ulysses* in his *ReJoyce.*

In the present context, however, it must suffice to note simply that the economy of language in *MF* suggests a far deeper economy related to the very structure of reality. For what it is given to Miles Faber to understand in the course of the narrative which bears his initials is that "the ultimate organic creation," through the voices of its riddling emissaries, declares: *"Dare to try and disturb the mystery of order.* For order has both to be and not to be challenged, this being the anomalous condition of the sustention of the cosmos. Rebel becomes hero; witch becomes saint. Exogamy means disruption and also stability, incest means stability and also disruption. You've got to have it both ways, man." Thus, just as this fiction conceived in the present from the perspective of the future reverberates with the same note of woe struck in the primal past, so too with that ultimate realization young Miles becomes one with "Swellfoot the Tyrant," the original MF.

Stephen Donadio. *NYT.* April 4, 1971, p. 4

Anthony Burgess's comic skill relies principally on the combination of the horrible and the absurd to achieve a proper effect. In the majority of the novels, horror and absurdity are balanced to achieve a comically appropriate moment. When the balance is tipped in favor of one at the expense of the other, the novel suffers. Comedy is, to say the least, the most difficult and most treacherous form in which a novelist can work, and the fact that Burgess has created a number of superbly funny books, ones in which horror balances absurdity in order for an underlying religious purpose to emerge cogently, is ample testimony of the fact that he is a master of this most difficult and elusive form.

Burgess admits to the influence of Evelyn Waugh on his work; but, in considering the overall effects and ultimate purpose, Waugh's influence seems less important to Burgess's method than at first appears. Exaggeration and absurdity serve Waugh well, especially in the early novels, from *Decline and Fall* to *Put Out More Flags.* Burgess's use of absurdity, although Waugh does indeed stand behind some of the hilarious scenes, relies more on Kafka's purpose and on Joyce's method than it does on Waugh's, principally because language is used to force the reader to an awareness of religious and/or metaphysical considerations. . . .

A. A. DeVitis. *Anthony Burgess* (N.Y.,
Twayne, 1972), p. 164

CAMPBELL, ROY (1902–1957)

To those who remember him, Roy Campbell usually appears an enigmatic figure whose frequent changes of loyalty are confusing and contradictory. His literary career was built around changing allegiances, publicly proclaimed, and usually accompanied by a change of environment. . . .

These changes in loyalty and outlook affect Campbell's writing. He never fully realized the promise shown by his first volume. The lyric power, so clearly evident from the opening lines of *The Flaming Terrapin*, continued to delight readers of his subsequent volumes, but his colourful and incisive talent became increasingly diverted into polemical and satirical writing as he grew older. By turning more frequently to polemic as his political and personal feuds multiplied, he neglected his distinctive lyrical gift which is at its best when capturing his inward reactions to stress or beauty. His later obsession with argument could only lead him away from the vivid expression of subjective values, and into statements and comments which are open to more objective assessment. . . .

The marked variations in tone and manner in the works themselves call for a careful separation between what is excessive and ineffectual in his responses, and that which gives the distinctive vitality and beauty to his best poems. When considered in relation to the events in his life, his beliefs and loyalties are less enigmatic than might at first appear. Without attempting to force his life and work into an oversimplified pattern, my study traces the effects of his colonial background, and his resulting sense of being an outsider from the time of his first contacts with English life. Once his unhappy return to South Africa seemed to cut him off from his native culture, his own feeling of isolation grew more intense. Many of his subsequent allegiances are an inevitable result of his steadily increasing alienation throughout the thirties. His need to justify himself and the values he had adopted became more acute.

Campbell's isolation affects his work in two ways. It drove him into self-justifying polemic, and finally to a predictable, public response. At the same time, however, it gives his writing a remarkable intensity when he uses his lyrical gift to communicate the personal tensions and values which lie behind the less successful, public poems. After he was finally accepted, albeit as an eccentric, on the English literary scene, his lyrical fervour left him. His last volume of original poems was published in 1946. . . . His distinctive lyrical power had gone, and his few original poems show none of the burning intensity which so distinguished his work during his long period of isolation.

Rowland Smith. *Lyric and Polemic: The*
Literary Personality of Roy Campbell
(Montreal, McGill-Queen's Univ. Pr.,
1972), pp. 1–3

CARROLL, PAUL VINCENT (1900–1968)

The best known of Carroll's recent plays is *The Wayward Saint* of 1955. In it, he returns to the Mourne Mountains and the Paul Vincent Carroll stock company. His Canon Daniel McCooey is a simple, gullible priest who like St. Francis talks to birds and animals, and who is a kind of male counterpart to Brigid of *Shadow and Substance*. However, the girl's part was played straight, whereas the Canon's is permeated by a charmingly humanizing faultiness. The devil, in the form of Baron Nicholas de Balbus, is able to play on the Canon's pride and to give him a droll self-importance about being a saint—a fact which suggests the influence of D'Alton's *The Devil a Saint Would Be*. Also, the Canon's saintliness is humanized by his willingness to trick his bishop, his housekeeper, and his grocer in ways not far distant from outright lies.

The play is nicely of a piece, and its pleasant humor never deserts it. Its main fault lies in the quality of Carroll's inventiveness. The Canon's miracles—stopping clocks, making lights blink, raising chairs—are pleasant theatrical devices, but not particularly fresh or striking. The play, even when compared with O'Casey's *Cock-a-Doodle Dandy*, seems imaginative, but the imagination does not seem first-rate. The piece is mildly charming, but never quite delightful, and Carroll's own wild mind seems muted in it. . . .

Despite his "rebel heart," Carroll has always been brought up short by authority. His strictures on the Catholic Church have always been blunted by his ultimate belief in the Church, and his irritation with realism has always been foiled by his debt to it. Just as he always follows a criticism of the Church by a eulogy of it, so technically does he follow up a tentative diversion into experiment by an example of total realism. The upshot is that his great artistic promise has never been completely realized. He has not developed as a thinker, but wavered between two conflicting impulses. He has not developed as an experimental playwright, but only tried furtive forays away from realism. He is a rebel who has never truly rebelled.

That seems to me an enormous waste, for, make no mistake about it, Carroll has a talent rivaling O'Casey's. O'Casey's genius was strong enough to hammer out an inimitable style because he was not afraid to be the conscience of his race. Carroll could never quite do that.

Still, he has made a rare contribution to Irish drama, and a larger one than he has so far been credited with. He must be remembered not only for the superb realism of *Shadow and Substance* and *The White Steed*, but also for the equally fine realism of *Green Cars Go East*, and for the beautiful lyricism of *The Old Foolishness*, and for the wild hilarity of *The Devil Came from Dublin*. In these plays, he was writing at the top of his form, and that top was very high indeed.

Robert Hogan. *After the Irish Revolution*
(Minneapolis, Univ. of Minnesota Pr., 1967),
pp. 62–63

With all his accomplishments and abilities, it is distressing that Carroll did not, particularly in the 1940s, achieve his potential. Curiously enough, his career in one basic respect parallels O'Casey's. They both successfully started with a gripping realistic play—*Things That Are Caesar's* and *The Shadow of a Gunman*; then they experienced two hit dramas, and then a decline from their two most important works. Unlike O'Casey, however, Carroll did not possess the lyrical and poetic qualities that would have given his secondary work more distinction. But, like O'Casey, he became caught up and waylaid by the siren call of symbolism and allegory and also, like O'Casey, he became too message-and-thesis conscious so that with the advent of *Kindred*, instead of the themes emerging subtly from the play, they too often seem to be the principal reason for the play's existence.

If Carroll is not so great a dramatist as he should have been, these are the reasons why. He came to allow his heart to rule his head, to preach almost unceasingly the nobleness of, and need for, love, dignity, tolerance, and understanding at the expense of retaining consistent dramatic control, clearness, and firmness. To say this, however, is not to ignore the fact that as long as the modern English theatre exists, Carroll's best dramas will be played, and these works, and the characters existing therein, are sufficient reason indeed for placing him in the pantheon of significant modern playwrights.

Paul A. Doyle. *Paul Vincent Carroll*
(Lewisburg, Pa., Bucknell Univ. Pr., 1971),
p. 110

CARY, JOYCE (1888–1957)

Joyce Cary's interest in Africa and primitive forms of life was close to that of modern anthropologists in so far as he saw it objectively in its societal-forming aspects and attempted to link these patterns with the forms of contemporary civilised society. It is interesting to note, for example, the number of points of agreement between his observations about primitive culture and those of Ernst Cassirer. A more important link between him and Cassirer is their mutual agreement with the Kantian dictum of the powers of the imagination, of the mind as an active creative and shaping force rather than as a tabula rasa on which sense data are inscribed. He most certainly would have subscribed to Cassirer's belief that "man's outstanding characteristic, his distinguishing mark, is not his metaphysical or physical nature—but his work." . . .

Cary was a profoundly religious spirit of that intensely individual and protestant kind which cannot find fulfillment in any corporate body; he had to carve out his creed by himself and for himself. Brought up as an orthodox Anglican, he lost all religious faith in early manhood to find a new one in mature life. It was not orthodox; it was not Christian in any substantial sense. Cary did not identify God with Christ or with any kind of personal spirit. But experience had convinced him that man's apprehension of beauty and of human love was inexplicable on any purely rational or materialist terms. It was proof of some transcendental spiritual reality with which a man must relate himself harmoniously if he is to find satisfaction. He did not hold this as a mere pious opinion. It burned within him, an intuitive conviction as strong as that of Preedy [in *The Captive and the Free*], strengthening his spirit and directing his actions. To be often in his company was to be aware of its presence. This strong faith was what enabled him at the end against appalling odds to win his tragic race with death.

Golden L. Larsen. The Dark Descent
(Joseph, 1965), pp. 17, 192–93

Cary did not want to forgo [the] sense of immediate life. He believed that life is in the living, here and now, in the flowing present, minute to minute. The Cary story moves quickly. We *see* as Jimson sees. We *feel* as Charley in *Charley Is My Darling* feels. Cary's imagination was empathetic, and the excitement experienced by a character electrifies the prose, illuminates a scene; it pleases, alarms, or terrifies.

As Walter Allen points out, Cary also intrudes, but not in the manner of George Eliot or Thackeray. He suggests or intimates. A delinquent character represents an aspect of all delinquency. His pedantic tutor suggests all pedantic tutors. His nonconformist politician says something general about the nonconformist mind.

Cary seems somewhere between the new and the old. The "modern" novelist tends to ask questions, not to give answers. The older novelists tended to give the answers: Society is like this; the legal system is wrong for this or that reason; and serving girls who are not circumspect can expect this! The modernist seems to say: Is this the way it is? Cary seems to say, Look, haven't you seen how certain types behave? Listen closely, and you'll hear that tone of voice that is heard all over the Empire. Or, that Mister Johnson, isn't he like impulsive, hard-driving, creative men everywhere? The generalizations are there, but they are tentative, not insisted upon.

The novelist's problem is the discovery of a satisfactory form. Cary was, in a sense, obsessed with that need. In *Art and Reality*, written for Cambridge lectures he was too ill to give, he spoke of two sorts of mind: the analytical-conceptual, and the intuitive-imaginative. Strong on theorizing, Cary would write an essay or give a radio talk at the drop of a hat. He was a great explainer. He was also an artist. Sometimes he saw a story swarm into being, coming up from some dark recesses in his mind; or he pushed his way, character by character, episode by episode, page by page, until he had a huge pile of manuscript. Sometimes, when he found the clue to form and meaning, he would cut out scenes, episodes, and even begin again, pursuing the "right sensation." He was like Lawrence in refusing to plot (anyone, he said, can plot) and in insisting on giving his demon its way. ("Trust the story," Lawrence said, "not the author.") Cary would have agreed. His problem was to keep Cary the analyst and Cary the theorizer in check, and to give Cary the intuitive-imaginative man as much freedom as he could take without fouling the reins.

William Van O'Connor. *Joyce Cary* (N.Y.,
Columbia Univ. Pr., 1966), pp. 4–5

Cary's works exhibit a continuing interest in history and historical development. *The Moonlight* and *A Fearful Joy* are both works whose primary purpose is to trace the changes brought by time into the sociological context and thus into the attitudes and reactions of individuals. This is also expressed through major themes of both trilogies and of *Castle Corner*, and is more than hinted at in other works. Superficially viewed, the works seem to make the point that history is a process of decay, with the passing of time bringing only the dissolution of an orderly past and the loss of firm moral standards. Perhaps such a view even corresponds to an attitude held by Cary himself. The full effect of the theme, however, is to show that history is always in a state of being created and that thus each moment contains the possibilities of either triumph or defeat. No moment is ever fixed, and none ever limits the individual's potential achievement. The standard of universal order which seems to belong to the past, therefore, is not a real one, but only one which the future superimposes on its memory of what has gone.

For Cary one standard nonetheless does exist, and it is the eternal, unchanging basic pattern of humanity. No individual is ever the same as another, but none is ever totally different from his fellows. Both the differences and the similarities—appearing as a fixed constant underneath changing events and under all the differences cloaking various societies—make for a strand of irony which insistently appears in most of Cary's work.

Jack Wolkenfeld. *Joyce Cary: The Developing Style* (N.Y., New York Univ. Pr., 1968), pp. 129–30

CHESTERTON, G. K. (1874–1936)

While some writers are more "difficult" than others and cannot therefore hope to reach a very wide audience, no writer thinks he needs decoding in order to be understood. On the other hand, nearly every writer who has achieved some reputation complains of being misunderstood both by the critics and the public, because they come to his work with pre-conceived notions of what they are going to find in it. His admirers praise him and his detractors blame him for what, to him, seem imaginary reasons. The kind of critic an author hopes for is someone who will dispel these pre-conceived notions so that his readers may come to his writings with fresh eyes.

At this task of clearing the air, Chesterton was unusually efficient. It is popularly believed that a man who is in earnest about something earnest. The belief is not ill-founded since, more often than not, this is speaks earnestly and that a man who keeps making jokes is not in true. But there are exceptions and, as Chesterton pointed out, Bernard Shaw was one. The public misunderstood Shaw and thought him just a clown when, in fact, he was above all things a deadly serious preacher. In the case of Browning, Chesterton shows that many of his admirers had misunderstood him by reading into his obscurer passages intellectual profundities when in fact the poet was simply indulging his love of the grotesque. Again, he shows us that Stevenson's defect as a narrator was not, as it had become conventional to say, an over-ornate style but an over-ascetic one, a refusal to tell the reader anything about a character that was not absolutely essential. As a rule, it is journalism and literary gossip that is responsible for such misunderstandings; occasionally, though, it can be the author himself. Kipling would certainly have described himself as a patriotic Englishman who admired above all else the military virtues. In an extremely funny essay, Chesterton convincingly demonstrates that Kipling was really a cosmopolitan with no local roots, and he quotes in proof Kipling's own words.

> W. H. Auden. Foreword to *G. K. Chesterton:*
> *A Selection from His Non-fictional Prose*
> (Faber and Faber, 1970), p. 14

What above all pervades these pieces [in *Selected Stories*], indeed the whole of his fiction, is Chesterton's inexhaustible fascination with the outward appearance of things, not only with the effects of light upon them, but with the things in themselves: landscape and seascape, streets, shops, gardens, the outsides and insides of houses, ornaments, knick-knacks of every possible kind, details of dress and costume—and, more than any of these, the lineaments of the human being inside the costume. Nobody, I think, would call Chesterton a great characterizer of the inner selves of men and women, but one would have to turn to a writer on the scale of his beloved Dickens to find a better representer of how they look. Of all the thousands of people who appear in his fiction, even those with the merest walk-on parts, not one recalls another in his face or body. Every time, the author rises exultantly to the occasion and draws someone new.

If Chesterton was an optimist (no bad thing to be anyway, I should have thought, if it can be managed), it was largely because he loved the world his God had made, and never ceased to enjoy that vitally important aspect of the entire creation: its surface.

> Kingsley Amis. Intro. to G. K. Chesterton,
> *Selected Stories* (Faber and Faber, 1972),
> pp. 20–21

CLARKE, AUSTIN (1896–1974)

Clarke lead[s] a parade of poets who find ways of being at once deeply traditional, in his sense, and authoritatively modern.

One of the most interesting aspects of his modern side is that Clarke's most recent book, a single narrative poem called *Mnemosyne Lay in Dust* (1966), approaches the spirit of confessional poetry as closely as any work that has yet appeared in the British Isles. Though written in the third person, this book has an autobiographical ring to it. It has to do with the hysterical breakdown and amnesia, hospitalization, and recovery of one "Maurice Devane," Clarke's relatively youthful protagonist. Formally, it represents a culmination of Clarke's entire development. After his early period of romantic work, he has for years cultivated an astringently compressed style employing certain rhyming and alliterative devices that appear eccentric in English but that are precisely that "influence of Irish versification" to which [John] Montague refers. The remarkable turn, achieved in old age, that *Mnemosyne Lay in Dust* represents is clearly the result of a fusion of resolutions, artistic and psychological. . . .

Though Clarke began his career under the influence of the Celtic renaissance, he always combined romanticism with harsh wit and realism. His major books between the *Collected Poems* of 1935, now long out of print, and *Mnemosyne Lay in Dust* are, like the latter, the work of his old age. *Later Poems* (1961) and *Flight to Africa* (1963) contain a good deal of satire of an unusual sort. It is the self-flagellant satire of a man of strong and compassionate feeling, and this is the root of Clarke's late confessional tendency. His identification with Ireland is as complete and unself-conscious as with his own family, and the criticisms he directs against her have the domestic authenticity, so to speak, of a man complaining of wife or mother.

M. L. Rosenthal. *The New Poets* (N.Y.,
Oxford Univ. Pr., 1967), pp. 268–71

The reader always gets a prose sense from a Clarke poem. The technique is submerged, and while one realizes afterwards that a strange music has been at work on the ear, one is not forced to quarrel with the prosody in order to find out what the subject matter is. When Robert Frost visited Dublin to receive an Honorary Degree from University College, he asked Clarke what kind of verse he wrote. Thinking of the strong man who used to perform outside St. Martins in the Fields in London, the Irish poet replied: "I load myself with chains and try to get out of them." It is clear to this reader that Austin Clarke, like the strong man, always wriggles miraculously free. . . .

W. B. Yeats took a long time coming to his poetic majority. So did Austin Clarke. Ours is a nation of late marriages and late development in the arts. At the age of seventy-four, Austin Clarke is in the prime of his poetic life. He is at that magical point where whatever he looks at can turn into poetry if he wishes.

Richard Weber. *MR*. Spring, 1970,
pp. 305, 308

COLUM, PADRAIC (1881–1972)

It is wholly proper that Padraic Colum is best known as a poet, for his poems are his most significant contributions to literature. . . .

Colum thinks of himself as one of the few authentic national poets of Ireland because his upbringing is rural and Catholic, as opposed to the Protestant ascendancy backgrounds of poets like Yeats, AE and Lady Gregory, whose links with the peasant people are at best studied and vicarious. Much of Colum's poetry retains its roots in the Catholic peasantry of the Irish Republic, dealing occasionally with the joys and aspirations of the people but far more with their sorrows, hopelessnesses and disintegration. Always, however, his people are uncomplicated and readily understandable and his language sparse and accurate.

Colum cannot be considered typical of any particular modern tradition. Hailed as a poet of the Irish Renaissance, his poems lacked the nationalistic didacticism which plagued other Irish poets. . . . During the years following World War I, a period of realism, surrealism, Dadaism, and naturalism, each with its own limitations on subject matter and emphasis on a particular variety of experiment, his poems bordered on the sentimental, and were more often about the beautiful, the remote and the wondrous than the ugly, the despairing and the hopeless. . . .

Any overall assessment of Colum as a dramatist would be less than candid if it did not admit that his chief contributions to the stage were historical rather than literary. While his importance to the Irish theatre cannot be overstated, his contributions were noteworthy because they were precedents rather than because they were destined some day to be recognized masterpieces of drama. Many of Colum's plays had merit, but none, in the final analysis, could be called great, as can a number of his poems. On the other hand, it has already been shown that his poetry has depended in large measure on his dramatic background and techniques, and to the extent that his poetry enters into his last plays it has improved them. It is difficult to imagine Colum not writing for the theatre. Without the influence and experience of his playwriting, we would have had a poet and storyteller of a vastly different and less important kind.

Zack Bowen. *Padraic Colum* (Carbondale,
Southern Illinois Univ. Pr., 1970),
pp. 25–26, 89

COMPTON-BURNETT, IVY (1892–1969)

Miss Compton-Burnett's novels have much in common with one another, far more than most writers' have. They have appeared fairly regularly at two- or three-year intervals, and the titles themselves have had a gnomic, often alliterative familiarity as novel has followed novel. Each title has told us something about the contents of the novel— *Brothers and Sisters*, for example, has six sets of brothers and sisters in it (the eldest pair of whom are also man and wife), while *A Family and a Fortune* concerns the effects of a large and unexpected inheritance which a dependent member of the household receives. In general the titles are not interchangeable, although *Men and Wives*, the climax of which is the murder of Harriet Haslam by her son Matthew, could with equal aptness, it would seem, be called *Mother and Son,* and *Mother and Son*, which is in part an account of courtship among certain middle-aged and elderly people, might almost as well be called *Men and Wives*.

Such similarities as exist among the titles are multiplied when we come to the novels proper. These similarities are what is initially most striking about the novels—similarities of mechanics and subject, what might be called veneer: what the novels look like. Every novelist adopts a set of conventions to serve as vehicle for his meaning—he chooses his settings, his point of view, characters, etc.—or, more accurately in most cases, they choose him. Miss Compton-Burnett's set of conventions varies much less from novel to novel than do other novelists'; to find a parallel, one would have to go to the drama, particularly the neo-classic drama, whether French or English, or perhaps the *pièce bien faite* of the late nineteenth century in France and in England. . . .

Rarest of all, especially in the later novels, is any physical description of action longer than an adverb or a phrase. When it does appear, it can be so effective that one marvels the more that a writer of such gifts should subjugate them to her greater aim. It is often what the classical author does not do that makes us admire what he does. . . .

Within the central house there is almost always a power figure like Sophia Stace—mother, father, aunt, grandmother, grandfather—and critics have agreed to call this figure the tyrant. His will is challenged, without much success, by his dependants. The first round of the battle may take place at the breakfast table, where more than half the novels open. The events proper may begin with an arrival, as stories always have; later in the events one or more members of the family may leave the household; they always return.

Charles Burkhart. *I. Compton-Burnett*
(Gollancz, 1965), pp. 25–26, 28–29

Ivy Compton-Burnett embodied in herself a quite unmodified pre-1914 personality, so that one was, in truth, meeting what one *had* encountered as a child. The particular interest and uniqueness of this is in relation to the immense individual revolutions and transformations that must, in fact, have taken place within herself, all without in the smallest degree affecting the way in which she faced the world. No writer was ever so completely of her books, and her books of her.

The Compton-Burnett novels deal with a form of life that has largely, if not entirely disappeared, though I suspect that even to this day pockets of something very similar could be found; perhaps not so much in the country, where the novels tend to be located, as in residential suburbs and seaside towns. As with all good writers, a fair amount of nonsense has been written about her subject matter, so that one hesitates to generalise for fear of adding to it, especially in these days when so many people are obsessed with the subject of "class."

However, let me risk suggesting that, between a still lively aristocracy merging effortlessly into an enormously proliferated middle-class, both keenly aware of what is going on round them, large gloomy moderately rich families in largish, though not immense, houses in the country, going as a matter of course to Oxford or Cambridge, interested in acquiring property or money, yet lacking almost all contact with an outer world, living in a state of almost hysterically inward-looking intensity, have become pretty rare. If we add to that the Compton-Burnett conditions that such families take little or no interest in sport, and none of the sons enter the army or navy, the field is again narrowed within the terms of reference.

Anthony Powell. *Spec.* Sept. 6, 1969, p. 304

It has long been known to admirers of Ivy Compton Burnett that she published a novel called *Dolores* when in her twenties, 14 years before the first volume of the recognised canon, *Pastors and Masters*. Most of her interviewers tried to draw on her to speak of this early work; many enthusiasts visited the British Museum Reading Room especially to read it, for it had long been out of print.

Dame Ivy herself preferred to ignore it as having no part in the long, homogeneous (though each subtly very different) line of novels which she saw as standing for her unique achievement. The novels of her maturity, which came late, after, it would seem, a good deal of personal tragedy and the finding of a fulfilling personal happiness, are so marked, despite their varying successes, by an absolute certainty of aim both in method and in meaning, that it is hardly surprising that she should have preferred to omit a single juvenile essay, the chief feature of which is its dependence upon the styles of other novelists and a marked conflict between the various levels of its moral teachings. . . . Its interest lies largely in showing what paths Dame Ivy did not follow in her maturity, only a little in its intimations of the one she did. . . .

The Last and the First, splendidly put together by Livia Gollancz from pencilled notebooks, is the last novel she left behind (her twentieth). Here we see her special powers pared down to their essentials, in part perhaps from weakness, in part from lack of time to revise (which for her must have meant to fill out), but, in fact, surely from a growing desire to present her theme without any of the trappings of realism. Description and action (even in her own peculiar interpretation of those terms) have gone: she simply gives us the stylised dialogue of a series of witty discussions of set themes among two families and their servants. . . .

The book is notable because it declares openly the compassion for wrong-doing that she asserted again and again in interviews. . . .

Angus Wilson. *Obs.* Feb. 7, 1971, p. 26

It is often said that Compton-Burnett characters have no bodies and no physical contacts, just as it is widely assumed that there are no descriptions in her books. Both these observations are inaccurate, although caresses are more often between children and parents than between adults. They may not kiss, but mothers constantly fold their arms about their daughters, daughters bury their heads on their mothers' shoulders, and small children have an endearing way of leaning against their parents' knees or of taking their hands for affection or protection. . . .

It is also frequently said that the Compton-Burnett novels are all alike, but this too is a fallacy. It is true that her admirers often choose a volume at random to re-read, but this is rather in the same way that a listener chooses at random a record by a favourite composer. Unlike as the works may be, the unmistakable signature of their creator is on them. It is interesting to analyse the idiosyncrasies that point her style, but each work is a new creation.

Many English writers contributed to the publisher's blurb for the American edition of *Manservant and Maidservant*. Among other tributes, Elizabeth Taylor wrote that "her books are for ever and ever," Storm Jameson said: "Take her to your heart or hurry her out of the house . . . she is not to be ignored," Rosamond Lehmann opined that she was "probably the purest . . . of contemporary English artists" and Robert Liddell declared: "It does not seem too much, or nearly enough, to claim for her that of all English novelists now writing she is the greatest and most original artist."

In England *Manservant and Maidservant* sold best of all her novels, and it had an excellent reception in the States. The *New York Herald Tribune* declared that "Miss Compton-Burnett is immensely unfair to most other contemporary British novelists. . . . Her apparently effortless skill shows them up. They seem to be breathing too hard by comparison."

Elizabeth Sprigge. The Life of Ivy Compton-
Burnett (N.Y., Braziller, 1973), pp. 121–22

CONRAD, JOSEPH (1857–1924)

Much of what Conrad initiated in fiction has been acknowledged: *Nostromo*, parent of the political novel as we know it; *Lord Jim*, parent of the psychological novel of today; *The Secret Agent*, forerunner of the intellectual mystery story. But he contributed, not only to fiction, but to a better understanding of the world that we, today, live in. The emergence of new nations in Asia and Africa has given a special timeliness, for the historical insights they provide, to his stories of the East, of the Congo. "If it has become an axiom of our time that 'no man is an ilande,' it has become even more forcibly apparent that no people, race, or nation is either," Morton Dauwen Zabel has written of the close relation between the world of Conrad's books and the world today. The interpretation given those books in 1917 was one Conrad quarreled with, and justly. In the light of the vast changes since then the writer too far ahead of his day may yet find the understanding he looked for.

His human commentary left out little, either of the outward, physical world or of the inner region of each man's private contest. He wrote of fear, greed, guilt, love, isolation, brotherhood, betrayal, death, honor, revolution, the peace of mind of the unaware, the heroism of those too bereft of imagination to know fear. He wrote above all about "the wound of life," loss of self.

Jerry Allen. The Sea Years of Joseph Conrad
(Garden City, N.Y., Doubleday, 1965), p. 312

Conrad's stake in the structures of experience he had created was absolutely crucial, since it was rooted in the human desire to make a character of and for himself. Character is what enables the individual to make his way through the world, the faculty of rational self-possession that regulates the exchange between the world and the self; the more cogent the identity, the more certain a course of action. One of the curious facts of history is that it is the compulsive man of action who feels the need for character more strongly than the man who is only on the verge of action. T. E. Lawrence, Conrad's notorious near-contemporary, has been described by R. P. Blackmur as a man capable only of creating a personality for himself: his failure to forge a character, Blackmur argues, is the secret of his life and writing.

Conrad's predicament was, I think, not unlike Lawrence's: he, too, was a man of action urgently in need of a role to play so that he could locate himself solidly in existence. But whereas Lawrence failed, Conrad succeeded (although at immense cost). This is another aspect of Conrad's life of adventure. To Conrad it seemed as if he had to *rescue himself*, and, not surprisingly, this is one of the themes of his short fiction. Marlow and Falk, to take two examples, are faced with the terrible dilemma of either allowing themselves to vanish into "native obscurity" or, equally oppressive, undertaking to save themselves by the compromising deceit of egoism; nothingness on one side or shameful pride on the other. That is, either one loses one's sense of identity and thereby seems to vanish into the chaotic, undifferentiated, and anonymous flux of passing time, or one asserts oneself so strongly as to become a hard and monstrous egoist.

It is important, therefore, to distinguish the dominant mode of Conrad's structures of experience: quite simply, it can be called their radical either/or posture. By this I mean a habitual view of experience that allows *either* a surrender to chaos *or* a comparably frightful surrender to egoistic order. There is no middle way, and there is no other method of putting the issues. Either one allows that meaningless chaos is the hopeless restriction upon human behavior, or one must admit that order and significance depend only upon man's will to live at all costs.

Edward W. Said. *Joseph Conrad and the Fiction of Autobiography* (Cambridge, Mass., Harvard Univ. Pr., 1966), pp. 12–13

[Conrad], who began with a virulent anti-democratic bias, came round to an extremist position against restrictive authority, not only in its blatant form in autocratic nations like Russia and Prussia but also in its relatively modest appearance in England, as we have observed. His early nationalistic sentiments have been seen to reappear throughout his career, yet to leave room for international solutions to national rivalries and for the ethos of European solidarity—this despite his continued doubts about international peace organizations and despite his insight into the decadence of European civilization.

The ambiguity of Conrad's thought on political questions is a necessary condition for the power of his political fiction. Nowhere did his complex political viewpoint enter into his fiction as fruitfully as on the subject of revolution. In order to gather the full measure of the art of Conrad's political novels, we need to be aware of how deeply he struggled with the issues of social change, how he remained committed to nationalist revolutions and declared social revolution a potential shortcut for the popular will, yet recoiled from the emergence of the anarchic forces which he knew to be latent and volatile in men. Not all his politics were ambiguous, however. Conrad retained throughout his career a straightforward attitude toward governmental abuse of power, particularly in the area in which such power was most flagrantly increasing human misery—imperialism. Imperialism became for him a consistent bête noire (although he mitigated his initial opposition to the English show of force in the Boer War), and a large part of his fiction is shaped by his outspoken, emotional response to it.

A letter from the close of his life may stand as typical of the complex play of feelings and values that marks Conrad's political opinions throughout his career. In May, 1924, under Britain's first Labour government, Conrad received one of the few official recognitions of his work, the offer of a knighthood. His letter to Ramsay MacDonald, the Prime Minister, declining the offer expresses several aspects of his political imagination. . . . First, it marks a symbolic act of renunciation of his own aristocratic tradition which, if not an operative political sentiment, was still an emotional influence on many of his political opinions. Second, the refusal to identify himself with the community by receiving a national title might suggest a departure from the idealization of the organic state . . . but . . . the letter makes an effort to reaffirm his tie with the social community. It would seem that Conrad conceived of the community as the fellowship of all working men, rather than as an abstract political symbol, the Crown. Third, by the lines addressed specifically to MacDonald, Conrad anticipates the possible interpretation of his action as a snub of a Labour government. By identifying himself personally with the working class, Conrad indicates an aspect of his political sympathies that cannot be ignored when dealing either with his essays or with his fiction.

Avrom Fleishman. *Conrad's Politics*
(Baltimore, Johns Hopkins Univ. Pr., 1967),
pp. 46–47

More interesting, in fact, than the presence of dream and fear [in Conrad's work] is their reciprocal paternity. Almayer, contemplating the renunciation of his egocentric ideas to follow selflessly his daughter and her Malay husband, catches himself up "in the sudden fear of his dream." More precisely, he fears his anti-dream, the negation of his own personal dream of power. Just as fear may inspire a dream to dominate frightening circumstances, so the dream may breed new fear that the dreamer will not be able to live up to it. Those who do not set much store by their own personalities, like Captain MacWhirr or the French lieutenant, digest their fear and act courageously. Those who are conceited are more dismayed by the prospect of inadequacy or helplessness than by death itself. Thus Brierly's suicide is explained by his old mate Jones with "a last word of amazing profoundity" to Marlow: "Ay, ay! neither you nor I, sir, had ever thought so much of ourselves." On the *Patna*, Marlow tells us, Jim is not afraid of death but of the emergency, which his imagination suddenly presents to his consciousness: the vision of a senseless catastrophe in which he will *not* be a hero. Kurtz penetrates the true nature of his original dream—a "power for good practically unbounded"—to an anti-dream summed up in his last words: "The horror!" Decoud is driven to suicide by the perception of himself helpless and humiliated under the eyes of the girl he meant to sweep off her feet. But the most explicit connexion occurs in *Under Western Eyes*, the novel that figures Conrad's own conflict in the most transparent metaphorical disguise. Conrad seems to have regarded his departure from Poland partly in the same light as Razumov viewed his enforced trip to Geneva. He wrote to Galsworthy in 1914:

> In 1874 I got into a train in Cracow (Vienna Express) on my way to the sea, as a man might get into a dream. And here is the dream going on still. Only now it is peopled mostly by ghosts and the moment of awakening draws near.

Razumov has very similar feelings on leaving Petersburg, accompanied only by Haldin's ghost:

> . . . Prussia, Saxony, Würtemberg, faces, sights, words—all a dream, observed with an angry, compelled attention. Zürich, Geneva—still a dream, minutely followed, wearing one into harsh laughter, to fury, to death—with the fear of awakening at the end. . . .

And the following section continues:

> "Perhaps life is just that," reflected Razumov, pacing to and fro under the trees of the little island, all alone with the bronze statue of Rousseau. "A dream and a fear."

It is not too narrow a view of Conrad to regard his work as an exploration of the possibilities of human experience between these two poles of force.

Paul Kirschner. *Conrad: The Psychologist as Artist* (Edinburgh, Oliver & Boyd, 1968), pp. 21–23

"Imagination, not invention, is the supreme master of art as of life." This statement from *A Personal Record* sums up the theory of creation so far as Conrad was concerned. "Invention," in the sense of making up or devising themes, plots and characters, had never been his method, which was generally one of close and imaginative analysis of his own experience (*The Shadow-Line*) or of the experiences of others which were closely linked to his own (*Lord Jim*, "The Secret Sharer"). In the latter instances, the observer/narrator figure would seem to be an essential part of the creative process, allowing Conrad to project himself, again imaginatively, into another's experience.

But in [*Heart of Darkness, Nostromo*, and *The Secret Agent*] Conrad can be seen moving further and further from his own experience and from the experience of others linked to his own. Kurtz, unlike Jim or Falk or the Secret Sharer, was not a seaman; Conrad had a mere glimpse of South America; he had no part in the world of the London anarchists. But this movement away from his own experience still does not turn him towards "invention," but towards an extension of the faculty of "imagination." More and more he is involved in an immersion of the mind and spirit in the experiences of others, in the history of peoples, and in the growth of ideas as he found them recorded in books. Increasingly, the absence of any direct personal experience made the process a more difficult and a more remarkable one. It is this initial stage of reading and total and sympathetic involvement that must have formed the beginning of the creative process for each book. Its completeness and its mentally exhausting nature is revealed in his Author's Notes to *Nostromo* and to *The Secret Agent*, in his letters, and also in his record of how a lady visitor interrupted him in the composition of *Nostromo* and he "jumped up from [his] chair stunned and dazed, every nerve quivering with the pain of being uprooted out of one world and flung down into another." The total nature of this immersion obviously accounts for his ability to construct a completely convincing fictional world. . . .

Norman Sherry. *Conrad's Western World* (Cambridge Univ. Pr., 1971), pp. 337–38

COWARD, NOEL (1899–1973)

Mr. Coward writes dialogue as well as any man going; it is seemingly effortless, surprising in the most wonderfully surprising places, and "true"—very, very true. He is, as well, a dramatic mountain goat; his plays are better made than most—but not in the sense of the superimposed paste job of form, but from within: order more than form. And Mr. Coward's subjects—the ways we kid ourselves that we do and do not exist with each other and with ourselves—have not, unless my mind has been turned inward too long, gone out of date.

Notwithstanding it all, Noel Coward can be a bore. He bores his admirers every time he gets within earshot of a reporter by announcing how old-fashioned a writer he is, how the theatre has left him behind, how he does not understand the—to use an expression vague and confusing enough to have become meaningless and therefore dangerous—"avant garde" playwrights of today, feels no sympathy with them.

It is difficult to imagine him wringing his hands and seeking reassurance when he says these things, and it is equally difficult to think that there is a smug tone to the voice, so I don't really know what Mr. Coward's problem is. . . . But let me stop being churlish. A man I know and like and whose opinion I respect, a man involved with the theatre, a man who has produced the work of such playwrights as Beckett, Ionesco, Pinter, Arrabal and Ugo Betti, said to me not long ago that he greatly admired Noel Coward's plays, that he thought Coward a better playwright than Bernard Shaw and that Coward's plays would be on the boards long after most of the men writing today had been forgotten.

Edward Albee. Intro. to *Three Plays
by Noel Coward* (N.Y., Dell, 1965), pp. 4–5

Noel Coward . . . made his first stage appearance in 1911. During the fifty-five years since then, he has been prodigiously active; and the range of his output has been astonishing. Even now, when he has as much fame as any man could desire, he is returning [with *Suite in Three Keys*] to Shaftesbury Avenue in the dual role of actor and playwright. Laurels, he manifestly feels, were made for wearing, not for resting on.

As a dramatist, Mr. Coward did not merely start young: he succeeded young. *The Vortex* won him, at the age of 25, golden opinions from all sorts of people. It also brought him attendant publicity. One particular photograph, he claims in his autobiography, that showed him looking "like a heavily-doped Chinese illusionist," caused him to be unfairly identified for many years after with a life of dressing-gowned degeneracy. The play itself, as a revival at Guildford last year showed, has a bitterness unusual in Coward and remains a scathing indictment of the vain, self-absorbed and neglectful mother. Yet a year later, in *Hay Fever*, Mr. Coward used exactly the same character-traits to make up the endearing comic figure of Judith Bliss.

The ease with which Mr. Coward switched from anger to approbation illustrates perfectly his most essential quality: sheer professionalism. If he were asked to dramatise the Book of Job, one feels that he would bring to it the same professional zeal that shines through his countless plays, his musicals and revues, his film-scripts, novels and autobiographies. Always dexterous, he is sometimes inspired: Think but of *Hay Fever, Private Lives, Blithe Spirit* and *Present Laughter*. Three of this luminous quartet have been revived in London recently with heartening success. Immaculate in their conception, they contain the sort of unfailingly funny situations that ensure them a long life in the theatre.

In recent years, Mr. Coward has added one more to his many roles—that of embattled controversialist. With downright zest, he has attacked the younger playwrights, the "scratch-and-mumble" school of acting and the incivility of certain critics. This, allied to the uneven standard of his later plays, has made him an obvious target of abuse for theatrical progressives. But even his detractors will have to admit that the arrival of a full-length play and a double-bill by Mr. Coward in the West End remains a major event.

Michael Billington. *PP*. March, 1966, p. 9

Baudelaire, Huysmans, Wilde, Yeats, James, even Chekhov, whose melancholy crew daydream in the provinces—the beginnings of modern art are the beginnings of artifice. The repertory has different accents, different programs, but throughout the underlying disgust or disenchantment with the common world is the same. With Coward, with the age of the entertainer, artifice became another aspect of the world, became, in many respects, *the* world: deluxe gossip, journalistic "profundity," scandal. Coward created his mark, his style, but it was also a creation of the day. His was a talent which could only have worked in a seller's market. What it had was the fortunate moment, the decisive conjunction between performer and audience. Looking at life as fabulous and heartbreaking, creating always without real reference to himself, without vulgar experience, Coward gave us characters who are not so much worldly wise as "world weary," who have about them something so sleek as to be a little inhuman, an inhumanity that became best expressed with the cult of "personalities" in public life and the press.

In Coward, of course, what you observe is the growth of a "personality," rather than that of a writer, a sort of glittering stasis. That the career, nevertheless, has been unique and exhilarating, that more than one generation of playwrights (including Osborne and Albee) have taken its lessons to heart, that an "evening's entertainment" by Noel Coward will be on the boards twenty years from now—who can doubt that?

Robert Mazzocco. *NYR*. March 14, 1968,

p. 31

In March 1966, against the advice of his Swiss doctors, Noel flew to London and started rehearsals with Irene Worth and Lilli Palmer for *Suite in Three Keys*. Of these three latest Coward plays, *A Song at Twilight* is the most important and also far and away the best; it is an earnestly moral drama about an aging, distinguished, petulant, bitchy and truculent writer who manages to conceal his homosexuality from the world at the cost of warping his talent and cutting off his human sympathies. Yet curiously enough *A Song at Twilight* started out in Coward's mind as a comedy; he had recently read David Cecil's biography of Max Beerbohm, which describes Constance Collier's visit to Max when they were both in their seventies and long after their friendship had ended. . . .

But gradually, as the play developed in Coward's mind, he realized that there could be more to it than just the meeting of a couple of Elyot and Amanda figures in their old age. What if the writer, unlike Max Beerbohm, had been homosexual for most of his life; and what if the woman brought with her letters that could incriminate him in the eyes of posterity? Slowly but surely this became the theme of *A Song at Twilight*: an old, queer author fighting off a threat to his "good name." Given that plot, it is not altogether surprising that many critics took the play to be firmly based on Somerset Maugham, an illusion which Coward fostered by making up to look curiously like him on the stage. But if Beerbohm and Maugham were the direct influences on the creation of Sir Hugo Latymer, there was also a certain amount of Coward himself in the character he had written and was about to play.

Sheridan Morley. *A Talent to Amuse: A
Biography of Noel Coward* (Garden City,
N.Y., Doubleday, 1969), p. 402

DAVIE, DONALD (1922–   )

The place of Donald Davie in the British poetic scene is an interesting one. His poetry, particularly the earlier work, strikes one at first as coldly intellectual and distant. His criticism responds to new currents, both British and international, without seeming to be deeply and significantly informed by them; though it is always intelligent and relevant, it tends to let go of issues before they are fully and sympathetically encompassed. Nevertheless, one grows to see that the "defects" of detachment have enabled him to cultivate a valuable openness at the same time. . . .

Davie has in *Events and Wisdom* begun not only to ponder Concrete but to use the confessional mode in a perfectly natural way. "Wide France" and "Across the Way" are poems of family turbulence, and the sequence "After an Accident" (about the effects of a terrible automobile smashup in which Davie was involved) is a serious effort to repossess a psychological state that was both traumatic and productive of painful private realizations. The stubbly thoughtfulness of most of Davie's other work holds one kind of spiritual independence, suggesting an intellectual honesty that refuses to preen itself on its virtues.

M. L. Rosenthal. *The New Poets* (N.Y.,
Oxford Univ. Pr., 1967), pp. 209–10

The thesis of . . . [*Thomas Hardy and British Poetry*] is that Hardy is the chief influence on 20th-century British poetry. It is a surprising thesis but, as you would expect from Davie—author of the best book written about Ezra Pound—it is worked out in exemplary fashion. The influence is of several kinds: he sees Hardy as, stylistically, a self-conscious technician (doing "a precision job" on stanza and meter), and politically a liberal "scientific humanist." He traces the influence of Hardy's attitude on British poets from Auden to the comparatively little known Roy Fisher. . . . Both in his description of general patterns in Hardy's poetry and in close analysis Davie is more accurate and more helpful than any other critic I have read. And I certainly end up persuaded that Hardy has been the central though least acknowledged influence on modern British poetry. . . .

Of course Davie is not only a critic but also, and more important, a poet. Part of him does certainly try hard to write like the sensible Augustan citizen he outlines near the end of his book. Some of the cruder early work in his *Collected Poems* consists of what I might call the Aesop's fable poem: an instance is described, a moral follows. And he is still, occasionally, capable of such a poem. Yet he also—and it is a constant theme—wants to write a poetry like sculpture, which is the reverse of all that is verbal, judgmental and abstract.

Indeed the common-sense moralist and the sculptor-poet are locked in struggle throughout this book, and there are abrupt fluctuations to be found in it, fluctuations of purpose, for example, which could be harmful in a sequence of poems but are not in a collected volume.

Thom Gunn. *NYT*. Jan. 7, 1973, p. 5

DAY LEWIS, C. (1904–1972)

The Room seems to me to be an advance on [Day Lewis's] last collection, *The Gate*, where I felt a certain stiffness and congestion. That is not to say there is any great difference in themes or in style. Always elegant, Day Lewis rarely pushes his poems far enough away from him, so that the reader seems too bound up in the poet's own nostalgia— he is nothing if not nostalgic—and there is a recurring dying fall about the rhythms that inclines to monotony. One wonders if he is ever going to be able to take the giant step forward that would make us see him as more than a fine lyric poet.

There are many good and moving poems in this new collection. The love poems in particular have about them the reflective grace and compassion that has always been one of the rewarding features of his work. In poems which explore a larger situation the lack of what might be called metaphysical conflict prevents them from being more than statements, however admirable, about the given subject. The longish poem "Elegy for a Woman Unknown" is deeply felt and moving and worth comparing with Stephen Spender's "Elegy for Margaret" which it resembles to an extraordinary degree. Read, for flavour, the excellent title poem and, perhaps even better, "Derelict."

John Smith. *PoetryR*. Spring, 1966, p. 41

I suppose the name "MacSpaunday" is now buried in literary history; it was Roy Campbell's satiric name for the composite English poet of the thirties; Campbell's way of saying that from the point of view of someone like himself, a right-wing traditionalist, there was nothing to choose between Auden, Spender, MacNeice and Day Lewis.

Even in those days that was not true, unless one took the line that their left-wing and generally "progressive" attitudes were all equally worthless; and time has sundered them still further. MacNeice is dead; Auden has completely changed his character as a poet; Day Lewis, who took his cue from Auden more mechanically than any of the others, now takes an entirely different set of cues; only Spender appears to me to be still on what is recognizably the same trajectory as he was then.

These reflections are prompted by reading Mr. Day Lewis' *Selected Poems*, a severely pruned selection from forty years' work. The author has had the good sense to realize that most of his rather large output has not stood the test of time, and yet it is a pity, in some ways, that he did not gather up his complete works and throw them at us, with all the absurdities and extravagances, rather in the manner of an unabashed roarer like Hugh MacDiarmid. Day Lewis' incredibly naïve Marxist poems of the thirties, for instance, with their blend of camp-fire heartiness and industrial imagery, do at least bring back the excitement of the period, whereas the well-bred and flavorless snippets, which are all he has allowed himself to salvage from those years, convey nothing at all.

John Wain. NR. June 24, 1967, p. 21

From most of the news stories about the appointment of Cecil Day Lewis as Poet Laureate of Great Britain, you would gather that he is one of those lyric dons who dash off an occasional detective story in their light moments. In fact the poet is, as "Nicholas Blake," a hard-working professional in crime, who has written a novel almost annually since 1935, and is also one of England's two or three leading reviewers of crime fiction. Blake's stature among mystery novelists is at least as high as that of Day Lewis among poets; he has excelled both in the straight detective puzzle and in the broader study of crime and character, as well as in happy blends of the two methods. And it seems particularly fitting that he should celebrate his laurels by publishing his best novel in a dozen years, *The Private Wound*.

The narrator, an Anglo-Irish novelist visiting County Clare in the disturbed year of 1939, says that his story "began as an idyll, continued into low comedy, and ended in tragedy." It is an intensely penetrating study of sexual passion (and, incidentally, a model of how to write sexy without writing dirty). It is also a powerful story of murder and its aftermath, strengthened by a subplot of Irish politics, and constantly illuminated by the author's lightning flashes of insight into the peculiar relation between the Irish and the English (he himself is both) and the even more incredible relation between man and woman, which few male novelists have understood so well.

Anthony Boucher. NYT. April 7, 1968, p. 20

As the Charles Eliot Norton lecturer at Harvard in 1964–65, Day Lewis delivered a series of essays later published as *The Lyric Impulse*. Like *The Poetic Image* of nearly two decades earlier, the lectures define a commitment which had come increasingly to be Day Lewis' great obsession and his ultimate strategy for turning poetry away from intellect and back to the emotions—or better, from the public back to the personal. The lectures define what is in effect his own retrenchment, his return at last to the native element of poet-as-singer which he had sought in his earliest verse. It is not that his poetry of recent years is not mature or technically more successful than his earlier work: maturity has only confirmed Day Lewis' powers as an imitative poet, one whose style is more the product of his "tradition" than of experiment. . . .

The Lyric Impulse, a strikingly casual book, is almost completely void of intellectual tension. Because it follows Day Lewis' last three volumes of poems rather than emerging from the immediacy of their creation, its argument is a kind of afterthought and apology. Or rather, we find in it the ultimate emergence of the residual conviction that earlier had prevented him, on the one hand, from embracing a Marxist poetics and, on the other, from any kind of experimental daring. As such, the book is an unimpassioned and direct plea for another counter-current in modern poetry: a return, as it were, to the primal origins of poetry in song and a repudiation of the self-conscious, intellectual tradition of modern poetry to which Day Lewis had earlier been party. . . . Ironically, the less cerebral his poetry becomes, the fewer spots of successful lyricism it contains.

Joseph N. Riddell. Cecil Day Lewis (N.Y.,
Twayne, 1971), pp. 116–17

DENNIS, NIGEL (1912–   )

When it appeared in England, Nigel Dennis's *A House in Order* was widely reviewed, and the reviews were neither cursory nor perfunctory. As might have been expected for a novel with a nameless hero set in an unspecified country at an indefinite time, most of the reviewers were puzzled. Peter Quennell wrote that "In a long career of reading and reviewing I have seldom met a book more suggestive and provocative, yet at the same time more oddly elusive. . . ." He decided that the book should considerably increase Dennis's reputation, but he had not said why. Frederic Raphael observed that Dennis often seemed to be deliberately composing "in some hippogriffic tongue," and frankly admitted that he did not get the point of it all: "I am bound to say that

I felt neither better nor wiser when the thing was done." Ian Hamilton described the novel as "an apparently bleak existential fable" in which a stoic salute to the passive was made with a smile exceptionally wry even for Mr. Dennis. And D. J. Enright concluded that the book must be an allegory, its sparseness, coolness, and single-mindedness preventing it from being anything else. He was willing to concede that it was as humane as anything could be which offered so little human foothold, and he considered that it "ought to make a quite superior play in the contemporary manner, since in the modern theatre our demands seem to be considerably less precise and strong than they still are when we read a book." . . .

Many other reviewers express admiration for the bleak and lonely central figure. Irving Wardle refers to the author as an ironist turned human; in his view, Dennis's compassion for the hero stands out. Martin Seymour-Smith refers to the narrator's "peculiarly attractive misanthropy," he considers that the book "brilliantly and sympathetically illustrates the solipsist aspect of our condition, and turns it—by means of the gardening—into something less terrible." Frank McGuinness sees the book as a fierce repudiation of those qualities which a competitive and bellicose society has decided are most laudable and a plea for us to revise our values in a more civilized direction. The tragedy of the hero is not that he is cowardly, but that his gentle virtues are mistrusted by the brutal herd around him: he is the odd man out in an army conditioned to the notions of duty and valour, and it is only when he seems to have abandoned his position that he is accepted. "Conform or be damned" is the cry of Left and Right alike in our society, and Dennis gives us a moving portrayal of the eternal outsider.

In my view, however, the central character is treated with a great deal of irony. . . . The hero is content to potter about his greenhouse and ask for an interpretation of his experience from someone who can respond only with clichés. Usually things go well enough with him. But is he a new and changed man? In the first paragraph of the novel, he was a panting, fearful figure—"choking and crying in a dusk that terrified me." In the last paragraph, he relates that sometimes when he crosses the paddock from his greenhouse to his bungalow "I feel suddenly a big, cold hand pressing my shirt against my back—and with fifty yards to go, I run and run." He remains what he was at the beginning—fear in a handful of dust. He possesses remarkable powers of endurance, but Dennis has left him as much a hollow man as the common soldiery he despises. Dennis has left us no way out; his fable is even bleaker and more pessimistic than at first appears.

D. J. Dooley. Critique. Vol. 10, No. 1, 1967,
pp. 95, 97, 99

Nigel Dennis devotes almost half of *Exotics* to his clean uncluttered version of the Gilgamesh Epic. It walks an even, sensible line between the archaic and the prosaic, eschews any recreation of mythic grandeur by lyrical density and wisely allows the exclusion of doubts and guilts to establish a pristine, amoral semi-divinity. The effect is, curiously, of a flight from the rationalism and evangelicalism which the public school confers on classical antiquity, and a search for a parallel myth, less spartan, more stoic, and, incorruptibly, aware of the injustice of things.

Yet a prefectorial stance is implied by the stiff-upper-lip tone (sometimes a meditative expansion of prose), the (too tentative?) hardheadedness of "Kinglake's Eothen," in the heavy satires on academic unworldliness, and the pointedly "stomachic" versions of Giusti's satires on the Italian bourgeoisie. Like other ex-so-called "angry young men," Dennis seems sometimes to dwell in a limbo, a no-man's-land, critical of "Englishness," yet bound to it. From this ambivalence, perhaps, the swerves between the fastidious and the full-blooded which render Dennis at once disconcerting and sympathetic. One seems to hear a voice: clipped, hurt, pointedly numb, briefly nostalgic, girding with ironic quotation marks such Nowhere Man locutions as "crack museum," "sport his snout," "Eh bien, ninnies," and "Most of the pep's gone out of the Pope." The effect of such disruptions on the satires is to render them distinctly odd to eye-reading. Vocal performance becomes mandatory; they gain greatly in a kind of pained, yet supercilious, strength. Ingenious yet somehow synthetic, they interested me less than the illiberal heresies quietly, cautiously celebrated in the Gilgamesh Epic and in the sadly cynical nostalgia for imperialist firmness.

Raymond Durgnat. *PoetryR*. Winter, 1970–71,
p. 366

● DEVLIN, DENIS (1908–1959)

Mr. Devlin, inheritor of the Irish poetic tradition, brings to his work its feeling for rhythm and cadence, Celtic mother wit and rich religious background. But he adds modern youth's re-examination of the past and awareness of the significant part that science now plays in man's universal orientation. Using greater economy of language than most of his Celtic forebears, he attains a strength of structure sometimes lacking in even the greatest of them. The bone structure of a philosophy is here more clearly defined than in other Irish poets, beneath that metaphorical process which is the flesh of all poetry.

"Lough Derg," the poem from which the book takes its title, is the story of an Irish abbey, ancient and famous as a place of religious pilgrimage. The reference to Dante in it is not merely metaphorical but historical: tradition has it that Dante once stayed in retreat there. "Est Prodest," one of the loveliest poems in the book, is full of the deeply religious background and demonstrates the view of modern occultists that praise is more efficacious than prayer. The poem "Annapolis" shows Devlin's keen observation of the American scene. In "Diplomat" and "Memo from a Millionaire," the poet becomes the social critic with a light touch. "The Victory of Samothrace" and "Venus of the Salty Shell" are effective poems on subjects that because of their triteness are difficult to handle, but which in this case are handled exceedingly well.

Inez Boulton. Poetry. Dec., 1946, p. 169

Like most Irishmen of his generation, Devlin had closer ties with France than with England, and his education in modern poetry was mostly French. The influence of Valéry is pervasive; and there is a little of Yeats. His originality is not spectacular; it is subtle and sub-dued, consisting in a slight modification of the language and conven-tions of his immediate elders. He wrote a few bad poems, many good poems, and perhaps three great poems. These are "The Passion of Christ," "From Government Buildings," and, above all, "Lough Derg," a poem that may rank with Stevens' "Sunday Morning," Eliot's "Gerontion," and Crane's "The Broken Tower." In all these poems, the poets are exploring the difficult region where doubt and faith have been conducting an inconclusive dialectic since the middle of the last century.

"Lough Derg" takes its title from that part of Donegal where annually Irish pilgrims gather to pray. The poem is composed of nine-teen six-line stanzas, rhymed *ababcc*, a modification of rhyme royal, or perhaps an adaptation of the stanza, *aabccb*, of "*Le cimetière marin*." In other ways the poem suggests a derivation from, but in no sense an imitation of, Valéry. Like "*Le cimetière marin*," it poses a universal religious conflict which, in Valéry, Mr. Yvor Winters has described as a sense of the "flaw in creation"; in "Lough Derg" the conflict moves within a definitely Christian orbit: a civilized Irishman of the Catholic faith meditates on the difference between the scepticism of faith and the simple, fanatical faith of the Irish peasant—with whom he partly identi-fies himself—praying at Lough Derg. It is a sufficiently commonplace subject, yet one that still seems to give rise to great poetry. . . .

Allen Tate and Robert Penn Warren. Preface
to Denis Devlin, Selected Poems (N.Y., Holt,
Rinehart and Winston, 1963), p. 13

Denis Devlin, who died in 1959 while he was Irish Ambassador to Italy, published widely and won the approval of several important tastemakers. . . . However, he has received scant critical attention for a poet so well introduced [by Tate and Warren]. He is, nevertheless, one of the most impressive poets to come out of modern Ireland. What may have kept Devlin from wider approval is what irritated Austin Clarke about his poetry: his similarity to intellectual poets of the Continent. Devlin has translated St.-John Perse, and his own progression has been from a surrealistic portrayal of disgust to a mythic celebration of love. In his presentation of a psychological reality, metaphor becomes reality. He searched for ontological relationships which could raise him above the enforced fears and the miserable squabbles of opportunists. . . .

Understandably, Devlin did not become one of the people he wrote of in "Lough Derg" for whom "all is simple and symbol in their world, /The incomprehended rendered fabulous." He was a civilized European who came to see the history of Ireland and the soul of man without the guilt-inspired fear and reticence so prevalent in his early poems. Yet he did achieve a complex and, I believe, more fabulous world than those who did not share his struggle. Though Devlin's inquiry and his desire for joy took him to beliefs that would be strange to many of his countrymen, he discovered the living divine within himself and those he loved. He does not seem to have abandoned Christianity. Like Charles Williams, whose magical writings about love resemble Devlin's, he sought in various cultures a belief founded on the permanence of the divine in the temporary body of humanity.

Frank L. Kersnowski. *SwR*. Winter, 1973, pp. 113, 122

● DOUGLAS, KEITH (1920–1944)

Douglas's poems fall into a number of distinct groups, and any later group is always more interesting and important than the group that immediately precedes it. The poems that he wrote at school are mainly important in that they show us a boy patiently learning his craft. The poems that he wrote at Oxford have more depth and subtlety, but they have something in common—both in their charm, and in their occasional weakness—with all undergraduate poetry. They are very "literary" poems. In the poems which Douglas wrote during his period of military training in England, we begin to feel that he is biting deeper into experience; or that experience is biting deeper into him. Finally, the poems written in the Middle East are, of course, Douglas's most important achievement. If we take these groups in turn, we shall get a fairly accurate picture of his development.

There is, however, one more group still: the group of poems Douglas was never able to finish. The most important of these is a poem, or a set of frustrated beginnings of a poem, called "Bête Noire." This, as it stands, is not anything achieved. It is a succession of hopeless attempts to grapple with an intractable subject, the subject of what Douglas called, in conversation and in letters, "the beast on my back." It is the subject of what any of us colloquially might call "the black dog on my back": or in more ambitious language, it is the subject of what Freudian psychologists call, or used to call, the Death-Wish and Jungian psychologists call the Shadow. I imagine a Jungian psychologist would say that Douglas was very much aware of his Shadow, in a sense at times almost obsessed with it, but that he had never properly accepted it, or come to terms with it, and that therefore, in spite of the impression he gave of being far more mature than his years, he was not, when he died, yet a fully integrated personality. There was, as it were, a crucial and painful experience still to come, of which he had a kind of poetic premonition.

G. S. Fraser. Proceedings of the British
Academy. Vol. 42, 1956, pp. 97–98

When [Douglas's] Collected Poems were first published in 1951 . . . he appeared primarily interesting, to most of his readers, as a "war-poet," and as such seems to have been largely forgotten. Now, twelve years later and eighteen years after his death, it is becoming clear that he offers more than just a few poems about war, and that every poem he wrote, whether about war or not, has some special value. His poetry in general seems to be of some special value. It is still very much alive, and even providing life. And the longer it lives, the fresher it looks. . . .

In his nine years of accomplished writing, Douglas developed rapidly. Leaving his virtuoso juvenilia, his poetry passed through two roughly distinguishable phases, and began to clarify into a third. The literary influences on this progress seem to have been few. To begin with, perhaps he takes Auden's language over pretty whole, but he empties it of its intellectual concerns, turns it into the practical experience of life, and lets a few minor colours of the late 1930 poetry schools creep in. But his temperament is so utterly modern he seems to have no difficulty with the terrible, suffocating, maternal octopus of ancient English poetic tradition. . . .

The war brought his gift to maturity, or to a first maturity. In a sense, war was his ideal subject: the burning away of all human pretensions in the ray cast by death. This was the vision, the unifying generalization that shed the meaning and urgency into all his observations and particulars: not truth is beauty only, but truth kills everybody. The truth of a man is the doomed man in him or his dead body. Poem after poem circles this idea, as if his mind were tethered. At the bottom of it, perhaps, is his private muse, not a romantic symbol of danger and temptation, but the plain foreknowledge of his own rapidly-approaching end—a foreknowledge of which he becomes fully conscious in two of his finest poems. This sets his writing apart from that of Hemingway, with which it shares certain features. Hemingway tried to imagine the death that Douglas had foresuffered. Douglas had no time, and perhaps no disposition, to cultivate the fruity deciduous tree of How To Live. He showed in his poetry no concern for man in society. The murderous skeleton in the body of a girl, the dead men being eaten by dogs on the moonlit desert, the dead man behind the mirror, these items of circumstantial evidence are steadily out-arguing all his high spirits and hopefulness.

Ted Hughes. Intro. to Keith Douglas, Selected
Poems (N.Y., Chilmark, 1964), pp. 11–13

With Keith Douglas, indeed, poetry and painting were twin preoccupations. Another Mertonian, Douglas Grant, has ventured the opinion that Keith "might have excelled eventually as the artist rather than as the poet." It was to nature, especially to horses and their settings, that he first applied his art and his fresh bright colours. Later, he used the same painter's skill to depict the turmoil and "nightmare ground" of the desert campaign.

Keith's character was, I believe, complex in the manner of many artists. Against his generosity and zest for life must be placed, if the portrait is to be (as he would have wished it to be) true to life, certain less endearing qualities—an impulsive and obstinate streak which was sometimes the despair of even his closest friends. His intellect was as I now feel on the verge of greatness. It is on this account that his poetry, and his poetry was not only the fruit of his war experiences, looks like answering the demand of his distant school predecessor Coleridge: the best poets utter a philosophy. Keith Douglas was (in the words of one of his schoolmasters) "one of the ablest of our History Grecians," and had formed his panorama of life and time out of his historical contemplations. His mythology was energetic, for he had not noticed that the classical world had been sent to Coventry. He was a young man who often did not notice such things.

Edmund Blunden. Intro. to Keith Douglas,
Collected Poems (N.Y., Chilmark, 1966),
pp. 18–19

Douglas would have approved of the brief, terse obituary note written by his friend Bernard Spencer for the little magazine, *Personal Landscape*, which we edited in Cairo: and to which Douglas had contributed a number of fine poems. It was as simple and bare as a war communiqué. Douglas, who above all loathed rhetoric and affectation, would have been grateful. Almost the only personal detail about his work was the phrase "He considered himself as being in the tradition of Wilfred Owen."

We knew that we had lost a poet of this high calibre but it is doubtful whether his companions-in-arms were aware of the fact; for them he was a brave and experienced officer of the line, a severe loss to a crack unit. This too he would have found completely appropriate and just. He was as devoted to his temporary profession as he was to his private gift and enjoyed both as fully as he was able in the short time allotted to him. There was neither self-delusion nor self-pity in his attitude. Life itself was so rich, so infinitely variegated, so full of sap, that he did not permit himself to think beyond the moment. How wise he was! He took things as they were, extracting every ounce of experience from them, and at the same time converting them into prose and poetry. Everything was enjoyable, even fear, horror and physical discomfort. Here and there in the poems he clearly previsioned his approaching death, but gaily and without reluctance. The only thing was time—would there be enough of it to enable him to capitalize on so rich a gift? Perhaps the very excellence of his work owes something to this sense of urgency; certainly it lends his prose an incomparable vividness and impact. Smooth, unhesitating and pointed, it conveys all his own enthusiasm and generosity: and it is the mirror of his conversation. . . .

It is not possible to know what Douglas would be writing today were he still alive; I suspect that the gradual maturing of this exceptional poetic gift might have given him by now an extra dimension, perhaps more metaphysical and less brilliantly impressionistic. But conjecture is fruitless. His work stands there in the niche he has carved for himself, perfect and self-subsisting. It is of the rarest quality and executed with an astonishing technical maturity. It is not the work of a

virtuoso but the early work of a real master. We have every right to
regret that his time ran out so quickly. He was a real loss to literature.

Lawrence Durrell. Intro. to Keith Douglas,
Alamein to Zem Zem (Faber and Faber,
1966), pp. 11, 13

● DRABBLE, MARGARET (1939–   )

A Summer Bird-Cage (quotation from Webster) is a sad but funny
little tale about the break-up of a marriage. Louise, a notable beauty,
marries for his money a rich but nasty novelist; the story is related by
her less beautiful sister, Sarah, in a colloquial, unpretentious, yet stylish
prose which is perfectly fitted to the narrative. The characters and
setting are entirely "contemporary," but Miss Drabble is neither a
beatnik nor a young-angry, and her pictures of girlhood have a charm
and tenderness which recall the novels of Rosamond Lehmann; yet
the book is without a trace of sentimentality. Its moral might be
expressed in the words of the heroine in the last chapter: "What fools
middle-class girls are to expect other people to respect the same gods as
themselves and E. M. Forster."

To call a first novel "promising" always seems a bit unfair, imply-
ing as it does that the author might have done better if he had tried a
little harder. Miss Drabble may write better novels in the future, and I
hope she does, but *A Summer Bird-Cage* seems to me a noteworthy
achievement and, considering Miss Drabble's age (she is twenty-four),
remarkably mature.

Jocelyn Brooke. List. April 11, 1963, p. 645

The British novelist Margaret Drabble has written a gravely intelligent
novel [*The Garrick Year*] on a familiar theme, the situation of the
contemporary young woman, well brought up, well schooled, with
enormous vistas promised to her by her family and by her society, who
finds her horizons shrunk to diaper-size, all her possibilities reduced to
a task that could, essentially, be done by any competent servant. This
dog-eared problem, this subject of the self-pitying outbursts of Doris
Lessing and the coruscating complaints of Simone de Beauvoir, is
treated here as freshly as if it had just come up for the first time. . . .

As stories go, it is not wildly eventful (until the end, when the
action moves like a speeded-up film). But is unfolded in such a way
that nuances of character and observation have all the surprise and

dramatic impact normally reserved for unusual external events. In short: it is written with extraordinary art. . . .

Yeats has said: "Of our conflicts with others we make rhetoric; of our conflicts with ourselves we make poetry." One of the reasons this novel is successful is that Miss Drabble understands her protagonist's conflict with herself. Emma's adventure, in the end, is not with her environment but with her own rebellious ego—and one sees that her rebellion is against a fate toward which she feels a strong, contradictory attraction. Out of that conflict, the author draws an act of the imagination, by which she defines, once again, what it means to be a woman. Her witty beguiling novel performs that act so quietly it seems, in retrospect, a conjurer's trick.

Here I am forced to a critical cliché. If you have a list, and on it appear such names as Elizabeth Bowen and Muriel Spark, add to it the name of Margaret Drabble. Her compass, as yet, is small: her publishers list only one other book, *A Summer Bird-Cage*. But in a world of disappointing behemoth, let us be thankful for the small and perfect.

Daniel Stern. *NYT*. April 4, 1965, pp. 4, 14

If a romantic novel is a novel that is essentially about the romance of love, then Miss Margaret Drabble writes romantic novels: and the point about her new one *The Waterfall* is that a harsh voice demands to know if every word within her romantic framework is the truth, and in the end rejects the framework itself. Her heroine is Jane, who like Rosamund and Clara before her, is refreshingly far from being open-legged for sex at the drop of a fly-zip. In creating Rosamund Stacey in *The Millstone*, Miss Drabble offered us a girl whose feelings about the prospect of sexual intercourse were more natural and more typical than the heroines of so much contemporary fiction—created by women as well as by men—have us believe. Rosamund, you may recall, had two boy-friends, each of whom assumed, as was her intention, that she was going to bed with the other: she remained, until she wished otherwise, a wise virgin. Clara in *Jerusalem the Golden* was more obliging, but she did have a way of keeping a book or two under her pillow to tide her over anything she might not care for.

Jane of *The Waterfall* is very similar to Rosamund and Clara, except that in her case Miss Drabble has delved more ruthlessly. . . . The dense introspective style that accompanies Jane when she's being truly honest sometimes reads like an argumentative thesis, but this is hardly a fault because Jane is a girl whose mind operates like that. Only once or twice does introspection seem unduly bothersome in this brilliant novel, and that's when it's too long indulged at a dramatic moment. Otherwise, *The Waterfall* seems to me to be a skilful, subtle achievement, a woman's novel that should be read, above all, by every man who's ever likely to have love for a woman on his mind. Contained within the limits of an everyday adulterous *affaire*, it is evenly perceptive and revealing throughout, and if it makes less compelling reading than some of Miss Drabble's earlier novels, that lack is more than compensated for by the greater riches of a greater truth. Miss Drabble's strength is that she never seeks to overreach herself or attempt what is alien to her imagination; and for that reason I believe it's unlikely that she has it in her to write a bad book. *The Waterfall* is built upon the foundations of all she has written before; what she builds upon *The Waterfall* may well be sheer magnificence.

William Trevor. *NS*. May 23, 1969, p. 738

Margaret Drabble's *The Needle's Eye* is an extraordinary work: It not only tells a story deftly, beautifully, with a management of past and present (and future) action that demonstrates Miss Drabble's total mastery of the mysterious form of the novel, but it succeeds in so re-creating the experiences of her characters that we soon forget they are fictional beings (perhaps they are not . . . ?) and we become them, we are transformed into them, so that by the end of the novel we have lived, through them, a very real, human and yet extraordinary experience. . . .

Each of Margaret Drabble's novels has been an extraordinary leap forward: from the well-written, entertaining, but not disturbing *The Garrick Year*, to the moral ambiguities of *The Millstone*, to the rather strange, disturbing *Jerusalem the Golden* and its remorseless "survivor," to the half-mad narrative of *The Waterfall*. Though I have admired Miss Drabble's writing for years, I will admit that nothing she has written in the past quite prepared me for the depth and richness of *The Needle's Eye*.

Joyce Carol Oates. *NYT*. June 11, 1972, p. 23

Margaret Drabble's bleak pessimism regarding love, marriage, and the casual disasters besetting the female locked into heterosexuality and a less radical life style is the focus of her first five novels, written since 1964. Published and praised in England, she seems little read in the United States, a transatlantic reader's loss since the currency of her vision is remarkable.

Bungled and achieved female self-definition is her consistent theme; her women might set out to pay homage to patriarchy's dearest forms but en route their increasing awareness of the absurdity of their sexual, social, and economic positions results in their befuddlement and defeat within the system. Only occasionally and in a limited sense do her women manage to infiltrate intellectually or economically the masculine milieu. Drabble turns to the novel to explore the various options of women today; she evidently lacks the idealism that active feminist politics demands while her awareness of human inequities needs no heightening through consciousness raising sessions. The conversion of the sexual protest into novels is what makes her interesting. The choices of artist over activist and imitation over frontal attack allow a subtlety and sensitivity that politics frequently precludes.

Margaret Drabble leisurely inspects patterns of female development and the nuances of both male oppression and sexual liberation; unlike her political counterpart who is sustained by a vision of a new order, Drabble's outlook is grim. Her conclusions are often nihilistic and suggest sexual tyranny is here to stay, a component of a deterministic universe. Neither a missionary, an idealist, nor a prophet, Drabble offers the reader practical imitations of the real world. The novels incisively diagnose female complaints while avoiding talky and dubious prognosis and treatment programs; rhetoric and wish-fulfillment are, mercifully, out of bounds in her work. Because the English novel has traditionally contributed to social reform through its criticism of social inequities, the enduring gains in woman's rights may as well be made by cautious and introspective artists, such as Drabble, as by the movement's activists and political theoreticians.

Virginia K. Beards. *Critique.* Vol. 15, No. 1,
1973, pp. 35–36

DURRELL, LAWRENCE (1912–   )

Lawrence Durrell is a man of infinite variety. But he's a man of marble constancy as well. The forms in which he has worked embrace the whole range of literary possibility. Yet the themes he has dealt with— even the images which carry those themes—display a simple kind of shining directness, mark out a clear path for his developing but remarkably consistent point of view. He is consequently one of our most protean writers and at the same time one of our most predictable ones.

It is variety, however, that immediately strikes anyone who does no more than glance through a stack of Durrell's collected works. . . . Even if one limits one's glance to works currently in print, something of Durrell's enormous range is bound to be suggested. He is author, for instance, of the espionage thriller *White Eagles over Serbia* (described by Durrell's American publisher as a book "for young persons"); of intricate poems (among them the sonnet of sonnets, "A Soliloquy of Hamlet") and bawdy ballads (Dylan Thomas's favorite being "A Ballad of the Good Lord Nelson"); of a trilogy of "travel books" which should perhaps more accurately be called island portraits (*Prospero's Cell, Reflections on a Marine Venus,* and *Bitter Lemons*); of three poetic dramas, startlingly different in tone—though not in theme; of the "solipsistic," raw fictional account of prewar London, *The Black Book*; of comic interludes about life in the diplomatic corps (*Esprit de Corps* and *Stiff Upper Lip*); of *The Dark Labyrinth,* a novel which Durrell accurately described to Henry Miller as "an extended morality, but written artlessly in the style of the detective story"; of literary criticism (*A Key to Modern British Poetry*); and—by far his most popular work—of the extraordinarily complex, expanding study of the emotional education of a hero and his friends, *The Alexandria Quartet.* He has also in his time turned out public relations copy, newspaper columns, and—presumably unavailable to the public—a whole series of confidential reports, the bulky stuffing of diplomats' bags and Home Office files. He has published some of his letters to Henry Miller and a smaller group of letters (to Alfred Perlès) about Henry Miller. He has acted as translator of prose (Emmanuel Royidis' novel *Pope Joan*) and poetry (Constantine Cavafy, not only in the body of *The Alexandria Quartet,* but elsewhere), anthologist, and magazine editor. He was for a while one of the principal script writers for the motion picture *Cleopatra*—and once, in his youth, a would-be composer-lyricist of popular songs. For years after the completion of *The Alexandria Quartet* he was reported as being engaged in work on "an enormous Rabelaisian comic novel."

His variety is, in fact, so spectacular that one suspects that, consciously or unconsciously, somewhere along the line Durrell must have toyed with the idea of being literature's Leonardo—the master of each literary form. So far as I know he has not as yet written the libretto of an opera—but give him time.

John Unterecker. Lawrence Durrell (N.Y.,
Columbia Univ. Pr., 1964), pp. 3–4

Whether it is imagination or fantasy that queens it over Durrell's world—basically, how "serious" a writer he is—is, I suppose, the key critical question about him.

One talks of bracketing off "the real world," but of course the creatures of Durrell's imagination or fantasy are very "real" to him and to many of his readers. . . . Part of the philosophy underlying *The Alexandria Quartet* is that there is a life-pattern inside all of us that will work itself out, comically or tragically, with certain variations, wherever we find ourselves. You take your basic character wherever you go with you, but a change of setting and circumstances can alter your fate. Durrell, I think, believes in fate, but in a fate loosely predetermined; a new setting can allow an apparently quite new aspect of character to flower. . . .

Durrell, to put this another way, is concerned in his fiction not with a growing change in character, in response to changing challenges, but with a process of self-discovery, a stripping away of layer after layer of the self of outward social habit, till a hard core is revealed, which was always there, and in a sense always half-known. In this respect, he is more like an ancient historian than a modern novelist. Collingwood, in *The Idea of History*, points out that ancient historians take it for granted that Tiberius was always very wicked but needed to become Emperor before he could show how wicked he really was, whereas the modern historian's picture of Tiberius would be that of a good soldier and public servant whose character slowly deteriorated under accumulating pressures of strain, disappointment, and fear. Durrell, in this sense if not in others, is a classical writer. A preoccupation with the mystery of self-identity lies at the core of *The Alexandria Quartet*.

G. S. Fraser. *Lawrence Durrell: A Study*
(Faber and Faber, 1968), pp. 22–23

For Lawrence Durrell, places are holy. Landscapes are as powerful as gods or parents; men are their creations. "We are the children of our landscape," he writes in *Justine*. "I can think of no better identification." *Spirit of Place*, the new Durrell collection, is a testament to his lifetime preoccupation with landscape. . . .

Durrell believes that the task of the travel writer is "to isolate the germ in the people which is expressed by their landscape." Travel becomes "a sort of science of intuitions," "the education of the sensibility." To be educated, the traveler must identify. . . . Identification seems simple, "for all landscapes ask the same question in the same whisper. "I am watching you—are you watching yourself in me?" Durrell's approach is that of the outsider and the romantic; places exist for his sake. They are—as titles of other works suggest—private countries, personal landscapes. . . . Durrell identifies with the mythic elements and *status quo* of a place, and closes his eyes to social and political problems.

Throughout his life, Durrell has been moving through foreign landscapes, mirroring himself in them and recording the interaction. Born in India he spent his childhood there, his adolescence in England, his young manhood on the Greek island of Corfu. During World War II he lived in Egypt. At the close of the war he returned to Greece, to the island of Rhodes. From Rhodes he went to Argentina, Yugoslavia, Cyprus. He now lives in Provence and still travels. Not all of Durrell's landscapes have had the same effect on him: "Everyone finds his own 'correspondences,' " he writes, "landscapes where you suddenly feel bounding with ideas and others where half your soul falls asleep. . . . Writers each seem to have a personal landscape of the heart which beckons them." For Durrell, landscapes seem to be either death- or life-giving. In Yugoslavia, Argentina, especially in England, and even in Egypt, he felt suffocated, uncreative. Durrell's landscape of the heart, the landscape that first nourished his art and that always seems to draw him back, is the Greek island.

Joan Goulianos. Nation. July 14, 1969, p. 56

With the publication of *The Alexandria Quartet* in the late 1950's, Lawrence Durrell, a prolific writer since the mid-1930's, suddenly achieved both commercial success and serious critical consideration. Despite its anomalous nature, such Janus-faced attention is not really surprising; for the world of Durrell's writing is something various and new, rich yet firm, as soaring and mundane as mountains or cities. It is a heady brew of poetry and prose to be imbibed in great rapid bursts of taste—and one falls invariably into purple passages in attempting to convey its flavor. It is, at the same time, the substantial fare of a major craftsman.

Durrell takes his place—with Proust, the early Joyce and Lawrence, Henry Miller—within the tradition of artist as autobiographer, as transmuter of transient personal experience into the mold of permanence. His life has been a kaleidoscopic pattern of jobs and places, of being press officer, public relations official, editor, teacher, lecturer on British poetry, and in such unlikely places as Athens, Cairo, Alexandria, Rhodes, Argentina, Yugoslavia, Cyprus. And no place he has resided in or visited, no job he has performed, no person he has known, no idea he or someone near him has held, it would seem, fails to be both retained and transmitted through the products of his art.

Perhaps the central impetus in the work is Durrell's inherent sense of deracination and his concomitant need to belong somewhere. Indeed, he would seem to embody the very pattern of the rootless wanderer imbued with a highly developed sense of roots; for, like most placeless men, Durrell worships place—it inspires a sense of comforting wholeness, an enduring context that implies the underlying and permanent basis for the world's unending temporality. Regionalist novelists find permanence and stability in the people and continuing traditions of an area; Durrell, who superficially resembles them, has sought values outside the social structure, in the more externalized world he calls "landscape"—a collective noun encompassing ambience, atmosphere, essence, a way of life, all the innumerable forces impinging on the writer during his stay in a given place, as well as all his imaginatively felt and reconstructed reactions to them.

> Alan Warren Friedman. *Lawrence Durrell and*
> *"The Alexandria Quartet"* (Norman, Univ. of
> Oklahoma Pr., 1970), pp. xiii–xiv

Nunquam is the second part of what Lawrence Durrell describes as a double-decker novel. At the end of *Tunc*, the first part, it is left as an open question whether Felix Charlock will be successful in trying to free himself from the golden tyranny of what is referred to in both books as "the firm." Felix is an inventor, his creations are used by the firm for its own purposes, but he is spectacularly rewarded for them. In marrying Benedicta, he has married into the firm, although he has not been successful in actually meeting Julian, its Western head. *Nunquam* now reveals that Felix's bid for freedom has come to nothing, and it is one of several disappointments provided by the new novel that both the narrative and the abstract implications of Felix's attempt to escape should be so weakly resolved. . . .

Durrell's interest in and use of ideas has always been more opportunist than rigorous. He enjoys the kick that can be got out of certain notions more than the disciplined conclusions that can be reached through them. The ideas that lay behind the Quartet had at least the merit of leading us back to the permanently interesting imponderables of personality and point-of-view. The more abstract concerns of the new diptych not only mean that Durrell's usual command of the sensually realized scene is mostly conspicuous by its attenuation: they are not even very coherently or persuasively worked out in their own terms.

> *TLS*. March 26, 1970, p. 328

Admirers of Lawrence Durrell's lavishly praised *Alexandria Quartet* will doubtless find the *Tunc* and *Nunquam* duet (or alternative?) equally excellent, and those who hated it will find them just as detestable. The two new novels cover much the same ground as the four old ones, and in much the same way. The main difference is the comparative brevity of the new work, which will be deplored or applauded according to taste. You can take your choice—king-size *Alexandria Quartet* or economy-pack *Tunc* and *Nunquam*.

The earlier work was based on the theory of relativity—at least this is what Durrell assured his readers when he announced his "four-decker novel whose form is based on the relativity proposition." Three sides of space, he said, and one of time were to constitute "the soup-mix of a continuum. The four novels follow this pattern." It is doubtful whether Durrell's readers would ever have guessed this if he hadn't told them, and the ambitious project of becoming the Einstein of the novel (a "word-continuum," no less) was always more apparent in the intention than in the performance.

The new, double-decker soup-mix (handi-pak) "tries to take a culture reading merely," says the author in a postface to *Nunquam*, and he adds "of course the poetic game is to try and put a lid on a box with no sides." Apparently, then, Durrell is still in there, playing games.

Richard Boston. NYT. March 29, 1970, p. 4

ELIOT, T. S. (1888–1965)

Eliot's contribution has been tremendous. Refusing easier expedients, he has concentrated on what in our time can make poetry of a high order; and in so doing has used poetry as a test for what is, and is not, valid. The complete canon, poetry and prose, may show a lack of harmony, of interlocking; neither state affairs nor dramatic action was artistically mastered. But Eliot's juxtaposition of disparate mind-adventures have had a clarity and a detonation that premature attempts at inter-relation—the danger is clear in the last plays—might have reduced; the impacts would have been softened, and unity bought, as it was perhaps in *The Cocktail Party*, at too dear a cost. No poet has been more deeply honest. The results are simultaneously personal in substance and impersonal in technique.

I write of Eliot as a poet, of his poetic self; and this self, I have argued, cannot be regarded as wholly, or even mainly, Christian: he has left no visionary statement so happily assured as "Marina." As a man he was, we know, a Christian; his conversion existed in the order of decision and life-action, not of art. The two orders are distinct.

G. Wilson Knight. *SwR*. Winter, 1966, p. 255

[Eliot] is not so great a creative power as D. H. Lawrence, who died in 1930—which datum doesn't all the same explain why, with my general themes in mind, it's Eliot I choose to discuss. It's by reason of the limitation attendant on the achievement that he lends himself to my purpose. You don't, where the Victorian age is in question, go to poetry for the kind of major significance that, as I've just suggested, characterizes Eliot the poet; we go to the novel, where the creative, or poetic, strength of the English language manifests itself. Eliot restores to poetry the capacity for major significance, and in doing it invites, in direct and pregnant ways that favour demonstrative economy, the discussion of those questions I've raised: In what sense has the past its life in the present, and what and where are the life and reality of English Literature? He has here, for my purpose, an advantage over Lawrence—he offers me one that Lawrence doesn't. This distinctive characteristic of Eliot as a great innovating poet is associated with the fact that his creative achievement bears a peculiarly close relation to his criticism.

Lawrence is a critic too—a greater critic than Eliot, just as he is a greater creative power. He is much more freely a critic—infinitely more, and a critic over an unlimited range. Eliot is not freely a critic at all; in fact, he lacks most of the gifts one thinks of as making a critic. He is a distinguished critic only over an extremely narrow range; his good criticism bears immediately on the problems of the "poetic practitioner" (his own phrase) who, in the years around 1920, when Swinburne pervaded the atmosphere and the Georgians were undertaking to occupy the field, was intent on proving that there might again be an important English poetry. He proved it—whether there has been any of importance since is another question.

F. R. Leavis. MR. Winter, 1969, p. 10

The "learning" in Eliot's earlier poems must be seen as an aspect of his Americanism. As scholarship it is wide-ranging, but often superficial and inaccurate. At one level, indeed, the enjoyment that he and Pound found—and successfully communicated to their readers—in exploiting their miscellaneous erudition is the same in kind, if not in degree, that every American pilgrim of our cathedrals, galleries and museums experiences. The appearance of literary scholarship parallels the tourist's apparent acquisition of "culture." When Eliot in 1920 prefixed to *The Sacred Wood*—facing the title-page—the phrase "I also like to dine on becaficas," he was merely showing off. Why should the reader recognize this line from Byron's *Beppo*? Why should he be expected to know that "becaficas"—which both Byron and Eliot misspell—are Italian birds that make good eating? In any case what is the relevance of this particular line of Byron's on the attractions of Italy as a place to live in to a collection of critical essays? This is tourist-erudition.

Such frivolities can be disregarded. Their interest—like that of "Burbank" (which has other interests too, as I have argued)—lies in the evidence they supply of a certain gaiety of spirit that Eliot never fully recovered after his nervous breakdown in 1921. For the poetry the significance of the "learning" is that it was an American supplement to the various attempts made by the best European poets of the time to escape from the *impasse* of Pure Poetry. In the end, of course, the expatriate American intellectuals—with the eccentric exception of Pound—had either to adapt themselves to their European surroundings or to return to America. Eliot gradually merged into the Anglo-French literary establishment, though with the poetic consequence that when (in and after 1927) he had formally become an English citizen the "learning" had lost most of its aesthetic *raison d'être*. He was no longer an American poet with a revolutionary new technique—as Poe and Whitman in their different ways had been before him. After *The Waste Land*, therefore, the learned allusions tend to persist only as a matter of literary habit. In *Four Quartets* (composed 1935–42) in particular it is noticeable how functionless most of the allusions, quotations and plagiarisms now are. The impression one has is of an essayist in the Lamb or Hazlitt manner eking out material that is subjectively and emotionally decidedly "thin." The one exception that occurs to me is the half-translation from Mallarmé in the beautiful Dantesque episode in "Little Gidding."

F. W. Bateson. In Graham Martin, ed., Eliot in Perspective (N.Y., Humanities, 1970), pp. 42–43

For Raymond Williams, belief in the possibility of a common culture is a belief in the capacity of "high" culture, when shared and re-created by a whole community, to be enriched rather than adulterated; it is also a belief that this wide artistic sharing can make sense only within the admission of the people as a whole to full participation in the making of "culture" as a way of life, in its social, political and economic forms. Eliot, of course, sees such an operation as disastrous, as the emotive force of his phrase "[to] put [art] at the disposal of everybody" reveals. But the difference lies partly in whether society is conceived of as static or moving, as a finished structure or an ongoing human creation.

Williams's belief in the possibility of a genuinely common culture is based on his recognition that the growth of literacy, industrialism and political democracy in Britain has been growth towards control by a whole society over its own life, a reaching for common responsibility through the struggles of a long revolution still far from finished. It is a process which has been faced at many points by the conservative response which Eliot represents; the urge to erect barriers, to draw the line before one's own feet and place culture, literacy, democracy on *this*, not *that* side, has been a recurrent reaction, and Burke's contempt for the "swinish multitude" has taken many subsequent forms. Each time, however, the revolution for wider participation and responsibility has continued; each grudgingly lowered barrier, each new form of incorporation, has been the cue for a further participation, until the whole process can only be denied or halted by replacing the images of growth with those of stasis. The conservative version of a stable and stratified society, with given degrees and relations of culture, and the "liberal minority" version, with its faith in the few just men sustaining a personal tradition within an impersonal and unchanging "mass" society, both end by doing this. Eliot's cultural work has been one major example of the conservative reaction, and as such is a challenge which must be met if a common culture in its fullest sense is to exist.

Terry Eagleton. In Graham Martin, ed., Eliot in Perspective (N.Y., Humanities, 1970), p. 294

The fiftieth anniversary of the publication of T. S. Eliot's *The Waste Land* is an obvious occasion for critical revaluation. Already we are separated from the great works of that *annus mirabilis*, 1922, by a distance in time and sensibility as great as that which separated Eliot and Pound and Joyce from their Victorian predecessors. In the late 1940's, when I first encountered *The Waste Land*, I could still read Eliot as if he were my contemporary: evidence both of the extraordinary impact of the "modernist" movement and of *The Waste Land*'s central place in that movement. Few works can have remained *avant-garde* for so long. But now that "modernism" has passed into the realm of literary history *The Waste Land* must pass with it, helped on its way by the recent discovery and publication of the original manuscripts and typescripts. *The Waste Land* and Eliot's other poems will never look quite the same again.

To me *The Waste Land* has always been the classic example of the "really new" work of art, as Eliot himself describes it in "Tradition and the Individual Talent": the radical achievement which enters the established order of literary works and causes a permanent shift in our perspective, so that the entire idea of a literary tradition is significantly altered. This position of *The Waste Land* as the central or normative statement of a new literary age was recognized from the start. In July 1922, three months before the poem's publication, Ezra Pound wrote to his former teacher Felix E. Schelling that "Eliot's *Waste Land* is I think the justification of the 'movement,' of our modern experiment, since 1900." Like Joyce's *Ulysses, The Waste Land* was acknowledged as a revolutionary document while still a work in progress. It was part of the propaganda, as well as the crowning achievement, of the "new poetry" of 1909–1922.

> A. Walton Litz. In A. Walton Litz, ed., *Eliot in His Time* (Princeton, N.J., Princeton Univ. Pr., 1973), pp. 3–4

As a Briton commenting on an Anglo-American poet, I am assuming that a little insularity will not come amiss. And in fact it can hardly be avoided, seeing that my particular concern is with those last poems— the *Four Quartets*—which were undertaken by a British citizen and completed in a Britain at war, and which allude continually to England's historic past and to what was then London's imperiled present. This is borne out by that one of the *Quartets* which seems not to fit my description; Eliot, when he herded all his American references into "The Dry Salvages," rather plainly meant, by thus honoring his transatlantic pieties in one delimited act of homage, to assert his right through the rest of the sequence to speak as an Englishman.

Eliot had undoubtedly earned the right thus to speak for his adopted nation; his patriotism is moving, and I have no wish to impugn it. Yet it is certainly to the point to ask how well he knew the country and the people that he meant to speak for. And if I read aright the mostly ungracious comments that may be culled from Englishmen of my own generation and younger, the consensus is that Eliot knew England and the English very imperfectly, after thirty years. Some of the evidence is too familiar to be worth dwelling on—such characteristically English voices as D. H. Lawrence's, Thomas Hardy's, William Blake's, Eliot showed himself more or less deaf to. But other features of Eliot's adopted Englishness may not be so apparent to a non-British audience; and in that sentence I have slipped in one of them already—"English" and "British" are not the same, and when Eliot welcomes "regionalism" in *Notes Towards the Definition of Culture*, this is not going to satisfy people who define themselves as Scottish or Welsh, let alone Irish. Among Eliot's British contemporaries we need think only of David Jones, Robert Graves, and Hugh MacDiarmid, to be reminded how there are other ways of tying historic Britain in with European Christendom besides the one that Eliot impatiently or blandly took to be the one right way—through Canterbury and Lambeth. Eliot's sense of Britain is offensively metropolitan—and not of Britain, but of England too; his England is to all intents and purposes London, or at most the home counties.

Donald Davie. In A. Walton Litz, ed., *Eliot in His Time* (Princeton, N.J., Princeton Univ. Pr., 1973), pp. 181–82

ENRIGHT, D. J. (1920–   )

A series of books by D. J. Enright shows one kind of partial solution to the characteristic problem of mere articulateness. Enright's form is usually very flat and conversational, approaching in a way the "minimal" style of Robert Creeley, and though actually the poetry is intellectually oriented the statement is kept as simple as possible. He sometimes sounds a more rational Lawrence, or a plainer Empson. A tremendous identification with the betrayed innocents of the earth marks his writing and, together with his tart self-knowledge, accounts for the basically sympathetic speaking character he presents. Enright's subject matter gives him a great advantage, for he has lived and taught literature in various foreign parts, particularly in Asia, and the hard-bitten realism of what he reports is intrinsically of the greatest interest.

In his most telling collection, *Addictions* (1962), the bitterness of his encounters with official repression in a "new" nation explicitly enters a number of the poems. His disillusionment—that of the Western radical with the developing, altered world which he himself has helped create—is all the more convincing because Enright, despite his own unfortunate experience, does not allow himself to condemn humanitarianism or social progress. It is, rather, the impersonality, the inevitable philistine indifference of political process to the ordinary person, and at the same time certain doubts about his own motives, that disturb him. An unusual sequence of poems (for Enright) in this same volume concerns a love-affair that has gone wrong in very much the same sense as modern history has gone wrong. Somehow, things went awry; the dreamt-of came to pass and yet was not what it should have been. In his highly candid and precise speech and his amateurish free-verse, he involves us, wearies us, stamps his personality on our sympathies.

M. L. Rosenthal. *The New Poets* (N.Y., Oxford Univ. Pr., 1967), pp. 222–23

Nearly all his academic life D. J. Enright has spent dedicatedly teaching Eng. Lit. in troubled foreign places. His personal commitment has been profound, and often courageous. But it has resulted in his verse becoming a sustained lament for the ineffectualness of art—"man's slight non-murderousness"—in a world controlled by politics and economics. It is hard to see how much more can be got out of this theme after the present volume [*Unlawful Assembly*], although the writing is as sensitive and likeable as ever.

Unlawful Assembly repeats the topics and attitudes of several earlier books, with little added and with rather less energy (the poems are less observant and pointed than they used to be). Enright continues to write appealing, but slightly tired, accounts of places and politics, casting wry glances at cultural foibles, shrugging off causes with sad, cultivated weariness. . . . No one writes on these things with a more compassionate perception, but it is sad to see an interesting talent standing still.

Alan Brownjohn. *NS.* Sept. 20, 1968, pp. 362–63

An editor of *Encounter*, an author of four novels and five books of essays, D. J. Enright is a rather anomalous figure on this side of the Atlantic—the man of letters as poet. We're suspicious: Is he or isn't he a poet? Does he take his poetic calling seriously? . . .

Art bitten by poetry longs to be freed from reason, Jacques Maritain once said. Enright is bitten by poetry, but he longs to keep his reason. Sometimes he keeps it without a fight, and the result is a snide hyena; but at his best he is our minor Dryden, whose art is in the service of reason, whose mordant poems wake us up to the temptations of the artist and the evasions of art. Nourished on confessional poetry, on the intensities of Plath and the dream-visions of Merwin, on poets with sensibilities as rich as cheesecake, some of us may find such plain English food flat; Enright's poems are neither ambiguous nor profound. But then he didn't want them to be.

Stephen Miller. *NYT*. Feb. 13, 1972, pp. 6, 18

Daughters of Earth includes some of the finest of Enright's mature poetry. The poems fall into three groups, Asian poems treating of oppression, war, poverty, and, as one would expect, a set of sardonic and comic poems, and a handful of strong, tragic and intensely personal utterances of private experience. What they have in common is twofold. For one thing they share an extreme precision so that the contour of each phrase, the centre of each image, the slightest rise or fall of rhythm, is defined with an unqualified accuracy. At the same time the line has all of Enright's characteristic mobility and vitality, moving with spontaneous, inward energy and with a variety which never flags. . . . If we put together this linear precision and this bounding rhythm, and join to it an attitude, the deep impulses of which are always on the side of liberality and generosity, so that even in the sharpest, most acid irony there is nothing pinched, mean or sour, we shall have the notes making up Enright's personal tone—"the accents of Enright," as it were. . . .

A lapsed Wesleyan and a lurching humanist, as he calls himself, he is also in one part of his sensibility distinctly oriental, an admirer and almost a possessor of a Chinese habit of mind, courtly, exact and ironic. But he is also one formed by a working-class childhood and memories of margarine and hissing gas mantles, an enemy of executives and industrialists, managers, chairmen and senior civil servants. He is without even the thinnest carapace of indifference and almost shockingly vulnerable in his sympathies for the cruelly treated. He is erudite and colloquial, a common man with an aristocratic disdain for moral seediness.

William Walsh. *D. J. Enright: Poet of Humanism* (Cambridge Univ. Pr., 1974), pp. 95–97

FIELDING, GABRIEL (1916–   )

Of the novels that have come out of England in the last fifteen years, none that I have read has made a more powerful impression on me than *In the Time of Greenbloom*, by the man who writes under the name of Gabriel Fielding. The book did not find a large audience in this country, though now that it is available in paperback it seems to be reaching more readers; and Fielding's reputation has grown very slowly, partly because his subsequent books have been so various in style and treatment that a reader who likes one of them may find the next not at all to his taste, but partly too because the books have been of decidedly uneven quality. But Fielding's new novel, *Gentlemen in Their Season*, is one of his better performances; certainly this is Fielding in his best vein.

The book is a study of lukewarmness. The main character, Randall Coles, is a middle-aged, middle-class man who calls himself a humanist. Neither happy nor miserable, he belongs to the army of those Eliot characterized as "living, and partly living," the army of dabblers. In fact it is his gift for dabbling that enables him to make a comfortable living and occupy a certain status in society; he can hold a fairly important job in the religious broadcasting division of the BBC for the very reason that he has no convictions to get in his way; he is tolerant of all the religious groups he must deal with and fair in allocating time among different beliefs because none of them matters in the least to him.

In human relations too Coles is a dabbler. . . . But Coles's most fateful dabbling is his "prison visiting." . . . The fact that Coles emerges from the whole experience essentially unscathed, his lukewarmness never varying by more than a few degrees either way, has to be revealed because it is the problem of the novel.

Fielding has tried a very bold experiment here; he has put at the center of his story a character whose sin is indifference, imperviousness to any genuine experience beyond the harm it may do his job or reputation or person. And the reader longs for some retribution that will damn Coles or some revelation that will save him, and when neither occurs the ending seems unsatisfactory. Yet on reflection one sees that Coles's damnation is all the greater because he is beyond retribution or revelation. Psychologically and morally Coles is a completely convincing character, a terrifyingly accurate representative of contemporary indifference, but he has little narrative interest, because narrative interest results from the interaction of character and event, and Coles cannot or will not interact with the events of his life except in a superficial, skin-saving way.

But the experiment of putting such a figure at the center of a novel was certainly worth making, and Fielding more than compensates for the irresolution of the narrative by his fine intelligence, his wonderful sense of how people really live, the depth of his moral concern, his supple literacy, and his comic gift.

Paul Pickrel. Harper's. June, 1966, p. 98

Although a great deal of critical attention has been devoted to the dramatic treatment of that view of life which is usually termed the absurd, the serious novel which has set out to explore the same theme has tended to be ignored unless it has innovated some startling form. . . . A novelist whose work so far, although uneven in quality, has concerned itself more and more with the individual in an irrational world, is Gabriel Fielding. His work has attracted the attention and gained the praise of several major reviewers and of contributors to one or two Catholic journals, but not of literary scholars; he is worth attention particularly for his novel *The Birthday King*, which won the W. H. Smith Literary Award when it appeared in 1962. . . .

In his introduction to some of the writings of Existentialism Professor [Walter] Kaufmann writes: "In the end, Rilke, Kafka, and Camus pose a question, seconded by Dostoevski and by Sartre's plays and fiction: could it be that at least some part of what the existentialists attempt is best done in art and not in philosophy?" He also brings attention to the general inauthenticity of English speaking philosophy which manages the rare feat of being "frivolous and dull at once." The work of Fielding so far, and particularly *The Birthday King* confirms the implication of Kaufmann's question and redeems the modern English novel by bringing to it a philosophic significance which with a few exceptions it has lacked too long. The epic sweep of Fielding's chronicle and the practical importance of his existential philosophy together with his skill in the novel give him a major significance and an unusual quality of universality.

Frederick Bowers. QQ. Spring, 1967,
pp. 149, 158

FIRBANK, RONALD (1886–1926)

Ronald Firbank is scarcely known to American readers of English novels, yet so eminent a critic as Edmund Wilson has called him "one of the finest English writers of his period" and added to that accolade the prediction that he was "one of those most likely to become a classic." Since Firbank's period coincided with, in part, the period of Virginia Woolf and D. H. Lawrence, to name only two, Wilson's appraisal assumes added significance. And Wilson is far from being alone in his admiration. Firbank's comparative obscurity is the result of such diverse factors as the unavailability (until recently) of most of his work, and a legend that has grown up around him which makes him into a late-blooming "decadent" flower, whose work belongs more to the "yellow 1890's" than to pre-World War I or to the 1920's, the periods in which his work was largely written. . . .

Firbank has usually been classified as a satirist by readers who did take him seriously, but to be a satirist the writer must exhibit a reasonably strong disapproval of those elements of society which he chooses to satirize, and Firbank does not. He led a life which was very much like that lived by some of his characters, and he led that life by choice and deliberate contrivance. Most of his characters live behind elaborate façades, which may lead one to believe that Firbank is satirizing the man beneath the façade; but the façade is so obvious, so exaggerated and contrived, that it becomes the character; and the man beneath the façade disappears into insignificance. Firbank certainly saw that life was very like the sideshows in Vanity Fair; if one wishes to take his men and women, all regular visitors to and participants in Vanity Fair, as satirical representations of society, he may do so; but such broad generalizations about the author's motives are unwise.

James D. Merritt. *Ronald Firbank* (N.Y., Twayne, 1969), pp. 13–14

In an amusing essay on Ronald Firbank, E. M. Forster cautions potential Firbank critics that "to break a butterfly, or even a beetle, upon a wheel is a delicate task. . . . The victim is apt to reappear each time the wheel revolves, still alive, and with a reproachful expression upon its squashed face to address its tormentor in some such words as the following: 'Critic! What do you? Neither my pleasure nor your knowledge has been increased. I was flying or crawling, and that is all that there was to be learnt about me. . . . I only exist in my surroundings, and become meaningless as soon as you stretch me on this rack.' " Conceiving Firbank as an insect, Forster facetiously implies that writing about him is altogether useless. Such casual advice can be safely ignored, however, especially since Forster himself ignores it. In dealing with Firbank, I have discovered that he is less a butterfly than a beetle and one, moreover, whose plucky resilience enabled it to survive my rack even when I was tempted to apply a gratuitous tweak.

Firbank's evanescent prose and his air of ephemerality place him among the most elusive of writers. Because of these baffling qualities, the diversity of opinion among Firbank's critics (each using a different rack) has been remarkable. Considered variously baroque and rococo, Catholic and pagan, amoral and immoral, decadent and robust, a minor classic and a major mistake, Firbank is some of these things maybe but not all of them.

Edward M. Potoker. Ronald Firbank (N.Y.,
Columbia Univ. Pr., 1969), p. 3

To quote Ronald Firbank in praising him would be to seem to lean on corollary facts more heavily than did Firbank himself. His facts are delightfully fictitious and they lean on each other very densely too, if the whole weight of them is uniformly light, evenly distributed. Dip anywhere into a novella of his and something "quotable" will turn up very quickly. He is one of the most quotable authors in all the world. But what *is* quotability? Merely, I think, the quality of hanging together, being of a piece, a good, really good piece. Yet this is just where one must be careful in Firbank's case: the pitch (in all senses) is so fragile. Critically defined, quotability might be thought a demerit; prose continually giving off sentences and passages of high calibre is to be suspected of ignoring that deep serious basis of life that means solidity and steadfastness for the mind, the eye and the ear, offering them no purple passages, no golden nuggets.

Firbank's enthusiasm for life does not wait for the logic of an idea to unite his stories, nor is the logic imposed late, or afterwards. His work shows no solid invulnerable front, no warning against taking it apart or cutting a flower stem. But then, suddenly tempted, one is brought up: "Why *spoil* it all? Don't." The spontaneity of the passing phase of life's energy is too precious to Firbank for him to calculate his story before the urge to tell it has seized, propelled his mind. Uninhibitedly, unembarrassedly "expletive," his dialogue flows down the page stringily but like a graceful waterfall. . . .

The prose as such is designed to be answerable to the dialogue like instructions on how to work a machine. Yet the dialogue works itself as if a very modern computer had been invented to mediate between author and reader. Conversational prose manner, as a way of animating narrative, is first a way of animating the narrow, but very extraordinary, mass of life Firbank found accessible, and pioneered. His narrative depends on the impulse to "use speech" as distinct from "writing prose." Today, forty years after his death, an audibly lifelike, running dialogue is far from being an unknown technique of making ideas about life organic to a story's movement.

Parker Tyler. *Prose*. No. 1, 1970, pp. 135–37

FORD, FORD MADOX (1873–1939)

After Ford's early fiction, *The Good Soldier* is both familiar and strange. It is so much like the other novels; it is so much better than they are. There is little need, now, to plead for its excellence. But there is still room for analysis—of its technique, of its psychology, of its vision of life. Even Mark Schorer's admirable Introduction to the 1951 edition, by far the best discussion of the novel to date, just begins to explore its intricate and inviting ways. . . .

The Good Soldier rests, I think, on a severe and wonderful achievement of self-criticism. If Ford's own psychic needs seem to contribute to the relatively indifferent quality of his apprentice work, they determine in part his good fiction as well. His preoccupation with guilt and shame, with the longing for innocence and the need for vindication, leads him at last to his great theme of romantic idealism. Perhaps predictably (if we recall the unexceptionable, and unconvincing, hero of *The "Half-Moon"*), perhaps necessarily, Ford works in his masterpiece by implication and indirection. He creates a series of romantic figures, each of whom aspires to be beyond reproach. He shares in, he draws with acute and sympathetic insight, their consistently motivated personalities, and the relationship between their personalities and their various ethical values. But he never suggests in *The Good Soldier* that the ego-ideals his characters follow may be achieved, save in their own imaginations, in their self-deceptions and illusions, or should be achieved. He never asks us to believe in an incredibly good hero or to assent to an ethic that would exalt that hero at the expense either of a whole unworthy world or of all moral obligations. Ford sympathizes with his characters in *The Good Soldier*, but he has learned to judge them for their immaturity, their egoism, their foolish rejection of things as they are, and their headlong pursuit of an impossible conception of themselves.

Carol Ohmann. *Ford Madox Ford, from
Apprentice to Craftsman* (Middletown, Conn.,
Wesleyan Univ. Pr., 1964), pp. 71, 111

Throughout his lifetime, Ford was faced with the problem of finding alternatives to a recurrently collapsing world. Because the social reality was so disheartening, he found himself conceiving such alternatives on individual terms—whether those of the artist or the "Small Producer" —and his tendency to think in these terms may well have been the factor that caused him to view the failures of the Victorians as individual ones, and therefore to condemn them so personally for not having come to grips with their world. And while he viewed the Victorian failure as one of individuals, and especially of the rhetorical public hero, Ford also saw his alternative as a private matter, centered around the self-sufficiency of the limited hero. The author thus tended to view his world through the circumscribed perspective of the individual, and his work showed both the strengths and weaknesses of this position.

It may be said that Ford's advocacy of the "Small Producer" and the Provençal way of life grew to seem increasingly hopeless in a world marked by inept politicians and dictators who pushed their opponents "up against a wall." In a sense, his ideas, read in the light of all the history that has occurred since his death in June, 1939, have an ironically empty ring. The sense of urgency which resulted in the weakness of Ford's final novels and their subordination to his "travel" books—a weakness and subordination that can scarcely at such a late stage in his life be attributed to literary apprenticeship—is in itself an indication of the irony that shadowed his final work. For he hardly had time to advance his position before it was lost in the welter of a second war.

And yet, Ford's late writings show that he was aware of the political realities of the 1930's and that he was becoming progressively concerned over their recurring manifestations. He chose, however, not to seek a solution in the very area of which these manifestations were a part. Therein, he thought, lay certain failure. Within the terms that Ford openly set for himself, his work shows a persistent attempt to grapple with the problems of his world. This world and its alternatives were rendered as he saw them, and this, too, was in accord with his view of the artist's role. The relevance of Ford's approach may be limited, but his plea for the limited hero is true to its own terms; and for the reader it at least recalls awareness of a private sphere that ought hopefully to underlie any public solution.

But it is really through its anguished sense of the bewilderment and attempted solutions which accompanied the historical crisis that Ford's work makes its strongest appeal. . . . The response of limited heroism offers a possible and limited resolution; but it is a resolution cradled in crisis, and in the final analysis, it is perhaps Ford's acute sense of this crisis that is most emotionally striking and intellectually significant.

Norman Leer. *The Limited Hero in the Novels
of Ford Madox Ford* (East Lansing, Michigan
State Univ. Pr., 1966), pp. 218–19

Largeness is the key word for Ford. He liked to say that genius is memory. His own was like an elephant's. No one admired more of his elders, or discovered more of his juniors, and so went on admiring and discovering till the end. He seemed to like nothing that was mediocre, and miss nothing that was good. His humility was edged with a mumbling insolence. His fanatical life-and-death dedication to the arts was messy, British, and amused. As if his heart were physically too large for his body, his stamina, imperfection, and generosity were extreme.

Ford's glory and mastery are in two or three of his novels. He also never stopped writing and speaking prose. He had a religious fascination in the possibilities of sentence structure and fictional techniques. About poetry, he was ambivalent. He had a flair for quoting beautiful unknown or forgotten lines, yet called poetry something like "the less civilized medium," one whose crudity and barbarism were decked out with stiff measures and coarse sonorities. Like Boris Pasternak, he preferred Shakespeare's prose to his blank verse, and thought no poetry could equal the novels of Flaubert.

He himself wrote poetry with his left hand—casually and even contemptuously. He gives sound and intense advice to a beginning poet: "Forget about Piers Plowman, forget about Shakespeare, Keats, Yeats, Morris, the English Bible, and remember only that you live in our terrific, untidy, indifferent empirical age, where not a single problem is solved and not a single Accepted Idea from the poet has any more magic. . . ." Yet he himself as a poet was incurably of the nineteenth century he detested, and to the end had an incurable love for some of its most irritating and overpoetic conventions. His guides were always "Christabel," the Browning of "My Last Duchess," the Rossettis, Morris, and the successors, the decadents. He is Pre-Raphaelite to the heart. Their pretty eloquence, their passionate simplicities, their quaint neo-

Gothic, their vocabulary of love and romance, their keyed-up Christianity, their troubadour heresies, and their terribly over-effective rhythms are always peeping through Ford's railway stations and straggling free verse. . . . Even in prose, except for *The Good Soldier* and *Parade's End*, he had difficulty in striking the main artery; in poetry, he almost never struck it. His good phrases and rhythms grow limp or hopped up with impatient diffidence, and seldom reach their destination. . . . His shorter poems are brisk, his longer diffuse.

Robert Lowell. Intro. to Ford Madox Ford,
Buckshee (Cambridge, Mass., Pym-Randall,
1966), pp. xii–xiii

Ford consistently proclaimed that the novel, as a form, could be a major cultural force by informing and reshaping public attitudes, that in its pages the concerned novelist might give his age some sense of where it stood in the long sweep of history by mirroring it against the perspective of its own historical past. In short, Ford's task as he conceived it was to show the Englishman what he had been and what he was now becoming. To accomplish this Ford sought for some satiric counter, some alien personality, with which to contrast the collective psychology of the Edwardian scene. It is this alien protagonist, and the struggle in which he is engaged, that provides the key to that curious similarity in the situations and fate of Ford's generous natures who always fall on evil times.

The word "protagonist" must be used here in a qualified sense, really for want of a more definitive term. Though these are the characters who most evoke the reader's sympathy and respect, as Ford intended, they cannot always be said to be the chief characters in the novels. Consequently, characters like Edward Ashburnham or Katherine Howard are not so much heroes and heroines as they are advocates or exemplars for past historical values in conflict with the social forces of their day, these social forces being the real focus of Ford's concern. For one to understand Ford's analysis of those forces it is necessary to recall briefly the milieu just preceding the Edwardian Age, for it was this that shaped both Ford's general view of history as well as his understanding of the mechanics upon which historical movement itself was generally thought to be based.

H. Robert Huntley. *The Alien Protagonist of
Ford Madox Ford* (Chapel Hill, Univ. of
North Carolina Pr., 1970), p. 8

To present in a few trifling words of introduction the monstrously variegated personae, masks and contradictory identities of that large,

large-hearted and in his own lifetime so much larger-than-common-life figure of Ford Madox Ford seems an impossible task. Not even H. G. Wells could come up with anything more definite than, "What he is really or if he is really, nobody knows now and he least of all." That was in 1934 and Wells, a hostile friend and friendly enemy from before the turn of the century, recognized that in Ford there walked the earth a creature so vast and diffuse and blurred at the edges into different people and other times that there could be no one adequate characterization of him. Ford then was sixty-one, a controversial literary phenomenon on both sides of the Atlantic, with five more years of life and some of his most lasting work still ahead of him. In the course of his career he had thrown up clouds of ink around himself like a cuttlefish. He existed somewhere behind the extravagantly dramatized personalities of the last Pre-Raphaelite, the Tory English gentleman, the simple kitchen-gardener or the literary pundit, the benevolent, omniscient headmaster of a whole school of writers in Paris and New York, indeed as D. H. Lawrence put it, "everybody's blessed Uncle and Headmaster."

Today, from the perspective of a time more than thirty years after his death, Ford's masks become a vast entertainment and in this assembly of autobiographies his bulky figure appears on the well-lit stage he prepared for himself, unencumbered by the acrimonious carping of contemporaries, a man of many parts free to speak his lines and address posterity. For it is for posterity as much as for his contemporaries that he wrote these chronicles of his life.

> Michael Killigrew. Intro. to Ford Madox Ford,
> *Your Mirror to My Times* (N.Y., Holt,
> Rinehart and Winston, 1971), p. ix

FORSTER, E. M. (1879–1970)

Circles, containers, hollows, and swellings are, with Forster, basic symbols. His fiction is thick with dells, grottoes, hollow trees, rings, pools, rooms, houses, and in this last and greatest novel [*A Passage to India*] with caves. . . . Expansion and contraction—functions of circular figures —are the prevailing motions of his art, and the prevailing images are those which arrest this motion and focus on it. Even the idea of flat and round characters may be seen as an expression of this same symbolism, as may the circularity of certain characters' experience—the self-return of a Philip or a Rickie after their timid investment in the active life.

Throughout his work, these feminine images operate in double roles—as prisons and as paradises, as dread enclosing coils and as cradles of an ideal, harmonious peace; they are obviously basic to Forster's fictive imagination. His work shows an increasing awareness of the elemental paradox that the tumescence of creation has always a dark underside of nothingness, that life lives on death. This vital awareness, part of Forster's matured private myth, is deeply embedded in the esthetic structure of *A Passage to India*.

The circle has an ancient symbolic lineage. In nearly all cultures it has stood for the cyclic unity of life, the inseparability of beginning and end, the eternal round of the seasons. The wheel of life and the serpent swallowing its tail are two of man's earliest imaginings; and an ancient phrase popular with Renaissance poets was "God is a Circle, whose Circumference is nowhere and whose Centre everywhere." The notion of the Circle of Perfection, the conception of a perfect correspondence between macrocosm, geocosm, and microcosm (universe, world, and man), was widely held as late as the Elizabethan period, but with the advent of science and more skeptical attitudes that metaphor was shattered. "For three hundred years," writes Marjorie Nicolson, "men have vainly tried to put together the pieces of a broken circle." One need not search far in modern literature to find evidences of the effort. . . .

A Passage to India is an attempt to put together the pieces of that broken circle; it is Forster's greatest effort to relate the broken arcs of his own experience to some final scheme of ultimate value. The book's fundamental structure consists of circle after circle echoing out from the caves at the center to the outermost fringes of the cosmos. Although the book teems with variety, it is contained by this unity.

> Wilfred Stone. *The Cave and the Mountain:*
> *A Study of E. M. Forster* (Stanford, Cal.,
> Stanford Univ. Pr., 1966), pp. 298–99

Four things may be said about the fiction of E. M. Forster: first, that his works are romance rather than novel; second, that symbolism is central to his achievement in the romance form; third, that the principal source of his symbols is ecstatic experience; and fourth, that through the power of ecstatic perception his symbols achieve archetypal significance and mythic wholeness.

What is eminently true of Joyce and Eliot [the use of myth to impose order on the fragmented and disjointed experience of twentieth-century man] . . . is not true of Forster. Forster's mythic or archetypal symbols are the heart of his fiction. They do not add up to a method; rather they constitute the substance and significance of his stories. Everything else exists to enhance their power and value either by serving positively as a reinforcement or negatively as a foil. Persons and objects take on archetypal power and value not because they can be assimilated to a literary or psychological tradition but because within the fiction itself they create an unqualified impression of objective and absolute existence. . . . They create such an impression because they are seen as objects of mystical or ecstatic vision. Thus it is the manner of their creation and presentation that renders such persons and objects archetypal. In addition, they may and probably will have counterparts in mythic tradition; but they need not, a point readily illustrated by the hay image in *Howards End.* Hay is not a traditional mythic symbol; it is rendered mythic solely by Forster's presentation.

George H. Thomson. *The Fiction of E. M. Forster* (Detroit, Wayne State Univ. Pr., 1967), pp. 13–15

Forster may be remembered by nonspecialist readers of future generations for only one novel, *A Passage to India.* For with time Forster's last novel, published in 1924, increasingly detaches itself from the rest of his work as incommensurably major. Wilfred Stone's book, *The Cave and the Mountain: A Study of E. M. Forster,* has the advantage of such critical hindsight—an advantage over Lionel Trilling's brilliant introductory study of 1943—in that it treats all Forster's work in order to show *Passage* as a culmination. . . . Given Forster's starting point in turn-of-the-century liberalism and estheticism, he says in *Passage* all he had to say and all perhaps that there is to say. Since then, he has wisely preferred writing criticism and biography to writing inferior fiction.

Actually, Forster has written two masterpieces—his last novel and his first, *Where Angels Fear to Tread. Angels* is on a much smaller scale than *Passage;* it is a perfect little comedy of manners. Such success at first try shows that Forster's talent is essentially comic; and criticism, which is better suited to talk about the ideas and symbols in the novels, has never done justice to their lightness and charm. Except for George Eliot in her lighter moments, Forster is the only English novelist in whom one can discern another Jane Austen. The question is why Forster was not content to go on writing comedy. Stone does not try to answer this question, though he identifies it in speaking of Forster's attempt to combine comedy with prophecy or vision.

The answer is that no writer of integrity, standing this side of the romantic and relativistic nineteenth century, can write for long like Jane Austen. To write like her, a novelist has to believe in his society, believe that its norms represent some ultimate truth and that the job of comedy is to correct deviations from the norms. Forster's characters have, instead, to be judged and to work out their destinies through shifting and inadequate standards. That is why Forster takes a comparative attitude toward cultures, and why his more enlightened characters work out their destinies between cultures. The lack of valid standards leads to a complex irony that criticizes not only English middle-class values, but the alternatives as well, and the very characters who seek the alternatives. The lack of standards leads also to concern with a mystical reality behind the shifting social surfaces. Hence the romantic emphasis on nature and imaginative apprehension, that assorts so oddly with the witty notation of manners.

Robert Langbaum. *SoR*. Winter, 1968,
pp. 33–34

The Forster elite, his central figures, are people of passion—without exception, I would say, were it not for *A Passage to India*: Adela, Ronnie, Fielding are cold fish. But then, there is Aziz. Very often passions are submerged or muffled; they need to be—they are outlaw passions. They are called upon, also, to bridge gulfs. *Howards End*, the most violent of the novels, surges with them: hostility, pity, sense of injustice, hunger for knowledge are among those rocking the book. The Forster passions are not invariably sexual, or directly sexual. *The Longest Journey* is governed by passions which are not: Stephen Wonham's passion is for the earth on whose breast he sleeps at the very end of the novel. . . .

Above the battle, guardians of morality, are the elderly women. They have a Fate-like quality: Mrs. Honeychurch, Mrs. Wilcox, Mrs. Moore. . . . The great three are not only creatures of temperament but inject a further degree of temperament into the books they severally inhabit; they continue to do so after their deaths. . . . They are capricious; they unaccountably veil themselves in huffiness. They are Nature. One passes directly from them into weather and landscape. "Landscape"?—I mean, the formidable, ever-amazing shapes of pieces of country. The concern is with what these shapes give off, what they do to man. What do they not? They impart the sense of existence, of how ancient it can be, how volcanic it can be, and of how it continues. These are, therefore, the dominants in the novels. . . . England, Italy, India, unlike, fascinating the pen as they do the eye by their singularities, have in common an underlying, impenetrable strangeness. In his unceasing awareness and awe of this resides, for me, no small part of the genius of E. M. Forster.

Elizabeth Bowen. In Oliver Stallybrass, ed.,
Aspects of E. M. Forster (N.Y., Harcourt,
Brace, 1969), pp. 10–11

Embarrassment has been the note among those who had been allowed to read Forster's secret novel [*Maurice*], the apologia for homosexuality which has lain unpublished, but frequently revised, since 1912. One's expectations have consequently been too low. To have set a burning topic in what is now an Edwardian period piece is awkward. It puts the fire out and leaves one with the uncomfortable impression that Forster complained of in Meredith: that he thought the Home Counties were the universe. Although the book has been many times revised in the course of 50 years, it must be said that the first 100 pages of *Maurice* are fossilised. After that, when he begins to tussle with his hero's homosexuality, the book comes to life. It has a good deal of Forster's tart gift for moral puncture, all his talent for not forgiving and for not shedding tears. It has always been engaging to see him using the stiff upper lip of pre-1914 manners, in order to loosen it in others and to persuade them of the vital necessity of losing it altogether. The grey, unconsoling sentences, so curtly dismissive, have the humanist's courage. . . .

Maurice is the male version of *Lady Chatterley's Lover*, written in 1913, long before D. H. Lawrence's book, and a similar criticism of English life, as Forster says himself, in a few pages of comment on the book, written some 10 years ago. There is the same preoccupation with snobbery and class consciousness, the same allegory of the stagnant condition of English life. Lawrence's tutelary sexual games are missing, and this is as well; for the early novelists of the sexual revolution had so strong a sense of sex as "the Cause" that they lost the stalking, primitive gaiety of the hunt, and the natural good humour of love. If Forster's own sense of Cause gives an unusual dry harshness and something very wooden to the book, it is to his credit that he shows Maurice emerging recklessly on the side of instinct. . . .

One cannot put *Maurice* beside Forster's other novels, for the story is a case; it is not his fault that the 1914 war pulled the carpet from under the feet of his characters or that today, after Wolfenden, if homosexuality is still a subject on its own, he would be able to write the same book without corseting it, like some 19th-century tract on the risks of adultery or the right to be a teetotaller in a society of hard drinkers.

V. S. Pritchett. *NS.* Oct. 8, 1971, pp. 479–80

Two male lovers going off to live in the "greenwood" is precisely the note on which Forster ends *Maurice*. It is the happy ending he attached onto an otherwise disappointing novel. *Maurice* is, moreover, disappointing in a variety of ways. Although it was not possible to have published the book in England till recently because of laws then extant against homosexuality, one feels that the high pornography crowd will find little to cheer them here, for *Maurice* is quite without descriptions of homosexual high jinks or of any scandalous content whatever. Nor is it likely to become a homosexual cult object of any significant kind, for it is altogether too subtle and insufficiently boisterous on behalf of the virtues of homosexuality for the political likes of the gay-liberation movement. And others, homosexual and heterosexuals both, who read novels for reasons apart from sexual excitement or sexual allegiance, will find *Maurice* disappointing on literary grounds, for even though Forster came freshly away from his masterpiece [*Howards End*] to compose it, it nonetheless falls well below the mark of his other novels.

What went wrong? "The affections are more reticent than the passions," Forster noted in his own voice in *Howards End*, "and their expression more subtle." *Maurice* is a novel devoted almost exclusively to the passions. In all probability coinciding with Forster's own homosexual coming out, it ought properly, I think, be looked upon as E. M. Forster's first novel, even though he came to write it fifth among his six novels. . . .

What we have, then, is an idyll, a homosexual fantasy. Lytton Strachey, whom Forster showed the novel, said upon completing it that in reality the affair between Maurice and his gamekeeper would not be likely to last more than six weeks. Forster, naturally enough, would have it differently. "A happy ending," he comments in his terminal note, "was imperative. I shouldn't have bothered to write otherwise. I was determined that in fiction anyway two men should fall in love and remain in it for the ever and ever that fiction allows, and in this sense Maurice and Alec still roam the greenwood." . . .

The writing of *Maurice* must have been part of an act of deep personal liberation on Forster's part—a novel that, for complex reasons, he needed to write, just as he may have needed to imagine a happy ending for a homosexual life. One likes to think that his own coming to terms with homosexuality ended happily, which it may well have, for he had an enormous talent for living an ordered life. Nor does having written one deeply flawed novel in any way invalidate all that is so very fine in the body of his work. The obvious nature of the flaws in *Maurice* somehow serves to make Forster seem even more human than before. *Maurice* after all, illustrates a very odd and very common point in the history of literary creation: in literature, psyche's gain is often art's loss.

Joseph Epstein. *NYT*. Oct. 10, 1971,
pp. 24, 26, 28–29

Apart from some that were destroyed, these [homosexual] writings consist of the novel *Maurice* and most of the present book [*The Life to Come*], though there may be some fragments still in store. Forster died in 1970, at the age of ninety-one, and after that it was decided to publish what was once unpublishable. . . .

In 1935, at the age of fifty-six, Forster set down in a personal memorandum the kind of resolution which a young man might make with regard to his hopes for adult life: "I want to love a strong young man of the lower classes and be loved by him and even hurt by him. That is my ticket, and then I have wanted to write respectable novels." In fact, it was already apparent to him many years before, when he embarked on his "indecent writings," that this was his ticket. . . .

What is striking is the extent to which the sexual program embodied in the stories—Forster's ticket—was determined by the class system of Edwardian England. It is almost as if in a less hierarchical society, a kinder society, his lusts would have been at a loss. He hated the treatment his lads received from their betters, but he himself was one of these betters, perhaps unavoidably. He was better than his lads, too, in a more literal sense—in certain respects which he could not convincingly have claimed were unimportant: in respect of truthfulness, for example, though there's an occasion in the stories when he does appear to claim that truthfulness is unimportant, in comparison with what a man looks like. His amorous dreams cherished and exaggerated the differences between himself and his lads: to that extent at least, the sadomasochistic element in these dreams entailed some submission to the class system he detested. . . .

Some have claimed that the publication of these stories is a disservice to Forster, but I think, on balance, that the decision to publish them was correct. Together with *Maurice*, they are bound to inject doubts into the settled admiration which his work has long commanded, but to withhold them could hardly have helped seeming cowardly and untruthful. He is a good enough writer to bear the weight of his failures, and in any case these failures are interesting and explanatory.

Karl Miller. NYR. June 28, 1973, pp. 9, 11

● **FOWLES, JOHN (1926–   )**

There are many things to admire in this first novel [Fowles's *The Collector*], and much to look forward to in future ones. There is the handling of the relationship between the two people, the long drawn-out anger, dread and frustrated longing interspersed with bouts of something like ordinary friendliness and that curious intimacy Sartre noted as existing between tormentor and victim. Another score is the way in which the fundamental goodness of the girl is agreeably conveyed, goodness being for some reason a difficult thing to make plausible and attractive. There is also, strange to say, a slender but rich vein of comedy running through it.

The best thing of all is that *The Collector* is a work of art, a work of the imagination. It both stirs the mind and satisfies it in a way that the chunks of personal experience nowadays masquerading as novels, however vividly written or deeply felt, can never do. My only criticism is that now and then Mr. Fowles seems to use a character as the mouthpiece for his own ideas, that it is he, not Miranda or her lover, telling us, "you have to be Left politically." He is too good for that sort of thing. It is early days to sound the trumpets, but it does look as if the new England has brought forth a novelist at last.

Honor Tracy. *NR*. Aug. 3, 1963, p. 21

In *The Collector*, John Fowles's admirable seedy thriller, Miranda, the Progressive Art Student captured by the psychopathic lower-middle-class Clegg, kept a Journal. To this she committed, sometimes, in numbered paragraphs, her views on Life and Art, her hopes of freedom, and her contemptuous, pitying and terrified reactions to the bone-headed Philistine who was keeping her mewed up in his cellar. It was the great merit of the book that Clegg was by far the most sympathetic character, his was the desperate situation; even when Miranda came out in spots and died, we could not think of him but as the victim of the kind of vapid, artistic, self-centred little cock-teaser who might be kidnapped and chloroformed any day of the week off the end of the queue outside the nearest art-cinema.

Now Mr. Fowles, in *The Aristos* (i.e., "the Best"), has also written down his views on Life and Art, entirely in numbered paragraphs, and it's interesting to see that it is Miranda's side he's on. In fact, Mr. Fowles and Miranda together give us a fascinating view of the mind of the contemporary and progressive artist, trying to evolve a satisfactory creed and all the time waiting for the messy, tasteless, money-mad public (Clegg had won £73,901 on the football pools) to burst in and start the rape. Mr. Fowles is, of course, brighter and more widely read than Miranda, and his book is dotted with references to Heraclitus, Tao Te Ching and René Clair. . . .

Perhaps it's having to care that produces works like this, just as it produces many a secret undergraduate notebook and much speculation as to the meaning of life among the Nescafé after midnight at Lady

Margaret Hall. The sad fact is that the meaning of life is not to be trapped in numbered paragraphs even with the aid of Heraclitus, Teilhard de Chardin and the Latin word for no one. Admire the "Aristos" as we will, shun the ISR [Illicit Sexual Relationship], care deeply and do our best to elevate the Many, there are still times when the meaning of life is inescapably Clegg, pursuing butterflies and photographs of stark women, with his plaster ducks and his cellar aired out for the girl from Woolworth's, his next reluctant guest.

Miranda may never accept this; but Mr. Fowles knows it. After all, he created Clegg. And he didn't find him in a guide to philosophy.

John Mortimer. *NS.* July 2, 1965, p. 16

No way but down, one would have thought, for John Fowles's third novel. In 1963 *The Collector* impressed the critics, sold in the millions and made a fine movie. In 1966 *The Magus*, much more ambitious, was almost as successful and won a special following among the under twenty-fives that bade fair to rival the simplistic and self-indulgent moralism of *Demian* and *The Lord of the Rings*. This new novel should also make a good movie, but it will probably appeal to very different kinds of readers, including many for whom the earlier works, for all their compelling readability, were, in the last analysis, pretentious grand guignol. *The French Lieutenant's Woman* is immensely interesting, attractive and human.

Fowles had already demonstrated his expert command of the traditional resources of the English novelist: from paying an initiated deference to the weather and decorating the literary landscape with flora and fauna whose names range over the intimidatingly scientific and the folksy-whimsical, to knowing how many of the solid continuities of English life are underpinned by one simple law—never let people ask why they are being punished.

Unlike many of his contemporaries, though, Fowles wasn't a Little Englander. Both the way he saw the world and the way he presented it flaunted, not his ignorance, but his knowledge of the postwar philosophical and literary scene. One's only doubt was how much he meant it all. Was there any deeper commitment than a currently fashionable nastiness behind the trapped isolation of the protagonists in *The Collector* or the mind-blowing manipulations of *The Magus*? *The French Lieutenant's Woman* largely exorcises this doubt: it is both richly English and convincingly existential.

Ian Watt. *NYT.* Nov. 9, 1969, p. 1

In his perceptive and laudatory review of *The French Lieutenant's Woman* on page one of the *N.Y. Times Book Review*, Ian Watt paused to ask, "Was there any deeper commitment than a currently fashionable nastiness behind . . . the mind-blowing manipulations of *The Magus*?" This question can be translated into the terms I have been using here to talk about orgastic fiction. In these terms the question asks whether Fowles's passion in *The Magus* is equal to his virtuosity, whether the book is merely sensational or truly meaningful. It is a fair and important question. . . .

It is interesting that what should be called into question is the presence or absence of ethical commitment to justify the esthetic virtuosity of *The Magus*, because it is precisely the relationship between the ethical and the esthetic which is the central theme in the book's structure of meanings. Speaking of his behavior at Oxford, the narrator observes,

> we argued about essence and existence and called a certain kind of inconsequential behavior existentialist. Less enlightened people would have called it capricious or just plain selfish; but we didn't realize that the heroes, or anti-heroes, of the French existentialist novels we had read were not supposed to be realistic. We tried to imitate them, mistaking metaphorical descriptions of complex modes of feeling for straightforward prescriptions of behavior.

The literary advice offered here is very important. The passage insists that French existentialist fiction should be treated as metaphor rather than as description. It implies, by extension, that we should be careful to take *this* book with *its* "anti-hero" in a metaphorical (or allegorical) way. And it presents succinctly to us the existential problem of its anti-hero, Nicholas Urfe: he is confused about the relationship between art and life. Nicholas, of course, is both the protagonist of the book and its narrator. As narrator he is no longer confused; in fact he can present his life to us fictionally, as a meaningful metaphor, precisely because he has learned the difference between fiction and existence. But the character Nicholas starts in confusion, and the narrative is the story of his education.

The distance between Nicholas as character and Nicholas as narrator is expressed in the double meaning of the word "enlightened" in the passage just quoted. Nicholas as character thought of himself as really enlightened, but as narrator he uses the word to mean something like superficial and dilettantish. Urfe may be related, as he tells us, to the historical Honoré d'Urfé, the author of the massive seventeenth-century pastoral romance, *Astrée*. Knowing this, we can see Nicholas-as-character victimized by his romantic vision of life as art, and we can see Nicholas-as-narrator accepting the conventions of orgastic romance sufficiently to prevent us from taking his narrative as a transcript of reality. But Nicholas the character is not merely confused about how to take his reading. He is also guilty of a more fundamental error: he uses his misreading of literature as an excuse for mistreating life as if it were art. In older language he is a cad, a Don Juan. He is Kierkegaard's seducer of women, using them and discarding them as one might use and discard a drugstore paperback book: "I mistook the feeling of relief that dropping a girl always brought," the narrator says of his earlier self, "for a love of freedom." Freedom is a word charged with meaning in the vocabulary of existentialism, and that word along with such others as "choice" reverberates powerfully throughout the book.

Robert Scholes. HC. Dec., 1969, pp. 3–4

Foppish, Frenchified, flashy and "very minor," the lavish figure who inserts himself into the final chapter of *The French Lieutenant's Woman*, looking back at Mr. Rossetti's house in Chelsea "as if it is some new theatre he has just bought and is pretty confident he can fill" and turning back time on his watch, is patently none other than a figure for the novelist John Fowles himself. He has, in fact, popped into the novel before, in several guises and voices, and we are used to his here faintly worried and there grandly confident, here contemporaneously nineteenth-century and there a-chronologically twentieth-century, presence. However, his final appearance in the guise of a stout impresario is not entirely creditable either to himself or to the ongoing novel, for it is as a confidence man he shows himself, a notably unresponsible intrusion that he makes and the small mechanical task he performs—setting the clock back a little in order utterly to transform the fortunes and futures of his two central characters, Charles Smithson and the French Lieutenant's Woman—he performs blandly, vainly, and trivially, out of an arrogant power and while en route for fresher pastures. He is the novelist in one of his less likeable guises.

Fortunately the writing continues in more reliable hands, for there is another John Fowles—a much more sober, sententious, and omniscient figure, capable of reporting and reflecting on events, and so of taking seriously the destiny of his characters and establishing with authority an ending which, however, may or may not have any authority whatsoever. The doubt arises because this narrator has already given us, in the previous chapter, one ending to his story. He has, for that matter, given us one two-thirds of the way through the novel, but that one he has rescinded in order to enforce deeper possibilities. But his two final endings have a different status. Both of them, we may say, are structured with all appropriate scruple out of the eventful plot; both of them are substantiations of the argumentative level of the book, or what used to be called its "sentiments," closing in an aura of Arnoldian humanism, existentialist authenticity, and Marxist history, all of which textures of thought and feeling have been part of the work as a whole. Authorial authority is relativized not in order to lighten responsibility for the characters, thrusting it on the reader, but rather to take full responsibility for showing their freedom, their faculty of choice. The book closes and the reader can fall back only on recognitions themselves duplicitous; here is the writer's great power both to set his characters free to act and choose as they like, and his power to make them his victims, to set them free from his plot but by withdrawing his power himself exposing them more vigorously than if he had fulfilled it. The trickster and the voice of fact and authority; the manipulator and the humanist concerned in all good faith over the fate and the individual freedom of his characters; the plotter and the plot-escaper—these are co-existent presences in the novel and they produce an extraordinary resolution to it, a resolution in which the substantial action seems to end in one world and the substantiating *machinery*, the technical modes and means, in another. [1970]

Malcolm Bradbury. *Possibilities* (Oxford Univ. Pr., 1973), pp. 256–57

Although *The French Lieutenant's Woman* seems as different from *The Magus* as that book seemed from Fowles's first novel *The Collector*, there are similarities as well. For Fowles, like many novelists, contemporary and otherwise, is a writer whose work reveals a continuing fascination with certain kinds of themes, characters, and situations as well as with certain literary strategies for revealing this material. His preoccupations have to do with the natures—intellectual as well as sensual—of sexual attraction, repulsion, and choice; with the relationship of sex to power, on the one hand, and fantasy, on the other, and of love to all three; with the existential notion that man creates himself anew when—and only when—he acts on a conscious decision about himself and his world; with the relationship of moral beliefs to artistic forms and of art to play.

One way or another, these concerns turn up in every book Fowles has written. They give resonance to what would otherwise be simply a sensational kidnapping in *The Collector* and substance to the nightmarish manipulations of character and action that occupy about two-thirds of *The Magus*. They are the overt subject of *The Aristos*, a collection of grouped philosophical axioms which Fowles calls his "self-portrait in ideas," and of Charles Smithson's dilemma in his latest fiction as well. . . .

His novels, then, are, in his own terms, curiously old-fashioned.

Moral epistemologies, they explore and attempt to affirm the premise that intelligence and goodness are, however fluid, nonetheless real, knowable, and enactable.

Fowles accomplishes his investigations by reworking the classic literary forms: the romance, specifically *The Tempest*, in *The Collector*; the *Bildungsroman* in *The Magus*; and the Victorian novel in *The French Lieutenant's Woman*. He uses the techniques of realism—tight plots, precisely observed and recorded data and phenomena, apparently mundane settings, and bourgeois characters—to raise questions concerning the very existence of that permanent reality which is generally assumed to lie behind the conventions for describing it.

Lee R. Edwards. *MR*. Summer, 1970,
pp. 605–6

● FRAYN, MICHAEL (1933–   )

Frayn qualifies for the satirical label because his pieces render recognizable characters and situations, once you've got the hang of it, ridiculous. His novel [*The Tin Men*] is very much a stringing together of pieces. It is ostensibly the story of the William Morris Institute of Automation, thrown into confusion by the impending visit of the Queen to open a new wing dedicated to the automation of Ethics. But the story, often hilarious, is only an excuse to satirize—there is no other word—various aspects of English society. Starting with a television magnate, Rothermere Vulgarian, we proceed through the various members of the institute who, intellectuals all, exemplify some weakness, some absurdity we can all recognize. It's farce from start to finish, without even a straight character against whom the weirdies can be compared. . . .

It contains some marvelous flashes, notably the description of computerized journalism, based on the constancy of certain types of stories and the incomprehensible ambiguity of headlines—a random selection by computer from a small vocabulary will produce headlines as acceptably meaningless as those in any popular paper. . . .

Yet the inventiveness which in Frayn's columns is sustained by not being overexposed does not support a novel. He succeeds in ridiculing a lot of not-so-sacred cows; but as they stand, comical nuggets barely connected by a thin tissue of incredible narrative, they fail to add up to anything substantial.

Peter Buckman. *Nation*. Feb. 7, 1966,
pp. 163–64

The Russian Interpreter . . . is successor to *The Tin Men*, Michael Frayn's first novel, which has won a Somerset Maugham Award. Although I do not agree with the claims of greatness which everyone seems to be staking for Mr. Frayn, and although I consider that his humour has not yet recovered from whatever went wrong when he moved from the *Guardian* to the *Observer*, I still think he is very very good. Of course, nobody will ever again be as funny as Thurber, and perhaps it is unfair to Mr. Frayn that this is the standard against which his talent must be measured. If it looks tiny, that is only because Thurber had enormous genius.

Mr. Frayn's lines look more impressive when he comes alongside smaller craft like Wodehouse, Saki and Waugh. His Proctor-Gould, a Cambridge man loose in Moscow, apparently promoting Anglo-Soviet trade and goodwill, but really mixed up in espionage or royalty-smuggling, is quite a Waugh character. There are eleven good belly-laughs, and the rest is trim and shipshape and elegant. The only complaint I have (and this also applies to Waugh) is that often the funny bits suddenly become darkest black in a surprising and rather disgusting way.

Bill Byrom. Spec. April 1, 1966, p. 410

"It's a very funny business, the newspaper business," one of the two focal characters in *Against Entropy* remarks, about two-thirds along the way in Michael Frayn's comic novel. And indeed it is, the way they still seem to practice it—or play at it—over in England. In this country, alas, especially from a New York City vantage point, poking fun at the daily press would be an exercise in black humor. The daily newspaper business here, which once provided the fertile backgrounding for many a novelist's and playwright's fancies, now seems to have become a vanishing medium, offering all the humorous possibilities of an abscessed liver.

But working with a Fleet Street Background, Mr. Frayn has created the sort of daily that would have made *The Boston Evening Transcript* look like *The East Village Other*, a richly dreary example of journalistic geriatrics where no one is ever fired—or inspired. It is a newspaper that seems to grind on through inertia, running its way downhill forever. The editor himself, whom the staff never sees, looks like "the sort of man who calls at newspaper offices carrying sheaves of brown paper on which he has written down messages from God or outer space setting forth plans for the spiritual regeneration of the world." . . .

A columnist for *The Observer*, Frayn has a wayward wit and a way with words. He also possesses to a high degree the essential humorist's knack: he knows how to cross over the bounds of reality without extending credulity to the breaking point. Any British novelist attacking on a newspaper front eventually has to face up to Waugh. *Against Entropy* is not another *Scoop*—but then what is? Until something better comes along—and, as I've said, the prospects from our side of the ocean seem dreary—it is the next best thing. And that is offering high praise indeed. But *Against Entropy* is a genuinely funny novel—something almost as rare as an afternoon daily newspaper in New York City.

Josh Greenfeld. NYT. July 16, 1967, pp. 28–29

Michael Frayn has long been concerned with what one might portentously call the nature of reality and, until now at least, he's always stood squarely opposed to those who've attempted to fob off the rest of us with alluring substitutes. Hence his rather puritanical obsession with pop culture and the mass media, with ignorant pundits, facile critics and, of course, the eternal PROs and admen. The novels, especially *The Tin Men*, have pushed the attack rather further than the journalistic pieces. Why not, he asks at one point, an eventual world in which computers play all the games, watch and appreciate each other playing the games and discuss the games afterwards on TV, watched by yet more computers? It's all very fanciful, and may seem frivolous to some, but there's a genuine anxiety somewhere behind it. What is happening, not just to people's ability to distinguish truth from pretence, but to their very capacity to feel? And what, if anything, does a "capacity to feel" mean or matter?

Frayn took his degree in moral sciences; and if anyone doubts that his interests are indeed essentially philosophic, he should closet himself with *A Very Private Life*, a novel that gnaws at the mind, like some maddening if nonmalevolent virus, and leaves it hot and irritated long afterwards; a subtle, rather difficult book, unusual by any criterion and easily the most original thing he, Frayn, has done.

Benedict Nightingale. NS. Oct. 4, 1968, p. 434

Amongst the wit and high spirits Michael Frayn brings to this tale [*Sweet Dreams*], the satire on Howard and his friends is firm, even harsh: yet, for satire, it is curiously indulgent towards the reader. With Frayn, it is not so much a question—as in Amis's or Enright's work—of tempting the reader to sympathise with some egotist and then deftly exposing his self-indulgence in doing so, as of asking the reader to make his own moral judgments from his own knowledge of the world. He has to do the work himself, if he is to interpret Frayn's picture of Howard in Heaven as a blow-up of the cocooned, self-satisfied, prosperous modern do-gooder. This is the kind of satire which makes the reader feel better as he reads, not worse—and consequently, in the end, worse rather than better, suffering from mild moral flatulence.

There is a powerful twist as the book nears its close: one of Howard's friends, Phil, has been creating Man, but when he puts on the premiere, everyone in Heaven is very disappointed. At the premiere, Man "told a series of long, rambling stories to which he forgot the punch-lines, conducted a hesitant affair with somebody else's wife, and announced half-baked plans for an ideal world." The reviews in Heaven's papers the next morning declare that Man has "a unique combination of vanity, greed and incompetence . . . his capacity for deceiving himself about his own motives would seem to be boundless." What is Howard, then, but a classic specimen of Man? Yet this shock, in turn, leaves the novel oddly flaccid afterwards. Howard, of course, never notices the comparison: he goes excitedly on to become chief assistant to God, then, just in time to avoid boredom, starts off at the beginning of the same cycle again. But we are left floundering: if Howard is absolutely no different from other men, the sharp, satirical distinctions the book has been making go up in a puff of smoke. We put the book down, a desire for the tangible ills of a claustrophobic world mounting again inside us.

Derwent May. List. Aug. 16, 1973, p. 224

Impossible not to overpraise Michael Frayn's latest novel, *Sweet Dreams*, I say to myself—and then ask myself, whatever do I mean? How could one overpraise so charming a book? It is lucid, intelligent, delightful, stylish, extremely funny, and I have no reservations about it at all. I recommend it wholeheartedly.

Michael Frayn has a most unusual talent. His books seem so deceptively simple, but they linger in the mind for years, and can be re-read with the greatest pleasure. *Sweet Dreams* is no exception. It is a fantasy, but let not that deter—there is nothing wild or difficult or provoking about it. As he assures us, it is a middle-class fantasy, and it is a sweet one. His hero, Howard Baker, is transported, while waiting at a green light in Highgate, to Heaven—which, American readers will be interested to note, bears a striking resemblance to a dream America. But Heaven contains all things—the past, the present, the glorious future. There, friends at dinner parties laugh at one's jokes in the right way, one gets the right kind of job promotion, one's wife and one's mistress and children prosper. There are, it is true, snags, but they can all be turned to glorious Good in the end.

It is also true that little sneak reminders of reality creep in— Howard Baker, who lands a good job designing the Alps, at first laughs to scorn the idea that the Matterhorn is a threat to life because people will try to climb it and fall off it—why ever should they? he says, laughing loudly. And when forced to admit they will, he has to construct a whole new ideology which contains the ideas of pain, trial and endurance—a whole new middle-aged philosophy.

The novel is a satire on modern fashions—clothes, houses, jobs, attitudes, beliefs—but it's more than that. It's an account of growing older, it's a comment on the nature of man. (One of the characters is designing not the Alps, but Man, and a poor job he makes of it.) The accuracy of Frayn's observation is dazzling; in a few words he creates a man, a room, a dinner party. What he does, he does precisely. And it isn't a small talent. Most satirists and writers of Utopias dislike people profoundly, but Frayn's work is informed with the most beautiful goodwill. It isn't innocence, because he is knowing (though one suspects he suspects that others suspect at times that he is an innocent). It is a kind of goodness. One of the rarest qualities, and how could one ever overpraise it?

Margaret Drabble. NYT. Jan. 13, 1974, p. 7

● FRIEL, BRIAN (1929–   )

One reason Brian Friel's new Irish play, *Philadelphia, Here I Come!*, is so likable may be that it so honestly assesses two unsatisfactory civilizations: inhibited and materially impoverished Ireland and its opposite, America. The playwright's view seems to be that Ireland's tragedy is the constant emigration of its best young people, and that the Irish emigrant's tragedy is that his achievement elsewhere is rootless and disconnected. For the play's entire action is its protagonist's sometimes humorous, sometimes sad, search for any reason to stay where his roots are.

To make this search more dramatic, Mr. Friel has employed the device of having one actor . . . deliver young Gareth's outward behavior, and another . . . portray the same character's private self. The latter argues and provokes, hopes and laments, underlines and comments, but surprisingly enough emerges as almost more real than the actual Gareth. . . .

While the author doesn't demonstrate a capacity for writing dialogue comparable to that of an O'Casey or a Behan ("You wait, says she, till the rosary's over and the kettle's on" is about as lyrical as he gets), his powers of observation permit him to recreate characters with telling accuracy. . . .

Furthermore, like *The Glass Menagerie*, this play expresses a tender awareness of how memory distills events, with the evening's nicest irony being that the uncommunicative father remembers his son through one past incident, while the lonely young man remembers his father through a different one. But the tragic fact is that neither can recall the other's incident.

Because it is such an honest piece of work the play ends inconclusively, and one feels that the playwright may have missed an opportunity to allow the private Gareth to stir us with a more passionate and poetic summing up. Nevertheless, *Philadelphia, Here I Come!* achieves great poignancy without pretension and deserves to be widely appreciated.

Henry Hewes. Sat. March 5, 1966, p. 54

Brian Friel is a quiet man. In a social gathering, while less gifted persons babble on, he listens and, it would appear, remembers with a tape recorder's accuracy. This unusual ability to keep his ears open and his mouth shut served him well in writing his poignantly touching play, *Philadelphia, Here I Come!*, with its faithful rendering of the speech patterns and portrayal of the personalities of a small Irish town. It serves him equally well in this volume of 13 short stories [*The Gold in the Sea*].

In these stories, as in the play, Mr. Friel is concerned with presenting "the human condition." (Incidentally, he thinks that *Philadelphia, Here I Come!* has been miscalled a comedy by the producer of its current Broadway run.) He does not have the same comic genius as Sean O'Faoláin and the late Frank O'Connor, though one story in the present collection, "The Death of a Scientific Humanist," ranks with the funniest they have written, and the dialogue in the title story, "The Gold in the Sea," will delight anyone who has ever listened to Irish blathering. His talent, rather, is for the bitter-sweet aspects of life and he excels at evoking them.

There is not much plot in any of these stories. Where the slice of life chosen by the author ends, there the story closes. But in each of these stories Brian Friel gives the reader a look into and a feel for life as it is lived, and for men and women as they are found, in his native County Tyrone, in County Derry where he now lives, and in neighboring Donegal.

It is all very Irish, but all very human and therefore universal. Readers who would enjoy short stories by an accomplished and sensitive literary craftsman will find this book more than entertaining.

Francis Canavan. America. Sept. 24, 1966,
pp. 359–60

At the moment, Brian Friel is Ireland's most important playwright and something of an enigma. He is a shareholder in the Abbey Theatre but has refused to give the Abbey any of his plays for production, and he is frequently criticized for his silence on Abbey policy. . . . He continues to publish occasional short stories that are indistinguishable in style and attitude from his earlier ones; yet in his plays he has deliberately avoided repeating himself. His reputation in America rests almost entirely on *Philadelphia, Here I Come!* and *Lovers*, and he is generally considered a light-hearted, sentimental writer, a comic writer easy enough to label *Irish*, and thus easy enough to dismiss between successes. But looking at his work to date, and with special concern for these most recent plays, one more and more senses the dark side, a developing tragic view that has not yet found a clear voice. There is still too much of the story teller in Friel, evident not only in his various experiments with narrators and commentators but more seriously in the anecdotal nature of his subjects. Only in *Philadelphia* did he find a way to give his play a greater density than that of an acted-out story, only in that play does one feel that form and content are seamlessly united. But the omens are excellent, particularly in *Crystal and Fox*, that Friel is moving beyond the role of entertainer. The number of his plays makes one forget that he is only in his early 40's, and he has, we hope, only begun to push beyond tasks that are relatively easy.

Milton Levin. Éire-Ireland. Vol. 8, No. 2,
1972, p. 136

Of [all the current] Irish dramatists, Friel has unquestionably the body of work most distinguished by its substance, integrity, and development, well able to stand with that of his English contemporaries. Their writing has a variety and intensity which, even where he does not particularly take to it, Friel much admires. . . . Nor is it easy to enter Friel into any of the Irish "schools." His plays are obviously not isolated from the Irish traditions; but he is a Northern Catholic, the first important dramatist from that background, which inflects his distinctive, personal voice.

"I would like," he has said, "to write a play that would capture the peculiar spiritual, and indeed material, flux, that this country is in at the moment. This has got to be done, for me anyway, at a local, parochial level, and hopefully this will have meaning for other people in other countries." This is a fair description of the plays Friel has already written, regarded as a composite, a single, continuing testimony. Their content has its own interest, but the content does not explain their force. Henry James asserted the supremacy of "the compositional contribution," which confers imaginative truth upon the unworked material. In each of his plays Friel achieves the process of dramatic organization, the conjunction of its parts, that discovers order in observed facts, and conveys their meaning. In each of them too, in R. L. Stevenson's phrase, he has varied his method and changed the point of attack.

This inventive command of design gives Friel's plays their excellence. He has remarked that when Shakespeare wanted to make a point he stated it bluntly, usually three times; in other words, he is sensible of the particular demands imposed by the passing traffic of the stage. Nevertheless, a play does not make its effects only on the large canvas. The totality of experience in the theater consists of accumulating particulars. . . .

What matters, however, is the ultimate end of such means, the convincing familiarity of character and event, bringing to mind the ways of life itself, just as dramatic speech, while it orchestrates, must hold the tune of the spoken word. The audience is to instruct itself from, to quote Friel again, "a set of people and a situation presented with a certain clarity and understanding and sympathy." Both his short stories and his plays supply the creative premises where writer and audience collaborate. In the plays his development has been toward a greater simplicity, but no less subtlety, of method. Friel will continue to find the dramatic forms that generalize, with humor and compassion, on his particular and regional veracities, where art begins.

D. E. S. Maxwell. *Brian Friel* (Lewisburg,
Pa., Bucknell Univ. Pr., 1973), pp. 109–10

FRY, CHRISTOPHER (1907–   )

Fry's admirers have emphasized the richly metaphorical, opentextured quality of his verse and the joyous acquiescence in mystery with which his characters respond to their inner divisions and perplexities. The greatest weakness of Fry's work is that it too often fails, like that of Wilder and Eliot, to embody the form and meaning in imagined human conflict. In using the commercial theater to include areas of sensation and emotion which the theater of prose realism has rigorously left out as irrelevant or unreal, Fry has relied heavily on witty, open-cast, often dazzling language to shoulder the burden traditionally assigned to plot and dramatic symbol. The most familiar charges against Fry, oversimplified as they may be, have concerned the supposed emptiness, superficiality, and derivativeness of his irregular blank verse, which had supposedly been exhausted of all flexibility and vitality by the Elizabethans. Fry's drama is most satisfying when it is most ironic: when the seriousness of his characters' problems is parodied by the whimsy of their verse, when their miraculous escapes carry the aura of a nightmare barely dissolved, when their recognitions of divine mystery are balanced against the decay of the body, both human and politic. He is so quotable that both his admirers and detractors find a wealth of aphorisms in his work to support their positions.

Fry uses the theater to develop a theme embodying what he considers to be the undiscussible truth. His antagonists tend to be weak or incredible, and his use of the *deus ex machina* has been much condemned, and justifiably so. Traditional forms of conflict—between man and men, a group or an idea—are replaced by a protagonist's resistance to love, to the Life Spirit. . . .

The best qualities of Fry's work arise where the characters' inner struggles—whatever the ostensible time and place—are firmly rooted in contemporary life. Either the moral conflict is fully developed in such a way that it cuts across most of the personal, social, and religious issues which agitate our century. Or it is articulated through irony—in conflict within an intensely divided character whose resistance to life and moral scepticism are expressed with vitality, nobility, and even tragic grandeur. . . .

Emil Roy. Christopher Fry (Carbondale,
Southern Illinois Univ. Pr., 1968), pp. 163–64

Christopher Fry's blend of verbal fireworks and vague Christian benevolence fitted in exactly with the post-war mood, and the public took him to their hearts. He supplied glitter and a sense of uplift without making anyone feel uncomfortable; qualities that instantly threw him into disfavour after the theatrical upheaval of 1956.

Since then no British playwright has suffered more critical abuse than Mr. Fry, and it would be pointlessly vindictive to renew it but for the publication (and Nottingham Playhouse production) of *A Yard of Sun* in which he goes back sixteen years to complete the quartet of seasonal plays that first made his name. Those pieces may have adopted a soft Christian line, and certainly gave Mr. Fry a sounder foothold in the theatre than Eliot ever had; but they were based, no less than Eliot's comedies, on what one may only describe as a contempt for the theatre and, even more, for its public. Each in turn, from *The Lady's Not for Burning* to *The Dark Is Light Enough*, took an absurd romantic fiction (on the assumption that audiences love to swallow such things) and proceeded to dress it up with fanciful language and underscore it with Christian symbolism. In those days reviewers were apt to talk about different "levels" of meaning, and that term applies all too appropriately to the naïve architecture of Mr. Fry's compositions.

In *A Yard of Sun* he reverts to precisely the same vein. And while this no doubt demonstrates his integrity, there are times when integrity looks like paralysis.

TLS. Aug. 22, 1970, p. 918

Poetic theater came to new life with Christopher Fry. . . . With *The Lady's Not for Burning*, Fry began a cycle of four verse plays portraying, to the accompaniment of the changing seasons, the course of human life. The first play, a cheerful work but with serious undertones, symbolized spring. It was followed by *Venus Observed*, representing autumn, and *The Dark Is Light Enough*, representing winter, in nature as in human life. Finally, after a long interval, came *A Yard of Sun*, the summer play.

Fry's plays of the four seasons brought new life to the stagnating West End theater. The monotony of the well-made play seemed at last to have been dispersed by the dramatic power of Fry's language and his soaring imagination. Behind the ambiguity of the word play and the images, the real and imaginary worlds lie side by side—which is not the case in the realistic theater of illusion. Fry has been criticized for putting too great a stress on language to the detriment of action and dramatic density. But others have felt that in his works language at last came into its own again on the stage. He is, in a sense, a successor to the Elizabethan dramatists.

Fry's plays, like Dylan Thomas's, have been based on individual experience and cannot be interpreted as direct statements about contemporary life. What Fry offers is diversion from the chaos of destruction, a reminder of the healing powers of nature, and, in his religious plays, a certainty about the consoling power of religion. He has not been primarily interested in experimenting with dramatic forms; he prefers to present a world view. For Fry, art is a catalyst through which the claims of daily reality can be transcended.

Horst W. Drescher. In *World Literature since 1945* (N.Y., Ungar, 1973), p. 73

FULLER, ROY (1912–   )

The title of Roy Fuller's new book, *Buff*, derives from the following snatch of dialogue, quoted from an old Forfeits Game:

> "Methinks Buff smiles"
> "Buff neither laughs nor smiles"

and it seems to embody what has always been a familiar warning, or misgiving, in Fuller's work; that we should not be misled into assuming that the poet has anything like the coolly authoritative command of experience that his elegant forms, his trim vocabulary, his wittily self-effacing parentheses, and so on, might seem to imply. Indeed, it is perhaps Buff's real distress that his expression should so readily invite this sort of misinterpretation, that the style he has to be content with is as insufficiently nourished by direct feeling as the personality, or state of mind, he wants it to express.

Although Fuller has admitted before that the "prim ego's guesses" are unlikely to encompass the "cesses of the Id," that the rational discursive manner cannot receive the full weight of imaginative experience and do very much with it except perhaps shrivel its mystery into a few punily inexact, if clever, propositions, he has nevertheless invariably preferred to rely on the certainties of what he calls an "austere miss" rather than on the possibilities of a "romantic woolly hit." Few poets, though, can so often publicly have found their own work to be as "boring" as Fuller seems to find his; time and again he has turned on what he has done and scoffingly dismissed it as inadequate to the real demands of the age, as pitifully falling short of what he sees as the traditional civilizing responsibilities of art. . . .

A child of the 'thirties, Fuller was not able to turn in his political disillusion to the contemplation of any "staggering equation/or mystic experience"; all system failed and his unsatisfactory refuge, always guiltily inhabited, has been precisely that life of the imagination which he has continued to wish might be shared by the oppressed and barbarous "common fold." The separation between his rarefied personal life and those regrettable "ordinary modes of being" which he is yet committed to, has become wider with age so that now—and this kind of honesty runs painfully through his new book—more than ever is it difficult to decide who is the more to be pitied, who is the more tragically deprived; the poet, neurotically withdrawn, beset by nightmares, symbols and impossible cravings, or his lost audience, philistine, exploited, briefly instinctual.

Ian Hamilton. *L.* June, 1965, p. 67

In Roy Fuller's fiction the hero tends to be a complacent or resigned man given a sudden jolt, presented with areas of possibility which he had counted out or had preferred to dismiss, entrenched in a routine that was comforting even when stultifying. One of the great strengths of these novels has been the author's ability to register the details of habit, and this authority helps to stabilize any more extraordinary episodes—this can be seen particularly clearly in the thrillers. But there seems not to be any true feeling of freedom, there is an ultimate holding back. . . . It is one of the most interesting features of this novel [*My Child, My Sister*] that this lurking impediment is brought out into the open. The price of doing this is making the hero-narrator a novelist himself. . . .

My Child, My Sister is a very accomplished work in its restraint of incident, its characters. . . . The narrating style itself is thoroughly *written*. . . . Nor does it seem to lack that sensitivity to time and place which have served Mr. Fuller almost too well in the past. And if it seems to have in the context of his career an unusual significance, it has in itself a distilled quality, as of a work that has confronted its own limitations and has refused to be belittled by them.

Stephen Wall. L. Jan., 1966, p. 97

If Truth is, as Yeats said, "an attitude of mind," then perhaps the central "message" of a collection of poems lies as much in its stance as in its conclusions. . . . [Roy Fuller's] new collection [*New Poems*] causes one to turn back through his work of the past thirty-five years and realize that he has steadily, and with ever increasing authority, established a stance of importance to our times. Early Fuller was, of course, sometimes limited by an over-addiction to neatness and wit. The voice was sometimes thin, even shrill, and there was more petulance than passion, more artifice than art. It is the mark of the major poet that he exploits his defects. In these *New Poems*, as in most of his work of the sixties, Fuller has enlarged ennui, self-disgust, complacency, petulance, nervous tension, and bourgeois anxiety into aspects of a representative man whose total vision is so inescapably human, so completely and easily aware of fallibility, so morally ambivalent, and so indestructibly speculative that he is more ourselves than we are. His ability to catch himself, and us, observing a "Girl with fat legs, reading Georgette Heyer," or noticing the face reflected in the window pane, "becoming ancestral," is accompanied by an ability to bring mythic ironies to bear upon those sensual minutiae, and a reasonableness that is tough enough to admit, mock, and revere the irrational compulsion, the jerk of the puppet at the crooking finger of some unpinnable ghost or god.

The style, the speech, in which these meditative wry confessions, these coffee-break soliloquies, these self-apostrophes of the middle-aged century, are presented to us is fluid and easy, modulating from vulgarity to pedantry, from matter-of-fact loquacity to rhetorical rigour, and from complacency to hesitance, with a self-indulgence that is central to the poems' intent and message. Quotation is unfair to these poems. There are few truly key passages. The extracted apothegm requires its whole context to have its ironic richness displayed, and the mastery of scale is such that to sample one line would be to attempt an evocation of the Sahara with a cup of sand.

Roy Fuller is now, without doubt, one of our most valuable poets and one of our most disturbing. He has taken on a territory that few others have risked, and he has refused to melodramatize his portrayal of man by the use of merely adventitious intensities, or the arts of symbolist ellipsis. It is a poetry of real integrity, for it pretends to none, admitting only a passion for speculation, a weakness for introspective self-indulgence, and a wry recognition that, for all the hectoring of our egos, we must remain unpersuaded of personal superiority, and aware continually of our desperate similarity to all those others moving, like footnotes to a dream, through the tangled back streets of our journey towards the recognition of the dim face in the glass.

Robin Skelton. *Poetry*. Sept., 1969, pp. 397–98

GALSWORTHY, JOHN (1867–1933)

For [Galsworthy] property was the English passion; convention disposed of the innocent emotions. You bought everything—from houses, pretty country, works of art, to women and children. Every human feeling had to pass through a more or less brutalising shareholders' meeting; it had somehow to pay and, if you had your losses, you put a soothing cream of sentiment over them. The foreigner brought up on Victorian impenetrability was ready for Galsworthy's inside view. It explained that peculiar foreign fantasy: the well-off, buttoned up, blue-eyed, blank-faced Englishman who was a sort of gun dog to a master called the Right Thing and trained to love life only when it was decently dead. In short, the Forsytes are "rum" because they are a theory. The theory works in *The Man of Property* because Galsworthy's anger is roused; once that dies, the *Saga* becomes a family charade and a hymn to crustiness. . . .

[Galsworthy] continued all his life to be indignant about cruelty and social injustice, but within the system. He became a very likeable kind of English crank and this crankiness found an effective outlet in his plays; but as a novelist he sank back into an ironical apologia for the class he represented. Soames, the villain, the only character of any account in *The Forsyte Saga*, becomes Soames the stoic, bearing the weight of his own dull, tragic compulsion to possessive love. That development is commendable. Galsworthy has at least seen that possessive men who put a money value to everything are not thereby cut off from tragic or, at any rate, pathetic experience: if Soames is mean, he is also emotional and, in stoicism, he gains a pitiable strength. But gradually Soames becomes Galsworthy's mouthpiece and that is a betrayal of the meaning of the first volume of the *Saga*. Galsworthy has not the talent, the vitality, the conviction to deepen an idea.

V. S. Pritchett. *The Working Novelist* (Chatto
and Windus, 1965), pp. 13–15

Taking Galsworthy's writings for the theatre as a whole, it can be seen that it was his misfortune to come on the scene with an initial delusion that a play was something less serious, or less important, than a novel at a time when the English stage was in the opening phase of a rebellion against the stagey, and against the exhausted conventions of the "well-made play." When Galsworthy offered *The Silver Box* to the Vedrenne-

Barker management at the Court Theatre and launched himself on the world as a dramatist, his offering was snapped up precisely because it was a structureless and anti-dramatic animation of the thesis that there is one law for the rich and another for the poor. Received by Harley Granville Barker on a Saturday, it was accepted by him on the following Monday. This instant collapse of the walls of Jericho apparently gave Galsworthy the wholly mistaken idea that he had no need to learn more than he already knew about the theatre, and that there was no important distinction to be made between the novelistic and the dramatic. He consequently never developed a feeling for the necessities of dramatic construction, and never reached the level of professional competence as a playwright. *Justice* and *The Silver Box* were his two happiest hits, and they are essentially amateurish. His most successful play from the commercial point of view, *The Skin Game*, now reads like a parody, and the majority of his plays are never far from it in their stagey extravagance of language and plotting.

It would, of course, be altogether unjust to deny the entire corpus of Galsworthy's work any merit apart from its value as inadvertent self-revelation. He set out to hold a reducing glass up to the world of middle class custom and aspiration that he knew, and attempted to capture its essences in his miniature. He did this so successfully that many people can still recognize themselves, their relatives, and the matter of their own lives in his stories. But Galsworthy was able to do more than to persuade his readers to identify themselves with his characters, he engaged their interest in what was to happen next. In the context of his time, he was, for his class, a master storyteller.

Anthony West. Intro. to *The Galsworthy
Reader* (N.Y., Scribner's, 1967), pp. xx–xxi

In England, the reputation of Galsworthy fell like a shot bird [after his death] and is only now, in the centenary year of his birth, rocketing up again: owing chiefly to a TV presentation in 26 episodes of *The Forsyte Saga*, both paperback and hardcover editions are selling like hot cakes. But in the U.S.S.R. it never slumped at all; he has always been read avidly there, in enormous editions, and it is hard for some Russians to understand why we refuse to rank him on a par with Tolstoy.

Now this is a very curious business indeed. The reason most commonly given in England, when the question arose as to why Galsworthy was so sadly in eclipse, was that he represented *fin de siècle* snobbery at its worst. To the best of my belief, the Russians never took this view, regarding his work as analytic social satire, which, basically, it is. There is a very fine piece of irony at the end of the Saga, when, by

Fleur's marriage to Michael Mont, the heir to a baronetcy, the Forsytes are dragged screaming (if one can imagine a Forsyte screaming) out of their bourgeois bastion and dumped down upon the dangerous borders of the upper classes. It is not for nothing that Michael apologizes facetiously to Soames for being "the son of a baronight."

To imagine that the Russians enjoy Galsworthy only because they think he exposes the hollowness of English society would be naïve. They feel, instinctively, that he is a superb social analyst, almost Marxian in his historical method, though within a very narrow framework. . . .

For English-speaking readers the real stumbling-block, where Galsworthy is concerned, seems to me a different one. There is not a single character in the entire Saga with whom self-identification is easily possible, unless it is with the unfortunate Soames. When we feel that all the dice are loaded against us, that we are integrally unlovable, that maybe our breath smells, it is then that Soames appears to us much in the comforting light of an anti-hero. And the truth is, that when we study the work as a whole, Irene emerges quite unmistakably in the light of a Female Cad.

Galsworthy did not intend this. Since she is never seen "from within," she must stand or fall as an ideal of earthly beauty, beauty to which all things must be forgiven. In *The Man of Property*, by far the finest volume in the series and the only one, I believe, that is going to be taken quite seriously while our literature lasts, her behavior is at least explicable, though it is difficult not to feel that it is mean.

Pamela Hansford Johnson. NYT.
March 12, 1967, p. 2

GOLDING, WILLIAM (1911–   )

It seems clear that *Lord of the Flies* should be read as a moral novel embodying a conception of human depravity which is compatible with, but not limited to, the Christian doctrine of Original Sin. To call the novel religious is to suggest that its values are more developed, and more affirmative, than in fact they are; Golding makes no reference to Grace, or to Divinity, but only to the darkness of men's hearts, and to the God of Dung and Filth who rules there. Simon is perhaps a saint, and sainthood is a valuable human condition, but there is no sign in the novel that Simon's sainthood has touched any soul but his own. The novel tells us a good deal about evil; but about salvation it is silent.

The Inheritors is Golding's most brilliant tour de force—a novel written from the point of view of Neanderthal man. Golding has set himself the task of rendering experience as it would be apprehended by this subhuman, subrational intelligence, and his success, within the severe limits implied, is extraordinary. But, being Golding, he has not assumed such difficulties simply to demonstrate his skills; *The Inheritors*, like *Lord of the Flies*, is a moral fable, and the quality of the observing consciousness employed is a part of the morality.

The Inheritors also resembles *Lord of the Flies* in the way it relates to a book out of Golding's childhood. *Lord of the Flies* used Ballantyne's *Coral Island*, not as a source of plot or character, but as the embodiment of an attitude—a symbol out of childhood of a whole set of wrong beliefs about good and evil. *The Inheritors* uses H. G. Wells's *Outline of History* in a similar way.

Samuel Hynes. William Golding (N.Y.,
Columbia Univ. Pr., 1964), p. 16

William Golding refuses to deal with conventional themes, characters, or situations. He avoids neat categories. He irritates us so much that we are tempted to label and forget him. Some critics have already done this (with great respect). Frederick R. Karl writes that Golding's "eccentric themes, unfortunately, rarely convey the sense of balance and ripeness that indicate literary maturity. . . ." James Gindin objects to his self defeating "gimmicks." V. S. Pritchett calls his last two novels, *Free Fall* and *The Spire*, "obscure, strained, and monotonous." But Golding remains a problem.

Perhaps we can respond freshly to his works—are they novels or fables?—only if we question our usual critical assumptions. Do novels have to deal with social issues? What is artistic maturity? Is language as powerful as gesture? Such radical questions are avoided by the three critics mentioned above, who accept vague definitions of novelistic "reality." Golding asks himself these very questions—in his novels. He presents the constant battle between primitive levels of response and deceptive consciousness, the beast and the human. Because he tends to view this conflict within one being, he does not portray complex social character. His heroes are more aware of elemental nature than of social adaptation. They are flat and stylized; they do not seem to belong in novels (at least the ones we are used to).

Golding's psychology shapes his novels. He wants to give us the "poetry of disorder" (Richard Chase's phrase), not the science of order. But the very words he uses are logical; they discipline elemental nature, destroying some of its violent, sudden beauty. How can he express his *vision* of our primitivism when this very expression mutilates it? Golding's strange novels are, by their very nature, suicidal because they cannot capture those ambiguous gestures which are below (or above?) language. To claim that he does not know what he is doing; to assert that he is unnecessarily eccentric—such statements assume the incompetence of Golding, whereas they confirm the limitations of his critics.

Irving Malin. In Charles Shapiro, ed.,
Contemporary British Novelists (Carbondale,
Southern Illinois Univ. Pr., 1965), pp. 36–37

All of Golding's novels have been concerned in one way or another with the Sphinx's riddle, but, as they have developed, the emphasis has shifted from the necessity of getting the right answer to the necessity of posing right questions, setting the riddle in the right way. As explanations have given way to explorations, fable has gradually been assumed into myth located in history.

Put in these terms, we might incline to regard Golding's achievement from *Lord of the Flies* to *The Spire* as a continual progress, in that in his last novel he seems to have found a satisfying shape for myth. In a way this is true, but we are saying less than we might think about the actual achievement in fiction. The solution of artistic "problems" is something that can be seen only in retrospect, and consequently it is an abstraction from the individual works of art. To think of "solutions" as synonymous with "achievements" would be to misunderstand the nature of the artistic process—to become, in fact, a pattern-maker without the imaginative strength of the art of fable. All we can say, as we look at the various transformations which Golding's imagination has undergone in the last twelve years, is that it would seem that *The Spire* marks the end of a phase in his work; the resolution established in that work is of such a kind that it is not easy to see how it can be extended. In saying this, the critic can claim no foresight. He can only try to learn to see what is there already, and what is there in Golding's case seems to be a body of work which has resolved what seem to have been its predominant tensions, leaving the artist free for further exploration.

Mark Kinkead-Weekes and Ian Gregor.
William Golding: A Critical Study (Faber and
Faber, 1967), pp. 256–57

To speak of Golding's achievement in the body of his work is a good deal easier than to generalize effectively about his development to this point in time as a novelist, for *The Pyramid*—so unpredictable, I think, in the light of its predecessors—appears to break decisively in technique and theme with what has gone before. Whereas four of the first five novels are grounded in a sequence of events that accumulate an enormous narrative charge (and even *Free Fall* depends on such a sequence in the central episode of Sammy Mountjoy in the concentration camp), *The Pyramid* feels much more loosely structured, with only the three sexual encounters between Oliver and Evie in the first part of the story affecting one as a sequence that advances narratively with something like the thrust of those in the earlier books.

In the earlier novels, as well, the subjective experience of main characters so various as the youthful Ralph or Dean Jocelin is richly imagined by Golding, and densely represented, too, in the case of Lok's sensuous apprehension of the world, or the existence which Pincher Martin has willed for himself, or the combination of remembered events with commentary through which Sammy Mountjoy re-creates his past; yet *The Pyramid* offers no such vital center in Oliver, whose inner life remains comparatively empty even while he tells us his story. Similarly, Golding's style itself in *The Pyramid* seems relaxed and colorless in comparison with the controlled symbolism in *Lord of the Flies*, the marvellous evocation of the world as sensed by a primitive in *The Inheritors*, the interlocking of the apparently substantial and the subjective in *Pincher Martin*, the rendition of a religious dimension in *Free Fall*, or the spare, taut verbal mode of *The Spire*. But . . . all of its technical differences may be viewed as consequences of an attempt to represent a presumably rather ordinary person so deeply conditioned by society that he is hardly aware of the ways in which it smothers him —which may be to suggest, once more, that Golding typically creates his fictional structures in the service of meaning.

Howard S. Babb. *The Novels of William Golding* (Columbus, Ohio State Univ. Pr., 1970), pp. 202–3

I have always thought since the days of *Pincher Martin* and, above all, *The Inheritors* that William Golding was the most original imagination among living English novelists. If he labors (and makes us labor too) in the scene he generally deals with, he dredges up unease from the muddy bottom of time, and the stuff has, at the crisis, a flash of cruel revelation. He deals in the primordial, not as if it were allegory or a scientist's guess, but as a throb of the pulse of primitive consciousness at the point of change. He has sunk himself far deeper than, say, Ballantyne in *Coral Island* or the journalistic idea-mongering of science fiction. When he sees the bubble breaking in the mud he knows that something is born. He is strenuous reading but dramatic when your eye gets accustomed to the genesis-like darkness.

The talent has one serious danger: if you are concerned with the moment when the bottom falls out of a torpid culture and a new life-force begins to blunder toward being born, then your anthropology is likely to become slangily instructive. The three short novels in this new book [*Three Short Novels*] do not altogether escape this. In the classic *The Inheritors* Golding was admirable in showing that the arrival of the new apeman was wretchedness for the unenlightened apes whose sorrow could come out only in grunts. His feeling was for the losers. . . .

Golding's strength lies in his image making; less, I think, in his dialogue, for that—except in the comic story—is an awful difficulty. In spite of its exhilaration, I find the middle one, "Clonk, Clonk," too close to fairy tale for my taste, but Golding is a wit.

V. S. Pritchett. *NYR*. Feb. 24, 1972, p. 13

GRAVES, ROBERT (1895–   )

Robert Graves is a minor poet of major proportions. In 1958 he esti-mated that up to then he had written close to five million words. He has since published another twenty books. A list of the first editions would include over one hundred thirty items. Among them are fifteen novels; a dozen books of criticism; as many volumes of biography and studies in myths and history; a dozen collections of short fiction and other miscellaneous writings; a half-dozen editions of other writers' poems, letters, ballads, nursery rhymes; translations from Greek, Latin, French, Spanish, German; a travel book; books for children; a handbook on English prose; a study of swearing and improper language; a book on dreams; and a couple of plays. He has published 824 poems that I know of. Most of them have come out in thirty-nine successive collec-tions. Only three of these books are dull.

But though he is a prolific, an imitated, and since 1926 a consist-ently good poet, he is not a major one, by choice, and according to his own definition of "major." "Minor poetry, so called to differentiate it from major, is the real stuff," says Graves. . . .

A major poet is himself a tradition. . . . But that is exactly what a number of his critics, starting with Edwin Muir, and swelling to a chorus during the fifties, have been claiming for him. Robert Graves, according to these critics, is now the most important poet writing in English and the best model for young poets seeking either to establish a new tradition or to recover the native one that "Franco-American modernism," as he calls it, is supposed to have set aside. . . .

George Stade. *Robert Graves* (N.Y., Columbia
Univ. Pr., 1967), pp. 3–4

Because *The White Goddess* synthesizes not only . . . [many] scholarly works and disciplines . . . but also unites the needs of a modern sensibility with the rituals of the ancient world, it makes possible a body of the most distinguished love poetry in the twentieth century. Whatever his shortcomings as a scholar—as the university considers scholarship—Graves discovered the identity of individual need with what was once the communal structure of myth and ritual devised to serve that need. He maintains, with some justice, that over the centuries the religious structures based on the propitiation of fertility were repressed and replaced with more abstract and intellectualized conceptions of the divine. Just as metaphysics is based upon physics, so theology is based upon the structure of society; and its main economic institutions—hunting, agriculture, or manufacture—are recognizable to anthropologists as the unmoved movers that determine the religious dispensations under which the society operates. Yet the human creature is biologically (and perhaps in important ways psychically) unchanged by the five thousand years of cultural development since the worship of Isis, Latona, Caridwen. Graves is grappling with latent dispositions of human character that have been overlain by a few dozen centuries of social life. Call his theory atavistic, yet none can deny that he restores to an indestructible and necessary part of human experience its original mystery, spiritual energy, guilt, and wonder.

The conceptual system of *The White Goddess* might, however, have made possible a wider range of poetry than that which Graves has actually managed to write. Not all the ingenuity and energy that went into his sometimes devious proofs could be transformed into the poetry his grammar of myth was designed to liberate. His mind ranges further than his sensibility, caught within the circularities of love. His principal application of his system is in the analysis of love in all its aspects he can know. The identity of the Muse changes in real life as the poet offers his fealty to various Muse-women in turn. But the conceptions which each of these women embodies remain constant, perpetual, while the poet is alternately the bringer of fruition and the sacrificed victim in the fertility ritual they enact and re-enact. It will be seen that these conceptions serve Graves somewhat as the idea of chivalric love served the courtly sonneteers and lyric writers in the Petrarchan tradition. They too addressed their plaints to a beautiful, disdainful Muse, and the sequences of their sonnets became the spiritual autobiographies of such lovers as Astrophel. But, as is plain from "Cry Faugh!," Graves spurns their Platonic love as fruitless.

Daniel Hoffman. *Barbarous Knowledge: Myth
in the Poetry of Yeats, Graves and Muir*
(N.Y., Oxford Univ. Pr., 1967), pp. 212–14

Critics who differ over the nature of Graves's poetic achievement seem to agree about its limitations. A common judgment is that in some way Graves has evaded the problems of the twentieth century, forsaking the arena of general concern, where, for example, Pound, Eliot, Empson, Bottrall and Auden have honourably fought, for the less demanding labours, albeit performed with incomparable skill, of the private garden.

It is true that his themes are not public and rarely topical, that his imagery, though exact, vivid and richly evocative, is uncomplicated, rural, and traditional and makes very little allusion to the realities of an urban, technologically sophisticated society or, except indirectly, to modern scientific and philosophic thought; he has, in fact, deliberately excluded from his collections those poems in which it does. But his poetry is no less fully engaged with the modern world for having these characteristics.

We have a right to expect a contemporary poet to be in some sense "modern"—that his work should bear the impression of the age in which it is written—even if he is profoundly at variance with the tendencies of that age; it is a question not of themes and images, however, but of sensibility. The quality of a poet's modernity can be gauged less from the amount of direct reference to contemporary history or direct indebtedness to contemporary thought than from the degree of (implicit or explicit) *awareness* embodied in his work of contemporary ideas and events, and the quality of his response to them. By this definition Graves's poetry is modern. He lives in spiritual exile from our civilization, but he rejects its values neither ignorantly nor irresponsibly.

Michael Kirkham. *The Poetry of Robert
Graves* (N.Y., Oxford Univ. Pr., 1969), p. 269

Of all poets of this time, Robert Graves is the one who, without solemnity but with total dedication, has kept the idea of poetry sacred and the idea of the poet true. He has always disliked the idea of poets using poetry ambitiously in order to assert claims of greatness and universality, whether these were made by Virgil or Milton, or (as he considered) by poets of his own day like Yeats or Eliot. His ideal of poetry is, I suppose, that of Catullus, in whose work the holy rage or passionate love in each poem seems exactly to equate the entranced but still measurably personal feeling—the situation of loving a girl or hating a rival out of which the poem arises. . . .

He has expressed with learning and wit ideas that often seem wildly eccentric—yet he is not in the least a man above the clouds or ignorant of the world. There are elements of egoism, rationalization and even absurdity in his writings, but in the end they do not matter. Reading these late poems [*Poems 1970–1972*] mostly written between his 75th and 77th years, one feels the calm of a lifetime justified by past results and by new results expressing that peace gained. . . .

All his life Graves has been indifferent to fashion, and the great and deserved reputation he has is based on his individuality as a poet who is both intensely idiosyncratic and unlike any other contemporary poet and at the same time classical. There is one short poem written in Latin in this book, and his work is the nearest thing we have to Latin poetry. These new poems are not his greatest work, but they are not imitations of past achievements either. They are mysterious, shadowy, gentle, sad, yet smiling and strong, with a humanity that he has rarely quite achieved before. If not a crown to his life's effort, they are a shining green laurel wreath.

Stephen Spender. *NYT*. March 11, 1973,
pp. 7–8

GREEN, HENRY (1905–   )

Nearly everyone who writes about Henry Green ends up calling him elusive. Nearly everyone who reads him understands why. Trying to come to discursive grips with his novels is rather like trying to pluck and pocket smoke rings; the attempt yields intimations of design, evanescent luminosities and pervasive fragrance, but precious little palpable residue.

Initially, our situation as we prowl through his verbal fugues attempting to pounce on meaning seems not unlike that of the cat who, entering the barn a moment too late, almost saw the mouse. But mice, although properly elusive, are not suitable symbols of significance in Green; birds are better. Whether on the wing, sitting, or dead, their presence in Green's novels seems somehow (and how that word hovers over one when thinking about Green!) to inform and order them, their swift elusive flights to suggest the delicate play of motifs, their occasional flocking the subtle clusterings of meaning. They both connect and spin off motifs, and contemplating their place in Green's ambiguous fictional world, one understands the plight of that speaker in one of Wallace Stevens's poems about complexity, who was finally astonished to discover that fluttering things have so distinct a shade.

Green's fluttering novels have been variously perceived and assessed. His work has been described as ambiguous, enigmatic, cryptic, excessively mannered, and brilliant. Green himself has done little to illuminate the enigmas which envelope him and his work. Like Wallace Stevens, he has led two lives, and they seem not to have over-lapped appreciably. An industrialist now retired, he has, in the past, written and said very little publicly about his work or that of other writers. His most recent published word to the outside world is suitably cryptic: he advises people in general to stay home, preferably in bed. While there seems little disagreement as to his importance or talent, there is considerably more as to the nature and beneficence of his influence. On the one hand, he is regarded as one of the central symbolist novelists of our time, in the tradition of Conrad, Joyce, and Virginia Woolf, one who has made important innovations in the modern novel. On the other hand, he has been condemned as a slick and decadent fooler-around with words and techniques, one whose verbal pyrotechnics, while dazzling, have cast their garish light along quite the wrong path for the novel to take.

Robert S. Ryf. *Henry Green* (N.Y., Columbia
Univ. Pr., 1966), pp. 3–4

GREENE, GRAHAM (1904–   )

The popular image of Greene as a master technician with a crucifix hidden behind his back (or up his sleeve) obviously will not do. But his work does not fit into the categories that orthodox literary criticism has evolved in its appraisal of serious modern fiction. While the mass media of entertainment have figured as the villains in most contemporary cultural discussion, Greene has not only enjoyed popular success as a writer of thrillers and stories (like *The Third Man*) designed for the movies, but has drawn extensively on their conventions in his most ambitious work. In a period when the most influential school of criticism in England has proclaimed the duty of the novelist to be "on the side of life," Greene has spoken eloquently on the side of death. Belonging by language and nationality to a tradition in the novel based essentially on the values of secularized Protestantism, Greene has adopted the alien dogmatic system of Roman Catholicism, and put it at the very centre of his mature work. Eschewing the "poetic" verbal texture, the indifference to "story," and the authorial impersonality of most of the accredited modern masters of fiction, Greene has cultivated the virtues and disciplines of prose, favoured involved and exciting plots, and reasserted the right of the novelist to comment on his characters and their actions.

The result of all this, one can't help thinking, is that Greene has represented for many critics a temptation of a kind to which criticism of the novel is always susceptible: the temptation to abstract from fiction the author's version of reality, measuring this against a supposedly normative version, rather than assessing the persuasiveness with which the novelist realizes his version. . . .

Part of the trouble, no doubt, is that Greene's *données* are often based on Catholic dogma and belief, on such assumptions as that there is such a thing as "mortal" sin, that Christ is "really and truly" present in the Eucharist, that miracles can occur in the twentieth century. The fictional endorsement of such ideas in the context of a pluralist and largely secular culture presents very real artistic problems. In seeking to convey to his non-Catholic audience a technical and emotional understanding of Catholic experience, the Catholic novelist risks arousing in this audience whatever extraliterary objections and suspicions it entertains about the Catholic Church as an active, proselytizing institution; while on his own part he has to grapple with the problem of retaining his artistic integrity while belonging to a Church which has never accepted the individual's right to pursue intellectual and artistic truth in absolute freedom. . . .

There is a good deal of evidence, internal and external, that in Greene's fiction Catholicism is not a body of belief requiring exposition and demanding categorical assent or dissent, but a system of concepts, a source of situations, and a reservoir of symbols with which he can order and dramatize certain intuitions about the nature of human experience—intuitions which were gained prior to and independently of his formal adoption of the Catholic faith. Regarded in this light, Greene's Catholicism may be seen not as a crippling burden on his artistic freedom, but as a positive artistic asset. [1966]

David Lodge. *The Novelist at the Crossroads*
(Ithaca, N.Y., Cornell Univ. Pr., 1971),
pp. 87–89

[*The Comedians*] astonishes and delights by its apparently effortless display of superb craftsmanship and its almost insolent ease and prodigality of invention. And it most vigrously displays that element in his work which is a main root of Greene's strength and originality as a novelist, his ability to write a sheerly exciting story of violent action and suspense, the element that, in isolation, is the staple of what he used to call his entertainments. . . .

Greene's way of seeing the world and the nature of men has remained constant. It is all there, at any rate by implication, in his first

novel, *The Man Within*. It is motivated, it seems, by two exceedingly
strong emotions that perhaps spring from a common tap-root. One is
boredom. . . . But there is the other, equally strong emotion; a horrified
pity for mankind. When Greene was a specifically Catholic novelist he
saw the grace of God as the only succour for man. . . .

What we have instead, in *The Comedians*, is a sort of intransigent
stoicism, a refusal to be borne down by evil without at least fighting
back. It is rather as though Greene now sees life as an endless, bitter,
desperate Resistance struggle against the elements in it that make for
evil. In its totality, the view of life and of the necessity for commitment
expressed in it, this novel seems to me not so very far from Conrad,
whose presence one has always felt close to Greene. *The Comedians* is
his most Conradian novel to date and his finest, I believe, since *The
Power and the Glory*.

Walter Allen. L. March, 1966, pp. 73–75, 80

English Catholics, even converts, are tempted by more heresies than are
the children of Mediterranean baroque Christianity. The greatest
temptation is provided by the British heresiarch Pelagius, a monk who
denied original sin, doubted the need of divine grace to achieve salvation, and thought that man could attain some sort of perfection by his
own efforts. His doctrines, which flourish in our mild air, are at the root
of both the major political ideologies of this country, though they are at
their more conspicuous in socialism. If an English Catholic does not
wish to be tainted by Pelagianism, he had better seek the exile either
of Evelyn Waugh's "idiosyncratic Toryism," which can properly
flourish only in a small manor cut off from the traffic, or of one of the
barbarous places of the world. Surprisingly enough, such barbarous
places take kindly to the heresies that have come out of France, a most
civilized place: it is easy to be Albigensian or (which is not so bad)
Jansenist in Cuba, Haiti, or the Heart of Darkness. But once a
Catholic lays open his soul to the corruptions of the great world of
commitment, he must accept a kind of empiricism if he is not to be
damned, drawing from the natural order what may conceivably further
the terrestrial ends of the supernatural order.

In Greene's fiction, however, there is little flavour of empiricism
(which, after all, has something of Pelagianism about it). There are
instead paradoxes and anomalies—the sinner who is really a saint, the
philanthropist who is really a destroyer. And there are dangerous
epigrams like "There is always an alternative to the faith we lose." No
significance need be attached to the fact that Graham Greene is now
living not too many kilometres away from Port-Royal. His beliefs are

his own affair; we are merely concerned with his fiction. And fiction, as we know, has to be stranger than truth. [1967]

Anthony Burgess. *Urgent Copy* (N.Y., Norton, 1968), p. 20

Travels with My Aunt will cause no one to change his overall estimate of Greene. It bears the undeniable stamp of his craft, his style, his obsessions. But it is an example of the later Greene and noticeably different, therefore, from the novels of his early and middle years. There is occasionally a metaphor that harkens back . . . the reflective aphorism . . . the jibe at old targets . . . the swipe at Americans . . . and the almost concealed *double entendre*.

But what is most noticeable are not the similarities but the changes in style and feeling. The language is pared down, unadorned; the quick nervous pace has given way to a sure continuous flow; and the feeling is closer to the more compassionate view that was emerging in *The Comedians* and to the amused urbanities of *May We Borrow Your Husband?* than to the angular and harsh view of the earlier novels. . . .

In his best novels and notably in this one, Greene has taken a genre that some judge to have reached the dead end of perfection, at least in English, with Joyce and James, has employed the traditional means of narrative, character and reliance upon the actual world and has presented life reflected through a modern sensibility. Not a pure art form, not an aspiration toward the condition of music, *Travels with My Aunt* is solid, mature, amusing and disturbing. As one who continues to hold in affection the loose, baggy impure thing we call a novel, I hope Greene continues to add to his past achievements and to develop and extend the view that in his work emerges clearly for the first time with this novel.

James Finn. *NR*. Feb. 14, 1970, pp. 27–28

Nowhere in Greene's work do human energies pulse more vividly than in his entertainments, or lighter fiction. . . . Greene's novels and entertainments are generically alike, as outcroppings of the same mind. But criticism must sometimes work from the genus through the species to study variants of the species. This sort of attention has not been given the entertainments. Even when critics discuss them, they do so perfunctorily, preferring to dwell on the novels. The remarks they do make are marred by the same faults they attribute to the entertainments when comparing them to the novels—loose interior logic, surface dash, scamped construction, and a giving in to topicality. Important questions about the entertainments have gone unanswered in the wake of this casualness. Is the chief difference between the novels and the entertainments philosophical or technical? Does the novel-entertainment division devised by Greene smack of lecturing the reader? . . .

Greene knows that controlling the reader's responses depends upon the ability to control one's materials. His praise of Ford Madox Ford's craftsmanship applies as much to himself as to Ford: "He [Ford] was not only a designer; he was a carpenter: you feel in his work the love of the tools and the love of the material." The tight economy of design and the clean narrative follow-through of the entertainments certify Greene a master craftsman, too. A seasoned professional, he roughs out a narrative curve and then fits his data into their proper place within the curve or sequence. He gives his minor characters personalities; he touches in local color vividly; he alternates pleasingly between dialogue and description; danger stabs out of his most commonplace situations. Everything contains the seeds of terror; everything is subject to sudden change. A character can unknowingly spark a series of events that reshapes other lives, the supreme example being the exertions of James Raven, the demonic harelip killer in *This Gun for Hire*, which prevent a European war. To blame Greene for mounting this kind of excitement is to blame him for not boring the reader.

A child pushed from a top-floor window, a man literally frightened to death, an amnesia victim driven to madness by his keepers at a mental hospital, "the smashed dreary city of Vienna" during the four-power occupation—these are some of the data making up Greene's entertainments. Although they fit no rigid pattern, the entertainments usually revolve around a male character with the chance to save. But the potential savior is not only a man with a mission; he is also a man on the run. The urgency of his situation—that of working alone with his life on the line—evokes the reader's sympathy. In *The Confidential Agent, The Ministry of Fear, The Third Man*, and *Our Man in Havana*, the hero's exertions carry the added reward of winning the girl. Yet this last-chapter concession to a happy ending is usually blunted. . . . The hero's exertions produce even less. At the most, they amount to holding actions or stalemates; the evil that spurs the hero to act remains basically untouched by his efforts.

Peter Wolfe. *Graham Greene the Entertainer*
(Carbondale, Southern Illinois Univ. Pr.,
1972), pp. 4–5, 8–9

For me . . . [Greene] is the largest English novelist alive. E. M. Forster was consistently deeper, though never as broad; but Forster is recently dead. L. P. Hartley, Christopher Isherwood (long an American citizen), Anthony Powell and Henry Green have sustained perfections denied to Greene, but again, in each case, the grasp and the quarry have been smaller.

Of older living English novelists, only Graham Greene seems now to have created (over 46 years, in 19 novels and . . . 40 short stories) the sort of world-in-language that has been the deducible ambition of a majority of novelists in Asia, Europe and America—a world which differs from the particular novelist's observable and appallingly rich world of time and place (which is more than an image of that world) in one respect only: that it yields *stories* to the patient witness. . . .

Since *Brighton Rock* (1938) Greene's fiction has been a search for the existence of that conspiracy at the center, a conspiracy on the part of a Creator God and His ministers (human and otherwise) to lure a renegade, reprobate creation back to Himself, toward rest. The instrument of Greene's search has invariably been *story*, the actions of men in specific time and place. And the fact that we experience the stories as natural and true, or manipulated and false, is the gauge not so much of the success of his search for knowledge and answers as of his strengths as a novelist, his power to console. (All enduring novels have offered consolation, however indirect.)

There are novels in which a divine plot is discovered by the characters and confirmed in their actions (*Brighton Rock, The Power and the Glory*), those in which a plot is suspected but not confirmed (*The Heart of the Matter, A Burnt-Out Case*), and those in which the fierce benevolence of God is not suspected but confirmed in credible action (*The Comedians, Travels with My Aunt, The Honorary Consul*). Since that analysis proceeds chronologically, it suggests not only a movement in time but a development in the skills of the searcher—in the honesty of his methods, the reliability of his findings. . . .

Reynolds Price. *NYT*. Sept. 9, 1973, pp. 1, 18

GREGORY, LADY [AUGUSTA] (1852–1932)

The base to Lady Gregory's personal theatre was the little community of Kiltartan, where through restricted dialect and characterization she managed to express her universal comic vision. Closer examination reveals two basic themes which are both universal and persistent: the idealist and his shattered dream. As all who knew her attest, and as can readily be observed from her writings, Lady Gregory had a deep sympathy with the "image maker," the rebel who must stand alone, apart from his community and yet bound to it by his dream. "To think like a wise man, but to express oneself like the common people" was her favourite quotation from Aristotle; perhaps she too felt the inevitable loneliness of the leader who must take his own way. For as Yeats has said, "always her wise man was heroic man."

It is not surprising to discover in her first folk-histories, therefore, an emphasis far more personal than historical in her examination of three "strong people of the world": the tragic heroines of Irish history, Gormleith, Dervorgilla, and Grania. . . .

It is perhaps inevitable that the celebration of the rebellious individual should appear under the mantle of tragedy, for in Lady Gregory's universe, as in Yeats's, such is the fate of those who take destiny into their own hands. But as one observes in Yeats's heroic fool, clearly the struggle is worth it, for only in controversy against inevitable Fate or overwhelming odds does he realize his full strength. This is the message of Grania, Gormleith, the penitent Dervorgilla; it is the message of Ireland's history. And when we turn from the tragic "tragi-comedies" to the "pure" tragedies, "MacDonough's Wife" and "The Gaol Gate," we find the same stirring call to inner strength and the independent spirit.

The world in which Lady Gregory's plays have reality is very much a people world, inhabited by characters who are all gifted with loquacity and infinite capacity to believe, their individuality a result of fertile imagination. Consequently she rarely scales the heights of heroic tragedy, for as Yeats pointed out, the spirit of laughter is a great deflater, and once Lady Gregory allows her little people to take on their wayward personalities, she is no longer in control. . . .

Ann Saddlemyer. *In Defence of Lady Gregory,*
Playwright (Dublin, Dolmen, 1966),
pp. 63, 72

Lady Gregory's use of character in her comedies is far from romantic; it is classical. She would subscribe to the Aristotelian view that character is present for the purpose of the action. In some ultimate sense, however, for her the action is there to present the static image of a world. One imagines that with the conclusion of one of her actions and with, say, the next morning's opening of the shops in Cloon square, all things and all people will be at the places appointed them in the original stage directions. This is obvious in such shorter plays as "The Workhouse Ward" and "Coats," least obvious but equally true in *Spreading the News*, where at the play's end certain things remain to be cleared up among the characters before the original situation is restored.

"The Workhouse Ward" (1908) has the quality of a tableau that is for a little while interrupted by a minor crisis resolved ironically. It invites a brief meditation on its scene—two old paupers endlessly wrangling in their separate beds. It is not surprising that Lady Gregory herself meditated upon the scene and observed, "I sometimes think the two scolding paupers are a symbol of ourselves in Ireland—'It is better to be quarrelling than to be lonesome.' " "Coats" (1910) offers the picture of two rival newspaper editors lunching at the Royal Hotel, Cloonmore. The action of the play is a confused argument between them over their respective obituary notices. It breaks the quiet of their lives, but is resolved. One imagines them sitting there again at the next noon, the next argument on another subject, but again resolved.

Lady Gregory's plays are very Irish, but they arise out of a conception that life is everywhere fundamentally the same and that the fundamentals do not change from age to age. This is the attitude of the folklorist and of one who is conscious of a tradition and seeking to preserve or restore it. Finally, it is one of an artist observing a society that has been conservative, isolated, and jealous of its privacy, suspicious of the invader.

Hazard Adams. Lady Gregory (Lewisburg,
Pa., Bucknell Univ. Pr., 1973), pp. 73–74

GRIGSON, GEOFFREY (1905–   )

New Verse, which Geoffrey Grigson edited from January, 1933, to the Autumn of 1938, seems a more astonishing achievement with every passing year. Grigson as editor now appears far more generous and catholic in his taste than he pretended at the time. Few other editors, I suspect, have kept their pages open to poets whom they felt to be talented, but whom they accused so vigorously of abusing their talents in the editorial and review pages. The poet's work and the accusation often appear in the same issue. Few editors, I also suspect, have produced a magazine of such obvious importance that contributors were willing to suffer this treatment.

Of Grigson's best literary battles there is still much to say—his refusal, for instance, to join in the mad wake for Dylan Thomas, a poet he had honored, published, and castigated often enough in *New Verse*.

It is as well, too, to remember his long period in the wilderness—another John—crying out against the excesses (and was there anything other than excess?) of the Apocalyptic School of the 1940's.

Of the pettier battles, too much has been made already. Grigson might have done well to ponder on his own essay on Landor's lines that begin "I strove with none, for none was worth my strife." The satirist who makes his targets look small is usually in some danger of diminishing himself. And, at times, Grigson has been too shrill to sound sensible. All this could now be forgotten, if only he would forget it.

In defending language and the intelligent use of language (in some of its worst days), he was always better. His voice was not altogether ignored, but, reading the last essay in *Poems & Poets*, "A Man of the Thirties," I began to wonder, not for the first time, what would have happened to English poetry in the 1950's if Grigson, rather than Empson, had been taken as a model by the many poets in England then struggling back to sense. Grigson's obsession with precision— precise observation matched with the precise language to describe it— might have saved a number of them from either affected obscurity or plain tameness. In too many cases, it now seems clear, the underdone was a poor exchange for the overdone. To put it bluntly, there are more ways than one of being soft-minded.

The lessons are still there to be learned, though some American poets (Denise Levertov is an obvious example) have, in the meanwhile, found their own very different ways to something of the same precision in language, and impassioned, but disciplined, observation.

Michael Mott. *Poetry*. April, 1970, p. 47

Most English of characters, Geoffrey Grigson has for several years made a second home in France. With his nose and eye for the unusual in the ordinary, he chose a village in Touraine, Trôo, far from the sea, a place partaking of the climatic changes of Northern Europe and the Mediterranean's summer heat. Trôo "is the hub of the odd country of these notes [*Notes from an Odd Country*], which is a country of the mind and a portion of France": "Trôo is my bright world of imagination, where I take my true holidays; and in that world truth is more true and the real more real." The book employs that form which may seem so easy to bring off but which in fact contains many fatal pitfalls, the domestic and spiritual journal. It is not enough to display "character" and learning, acute observation of nature and people, to reveal the right (i.e. non-embarrassing) amount of personal intimacy. Grigson does all this and it would serve extremely well for journalistic purposes; but he also adds binding and preservative ingredients which I guess will make this a bedside book for a long time to come. In brief, he is a true poet, as we know from the persistence and constant renewals of his verse, and he reveals it here—perhaps most in his convincing us that he has earned his ripeness, his enjoyments, by having weighed, by constantly weighing them against the worst.

This position we now see, too, in Grigson's early hero Auden, also in his mid-sixties, but in Grigson it is more securely—and for me more congenially—underwritten by springing from a secular and, indeed, irreverent mind. "Why can I accept the Christianity of George Herbert —though 'accept' may beg the question—and not the Christianity of Eliot or Auden, or Claudel, or any television apologist?" runs one of Grigson's notes. "Because Herbert had no option. He had no possible, no sensible alternative. It was his inevitable mode of evaluation." This comes from a series of reflections on Claudel, remarkable for their measured denigration. The same process may be seen in Grigson's dealing with other villains, such as Roy Campbell. It is part of the ripeness and the weighing process. Often, quite rightly, the measure is missing, as about "the public posturing of some baboon of a blunt Bradford novelist" or the inflating of "American names inflated already in America, and elsewhere, by America's cultural propaganda agents, for American *amour-propre*."

But this book is not a *sottisier*. Neither is its interest mainly for *littérateurs*—although one of the binding ingredients is Ronsard (who Grigson did not at first realise had been born only a few miles from Trôo, and whose life and work he re-creates throughout the book in an extraordinarily vivid way), and there are many wise literary passages (the remarks on page 199, for example, about the use of poetry are classic in their spareness and accuracy). It is essentially the presentation of a mind—not in the round, the mind is too quirky for any simple shape, but well-stuffed, with delicate appendages. Perhaps what Grigson does best, what are most memorably fixed after a first reading of the book, are the descriptions of nature: "The slope of stubble rising towards a moon of polished grey, lopsidedly short of roundness and fullness." As he truly says, the "revelation of the various visual qualities of our world is a lasting value in art."

Roy Fuller. *List*. Sept. 3, 1970, pp. 315–16

GUNN, THOM (1929–   )

The writing of poems about pictures—though it has honest precedent— holds out little more intrinsic promise than relating poetry to jazz. In either case, if the poems are any good they can stand on their own feet; if they're not, they are merely a liability. In the early 'forties, Dylan Thomas achieved some memorable images by setting a group of photographs to caption in verse for *Lilliput*, but apart from this and the scattered poetry and prose written as accompaniment to Izis's photographs in *Gala Day, London,* there has been next to nothing.

Positives, an enterprising family collaboration, contains forty photographs by Ander Gunn, with verse text by his brother Thom. It is legitimate to suppose that, in this instance, the poems would not have been written had the photographs not existed. Thom Gunn, provided with an urban setting—streets, pubs, building sites, park benches —and a sequence of portraits ranging from infants and brides to sweepers and old crones, has made a good job of it. The photographs, in themselves on the dull side and moderately reproduced, are thematically near enough to the kind of poetry Thom Gunn writes anyway, for there to be none of the usual sense of strain. Rather the reverse; one feels the poems growing naturally out of the pictures, a logical extension of theme. Had the photographs been more self-sufficient or arresting, captions of any kind would have been unnecessary. As it is, these fairly arbitrarily related studies of childhood and decomposition, of revving motorcyclists and guitarists, waitresses and barmaids, which on their own scarcely delay the eye at all, act as neat decorations to the genuine poems they have themselves inspired. . . .

Picture and poem, and a relaxed, informal level, complement each other rather than compete. The overall effect is low-toned, a shade muzzy; but the whiff of beer and smoke, exhausts and dead leaves, is real.

Alan Ross. L. March, 1967, pp. 113–14

Gunn's increasing ability to allow his general meanings to emerge from physical process, without manipulating that process either to replace or merely exemplify human significance, leads in this new volume to an interesting shift of moral emphasis, summed up in the book's title [*Touch*]. Human touching is seen as a difficult and precarious gesture, an unlocking of that sharply defined firmness of self-possession which is Gunn's vigilant stance towards chaos, a disintegration of that stance into an embracing of the amorphous mind and dust from which it was salvaged; but now there is also criticism of this rigidity, a wryly ironic sympathy with indeterminacy, and a doubt about where, precisely, the edge between self-possession and the dissolving fluidity of human contact occurs.

Terry Eagleton. Stand. No. 3, 1968, p. 67

Perhaps it is not very flattering to compare a poet with Lord Byron these days. But I think that it is there that one has to begin to describe Thom Gunn's work. He is the same kind of poet, with many of the same faults, though with a good many more poetic virtues too, it should be said. Like Byron, Gunn thinks of the poet as *one who acts*; he does not think like a philosopher, because his thoughts take the form of action, of a doing something—they are immediately expressed as deeds. To be sure, these deeds are of a special kind; they are poems. They differ from the poems of other men in this way: the reader feels that in writing them the poet has committed himself to what he has to say in such a manner that he is irrevocably changed by it. The poem is an action, because it represents an attempt to form or to transform the poet's identity. . . .

Both poets exercise over us a command of personality, a force which Hazlitt describes as "genius." We would not; we have misgivings about that word which are surely justified. Yet Gunn's poetry, by contrast with Byron's, reminds us that poetry can usefully serve to realise for us the idea of a character made strong by the candour with which its conditions of life are regarded. Byron's adversities are largely self-willed, and strike us as though he had in the first place brought them into being, yet is now only half-conscious of the fact; Gunn's really do exist, not only for him, but for all of us, though we are not necessarily continuously aware of them. This marks a very large difference between the two poets. What we feel to be a fine phrase when applied to Byron—"he grapples with his subject, moves, penetrates and animates it with the electric force of his own feelings"—is seen simply to be true when applied to Gunn. In the one case, the active imagination drove Byron further and further into a world of animated fantasy; on the other, it has brought Gunn further and further into the world of all of us, where there really are substantial powers to be grappled with.

Like Bryon and unlike: of course. Any account of Gunn's work must deal with the movement away from fantasy in his verse which distinguishes him so clearly from the author of *Childe Harold* or *Don Juan*. Nevertheless, it seems good to begin with an account of the personality felt to underlie all the poems, that is, with the part of Gunn which we may imagine to have set his poetry in one direction rather than another, and to have made of his poems more than receptacles of thought—to have made them that kind of poetic act of which a description has already been attempted. The conviction is strong that the valuable quality in Gunn's work lies in the *whole* of it rather than in those moments of success that we often believe it is a critic's first duty to sort out. A good deal of Gunn's excellence, that is, has to do with his general aim in writing poetry, and this quality, whilst not blinding us to his defects, can lead us to see merit in those very defects.

Martin Dodsworth. In Martin Dodsworth, ed.,
The Survival of Poetry (Faber and Faber,
1970), pp. 193–94

Thom Gunn's new collection [*Moly*] is welcome for two reasons: he has returned to a traditional prosody, and the poems establish a personal concern and a particular locality in which he can investigate his chosen subject, the escape from the body. There is, too, a renewed concretion and vitality of language. It is rare to find the old calculated abstractions, and when one does (as at the end of the sonnet about flooded meadows) they seem the more meaningful for this rarity.

Gunn's theme is set out in the title-poem, spoken by one of Circe's pigs in a slightly comic tone. . . . This is presumably an allegory of the acid head. The herb is shown to be real, and the myth directs one's feelings about it, though these feelings are rather different from the traditional ones where moly could represent moral philosophy, or at least something rare and splendid that could stop you turning into a pig. If we are really all pigs already, then I agree that it would be worth looking for moly, but not even Gunn's scrupulous accounts of what taking LSD is like could persuade me that we are. It is much more likely that LSD is what the enchantress herself has to offer. But, of course, Gunn doesn't stop here. . . .

It is this sort of sport (though with serious conclusions) that makes *Moly* seem a particularly alert and well-unified collection, with a new freshness of feeling in it.

John Fuller. *List.* March 25, 1971, p. 381

HANLEY, JAMES (1901–   )

It requires no great courage to maintain that [Hanley] is one of the three or four most important British novelists of his generation, perhaps the most important of all. Some of his earlier work revealed clearly enough the influence of a number of writers, both of the nineteenth and of the twentieth century, both novelists and dramatists. But that he is fundamentally original is suggested, I think, by the very diversity of the names invoked by the critics in an attempt to define his special qualities. Hanley has been compared (and the list is probably not exhaustive) with Dickens, Hardy, Conrad, Lawrence, Joyce, J. C. Powys, O'Casey, O'Flaherty, Henry Green, Beckett, Dylan Thomas and Pinter; with Melville, Bierce, London, Dreiser, Lewis, O'Neill, Faulkner, Wolfe, Farrell and B. Traven; with Balzac, Maupassant, Zola, Mauriac and Simenon; with Dostoievsky and Strindberg and Kafka. Most of the parallels are valid enough, but, at least from the mid-1930's on, it is not a question of imitation, but simply of a natural temperamental affinity between Hanley and other writers who see life tragically, who are aware of cosmic absurdity, who understand human misery, isolation and obsession, who are more interested in the fringes and limits than the norm of human experience, who know that human beings are grotesque and mean and violent and rapacious—and yet capable of love, heroism and self-sacrifice. . . .

Hanley has always kept aloof from literary societies, sets, cliques and coteries. He has always gone his own way, following no line but his own, with the complete absorption of a dedicated artist. It is therefore all the more remarkable that, working in virtual isolation as he has done, he should have developed so strikingly. The sometimes sickening and melodramatic violence of his earlier work was eliminated without any loss of real power; the clumsiness and crudity, the over-emphasis and turgidity of the earlier work gave way to a style spare, strong, disciplined, but flexible, evocative and individual. . . .

Hanley (to end with specific rather than general claims) has written, in the first four Fury novels, what seems to me, despite many faults, the finest large-scale study of a family, with all its obsessions and fears, longings and hopes, enmities and loyalties, to appear in the last three decades. He has written, in *Hollow Sea, The Ocean* and *Sailor's Song*, the three finest novels of the sea since Conrad. He has written, in *No Directions*, one of the finest evocations of the horror, the monstrous beauty, the shattered nerves and the casual heroism of the blitz. In *The Closed Harbour, Levine, An End and a Beginning* and *Say Nothing* he has written four of the most compelling modern studies of spiritual claustrophobia and psychic self-imprisonment. Despite the extraordinarily widespread ignorance of his existence (even among those who are familiar with the work of Graham Greene or C. P. Snow or Angus Wilson or Elizabeth Bowen or Iris Murdoch) which has driven him at last virtually to abandon the novel, few if any of his British contemporaries have equalled his achievement.

> Edward Stokes. *The Novels of James Hanley*
> (Melbourne, Cheshire, 1964), pp. 201–2

James Hanley's writing is succinct as a telegram, nude, yet terrific. He speaks of love in various forms and of madness, love's cousin. The style is idiosyncratic and special. Human archetypes glide, strong specters, through the novel. It's as if the subconscious were worn outside. *Another World* is a masterly book.

There are five important characters; three or four loves between them. They dwell in Garthmeilo, a plugugly Welsh seaside resort that keens with February desolation: a song for the working out of passions. The body is indoors, made senseless by rain and chill; the subjective cannibalizes itself, monasteried there. The characters are each injured or deficient. The warmth they clumsily strike from their obsessions is electric and self-consuming. Garthmeilo is Hanley's controlled environment, a weathering test.

Descriptive passages seem only functional here. Tension concentrates in the dialogue. Hanley's words are crammed with meaning. Voices that prate imaginatively in the dark, scaring themselves, full of intuitions they can't wholly comprehend. Perhaps there is a Celtic rhythm in it. Even the most casual remark impends: mystery, emblems, violence. There is an italicization (real and implied) in the talk, a viewing beyond, as though articulate sounds were a poor adjunct to some heightened, extrasensory communication. Jamesian dialogue but more savage than in James; the people wear no careful dress, inhabit no precise social neighborhoods. . . .

Names weigh: Jones, Mervyn, Margiad, Gandell, Vaughan. They have no inherent allusive powers: not certainly the power of Antony crying out at last to his servant Eros. They are repeated in conversation by Hanley's characters with the awed trust of primitives who cannot separate symbol and symbolized. After 100 pages they have an adjectival force. Hanley will write, "The Jones touch," "The Gandellian thoughts," as if name were inseparable from physiognomy, were sufficient description. Hanley's names abstract so that they can specify more conveniently and widely—in the same way that *tense* distances while giving a fresh and more suggestive emphasis.

Yet the people survive and have tremendous value. Hanley ekes them out. Creatures of a single passion, more energy than flesh, they are still elaborate. They have possibilities, they surprise. Not many novelists could achieve this; perhaps not many would care to. James Hanley is past 70, with more than 40 books behind him. Yet he remains *tense*. His effects are economical and sure and profound. A unique performance. Peculiar, alive.

D. Keith Mano. *NYT*. Aug. 27, 1972, p. 2

HARDY, THOMAS (1840–1928)

As a writer of novels Thomas Hardy was endowed with a precious gift: he liked women. There are not, when one comes to think of it, quite so many other nineteenth century novelists about whom as much can be said. With some, the need to keep returning in their fiction to the disheveled quarters of domesticity causes a sigh of weariness, even at times a suppressed snarl of discontent; for, by a certain measure, it must seem incongruous that writers intent on a fundamental criticism of human existence should be sentenced to indefinite commerce with sex, courtship, adultery and family quarrels. Hardy, by contrast, felt no such impatience with the usual materials of the novel. Though quite capable of releasing animus toward his women characters and casting them as figures of destruction, he could not imagine a universe without an active, even an intruding, feminine principle. The sexual exclusiveness of nineteenth century American writing would have been beyond his comprehension, though probably not beyond his sympathy.

Throughout his years as a novelist Hardy found steadily interesting the conceits and playfulness of women, the elaborate complex of stratagems in which the sexual relationship appears both as struggle and game. He liked the changefulness, sometimes even the caprice, of feminine personality; he marveled at the seemingly innate capacity of young girls to glide into easy adaptations and tactical charms. And he had a strong appreciation of the manipulative and malicious powers that might be gathered beneath a surface of delight. Except perhaps with Sue Bridehead, he was seldom inclined to plunge into the analytic depths which mark the treatment of feminine character in George Eliot's later novels; but if he did not look as deeply as she did into the motivations of feminine character, he was remarkably keen at apprehending feminine behavior. He had observed and had watched, with uneasy alertness. The range of virtuosity which other writers had believed possible only in a stylized high society or sophisticated court, Hardy, in his plain and homely way, found among the country girls of southwest England.

Irving Howe. *Thomas Hardy* (N.Y.,
Macmillan, 1967), pp. 108–9

Although the theories and assumptions which constitute Hardy's "philosophy" are still alive, they are also to some extent "historical" and will become increasingly so. They will, therefore, lose much of their power to irritate, but also their full and immediate impact on the mind and spirit. His readers will have to rely increasingly upon notes, commentators and background reading, and so he will come to the public on the same footing as his great predecessors whose work and reputation have overcome similar obstacles. He will, of course, always have some readers whose contact with his work is a kind of naked encounter, creating sympathy and comprehension without the need for intermediaries. It seems likely, too, that in the future, as in the past, their number will be increased in times of stress. The First World War was one such period when Hardy's stock rose and there was a similar, if less marked, movement during the Second. . . .

Conversely there will always be readers whose temperaments will clash with Hardy's. Any kind of self-satisfaction is likely to produce this, the situation then being as he described it in "In Tenebris II." Furthermore, despite his reputation for intrusive and repeated expression of ideas, the true Hardy is a poet of the intimate whisper; and it is very easy for some people to get the tone wrong. . . .

Ultimately, however, the reader who is trying to enjoy what Hardy has to offer will have to make the effort . . . to see the poems as the poetic unity that many of them are, to be in contact with the poetic persona revealed here. . . .

It is a truism that great literature is in the last resort ineffable; Pound must have felt this when he was discussing Hardy [in *Guide to Kulchur*]. . . .

Kenneth Marsden. *The Poems of Thomas
Hardy* (N.Y., Oxford Univ. Pr., 1969),
pp. 220–21, 223

[The] revelation of the truth of things is the poet's contribution to the universe. [Hardy's] patient registering of the facts is a defiance of the Will, but in its proof that things do always turn out for the worst, his art is, paradoxically, a happy one. It demonstrates the eternal fitness of things. Each man gets what the prescient expect and even what the knowing want. Moreover, Hardy's recording of the fated course of a life, his following of one strand in the web through to its happily unhappy end, turns numb suffering into the symmetry of art, that high form of art which is objective recording of the way things are. Writing *Tess of the d'Urbervilles* or *The Mayor of Casterbridge*, like singing Watts's "And now another day is gone" in the face of the red wall at sunset, transforms the fated into art and therefore transcends the power of the Immanent Will.

Such an art finds value and meaning in a world previously without them. If time is a sequence of moments which are born and die, so that each instant, with all its experiences, is swallowed up by the vastness of eternity as soon as it occurs, only the consciousness of the poet with its breadth and clarity of vision can hold the moments of time together. The pattern time makes is uncovered through art, and art is therefore a victory of consciousness over suffering. It is a sly and evasive victory, surely, for the poet only stands back and watches, recording what he sees from his distance, but it is an authentic victory nevertheless. The poet's mind is the world turned inside out, transformed into words, all existence concentrated in one place and time, an aeon in an hour. Hardy's writings are the verbal embodiment of a cosmic memory, or, one might better say, this memory is generated and maintained in being by the words he writes. When things have happened and have fallen into the past they are resurrected into that space of continual repetition which is the poet's mind.

> J. Hillis Miller. *Thomas Hardy: Distance and Desire* (Cambridge, Mass., Harvard Univ. Pr., 1970), pp. 262–63

Hardy's respect for James as an artist sprang from a profound artistic engagement of his own. Raymond Williams has demonstrated the inadequacy of identifying Hardy with a "peasant" viewpoint, and it is equally misleading to think of him as a kind of natural rustic genius, untutored, unreflective, divinely spontaneous. Although he seems essentially to have felt, as he told Galsworthy in 1909, that "an ounce of experience is worth a ton of theory," surviving notebooks and published essays testify alike to his interest in contemporary debates about realism and naturalism and, as Morton Dauwen Zabel pointed out, to his need and capacity to evolve some kind of personal aesthetic.

Hardy is best seen as striving—consciously enough, but without great clarity of conceptualisation—towards perceived goals quite different in kind from those of James and Meredith. His techniques are lacking both in refinement and in consistency. Eclectically and even opportunistically adopted, they are as likely to be drawn from poetry and the drama as from the novel as traditionally understood—though some of them can perhaps be traced to Hawthorne and other romance-writers. His violent and melodramatic plots, as Virginia Woolf observed in the eloquent essay she wrote on the occasion of Hardy's death, "are part of that wild spirit of poetry which saw with intense irony and grimness that no reading of life can possibly outdo the strangeness of life itself, no symbol of caprice and unreason be too extreme to represent the astonishing circumstances of our existence."

Hardy, like his hero Shelley, is very much the romantic artist, bold in scope and expression, working through broad effects for intensification of emotional immediacy. His best novels do not accommodate themselves to a design, whether aesthetic or moral, but strike outwards from a core of experience, reverberate from a single cry of pain.

Michael Millgate. <i>Thomas Hardy: His Career
as a Novelist</i> (N.Y., Random House, 1971),
pp. 358–59

What defeats the attempt to discriminate the better from the worse among Hardy's poems is not just the great number of the poems, and their variousness. It is not even the impossibility, for the most part, of categorizing the poems as "early" or "late"; nor the almost equal difficulty of categorizing them according to genre, except in the broadest and most impressionistic way. These impediments to taking Hardy the poet as a whole, the good with the bad, do not come about by accident. Behind them is the curious paradox that Hardy, who imposes himself so imperiously upon his medium, imposes himself on his reader hardly at all. On every page, "Take it or leave it," he seems to say; or, even more permissively, "Take what you want, and leave the rest."

This consciousness of having imposed on his reader so little is what lies behind Hardy's insistence that what he offers is only a series of disconnected observations, and behind his resentment that he should be taken as having a pessimistic design upon his reader, when in fact he so sedulously respects the reader's privilege not to be interested, not to be persuaded. It is on this basis—his respect of the reader's rights to be attentive or inattentive as he pleases—that one rests the claim for Hardy as perhaps the first and last "liberal" in modern poetry. And it is because we are so unused to liberalism as a consistent attitude in a poet, that we have so much difficulty with the poetry of Hardy.

But the outcome is that every new reader of Hardy's poetry finds there what he wants to find. And in the event this means, for the most part, that each reader finds in the poems what he brings to them; what he finds there is his own pattern of preoccupations and preferences. If this is true of every poet to some degree, of Hardy it is exceptionally true.

Donald Davie. *Thomas Hardy and British Poetry* (N.Y., Oxford Univ. Pr., 1972), pp. 28–29

HARTLEY, L. P. (1895–1972)

L. P. Hartley is neither an experimental novelist nor a fully traditional one. Equally dissatisfied with both the nineteenth-century objective novel of society and the subjective, stream-of-consciousness techniques used by many twentieth-century experimentalists, he has found a middle way, a way of retaining both interests—the psychological and the social. He probes the minds of his characters, articulating their subconscious desires by means of daydream, nightmare and the introduction of fantastical elements into the basic verisimilitude of realism, but at the same time he continues to see his characters from the outside, viewing them not only as isolated psyches, each with its internal conflict, but also as members of society who are in conflict with other human beings. Then he capitalizes on the dual interest by pitting fantasy against reality, symbol against object, the private self against the social self.

Though he uses themes which may be encountered over and over again in English novels, Mr. Hartley is able to individualize these themes because of this grafting of the subjective, psychological interest —his constant preoccupation with "heightened sense of being"—on to the root stock of the novel of manners and morals. And this technique is not arbitrarily imposed, but parallels his deepest aims. When Mr. Hartley introduces fantasy, mysticism, horror and the most involved types of symbolism into stories of polite society—introduces them so dextrously that they hardly seem to intrude—he is employing the technique best suited to his artistic goal, which is to *heighten the mystery of existence while still remaining true to ordinary life*. This goal, in turn, is a product of Mr. Hartley's sensibility. The best of his work is imbued with this sensibility; it bears the mark of the author's essential self. Thus Mr. Hartley does what every true artist must do, but which nevertheless is all too rarely found: he allows us to peek into the hidden, mysterious core of a human being.

Peter Bien. *L. P. Hartley* (Chatto and Windus, 1963), pp. 9–10

Poor Clare is one of those dry wafers of perfection L. P. Hartley does so well. Published as a slim novel, it is really an extended short story, an elaboration on a single theme. Gilbert, passionate and tortured composer, gives away Aunt Clare's legacy of paintings to pay off friends he wishes to abandon. The friends, among them the narrator Edward, are first grateful, then hurt as they understand his motives, and the repercussions of this act of twisted generosity are the theme of the book.

This is Mr. Hartley at his coolest. There are hints, as always in his work, of darker thoughts, a moral world elsewhere which the characters, absorbed in their formal dance, glimpse and will never quite forget. . . .

L. P. Hartley has always admitted a preference for the shorter form, an inclination justified by his collection of short stories [*The Collected Short Stories*], also published this week. From the early twenties to the sixties, these show a remarkable consistency of skill and quality, but most of all of attitude. Coolness, yes, and the same obsession with perfection—not only in form but in the objects (buildings, vases, churches) he chooses to describe: never in people, because people, in Mr. Hartley's view, while vaguely desiring perfection, never achieve it; rather they submit to or bring about their own destruction. In the ghost stories (which I tried to skip but couldn't stop reading) they call up from within themselves, or from outside, the evil that brings them down. . . . I can see now, having read this thick volume, that the coolness is not the coldness of the misanthrope but the irony of someone who can hardly bear the waste that people make of life and of themselves.

Janice Elliott. NS. Oct. 25, 1968, p. 552

Art had not gone back on [Hartley], though *The Love-Adept* is too contrived to be a valid new experience. Heaven forbid we should always be asking for what is congruous with present trends ("trendy" isn't nearly enough the dirty word it ought to be), yet this story about an author in comfortable circumstances (of course), inviting several friends of his, who all happen to be called Elizabeth, to discuss the dénouement of the novel he is writing . . . is altogether too irrelevant to the human situation, and far too *cosy* for the times we live in.

The book, with its discursions on the theory of novels as an art form, goes to show that anything which more or less convinces may be allowed to pass, but hardly reinforces the essential truth: the greatest novels, bar some half a dozen, are written as if they were about things that really happened to men and women and were worth writing about.

Though in *My Sisters' Keeper* (1970) Hartley sticks his neck out more than ever before, this is a much more considerable book. "Though" is deliberate; "because" would not suit. It just is not true, as La Rochefoucauld claimed, that we bear other people's troubles philosophically. Far from it: there is so often someone near or dear to us whose woes or inadequacies torment us as much as they do them, or more so.

Curiously enough, the story of Basil Hancock's matchmaking activities on behalf of his three sisters . . . does not really illustrate the point, as presumably by hypothesis—viz. the title—we are meant to expect it to do. The sisters are not unmarriageable, and Basil is not, like Eustace, particularly concerned to find them *partis* eligible in the worldly sense. The theme could be intended to remind us that nobody can live anyone else's life for them—as perhaps to the end of time it will be difficult to persuade many parents (brothers aren't so often involved). But no; the question here is not "why couldn't Basil's sisters manage for themselves"; the question is "what's wrong with Basil," and the chief interest of the book may come to be thought the opportunity it offers for examination of the author's analysis of Basil's "sisteritis."

Paul Bloomfield. *L. P. Hartley*, rev. and enl. ed. (BC/Longmans, 1970), pp. 30–31

[Hartley's] best novels are the *Eustace and Hilda* trilogy, *The Boat*, and *The Go-Between*, three of the most significant works published in our century. Though it is better than *A Perfect Woman* or *The Hireling*, Hartley's recent duology—*The Brickfield* (1964) and *The Betrayal* (1966)—does not seem to me to be as good as the three I consider Hartley's best. *The Brickfield*, an experiment in handling a tale within a conversation, is an illuminating variation on the theme of *The Go-Between*. *The Betrayal*, which shows the consequence of overtrusting and misunderstanding the conversation of *The Brickfield*, reveals many interesting things about Richard, the not-hero, but is structured loosely.

Hartley's three most distinguished works do not make their claim to permanence in an obvious way. (Except in *The Brickfield*, one does not find startling stylistic innovations in his work.) Though he has learned the lesson of Henry James about a central point of view defined clearly, he allows himself liberties that suggest the "old fashionedness" of E. M. Forster and the nineteenth-century English novelists. His style does not call attention to itself as frequently as that of, say, Virginia Woolf, because it is submerged in substance. Though he has read widely and has lectured often about the novelists of the past and present and has absorbed more about depth psychology than many psychiatrists, he never gives a pyrotechnical display of what he knows, as Aldous Huxley upon occasion does. His apparent scope is not a great deal wider than that of Jane Austen or Ivy Compton-Burnett. Like them, his method is to suggest the great world by intensively representing the smaller world most individuals habituate. With Hartley, substance is the main thing and even this he approaches cautiously, circuitously, more like a birdwatcher than a hunter. . . .

How long his best work will endure neither I nor anyone knows. To me now it seems that he can take his chance with the Fielding who wrote *Amelia* and the Thackeray who wrote *Vanity Fair*. But such speculation is ultimately foolish. For those who believe it important to understand twentieth-century man in both his mistakes and his potentiality, for those who want to know how novels that *make* nothing happen can cause us to be more aware and less likely to make our world a mess than our predecessors did, the best of L. P. Hartley is required reading for survival.

Harvey Curtis Webster. *After the Trauma:*
Representative British Novelists since 1920
(Lexington, Univ. of Kentucky Pr., 1970),
pp. 154, 167

● HEANEY, SEAMUS (1939–   )

Seamus Heaney's *Death of a Naturalist* is a first book of verse and, as such, many of its poems are explorations of the poet's roots, attempts to define the rural life of Ulster he was once part of. The title of the book indirectly refers to this earlier rootedness in a way of life grimly dependent on making the best of the soil; but it also defines an autobiographical difference with which several of the poems are concerned. A "naturalist" is one who studies nature by observation, and not one who labours with it to exact from it a subsistence. Thus Heaney's father and grandfather cut peat and dug potatoes; and although to see and to smell what is dug reminds him of what was once a common way of life, its damp, truculent activity now divides him from them. . . . Their activity defines for the poet the difference between them and him. Unlike them, the poet's concern with nature, although vivid, and alert, is a naturalist's, one whose connection with it is not intimate any more since not dependent on it. . . .

The last two lines of the title poem, with their clinching rhyme, instance a different aspect of Heaney's language—a desire for incisiveness, which tends towards an over-neat epigrammatizing quality. This is already familiar to us through some of the poems in the first of the *New Lines* anthologies, and through the rather precocious *dicta* that surrounded its appearance in 1956. Yet although this incisiveness does not express the sharpness of feeling that one supposes Heaney wants to convey in his love poems, its bitter, reprimanding quality is the very instrument for the poem concerning The Great Hunger. . . .

Jon Silkin. Stand. No. 4, 1967, p. 69

It was not until he began to teach that Seamus Heaney discovered contemporary Irish literature, and with it, the possibility of exploring his own background—a small farming community in Northern Ireland. He said in his interview with Peter Orr that he found in the work of Patrick Kavanagh "what I took to be archaic subject-matter . . . treated in a modern way, in a way that made it universal and tragic, especially in this poem 'The Great Hunger,' which I think is a great poem." He turned also to Clare, Edward Thomas, Hardy, and Robert Graves— poets who stand in opposition to, or at least outside, the tradition of Anglo-American modernism that dominated English verse during the first half of this century. . . . He acknowledges the effect on his diction of Ted Hughes's work. . . . The curt, abrupt, elliptical movement of the verse unmistakably derives from Hughes. . . .

It is in the poems based on an anecdote, or grounded in a moral observation, that Heaney's strongly individual voice is heard. The tone of these poems is often Wordsworthian: Heaney shares Wordsworth's recognition that suffering and fear may play a valuable part in chastening and subduing the human spirit, and that a child is nurtured by terror as well as by beauty. But he faces the fact (and here he differs from Wordsworth) that, judged by human standards, Nature is sometimes malign and disgusting. . . .

John Press. SoR. Summer, 1969, pp. 681–82

[Heaney] talks about the cloud of unknowing, about what Patrick Kavanagh, an older Irish poet who died a few years ago, called the fog, "the fecund fog of unconsciousness." Kavanagh said that we have to shut our eyes to see our way to heaven. "What is faith, indeed, but a trust in the fog; who is God but the King of the Dark?"

What is acceptable in aesthetics may be a little off-putting in theology, if, that is, one at all desires a theology, and Heaney here may be a conscious victim of an Irish obsession which he can describe so well. For his childhood and adolescence, the equivalent of the dark Gallarus was the confessional, the Irish Catholic sense of sin, "a negative dark that presides in the Irish Christian consciousness," and, "the gloom, the constriction, the sense of guilt, the self-abasement." Every creed has its own creepy methods and for Irish writers, as witness O'Connor and O'Faolain, the confessional, for facetious and other purposes, has, so to speak, paid its way. "Penance," says Heaney, "indeed was a sacrament that rinsed and renewed—you came out light-footed and alert as those monks—but although it did give a momentary release from guilt, it kept this sense of sin as inseparable from one's life as one's shadow."

Waking or sleeping that King of the Dark would be just as uneasy a companion, or a master, as the capricious Something that Alexander Kuprin sensed at work, a spirit neither of good nor of evil, just an irresponsible and sometimes nasty Sense of Humour, writing at its worst moments Newman's scroll of lamentation. In a poem, "Against Blinking" (not yet collected) Heaney meditates on the folk-belief that an ill-disposed person could, merely by looking at it, "blink" a cow so that its milk would yield no butter. Is God the Blinker, Kuprin's law of logical absurdity?

Of all this, as I've indicated, Heaney is perfectly aware with the strong, balanced, humorous mind that he displays in poetry, in talk and in comment. . . .

Benedict Kiely. *HC*. Oct., 1970, pp. 10–11

Seamus Heaney's earlier books, *Death of a Naturalist* and *Door into the Dark*, were better received than all but a few during the past ten years. What almost everyone has commented on has been the sharpness and immediacy of his physical images, and the fastidious precision of his language. The actual substance of his first book—the sights and smells of a remembered childhood on an Irish farm—seemed to have something of the appeal of Laurie Lee: not cider with Rosie, exactly, but taties with Paddy. Nostalgically earthy emotions were appealed to, redolent of days behind the plough, shooting snipe, digging peat, lifting potatoes, peering down wells. And all these activities (not, one would have thought, the stuff of which metropolitan literary critics are made) were summoned up and transmitted with a sensuousness so neat that it was almost dandified.

Mr. Heaney's second book had plenty of bogs, bulls and buckets, but it was remarked that human beings were getting a bit more of a showing; and the thatchers and eel-fishermen, though less lovingly re-created than the thatch and the eels, gave promise that his marvellously apt mimetic skills were going to be used in ways that might stretch the mind as well as the senses. As the grim situation in Mr. Heaney's Ulster became grimmer, a different kind of poem began appearing above his name in periodicals—recognizably by the same man, but speaking from the centre of a bitter, and bitterly present, conflict.

But what has happened to these harsh and compassionate new poems? *Wintering Out* carries such a piece as a preface or dedication . . . but much of the rest of the book is "Thigh-deep in sedge and marigolds," to use one of Mr. Heaney's lines. . . . The bog oak, turf-banks and cobbles prevail, and no one is plucking up the latter to throw them at anyone. What *is* new, and interestingly so, is a desolate sense of the remote past, conveyed through such images as flints and Tollund man. . . .

TLS. Dec. 15, 1972, p. 1524

HEPPENSTALL, RAYNER (1911–   )

A student of the English novel who has been struck by the brilliance and originality of Rayner Heppenstall's *The Connecting Door* and *The Woodshed* (both published in 1962) may well wonder how it is that this writer seems to have enjoyed such scant recognition from critics and scholars. To a French reader, whose thinking about the novel has been influenced by the achievement of the *nouveaux romanciers*, Rayner Heppenstall appears to be one of the few English novelists who have done truly experimental work, one of the very few who can—and wish to—compete with, say, Michel Butor or Nathalie Sarraute, on their own difficult ground. The scarcity of serious critical attention to Rayner Heppenstall's recent fiction is all the more surprising as both *The Connecting Door* and *The Woodshed* are obviously "critics' (and professors') meat" (as Heppenstall himself calls *Ulysses* in *The Fourfold Tradition*, p. 153). . . .

Among Heppenstall's personal characteristics are to be found a number of "pet abominations," almost Ruskin-like in their vividness, but these on the whole contribute less to his writings than the things he significantly likes: sex, places, objects, time, language. His interest in sex and his Lawrence-like frankness about its details were first brilliantly advertised in *The Blaze of Noon*, a fact which did not escape the more hostile reviewers in 1939. In the later novels, there is less insistence on sexual expertise and prowess, though the reader is made to understand that the narrator, Harold Atha, is an efficient lover of his wife (variously known as "Blod" and "Old Flowerface") and occasionally of other women as well. He even goes out of his way once in each book to put in a little piece in rather questionable taste: in *The Con-*

necting Door there is an elaborate paragraph about his drinking sherry out of Blod's navel and in *The Woodshed* a reference to the fact that the number of "intimate occasions" with her "must by now approach four figures." Poor Blod!

Heppenstall's interest in objects and places is evidenced by the wonderful, Robbe-Grillet-like accuracy of his descriptions. His talent in this respect can unfortunately not be illustrated by brief quotations taken out of their context. I must merely record here that the streets and houses of Strasbourg (*The Connecting Door*) and Hinderholme (*The Woodshed*), as well as the outward appearance and the very clothes of the characters assume in the reader's eyes a concrete presence.

His interest in time, like that of several major French novelists, Marcel Proust and Michel Butor among others, is intense. Much of his originality as a novelist depends on his ability to manipulate the events of his narrator's life out of their chronological arrangement while gradually and efficiently suggesting to the reader the order in which they actually happened. He has thought much and written well about the functioning of memory. . . . In a magnificent passage of *The Connecting Door*, the narrator is shown as simultaneously seeing the Strasbourg cathedral in the present (1948) during a concert and perceiving its past existence through many centuries.

Sylvère Monod. In Maynard Mack and Ian
Gregor, eds., *Imagined Worlds* (Methuen,
1968), pp. 461, 464–65

● HIGGINS, AIDAN (1927–   )

John Calder [the publisher] introduces a young Irish writer of uncommon talent, joined in these six stories [*Felo de Se*] to a hopeless *Weltanschauung*. (German words abound.) Devotees of Beckett may find the combination fruitful rather than frightful. The similarity is inescapable and it is hard to see where Mr. Higgins will proceed, unless he follows the master and deprives his characters of arms, legs, hearing and sight. Already they are sadly afflicted. Baldness before thirty (in a lady), a stench of decay, a part-paralysed face, discoloured veins, rheumy eyes, a snout, a fractured spine, deafness, blindness, a discolouration under the right eye and hypertrophy of the prostate are a few of their difficulties.

A lifetime, we gather, is simply the process of corruption, physical and moral; and these stories are about people who undergo this process more rapidly than most. Ireland is the favoured spot, both inland and by the sea. Dublin Bay is calling again; though Mr. Higgins's strands are further south than the Sandymount and Dollymount of Joyce and Beckett. I believe I recognize Killiney and Greystones. However, his characters also listen to the waves in the North of England, Germany and South Africa. The sound of the sea obliterates, and these people are bent on obliteration. . . .

Michael Campbell. L. May, 1961, pp. 91–93

There were outcrops of huge talent in his first book, *Killachter Meadow*. In those dark stories lone individuals, often bizarre or grotesque or gigantic, are seen at large in settings cramped or limitless, working out dooms whose causes Higgins all but ignores. These people are fixed not so much in their ominous Irish, German, English, or South African landscapes as in the process of their fates. One remembers them almost as impersonations of nonpersonal lines of force. But Higgins' rather heavy craft and erratic tones indicate that at that stage he had yet to accommodate various techniques he wanted to use. Except for the long story "Asylum" (refuge, tomb) with its uncanny coupling of diurnal document and a Dinesen-like sub-patterning of occult vectors, *Killachter Meadow* is most promising in the melancholically sluggish, doom-dark pieces that grope for an indefinite ground between mood and action.

In Higgins' novel, *Langrishe, Go Down*, that promise is patiently fulfilled. If in 10 years this book is seen to have been a genuinely new work, perhaps the reason will be that by subtle differences in seemingly stock materials and an economy of balances Higgins makes a whole mysteriously unlike its parts. . . .

In his style, phenomena are held as if between the subject's response and some existence independent of an observer—perhaps in that perceptual silence Beckett says it is the function of objects to restore.

The Beckett influence is strong. . . . But despite the entropic mono-focus of *Langrishe, Go Down*, Higgins is much less mannered than Beckett. And despite the conscious linguistic variety . . . Higgins has nothing of the exhibitionist self-indulgence to be seen occasionally in Nabokov or Grass. Time will tell whether the comparison that makes most sense is with James Joyce.

Joseph McElroy. NL. Sept. 25, 1967,
pp. 18, 20

Balcony of Europe is Aidan Higgin's second novel. His first, the award-winning *Langrishe, Go Down*, was published in 1966, which leaves a six-year silence interrupted only by a slim but extremely good travel book, *Images of Africa*. The indications are that Mr. Higgins is one of those exceptionally careful and craftsmanlike writers who are today such rare birds—writers whose work, sometimes verging on the monumental, springs from the sort of aesthetic ambition we associate with the founding fathers of the modern novel. More so even than *Langrishe, Balcony of Europe* is an intensely serious and wonderfully sustained piece of writing. Mr. Higgins is an artist, in the full Joycean sense, and if he falls short here of giving us a completely satisfying work of art, he does so by reference to the most exacting standards. By any other standard he is, in company with only a few, well ahead of the field.

"A magnificent failure" is the phrase that springs to mind—yet this estimate may be premature, for *Balcony of Europe* reads like one of those books which demand return visits. Described as "a novel," it isn't quite that. Expectations of an intricately wrought structure will be disappointed. It's more episodic, falling somewhere between diary and *Bildungsroman*. . . .

The chief delight of the book is Mr. Higgins's prose itself, which is, as the French say, infinitely flexible—a precision instrument. If there is unreality, intentional or not, in the relations of the characters, there is more than adequate compensation in the (appropriately, for a painter) almost tangible presence of the contingent world. . . .

TLS. Oct. 6, 1972, p. 1185

● HILL, GEOFFREY (1932–   )

Of all our present poets, Geoffrey Hill is the one who most persistently tackles the problem of what to do about dead language, clichés, the phrases which have gone sour, flat, or heartless on us. Of course there are good poets like Philip Larkin whose approach and style make it appropriate for them to take no notice. And again there is Donald Davie who, after providing the best modern criticism on the subject of dead metaphors, has now come to believe that the worst enemy just now is not such deadness but frantic liveliness, verbal fidgets, a high-pitched buzz of interference. Yet all the same the restoration of clichés is by no means a form of antiquarianism. Conspicuous consumption and planned obsolescence are features of the linguistic as well as the social scene. . . . We ought to take particular notice of a poet like Mr. Hill who persists in his renovations with intelligence and passion. (And who writes some excellent poems meanwhile.) . . .

One says "renovations," because the poems in Hill's *For the*

Unfallen and *Preghiere* are very different from those that simply incorporate clichés in order to be matey. Like everyone since Wordsworth, Hill agrees that it is necessary for poetry to be in vital relation with the living speech of its own time. But he has argued, quite rightly, that this is not at all the same as believing that poetry need be chatty or full of gnarled rusticities. . . .

The distinguishing characteristic of Hill's poetry is that it uses cliché for tragic rather than comic purposes. This is not to deny his strong vein of sardonic humour, which he shares with the writers he most admires: Ben Jonson ("profound parody"), Isaac Rosenberg ("macabre comedy"), Allen Tate ("dry pun") and Robert Lowell ("the lampoonist's art"). In his best poems there is a largeness of ambition at one with an amplitude of phrasing (lines which it is a pleasure to mouth)—qualities which are rare these days. Yet the largeness is saved from mere orotundity by the persistent invoking of our seedier world. Hill achieves dignity by rising above cliché; he achieves truthfulness by not eschewing cliché. What fascinates him is the appalling gulf between the way we usually mutter such-and-such a phrase and the way we might use it if the doors of perception were cleansed.

Christopher Ricks. L. Nov., 1964, pp. 96–97

[*King Log*] is Hill's second book. His first appeared in 1959 and was rightly praised, though a certain bookishness brought it into disfavour with some. *King Log* is even more bookish, even more compactly phrased, even more stubbornly unbending, more rigorously assertive than its predecessor. The collection is introduced, significantly, by a quotation from *The Advancement of Learning*: "From moral virtue let us pass on to matter of power and commandment. . . ." Hill does pass on to these matters and he speaks of them with an authority and a kind of spiritual ruthlessness that is intimidating and almost medieval. And yet most of the poems are, while assertive, also masked; they are distanced by devices of title and rhetoric.

Three poems are called "Three Baroque Meditations" as if they are to be read as documents from a distant sensibility. A long sequence "Funeral Music" is based upon the deaths of three Elizabethans, and an accompanying "essay" tells us what the poem is trying to do, and displays the poet's familiarity with the savagery and confusion of the period. Other titles are: "A Letter from Armenia," "A Song from Armenia," and "The Songbook of Sebastian Arruz." This formidable "impersonality" extends to the language which never descends into the easily colloquial, but retains a formal elegance, a savagery of rhetoric that never permits us to forget the presence of singing robes. The personae are, throughout, both agonized and masterful. . . .

The landscape of Geoffrey Hill's poetry is one of the damned. He carries his books through Hell; his poems are strangulated wisdoms of the torn body, the racked soul; there is no, or little, time for nostalgia or courtesy. There is total commitment to an awful vision. And yet there is a strange hiding from the light also; there are misdirections and obscurities. A poem "To His Wife" is followed by the date, in brackets, (1921): Hill was born in 1932. The "Poems of Sebastian Arruz" do not need the mask of their apocryphal author, any more than they need the note that the poems "contain no allusion to any person living or dead." The tone of the book is authoritative to the point of arrogance. Its insights are convictions, and its convictions immovable as dogma. Every poem "moves grudgingly" as if carrying an immense weight; every poem ruthlessly excludes any self-indulgent slackness, any "improper speech." Every poem is wrenched into decorum. It is an unbearable, bullying, intransigent, intolerant, brilliant book.

Robin Skelton. Poetry. Sept., 1969,
pp. 398–99

The thirty prose poems that make up Geoffrey Hill's [*Mercian Hymns*] are called "hymns" but they are more like excavations: tiny, fascinated diggings-up not just of history and legend but of the poet's buried childhood self.

The central figure of the sequence is Offa, the eighth-century king of Mercia, a brutal and bloody despot who established the West Midlands' supremacy in the England of his day. . . .

The book carries an epigraph from C. H. Sisson about the need for men of power to square, with honesty, their private feelings with their public acts, and by removing Offa from his historical situation, by allowing him to move around, with figurative anonymity, among the centuries, and also by feeding into the king's imagined consciousness dark and eccentric private fantasies, Hill does achieve a striking and often subtle dramatisation of this obvious and ancient conflict. He also gives it a location. By accumulating, to the point of excess, images of plants, metals, stones, dead animals, he attempts to endow the poems' acts of archaeology with a vivid literalness. The poems really are digging, the problems are rooted. . . .

I'm not at all sure that Hill has allowed himself sufficient room to effect a convincing interpretation of these public and private concerns. . . . But given its small compass, the book is an impressive model for some envisageable later work, and it suggests too that Hill can relax his terror of the ordinary without sacrificing grandeur.

Ian Hamilton. Obs. Aug. 29, 1971, p. 23

Restlessness of forms is not something one would normally associate with Hill's work, but this is probably because the voice is unusually present and distinct. Sometimes it becomes over-distinctive, and this is usually the result of the formal means degenerating into mannerisms. Even so, a voice cannot itself provide more than a spurious unity, and to put on it work that is beyond its proper capacity produces the strain that exists in a fraction of Hill's work. This "mannered" and "mild humility," however, is more often disrupted by the variety of forms. Is it imaginative experimentation, or an inability to find one embracing and therefore controlling mode? It could be argued that such unity is undesirable, but I am suggesting that for a poet such as Hill, unity of form, as of thought and response, are important. This is why we have such apparently absolute control within each poem (or form) but such variety of form over the spread of his work so far. Each fragment of absoluteness represents a pragmatic concession to the intractable nature of the matter and response to it in each poem. One is glad that it is so, and it reflects the ongoing struggle between form, expressiveness, and the scrupulous attention Hill usually gives to his material, even when it is struggling against that oppressive attention so as to return an existence (in life) independent of his own.

Hill's use of language, and choice of words, has been noticed, often, one feels, to the detriment of his themes. One sympathises with the reviewers. The compressed language is intimately bound up with what it is conveying. This is true of many poets, but true to an unusual degree with Hill. It is true in another sense. The language itself is unlike most other writing current, and coupled with this is an unusually self-conscious pointing on the part of the poet to the language. This is not because he wishes to draw attention to it for its own sake, but because the language both posits his concerns, and is itself, in the way it is used, an instance of them. Moreover, his use of language is both itself an instance of his (moral) concerns, and the sensuous gesture that defines them. It is therefore difficult to speak of his themes without coming first into necessary contact with the language.

Jon Silkin. In Michael Schmidt and Grevel
Lindop, eds., *British Poetry since 1960:*
A Critical Survey (Oxford,
Carcanet, 1972), pp. 144–45

● **HINDE, THOMAS (1926–   )**

In a mood to go out on a limb, or at least a twig, this reviewer would guess that Mr. Thomas Hinde's first novel, *Mr. Nicholas*, is the best first novel (with one exception) ever written by a novelist of his age. Mr. Hinde is twenty-five. Dickens was twenty-four when he was writing *Pickwick Papers*. Mr. Nicholas is, of course, nothing like Mr. Pickwick. And yet, if the eighteen-thirties had been more like the nineteen-fifties, Dickens might have been more like Mr. Hinde; or to put it another way, the portly Pickwick of the Victorian dawn might have been replaced by the neurotic Nicholas of the Second Elizabethan. . . .

Mr. Nicholas would have made an outstanding novel if it rested on the title-character alone, but Mr. Hinde has been equally successful with others. . . .

[The] prose . . . is searching and sometimes intricate without reminding one in the least of Henry James. . . . *Mr. Nicholas* is far more than a bravura performance; it is achievement of a kind that begins beyond the point where many mature and accomplished novels leave off.

James Hilton. NYHT. May 24, 1953, p. 7

Mr. Nicholas, although confined in its scope, is because of its acute discernment and the understated power of its prose one of the few really distinguished post-war novels, and was an arresting though lonely cry of dissentience when it came out five years ago.

Last year Hinde published his second novel *Happy as Larry*. During the intervening years [Wain's] *Hurry On Down* and [Amis's] *Lucky Jim* had appeared, with them a new sort of hero far less genteel, well-bred and good-mannered than Peter Nicholas, a hero who had never even visited in the rich sham-rustic dormitories. Perhaps that was why in *Happy as Larry* Hinde came through the wattle curtain. . . .

Happy as Larry ends on a faint lap upward of hope, but the future is not frightfully convincing. Certainly he is no closer to dignity and consistency, although there is the implication that perhaps now he does not dismiss them as valueless. . . . Hinde's writing is meticulous, calm and reserved. The awfulness of the life that he observes, like someone flickering a torch in the Kensington fog, is never anything but natural and true. I think *Happy as Larry* is the nearest expression of Beckett feeling that we have in English, not so totally out of life, for the Beckett creatures have stepped off the edge, but Larry and Sasha and those of the eight millions they have brushed against are wandering along the brink. . . . They are paralysed people who have not so much rejected society or protested against society as been capsized by it. Comparatively, Wain's heroes, and certainly Amis's, are living on the sunny side of the street.

Kenneth Allsop. *The Angry Decade* (N.Y., British Book Centre, 1958), pp. 70, 72–73

Thomas Hinde is a highly original and gifted writer, but I sometimes wish that his talents were not quite so totally committed to the madhouse. As it is, paranoid delusion has become such a stock feature of his work that an abstracted reader might be forgiven the occasional panic-stricken thought that he has lost grip on things himself and picked up a book that he has already read. Not that this should blind us to the delicate skill with which the author consistently re-creates the fluctuating world of the insane or the deep insight and compassion he brings to the task. The least of his novels commands interest and his finest *The Day the Call Came* was a brilliantly imaginative feat that must have left even the brashest of us somewhat more sympathetic to poor Aunt Maud's lunatic fears and fantasies. But an excessive preoccupation with madness can be as crippling to a writer as an undue obsession with sex and will eventually reduce his novels to something little more than trumped up case histories on which the reader is called for a second opinion.

The slightly mechanical air of both the stories contained in his latest volume *Games of Chance* indicate that this could well happen to Mr. Hinde and put paid to our hopes that he might one day produce a novel to match the desperate agony of Gogol's study of madness or even explode our very concept of sanity as Camus would have done. They suggest that the writer may have exhausted this particular theme and reached the stage where he is writing strictly to formula. This is, I think, particularly true of *The Investigator*, the inside story of a man's paranoid plunge into fantasy and madness.

Frank McGuinness. *L.* Dec., 1965, pp. 89–90

High is about the most romantic version we have had so far of that pressing new English species: the Jamesian international novel in reverse. It's also a comment on the species in a book about books and writing—and the new mythology. Now the English man is the innocent, the voyage goes west, and the Eldorado of freedom is the tribal, youthful community of the perfect post-domestic orgasm, the ideal liberation beyond shame and guilt, getting away getting high. But, like all half-borrowed myths, this one has its problems—the problems of finding an appropriate language and tenor between the registers of English and American speech, English and American literature, English and American views of art.

The fables have been coming for quite a long time. The ur-version is *The Loved One*: the English writer goes to the States, a country of advanced and plastic modernity, and falls in love with, it seems, easeful death, romanticism. But art encourages withdrawal, back to classicism. . . .

The difficulty seems in fact to centre around the degree to which the book is concerned with scepticism and parody—a fictive farce in which *Stepping Westward* or whatever meets with *The American Dream*—and to what extent with pastiche, which just helps the action along towards its end. In short the book doesn't really quite answer to the kind of apparatus that surrounds it, though one can see how seriously and with what good reason the questions about mode and fictiveness are being asked. Even so, that leaves us with some brilliant episodes in the telling, tour de force performances. . . .

Malcolm Bradbury. *NS*. Nov. 8, 1968,
pp. 638–39

[*Generally a Virgin*] is Thomas Hinde's twelfth novel: a productive record, even for somebody who started as an undergraduate. But his books oddly—even perversely—refuse to add up to an oeuvre. One can't speak of a Hinde world or a Hinde character, while one can for such not necessarily more talented contemporaries as Frederic Raphael or Edna O'Brien. He remains obstinately locked in the ventriloquist's rather than the divine creator's role, inhabiting the sympathy now of a middle-aged loser (Mr. Nicholas), now of a gangster's moll (Bird). He withholds not only moral judgment, but the narrator's personal tone under which judgment is so often smuggled. He remains an elusive fish for critical rods, with little sign of unease about the fact.

Yet he is the opposite of an artless writer. *Generally a Virgin* is a mere 185 pages long and has a bare fistful of characters. But its subject is nothing less than America's Problem. And if that sounds like a sophomore's theme, the novel is not only set on campus, but behaves like a campus modernization of one of the World's Eternal Legends. . . .

Unfortunately one of Middle America's notorious failings is its inability to speak plainly about itself. Mr. Hinde has opted for a style which represents not so much raids on the inarticulate as a series of frenzied incidents on its frontier: a matter of jump-cuts and unfinished sentences suggestive of a painful collaboration between Ken Kesey and Ford Madox Ford.

TLS. June 9, 1972, p. 649

HOPKINS, GERARD MANLEY (1844–1889)

In assessing the profound influence of Hopkins's religious life upon his poetry, we must give due weight to that section of the *Exercises* which is called "Particular Examen." This deals with a rigorous method of daily self-scrutiny to rid the soul of sin. Important too, for an understanding of the later sonnets, is the Ignatian account of "consolation" and "desolation," the former being "any inward joy that calls and attracts to heavenly things and to the salvation of the soul," the latter being "a darkening of the soul, trouble of mind, movement to base and worldly things, restlessness . . . moving to distrust, loss of hope . . . when the soul feels thoroughly apathetic, tepid, sad and as it were separated from her Creator and Lord."

Modern psycho-pathology can no doubt trace the immediate causes of many such states, but it cannot explain away their spiritual significance. If all disturbing spiritual aspirations and depressions could be "conditioned" out of existence, so that we all lived like the decently regulated animals so dear to Walt Whitman, the value of Hopkins's poetry would disappear. But not anticipating such a calamity, we now consider the facts in the light of universally accepted values. "Desolation," then, is by no means incompatible with the highest religious ecstasies, even with mysticism. . . .

It is natural that the intense meditation and contemplation induced by the *Spiritual Exercises* should influence the poetic imagination. Many of Hopkins's mature poems are spontaneous yet conscious illustrations of the Jesuit ideal, vivid personal commentaries on certain passages in the Ignatian rule.

W. H. Gardner. Gerard Manley Hopkins, 4th
ed. (Oxford Univ. Pr., 1966), Vol. I, p. 17

[Hopkins'] poetry should now be allowed to sustain serious critical examination, rather than being apologized for or extravagantly defended as a whole. If there are difficulties now in a serious reader's appreciating this poetry, the difficulties probably have to do not with his prosody but with his psychology, not with his unorthodox technique but with his orthodox faith. And for the non-religious reader who can grasp and enjoy Herbert, Donne, or Milton, these need not be too great.

They need not be more, at the most, than grounds for qualifying judgment. We are no longer likely to write or read unqualified judgments of Hopkins: such a sweeping condemnation as Yvor Winters', asserting that the poet expresses overwrought emotion instead of making lucid statements about human experience, sounds as odd as Leavis' praise might have sounded twenty-five years before it. But Geoffrey Hartman's recent essay, suggesting that, in comparison with Browning or Crashaw, Hopkins seems narrow, poses a real question. It is the question whether Hopkins' range of experience and thought is not so small as to limit sharply his importance. The poet whose moods are contemplation, ecstasy, and spiritual dryness, whose subjects are natural beauty and supernatural grace, both strictly defined, lacks the dramatic vigor, the ironic humor, and earthly passions, the sense of moral indignation and the sense of honest and despairing doubt that mark much of nineteenth and twentieth-century art.

Wendell Stacy Johnson. *Gerard Manley
Hopkins: The Poet as Victorian* (Ithaca, N.Y.,
Cornell Univ. Pr., 1968), pp. 168–70

Gerard Manley Hopkins was born out of his time. Only a handful of his poems were printed in the nineteenth century, since his friend and mentor Robert Bridges, later Poet Laureate, did not feel them technically or even emotionally suitable for the times. His poems were eventually issued by Bridges in 1918. This Victorian poet has influenced and is still influencing the development of English poetry to as great a degree as Ezra Pound, T. S. Eliot or W. B. Yeats. Hopkins was a Jesuit priest and teacher who partially shared the official view of his Order that the writing of poetry might well be regarded as a terrible self-indulgence—an expression, perhaps, of things about the self that were better left to God, and not dwelt upon. Only his close friend Canon R. W. Dixon, himself a graceful minor poet, showed Hopkins any real comprehension or sympathy during his lifetime, although Bridges, a vastly inferior poet, did his best. Hopkins lived a difficult, piously devoted, unhappy life, subject to moods of elation (about which he suffered theological guilt) followed by depression.

James Reeves and Martin Seymour-Smith.
Inside Poetry (Heinemann, 1970), p. 80

HOUSMAN, A. E. (1859–1936)

One index of a poet's worth lies in his ability to escape the tenure of academic professionals and to serve the needs of the market place. Housman had a healthy distrust of the cloistered critic: he named bibliophiles "an idiotic class"; and he rejected his colleagues' high praise of him because they offended his judgment in their praises of one another. On the other hand, he never catered to the public, but he did want his poetry to become popular and he did not demur when it sometimes served decidedly unliterary ends. . . .

Many of Housman's picturesque turns of language are returning, touched with a new aptness, to the mainstream of popular speech—one of the chief fountainheads of his own poetic diction. Somewhat as his scholarly reputation has for a half-century and more made his name a byword for accuracy and thoroughness, so many of his pithy, keen-edged phrases have been picked up by Everyman and made to serve many and various causes. This is the way of poetry that lives. Such expressions as "proud and angry dust," "a word I never made," "shoulder the sky," "with rue my heart is laden," "to see the cherry hung with snow," and "land of lost content" are now firmly established commonplaces of everyday use wherever English is written. "And long 'tis like to be."

Books are perpetuated by books, and it is instructive to observe Housman's influence on authors who follow the amiable habit of naming their own productions from the writings of others. . . . Since 1920, when Storm Jameson's *The Happy Highways* appeared, about eighty books—poetry, novels, collections of short stories, plays, autobiographies, and anthologies of different kinds—have been published under titles chosen from Housman's poetry. . . . It is abundantly evident that writers of books in English are joined in a kind of free conspiracy not to let A. E. Housman out of their sight or others'. This is fame.

Tom Burns Haber. A. E. Housman (N.Y.,
Twayne, 1967), pp. 176–78

The author of *Poems by Terence Hearsay*—a collection now better known as *A Shropshire Lad*, the title suggested by Housman's friend A. W. Pollard of the British Museum—was also the Professor of Latin at University College, London. By the time *Last Poems* came out in 1922 he was the Kennedy Professor of Latin at Cambridge and a Fellow of Trinity College in that university: a man, in short, at the top of the academic tree. It is natural, therefore, for the critic of Housman's poetry to ask what connection there is, if indeed there is any at all, between the pseudo-Salopian Terence, who put down "Pints and quarts of Ludlow beer" and whose best friend murdered another farm labourer called Maurice (*A Shropshire Lad*, viii)—and the acidulous scholar who freely admitted that he had never actually spent much time in Shropshire. The question is more insistent in Housman's case than in that of such other scholar-poets as Milton or Gray, partly because of the wider gap between the particular poetic persona he adopted and the man himself, and partly because of the element of autobiography, usually veiled though often unconcealed, that is present in his best poems. . . .

But a critic's first concern is with the poems as poems and not with the neuroses of his poet. At least twenty of Housman's poems are likely to live as long as the language. If these poems continue to tease and fascinate the critical reader today, as I think they do, he will want to define to himself the special *literary* quality that they have. It is a quality almost unprecedented in English poetry that can, I think, be shown to derive from Housman's exceptional sensitivity to both English and Latin considered simply as languages. . . . It would be absurd, of course, to suggest that Housman became the foremost Latinist of his generation simply in order to improve his English. What can be said, however, is that his expertness in the Latin language left an indelible imprint on both his English prose style and his poetry.

F. W. Bateson. In Christopher Ricks, ed.,
*A. E. Housman: A Collection of Critical
Essays* (Englewood Cliffs, N.J., Prentice-Hall,
1968), pp. 130–31

People often say that Housman's romantic poetry was a kind of protest against the austerity of his life of scholarship. From a different point of view, Housman's life of scholarship can be seen as a kind of protest against that tyranny of "sub-Tennysonian taste" which he from his earliest years found all around him. . . .

Housman read widely in several literatures and keenly appreciated the quality of many different kinds of verse, even though his romantic dogmatism, tenacious as a Calvinist's belief in hell-fire, always prevented him from according any but a little of it the title of true poetry. As the reader of these three amazing volumes [*The Classical Papers of A. E. Housman*] admires the writer's powerful intellect and revels in his wit, he cannot help asking himself what would have happened had Housman by some lucky accident ever thrown off the chains of the rigid romantic prejudice which restricted his attitude to literature. If he had been able to employ his strong and supple intelligence in unison with his imaginative powers, might he not have become a major instead of a minor poet?

TLS. Feb. 9, 1973, p. 138

HOWARD, ELIZABETH JANE (1923–   )

[*After Julius*] is Elizabeth Jane Howard's fourth novel—time to ask where one of England's most talented writers is going. Miss Howard has been called "promising" so often the word must make her shudder. She has also been pinned as a "lady novelist"—fit companion for such quivering stylists as Rosamond Lehmann.

I suspect Miss Howard does not accept this description of herself. *After Julius* has a mother named Esme who rereads Jane Austen constantly—and a sweet, simple daughter named Emma, who has a complex, bitchy older sister named Cressida. Is Miss Howard tired of being hailed for her exquisite sensibility? Does she want us to notice that she also has quite a bit of sense in her books?

At bottom, all the characters in *After Julius* are working out a dilemma that has muddled middle-class lives in England and America for generations—how the do-good tradition of loving "humanity" in the large permits people (especially men) to fink out on loving people individually. Women, of course, are the inevitable victims of this masculine malaise. . . .

Miss Howard handles this story pretty much in the manner of her previous books—shifting points of view between the major characters. The style is superb, as always. The sensibility still casts a glow. Beautiful Cressida, endlessly analyzing her failures at love is a fascinating, totally believable character.

However, the same jarring artificiality remains. Asking us to believe Esme and Felix have remained in emotional limbo for 20 years while waiting for their confrontation is a bit creaky. The proletarian poet is just a little too simple. And at the end, when 27-year-old Emma decides to marry him, her uncle informs her—for the first time—that there is a legacy of £3,000 to keep them alive. Jane Austen could get away with it—but you have too much sense, Miss Howard.

Thomas J. Fleming. *NYT*. Jan. 9, 1966, p. 36

There is a moment halfway through Elizabeth Jane Howard's new novel [*Odd Girl Out*] when Edmund Cornhill, predictable, inhibited, dependable and dull, longs to provoke a nasty scene. He is even ready to wallow in "every cliché about the *ménage à trois* that every *ménage à trois* has been through" in order to communicate. But although, on the final page, his wife Anne feels that the air has cleared, it is hard to believe that Miss Howard expects us to accept their experience as cathartic. Rather, we are left—perhaps deliberately—wryly observing how very little these characters have dared, how little they have learnt or suffered, how little difference the events she describes have made to their lives. Except to one life, a fringe casualty, abandoned in despair and unnoticed, merely another piece in Miss Howard's ironical jigsaw of relationships.

TLS. March 24, 1972, p. 326

HUGHES, RICHARD (1901–   )

The Fox in the Attic, the first volume of Richard Hughes's planned trilogy, *The Human Predicament*, was published in 1961. In it, the scope and nature of the whole work was established: a novel about the years between the two world wars, which combines the fictional experiences of members of an upper-class family, their servants and their friends with real political events in England and Germany. *The Wooden Shepherdess* takes the same cast from 1924 to 1934. The leisurely pace has been abandoned for a packed style suggestive of the panic of those years, and the story of Hitler's rise to power is allowed, by the end of the book, to engulf the episodes in peacetime England and the wanderings of the central character, Augustine. . . .

The prose has changed in this volume, too, into something very like verse; doggedly rhythmical, full of inversions and tricks and rhetorical questions which seem there to encourage the reader's acquiescence in the inevitability of such mistaken, partial views of history. It is interesting that Mr. Hughes is so good at writing about children, who become much more than their parents' offspring. For them a partial view is inevitable and accords with their own reality. Where the adults often seem muscle-bound, rigidly the creatures of destiny, the children move with a sense of their individuality and still undefined promise, like fish among rocks.

Mr. Hughes is rightly admired for the size and the density of his novel, yet it seems clear that he has landed himself with more difficulties than simply the one of welding fact to fiction. It is impossible not to think of the expansiveness which Scott might have brought to such an undertaking. The tight rhythmical prose here produces monotony and smothers its best effects.

TLS. April 6, 1973, p. 369

Hughes's novel [*The Wooden Shepherdess*] is neither solemn nor heavy. He has somehow managed to embody his thesis in the common events of human life, sparkling with vitality and delight. If evil were really all-powerful instead of just seeming so in one bad time or another, there would be no answer to it and we should go down, would have gone down long since, in the muck and blood of banality. But life itself is evil's adversary, life and the joy which assures us of the unsayable truth, beyond any creed, that there *is* worth in living, that even a tale told by an idiot is somehow the vehicle of a significance we may never grasp but yet can feel.

So much is condensed in this novel by Hughes's art that we can understand the effort his mastery demands and, thus, the long span of time which elapsed between publication in 1961 of *The Fox in the Attic* and this second volume. We can only hope that Mr. Hughes has now subdued his dragon-theme enough to let us have his third volume before 1985. We end here on a confrontation between good and evil, on the details of the round-up of political and personal victims in the purge of June, 1934, of casual slaughter and destructive malice; and then, in the nun's cell, filled and overfilled with the presence of God almost past bearing, girding her up, it seems to her, for some future encounter with Satan. The limits of the human predicament are the limits of what humanity can experience. In this stunning book we are shown the range of what is possible to us, a seamless web reaching to the infinite but grounded in everyday events as familiar as the miracles of breathing and eating and seeing.

Elizabeth Janeway. *NYT*. Aug. 19, 1973, p. 3

HUGHES, TED (1930–   )

[Hughes] rarely writes coolly, but always with passion and power. In calling his book *Wodwo*, he reminds his readers of the lines from *Sir Gawaine and the Green Knight* and of the wodwos there, the wild men of the woods. And there is, indeed, a barbaric and elemental quality about many of these poems, as if they had sprung from the earth itself, wet and glistening, half-animal, half-human. They are the very stuff of nature, but not coy and nostalgic nature poems. They are savage and tender poems at one and the same time. Even when Ted Hughes writes about such everyday things as thistles, ferns and grasses he succeeds in giving them their own life so that we, with him, become part of them.

The book also contains some stories and a play which should be read alongside the poems. One of the stories, "The Rain Horse," is a magnificent piece of work, highly imaginative and compulsive. But one comes away from this remarkable book with the howling of wolves in one's ears and with a premonition that the world has been blasted and will only ever recover its innocence and beauty when man returns to his roots and discovers his exact centre.

Leonard Clark. *PoetryR*. Autumn, 1967,
p. 259

The introduction into a poem on thistles of the imagery of "splintered weapons," of Vikings and "Icelandic frosts" suggests some lines of thematic continuity in Hughes's work. Clustered together here, like thistles in a clump, are bristling images of brute nature, of warfare, and of the archaic human past. These comprise three of his constant themes. If *Wodwo* is Hughes's most powerful book thus far, the trajectory of his career—unlike that of the best American poets who, like him, started out in the fifties—is marked by the consistent intensification of his original position, rather than by sharp discontinuities. Hughes's style is much more flexible now than in his first book, he has all but abandoned the conventions of stanzaic and rational structure with which he began, yet the imaginative thrust of his work is toward a similar conception of experience.

There is a variety of forms in *Wodwo* which may be initially confusing. Interspersed . . . between an opening and a concluding set of poems are half a dozen short stories and a long play for voices. Compared to the fairly obvious connection between Lowell's poems and the autobiographical fragment in *Life Studies*, the congruence between Hughes's prose and verse is not so evident. Yet he insists on the unity of his book, saying that the prose "may be read as notes, appendix and unversified episodes behind the poems, or as chapters of a single adventure to which the poems are commentary and amplification." I don't propose that *Wodwo* is a code to be cracked, but it does take some doing on the reader's part to grasp its implicit unification. The "adventure" is revealed by sharp thrusts of consciousness, sudden gulps of knowledge wrested painfully from intractable experiences. The process begins with *The Hawk in the Rain*, for the "single adventure" in Hughes's work is a continuous one.

Daniel Hoffman. *Shenandoah*. Summer,
1968, p. 51

Looking back at his work as a whole, so far, it is as a *mime* that it is perhaps most useful to consider Ted Hughes. Though he is a traditional poet of the written word, and the normal action of the meanings of words is essential to his effects on us, he has an exceptional gift for making words act out the processes they are describing. This is a particularly important gift for a writer with Hughes's themes. (One must suppose, in fact, that this is not entirely fortunate coincidence, but that his preoccupations and his gifts have some common origin in his own nature: however that is a matter about which one can only surmise, if one is dependent simply on the evidence of his poems.) At any rate, the kind of instinctual, physically responsive life that Hughes has a particularly strong feeling for is displayed in action in the best of his work rather than simply argued for. He argues for it, too: but as I have tried to show, though he does this with wit and aplomb, he never really makes a case until he goes back to the poems in which he "imitates" and embodies it.

The best of his poems till lately are, in my judgment, the ones that in this way reveal clues to possible joys and satisfactions for man in the life of nature. It is only in his most recent work of all that another sort of largely instinctual life is insistently put on show for its attractions: Crow's refusal to be beaten in any circumstances, his determination to pounce and disarray first whenever there is any danger of his suffering that fate. Hughes has never gone far in trying to offer solutions to the more intricate moral and emotional perplexities of modern life, and his comments on the social scene have been pungent but perfunctory. But it seems no more proper to reproach him with this when he writes of Crow than when he writes of the skylarks. What he can offer is a confidently presented and beautifully judged demonstration of certain needs that are known to him being fulfilled. This, in a sceptical age, seems a starting point worth having.

Derwent May. In Martin Dodsworth, ed., The Survival of Poetry (Faber and Faber, 1970), pp. 162–63

In an illuminating interview about *Crow*, published in *The London Magazine* (January, 1971), Ted Hughes, commenting on the poetry of Vasko Popa, remarks: "In a way it's obviously a pervasive and deep feeling that civilization has now disappeared completely. If it's still here it's still here by grace of pure inertia and chance and if the whole thing has essentially vanished one had better have one's spirit invested in something that will not vanish." . . .

Whereas Eliot and Auden, although also accepting what Hughes earlier calls "the whole hopelessness of that civilization," thought that they could nevertheless reconnect with the sacred on the Holy Ground of the Augustan Eternal City of God (which is not liable to the destruction overtaking the temporal City), Hughes rejects such faith—evidently because he sees the churches as products of the same finished-and-done-with civilization. We have therefore to find a "new divinity," though I suppose Hughes would not claim that he has found one in Crow any more than John Berryman, presumably, would advertise his Henry as John the Baptist.

What Crow really represents is consciousness in a Last Ditch situation. He is like some new mutation—radiated and thalidomided —which grotesquely survives the concentrated fire upon its person of all the effects of atomic warfare, detergents, frozen foods, and tranquilizers. Crow is the spirit of survival incarnate. And the suggestion implicit in this is that the poet / anti-poet should be the prime example of such a survivor, whose final *reductio ad absurdum* aim is to verbalize a strategy against the results of war-game programming.

Stephen Spender. *NYR*. July 22, 1971, p. 3

The word Orghast is perhaps familiar now to those who like to keep a weather-eye open on the arts. It has two applications: it is the title of the new work created and performed by Peter Brook's International Centre for Theatre Research, and it is also the name of the language in which most of the work has been written. The author of *Orghast*—text and language—is the English poet Ted Hughes. . . . What are the impulses and the disciplines which he might claim for his new language so that it may be saved from the arbitrariness and fatal privacy of a random cipher? . . .

The premise in its simplest form is that the *sound* of the human voice, as opposed to language, is capable of projecting very complicated mental states. That it is capable of projecting very simple mental states is not a matter of argument. The sound "Help me" can be varied to project the mental state of a man in a burning building or that of a man trying to carry three suitcases. But my example compromises the real audaciousness of the Brook-Hughes opus, which does not rely on such eloquent situations to define the meaning of the sounds. The action of *Orghast* is simple, ritualistic, and at times hardly more informative of what is being said than is the disposition of an orchestra informative of what is being played.

This analogy with music is timely, because it should be stressed that although Orghast has a word-to-word relationship with English and thence to any language, Mr. Hughes does not expect or intend it to work on an audience in the way that a foreign language might, dropping philological clues here and there to be picked up with varying success according to the varying capacity of its hearers to make use of them. Orghast aims to be a leveller of audiences by appealing not to semantic athleticism but to the instinctive recognition of a "mental state" within a sound. One can hardly imagine a bolder challenge to the limits of narrative.

Clearly this is not Ted Hughes the poet. . . . The impetus of Orghast came from a dissatisfaction with English as the visible part of a barbaric, mythic formation. Every word came loaded with sophisticated associations and dog-eared with over-use. . . .

But it is not just a case of the actor giving meaningful life to an arbitrary sound, and here the water gets choppier. Because—crucially —it is Mr. Hughes's conviction, indeed the point of Orghast, that hypothetically there are *some* meanings, basic mental states, for which there is an optimum sound irrespective of the audience, Arab or Eskimo; and that in the absence of radical differences of culture, in a given situation, for *any* meaning there is an optimum sound. In short, it was Mr. Hughes's task to offer the actor the sound which he felt was *best* suited to convey a given meaning. These offers were invariably accepted, except, neatly enough, in the case of the Japanese actor and, less so, the African actor, who offered improvements. . . .

Tom Stoppard. *TLS*. Oct. 1, 1971, p. 1174

Ted Hughes is our first poet of the will to live. Lawrence wrote of animal joy, a lighter, perhaps more fanciful thing. Robinson Jeffers picked up the topic occasionally, a hawk on his wrist, but was too eager, too clumsy, to master it. Hughes is its master and at the same time is mastered by it. The subject owns him, he is lord of the subject.

The will to live might seem the first and healthiest of subjects, but in fact it is almost the last and most morbid. Men come to it after the other subjects have failed. It is the last stop, waterless and exposed, before nothingness. Civilization blows off, love and utopia evaporate, the interest the human mind takes in its own creations washes out, and there, its incisors bared, stands life, daring you to praise it. . . .

His first two volumes vigorously championed animal triumph. They represented a vomition of the human, of death. Hughes perched and gloated with the hawks, ran with the eaters not the eaten. To be sure, even so he could not outrun himself. His human weakness nagged like a teary child stumbling behind. He was only a partisan, not one of the elect. In an unguarded moment, he even turned up his love of will and disclosed its masochistic undersides. . . .

All the same, life in these poems kept its pride. Life was the side to be on. . . .

In Hughes's two most recent volumes, by contrast, the pride has given way. Rigid and unliving, it was never more than a support to hold up the tunnel while the creature passed. Now the creature halts, terrified of the weight overhead. Living things begin to feel small. Even savage animals no longer save Hughes from himself; rather, his own frailty seeps into them. Hughes has gradually given himself up to his human problems, rather brilliantly. . . .

In sum, though the contents of *Crow* are far from being realized past change, the volume itself goes beyond what anyone else would be likely to conceive, let alone bring off. It has an impact that only a very remarkable and inventive talent could create.

What will Hughes do now, having worked his subject so near to the philosophical bone? It is impossible to say; it cannot be an easy position to be in. Yet he has it in his favour that he he has already displayed, several times over, a cunning for changing and still surviving as a poet—as if some aesthetic form of the will were ruthlessly pushing him on.

Calvin Bedient. CQ. Summer, 1972,
pp. 103, 108–9, 121

HUXLEY, ALDOUS (1894–1963)

With the possible exception of Evelyn Waugh, Huxley is the great prose satirist of the century. Among the re-readable passages from his novels, surely the saga of Hercules the Dwarf in *Crome Yellow* is unforgettable for its blend of satire and pathos. Nor should one overlook Mr. Scogan in his disguise as a fortune teller. He predicts to an attractive customer that next Sunday if she lingers by a certain stile along the footpath she will meet and make love with a fascinating man named, of course, Scogan. In *Those Barren Leaves*, the naïve Irene offers the observation that contraception has rendered chastity superfluous. The same novel also contains pointed criticism of Dickens and two fine spoofs of Dickensian situations: the boarding house scenes at Miss Carruthers's and the wooing of Miss Elver by the designing Mr. Cardan.

In the bizarre world of Huxley's novels, Swiftian ironies and Dickensian zaniness alternate with more terrifying prospects. There are Neo-Pavlovian Conditioning Rooms in *Brave New World*, but these are balanced against the confrontation scene in which the Director of Hatcheries learns he has a natural son by a wife who is an old-fashioned mother. In *Point Counter Point*, Lord Edward can be telephoned in the lab by his crippled brother who insists he has "just this moment discovered a most extraordinary mathematical proof of the existence of God. . . ." Or consider the scene in *Ape and Essence* where the Arch-Vicar offers the already outraged Dr. Poole a pair of binoculars so he can see the annual orgy more clearly.

These scenes, and others much more savage in tone rest on Huxley's conviction of the importance of satire for the twentieth-century novel. Though capable of skilful use of such modern techniques as stream of consciousness—especially in *Eyeless in Gaza* where he keeps switching from the mind of the newly widowed John Beavis to the reflections of James and Young Anthony—Huxley's primary concern is with satire. Even the essay-like *Island* can be seen as an attempt to re-emphasize the satire *Brave New World* directed against the society of Mustapha Mond. Pete Boone, in *After Many a Summer Dies the Swan*, underlines Huxley's main concern when he recalls Mr. Propter's opinion of satire. "A good satire," Propter stated, "was more deeply truthful and, of course, much more profitable than a good tragedy." And yet, Propter continued, few satires have been effective "because so few satirists were prepared to carry their criticism of human values far enough." Huxley, however, never hesitates. He questions twentieth-century ideas of the individual and national ego, of sexual ethics, and of religious practice and belief.

Jerome Meckier. *Aldous Huxley: Satire and
Structure* (Chatto and Windus, 1969), pp. 7–8

The letters of Aldous Huxley form a kind of autobiography, like any such collection. They were written by a man of extraordinary intellect, who during his life, being constitutionally disinclined to devote himself to any branch of art or science, acquired the mastery of many. They illustrate in profusion the analytic powers of the literary and social critic and the synthetic powers of the creative artist and idealist. If, as some psychologists have argued, intellectuality is proportionate to the ability to think analogically, the mind of Huxley was superior to a pitch beyond the average man's imagining. This trait may appear, as certain emotional hard edges in his writings have appeared to some, a little "inhuman."

The truth is that reason and imagination only graduate man above the sub-human creation, man being the *thinking* animal. And, because by the same token he is the thinking *animal*, the qualities of gentleness which we honour as "human" are part of the animal residuum. The virtuous emotions, equally with the savage ones, stem from the beasts. Huxley, who was a humorous man with strong physical emotions, always had a vivid sense of this connection. His bias towards intellect, along with purely cultural habits, disposed him to rebel against the gross passions and to satirize them, but he was too affectionate to be coldly intellectual and too candid for intellectual pride.

Living aware of man's duality, he made it a theme of his works; in effect it was something he enjoyed.

Animal enjoyment of the human state pervades his letters. Though often tinged with a profound instinct to weep for life, it—and by no means the sadness of *lacrimae rerum*—is Huxley's hallmark. He must be recognized as one of the most human of men and letter-writers; and this was precisely because in his nature feeling was as highly developed as mind. Always in Huxley compassion and scorn, revulsion and tenderness, strove together and, as it were, through a dialectic of emotions regulated by intelligence, produced his multivalent attitude towards the world.

We cannot read Huxley's works of fiction and drama without meeting the scientific philosopher, nor his essays on men and ideas without meeting the artist. He was more interested in life than in art, and in art only as a function of life.

Grover Smith. Preface to Grover Smith, ed.,
Letters of Aldous Huxley (N.Y., Harper &
Row, 1969), p. 1

The work of Aldous Huxley developed through four of the most interesting decades in the history of Western Man and he responded all the time to what was going on around him: the breaking of Europe, the knowledge explosion with its technological revolution, the population explosion with the appearance of Mass Man, the economic revolution with its tantalising promise for poor men everywhere. During these decades violent oppositions came into being. It became possible for whole populations to be properly fed, clothed and housed; it became possible for them all to be destroyed together in a few minutes. The aeroplane and mass communications developed until what seemed a spacious world became a confined space in which the multitudes jostled one another. For the first time, on the other hand, it became possible to relieve mankind of its secular pain and anxiety.

Huxley was always sensitive to these oppositions, the eternal balance between good and evil in nature and in human societies. He was prepared to take a full look at the worst; but he spent more time in exploring the new possibilities of advantage to man. He believed in the individual, and he saw the possibilities of greater awareness for the individual. He believed that the balance could only come right if a sufficient number of individuals acted with steady good purpose. It is the Existentialist reaction in a time of flux, the Stoic attitude modified for the times. The unbelievably wonderful possibilities for good were frightening because they could become equally powerful possibilities for evil. But they had to be faced.

To all this Aldous Huxley reacted sensitively and energetically. He could not escape from his heredity, on the one side the Huxleys, on the other the Arnolds, two of the great intellectual families of the nineteenth century, when the responsible use of knowledge seemed to be replacing religion in the control of human societies. When Huxley was a boy, men believed in the steady progress of human betterment. The belief was based on the stability of society and it foresaw our knowledge explosion but not the breaking up of European societies. With his family background and the educational advantages of Eton and Balliol, Huxley could feel he inherited this world of progress. But he was born in 1894, and would have gone to war if he had not been nearly blind. The rich creative years of early manhood were spent in a society which was trying to forget the horrors of war, and the social earthquakes it had brought. He began with books of verse and intellectual satirical novels. The verses showed promise but never said much; a characteristic of most verses in England ever since. The prose was witty and ran clearly and nimbly. He discovered immediately a gift of style, which is a gift frequently denied English novelists.

Laurence Brander. *Aldous Huxley: A Critical Study* (Lewisburg, Pa., Bucknell Univ. Pr., 1970), pp. 11–12

To one school of ontology the world as a whole is unintelligible, whatever order we may discern in its parts. It has been said that there is no evidence that "all the systems and structures which we discover . . . are parts of a single system." From *Eyeless in Gaza* on, Huxley assumes the opposite. He takes it on faith that there is a Nature, an Order of things, which we must both assume and within our limits try to grasp. We can confirm this immanence in our day-to-day existence if we are willing to use all our available resources, and subject all but the basic assumption to a pragmatic, existential test.

Island is Huxley's equivalent to Yeats' *Vision*. Both writers began as divided men, and poets; both were alert to contraries for most of their lives; both were ultimately reconciled to them; both were able to make final assertions of joy. *A Vision*, however, is a more symbolic work, *Island* a far more literal one. Both symbolize a belief in ultimate order, but *Island* offers a human order here and now. Contraries are resolved on the plane of the divine, yet the divine resolution can be—it really is—immanent in our lives. Even the least appealing heterodoxies urge us to examine cultural pressures and to withstand the destructive ones, however strong. Mankind may not be able to withstand them, but *Island* claims that if it has the will, it can. It denies that one thinker or one method can provide complete or final answers.

It prophetically suggests "new psychophysical sciences" and affirms that answers are available if men will use a responsible intelligence, and look. Huxley's ideas, his whole adventure should become not a subject for dismissal on logical grounds, but instead what Whitehead calls a "lure for feeling." They should incite us to use our critical faculties toward greater usefulness and a larger understanding.

In Huxley's last book, *Literature and Science* (1963) and last essay, "Shakespeare and Religion" (1965), there are signs that his pluralism might have found more unified form. He sees both scientists and writers as purifiers of language, one for public and the other for essentially private truth. The scientist can learn from the artist's intuition while the artist should recognize the increasing accuracy of scientists who study aspects of the destiny of man. But theoretically a total unity is involved, since scientific observation is now recognized as a dialogue with nature, no longer involving a subject-object division. . . . Huxley never could have engaged in the analysis he mentions, or worked out the philosophy for an existential religion. Driven even more by personal need than by his inquiring mind, he was little interested in Whitehead's speculations about God, or even in those of Julian's friend, Teilhard de Chardin. He could never emulate the scholarship of a Northrop, a Toynbee, or a Tillich. He knew, however, at least as well as they, that the West must be alive to the ways and riches of the East, that man cannot live without both science and art, that knowledge must serve a lived acceptance, or faith.

Charles M. Holmes. *Aldous Huxley and the
Way to Reality* (Bloomington, Indiana Univ.
Pr., 1970), pp. 199–200

Given his desire to apprehend the truths that art finds only unconsciously, Huxley would not have shared the idea that once he had reached the Divide of his career, the journey was downward. Rejecting the aesthetic criteria that would make inevitable such an admission, he chose to see himself travelling along the ridge, with the chance of climbing more than one peak of insight before he reached the end of his journey. He had not entered these mountains of speculation to become a hermit, like Calamy in *Those Barren Leaves*. On the contrary, he found the views stupendous and revealing, and because of the greater understanding of the world and its problems which his new path gave him, he felt he could reveal more clearly the dangers that beset mankind through the retention of moral and political errors and through the destruction of an environment in which man had his proper place and no more.

Huxley perceived no real division between his views of the life of the spirit and his ideas of what should be done by sensible beings in the phenomenal world. He saw both as projections of man's dual nature; it seemed to him that the intuition leading to the knowledge of divinity was no less rational than the intelligence that sought to reshape existence so as to reach the limit of human happiness.

Certainly, though a perceptible decline in Huxley's powers as an imaginative writer cannot be denied, there appeared little loss, to the end of his life, in his power of argument and exposition. His remarkable intelligence, differently deployed than in his youth, remained acute as ever; his knowledge as broad, though otherwise channelled; his power of fertile generalization even more impressive than in the past. The retreat into a religio-political conservatism resembling that of his friend T. S. Eliot which was expected by those who were troubled by *Eyeless in Gaza*, did not materialize.

Indeed, on many issues Huxley worked ahead of his time. Long before the Civil Disobedience movement changed American society in the 1960s, he had accepted the transforming power of non-violent rebellion. World problems like population growth, the exhaustion of resources, the destruction of the environment, now subjects of urgent public discussion, might have been solved if men had listened to Huxley's warnings twenty years ago. The decentralist society which fashionable anarchists like Paul Goodman and perpetual student rebels like Tom Hayden now advocate he had already sketched out before the end of the Thirties.

George Woodcock. *Dawn and the Darkest Hour: A Study of Aldous Huxley* (N.Y., Viking, 1972), pp. 23–24

ISHERWOOD, CHRISTOPHER (1904–   )

One of the attractions of Christopher Isherwood's new short novel [*A Meeting by the River*] is that it changes as one reads it. In that sense it is like one of those optical-illusion drawings—a picture that seems like white squares on a black background until, after a while, it changes to black squares on a white background and ultimately becomes a mosaic. This novel makes its way to a rewarding complexity through the addition of simplicities.

I started with a prejudice against the book. The jacket-flap tells us that the river in the title is the Ganges and that Hinduism is prominent in the story. I knew of Isherwood's personal involvement with Hinduism, and I suspected a propagandistic work—not without art because nothing he does could be clumsy, but basically antipathetic to one who regards Hinduism as among the cruelest of religions: crueler than Christianity in its disregard of life and its exaltation of afterlife and without even an equivalent of the crucified Son of God as its central poem. Yet, not compromising his beliefs in the slightest, Isherwood has made a novel that is credible, moving, and ultimately ironic. He happily disappoints our fears of proselytism, and he also surprises our expectations in story. . . .

The novel's considerable work is accomplished with beautifully spare means, seemingly easy but possible only to an artist who has always been good and who has lost no refinement. The very form of the book—letters by the two brothers and excerpts from Oliver's diary—emphasizes the theme: closure from one another; discreteness. Each segment of the book is a statement by one of the two principal persons, reflecting events as seen through his eyes only. This form in itself underscores that neither is having the effect on the other that he thinks, and it also makes more trenchant the wry truth that it is the religionist who doubts and the non-religionist who never wavers.

Stanley Kauffmann. *NR*. April 15, 1967, p. 22

Since Christopher Isherwood has been denied, or spared, the gifts of widespread fame or fashion, it is appropriate to begin with the pronouncement that he is the best British novelist of his generation. "Generation," to be sure, must be conceived in its narrowest sense: those born in the twentieth century before World War I. Neither as witty as Waugh's nor as intense as Orwell's, his fictions have achieved the integrity of art while illuminating the human tensions of our time. Muted in tone, self-effacing in manner, his works continue to make a quiet but persistent claim on our attention. One wishes him to be better known, not for his sake, but for ours.

"Once you care about what he writes," Angus Wilson has written, "you care strongly enough to read everything that he produces." To read, for example, his "autobiographical" *Lions and Shadows*, is to find oneself not only committed to the reading of all his other books but surprised into an appreciation of the rarest literary conjunction of our times: readability and high intelligence. Cyril Connolly has referred to Isherwood's "fatal readability": nothing which can be read with such ease and pleasure will be accorded high marks. Readability is usually allied with superficiality, best-sellerdom, or, at best, competent nonfiction, and there can be little doubt that Isherwood's readability has preserved him from academic sanctification. It is difficult to be properly serious about a writer in whose literary presence one feels so relaxed.

Frank Kermode's is a typical attitude: "I remember," he has written, "the excitement when *Sally Bowles* came out, and my despondency when it lasted no longer than the lecture during which I read it. It is still read in the same way, for fun. And Mr. Norris is, so far as I know, the only character of thirties fiction with any of the old Dickensian extra-fictional prestige." But, Mr. Kermode adds: "Mr. Isherwood is not serious." Isherwood's friend W. H. Auden has spoken of the necessity for the artist to combine frivolity and earnestness, since "without frivolity he becomes a bore, without earnestness an aesthete." *With* frivolity, however, as both Auden and Isherwood must have learned, a writer runs the danger of being considered not serious at all.

Certainly the effect of ease in Isherwood's writing is deluding: it persuades the reader to overlook the enormous skill of his prose. Carefully wrought prose is of two sorts: Joycean, artistically contrived to force the reader into attention and linguistic discovery; and documentary, allowing the reader ease, even inattention, until he is struck by the emotional and moral implications of what he has passively absorbed.

Carolyn G. Heilbrun. *Christopher Isherwood*
(N.Y., Columbia Univ. Pr., 1970), pp. 3–4

Everything is here, except for the locks of hair. *Kathleen and Frank* is a family album, and Isherwood's linking commentary has rather the flavour of those notes, in white styptic pencil and capital letters, that go beneath otherwise incomprehensible and yellowed photos in auntie's scrapbook. There's a cunningly quaint air of genealogist's pedantry, a narrative tone that is at once bald and stuffy.

From 1883, when she was 14, Isherwood's mother, Kathleen Machell Smith, kept a journal, and this, along with Frank Isherwood's letters, family gossip, and quotes from local and regimental histories, is the book's centrepiece. As family historian, working firmly within the convention of the clerical amateur, Isherwood himself is merely "Christopher," the most shadowy of all the characters, yet the one whose fortunes we as readers are most concerned to follow. It is a detective story in which suspicion comes more and more to rest on the person of the self-effacing narrator. For *Kathleen and Frank* is also the social pathology of a style. It allows a dead society to come to life again in its own terms—a society whose chief victim and whose finest product was "Herr Issyvoo," that evasive character who likened himself to the eye of a camera, and who came to life in a style of extraordinarily sharp transparency. It is a book whose own meticulously impersonal narration contrives to tell, by implication, how a narrator—someone whose sole vocation is to watch and tell—may be born and become, in the end, his own hero.

Jonathan Raban. *NS.* Oct. 22, 1971, p. 546

● JACOBSON, DAN (1929–   )

To make every single element in a work of fiction serve its exact purpose, as Mr. Jacobson does, and yet to make of each something that has its own reality, that exists, that persuades, that moves, all by itself —this is art of a very high order.

Still—with the proof of the pudding on one's very tongue—it is difficult not to feel that the unfailing detachment, precision, and self-control of all Mr. Jacobson's work (particularly [*The Price of Diamonds*], since it is the most "relaxed") point to something more than the operation of his literary intelligence. In the whole of his writing there is not a single gratuitous detail—thrown in for love or even just because it has occurred to him—not a gesture, not a response that does not have its exactly defined place in the whole. And obversely, not one thing any of his characters ever does or says is done or said without being carefully accounted for and predicted, not only by the kind of person he is made to be, but by something explicitly referred to in his history. *Diamonds* is a book almost frightening in this regard. It cannot be that Mr. Jacobson is incapable of making mistakes; the kind of irony with which he touches his material is as capable of mistakes as is passion. The truth of the matter is that Mr. Jacobson works almost as much by a principle of evading the "wrong" objects and perceptions as by finding the right ones. The principle of evasion is for him an honorable, not a cowardly, one, and one that must cost him a great deal of anguish and self-effacement; for clearly what he is pushing away, excluding, at every moment he writes is the chaos he does not yet feel adequate to—the chaos of things gratuitously ugly and mean and of the feelings in himself for which he has no respect. He does not permit himself, or his characters, the rage that might contradict his ironic, humane intelligence. . . .

But the gentleness of *Diamonds* is deceptive. There is a kind of fury in the close arrangement of the writing which comes not from the knowledge that "there is nothing in the world except what we make" but from the sense, the South Africa-born sense, that there is much too much in the world we have not made and can do nothing about. This sense, too, is part of Mr. Jacobson's vision, the part, if he let it, that could spur him to move beyond the limits he sets for himself to be a writer of "big" books—and a major novelist.

Midge Decter. *Cmty*. June, 1958, p. 542

Dan Jacobson's writings have won golden opinions from the critics, and yet it may be doubted how familiar his work is to the general public. Few contemporary authors, however, so deserve to be thoroughly well known and appreciated, for his qualities are rare and his perhaps deceptively quiet voice conceals a great and invaluable inner strength.

Certainly, he can move me deeply. I think this is not just because he expresses so finely—in particular in his latest novel, *The Beginners* —those dilemmas of the modern spirit which concern the "mystery" of Jewish uniqueness for "those of us without religious belief who yet continue to be Jews," but also because he knows how to relate those dilemmas to what is universally human.

He is typical of one aspect of the fifties and sixties. These years have frequently been marked by a suspicion and total lack of understanding for any form of romanticism or grandeur. Plain speaking, the stripping away of illusion, the declared absence of affectation carried sometimes to the point of affectation, have won the day.

Dan Jacobson shares in the prevailing ascendancy of common sense, blunt realism and plain dealing, but he contributes also a refinement of sensibility, a poetic delicacy of response to the manifestations of nature and to manifold subtly changing human relationships. Nature plays a vital role in his work. It is not merely the setting for the mood of his characters, but the very mold that has shaped them. Here is no pathetic fallacy, but a vast, impenetrable, indifferent force against which his characters meet in friendship and enmity, in misapprehension, in love. Significantly, he once criticized Kafka because, he felt, he showed no interest in nature, the delights of the senses, family affection or the joys and sufferings we experience, in the purely human so thoroughly explored in *The Beginners*.

He himself belongs with the consolidators rather than the innovators. There is nothing *avant-garde*, experimental or sensational about his work from a technical point of view. Yet his apparent traditionalism, his eloquence, his evident pleasure in formal harmonious arrangements are almost a smoke-screen for his acute individuality. If he could not have written as he does without the great nineteenth-century Russians, and especially Tolstoy, without James, Conrad and Forster (and I am not making odious comparisons), nonetheless his tone of mingled coolness and warmth is peculiarly his own.

Renee Winegarten. Midstream. May, 1966, p. 69

Dan Jacobson, who although a South African is representative of prevalent English attitudes, appears to have had a less profitable experience of teaching in American universities than Thomas Hinde. In an article called "Muffled Majesty," published in the *Times Literary*

Supplement in October 1967, he objected to the idea, which he found still academically dominant, that novels should be impersonal, wholly dramatised structures, with everything "shown" rather than "told," and the author conspicuous by his absence; the kind of fiction, in fact, that can be associated with the precept and practice of the late James and of Joyce. Jacobson argues, very plausibly, for a return of the author as narrator and commentator, with a right to let his own voice be heard, and for a restored place for "telling" as well as "showing" in fictional narrative.

Yet it is surprising that Jacobson advances these ideas as if they were wholly new and subversive, as though the dominance of the critical orthodoxy of impersonality in fiction were total and unchallenged. Perhaps it was at the American university where Mr. Jacobson was teaching; nevertheless, during the last ten years there has been a general acceptance in the academic criticism of fiction of the ideas he advances. A crucial work in this process was Wayne C. Booth's *The Rhetoric of Fiction*, published in 1961: it is sad that Jacobson showed himself so unaware of the arguments put forward in this book, and the subsequent critical response to them. Nor is this a purely academic development: the role of the narrator and the relation of the narrator to the author have been most interestingly opened up in a number of recent novels.

Bernard Bergonzi. *The Situation of the Novel*
(Pittsburgh, Univ. of Pittsburgh Pr., 1970),
pp. 70–71

Dan Jacobson has made a remarkable novel [*The Rape of Tamar*] out of . . . the rape of King David's daughter Tamar by her half-brother Amnon. In Jacobson's hands, the few lines in *2 Samuel* recording the event have grown—with a push, probably, from their elaboration in Josephus—into a wonderfully cogent study of the psychology of the powerful. The narrator of the story is Yonadab, a minor kinsman of David, whose father is a flunkey at the court. . . . The most moving moment . . . is . . . a moment of terrible and unassailable insight: that of the simple Tamar, on the morning after the rape, when she knows there is only one role for her in life now, that of heroine-victim, and she goes bedraggled and bloody into the streets of Jerusalem that she has never even stood in before, to shout her name to everyone. All this is told by Yonadab with a swift, unfaltering intelligence that one hardly associates with novel-writing any more. . . .

With *The Rape of Tamar*, Dan Jacobson establishes a place among the best of living imaginative writers in English.

Derwent May. *Enc*. March, 1971, pp. 72–74

JAMES, HENRY (1843–1916)

The 1950's brought a great change in Jamesian criticism. At the end of the 1940's there had appeared Simon Nowell-Smith's witty collection of anecdotes, *The Legend of the Master*, with their penetrating analysis of how legends are created. F. W. Dupee drew upon this for his lively critical study of James written for the American Men of Letters series. This small volume served for almost a decade as an easy and lucid résumé of the then-known facts of James's career and a discussion of the principal works. Too brief to be a vade mecum, it filled that role in the absence of a larger and more systematic study. . . . The most puzzling work of the decade . . . [by Quentin Anderson] sought to make of James an allegorist and a Swedenborgian, an acolyte of his father. Anderson neither offered historical evidence nor utilized traditional scholarly method. His work belongs to those recurrent speculations by which Bacon becomes Shakespeare or ciphers are discovered conveying the Bard's hidden messages to posterity. Anderson conceived of James's final novels as constituting a "trilogy" and a "divine novel" embodying the elder Henry James's religious beliefs. He boasted in his preface that he had "given the novelist a father and a past" forgetting perhaps that the novelist himself had written *Notes of a Son and Brother*.

That James used religious symbols in his works everyone knows; they are there, the signs and emblems of the fabric of civilization out of which the novelist built his last novels. However, James was by nature a realist of the school of Balzac; and late in life, rereading Balzac, he discovered what he had earlier overlooked: that if the people and places were real in Balzac's work, the actions in which he engaged them were pure imaginings of the most romantic sort. James, in the end, himself became this kind of romantic-realist: one who believed above all in the reality of his imaginings. He held allegory in particularly low esteem. Anderson's book, however, seeks to read into each of the late novels a religious allegory with a minuteness that flies in the face of all that we know about James's personality and his creative imagination. Anderson's thesis inaugurated in the 1950's that school of criticism which reads more *into* James than out of him, and this has been true of the attempts to discover a Garden of Eden archetype in *The Turn of the Screw*, a "night journey" in *The Ambassadors*, or ambiguity in narrators who reveal themselves with crystal clarity in their narratives.

The consequence has been a state of anarchy in Jamesian studies, particularly in the universities.

Leon Edel. Intro. to Leon Edel, ed., Henry
James: A Collection of Critical Essays
(Englewood Cliffs, N.J., Prentice-Hall, 1963),
pp. 8–9

Edmund Wilson once speculated that the ambiguity of *The Turn of the Screw* (1898) may be a consequence of psychological insecurity in the author himself, as James pulled himself out of the disappointment and failure of his years in the theater. . . . I suspect, rather, that the ambiguities of *The Turn of the Screw* have the same origin as those in *The Sacred Fount*. Both stories are complicated by a transferal of James's interest from the *donnée* to the observer rather than by a confusion of outlook. But the resultant ambiguities are appropriate to the ghost story, they enrich its effect, while they obscure a narrative which James was to ground much more firmly in the explicable.

In any event, there is no self-deception in the author's attitude toward his character in *The Sacred Fount*. James's estimate is patently negative, as the reader's is meant to be. And the inconsistencies and ambiguities of this novel seem most explicable as a consequence of its being written while James's own mind was in a climactic state of assimilation and ferment just prior to the creative outpouring at the turn of the century. *The Sacred Fount*, more than any other book of the experimental period, appears to reflect this transitional state of mind. It is mixed in tone, tending to fluctuate between high comedy and the sinister. It is excessive in its technical virtuosity, for it carries the scenic method to an experimental extreme. And it might have become any of several stories and have had any of several themes, as I have tried to demonstrate in this survey of analogues. It was constantly outgrowing imposed limits, as James intuitively worked toward a deeper and more expansive rendering of the implications of his material. In spirit he was well into *The Ambassadors* before he put down the manuscript of *The Sacred Fount*.

Jean Frantz Blackall. Jamesian Ambiguity and
"The Sacred Fount" (Ithaca, N.Y., Cornell
Univ. Pr., 1965), pp. 173–75

The proliferation of the comically observed or psychopathic hero, the isolated voyeur, who controls our vision in modern fiction is perhaps the result of the crumbling of the social pillar of the classical novel, tradi-tionally shaped by the tension between the society and the individual. The antagonism has necessarily shifted to abnormal individual versus a death-like norm, character has shifted from unique complexity to archetypal extremism, and dominant tone from irony to farce. With no moral anchor, the Lucky Jims and Billy Liars use people with few guilty hangovers. Their fantasies hurt. The morality of relationship, the heart of the James novel, seems to belong to another era. . . .

Granted his prejudices, James assures us of at least one fit life-boat. The question that he inevitably leads us to ask is a vital one: "Ultimately, without a concern for the deeply human and conscious relationship at its center, can the novel 'help us to live'; will it become, otherwise for us, both useless and boring?"

Naomi Lebowitz. *The Imagination of Loving:*
Henry James's Legacy to the Novel (Detroit,
Wayne State Univ. Pr., 1965), p. 157

It has often been suggested . . . that Henry James came to allow his interest in the predicament of Americans in Europe (and, to a lesser extent, of Europeans in America) to distort or divert the genius he had already shown, in his early tales and novels, for a loving preoccupation with the general human predicament. "National" characteristics loom as large in much of the work of his early maturity as "social" charac-teristics loomed large in the work of his latter years; and readers who happen by chance upon these stories rather than upon those in which his concentration on "personal" characteristics is least distracted, may be forgiven if they find him tediously prone to national caricatures animated against a travelogue, or social caricatures animated (barely!) against a series of trivial and complacent salons. It should, however, be a simple matter to show how his interest in society grew out of his inter-est in the conscious behaviour of individuals *in* society—and Proust could be adduced as a fashionable witness in sympathy. Similarly, it can readily be held that Henry James's preoccupation with the interrela-tions of the representatives of trans-Atlantic cultures sprang only from his attempt to externalize or universalize his own deep personal concern with his own reactions as an American plunging willingly into the Euro-pean scene.

The notion of Henry James as a being enslaved from earliest child-hood by a preternatural nostalgia for Europe is too well established to need much stress (people who have not ventured beyond *The Turn of The Screw* and the dramatized version of *The Aspern Papers* seem qualified to endorse this account), and in many important ways it is too accurate a notion to require much modification.

S. Gorley Putt. *A Reader's Guide to Henry James* (Thames and Hudson, 1966), pp. 57–58

The major wonder of *The Portrait of a Lady*, almost all critics agree, is the portrait itself—Isabel Archer. Always talented with titles, James was never happier than with this, for it precisely describes his method, even as it presents his subject. Whatever else the novel is, it is first and foremost a picture—a picture, moreover, composed before our eyes and minds by the novel itself and completed only with the last period of the last sentence of the last page.

Everything of consequence in the novel *is* of consequence only as it relates to the total picture of Isabel. . . .

Critics of the novel, often taking their cues from James's own comments to himself, have most often questioned the compositional effect as it relates to two particular parts. The far more widely discussed one has been on the extent to which the portrait is indeed complete. James himself foresaw the criticism even as he rejected it. "The *whole* of anything," he wrote, "is never told; you can only take what groups together." Readers have had sharply differing views about the matter, and the issue continues to be hotly contested. . . .

William T. Stafford. Intro. to William T. Stafford, ed., *Perspectives on James's "The Portrait of a Lady"* (N.Y., New York Univ. Pr., 1967), pp. xii–xiii

Henry James characteristically saw life as tragic. His letters, both published and unpublished, abound in expressions of its grimness as a fact to be acknowledged and somehow dealt with. In a letter of sympathy to Edith Wharton he writes, "but life is terrible, tragic, perverse and abysmal" (*Letters*, II, 91). The adjectives which surround "tragic" help to define it. The tragic emotion of terror and the sense of a fate which deals perversely with man lead to the climactic "abysmal." The feeling of the abyss most of all relates the suffering James is talking about to that of tragic drama, which is not only extreme in itself, but arises from situations which push man to the limits of his manhood—what Richard Sewall calls "boundary-situations." In life, as in art, the people who most interest James are those who are capable of such suffering, those, "habitually ridden by the twin demons of imagination and observation," who because of their lucidity are responsible moral agents and capable of decisions which are as irrevocably tragic as the surrounding circumstances are ironic.

In James's letters, the awareness of tragedy is relieved by the rich play of wit and comic invention. Often the gaiety seems dictated by a sheer sense of fun; but often (as in letters written during illness) it is quite openly used as a way to bear suffering.

> Ellen Douglass Leyburn. *Strange Alloy: The Relation of Comedy to Tragedy in the Fiction of Henry James* (Chapel Hill, Univ. of North Carolina Pr., 1968), pp. 168–69

● **JELLICOE, ANN (1927–   )**

The Sport of My Mad Mother . . . recently in repertory at the Royal Court, shared the third prize in the *Observer* play competition and is the first of the prize-winners to be produced. Here one feels the atmosphere of a drama school "original." The play presents a group of teddy boys and girls, led by a not very persuasive Life Force with a long red wig and full womb, an Australian girl named Greta. Into this group's alley hangout wanders a young American with dark-rimmed spectacles and a need to understand whatever he encounters. Tension grows between the American's feeble but persistent Mind and the Life Force's cruel, unpredictable vigor. ("All creation is the sport of my mad mother Kali," says the program, quoting a Hindu hymn.)

What makes this play interesting is not its stock of ideas, needless to say, but rather its use of techniques of formalization. The treatment of language, except for some rather witless lyricism at intervals, may recall Eliot's jazz refrains in *Sweeney Agonistes* (this is the suggestion of Kenneth Tynan, and it seems just). For Miss Jellicoe, too, tries to present the current ills of our world, this time through the symbols of frightened, fidgety, aggressive adolescents. And she uses their East London idiom and their gawky but busy gestures as devices for catching the uneasy excitement of all of us. These characters are ready at every moment to bring overcharged nerves to playing with a home permanent kit (chanting the instructions in a jazz tempo and falling into a dance as they do) or to carrying on a suddenly terrifying interrogation of the strange American in their midst. Three of the adolescents were beautifully played, and there seemed to be at least a dazzling one-act drama lost in this rather pretentious and directionless full-length play. By the time Greta is delivered of the Future, or what you will, the audience is cringing too hard to listen to the Theme.

> Martin Price. *MD*. May, 1958, pp. 58–59

Whole sections of the text [of *The Knack*] make no noticeable sense in themselves, because it is always what is going on, and what the audience apprehends from participating in what is going on, that counts. Often the dialogue is simply a series of disjointed *non sequiturs* or uncomprehending repetitions, and in one key scene, where Colin and Tom gradually draw Nancy into their fantasy that the bed in the room is actually a piano, of "pings" and "plongs" variously distributed and extending virtually uninterrupted over some three pages of the script. The most remarkable quality of the play, in fact, is the sheer drive of the action, physical and emotional, right through its three acts in one unbroken movement; in the theatre not only does the play not demand rationization on the part of its audience but, unlike *The Sport of My Mad Mother*, which is by comparison sometimes uncertain and immature (the last act in particular fails to cap the previous two conclusively), it positively forbids it: the spectator is carried along irresistibly by the verve and ebullience of the play, and at the end, even if he does not know what, stage by stage, it means, he certainly knows vividly what it is about.

In the five years between *The Sport of My Mad Mother* and *The Knack* Ann Jellicoe has matured and developed extraordinarily as a dramatist while continuing obstinately to plough her solitary furrow (her translation, during that time, of two Ibsen plays, *Rosmersholm* and *The Lady from the Sea*, has had no noticeable effect on her writing). Her plays are quite unlike anyone else's, and even in a generation of dramatists distinguished above all else for their sure grasp of practical theatre her work stands out by virtue of its complete command of theatrical effect. Her plays are difficult to stage, undeniably, since they depend so completely on their theatrical qualities and the sensitivity and accuracy with which the director can cover the bare framework of mere words with the intricately organized architecture fully drawn out in the creator's head. But once staged, and staged well, they infinitely repay the trouble. . . .

John Russell Taylor. *The Angry Theatre*
(N.Y., Hill and Wang, 1962), p. 71

Shelley is in his room at Oxford, his furniture madly collected into the middle of the room in the shape of perhaps a boat. His desk is attached to the ceiling by a rope which passes through a tinder box, which later explodes. Upon the bridge stands "Mad Shelley." "I'm making an experiment," he cries to his friend Hogg. Dimly the necessary symbolism shimmers: rearrangement of established dogmas, intellectual dependence on religious doubt for inspiration, the break, the boat-life.

Once the spoonful of castor oil has been got down, a straight enough reconstruction follows of Shelley's brief downhill run into exile and death. It is done by a skilful tableaux montage, with only the faintest shading here and there to betray an author's hand as distinctive as Ann Jellicoe's. It might almost have been written as a fast after the indulgencies of *The Knack*.

The subject seems to have been taken on as a Bible story might be, "because it is there," rather than for any sympathy the author may have had for Shelley's beliefs as listed in the programme. Subject and treatment would seem aimed at the film men, were it not for the unheroic, deadpan allegiance to the facts of Shelley's life. Facts which no director could afford to take seriously.

Shelley has long been the god-head of youthful poetic genius overwhelmed by personal tragedy. At first glance he is the easiest character to identify with in moments of romantic self-pity. When we hear he was called "Mad Shelley" at Eton, we are up there beside him in madness. Not so Ann Jellicoe. She is down among the commentators in the cold light of day. Here is a Shelley who could lay down the pompous "Declaration of Rights," yet here too is a Shelley noble enough to stand by them—not till death, for he forgoes them before then, but until social ridicule and hate force him out of the country. It is a Shelley at once too boring and too wonderful to suit our need.

The play goes diligently ahead with its moulding. Anyone who could take himself so seriously, "A man has not only a right to express his thoughts but it is his duty to do so," must surely be humourless, it reasons. But that is not human nature. Shelley's humourlessness is too consistent. It is not until the end of the play, when disillusionment has arrived and he starts to twist his ideals to salve his conscience, that a human being emerges. . . .

The emphasis of the play is on historical fact, not characterization. The characters are depicted, as everyone dreads their own will be, by what they have done, rather than what they were like. In a life-story so complete there was no time for fancy. The actors play the parts of chessmen on a board. They have little to disguise themselves with, so their own personalities are inclined to show through like bare skin. As each of them plays several parts, this is unfortunate. One sometimes can't tell one from another.

Hugh Williams. L. Jan., 1966, pp. 66–67

The Knack is about three boys and the girl whom two of them are trying to seduce. The most likely to succeed is Tolen, a ladies' man who claims to have mastered the art of seduction and, if he is to be believed, is in constant practice of that mastery. The least likely is Colin, a meek, awkward and gallopingly nervous school teacher. While Tolen is sexual in a crudely esoteric way ("There is little charm and no subtlety in the three-minute make"), Colin is a novice at casual (or any) erotica. Mediating between them is Tom, a very bright, very articulate boy with a sensitivity to shapes, movement, colors and size. . . .

Their victim-bait-test tube is Nancy, lately from the provinces and swept into the trap on her way to the YWCA. Whether she is really seeking a Tolen, whether she is really seeking a Colin, whether she is too willing a seducee or whether she is merely an innocent at the mercy of circumstance is one matter of the play. But there were more things on Miss Jellicoe's mind. For *The Knack* was as much about international politics as it was about interpersonal relationships, although the author rightly considered neither matter of greater importance than the other. . . .

Jellicoe will not restrict herself to a temporal political situation. The behavior of nations is analogous to the behavior of individuals and humans have always attempted to get control of other human beings. The situation of Colin, Tolen, Tom and Nancy remains human and pitifully illogical. Force is force and is always terrible. Weakness is eternally ineffectual. Decency is inevitably trapped in the middle and is without even the victim's sympathy.

Martin Gottfried. *A Theater Divided* (Boston, Little, Brown, 1967), pp. 219, 221

JENNINGS, ELIZABETH (1926–   )

The Mind Has Mountains (the title is from a poem by Gerard Manley Hopkins) is an unusual and disturbing book. It consists of a series of poems which Elizabeth Jennings wrote as the result of mental breakdown, and while she was recovering in hospital. Most of them deal with her mental condition, with suicides, illusions, derangements, and hysteria, and all are written with the same kind of understatement usually associated with her work.

For all their grim subject-matter, they are the poems of a quietist, of one struggling for the light of reason, and for some kind of release, in brilliant moments of lucidity. They have not the frustration of Clare, the high electrical passion of Hölderlin, or the torment and splintered coherence of Ivor Gurney, all of whom were touched by madness in one form or another. Their feet are on firmer ground, they are more analytical and less protesting, the people and the happenings they mention are minutely observed and assimilated. But they are very painful poems to read, largely because they do not concentrate on self-pity but rather on resignation and acceptance. Yet, for all their restraint, they are very self-conscious and may well mark a state in Elizabeth Jennings' development. Since they are poems of recovery they represent her triumph over adversity, but, in the end, she may well discard many of them for some lack the inner tension of her former work, and others read as drably as the unhappy condition they describe.

Leonard Clark. *PoetryR*. Spring, 1967, p. 52

Looking at the whole collection [*Collected Poems*], there are immediately available qualities: the dedication of the craftsmanship, the serious, uncompromising honesty, the refusal of cheapness (although, on occasions, at the risk of preciousness). Miss Jennings has written over the years a severely limited poetry, sometimes pressing a stiflingly orthodox form to the limits of its suppleness and intelligence, but remaining on the whole within its conventions, with both creative and damaging consequences. Her mind works in exact congruence with the poetic structure she uses, so that this pared, precise, aesthetic yet morally sensitive structure seems to reproduce the structure of her thinking and feeling.

It is this exact congruence which is both her strength and weakness: in her best poems, the marriage of form and substance is compelling, but elsewhere the absence of *tension* between the two results in a passive, abstract and energyless verse. Since she seems deliberately to inhibit her feeling, the tension which can't be got from a conflict of substance and technique can't come, either, from the structure itself: instead, she strips down its elements to create a cool, pure space, within which the idea moves like a dance, always coaxed through with precise fidelity, allowed to emerge logically and as it were inexorably through the balanced working-out of rhythm, in a process which can never be quickened or short-circuited.

Again, this has a strength and weakness simultaneously. The poetic structure stays strikingly faithful to the experience it negotiates, but only at the expense of a drastic limitation of range and feeling, of a kind of monotonously aesthetic arrangement of small items into ironic apposition, paradox and aptness so that wistful "truths" may mutedly emerge.

Terry Eagleton. *Stand*. No. 3, 1968, p. 69

● JOHNSON, B. S. (1933–1973)

In Mr. B. S. Johnson's highly experimental first novel [*Travelling People*] eight different techniques are used, one in each chapter. The first and last chapters are the only ones involving straight narrative and conventional dialogue. For the others he uses: interior sense-impressions; indirect speech; a letter; a film script; a journal; an interior monologue; and an omnipotent author. In between the chapters there are "interludes" and "interruptions," ranging from a passport-description of the hero to excerpts from Hakluyt.

Through these approaches we meet Henry Henry, a graduate of philosophy and an experienced hitch-hiker. As a result of a picaresque encounter he is offered a job as a barman at the Stromboli Club in North Wales, a Club for Exclusive People, offering *inter alia* a Beautiful Garden of Gorgeous Hydrangeas and, as its Speciality, Stromboli Pizza. Into this neon atmosphere Henry descends, and is soon entangled in the incestuous group responsible for managing the place. There is Maurice, the owner, fiftyish but behaving like an adolescent, Kim, his undergraduate mistress and cook, Trevor the villain, and Mira the pianist, forever ogling Henry Henry.

Although there is a surface-story moving through farce to tragedy (culminating in the impressive monologue of Maurice which leads up to the point of annihilation) the author's chief concerns are with the conflict between illusion and reality. He is anxious to assure the reader that he is only reading a book on his knee, that the "characters" have been sprung into birth at an arbitrary time and in an arbitrary place. The title reminds us (although the novel is only incidentally about travelling) that any "story" is a falsification of reality, that any situation is pregnant with possibilities, and that this is only an illustration of one.

I admire Mr. Johnson's bold and frontal attack, but his philosophy threatens to browbeat his art (and he is responsible for a division I should not care to make). His concern with reality outside the novel is such that those inside suffer; his characters (to use an old-fashioned term) get the worst of both worlds. Wallace Stevens wrote much flat poetry for the same "truth." The process is one of constant fluctuation: the pressure of reality and the resistance of the imagination, between which acceptable convention flutters like a trapped bird. So Mr. Johnson's comedy does not come fully alive because it is neither firmly in the novel nor clearly out of it. And for the same reason, the gap between the omnipotent author and the "I" of Henry wavers, so that Henry eludes our focus. But despite this, *Travelling People* is a novel which tackles, head-on and with intelligence, the problem of being a novel and not some stale copy of previous work.

John Daniel. *Spec.* April 26, 1963, pp. 544–45

B. S. Johnson's Somerset Maugham Award-winning *Trawl* would certainly take precedence over, as Mailer would say, the available talent in the room. It represents a very considerable advance on his earlier books. *Travelling People*, for instance, with its wilful and slightly pathetic attempts to be formally and typographically with-it, seemed paradoxically dated. Unfortunately, it is once again a kind of spurious, tacked-on contrivance of style that mars his newest novel. The recurrent obeisances to Joyce and Beckett . . . stick out like new skin grafts on the flesh of what was nearly a fine book. . . .

On the credit side for *Trawl*, it should be said that the "straight" passages of description of the trawling, and of the pains of childhood and wartime evacuation are finely handled, with a poet's concern for the weight and value of every word. There's a poignant immediacy in these passages which informs the main character's responses to both his past and his present experience. What seems to me to vitiate the total impact and achievement of *Trawl* (in addition to the stylistic false notes I've mentioned) is the deliberate, almost obsessive emphasizing of the symbolic value of "trawling" the subconscious for its memories, probing the mental sea-bed for an emotional catch: "Why do I trawl the delicate mesh of my mind over the snagged and broken floor of my past? . . ." and so on. Johnson's continual explicit underlining of how symbolic everything in *Trawl* is of Man Alone, of how the action of the book is a paradigm of the human condition, a Proustian search for truth and salvation in the past, comes between the reader and the organic movement of the novel itself.

Rodney Pybus. *Stand.* No. 1, 1967, p. 73

The non-fiction novel . . . is like fabulation, often associated with . . . disillusionment [with the novel as a literary form]. A case in point is the young English writer B. S. Johnson, whose break with the conventional novel was very explicitly made in *Albert Angelo* (1964). This, for about three-quarters of its length, is the story of a young architect who is unable to practice his profession, and is obliged to earn his living as a supply teacher in a number of tough London schools. He is a fairly familiar kind of English post-war hero, or anti-hero: young, frustrated, classless, mildly delinquent, disappointed in love. Though Johnson uses a number of experimental expressive techniques (simultaneous presentation of dialogue and thought in double columns, holes cut in the pages so that the reader can see what is coming), the narrative reads like realistic fiction. Then at the beginning of the fourth section, comes the shock. . . .

Johnson goes on to expose and destroy the fictiveness of the narrative he has elaborately created, telling us the "true" facts behind the story—for instance the real name of the girl and the fact that while in the novel the girl jilted Albert, in actuality Johnson jilted her. Of course, one has to take the author's word that he *is* telling the truth in this section; but even if one doubts this, the story of Albert has been drastically stripped of what Henry James called "authority." It is an extreme strategy for achieving an effect of sincerity and authenticity, though coming so late in the work it is more of a gesture than an achievement. Having blown up his fictional bridges behind him, the author stands at the end of the book defiant and vulnerable on the bare ground of fact. And there in his subsequent books, *Trawl* and *The Unfortunates* he has remained, taking the fundamentalist Platonic position that "telling stories is telling lies," but at the same time experimenting with form to bring writing into closer proximity with living.

The Unfortunates, for instance, consists of twenty-seven unbound sections, in a box. The first and last sections are marked as such, but the rest are in random order, and the reader is invited to shuffle them further if he so wishes. According to the blurb, this unconventional format is designed to "represent the random workings of the mind without the forced consecutiveness of a book," but this is not in fact the case. The random flow of sensation and association in the narrator's mind is imitated by the movement of the words, clauses and sentences *within each section*—a stream-of-consciousness technique in the manner of Joyce. The randomness only affects the narrative presentation of this consciousness in time. It makes explicit the almost infinite choice a writer has in representing a particular sequence of events by refusing to commit itself to any one choice. Such is the nature of the human mind, however, that working with the key of the marked first section, we mentally arrange the events of the book in their chronological order as we read; and the puzzle or game element thus introduced into the reading experience has the effect (ironically, in view of the author's declared intentions, but also advantageously in my opinion) of putting the painful, personal, "real" experience of the book at an aesthetic distance, making it read more like fiction than autobiography.

David Lodge. *CQ*. Summer, 1969, pp. 113–14

The idea that fiction is lying, and in other respects undesirable, has been propagated by . . . B. S. Johnson, whose considerable talents seem to me unnecessarily limited by his doctrinaire attitudes. For an English writer Johnson is remarkably conscious and theoretical in his ideas about what he wants to do. . . .

Travelling People is an extremely entertaining novel with an obvious debt to Sterne in its typographical eccentricities: as, for instance, when one character has a heart-attack and Johnson illustrates its effect with a blank page printed entirely in black. The novel contains a lively parade of stylistic improvisations, including passages printed as letters, a television script, extracts from obscure early writers, and interpolated digressions by the author. If its manner is fairly dazzling, the matter tends to be thin: in essence *Travelling People* is a familiar kind of first novel about a young man's picaresque adventures, in this case set in a shady country club in North Wales. There is a lack of conviction about the more conventionally narrative section, and it is evident that much of Johnson's energy went into the stylistic innovations. Yet this novel showed that Johnson had unusual talents and some disconcerting and provocative ideas about the novel; unlike most young English writers he had learnt a great deal from Joyce and Beckett and was trying to move beyond the conventions of realism. In his stress on the formal and artificial elements in fiction, and his preoccupation with eighteenth-century models, Johnson has something in common with John Barth, although he comes nowhere near Barth in intellectual stamina and obsessive power.

Bernard Bergonzi. *The Situation of the Novel*
(Pittsburgh, Univ. of Pittsburgh Pr., 1970),
pp. 204–5

Mr. Johnson knows everything, and has a tiresomely indiscriminate appetite for jokes of every kind—pedantic, scatological, schoolboy, pub bore. His fiction is naughty, brutish, and short. *Christie Malry's Own Double-Entry* reads as if it had been written with *The Bluffer's Guide to Laurence Sterne* at one elbow, and *101 Things for a Boy to Make and Do on a Wet Afternoon* at the other.

It is an overstretched, under-explored gag which might have led a previous, more persuasive if less elevated existence on the Morecambe and Wise show. Christie Malry (you may, on a wet afternoon, rearrange his name to make SMIRCH REALITY, or CHRIST MARY LIE, and no doubt many more amusing things) starts an account-book to keep a tally of his score against society. Not being very bright, or particularly happy in his work, he soon finds that society's debt to him is rather large, and even after such sidesplitting japes as killing off 20,479 West Londoners by dumping cyanide in a reservoir, he cannot make his figures balance. . . .

Waugh Minimus has already offered the Nobel Prize for literature to Mr. Johnson on the strength of this uncompelling little giggle, and the book comes larded with an encomium (among others) from a real Nobel Winner, Samuel Beckett. And it does have some evident, though I feel they are easy, virtues. It is lightly, readably written in the joke-pedantic style popularised by Anthony Burgess, including Burgessiologisms such as "helminthoid" and "cryptorchid" and "fastigium." Johnson is always gleefully reminding the reader that this is all fiction, a card-house of lies, and that he is manipulating his puppet-characters for a strictly didactic purpose; none of your *trompe l'œil* nonsense here. So we may, if we wish, treat the book as a novel about writing novels, as essay on the relationship between authority and authorship, on Mr. Johnson as the unjust god of his tiny world. (The problem here is that it takes only a very little ingenuity to argue the same point about every novel ever written; a few beers, and *Barchester Towers* turns into a masterpiece of the fiction of fiction—you start with "towers" as a metaphor . . .) More seriously, perhaps, *Christie Malry* rejects a class as it rejects a literary tradition. Social and literary economics are seen to be aspects of the same thing, and Johnson's cut-down comic-strip prose stands for a new kind of world in which moral vision is unimpaired by the commodities of the world we actually inhabit. But novels like this, because of the very slightness of their texture and detail, are invitation cards to an orgy of speculation. They are as good, or as bad, as the critic's capacity to make something of them, DIY kits for building cathedrals out of a few strips of balsa wood and a scrap or two of cellophane paper.

Jonathan Raban. *Enc.* May, 1973, pp. 82–83

JOHNSON, PAMELA HANSFORD (1912–   )

Miss Hansford Johnson is a novelist of varied method and versatile talent. The most impressive of her earlier works, *The Humbler Creation*, dealt seriously with the problems of an English clergyman and his abominable wife. In later books she has turned to comedy, commenting directly upon sorrow and silliness rather than depicting them plain.

Her latest book, *Cork Street, Next to the Hatter's*, contains, as all good comedies should, a portion of pathos and of the materials of tragedy. It also contains a much larger portion of commentary on society and morals. Morality is the author's chief concern, and her position is one that might be described (and is indeed described by her more odious characters) as reactionary. She espouses with spirit views at present unfashionable, at least among novelists.

For one thing, she believes that vice and crime are boring and that sinners are generally commonplace people, and to prove the point she produces a marvelously wicked and marvelously insipid murderer. But while sin is dull, she believes that the incessant portrayal of depravity in books, plays and films can make the public depraved. The main part of her story concerns a play, unspeakably disgusting, obscene and blasphemous, written by one of her good characters in an unsuccessful effort to prove to himself that there is some limit to the amount of repulsiveness the public will swallow. . . .

She is not merely wholesome, she is didactic. And her conservatism is irascible; she might with exactitude be called an Angry Middle-aged Woman. But her weapons are up to date. She writes with superb urbanity, and her wit reeks of sulphur. *Cork Street, Next to the Hatter's*, the reader may feel, is very much what might happen if Mary McCarthy were suddenly to embrace the *Weltanschauung* of Louisa May Alcott.

It is a novel of flashing juxtapositions, contemporary depravity displayed against timeless virtue.

Laurence Lafore. *NYT*. Nov. 14, 1965, p. 61

Pamela Hansford Johnson is untypical in that she deals with situations that are untypical, "unfictional" in the sense that they have not the neat, ready-made air of so many chosen by novelists. Her lovers, for instance, are not necessarily young or attractive; people of many varied ages can love, depend on one another, desperately need one another; good people may need bad ones, worthy people be infatuated with wastrels (from Sid in *The Trojan Brothers* to Helena or Charmian in the trilogy, the decent person obsessed with the indecent, with the totally unworthy object of love, is a recurrent figure in her novels). Even in the first novels, when almost inevitably it was a case of boy meeting girl, there were no conclusions, solutions, or happy endings. Even when she was still at an age to be moulded by it herself, Miss Hansford Johnson could stand outside the ideas of her time and background, criticise the sort of education (or lack of it) that made a girl totally unready for marriage.

The ability to "belong," atmospherically, to a particular place, class or age-group never means that she is confined to the standards of that particular group: time and distance become integral parts of the action, so that, while one has a vivid sense of a particular moment, one has an equally strong sense of a later judgment, a distancing and re-living of what happened then. Even in the earliest books everything was seen as fluid with possibilities, the present opening into the future; life was never a series of compartments, fixed and sealed by a particu-

lar situation. Things were always relative, becoming unfinished, open
to every sort of possibility.

Isabel Quigly. *Pamela Hansford Johnson*
(BC/Longmans, 1968), p. 8

Miss Hansford Johnson's latest novel [*The Survival of the Fittest*] is,
paradoxically, vaguer in outline and more naked in feeling than her
earlier books. It is a deliberate attempt at a large novel—408 pages of
the emotional lives of a large group of people, in detail, from the
1930s to the 1960s. . . . Pamela Hansford Johnson is one of the very
few living (or indeed dead) women novelists who is able to describe
sexual happiness in women with interest or conviction. . . .

Miss Hansford Johnson does seem a novelist of whom it is meaningful to say that she is creative. Not particularly inventive—her
invention often flags, and the much-praised comic novels seem to me
often put together with effort rather than glee. But in the trilogy, and
the patient, serious novels of the Fifties—*An Impossible Marriage, The
Last Resort, The Humbler Creation*—she seemed able to create solid
dramatic life, independent of her own circumstances. She seemed to
write out of an emotion which appeared then one of her own primary
responses to life—a greedy curiosity, detached yet sympathetic, about
other people's passions. As the novelist-narrator of *The Last Resort*,
her most finished and immediately passionate book, said of herself, she
is aware of the automatic slight sexual tensions by which almost anyone
relates, or refuses to relate, to almost anyone else at any given moment,
and can construct from these clues a complete image of their needs,
drives and fates. She specialises . . . in odd loves—a rich spinster's
marriage to an ageing homosexual, a vicar's sister-in-law's physical
passion for a drunken journalist, a 70-year-old's passion for an amor-
phously subservient young man. She also specialises in the quiet creation of real pain—and both love and pain are made sympathetic and
solid through the ability to recreate the basic obsessions which produce
them.

As a primary impulse, curiosity, rather than confession, is a great
advantage to a novelist, but it follows that to be intensely personal
about the non-autobiographical is easier than to confront or recreate
one's own world. *The Last Resort* is so good partly because the sexually
happy novelist and the created heroine in pain are both real, and the
novelist's curiosity is part of the plot and focus for it. In *The Survival
of the Fittest* attention is dissipated, not concentrated by movements
of memory, shifts of point-of-view between several characters, all
partial. The book is slightly shy. On the other hand, the sense one
occasionally had in the past that art was labouring to cover the effect

of artifice, that a character was converted by pure will from a grotesque to a person, is missing. . . . The book as a whole, if without urgency and solidity, has gained in ease and certainty. Miss Hansford Johnson is still a finished and unassuming artist.

A. S. Byatt. *NS.* May 17, 1968, pp. 654–55

JOHNSTON, DENIS (1901–   )

Johnston's plays have not had the popular impact of O'Casey's or Carroll's or Behan's, for none of them has a simple theatrical theme as even the best plays of O'Casey do. His plays are not obscure in the way that Beckett's are, for Johnston is not, I think, an ambiguous writer. He does use the drama as an intelligent rather than as a simple-minded art. To that extent, he is at war with his form; this conflict makes him both interesting and somewhat unproduced.

Perhaps the best way to make sense out of his diversity of styles is to note how in succeeding plays he seems to be searching for a compromise between significant statement and theatrical necessity. His first play, *The Old Lady,* is his most unbendingly intellectual. It is perhaps a young man's play, because of its brilliance, its brittle ironies, its dazzling reliance upon allusions, and its uncompromising demand for an amount of information no audience has ever collectively had. As Johnston became more a man of the theatre—came to know more about audiences, acting, directing, set design, theatre construction, the college and the commercial theatre—he became less willing to settle for excellence *in vacuo.* A play in the theatre must touch its audience constantly, and his later plays attempt to do just that. However, they attempt to touch the audience not merely emotionally, as O'Casey and Behan do, but more fully—both emotionally and intellectually. This poses a knotty problem and is probably the reason Johnston once remarked, "The variety of style that the plays disclose is simply a reflection of my search for an adequate means of communication." He has certainly not reached the end of his search; but in an ideal theatre in an ideal civilization, with an audience composed of Shavian He-Ancients, Johnston might appear a better playwright than either O'Casey or Behan who, despite their excellences, used the stage as a primitive and naive art.

Robert Hogan. *After the Irish Revolution*
(Minneapolis, Univ. of Minnesota Pr., 1967),
pp. 134–35

JONES, DAVID (1895–1974)

The special flavour of [Jones's] poetry has continually become more intense, but it was already unmistakable in his long poem about the 1914 war. Since then his subject matter has ostensibly widened, he has become obsessed with the past, with prehistory, with human tradition and with local *numina*; the 1914 war, the Roman empire and mediaeval Wales have each of them furnished the raw material of his poetry; these themes have been important to him because they are the most present to his understanding of history and of modern life; his poetry is in a way a struggle to talk about the history of the world.

He is not the only modern writer to have wrestled with these gigantic and powerful ghosts: in their different ways St. John Perse, Pound, Carlos Williams, Lowell and even Yeats have all done the same. Perhaps some theme of this kind was inevitable for a writer of the last fifty years who is still to command our most serious interest. These themes are fundamental to us just as certain themes were fundamental to the contemporaries of Aeschylus.

What is special to David Jones is the extraordinary variety and particularity of his language. It can be looked at in two ways: as an expression of all those local and historic diversities which his intelligence sets out to comprehend, and which his poetry does against every convention express, or simply as language, as the construction of a moral context as demanding, as multiple and as strong as that of Jonson's theatre, a concern with the texture of words and their effect on each other like that of figures and colours on a painting in progress, so that it has not been by chance that probably no writer since the time of Shakespeare has brought to bear so wide a range of the English language and such different levels of it inside a few pages.

Peter Levi. Agenda. Spring–Summer, 1967,
pp. 81–82

The supreme quality of [Jones's] art—using the word in its inclusive sense, for it would be impossible, so closely related is the technique of his drawing to that of his use of words, to say that David Jones is an artist who also writes, or the reverse—has long been apparent to an inner circle of his friends, which included T. S. Eliot; but he has never at any time been a widely-read, still less a fashionable writer, nor is he ever likely to become so, for his work is too subtle and learned for popular taste.

It was for a time possible for my generation to persuade ourselves that "the late Yeats" was a different and incomparably better poet than "the early Yeats" in order to justify what was really a change in ourselves and not in the poet. In the case of David Jones nothing of the kind would be possible. In the current number of *Agenda* there are several pieces of recent writing (or recently completed, for David Jones has a habit of laying aside pieces of work for years and then getting them out and working over them), but these are not technically different from, or necessarily better or worse than *In Parenthesis*, his poetic novel, or epic poem, of the first World War. At most the late writings are more richly complex, more finely wrought; but the matter, the vision, and the craftsmanship are essentially the same throughout. His work stands as a whole, beautiful in its coherence.

Kathleen Raine. SwR. Autumn, 1967,
pp. 740–41

There are those of us who consider that, since the passing of the late T. S. Eliot, David Jones is by far the most eminent, possibly the only great, poet now living and working in these islands. At any rate, with Pound, and perhaps one or two others, he is a survivor of the heroic phase of the modern movement in English poetry, "the protagonists of a new style" in Bateson's phrase. As in the work of Joyce, Pound and Eliot his method is to give a sense of dimension by relating contemporary subject matter to mythical and historical archetypes and prototypes, and vice versa. Eliot recognised this, in his preface to the second edition of Jones's *In Parenthesis*, but pointed out that while he himself, Joyce and Pound were in close touch with one another during the critical period of their writing, Jones developed the method quite independently.

Jones's "writings," he will not call them poems, consist of *In Parenthesis, The Anathemata*, and a series of further poems, related in theme, but not yet unified to form a third single work—though that may eventually prove to be the author's intention. "The Tribune's Visitation" belongs with these, and Jones himself particularly relates it to "The Fatigue" and "The Tutelar of the Place." "The Fatigue" has as its subject the Roman soldiers who carried out the Crucifixion of Christ. They are seen in terms of the soldiers of the 1914–18 war. Jones's own experience of this conflict clearly proved both traumatic and creative, and formed the basis of *In Parenthesis*. "The Tutelar of the Place" was more related to *The Anathemata*. In these poems Mr. Jones writes as a Catholic who sees the Church as taking over and giving a new value in its rituals to the immemorial, quasi-instinctive pieties of an early man. The Tutelar of the Place is the goddess who presides over these pieties, which are threatened by the Ram, who stands for the materialistic and mechanistic and abstract ways of looking at the world, which Blake embodied in the figure of Urizen.

John Heath-Stubbs. *PoetryR*. Summer, 1970,
p. 168

What little reputation Jones has in America seems to be chiefly as Welsh or Roman Catholic cult hero. But Jones has none of that passion for exclusiveness that has marred his church at her worst. In calling his most ambitious work *The Anathemata*, Jones surely means to redeem the word from its association with the medieval formulas. For Jones, though his devotion to the Church is plain enough, participates in no excommunications: instead, his central effort is to restore communion, to include rather than exclude, to share memories, devotions, pieties. His key word *anamnesis* (familiar now chiefly in its psychoanalytical use) Jones defines to mean not merely "unforgetting" but " 'recalling' or 're-presenting' before God an event in the past so that it becomes *here and now operative by its effects*"; the greatest and most common example is the mass. Poetry "is a kind of *anamnesis* of, i.e. is an effective recalling of, something loved." Hence poetry is at the opposite pole from any kind of curse. Speaking of Christopher Smart, Jones remarks: "if poetry is praise, as prayer is, it cannot co-exist with any malignant and persistent criticism of the nature of things. . . ." The poet, however, is no prophet or seer; in the preface to *The Anathemata* Jones describes him thus: "Rather than being a seer or endowed with the gift of prophecy he is something of a vicar whose job is legatine—a kind of Servus Servorum to deliver what has been delivered to him, who can neither add to nor take from the deposits." . . .

Jones's long poems demand comparison with Pound's *Cantos*, similar in so many respects: in length, scope, "mythical method," and fragmentariness, and in attempting to be at the same time tribal remembering, a personal testament, and a rendering of the modern world in terms equivalent to those of the classical epic. But the *Cantos* become, after the first few, increasingly uneven, eccentric, and idiosyncratic; to an increasing extent, they seem lacking in awareness of the present and irresponsible intellectually and morally. (These strictures do not apply to the *Pisan Cantos*, however, where Pound comes to himself in every sense.) Jones, in contrast, never seems capricious or self-indulgent; he is personal chiefly in that he regards himself as an intersection of channels whose archetypal significance he explores as he traces them to their confluence with central streams of myth and history. Pound laboriously discovers (if he does not invent) meanings for his Sigismundo and his minor American and Chinese statesmen; Jones remembers well-loved places, people, poems, stories. The *Cantos* range in an ultimate cosmopolitanism over all times and places; Jones's poems deal only with what he has himself participated in. Hence Jones perhaps comes as close to success in producing integral modern epics as is possible in our time.

Monroe K. Spears. *CL*. Autumn, 1971,
pp. 403, 419

What is the nature of David Jones's achievement as a poet? Where can he be placed in relation to other 20th century poets? and what sort of position does he occupy in the long tradition of literature in the English language? These questions are not susceptible of an easy or straightforward answer, but some attempt has to be made to provide at least a starting point.

Part of the problem lies in the fact that the lyric or short poem is the dominant poetic form and that by and large it currently contents itself with circumscribed pirouettes around the surfaces of personal triviality. The situation has been set out clearly enough in Kathleen Raine's recent book *Defending Ancient Springs*, where it forms the background to her discussion of a number of poets who she feels are faithful to the spiritual depth of "true poetry" and find new ways of exploring and expressing it. David Jones is not explicitly dealt with in this study, though he is mentioned on several occasions, but like Vernon Watkins, Edwin Muir, David Gascoyne, Yeats and St. John Perse he is one of the defenders of the "ancient springs." Add to these names those of Pound and Eliot, Hopkins, Joyce, Blake, Hugh MacDiarmid and (despite all the decrying that she is at present subjected to) Edith Sitwell, and one probably has a fair context, and a diverse enough one, for David Jones's work.

Vernon Watkins is the Welsh poet with whom he has the closest affinity; St. John Perse he explicitly recognizes as a kindred spirit; and Pound, together with the Eliot of *The Waste Land*, is the person whose technique of poetic collage most nearly resembles his own. Hugh MacDiarmid seems to me to possess a similar toughness and exactitude of language, a delight in particularity, and an even greater range of literary and cultural continuities, while Edith Sitwell expresses in much of her later poetry a kind of mystical numinosity, a sense of involvement with the obscure sufferings of the world, and an incantational element that derives ultimately, in the West, from the rites and insights of Catholicism.

It is possible, however, that the most important of all these literary affiliations or correspondences is to be found in Joyce. Not so much the Joyce of *Ulysses* as the Joyce of *Finnegans Wake*. David Jones doesn't go in for the Joycean pun (or at least not on the same, bewildering scale), nor does he share the negative side of Joyce's obsession with Catholicism, but his use of language is motivated by a similar kind of philological delight and he employs its cross-fertilizing powers. Moreover, what he has to say is based on a comparable perception of the permanence of mythological structures. This similarity has been remarked on before by such critics as Kathleen Raine and Edwin Muir, and it is probable that David Jones would confess to Joyce as a "master," while rejecting any other specific influences. *The Anathemata* could be regarded as a counterpart in the field of poetry to *Finnegans Wake*, though whether the common distinctions of poetry and prose have much relevance here is a matter open to dispute. *The Anathemata* is certainly more readable.

David Blamires. *David Jones: Artist and Writer* (Toronto, Univ. of Toronto Pr., 1972), pp. 193–94

JOYCE, JAMES (1882–1941)

Joyce cannot resist the lure of parody in his later work, and in yielding to this he is forging much more than the "uncreated conscience" of his race. His use of the misspelling, "hesitency," throughout the work—the classic error of a forger through which Parnell triumphed over Piggott —is a continual warning that he is up to his tricks in this respect.

But what then is he parodying in presenting us with this odd amalgam of false clues? The answer may lie in the other element that I have yet to mention—Joyce's return to religion in this, his final work [*Finnegans Wake*]. While the first half of his life is devoted to denial and doubt, there is every indication in the Wake that the Joyce of later middle age was not only a Gracehoper but was profoundly concerned, maybe not with a heavenly life-hereafter, but with the eternity of this life. Hence the significance to him of the river as an image or model of a working Viconian cycle—a phenomenon that is being born in the hills, that flows and grows, and is finally lost in the sea, from whence it returns once more to the hills. And here's the point—there is no mutual exclusiveness in all of these phases. They are all happening "Now." Finn again and again and again. What a hell for the damned, as Sartre has since pointed out. But Joyce is not damned, for all his *Non Serviams*. He has got the mysterious gift of Grace, as even Clongowes will agree nowadays. . . .

In spite of the fact that it is one of the dirtiest books in public circulation, Joyce shows a far greater sense of religious purpose in the Wake than in anything else that he has written. Why he has to be so secretive about this fact is one of the charms and peculiarities of the man. Why he feels bound to conceal the message of his newly-born Penelope in the pidgin English of page 611 is perhaps an expression of his arrogance, or maybe it is a feature of his Irish love of a secret, or indeed of his Irish fear of a nasty laugh wafting out of Davy Byrne's. [1964]

> Denis Johnston. In Robin Skelton and David
> R. Clark, eds., *Irish Renaissance: A Gathering*
> *of Essays, Memoirs and Letters from the*
> *"Massachusetts Review"* (Dublin, Dolmen,
> 1965), pp. 126–27

Eugene Jolas, who knew Joyce well from 1927 on, once characterized him as "never an ebullient man. His moments of silence and introspection frequently weighed . . . on his immediate surroundings. Then a profound pessimism, that seemed to hold him prisoner within himself, made him quite inaccessible to outsiders. Usually, however, among his intimates, there finally came a festive pause, when he would begin to dance and sing, or engage in barbed thrusts of wit; when he would show flashes of gaiety and humor that could, on occasion, approach a kind of delirium."

It is almost as though Mr. Jolas were describing Joyce's books along with their author. That "profound pessimism" manifests itself first in those studies of Irish moral paralysis, the *Dubliners* stories, written in a spare, almost reticent prose, which Joyce himself termed a style of "scrupulous meanness." When the snow begins to fall upon all Ireland at the close of "The Dead," falling, "like the descent of their last end, upon all the living and the dead," an icy Joycean pessimism descends simultaneously upon us, and as we look back over the sorry lot of Dubliners just encountered—the paralyzed and perverse alike—we may be tempted to reflect upon the bleakness of the moralist who created them. In the *Portrait* that same pessimism, expressed this time in a different style, lurks beneath the many passages of soaring, silvery romanticism. . . .

But just as in Mr. Jolas' characterization, "there finally came a festive pause." Enter Bloom, and with him Joyce's barbed wit, humor, and sometimes delirious comic satire. Enter Molly Bloom as well, and later Earwicker and Anna Livia and certainly "the twins that tick *Homo Vulgaris*," Shem and Shaun.

Joyce's pessimism, of course, is never banished: but it requires redefinition, revaluation. It dresses now in cap and bells, covering a sad heart with a gay costume, even as a Shakespearean Fool. It is resigned to the doubleness or duplicity of life, recognizing the common reality co-existing with every vision of beauty, but choosing to laugh rather than to rail at life's irreducible antinomies. Adopting this ironic stance, Joyce directed his comic satire against a wide range of human follies, some truly reprehensible and others merely amusing.

Darcy O'Brien. The Conscience of James Joyce
(Princeton, N.J., Princeton Univ. Pr., 1968),
pp. 240–41

As a native of Ireland, Joyce has often been accused of being a middle-class author whose work is a denial of history and attempts to make itself a mediaeval *summa* rather than a realistic portrayal of his times. It is true that Joyce wrote no historical novel, and it is true that *Finnegans Wake* is an encyclopedia of mythology; but Joyce is profoundly an Irishman and his work is truly the product of his own inner Ireland. Joyce's Ireland is not that of Yeats and perhaps even less that of Eamon de Valera.

What he retains from it is less its legendary past or its political future, than its present, that of the beginning of the twentieth century; from a reading of *Dubliners* and *Ulysses* one can discover all urban Ireland and Dublin society. As a social document it still retains its value today. But that is only the framework for the story of a developing consciousness, that of the artist, and, in *Ulysses*, that of an ordinary Dubliner—and by extension that of Dublin itself. There will always be a realistic basis to this spiritual or intellectual history, but neither is it presented objectively, nor does it distort the real; in the center of the work Joyce places individuals, and around the individuals, the three circles of family, homeland and Church are interpreted by those whom they surround and who at the same time serve to define them.

The family, the economic and social problems, are thus both concrete elements of surrounding reality—an end in itself, but limited—and the means by which the artist's mind is sharpened. In this, any realism is at once overtaken and assimilated, to become the surface of a symbolism which is made less and less publicly significant as it is more and more charged with personal meaning, until, with *Finnegans Wake*, it becomes a Joycean form of occultism, initiation to which is achieved by a progress *through* Joyce enabling one to reach reality.

How far and to what degree can one speak of "realism" in Joyce's art?

When Joyce writes *A Portrait*, he already possesses that "double consciousness of one watching himself live" (J. J. Mayoux, *Joyce*,

p. 44), which enables him to reconstitute by memory a time which is experienced and now past. This retrospective glance at his own history reveals both the *image* he has of himself (not himself), and the exterior forces which have caused him to develop in opposition to them; what he sees is the social alienation of his family and of Ireland to which he has responded by withdrawing, by declaring his *difference,* while still, in the tones of the romantic and idealistic *fin-de-siècle* artist, claiming the role of moral reformer within this very society that he rejects. [1968]

Hélène Cixous. *The Exile of James Joyce*
(N.Y., David Lewis, 1972), pp. ix–x

This elaborate little volume [*Giacomo Joyce*] is a monument to the irony of Joyce's publishing history: the contrast between his difficulties in finding an audience for his major works, and the increasingly easy flow of Joyceana during the quarter-century since his death. Sixteen pages of manuscript are here transcribed line by line, also reproduced in photographic facsimile, and interpreted by our leading Joycean, Richard Ellmann. In his admirable biography, Mr. Ellmann made previous use of the material, printing about half of it and commenting on the rest sometimes more explicitly than here—notably, in identifying the heroine. His new presentation stresses, perhaps unduly, the artistic merits of this autobiographical document. Whether or not it is "a great achievement" may well be arguable. That it should be described as a novel is, I think, an unwarranted source of confusion. Mr. Ellmann did much better by it in *James Joyce*, when he referred to it as a prose poem.

Though we exaggerate to call it a story, it is indeed a fascinating record, especially for those who wish to follow the interplay between a writer's career and his literary expression. The two are brought together rather arbitrarily by the present title, which is simply the name inscribed on the cover of Joyce's notebook in another hand. The editor argues that the Italianized forename conveys the ironic self-depreciation of a would-be Casanova. Conceivably; but it is hard to believe that these jottings, although carefully recopied by Joyce himself, were ever intended for publication. The transmutation of life into art, as no one has shown more impressively than Mr. Ellmann in his *James Joyce*, involves a process of far greater complexity. *Giacomo Joyce* derives its interest from its very closeness to unmediated experience, on the one hand. On the other, it enables us under expert guidance to retrace the development of motifs and cadences which appear in Joyce's finished work.

Harry Levin. *NYT*. Jan. 21, 1968, p. 22

There is no doubt that Joyce has played an important part in the development of the twentieth-century novel. His influence on other writers cannot be overrated. It is always a certain aspect of a work of literature which has an influence—and this influence is often based on a misunderstanding. In the case of *Ulysses*, it is to be found in the technique of the interior monologue, which, so Joyce says, he took over from Dujardin. Arthur Schnitzler had already used the technique before Joyce, but only after *Ulysses* did it become a common literary device.

Joyce's whole literary unconventionality had a very strong effect: his work encouraged writers to experiment more and more freely. This does not mean that Joyce's influence was necessarily all for the best. One might ask: Did not the so-called "decadence of the novel" begin with Joyce? Conrad felt the demonic evil of his time but was satisfied in portraying it objectively. Lawrence, on the other hand, warned and fought; he was the prophet with a solution. Joyce took pleasure in destroying in advance what would have collapsed anyway. Destruction and decadence, as he knew from Vico, are necessary steps in the course of things. Joyce was the one who advanced furthest and most boldly toward the abolition of the kind of literature and art which humanity has known since the time of Aristotle. It would be difficult to imagine a work of literature on the other side of *Finnegans Wake*.

Sometime, maybe, an author will find that only by writing in a new alphabet can he do justice to his thoughts and feelings, or he will throw away his pen and sell his works in the form of x-ray films of his brain at work. Then, of course, *Finnegans Wake* will look quite old-fashioned. In the meantime, Joyce's works will be on the shelves of anybody interested in modern literature; his first books will be read with pleasure, *Ulysses* and *Finnegans Wake* either with laughter or with antlike industry; all are essential documents of the literature of our time.

Armin Arnold. *James Joyce* (N.Y., Ungar,
1969), pp. 112–13

● KAVANAGH, PATRICK (1904–1967)

Nothing is easier to describe than a commonplace autobiography, few things more difficult than a good one. *The Green Fool* impresses one as a book of great distinction, but it is very hard to analyse the qualities which contribute to its effect. It describes the childhood and adolescence of a young man brought up in a part of Ireland where the traditional ways of life still subsist little diluted with modern habits, where a first visit to the urban world of Dublin, though the city is only fifty miles distant, is still considered an adventurous expedition into Wonderland. To a reader unacquainted with Ireland its chief attraction may be that it describes vividly a community retaining conventions, superstitions, beliefs which are altogether outside English experience; to anyone who knows Ireland well it attracts as a record of a way of life which, unless the nature of the Irish countryman is even more tenaciously conservative than it seems, must soon be submerged in the process of the country's development. For neither type of reader will this achievement be by any means the single attraction of the book.

Mr. Kavanagh is the first writer of his generation in Ireland to paint a picture of his country. . . . If this book had no other distinction it would possess that of having caught more exquisitely than any other recent book the rhythms and phrasings of Irish country speech. Anglo-Irish has been made by its exploiters a justly suspect tongue. But in its natural state it nevertheless remains a vivid, expressive and poetic form of speech. Recorded as fastidiously as it is by Mr. Kavanagh, it enchants as it does in life. . . .

Mr. Kavanagh's lyrics are for the most part slight and conventional, easily enjoyed but almost as easily forgotten. His prose is distinctive, possessing great vitality and braced on every page by some memorable image or observation. *The Green Fool* is a book of so many qualities that it is difficult to write of it with restraint. It is, of its kind, almost perfect; and the kind is worthy. It is a book which no one who opens can fail to read with pleasure.

Derek Verschoyle. Spec. June 3, 1938,
pp. 1022–24

In Patrick Kavanagh peasant Ireland has a poet. But "peasant Ireland" needs an explanation. . . . The older poets took their matter from a folk; today's poets take theirs from the individual peasant.

Patrick Kavanagh writes under this new dispensation. His verse has no longer a traditional lilt with the overtones of folk-poetry: again and again we catch a rhythm that recalls *The Waste Land*. But *A Soul for Sale* is of the Irish countryside, and its figures are recognizable as the farmers and priests, the boys and girls of a parish. . . .

Perhaps it is because he belongs to a transition period that this poet is so unequal: Patrick Kavanagh has not made up his mind whether he should celebrate or satirize. In *The Great Hunger* he attempts to give monumental treatment to the peasant. But he also wants to satirize the joylessness of the countryside: to do this he has to give his Pat Maguire an extra raw deal by giving him a vinegary sister as well as a dominating mother. When Patrick Kavanagh is wholehearted he writes poems that have the tang of sloes pulled off the bushes. . . .

Padraic Colum. *Sat.* Sept. 20, 1947, p. 24

[*Tarry Flynn*] is the tender and touching tale of a poor Irish farm and a young peasant, who dreams of the winged Pegasus as he follows a plodding plow horse over his mother's scraggy field. It is told with insight and sensitivity by Patrick Kavanagh, a talented new Irish novelist. . . .

Within the simple framework of this story, Kavanagh, who once was a farmer in a town with the odd name of Mucker, presents a vivid and realistic picture of the fierce struggle for existence waged by Irish peasants. He writes of the earthy people of the farmlands with humor and compassion, and one character, Tarry Flynn's mother, is truly memorable. Even while praying, this old woman cannot forget the demanding business of living, as witness [the] prayer in which she rolls one eye heavenward and keeps the other cocked on the earth. . . .

Richard Harrity. *NYHT*. Nov. 13, 1949, p. 32

The career of Patrick Kavanagh presents extraordinary features completely outside the usual literary framework. His *Collected Poems* reveals an astonishing talent—according to some enthusiasts, the finest not only in Ireland but in all English-speaking areas—that has kept on renewing itself not so much by a process of orderly growth as by a continual breaching of boundaries. Judging by his recent poetic practice as well as his comment on that practice, it is clear that Kavanagh now stands free of all obligations except the deepest and most demanding claims of the open imagination.

The early work of this poet, born in 1904 in the Irish countryside, reflects a life close to the pieties and rude circumstances of the agricultural laborer. His disillusion with the lot of the Irish countryman came into being only after he had described that lot—in *The Great Hunger* (1942)—with mixed affection and loathing. His subsequent descriptions of Dublin literary life and politics were again filled with the blackest disillusion. Kavanagh's chief object of detestation has come to be the coat-trailing, charming, Irish semi-clown—a tragicomic caricature designed, according to the poet, for the foreign trade. Behind Kavanagh's intransigence stands a thorough understanding of modern traps laid on all sides for the bafflement of human dignity, as well as an unfaltering sense of some human innocence, marred but indestructible.

His satire, cutting close to the bone, spares neither cause, nor institution, nor individual. He names person and place, and he can be as scathing in a sonnet as in a piece of parody or a stretch of doggerel. Since, as he frankly states in his introductory author's note, written in London in 1964, he now dislikes much of his early verse, the selection of the poems in the new volume, of nearly two hundred pages, was left to his friend Martin Green, who has carried out his task admirably. To come upon Kavanagh's spontaneity is delightful, and one understands the sober reasons that have kept him from being listed among the more official and solemn post-Yeatsians. Far from officialdom of any kind, Kavanagh survives and flourishes in that invigorating region where, without respectable let or hindrance, the wild rivers run and the wild timber grows. [1965]

Louise Bogan, A Poet's Alphabet (N.Y.,
McGraw-Hill, 1970), pp. 271–72

Patrick Kavanagh, who died last year in Dublin, was probably the most considerable poet to appear in Ireland since the death of Yeats. He was certainly the most original. His strong epic, *The Great Hunger*, conjured a new mood. Its impact on the Irish scene in the 1940's had some of the force *The Waste Land* had on English-speaking writers in the 1920's.

Paul Potts in one of the more percipient obituaries suggested that Kavanagh stands to Yeats in twentieth-century Ireland as Davitt stood to Parnell in the nineteenth. Yeats and Parnell emerged from the Anglo-Irish ascendancy, Kavanagh and Davitt spoke for the downtrodden peasantry. The stink of the barnyard is seldom absent even in Kavanagh's city poems. It is not "nice" poetry. If Yeats's lineage reaches back through Blake and Dante to seek the courtly tradition of Byzantium, Kavanagh's runs through Whitman and Melville to *Piers Plowman*. Yet he had in common with Yeats his resolute refusal to tread the nostalgic road of exile and merge his work with a non-Irish tradition. His strength, and a portion of weakness, connects with the fact that on a London street or an Illinois campus he remained a

Dublin peasant. In common, too, with Yeats he never qualified his championing of the poet's claim to be supreme repository for spiritual truth.

Gratan Freyer. Éire-Ireland. Winter, 1968,
p. 17

There are certain poets of whom it can be said that they have a unique personal vision—Blake and Yeats for example—and one knows immediately what is meant. They have a new, inimitable, disturbing way of looking at life and, at their best, they communicate this vision successfully. In twentieth-century Ireland, one poet (apart from Yeats) possesses such a vision—Patrick Kavanagh—who, for some unaccountable reason, is one of the most misunderstood and under-valued poets of our time. It is with Blake and Yeats that Kavanagh must be compared, for he is a visionary poet and towards the end of his life he claimed that he had achieved a truly comic vision. . . . Comedy . . . meant for Kavanagh something very definite and pro-found, but sometimes what is perfectly clear to a poet is confused to a critic because the poet lives poetry and his discoveries are inevitable and organic. They are one with the beat of his blood. . . .

Fewer modern poets have undergone such a deep, dynamic devel-opment as Kavanagh. . . . His was one of the most moving, coherent and profound visions in modern poetry.

Brendan Kennelly. Ariel. July, 1970, pp. 7–8

● KINSELLA, THOMAS (1928–   )

All but all of Thomas Kinsella's book [*Moralities*] consists of seven-teen poems of eight lines each in divisions labelled Faith, Love, Death, Song. There is not much room for development in eight lines, so one expects something "lyrical" or gnomic or epigrammatic—or anyway reverberative. Two I'm not sure I understand, so maybe they are the gnomic ones. The others speak in a sort of grave rhetoric, in language which is personal and alive, and they satisfactorily complete their own forms. None of them, short as they are, are flimsy. And though few of them make us aware of hinterlands of meaning as wide as those in the best of Charles Tomlinson's poems, there are some that do explode in one's face—not a huge explosion, but an explosion all the same. Some-times the rhetorical last line seems overmuscled for the weight it is lifting, and in some instances, indeed, there is precious little weight to lift, when Mr. Kinsella is "throwing skin about a puff of smoke" (a phrase of his own). But the good ones avoid that fault and this deficiency.

Norman MacCaig. *Spec.* Aug. 5, 1960, p. 223

The considerable talent that Thomas Kinsella brings to poetry is apparent, at its least complicated, in one of his shorter poems, "The Monk" [in *Poems and Translations*]. . . .

Kinsella is never a smooth writer; and his virtues are usually associated with this lack of smoothness. His poetry at best "resists the intelligence almost successfully," at worst only too successfully. There is a close connection, indeed, between that best and worst: if we feel his happiest epithets have been carefully sought, we can find an equal number of unusual words where we are more aware of the strain in the search than of the success in the finding; and if his power lies in the portrayal of the concrete, his distrust of abstractions is so great that whenever he has need of them he will permit them on the page only as monstrous personifications.

Yet two of his most ambitious poems, "Baggot Street Deserta" and "Thinking of Mr. D.," almost succeed as wholes because our exasperation at the incidental defects is less than our admiration for the central virtues. . . . It is another matter altogether whether Kinsella will ever write a perfect poem: when he is most ambitious both his best and worst instincts are at work, and I strongly suspect that he considers opacity a good in itself.

Thom Gunn. *YR.* Spring, 1962, pp. 486–87

Kinsella is . . . a moralist, but not a humanist. His moral concern stems not from a concern for human order but from a belief in struggling toward a conviction of the necessity of Divine Grace. His moralities lead to no other convictions; he may hypothesize, but he does not judge. He questions even the apparent clarity of positive good. His faith, his humility, his self-torment and self-ridicule, permit him no certainty. He records suffering without animus, and celebrates the necessary abandonment of the ego by despair. His personae are often similar to those of Graham Greene, whose faith permits few certainties, and whose self-destructiveness is itself a positive recognition of the need of Grace and of its incalculability.

Kinsella's first publication was issued in 1952. *Wormwood* appeared in 1966. In these fourteen years he has developed a poetic personality unique in our time. His use of gothic and romantic elements sets him apart from the majority of his fellows, and his moral concern and religious passion give his work a rigor and a symbolic toughness none can emulate. Kinsella may or may not be, as he has been labelled, the "successor" of Yeats. He is, however, clearly a poet of stature and at the height of his powers. It will be interesting to see his future development.

Robin Skelton. Éire-Ireland. Spring, 1968,
p. 108

I think [*Nightwalker*] is Kinsella's most accomplished book, and that is saying a good deal. Kinsella had to convince himself that he could do what the poets he admired did. He set himself to learn how to handle the metaphysical conceit, how to combine the familiar and exotic, how to use myth while ironically questioning it. He worked at putting the old themes of song into strict patterns of rhyme and meter. Among the masters he schooled himself in are Donne and Herbert and Marvell, Keats and Wordsworth and Arnold, Yeats and Eliot and Auden. And his debt to the old ballads and carols, and to the wisdom and folk poetry of Ireland is obvious. But I am not competent to judge the effect on his work of his Gaelic heritage. At least on the evidence of his own poetry, he has not much interest in the techniques of association or the theories of correspondence developed by the French symbolists or in the free-flowing inclusiveness of Whitman and his latter-day followers. He likes a poem to focus its meanings, even when these are logically inconclusive or emotionally unsettled, with force and lucidity. His quest for form in poetry mirrors, or parallels, his quest for order in life. If his earlier poetry could be said to choose its occasions for their adaptability to styles of traditional lyric, the later poetry, by contrast, may be said to seize its occasions from whatever is most pressing in the poet's life as though confident that, however grim the subject, the words could be relied on to perform their poetic duty.

This diagrammatic contrast is of course false if taken too literally, but it is indicative of what I have in mind in speaking of Kinsella's accomplishment. His art has come to seem unpremeditated, and this at the very time when the life his poetry so frequently describes seems threatened with collapse. One feels more pressure on the poetry to justify itself in human terms, and this perhaps accounts for the special attention given to the theme of art and life, not a new subject for Kinsella but one never so fully developed in his earlier work.

John Rees Moore. HC. Oct., 1968, pp. 11–12

As in *Butcher's Dozen*, the first pamphlet in this series, in which Mr. Kinsella commemorated the thirteen people killed in Derry by British paratroopers last January, *A Selected Life* depends for a good deal of its effect upon the shock of the event. Kinsella has a deserved reputation for the gravity, the sense of weight and mass which he can impart to his poetry even, perhaps especially, at his freest, most lyrical moments. This is partly the result of a penitential, almost liturgical rhythm in a language which is puritanical in its discipline, avoiding the risks of sentimentality with a disdain that sometimes becomes hard-boiled, veering instead towards an idiom of invective and bitterness.

A Kinsella poem very often manages to communicate emotional stress as a somatic experience. Love is a war of attrition, a matter of heroism; death a blow that can only be overcome by the rigorous capacity to endure it; and the endurance is supported by the stiff violence of that peculiarly stylized natural world that forms the landscape to much of his poetry.

TLS. Dec. 8, 1972, p. 1481

KIPLING, RUDYARD (1865–1936)

Certainly it is difficult to get a unified idea of Rudyard Kipling's complex and enigmatic personality. Reading through his fictional works you find, outstandingly, that he is a writer who can compel your imagination to accompany him from arid villages in Afghanistan to the rich downs of Sussex, from the plains of India to the wildest of Atlantic seas, from Arctic ice to the sweltering African forests. He can impart the chatter of journalists in London, the energy of pioneers in Canada, or the terrible isolation of a lighthouse-keeper. Here is a man who can horrifyingly reveal shocking depths of humanity, show it at its most tender and compassionate, or flash to you a queer vision of an archangelic world. He can go back to ancient Rome, even to pre-history, and forward to the year 2065. His variety is astonishing. It is of no use to read a few stories of one kind and put him in a certain category: you cannot pigeon-hole Kipling—he will catch you unaware. In the same volume a story of deep tragic significance may be followed by one of outrageously extravagant farce. What seizes you continually is the overflowing vitality that gives you the sense of being just there. And through the fiction, the lectures and the letters, there run threads of certain dominating ideas or intuitions, each, perhaps, simple in itself, but which woven together form an intricate, patterned tapestry.

Bonamy Dobrée. *Rudyard Kipling: Realist and Fabulist* (Oxford Univ. Pr., 1967), p. 3

The late-Victorian adulation of Kipling as an inexplicable literary miracle and the post-World War denunciation of him as an inveterate imperialist are both extreme attitudes in evaluating his complexity. These divergent critical perspectives drastically reduce the nature and quality of Kipling's achievement to highly simplistic categories. Consequently, the central reality of Kipling's cosmos, in which contraries such as the real and the ideal, the physical and the spiritual, the cruel and the compassionate are harmonized into art, is overlooked.

The core of Kipling's complexity as an artist lies in his alienated activism. As E. San Juan, Jr. has perceptively pointed out, Kipling is essentially a spokesman of activism which is a significant strand of Victorian thought. In its simple form "activism" may be described as "the doctrine or policy of being active or doing things with energy and decision." It postulates a life of vigorous, dynamic action committed to the belief in man's ability to transform society through this action. Though activism as a doctrine can be traced to the adventurous spirit of the Victorian age, it was also embodied, earlier, in the Faustian motif of the endless quest for experience and action. In this regard, the spirit of Faust, immortalized by Goethe, is symbolic of the growth of European civilization with its irrepressible longing for action, adventure, and knowledge.

Vasant A. Shahane. *Rudyard Kipling: Activist and Artist* (Carbondale, Southern Illinois Univ. Pr., 1973), p. 22

● KOPS, BERNARD (1928–   )

It is hard to say which piece of news is the best: that Bernard Kops should have written this remarkable play [*The Dream of Peter Mann*], that it should be produced, or that it should be published in a popular edition. All three events are signs of the extraordinary and unlooked-for rejuvenation of the English theatre that is still quickening its pace. . . .

This is a play of bold ambition, which enormously extends the dimensions of common life. The large forces that mould or menace our world are made to impinge directly on the characters. As in some other recent plays, people speak of the hydrogen bomb. Real people, maybe, don't do this except at political meetings, but they feel continually the presence of the bomb. Kops has given them words for that feeling, and the open-eyed courage to face and overcome it. This is not a play "about" the bomb; it is a play about living in a world that has the bomb.

There is another reality, more central to the play, which we commonly ignore even for a lifetime and of which these characters are made painfully but triumphantly aware. A curtain of incomprehension, thickened by pretence, divides one real self from another. Early in the play, Peter Mann says to the girl he wants to marry: "Isn't that strange we've lived here all our lives together and now we're strangers." How many young men and girls do in fact get married without ever daring to say or even think that? In plays by some of the new dramatists, the persistence of this barrier is a theme for tragedy. In others, the drama derives from a difficult and unresolved struggle against it. But in *The Dream of Peter Mann* the break-through is ultimately effected, giving at the end a justly earned sense of exaltation. By this the play stands or falls, and I think it stands as a wholly satisfying work of art.

For, despite its candid portrayal at the necessary moments of misery and terror, this is finally a joyous play and an affirmation of the love of life. The quality of this affirmation is often realized through humour. This humour is never a diversion, a whistling in the dark, an attempt to shrug off unpleasant truths. On the contrary, these very truths are faced and illuminated by humour. As G. K. Chesterton said, all the really good jokes are about serious things.

Mervyn Jones. Intro. to Bernard Kops, The
Dream of Peter Mann (Harmondsworth,
Penguin, 1960), pp. 9–11

The central character of *The Hamlet of Stepney Green* is David Levy, a dreamy young man with an urge to croon. This character, more or less, recurs in all Kops's plays, along with the Oedipal situation in which he is enmeshed; all Kops's heroes are tied emotionally to their mothers and all are dreamers obsessed with some fixed idea. In only one case does the dream show signs of winning out (*Change for the Angel*), but elsewhere Kops seems to advocate coming to terms with the realities of normal human life and recognizing that dreams may be delusions which prevent one from seeing the truth instead of insights into the truth denied to more mundane creatures. In this conclusion he avoids one sentimental stereotype, the dreamer-poet-rebel who is an unacknowledged legislator of mankind, only to fall into another: reliance on the good sense and solid values of warm-hearted, simple people to pull us through. Given this tendency, though (which in a primitive is not hard to accept, since one does not expect a sophisticated or subtly reasoned world-picture), it may be felt that Kops's work is at its best when it is most unashamedly simple and sentimental, as in *The Hamlet of Stepney Green*, rather than when, as in one or two of his later plays, he tries to reason and philosophize.

In *The Hamlet of Stepney Green*, fortunately, there is almost no overt philosophizing at all. . . . The plot is evidently pretty naïve in outline, and the main strength of the play is that it stays naïve and unspoilt all through.

John Russell Taylor. *The Angry Theatre*
(N.Y., Hill and Wang, 1962), pp. 123–25

The real power in the Jewish family resides with the mother, and young men like Bernard Kops and Arnold Wesker, who have been brought up in traditional Jewish families, usually grow up with what is best described as an unwhelped Oedipus complex: runny-nosed mama's boys looking up worshipfully at the all-encompassing Mother Earth figure. A few trips to those Yiddish theaters still remaining will convince anyone of this. The mothers are always large-bosomed, domineering figures and the fathers hollow-chested, runty little men skipping along behind their wives like coracles towed in the wakes of galleons. Watching Yiddish drama one wonders how the children were ever begot.

If Arnold Wesker demonstrates the disastrous consequences to the potential playwright of being formed in a traditional Jewish household, Bernard Kops demonstrates his possible salvation. This salvation lies in humor: if you can laugh at your heritage, you can transcend it.

This is precisely what has happened to Bernard Kops, another one of the promising young sparks of the "New English Dramatists" movement. Kops's work, like Wesker's, has been entirely determined by his Jewish heritage. So far he has published three plays: *The Hamlet of Stepney Green, The Dream of Peter Mann,* and *Enter Solly Gold.* Of these the second is an unfortunate attempt at writing a Jewish folk play in expressionistic style, while the other two are simple Jewish folk plays set in contemporary London but modeled on the type of Jewish folk literature written by Sholom Aleichem or Isaac Babel.

The Hamlet of Stepney Green and *Enter Solly Gold* are opposite sides of the same coin. In the former, Kops takes himself seriously and fails; in the latter, he does not take himself seriously and succeeds. It is as simple as that, and the lesson for the Jewish playwright is inescapable. The Jew is apt to be extremely emotional and to have a sharp, self-critical sense of humor. Extreme emotion is dangerous on the stage at the best of times. It is successful only when it is entirely impersonal and objective, as in Shakespeare and in the Greek drama. The Jewish form of emotion, as portrayed by Kops, is, however, strictly of the breast-beating, *mea culpa* type, sung solo with wailing-wall chorus obbligato; and this makes for embarrassed rather than sympathetic audiences.

Another drawback to Kops's serious plays is that serious plays require some sort of philosophical orientation. When a man writes a serious play he has to take a definite position with respect to his view of reality. Now, Kops, though a first-class humorist, is anything but a thinker. He feels that the world is really a wonderful place and that everything would be all right if people would only jiggle around flapping their arms and smiling through. To Kops reality is one long, manic vaudeville act.

George E. Wellwarth. *The Theatre of Protest and Paradox* (N.Y., New York Univ. Pr., 1964), pp. 244–45

The talented English playwright and poet Bernard Kops, whose development as a novelist has been an intense, protracted effort to bring his gifts to full maturity, has achieved that goal with his fourth and latest novel. *By the Waters of Whitechapel*, first published in England last year, is an enormously funny, macabre, and affecting account of how a pathetically trapped man wins freedom at the paradoxical cost of assuming the role of self-jailer. Kops writes here with greater artistic discipline and more stringent concern for the necessary precision of poetic language than ever before. He has attained a toughness of vision that enables him to evoke significant compassion rather than a mawkish sentimentalism such as that which mars some of his previously published writing, especially his first novel, *Awake for Mourning* (1958).

Kops deals again with material explored by him in drama and fiction—the past and present of Jewish immigrants in London's East End slums. Fortunately, he has reperceived these potentially redundant characters. They have been invested, accordingly, with a unified clarity, sympathy, and significance that elevate *By the Waters of Whitechapel* above the currently omnipresent kind of novel in which ethnic experience is opportunistically trotted forth as almost wholly vaudeville frolic, obsessively castigated as almost entirely traumatic nightmare, or otherwise reduced to misleading caricature. . . .

The central characters of both [*By the Waters of Whitechapel* and Philip Roth's *Portnoy's Complaint*] are inordinately preoccupied with their respective mothers and equally frustrated in attempts to achieve sexual satisfaction in any form. Nevertheless, Kops and Roth are fundamentally different writers, the former being essentially a poetic lyricist and the latter a social realist. Furthermore, we should not hastily conclude that Kops has imitated, for venal or other reasons, the sensational elements of Roth's best-seller. Oedipal fixation is a long-established Kopsian theme, appearing as far back as 1956 in his first play, *The Hamlet of Stepney Green*, and the adolescent rebel in *The Dissent of Dominick Shapiro* (1966), Kops's third novel, found solace of a sort in onanistic behavior several years before *Portnoy's Complaint* was even published. . . .

By the Waters of Whitechapel is a striking creation which should bring its author—best known in this country for his autobiography, *The World Is a Wedding* (1963)—wide recognition as an important writer.

Brom Weber. *Sat.* May 2, 1970, pp. 29–30

Katz, the aging hero of Bernard Kops's latest novel [*Settle Down Simon Katz*], likes to pretend that his long deceased spouse not only listens to him but also pops into his bed from time to time. He was cast from the mould marked "lovable old reprobate"—a mould someone should have broken years ago—and true to form he makes his first appearance in a whore's bedroom, later escaping without paying for the goods. . . .

Mr. Kops's intention, it seems, was to infuse Simon's escapades with a roguish (and Jewish) good humour, presenting his hero as an anarchic, slightly reprehensible old character with just enough sadness about him to show that those who cock a snook at convention might harbour Deeper Reasons behind the bluff outlandishness. Unfortunately, the humour is not good enough. Simon is too much of a stereotype to convince, and his episodic adventures are calculated without being much inspired.

TLS. May 18, 1973, p. 545

LARKIN, PHILIP (1922–)

On its appearance in 1955, Philip Larkin's *The Less Deceived* was praised most of all for its tone and style: its irony, its lack of sentimentality, and its strict formal control recommended it as an epitome of the reaction of the 1950s against earlier poetic excess. The fashion in the novel was for the anti-hero, the Chaplinesque "little man"; Larkin's poetic persona was that of the ordinary, rather unsuccessful, man equipped with a wry, out-of-the-ordinary awareness of his limitations. This persona was emphasized by the photograph of Larkin on the sleeve of his recording of his poems (issued by The Marvell Press in 1958): as if in illustration of "Church Going," the poet stands in a grass-grown cemetery, wearing an old mackintosh and cycle-clips and propping up a pushbike, and gazes glumly at stone angels and monumental masonry.

More recently, instead of praising Larkin's manner, critics have commented adversely on his matter, more particularly on his concern with humdrum "scenes from provincial life," his wariness of commitment to love or marriage, and his pessimistic awareness of the passage of time and the decay of human hopes. They wonder how much his melancholy is conditioned by a willed narrowness of experience: the key phrases are "Little Englandism of the Left" and "lack of nobility."

Both the praise and the blame do Larkin little, or at least incomplete, justice. The publication of *The Whitsun Weddings* in 1964 and the welcome reissue in 1966 of the first of his publications, *The North Ship* (1945), provide a frame for *The Less Deceived* and enable one to see Larkin's work in a wider perspective than that provided by the poetical fashions of the fifties. That an attempt to describe his subject-matter is not premature is attested by his statement, in an interview in 1964: "I don't think I want to change, just to become better at what I am." . . .

Charles Tomlinson has spoken disparagingly of Larkin's poetry as the embodiment of "his own inadequacy" and a "tenderly-nursed sense of defeat." If there is such a sense, it springs from clear-sighted observation of the amount of sadness and disappointment in life, and the determination not to burke its expression: far from being "tenderly-nursed," it is unflinchingly admitted. And what Tomlinson sees as Larkin's personal inadequacy can surely rather be said to be the statement, not only of his own, human limitations in a deterministic universe, but of the limitations of many. To find the expression of such limitations unpalatable is not to invalidate them; and even if Larkin's ideas are open to the counter-arguments of Christian belief, that is not to deny the poet his right to put down what he honestly sees.

Larkin's own claim, expressed with characteristic moderation, is that his expressions are *not* a special case but have a general relevance. . . . Those . . . who recognize their own faces in [his] mirror will admire Larkin for his scrutiny of their daily situation, and his expression of it in language that, in blending the contemporary with the dignified tradition of elegiac poetry, raises that situation to a higher power.

Philip Gardner. *The Dalhousie Review*. Spring,
1968, pp. 88, 98–99

The case against Larkin, as I have heard it, seems to boil down to "provincialism" (Charles Tomlinson), "genteel bellyaching" (Christopher Logue), and a less truculent but rather exasperated demur that any poet so negative can be so good (A. Alvarez).

Well, he is provincial in the sense that he doesn't subscribe to the current cant that English poets can profitably learn direct lessons from what poetry is going on in Germany or France or Hungary or up the Black Mountain: poetry is, thank heaven, a long way from falling into an "international style," such as one finds in painting, sculpture, architecture and music, and such validly "international" pieces as I *have* seen (e.g. in concrete poetry) are at best peripherally elegant and at worst boring and pointless.

"Genteel bellyaching" and "negative" are really making the same objection, the first more memorably and amusingly than the second. There is a sense in which Larkin does define by negatives; I have made the point already. He is wary in front of experience, as who should not be: one doesn't put in the same set of scales Auschwitz and the realization that one is getting older, or the thermo-nuclear bomb and the sense that most love is illusory. Yet the fact that Larkin hasn't, in his poems, confronted head-on the death camps or the Bomb (or Vietnam, or Che Guevara) doesn't make him, by definition, minor. His themes— love, change, disenchantment, the mystery and inexplicableness of the past's survival and death's finality—are unshakably major. So too, I think, are the assurance of his cadences and the inevitable rightness of his language at their best. . . .

I think that Larkin's work will survive; and what may survive is his preservation of "the true voice of feeling" of a man who was representative of the mid-20th century hardly at all, except in negatives—

which is, when you come to think about it, one way in which to survive the mid-20th century.

Anthony Thwaite. In Martin Dodsworth, ed.,
The Survival of Poetry (Faber and Faber,
1970), pp. 54–55

In the 50s, Larkin, contributing to a Movement manifesto, wrote that he didn't know why most poetry had to be written. This might be the crash of a new wave, its puritanism and purism. I didn't think, though, that he was just applauding the Movement, its low-voiced insularity and lack of pretence. No style or school could have given his words their poignant severity, the music of Herbert, afflicted, amused, clear accents stiffening colloquial informality. What is technique with nothing said? We cannot do metre or speak to God as Herbert did. Larkin, like some other moderns, is particularly good at finding words for the instants of action, a person in his instant of time and place, colours that come once only.

This anthology [*The Oxford Book of Twentieth-Century English Verse*] took six years; one might dread such leisure for industry. But it's a work of salvage, almost of beachcombing. All choice is a bias; here it seems softened by impartial tolerance and unhurried care.

Robert Lowell. *Enc.* May, 1973, p. 68

● LAVIN, MARY (1912–   )

To me [Mary Lavin] seems reminiscent of the Russians more than of any other school of writers and, with the exception of the gigantic Tolstoy, her searching insight into the human heart and vivid appreciation of the beauty of the fields are worthy in my opinion to be mentioned beside their work. Often, as I read one of her tales, I find myself using superlatives, and then wondering if such praise must not necessarily be mistaken, when applied to the work of a young and quite unknown writer. And yet are not such doubts as these utterly wrongminded? For if there is no intrinsic thing in any art whatever, irrespective of its date or the name or age of the writer, how then can there be anything in good work at all? How, if we cannot recognize great work when we come across it unexpectedly, have we any right to say that even Shelley or Keats wrote well? Should we not rather say in that case: "I have been told that they wrote well"? I know people who can never tell a beautiful piece of silverwork or furniture until they have first found out the date of it. If it is over a hundred years old they think it is bound to be good, and if it is made in this century they think it is bound to be bad. Often they are right in both cases, but they have no judgment whatever and, though they are quick to find out the date of a Chippendale chair or the hallmark on a piece of old silver, and will praise their beauty immediately after doing so, nevertheless the emotions that should respond to beauty can only be awakened in them by the aid of a catalogue. That is a very sorry state to be in.

Let us therefore always praise intrinsic beauty whenever we see it, without concerning ourselves with irrelevancies, such as the age or name of Mary Lavin or how on earth she came by her astonishing insight.

Lord Dunsany. Preface to Mary Lavin, *Tales from Bective Bridge* (Boston, Little, Brown, 1942), pp. ix–x

Don't let anybody tell you that Mrs. Lavin, who was born in Massachusetts, looks upon the Irish scene with alien eyes. With this distinguished novel [*The House in Clewe Street*] she takes her place among the best writers Ireland has produced in a hundred years. . . .

As a novel, *Clewe Street* is probably too long; it runs to 530 pages. But tragedies told briefly are six for five cents in your daily newspaper. Again, time passes slowly in Trim, and how else than by a piling up of detail is a novelist to convey the sense of slowly passing days? How else, indeed, can one give power—as Mrs. Lavin certainly succeeds in doing—to what must otherwise have been a rather trivial story? . . .

I must pay tribute to Mrs. Lavin's quite exceptional talent; here is some of the finest writing that has come out of Ireland in many a year, and though there is great and laudable honesty, there is no vulgarity in this book. Other reviewers, I am aware, have thought the characters wooden, but that, I think, is a very wrong idea. I have not in years come across a portrait so appealingly true as that of Aunt Theresa. It is the case, however, that the lyrical note is strong in Mrs. Lavin's prose; and her characters, though sharply and firmly conceived, are infused with a kind of poetic intensity that carries them, I suppose, to the point of verging on abstractions; so that you can, perhaps, forget at one moment how real these people were the moment before. But you won't have any trouble of this sort, be sure of it, if you happen to have any Irish relations of your own.

David Marshall. *Com.* July 20, 1945, pp. 340–41

Miss Lavin's novel [*The House in Clewe Street*] was partially published in serial form in America as *Gabriel Galloway*: the change of
title points to the weakness of the book. If the central subject is the boy
his fortunes do not really begin to unfold until about a third of the way
through—on page 149 he is not yet quite seven: if the theme is the fortunes of the house then that drops out of the picture not much under a
third from the end. This frailty in forming the central concept, the
"What-is-this-I-am-at-exactly?" also affects our pleasure in Miss
Lavin's stories which equally charm us by their delicacy and puzzle by
their dissipation.

This may be purely a matter of a technique that is not as yet
quite surefooted, and the timing all through *The House in Clewe Street*
is possibly mainly responsible for it. Thus the death of the child's father
is given a slow treatment, although Miss Lavin agrees that the boy will
hear of this past only in gossip about lives before his own "that will
not provide any depository of experience from which he can supplement his own inexperience": whereas the death of the grandfather
occurs in a flash, although of the boy's consideration on death *that* night
she says: "Leaf by leaf, petal by petal, our impressions are laid down":
and just before that he has had a slowly-told day in the fields with a
poor neighbour's children—ending, it is true, in a graphically-pictured
mimicry about what dead people look like, but, surely, taking a
disproportionate time to get to that point, if that is the point?

The pleasure of the book, as by corollary, is that it contains a great
many separate delights; whether she is describing a girl letting out the
tucks of her dress; or swans on the river—"one had to glance at the
banks along which they passed in order to perceive that they were in
motion; nothing about their compact, calm demeanour suggested the
furious activity of webbed feet that propelled them forward": or a girl
opening her umbrella—"such gestures at once familiar and unfamiliar
pierce the heart like a shaft."

She is, however, herself alone responsible for our impatience with
her faults, natural in a first novel. Hers is a quality that demands to be
judged by the highest standards: she is, obviously, the most promising
young Irish writer of our time.

Sean O'Faolain. The Bell. April, 1946,
pp. 81–82

[*Mary O'Grady*] is a novel of motherhood which tells the story of
Mary O'Grady from the time she leaves her native Tullamore to marry
a Dublin man to the day of her death some forty years later.

Miss Lavin, a talented Irish writer with a fine knowledge of the
human heart, succeeds in making Mary O'Grady a character of depth

and dimension, yet paradoxically she fails to make this somber chronicle of a mother come fully to life. Where Mary O'Grady's story should be moving it is often monotonous, where it should be simple it frequently seems contrived, and where it should ring with rich Irish laughter it is, alas, strangely lacking in humor. Furthermore, while Mary O'Grady and, to a lesser degree, her three daughters are well realized, the men, including Tom, the husband, and the two sons, Patrick and Larry, seem blurred and fuzzy. . . .

Disappointed in her hopes for her children Mary, alone in her shabby and disordered home, finally finds peace in her memory of the love she has known and given and in her dreams of meeting her husband and children in the next world. Miss Lavin's portrait of an Irish mother has warmth, loyalty, understanding and pride. But somehow the feeling aroused by the series of tragedies which befall Mary O'Grady is one of mere sadness rather than deep compassion.

Richard Harrity. NYHT. Jan. 29, 1950, p. 10

Miss Lavin is much more of a novelist in her stories than O'Flaherty, O'Faolain, or Joyce, and her technique verges—sometimes dangerously —on the novelist's technique. That has its advantages of course. In her later stories there is an authenticity and solidity that makes the work of most Irish writers seem shadowy; not the life of the mind interrupted by occasional yells from the kitchen, but the life of the kitchen suddenly shattered by mental images of extraordinary vividness which the author tries frantically to capture before the yells begin again. The only story in which she deliberately eschews the physical world is the fable of "The Becker Wives," which she sets in a capital city that might be either Dublin or London, and among merchants whose names might be Irish or English, and, for all its brilliance and lucidity it seems to me only the ghost of a story, a Henry James fable without the excuse of James' sexual peculiarities. She has the novelist's preoccupation with logic, the logic of Time past and Time future, not so much the real short-story teller's obsession with Time present—the height from which past and present are presumed to be equally visible. Sometimes she begins her stories too far back, sometimes she carries them too far forward, rarely by more than a page or two, but already in that space the light begins to fade into the calm gray even light of the novelist.

She fascinates me more than any other of the Irish writers of my generation because more than any of them her work reveals the fact that she has not said all she has to say.

Frank O'Connor. The Lonely Voice
(Cleveland, World, 1963), pp. 211–12

It is a truth not universally acknowledged, that the short story is so subtle an art form, and at the same time so independent of its surroundings, that a reviewer does violence to any collection if he reads it straight through, as he would a novel. Only frail, meagerly developed stories profit from such an approach; the accumulative momentum, then, provides assurance from story to story that the author has really constructed a world for us. The richer and more demanding the story, the more it forces us to participate in its imaginative drama; to read too swiftly a number of stories that require us to think and feel—like Mary Lavin's superbly artistic stories—would result in exhaustion that might wrongly be attributed to the stories.

A Memory is Mary Lavin's fifteenth book, and her thirteenth collection of short stories. She has long been recognized as one of the finest of living short-story writers. Uninterested in formal experimentation, she has concentrated her genius upon certain archetypal or transpersonal experiences as they touch—sometimes with violence—fairly ordinary people. The five stories in this collection emphasize the universality of certain experiences—love, self-sacrifice, the need to relinquish the world to those who follow us—but never at the expense of the particular. Mary Lavin's ability to transcribe the physical world, especially the green damp world of rural Ireland where many of her stories are set, is as remarkable as ever. She rarely strains for metaphors, yet her prose is "poetic" in the best sense of that word; if her people talk perhaps more beautifully than might seem credible, that is what art is all about.

Joyce Carol Oates. *NYT*. Nov. 25, 1973, p. 7

LAWRENCE, D. H. (1885–1930)

I believe that this failure [to reconcile his "male" and "female" impulses] . . . was the fundamental determinant of the direction [Lawrence] took in the large enterprise of the novels. *Sons and Lovers* gave him both the knowledge and the confidence of his power as a writer, and was the fullest expression in his early work of that opposition between the spirit and the flesh which was to continue to be of prime concern to him. The opposition, of course, is a basic instance of the male and female principles, of which he was to write at length in the Hardy essay; and it was of such concern to him not only because it was externalized in the conflict between his mother and father and in his own relations with Jessie Chambers, but also because it projected a violent clash within himself.

In *The Rainbow* Lawrence made his most strenuous effort to show how the male and female principles could be reconciled both within the individual psyche and within marriage. I think that this is Lawrence's finest novel, less flawed than *Women in Love*, if not more profound; and I do not believe it is coincidental that in it he succeeded in depicting an individual who was able to achieve a full reconciliation between the two principles. It is perhaps not without significance that the individual should have been a woman, that the task, as it were, was to balance an inherently female disposition with "male" qualities. In *The Rainbow*, however, no man was found to match Ursula's achievement, and in *Women in Love*—the most remarkable of the novels in its scope —her marriage to Birkin proved to be a marriage on essentially "female" terms. In it, moreover, Birkin persuaded Ursula to withdraw with him from the "man's world," and this withdrawal, I believe, necessitated the ensuing effort to redefine the meaning of "man-being" and to explore alternative ways of effecting a return to the world of men.

This effort led to the compensatory male assertion, of which there was already some evidence in *Women in Love*, that characterized the novels of the third period, and that drove Lawrence through *Aaron's Rod* and *Kangaroo* to the cul-de-sac of *The Plumed Serpent*. These novels are the worst of Lawrence's mature work. The decline in artistic achievement, in comparison with *Women in Love*, which preceded them, is marked; and it would seem that, in trying to establish a new kind of "male" significance and to assert a desire for male domination, Lawrence wrote so badly because he was writing against his own deepest values. In *Lady Chatterley's Lover* he succeeded in giving full and vivid expression to those values and in producing a novel that is only a little inferior to *The Rainbow* and *Women in Love*. To the end, however, he could not reconcile the male and female elements in himself; and his attempt to balance the overt "female" tendency of the novel by asserting a covert "male" significance resulted in its major blemish.

> H. M. Daleski. *The Forked Flame: A Study of*
> *D. H. Lawrence* (Faber and Faber, 1965),
> pp. 310–11

The nineteenth-century vision had certainly perished in the hands of Galsworthy, Bennett and Wells. Lawrence breaks out simultaneously from the nineteenth-century aesthetic and metaphysic to new shapes and new patterns of perception, thought and feeling. But however much we talk about the originality of *The Rainbow*, an amazing and far-reaching originality, we must not lose sight of the fact that it would still be among the greatest English novels without that originality (something which could not be said for *Women in Love,* where the original elements take over almost all functions). It is a realistic novel, perhaps even, where human relationships are concerned, *the* realistic novel.

Lawrence's mature prose gives us the tangible presence, the visible aura of real life, together with his own deep perception of inner realities and subtle relationships, so that the total presentation of the courtship of Tom and Lydia, the childhood of Anna, her honeymoon, the childhood and innocence of Ursula, is more real than anything we experience in the actual world except in the rarest moments. Here Lawrence gives us the very consciousness of the unintellectual farmer, the wilful child, the pregnant woman, the adolescent girl; the very quality of living—in the fastnesses of the inviolable self, in the straining intimacies of familiar relationships, in the pressures of an authentic environment—region, class, tradition, change; above all the poignancy of the real, possible (indeed *normal*) innocence, beauty, gladness and fearful strife of love.

Keith Sagar. *The Art of D. H. Lawrence*
(Cambridge Univ. Pr., 1966), p. 71

Lawrence was obsessed with apocalypse from early youth, and he remembered the chiliastic chapel hymns of his childhood. During the war the apocalyptic coloration of his language is especially striking; sometimes it strongly recalls seventeenth-century puritanism. He considered the world to be undergoing a rapid decline which should issue in a renovation, and expected the English to have some part in this, much as Milton put the burden on God's Englishmen; Lawrence, however, dwelt more on the decadence, and seemed to think the English were rotting with especial rapidity in order to be ready. He spoke of the coming resurrection—"Except a seed die, it bringeth not forth," he advises Bertrand Russell in May, 1915. "Our death must be accomplished first, then we will rise up." "Wait only a little while"; these were the last days, the "last wave of time," he told Ottoline Morell. There would be a new age and a new ethical law.

The nature of Lawrence's pronouncements on the new age and the new ethic is such that he can very well be described as a "moral terrorist," Kant's term for historians who think that the evident corruption of the world presages an immediate appearance, in one form or another, of anti-Christ. But he was also what Kant, in the same work (*The Disputation of the Faculties*) calls an "abderitist," namely one who explains history in terms of culture-cycles. More specifically, and perhaps more recognisably, he was a Joachite.

Where Lawrence, who was to call himself Joachim in *The*

Plumed Serpent, got his Joachitism from one can only guess. A possible source is Huysmans' *Là-Bas* ("Two of the Persons of the Trinity have shown themselves. As a matter of logic, the Third must appear"). But Joachitism is a hardy plant, and as Frank E. Manuel says in *Shapes of Philosophical History*, it was particularly abundant in the literature of the French decadence and so could have formed part of that current of occultist thinking to which Lawrence was so sensitive. The doctrine varies a bit, but broadly it postulates three historical epochs, one for each person of the Trinity, with a transitional age between each. The details are argued out of texts in *Revelation*.

Frank Kermode. In C. B. Cox and A. E.
Dyson, eds., *Word in the Desert* (Oxford
Univ. Pr., 1968), pp. 16–17

The first volume of Lawrence's posthumous papers [*Phoenix*] was published thirty-two years ago, and now, with yet another volume to companion it [*Phoenix II*], this important collection has been handsomely reissued. There are no letters, poems, or plays, but otherwise the total range of Lawrence's writing is represented: articles, reviews, translations, travel sketches, stories, religious and philosophical effusions, prefaces to his own poems, autobiographical snippets, forewords and fragments, from every period and of every quality except flat.

Lawrence may weary his reader with his railing, but his work is never lifeless; he is fully there in every line, for they are cries of his, these lines, and they are as he is, and go as he goes, whether well or ill, precisely. Nowhere in these pieces does he touch bottom as he does in parts of *Kangaroo* or *The Plumed Serpent*; nowhere is he as sick as he was when he wrote "The Woman Who Rode Away"; seldom is he as silly as when he did parts of *The Fantasia of the Unconscious*, though portions of his book on Hardy are; rarely, also, did he write with such luminous and original beauty as he manages in "The Flowery Tuscany," or "The Flying Fish," or display his remarkable powers of characterization more completely than in his Preface to Maurice Magnus's *Memoirs of the Foreign Legion*, and never, I think, is he as sane and cogent in argument as in the essay, "A Propos of *Lady Chatterley's Lover*." The set is certainly superbly titled, for Lawrence lives, as the kids say; bright, burning, acrid, and smoky. . . .

Much of Lawrence's writing, it seems to me, is symptomatic speech, controlled only by his inner reality, and measurable by little else. His work cries out to the world: accept me! and sotto voce: maybe then I can accept myself. And just as Nietzsche, sick too, overwomaned, powerless to put into the world the power he knew, within, he had, was driven to work his will, instead with words; so Lawrence wrote novels, stories, essays, of challenge and revenge, composed elaborate and desperate daydreams, disposing of his problems and his friends, recreating himself, renewing his forlorn history. Still, at night he had other dreams. "I hate your love," he once shouted at Murry, "I *hate* it. You're an obscene bug, sucking my life away."

William H. Gass. NYR. Aug. 1, 1968, pp. 3–4

Lawrence's writing was guided always by his desire to break down the barriers to spontaneity and to reintegrate our submerged, fundamental selves with our overt lives. The integration and destiny of essential human identity, across centuries or generations or within single life-spans or in brief moments of vitalization, interested him more than the circumstantial and conscious developments in the lives of his characters. His art, however fully it represents objective details of historical and personal life, focuses chiefly upon the recesses of individual consciousness, where his characters encounter their generic, natural self and must make a crucial adjustment to it.

In writing to remind people of their fundamental identity—"we never know that we ourselves are anything"—Lawrence's stance is sometimes prophetic and visionary with apocalyptic utterances, but he is almost always hortatory to some degree, as even his letters illustrate. He felt that art could serve man's urgent need to reclaim his essential being. The integration of character which Lawrence understood as necessary could come about through freeing our emotions from the tangle and oppression of our rational thought. Apart from the possibly restorative powers of passional experience, as in sexual intercourse or deeply felt encounters with death, only the strong feelings of an aesthetic response can renew man's awareness of his sensual identity and direct him toward acceptance of his whole self.

Literature and painting, the arts which Lawrence practiced and wrote about, have a corrective moral effect; by reviving the individual's capacity for direct, pre-mental responses, great art works can tear a hole in the curtain of mental consciousness and alter the way men recognize their lives thereafter. No protagonist in Lawrence's fiction has his sensuality revivified by reading a good book or attending an exhibition, but Lawrence assumed that his readers might profit from opportunities that his characters go without. The novel particularly, Lawrence came to feel, "can inform and lead into new places the flow of our sympathetic consciousness, and it can lead our sympathy away in recoil from things gone dead."

David Cavitch. D. H. Lawrence and the New World (N.Y., Oxford Univ. Pr., 1969),
pp. 5–6

Perhaps a major reason for the prolonged neglect of Lawrence's verse is that while his theory of the novel falls within a definable and acceptable tradition, his view of poetry was the exception rather than the rule in the earlier part of this century. He himself was well aware that as a poetic theorist he consistently opposed contemporary critical opinion and, to a lesser extent, prevailing poetic practice. For one thing, his view of a poem as a pure act of attention, an act of absolute surrender to the visionary image, was very much at odds with the emerging belief of critics—and of many influential poets—that the essential qualities of poetry are irony, ambiguity, and paradox.

The faith of the first half of the twentieth century, at least in England, America, and France, was in double vision. In fact, Lawrence's definition of the novel as "the highest example of subtle interrelatedness that man has discovered" would come close to Eliot's or Empson's definitions of poetry. Lawrence's definition of poetry, on the other hand, implies a kind of whole or single vision. While he never rejected irony, ambiguity, and paradox as literary techniques, he did not regard them as essential, especially not in poetry. For him, poetry, unlike the novel, did not involve elaborated relationships. On the contrary, he believed that its essence was single rather than double vision or, as he put it, "naiveté." For the act of attention was not only an act of intensity but, more important, an act of "the intrinsic naiveté without which no poetry can exist, not even the most sophisticated. . . .

Lawrence's poet of naiveté, then, consciously choosing the path of visionary awareness, must be "sufficiently sophisticated to wring the neck of sophistication." He must be anti-formal and anti-traditional, as well as anti-ironic, not out of ignorance or literary incapacity—two faults of which Lawrence himself has often been accused—but because he deliberately chooses to go beyond or beneath technique to the naiveté at the heart of the artistic impulse.

Sandra M. Gilbert. *Acts of Attention: The Poems of D. H. Lawrence* (Ithaca, N.Y., Cornell Univ. Pr., 1972), pp. 9–11

Lady Chatterley is back.

Her reappearance calls for a bit of history. Between 1925 and 1928, D. H. Lawrence wrote three versions of a novel; and in the last year published the third of these in Europe as *Lady Chatterley's Lover*. No publisher in the English-speaking world dared touch it. Copies shipped to England and America were seized by customs officers who, Lawrence suspected, were selling them on the sly for a tidy profit.

The book was also pirated. This prompted Lawrence to write "My Skirmish with Jolly Roger," later expanded into "A Propos of *Lady*

Chatterley's Lover," a vigorous defense of his approach to the erotic and of what he considered his therapeutic use of four-letter words.

Lady Chatterley's Lover was at last published in the United States in 1959 and was victorious in courtroom battles against those who tried to suppress it. Similarly the earliest draft of the novel, in 1942, brought out as *The First Lady Chatterley*, had won its right to be heard.

Now we have the second version, which has previously appeared only in Italian translation. The present American and English publishers have used the title *John Thomas and Lady Jane* because Lawrence had once intended to give that name to his book, in reference to the male and female sex organs. As so often, his attitude in this matter was both serious and mischievous. . . .

Those of us who have liked *Lady Chatterley's Lover* with reservations may find ourselves preferring *John Thomas and Lady Jane* and may wonder why Lawrence went beyond it, making various additions and subtractions. But not every reader will favor the second version, though it seems to me that in most ways it presents the story more intensely, in general more satisfactorily, and that the characters in it are at once more believable and more vital.

Harry T. Moore. *NYT*. Aug. 27, 1972, p. 7

LEAVIS, F. R. (1895–   )

That F. R. Leavis is a first-rate critical personality is certain, but that is by no means the same thing as saying that he is a first-rate literary critic. No doubt he has at times achieved that stature; at other times not at all. I am here primarily concerned with him as a critic, not with his reputation as a formidable teacher, nor with his educational theories, nor with his standing as the charismatic head of the sectarian *Scrutiny* group, consisting in the later years of that periodical mostly of epigones who have for some years now acquired positions of influence in the British schools. In the America of the late 1940s and early 1950s the "new critics" tried to annex him by gratuitously referring to him as one of their own, a comrade-in-arms. That was a mistaken assessment, if not something worse.

Actually, the peculiar combination of formalism and traditionalist ideology (*à la* Eliot), characteristic of the "new criticism," has always been foreign to Leavis. He has never committed himself to any kind of religiosity (covert or overt) and he has explicitly repudiated the formalist position. . . . Happily, their dominance of the American literary scene in the immediate postwar period is a thing of the past now and virtually forgotten; and my aim in recalling them in this discussion of Leavis is simply to set the record straight.

What I chiefly like about Leavis's work are its Johnsonian qualities: the robustness, the firmness, the downrightness. He is not one to beat around the bush, to play the diplomat, to cultivate ambiguity, or to shun controversy. A critic in the Arnoldian tradition, he aspires, in his own words, "to the highest critical standards and the observance of the most scrupulous critical discipline"—an admirable aspiration in the attainment of which, however, he has, to my mind, failed quite as often as he has succeeded. For he is plagued by all the defects of his virtues. What I have in mind is not his plain speaking, of course, but rather the *esprit de sérieux* animating many of his critical pronouncements. It expresses itself in a kind of provincial moralism (by no means to be equated with the "marked moral intensity" he so esteems in his literary preferences), a protestant narrowness of sensibility, basically puritan, resulting in what seems to me the thoroughly unjustified rejection of Flaubert, Joyce, and other important literary artists of the modern line, a tendency to elevate "English studies" to the status of a major force in the shaping of culture if not of society itself, and his endless and tiresome fulminations against Bloomsbury, the "London literary establishment," the "system of personal and institutional relations" that appears to him to dominate the British literary world and to obstruct the free play of the critical mind. . . .

Philip Rahv. *NYR*. Sept. 26, 1968, p. 62

The question of what social conditions most make for the strengthening, enriching, and fructifying of the psyche is not a new one, of course: it was Carlyle's question, Ruskin's question, Morris' question, Chesterton's question, Lawrence's question; and it was one of the questions too, though far less confidently answered, of Cooper, Hawthorne, Thoreau, Melville, and Twain. And if one were to say that Leavis in certain places points one toward the conclusion that in principle the best conditions are those which permit not only a wide range of intelligently ordered experience for the individual but also the participation of a wide variety of people in a common culture, one might not seem to be saying very much. . . .

Of course, T. S. Eliot's remarks about the dissociation of sensibility preceded Leavis' first significant publications by a number of years. But of course, too, if we *are* so conscious of these matters it is in part owing precisely to Leavis and *Scrutiny*; and in fact Leavis was engaged in something significantly new even where the dissociation of sensibility was concerned. For what he did was not only to go much further, *qua* literary critic, into the complexities of individual consciousnesses than did the social commentators I mentioned. He also diagnosed much more fully than Eliot a kind of cultural and psychological splitting that still goes on today. He drew attention to the losses involved not only in the actual disintegrating of, but in the averting of polite eyes and minds from, the sort of culture to be found in Bunyan—an averting, in fact, in which the very use of the term "culture" at all in such a connection seemed inappropriate.

He pointed likewise to the losses attendant on the post-Jonsonian tendency to think of the "classical" in terms of forms, rules, and decorums rather than of psychologically enriched and strengthened modes of being. And he bore down upon the yearning to escape into worlds that were idiosyncratic and arbitrary (whatever use might be made in them of ostensibly familiar classical or religious materials) and removed, both in action and language, from that "common" world to which *The Pilgrim's Progress, Macbeth,* "The Good-Morrow," and "An Horatian Ode" all belonged—and to which, manifestly, *Paradise Lost* and *The Faerie Queene* didn't belong. And a major part of his thrust where later literature is concerned—indeed, perhaps *the* major thrust—seems to me to have been toward illuminating those writers who in one way or another were aware of a related impoverishment in their own culture and psyches and were trying to correct it.

John Fraser. *SoR.* Autumn, 1971, pp. 969–71

LESSING, DORIS (1919–   )

The Four-Gated City is bulkier by far than any one of the four preceding novels in the series known as *Children of Violence* (*Martha Quest,* 1952; *A Proper Marriage,* 1954; *A Ripple from the Storm,* 1958; *Landlocked,* 1965). Like them, it is a chronicle of change, a *Bildungsroman* of character and history. Unlike them, it charts not only a decade and a half of the recent past (the previous four volumes together cover about two earlier decades) but moves on to view the apocalyptic years that will conclude this century. It is thus not only narrative and history but a stab at prophecy as well. For that reason and one other, *The Four-Gated City* is more important than its four predecessors.

The other reason has to do with turning a corner into mostly uncharted regions. Here, the concluding novel reminds me of *The Golden Notebook*, published in 1962 and generally considered to be the best of Lessing. As in that book, the immediate scene is England in the fifties. In both novels, the heroines move toward a descent into madness and then release from it, though the terms and values of the experiences differ significantly.

As in *The Golden Notebook*, mental breakdowns of all kinds are, in part, a response to the politics of the West, the bureaucratization, the incipient fascism, the irrational violence, and to the dehumanized, progaganda- and drug-addicted culture we live in. But for Mrs. Lessing in 1969, madness is not merely a debilitating affliction or an escape, or even a novelist's tool. Developing particular forms of what Western man calls "madness" may be the only way out of his afflicted culture. Can anything—any persons or organizations—Mrs. Lessing asks in this novel, call halt to the inevitable destruction to come, given the growth and movement about the earth of mad machines, on the one hand, and the lack of internal human commonsensical and moral controls, on the other? Her answer is unequivocally No. Our dulled apathy to the condition of daily life and to the cries of war signals what Robert Bly has called "the deep longing for death," a suicidal rush to annihilation, as though the half-drugged of us were longing for total immolation, for the relief of the end. Mrs. Lessing, on the contrary, envisions a struggle toward life, through the use of extraordinary sensory powers by intelligence and a moral consciousness.

Florence Howe. *Nation*. Aug. 11, 1969,
pp. 116–17

To read a great deal of Doris Lessing over a short span of time is to feel that the original hound of heaven has commandeered the attic. She holds the mind's other guests in ardent contempt. She appears for meals only to dismiss the household's own preoccupations with writing well as decadent. For more than twenty years now she has been registering, in a torrent of fiction that increasingly seems conceived in a stubborn rage against the very idea of fiction, every tremor along her emotional fault system, every slippage in her self-education. *Look here*, she is forever demanding, a missionary devoid of any but the most didactic irony: *the Communist party is not the answer. There is a life beyond vaginal orgasm. St. John of the Cross was not as dotty as certain Anglicans would have had you believe.* She comes hard to ideas, and, once she has collared one, worries it with Victorian doggedness.

That she is a writer of considerable native power, a "natural" writer in the Dreiserian mold, someone who can close her eyes and "give" a situation by the sheer force of her emotional energy, seems almost a stain on her conscience. She views her real gift for fiction much as she views her own biology, another trick to entrap her. She does not want to "write well." Her leaden disregard for even the simplest rhythms of language, her arrogantly bad ear for dialogue—all of that is beside her own point. More and more Mrs. Lessing writes exclusively in the service of immediate cosmic reform: she wants to write, as the writer Anna in *The Golden Notebook* wanted to write, only to "create a new way of looking at life."

Her new novel, *Briefing for a Descent into Hell*, is entirely a novel of "ideas," not a novel about the play of ideas in the lives of certain characters but a novel in which the characters exist only as markers in the presentation of an idea. . . .

So pronounced is [the protagonist Charles Watkins's] acumen about the inner reality of those around him that much of the time *Briefing for a Descent into Hell* reads like a selective case study from an R. D. Laing book. The reality Charles Watkins describes is familiar to anyone who has ever had a high fever, or been exhausted to the point of breaking, or is just on the whole only marginally engaged in the dailiness of life. He experiences the loss of ego, the apprehension of the cellular nature of all matter, the "oneness" of things that seems always to lie just past the edge of controlled conscious thought. He hallucinates, or "remembers," the nature of the universe. He "remembers"—or is on the verge of remembering, before electro-shock obliterates the memory and returns him to "sanity"—something very like a "briefing" for life on earth.

The details of this briefing are filled in by Mrs. Lessing, only too relieved to abandon the strain of creating character and slip into her own rather more exhortative voice.

Joan Didion. *NYT*. March 14, 1971, p. 1

The most considerable single work by an English author in the 1960s has been done by Doris Lessing, in *The Golden Notebook* (1962). It is a carefully organized but verbose, almost clumsily-written novel, and if we were to view it solely as an aesthetic experience, we might lose most of its force. The book's strength lies not in its arrangement of the several notebooks which make up its narrative and certainly not in the purely literary quality of the writing, but in the wide range of Mrs. Lessing's interests, and, more specifically, in her attempt to write honestly about women. To be honest about women in the sixties is, for Mrs. Lessing, tantamount to a severe moral commitment, indeed almost a religious function, in some ways a corollary of her political fervor in the fifties.

While the English novel has not lacked female novelists, few indeed—including Virginia Woolf—have tried to indicate what it is like to be a woman: that is, the sense of being an object or thing even in societies whose values are relatively gentle. For her portraits, Mrs. Lessing has adopted, indirectly, the rather unlikely form of the descent into hell, a mythical pattern characterized by her female protagonists in their relationships with men, an excellent metaphor for dislocation and fragmentation in the sixties. Like Persephone, her women emerge periodically from the underworld to tell us what went awry—and it is usually sex. Within each woman who tries to survive beyond the traditional protection of housewife and mother, there exists a bomb which explodes whenever she tries to live without men, as well as when she attempts to live with them. Her dilemma is her personal bomb.

Frederick R. Karl. *CL*. Winter, 1972, p. 15

Doris Lessing is a prophet who prophesies the end of the world. She is much read but not perhaps much heeded, for there is very little that can be done, in her view, to avert catastrophe. Why, then, does she continue to write for a posterity that does not exist? Because, she says, we must continue to write and live *as if*. She is used by now to living on the edge of destruction, though her conception of it has changed over the years: now she foresees a world polluted and ruined by nerve gas and fallout, with England "poisoned, looking like a dead mouse in a corner, injected with a deathly glittering dew," whereas she used to foresee revolution. One of her characters, contemplating her miserable marriage in the war years, comforts herself in these terms: "I'm caught for life, she thought: but the words, 'for life,' released her from anxiety. They all of them saw the future as something short and violent. Somewhere just before them was a dark gulf or chasm, into which they must all disappear. A communist is a dead man on leave, she thought." And that is how she continues to write, though no longer a communist: a dead man on leave.

If her prophecies are listened to, it is with helplessness. Her literary prestige in England could not be higher, though she cares little for the literary world. She also has real readers. She is the kind of writer who changes people's lives: her novel *The Golden Notebook* has been described as "the Bible of the young," and although I don't think she'd care much for the portentousness of the phrase, it certainly catches the feeling of converted emotion that she arouses.

Margaret Drabble. *Ramparts*. Feb., 1972, p. 50

One of the great rewards of reading Doris Lessing's novels has always been a sense of sharing with the writer herself the experience of growing older, of discovering new ideas and questioning old values. This is not merely to say that, in her best-known and most substantial books (the Martha Quest series and *The Golden Notebook*) Mrs. Lessing has given us an unforgettable account of her generation's involvement in world violence and a good deal of insight into her own writing experience; it is her peculiar gift to write with the kind of honesty and generosity that suggest to the reader he is privileged to be a friend, to feel he knows something of the true ideals, the private agonies and delights, that have inspired her writing. And, like any real friendship, this appreciation is more acute where those ideals are shared and the brave spirit of inquiry and challenge that Mrs. Lessing's work always shows seems to the reader in itself a wholly admirable thing.

Although a collection of short stories is not normally the form in which one finds integrated self-revelation, Mrs. Lessing's new volume [*The Story of a Non-Marrying Man*] is quintessentially part of her sharing of experience, a marvellous scrapbook of old and new memories and discoveries. Whether she is simply describing, in three short vignettes of solitary walks round Regent's Park, how a moorhen's nesting or the falling leaves seemed heavy with meaning and the images infinitely precious; or chronicling the bizarre chance that led a Rhodesian post-office clerk of thirty years ago into political prominence; or accompanying old Hetty Pennefather and her cat with their pramful of rags to a derelict's death in Hampstead; or imagining the reactions of interplanetary reconnaissance officers to a pop group in Cornwall—without obtruding, she leaves us in no doubt what, for her, gave a particular experience its paradoxical, often bitter, significance.

TLS. Sept. 22, 1972, p. 1087

More than most of the writers concerned with the emancipated woman in the complex modern world—Mary McCarthy and Simone de Beauvoir readily come to mind—Mrs. Lessing is not content merely to bemoan the pressures of the world that can affect a woman's personal evaluation of herself, nor to describe as completely sterile whatever "personal relations" she may have. Rather, Mrs. Lessing, in all her fiction but especially in *The Golden Notebook* (1962), clearly advocates a personal commitment on the part of the individual which will enable that individual to relate meaningfully to others and to the world. And although this commitment can take various forms for various humans, it frequently becomes an allegiance to or enthusiasm for the struggles for racial freedom and integrity; political, usually Communist, affiliation and activity; love and/or marriage; and, ultimately the most important of all, the creative act of reading and writing as means of achieving the most lasting and significant commitment of all, commitment to personal freedom.

> Paul Schlueter. *The Novels of Doris Lessing*
> (Carbondale, Southern Illinois Univ. Pr.,
> 1973), p. 2

Doris Lessing's relation to the women's movement, especially in America, has been an awkward one. After reading her novels, many radical feminists wanted to appoint her their wise-woman, but she has resisted this honor. The serious, intense crowds who welcomed Mrs. Lessing on her last trip to New York were disappointed and even angry to hear her say that *The Golden Notebook* was not about or in favor of war between the sexes. In fact, she also explained later in print, "the essence of the book" was "that we must not divide things off, must not compartmentalize." Moreover, though she supported Women's Liberation, she didn't believe it would have much effect. . . . Yet while making such discouraging, even patronizing, statements, Doris Lessing goes on writing novels and stories that seem to speak directly to and about women's liberation, at least in the lower-case sense. . . .

The intelligent middle-class housewife whose children have grown up and whose husband is tired of her is a staple of recent fiction (and life), but she has never been described better than in *The Summer before the Dark*. The movement of the book takes Kate Brown, age forty-five, from a last moment of domestic security, or blindness—afternoon tea on a suburban lawn—through a series of changes and crises that alter her perception of herself and the world. . . .

The Summer before the Dark, part of which has already appeared in *Ms.*, is sure to be read by liberated and slave women all over the world. And to judge by the attitudes of my own not very radical rap group, which is already lining up for my copy, they will read it like a prophetic book, to find out, first, How it really is, and second, What to do about it. If Doris Lessing tells them that nothing can be done, the slaves will be sourly satisfied; the rest, bitterly disapppointed.

> Alison Lurie. *NYR*. June 14, 1973, pp. 18–19

Doris Lessing, whose position as one of the major women writers of the twentieth century would now seem assured, stands quite apart from the feminine tradition of sensibility. Her fiction is tough, clumsy, rational, concerned with social roles, collective action and conscience, and unconcerned with niceties of style and subtlety of feeling for its own sake. She is, nevertheless, fully aware of the bifurcation between sense and sensibility and the meaning it presents to women, and it is with an awareness of the terms that she makes her choice. In the preface to *African Stories* she writes, "*The Pig* and *The Trinket Box* are two of my earliest. I see them as two forks of a road. The second— intense, careful, self-conscious, mannered—could have led to a kind of writing usually described as 'feminine.' The style of *The Pig* is straight, broad, direct; is much less beguiling, but is the highway to the kind of writing that has the freedom to develop as it likes." The latter part of this statement is ambiguous enough; suffice it to mean that Lessing finds her freedom in a realm apart from the traditional feminine resource of sensibility.

Lynn Sukenick. CL. Autumn, 1973, p. 516

LEWIS, C. S. (1898–1963)

Most of us modern Christians are poor weak creatures, and tend to be over-conscious of two thousand years being a very long time; even if we have not been trained in scientific thinking we have unconsciously absorbed some of the half-baked and one-sided thinking that floats uneasily around in this most unhappy age, and we tend to see Christ as pictured and static and *past*. I do not believe that Lewis was thus hampered. I believe that his reading in medieval literature and his painfully-acquired faith conspired to give him a personal feeling for Christ and an intellectual conception of His immediacy that was exceedingly strong; it would be a commonplace, to Lewis, to conceive of Christ under the likeness of a Lion, a Lamb, a Fish. In the interplanetary stories he dares to give Him another name—*Maledil*. . . .

Thinking it out, I was no longer shocked by the symbol of Christ as a mightly golden Lion, combining majesty and tender fatherly comfort. It is a child's picture, this dazzling golden heraldic Beast on fire with Divine Love that yet can be nestled up to, and perhaps the true shock comes from picturing the contrast between the enormous creature's power and its gentleness when it calls the child "dear heart."

This is very bold. Its boldness makes that of some contemporary writers look inept. Yet I confess that I do not altogether *like* it, and it could be argued that the tremendousness of the allegory mars the tale [*The Last Battle*]. I imagine the accusation would pass Lewis by completely. He would not have thought that it mattered.

Mr. Leavis, the critic, has rebuked readers and other critics for crediting writers with possessing genius because they can "make a world," and none of us like to be rebuked. Still, I feel that we shall continue to credit writers thus, and perhaps we may remind our mentor that it is not every writer who *can* create a world.

C. S. Lewis did, a beautiful and dangerous world lit by hope. I suppose that in his imaginative writing he might be accused of ignoring the travails and discoveries and ethos of the contemporary scene. In my opinion at least, it is all, as an imaginative writer, that he can be accused of.

Stella Gibbons. In Jocelyn Gibb, ed., *Light on C. S. Lewis* (N.Y., Harcourt, Brace, 1965), pp. 100–101

The use of the Augustinian City . . . shows Lewis' distrust of the science-oriented civilization in which he finds himself, and it is his essential concern with his own age, as well as his urgency, which separates him most sharply from Charles Williams. For if Williams often reaches and maintains mystical heights of vision into the life of things beyond the reach of Lewis (and this may be, remember, at least partly a matter of style), Lewis possesses an immediacy and a kind of evangelical demandingness that Williams lacks. Oversimplifying the matter vastly, one might say that while it is certain that Lewis has brought many converts to the confirmation classes of the Church of England (and presumably other churches as well), it is not at all certain that Williams' writings generally work towards a similar result. I expect that it is possible to be tremendously stimulated by Williams' thought without feeling the necessity or even the compunction of committing oneself to any sort of religious action.

To read Lewis, on the other hand, is to be constantly moved to action by the urgency and immediacy of his tone. Lewis' ideas are less complex (though no less profound) than Williams', and their simpler forms and phrasings cannot help stimulating the faith, and the right intellect, of the reader. It is thus not difficult to see Lewis as another Augustine, fighting a modern Pelagianism which, like its progenitor, feels that man somehow may do without grace and may eventually succeed to the throne of the universe. And like Augustine, Lewis turns quite naturally to the image of a City in order to frame and clarify his position.

Charles Moorman. *The Precincts of Felicity: The Augustinian City of the Oxford Christians* (Gainesville, Univ. of Florida Pr., 1966), p. 83

Even by the standards of fiction, Lewis's religious writings are his greatest because their character and their story are the greatest. His religious achievement finds a surprising parallel, I believe, in Kierkegaard: surprising because Lewis is far too objective and rationalistic to be labeled an "existentialist," but parallel for a number of reasons.

First among them is the fact that Lewis, like Kierkegaard, lived and wrote according to the maxim "purity of heart is to will one thing"; and that "one thing" was "mere Christianity" for Lewis as it was for Kierkegaard. Like Kierkegaard, Lewis disdained the Hegelian attempt to "go beyond" Christianity and to relativize it. The paradoxical result is that the apparently narrower, "mere" Christianity turns out to be so large as to be ubiquitous. Lewis need not venture out of it into more inclusive realms because he finds it inclusive of other realms. . . .

What Christian makes Christianity more morally compelling, more imaginatively moving, *and* more rationally convincing? Having many strings to his bow improves the tone of each one: professional preaching, for example, is nearly always bad preaching. And because of Lewis's unprofessional, many-sided excellence he is one of the few religious writers who is read by lowbrows and highbrows, poets and philosophers, conservatives and liberals, Catholics and Protestants, Christians and non-Christians. Though many communicate to a larger audience, few communicate to a more diversified one.

Modern man's crisis, all seem agreed, is one of disintegration, of alienation. He has split his own being, having split it from its source and center; and he finds his reason detached from his heart, the sciences from the humanities, analytic philosophy from existential philosophy (the navigators have crossed the Channel and forgotten to take their ship), producing more and more men who are either computers or psychedelomaniacs. Lewis's romantic rationalism shows that the two mental hemispheres *can* coexist happily and fruitfully in one man and one philosophy.

I am sure Lewis himself would insist that his most important single achievement is his *least* original: his re-presentation of "mere Christianity" to an age so eager to build contemporary Christianities that it seems bored with the foundation of the buildings. In an age of religious mixed drinks, Lewis takes his straight; he opposes "Christianity-and-water." In an age of religious pioneers and frontier Christians, Lewis is the most intelligent and imaginative tender of the home front, and nearly the only refutation of the gibe that a twentieth-century Christian can be honest, or intelligent, or orthodox, or any two of the three, but not all three.

Peter Kreeft. *C. S. Lewis* (Grand Rapids,
Mich., Eerdmans, 1969), pp. 40–41

LEWIS, (PERCY) WYNDHAM (1886–1957)

Lewis' effort to imagine, to invent, to look beyond and make up a story about Man is of more compelling interest than biographical speculations about what the author really believed in his last years. So far as anyone knows, he did not become a Catholic; neither does his hero, James Pullman. For our purposes, what Lewis believed is in the pages of *The Human Age*; and perhaps all they tell us is that the impulse, the gesture, is directed out from the self in an effort at inclusive sympathy and awe—as much as any one might demand of a novelist.

Despite his wishes, it is unlikely that he will be remembered for *The Human Age* more than for his other books; and we may take the Tolstoyan discounting of earlier work not as a final attempt at repentance, but as the inflection of a truly creative artist so engaged in making one more raid on the inarticulate that nothing finished and in the past mattered very much. Lewis died before his most ambitious literary flight—to heaven itself—was completed; yet the book, like his career as a whole, seems anything but unfinished.

William Pritchard. *Wyndham Lewis*
(N.Y., Twayne, 1968), pp. 164–65

There is a contradiction inherent in these three novels [*Snooty Baronet, The Revenge for Love, The Vulgar Streak*] which is not present, or is much less obvious, in Lewis's more plainly satirical or allegorical fiction. All of them are essentially critiques of meaningless, mindless "action" which, as he said over and over, causes human suffering and unhappiness and, in its drive towards the application of totally destructive energy, is also the enemy of art, which is something permanent and hieratic. We are confronted, however, by the inescapable fact that the novels are the work of a man fascinated by the violence he condemns, and that scenes like those in which Snooty shoots Humph or Victor and Margot make their drive to death are at the heart of the books in which they occur. It could even be said that Lewis's style, ejaculatory, assertive, loaded with images and jokes, is an embodiment of action, and certainly it is active rather than passive like the styles of most novelists.

Similar contradictions often appear in the social or philosophical books, which are never all of a piece or totally systematic, but where they are damaging to the argument of such a book as *The Art of Being Ruled* they add richness and depth to the novels. His achievement in them rests precisely in the writer's involvement with the action he describes, joined to the capacity to stand aside and comment on it. The effect is rather as though *A Passage to India*, say, had not been written by a gentle liberal but by a man passionately dedicated to Imperial superiority who was nevertheless aware that all the arguments advanced in its favour were wrong.

George Orwell said that Lewis, while able to put ideas into a single work of fiction that would have served other writers for half a dozen books, lacked nevertheless some basic ingredient of a novelist. The remark is shrewd, but it does not really apply to these books of the Thirties in which Lewis tried to work within the ordinary conventions of a novel. *The Vulgar Streak* is a failure, although one more valuable than the successes of lesser writers, but *Snooty Baronet* is unique in its blend of comedy and philosophical argument (the comedy itself was not inimitable—the Samuel Butler manner adopted by Snooty when visiting Val finds its echo in the faces pulled by Lucky Jim Dixon and perhaps has influenced the Angus Wilson of *No Laughing Matter*), and *The Revenge for Love* in its scope, its satirical energy and its quite unliberal reluctant humanism, is Lewis's finest achievement in fiction and one of the few great novels of the twentieth century.

Julian Symons. Agenda. Autumn–Winter,
1969–70, pp. 47–48

The Roaring Queen has the role of a farcical footnote to [*The Apes of God*], a footnote in which he takes satirical swipes at the trends in literature and society that he disapproves of, the cults of the detective novel, the tough Western, the homosexual novel, the youth cult, the Negro cult. All are summarily parodied; as too is the form of the novel itself, which is the Peacockian novel of Aldous Huxley.

As a novel, *The Roaring Queen* obviously has no great distinction. It is a *jeu d'esprit*, a squib, but it is authentic Lewis, and only he could have written it. It goes along at a spanking pace and it is very funny, not only as a cartoon of the book world of the day but, more precisely, as a caricature of one of its most famous inhabitants. Shodbutt is in character throughout, and in his rendering of him Lewis reaches considerable comic heights.

Walter Allen. Intro. to Wyndham Lewis, The
Roaring Queen (Secker & Warburg, 1973),
pp. 12–13

Lewis's work can be read as a defence of Western Man against the forces of the anti-Enlightenment which, he felt, so many of his contemporaries espoused. Were Lewis alive today he would find the post-Beckettian withdrawal into a near solipsistic silence as inimical as were the consciously "irrational" extravagances of Dada or the atavistic primitivism of Lawrence. Much of what Lewis detested and opposed has, in fact, come to full flower in the post-Modernist era: "random authors" like Brion Gysin and William Burroughs, who believe that "to speak is to lie" and who exalt the psychedelic *objet trouvé* into an art-form, represent a realization of the Bailiff's worst literary excesses. Jean Genet's submissive cry (in *Our Lady of the Flowers*) epitomizes one aspect of this philosophy of abandonment: "The only way to avoid the horror of horror is to give in to it." One might take all of Lewis's work as an attempt to face up to existence—horror and all—and to create meaning, discover values, in the phenomenal chaos: one must *never* give in to it.

As a satirist, Lewis is in the tradition of Pope and Swift; he is, indeed, the only satirist of modern times who can stand the comparison with these Augustans. Like them, Lewis attacked individuals as well as vices, and his most memorable satiric fictions are those—like *The Childermass, The Apes of God* and *The Revenge for Love*—in which he sets up satiric victims and then, with imaginative viciousness, proceeds to destroy them. Alongside this demolition work runs a strong sense of the satirist's duty to society. Lewis would have agreed with Shaw that "the salvation of the world depends on the men who will not take evil good-humouredly, and whose laughter destroys the fool instead of encouraging him." Lewis's "Enemy" attitude carried over into life the traditional *persona* of the satirist. . . .

In addition to the castigation of the especially wicked or the peculiarly foolish, satire was for Lewis a way of looking at humanity. Man, that animal with the word-habit, was an endless source of fascination, and man's self-pride was an endless source of satirical material. From *The Wild Body* to *Rotting Hill*, Lewis sardonically presents both individual psychologies and group dynamics for our instruction, delight and scorn.

Robert T. Chapman. *Wyndham Lewis:*
Fictions and Satires (Vision, 1973),
pp. 184–85

● LIVINGS, HENRY (1929–   )

Stop It, Whoever You Are has proved one of the most controversial of recent additions to the new drama—as far as the critics are concerned at least; some found it both profound and riotously funny, others determinedly found it neither. It is certainly uneven, and still rather undisciplined, but at least it implies a powerful individuality at work, and as it progresses it gradually gathers a wealth of subsidiary meanings without ever (and herein lies the author's artfulness) departing from the farcical tone in which it began, so that by the time we reach its extraordinary final scene we suddenly discover that the apparently simple artless North Country farce has taken on the force and intensity of a parable. . . .

Big Soft Nellie carries Livings's characteristic disregard of normal plotting much farther than *Stop It, Whoever You Are*; indeed, in it there is virtually no plot whatever, only a series of incidents in the back room of an electrical appliances shop. . . . In this play, plot being reduced to the absolute minimum, we can study Livings's individual techniques in their purest state. Basically, like so many of the new dramatists, he seeks just to show people together, interacting, existing. He carries his interest in this—at the expense of normal dramatic construction—far further than most, however, and in this play comes perhaps closest to an otherwise very different dramatist, Ann Jellicoe. Like her, he writes in terms of a total stage action rather than simply in words; much of what his characters say is merely a gloss on what is happening, and often an apparently completely random exchange in a sequence of *non sequiturs* makes sense only when we see the actors together and understand the relationship between them at that particular point. . . .

John Russell Taylor. The Angry Theatre
(N.Y., Hill and Wang, 1962), pp. 130, 133–34

According to the National Theatre's programme notes for *Hay Fever,* Noël Coward has influenced many unlikely playwrights, including Harold Pinter. Would that his breath had, however fleetingly, prickled the back of Henry Livings's neck. Mr. Livings has achieved fame on slimmer grounds than any other playwright in the history of Western theatre. *Stop It*, etc., had some good, rowdy humour, the usual enigmatic characterization laced with kookie insights, and that insubstantial vagrancy ("action or fact of wandering or digressing in mind, opinion, thought, etc." O.E.D.) which distinguishes his work. *Nil Carborundum* was as tenuous as a play can get without disappearing into air, into thin air. And now comes *Eh?*, so thin and so tedious an entertainment that one wonders how it passed the scrutineers of the usually exacting Royal Shakespeare Company.

Livings usually has at the core of his play an amiable, feckless, anarchic nonconformist who drives conventional persons dotty. This idea, through over-use, has in these vintage years of cinematic and theatrical rebels lost so much of its original force that it is badly in need of a rest. His hero does not claim our attention strongly enough: mildly amusing, moderately charming, but long before the explosive ending, a bore. He is not in his individuality individual enough to stand our hair on end; he is not in his unorthodoxy really radical enough to disturb. He is wet. Mr. Livings has sent this boy on the man's errand of rousing our delight in ragged individualism, stirring scorn for all authority. The character as created is not interesting enough to carry this burden and the play, grinding dully on and on, makes one long for the huge, fake boiler which dominates the stage to explode in reality and wipe all the guilty collaborators off the boards once and for all.

Aggression, as you can see, is unleashed by prolonged exposure to Henry Livings, and as this usually means that one has been somehow stirred in spite of oneself I have tried to analyse the reason for my hostility and find, I think, it has sprung from impatience, an impatience amounting to exasperation. *Encore* has reminded us that the serious theatre has been latterly more concerned with "essence" than with "events". In dispensing with narrative, however, our playwrights must really squeeze and squeeze until the essence of their chosen characters or situation has been extruded. *Eh?* does not squeeze enough; it achieves no illuminating analysis of why and how non-conformists and conformists in a society create pressure upon each other. We know little more of the protagonist at the end than we knew before the boiler began to throb.

Alan Seymour. L. Jan., 1965, p. 70

[*Eh?*] reflects the avant-garde tendency toward desultory movement or faint progression of scene fragments in lieu of tightly knit plots to be found in advanced English as well as the American theatre today, very much as it was present forty or more years ago in the frantic pace and verbal explosions of German expressionism in the manner of Kaiser's *The Coral* and *Gas* and Toller's *Masse-Mensch*. In *Eh?* this tendency appeared quietly and unhurriedly rather than very noisily and rapidly in the distinctly more dynamic American experiment *Viet Rock*.

Nevertheless the agglomeration of mere particles of plot and idea was the main feature of this British satire on the debilitation of man by modern technology. . . .

Ultimately, the hero and the other characters, who have all seemed more or less superfluous to the machine that virtually runs itself, escape the cramping and dreary world of modern industry, in which they are variously lost, and they do so by partaking of the vision-giving mushrooms he has cultivated in the boiler room. All this makes a proper travesty on the machine-age and the persons trapped in it. But in the aggregate these details either fail to cohere, or cohere too slowly and incompletely. By the time one has put the pieces together, much of the governing idea along with a good deal of the fun has escaped in the interstices of the wobbly dramatic edifice. One cannot but recall how much more pointedly the man-versus-machine theme was presented in the Chaplin motion picture *Modern Times*. In addition to having Charles Chaplin, that film had not only a more unitary story-line but a unifying cinematic technique that by the very nature of the medium makes details cohere with the speed of the camera-eye and the vivifying power of that "eye" to show instantly what the play *Eh?* elaborates with too much talk and too little action on a static one-set stage.

Considering the difficulty presented by the lethargic and random technique, it is, in fact, remarkable that *Eh?* should have any fascination at all. It does have some, and it possesses, perhaps, as many as a dozen markedly amusing details such as the despair of the charmingly played girl-bride who must share her young husband's love with his inept attentions to the machine and his solicitude for his mushrooms. And there is some humor in the latter's confusion as he tries to oil the machine and fertilize the soil in which he is growing his mushrooms with an oiling can containing liquid manure. If the results can nevertheless be considered less than satisfying, the reason lies at least partly in the marriage of leisurely realistic style to the play's absurdities. The mismatching of styles makes for a fundamentally unfruitful marriage. It has proved a dubious combination in a number of minor British plays. I have found it successful only in Pinter's plays, in which the suspense or the often threatening atmosphere matches the irreality of a factitiously naturalistic action. But *Eh?* is one more play that should call attention to the importance of providing maximal structural support for the clever notions, the satirical distortions, and even the "anti-play" bias of present-day dramatic nonconformism.

John Gassner. ETJ. March, 1967, pp. 82–83

Like many of the new English dramatists, Livings draws heavily on his working-class background, and in his own fashion, he is as militant a champion of working-class values as Arnold Wesker and the early John Osborne. Indeed, it is due to some extent to the plays of Livings that terms like "kitchen-sink" and "chamber-pot" (he has featured variants of both in his works) have come to be used in describing the English drama of the last decade. Unlike most of his theatrical contemporaries, however, Livings has written primarily for the working classes. His earliest successes were in television—a medium still considered somewhat suspect even in England, where the TV fare is generally superior to ours. Another possible cause of Livings' critical neglect involves the unwillingness of many commentators to take him seriously: in the eyes of many, he is an "entertainer," not an "artist."

Most of his plays incorporate the imagery of popular culture, a practice common to most of the new dramatists. Unlike them, however, Livings does not "transform," satirize, or dignify this imagery. Nor does he seem apologetic for employing traditionally "low" comic devices: stereotyped characters, implausible situations, corny working-class humor. Indeed, Livings' works seem more indebted to the films of the Marx Brothers and their lesser TV progeny than to any strictly "literary" sources. Like many American films of the 20's and 30's (and many present-day TV situation comedies), there is a sense of the world gone mad in Livings' plays—a theme particularly suited to farcical treatment.

The hostility to farce as a "serious" genre is still a common prejudice among many dramatic critics. This hostility, combined with Livings' "declassé" successes in TV, and his casual attitude towards dramatic structure, have effectively excluded him from most serious discussions of the contemporary English theater. However charming these earlier plays may be, their critical neglect, though perhaps unfortunate, is at least understandable. The plays do not, in fact, pretend to be much more than entertaining vignettes of working-class life, strung together by a most tenuous concept of dramatic unity. Livings' recent work, however, is a different matter entirely. *Eh?* and *Kelly's Eye* represent two of the most sophisticated (and successful) experiments in the entire range of the new drama in England.

Eh? is probably the best English farce since the death of Shaw. It is also the only play by Livings which has been produced commercially in America.

Louis D. Giannetti. *MD*. May, 1969, p. 39

Like other playwrights of his generation, Livings is also an actor; and from artists as otherwise dissimilar as Osborne and Pinter we should by now have learnt what that implies. It means a reliance on physical effect: it means starting from the theatrical end, on the assumption that a succession of sufficiently powerful images will discharge enough energy to carry the action along and generate their own intellectual coherence. This is the thunderstorm method: the idea that if lightning strikes often enough it will keep the landscape continuously illuminated. Pinter does achieve such an unbroken effect, with each flash coming before the last has died away. In Livings there is a distinct gap in between, so that his plays generally consist of isolated turns, brilliant self-contained oases of theatrical vitality with an arid trudge from one to the next.

He once rationalized this habitual limitation in the form of a dramatic theory displacing responsibility on to the spectator. Audiences, he said, were capable of a consecutive attention-span of no more than 10 minutes; so accordingly he wrote in 10-minute episodes. But however limited their immediate powers of concentration, audiences also need to grasp the whole curve of a play. Even in the music hall you know how many numbers there are on the bill; whereas in some of Livings's work you never know how many more episodes are coming and the spectator is apt to get lost.

This is not true of *Honour and Offer* where he has made a determinedly schematic attempt to create a cohesive action with throughlines of character and motive. Even Henry's long wait for breakfast is justified as a connecting thread leading to his murderously frustrated final entrance with a smoking frying pan and a shot-gun. The separate episodes are still there, bringing about tonal variations between satire and farce, but they are locked into the surrounding context, encouraging the pedagogue-reviewer to award marks for effort.

Effort, however, is not the quality that has fired Livings's best work. If there is one thing that sets his plays apart from those of his contemporaries, it is they seem to have been enormous fun to write; and that, for all their leaden stretches of linking material, they repeatedly communicate that fun to the audience. *Honour and Offer* may be easier to follow than *Nil Carborundum* and *Eh?*, but it purchases clarity only by subduing Livings's gift for explosive comedy. As an anarchic comedian, it goes against his grain to work inside formal limits.

Irving Wardle. *TL*. May 17, 1969, p. 19

LOWRY, MALCOLM (1909–1957)

With the publication of [*Selected Letters*], Lowry's reputation should increase considerably among scholars and laymen alike—for they reveal, along with much clear insight into writing, some brilliant insight into the human soul: into the area of the psyche where all great joy and agony reside. In these letters one finds all the despair and disaster, all the humour and happiness that one would expect from the author of the masterpiece *Under the Volcano*. The individuals addressed are publishers, writers, friends, critics—but there is frequently the feeling, which one finds in the greatest letters, that the author is writing for a wider audience. The editors have supplied several appendices with letters written to and about Lowry; the result is a complete and moving literary experience.

At their most poignant moments the letters read like the journals of a seer—of one who left the arbour of his work only to penetrate the arbour of nature. Both worlds Lowry knew considerably, yet both worlds (his art, nature) were able to terrify him. At times he entered the inner torment of self as though he were descending into hell. But then it was primarily the infernal regions of the soul that he wanted to write about. . . .

All the themes (the images even) that are worked out in the novels and in the stories can be found gestating in these letters. Only the all-too-real theme of dipsomania is played down. The letters seldom do more than allude to Lowry's drinking; and although there is considerable space for reading between the lines, we must read the final stories to imagine the kind of self-destruction he had to fight.

Matthew Corrigan. The Dalhousie Review.
Spring, 1966, pp. 118–19

Once in writing about Lowry I stated dogmatically, "Novels are about people. They may be about other things as well, but they stand or fall ultimately on the success with which they present the human relationship of their characters." Then I went on to say that *Under the Volcano* stood the test of this criterion. I do not think that I would be so generally dogmatic now, but I am more firmly convinced than ever that *Under the Volcano* succeeds as a novel wholly (though not, of course, exclusively) on the literal level, as a story about recognizably human characters. . . .

The novel may not attain the stature of great tragedy, but I think that the richness of its existence on this level entitles it, at the very least, to Walter Allen's claim that it is "the finest and profoundest work of fiction written by an Englishman" during the 1940's. There is some justification, I dare say, for expanding the chronological limits of Allen's statement to include the whole of the post-World War II era in fiction.

Dale Edmonds. *TSE*. Vol. 16, 1968, p. 105

I have never been an admirer of Malcolm Lowry. I find him too soft centred, and *Lunar Caustic*, this novella about life in New York's Bellevue Hospital for drunks, seems to have all the faults I have found distasteful in Lowry's masterworks and then some. His DTs are almost always too poetic to ring true, and here we have again visions like "a large scorpion . . . gravely raping a one-armed Negress." And, to paraphrase S. J. Perelman, did you once see a scorpion plain? And when the hero, Bill Plantagenet, complains that he is a failed piano player because his hands are too small to stretch an octave, it is the maudlin, mawkish drunk in Lowry that has the doctor answer: "Perhaps it was your heart you couldn't make stretch an octave."

Still, Lowry has his following, and one should like to see his shade done justice and a collection of his poetry produced in England. The only one obtainable is a 1962 edition produced by City Lights of San Francisco, and a trip to any bookshop will show you how esoteric that volume is.

Stanley Reynolds. *NS*. Feb. 23, 1968, p. 243

Lowry was a drunkard of such monumental compulsions that it took a huge act of will for him to write anything at all, let alone bring it to the consummation he achieved in *Under the Volcano*. Yet for all the bottles—in spite of the thousand hangovers, the several hospitals, the real despairs by which he was hounded—Lowry remained as compulsive about his craft as his boozing. In fact there was a kind of heroism in it, considering the circumstances. More than once, through disaster or irresponsibility, he lost manuscripts of entire novels-in-progress. Yet at his death there remained thousands of additional pages, including still other novels in fragmented versions of two or three or even four drafts.

One of these [*Dark as the Grave Wherein My Friend is Laid*] has now been published, edited (collated is perhaps the better word) by Lowry's widow and Douglas Day. As Professor Day says, in an acute and necessary introduction, the book is hardly another *Under the Volcano*. Yet, tentative and flawed as it is, one is hard put to name contemporary novelists whose ostensibly "finished" work is as richly suggestive.

A mere summary sounds banal: A writer-protagonist, Lowry himself, returns with his second wife to Mexico, the scene of his recently completed autobiographical novel; there he seeks out a friend who had figured in the book, now discovered to be dead. But if this is virtually all, from Lowry it is virtually all we should expect—nothing "happens" in *Under the Volcano* either.

What occupies Lowry instead is what was always his most persuasive concern—consciousness under stress. In *Under the Volcano* he brought to that subjectivity such richness of texture that the tragedy became as inevitable as an Elizabethan drama. If the same thing cannot be said of *Dark as the Grave*, the beginnings of an interior dialectic are there—the tensions between good and evil, guilt and redemption, sorrow and joy, in most human terms.

For the happy few *Dark as the Grave* is a gift from the grave—even if it must render all the more poignant the realization of our loss.

David Markson. *BkWd*. June 30, 1968, p. 8

Why is it . . . that a novel like *Under the Volcano* is so easy to enter yet so difficult to endure? No, it is not an image of the human condition. That's far too easy. It does not first address, then mail itself to some abstraction. It does not say the wind is cold, that life is hard, that Clifford is timorous and beastie. Beckett's books do not assert that life's absurd. Does that news pain me? I'm sick already if it does. The novel does not say, it shows; it shows me my life in a figure; it compels me to stare at my toes. I live in a suburb of Cincinnati, yet the Consul's bottled Mexican journey is so skillfully constructed that its image fits me—not just a piece of it with which I may identify, such sympathies rend the fabric, but the whole fantastic dangerous country, the tale in its totality.

How does it feel to be the fore-end of a metaphor, especially one so fierce and unrelenting? And how does it work, exactly—this book which takes us into hell? The philosophical explanation is complex. Here I can only suggest it. But you may remember how Kant ingeniously solved his problem. Our own minds and our sensory equipment organize our world; it is we who establish these *a priori* connections which we later discover and sometimes describe, mistakenly, as natural laws. We are inveterate model makers, imposing on the pure data of sense a rigorously abstract system. The novelist makes a system for us too, although his is composed of a host of particulars, arranged to comply with esthetic conditions, and it both flatters and dismays us when we look at our own life through it because our life appears holy and beautiful always, even when tragic and ruthlessly fated. Still for us it is only "as if." Small comfort for Clifford, the metaphorical mouse.

William Gass. *NAR*. No. 10, 1970, p. 64

Those who do not care for visionary fiction may not agree that Lowry was a literary genius. I should like to suggest finally that, considerations of his work aside, Malcolm Lowry was quite another sort of genius as well: the true innocent, the Fool of God, the man who desires simply and wholeheartedly to be *good*. I do not mean to suggest that he was a saintly man. Far from it: when in one of his depressed periods, he could (as we have seen) be cruel, even dangerous. Or that he was a simpleton: for his intelligence was both lofty and subtle. Or always a buffoon: for he could be dignified, even austere. I mean that he was a man of simple and uncritical good will. He attributed the best of motives to everyone—at least until they had cheated him past ignoring. Most of what he touched became a muddle, but he would very much have preferred to do things well, so as to please others. He was a nuisance, a disgrace, a constant burden to those who cared for him. He could fairly roll in self-pity. He could strike tragic poses that at first amused, then annoyed. He could be, in short, impossible. But we must always hear him saying, sly grin on face, "Do not take me quite so seriously."

He was, we must remember, a most loveable sort of man, in spite of (and perhaps because of) his many flaws. His friends speak of him today as though he were still with them, laughing and talking endlessly. He was able to inspire the most astonishing affection and loyalty on the part of almost everyone who came to know him. Crusty and irascible old men smile when they remember him. Mothers, maids, and wives of friends cared for him as though he were their own. Harvey Burt is as aware as any of Lowry's many exasperating defects, and will brook no romantic myth-making about the man; yet over Harvey Burt's mantelpiece in Dollarton hangs Lowry's old ukulele, and the eagle feather that Jimmie Craige once gave him. And we must remember the anonymous voice in a bar, saying of Lowry that "The very sight of that old bastard makes me happy for five days. No bloody fooling."

I imagine that most of us would be rather proud to be the sort of man of whom such a thing could be said.

Douglas Day. *Malcolm Lowry: A Biography*
(N.Y., Oxford Univ. Pr., 1973), pp. 471–72

The author of *Under the Volcano* built from transformed memories, shaped by the craft of earlier masters in words; the blend of experience and craft is at its densest here. While technically unfinished, the best of his late works capture—in the "gaps"—the disruptive struggle, the receding of continuously deepening vision which is their theme.

If Lowry's two "Tyrannies," as he termed them, the pen and the bottle, possessed him utterly at times, he succeeded in building a life of allegory; in spite of the obvious relevance of his history to his artefacts . . . Lowry thus becomes the best possible interpreter of Lowry. Since events can be significant only in the context of his art, the purpose of these pages is to establish the conventions of the art itself. For his later life, Lowry's letters form his own chronicle; his early life, which was progressively recovered and blended into the deepening vision of his latest works, can be traced from its transient historic form only through partial records and memories; but these suffice to show its continuous presence, though in a subjective form, i.e. Lowry's recovered past is always a symbolic past. . . .

Lowry's conflicts and achievements can be traced to the time when at the age of sixteen he became absorbed in weaving a blend of recollection and fantasy, and dropped out of the competitive world of sport and social conformity. By this time too, at least one of his contemporaries had observed that drink had taken a firm hold of him. His first novel, *Ultramarine*, established the theme of conflict between home and exile, in terms of a quest. *Under the Volcano* transforms one of the two "Tyrannies," the tales of Sigbjørn Wilderness the other. At the deepest level, *October Ferry* returns to the linked themes of exile and suicide; the development of Lowry's work therefore show the unity he claimed for it, when he named the whole sequence *The Voyage That Never Ends*—a unity of the "aeolian" kind, exemplified in minuscule in his collection of short stories, *Hear Us O Lord*.

M. C. Bradbrook. *Malcolm Lowry: His Art &
Early Life: A Study in Transformation*
(Cambridge Univ. Pr., 1974), pp. 17–18

● MACBETH, GEORGE (1932–   )

The Broken Places is divided into three sections. The middle one, consisting of apparently autobiographical poems, is written in a manner a child could understand. Not so Section One. (Section Three comes, in this respect, in the middle.) Which of his styles is his natural one? Several of these poems can be no more than intellectually contrived experiments. Is Mr. MacBeth a writer with a compulsive interest in techniques because he has no compulsive themes? Or are his compulsive themes so difficult and personal that he's having a job finding a way to express them, that he is in fact an author in search of a style?

Interesting techniques are interesting; but they're justified only if they don't get between the reader and the poem. On my first reading of these poems I was often so distracted by finding out just what he was up to this time, in the way of rhymes, rhythms and metres, that I had a job in getting a finger-and-toe hold on the sense. Often I fell off. There seems to me something wrong here. Technical subtleties ought to emerge later, or at least not take charge. On further readings none of this bothered me—except that I still get no pleasure from syllable metres in English. They seem foreign to the nature of such a stressed language, are unnoticeable to my ear—I don't believe anyone can be aware of 17 syllables in line one and 11 in line two—and when used as ruthlessly as Mr. MacBeth uses them they are apt to tease the eye and interfere with the sense.

All the same, a number of these difficult poems give intimations of passionate feeling and belief that couldn't be circumscribed in intellectual doodles. The easy ones in Section Two are too easy, contented with too little. I prefer the others, however tortured, extravagant, even grotesque, they sometimes are. The blurb says they're in the tradition of Hogg and Stevenson—a stupefying remark.

Norman MacCaig. *NS.* June 7, 1963, p. 871

Mr. MacBeth is a useful poet to have around. He specializes in the well-written verse of a raving lunatic. Or so it often seems at first sight; and I daresay that may even be the impression he would like to make. However, there is a lot of method in his madness (even perhaps too much). Cryptic, obscure, oblique, sick, unpleasant, sadistic—most of the pejoratives in the critical book have been thrown at him; yet he still occupies his own black eminence among present-day poets.

A Doomsday Book is a bit different from *The Broken Places*, Mr. MacBeth's first book. Syllabics are dropped, as a major vehicle for the thought. Pathos is out—well out (it crept in once or twice in *The Broken Places*)—except perhaps in "The Return." And a sort of gallows humour is in, with occasional crypto-sadism. But these poems are original and technically extremely adroit. According to his Foreword Mr. MacBeth "believes that it [the book] may brighten the gloom of paranoia with a warm and cheerful glow. As the storm beats at the window-panes, and Death comes down the chimney dressed as Santa Claus, there will surely be something within the covers of *A Doomsday Book* to soothe the nerves." This may well be so.

Gavin Ewart. *L.* Oct., 1965, pp. 104–5

MacBeth is an extraordinary phenomenon, but his real "presence" as a poet rather than a performer has yet to be demonstrated—he is the Unidentified Flying Object of British verse. . . .

MacBeth's mixture of grotesque humour and grisly seriousness with a buoyantly active style is a welcome addition in British poetry and cannot but have a liberating effect. His dead-serious poems, on themes involving the horror of war, the meaning of Eichmann, private suffering—all, once more, suggesting a Lowell influence at a certain remove—gain in sheer intelligent effervescence from his capacity for comic fantasy but by the same token lack a final conviction. Mind, sensibility, phrasing are pyrotechnically exploited; but the bright contriving that makes MacBeth's buffoonery so welcome also makes his more serious writing seem hollow, as though its conception were not truly his—not yet, at any rate. At this writing, he is thirty-three years old, one of the youngest and most prolific poets of some distinction in England, and very much in the midst of a rapid development.

M. L. Rosenthal. *The New Poets* (N.Y.,
Oxford Univ. Pr., 1967), pp. 260–62

George MacBeth's *Collected Poems: 1958–1970* affords a wide-angle view of one of the more versatile poets writing in Britain today. And, although MacBeth has previously published six volumes of verse, this one, which gathers the poet's choice of his earlier work as well as some new poems, is the best showcase to date for his far-ranging talents. Here one finds both searing portrayals of modern love—detailed down to the lady's mole—and soap-bubble poetic jokes which, as MacBeth says, were "written for those who (like myself) regard themselves as children." Forms range from the exploded typography of "op" to such traditional forms as the sonnet. But the tonal reach of these poems is perhaps their greatest surprise. This man can gear language to whatever effect he wants: humor, satiric wit, liturgical solemnity, or psychological horror.

MacBeth's metrical virtuosity is such that he seems equally at home in almost any form. In his lighter poems he often uses free verse, rhymed couplets, or ballad stanze; in his more serious poetry he may turn to tradition for Petrarchan sonnets or blank verse, to his contemporaries for that stress-scanned line so frequent since William Carlos Williams. MacBeth's experimental poems are most interesting for their tendency to play in rhythm, as seen by his use of rock-music beat in "Lady Dracula" or "The Auschwitz Rag," as well as by his pure-sound experiments. Some of these experiments rely on rhythmic chanting of nonsense syllables; MacBeth accompanies others during his readings by drumming a small stick against the lectern. But none make any sense on the printed page. Mercifully, the pure-sound experiments occupy few pages.

In MacBeth's light verse and experimental poetry anything goes, including the detached typography of the Concretists and strange do-it-yourself poems that one is supposed to paste upon playing cards and deal out to partners for reading. If a number of these are wearisome, others are genuinely entertaining but, for all their cleverness, they are not what MacBeth does best. What he does best is to write a poetry of psychological inscape so intense, yet so bleak, that the "fun and games" section of his book may be seen as a retreat, a place to gather one's senses before passing on to some new vision of hell.

MacBeth's serious verse gains its effect through a massing of details, and it is his prowess here that, combined with his considerable dramatic instincts, his ability to get inside his characters and bring their thoughts alive, accounts for his success in the dramatic monologue. . . .

Patrick J. Callahan. Sat. April 15, 1972, p. 71

In the better poems in George MacBeth's new collection [*Shrapnel*] one senses that the real life of the poems moves on a level quite separate from the aspirations of the language. The personal poems that conclude the book are sustained by moments when Mr. MacBeth edges towards a conversational tone: for instance, his parents are imagined in death. . . . This is a new tone in his work, and almost stifled at birth by habits of style: a fallen calf lies "on stones of unconcern"; a friend's phone call comes "through troubled iron of my own concerns." . . . How much better these poems could have been if their candour was not at the mercy of grandiloquence. Even so, they represent an advance.

Just how great an advance is emphasized by the book's first section, "Love Prayers," where we are plunged back into the sanctimonious gloom of MacBethesda, that lugubrious suburb on the outskirts of Bathos . . . where nothing is allowed to be just itself. In the middle sections of the book, past successes are reworked, with encyclopedic zeal, but considerably less verve. In "Soil Kings," however, a gallery of fantastical vegetables, there are some poems that work, not by perverse imagery or verbal frenzy, but simply by allowing the idea to move through uncluttered language.

TLS. March 9, 1973, p. 270

MACCAIG, NORMAN (1910–   )

Reading these poems [in *Measures*] is, for the most part, as temporarily reviving as a Scottish holiday: the landscapes are peeled off like pages from a photographic calendar. Only where photographs merely record, MacCaig interprets and invents images that are themselves outside the camera's range. No one has written about Scotland more freshly and originally nor with such rare detachment. The detachment, perhaps, is why his poems stand up better individually than in bulk. Is reading a book straight through a fair test, though? In MacCaig's case the country, and the language in which it is conveyed, never let one down, but he himself continually eludes. The result is equivalent to a long car journey in the company of an elliptical, clever, but enigmatic man. The silences allow one to look about without distraction, but no relationship has developed at the end of it.

Alan Ross. *L.* July, 1965, p. 103

Mr. MacCaig [in *Surroundings*] stalks the elusive images and as usual, brings home some eye-catching specimens: the sea a "fat-fingered lace-maker" on the beach, frogs as free-fall parachutists. His cult of the object precipitates a Keatsian unravelling of the self into the various components of a landscape. He becomes excited at the prospect of union with a Scotch mist, and gives his ingenuity a pleasant run. The tone, though, cannot always keep up, and the lines begin to titter at their own whimsicality. The modification of object by observer offers another sidetrack for speculation. Mr. MacCaig prods, a bit laboriously, at the difference between water trickling down a wall and a wall being trickled down by water.

Some of his new poems undertake social comment. In one, "King of Beasts," whimsy intervenes again, and leaves it hopping around between soap-box and nursery. But others find a genuine direction and follow it sharply. The best is about a dwarfish cripple begging outside the church at Assisi while a priest explains to tourists how clever it was of Giotto to make his frescoes reveal God's goodness to the illiterate.

John Carey. NS. Oct. 28, 1966, p. 633

Norman MacCaig started writing poetry when he was sixteen, forty-two years ago, and he is now escaping from the truth of the cliché that Scottish poets are without renown in their own country. The last two volumes of his poetry, *Surroundings* and *Rings on a Tree*, cannot be got for love or money in Edinburgh. As soon as they appear they are snapped up by, in the main, the young. . . .

Though MacCaig calls himself five sixths of a Gael, "My mother came from Harris and my father from Dumfries. They collided in Edinburgh and I was part of the fall out" and though he can read Gaelic, he has never written in Scots dialect or experimented with Lallans or in any way written peculiarly Scottish poetry. Yet he has been called a "writer in English with a Scottish accent of the mind." . . .

Though MacCaig's poetry is unarguably classical now it was not always so. "Until I was thirty-six I wrote absolute rubbish. I was a member of a movement called, I regret to say, the New Apocalypse and if I could get every copy of the two books of mine published then I would make a bonfire of them. At that time I wrote poems which were surrealistic conglomerations of images which I presume at the time I understood—and it was only when I came to my senses, all five of them, and decided this was useless that I began to write something that was communicable." . . .

A lot of his poems are about . . . mountains and the sea . . . and, a recurring theme in his work, the poet's relationship with the natural world. "I only write about things I know—first because I have absolutely no powers of invention and secondly because I have absolutely no imagination. So every poem I've ever written has been about something which I've noticed, observed or experienced."

This means that he never touches the huge issues which burn the young and the unhappy—the Bomb, war, alienation. "I leave all that," he says, "to the youngsters, who are brasher than I." And to any timorous suggestion that this refusal to touch such immediate subjects, combined with his classical canons, might mean a holding back of something essential from his poetry, he says that of course something must be held back—"poetry is not public vomiting."

Lindsay Mackie. G. July 17, 1969, p. 8

MACDIARMID, HUGH (1892–   )

It's impossible to talk about contemporary Scottish poetry without talking almost all the time about Hugh MacDiarmid. After nearly two centuries, during which hundreds of tiny poets wrote thousands of tiny non-poems, imitating the worst of Burns and never taking a peep over the Kailyard wall, he took the Scots language by the scruff of the dictionary, reviving words that were obsolescent or obsolete, and sent them out, fat and lively again, to discuss matters that had lain outside the scope of Scottish poetry for centuries and to introduce others that the old Makars had never heard of. The point is, in his best poems, and there are a lot of them, there is no whiff of *pedantry*. The language is alive and lively. And what it deals with is of a range and scope unparalleled in Scottish writing.

When he had done what he wanted to do in Scots, he took on English. Here again, linguistically and thematically, his range is extraordinary. An all-inclusive "poetry of ideas" is what he is after and he, who first made his name with tiny lyrics in Scots, has pursued that aim in a number of enormously long poems in English.

He is a good man at making enemies as well as friends, so it isn't surprising that, while many literary sleepwalkers in Scotland got very rude awakenings indeed, others were stimulated by his atrocious energy to find out what they could do themselves. The result has been called by a big name, the "Scottish Renaissance," and if it's big, it's not altogether absurd. One would have to go far back to find a time when the level of Scottish poetry was as high as it has been in the last thirty years, in two important respects, and this is due to MacDiarmid. He demonstrated the importance of technical expertise, and showed that to be Scottish was not enough—one had to be international as well. He says "Back to Dunbar!" But he also preaches the necessity to look abroad, to know what is being done elsewhere, to extend the range of one's informations and responses, to be the opposite of parochial.

Norman MacCaig. *PoetryR*. Autumn, 1965,

p. 148

The *Collected Poems of Hugh MacDiarmid* contains, the author states in an introductory note, by no means all the poems he has written but only those he thinks worth including in a definitive edition. The volume, with glossary and index, runs to 498 pages and is in general chronologically arranged—1923 onward; twelve books have been drawn upon and a number of uncollected poems have been added. The early poems, chiefly lyrical, have great charm, in spite of the fact that they are written for the most part in a mixture of Scottish dialects—in a vernacular that at some point or other took to itself the name Lallans.

Like the Chilean Pablo Neruda, MacDiarmid has applied himself, in a perfectly open and often rather compulsive-seeming manner, to subjects that at present are neglected and even shunned by the majority of English and American poets and audiences. Both Neruda and MacDiarmid bring patriotic and political poetry again into view; they occasionally resemble not only Whitman at his most optimistic and orotund but Victor Hugo at his most grandiose and bardic. Both are capable, too, of mingling the emotions of nationalism with the philosophy of the international class struggle; Neruda has made no secret of his allegiance to Communism, and MacDiarmid's early intense admiration for Lenin has never lapsed. And neither poet has ever considered restraint a virtue. Both have written endless variations of their favorite themes; their allegiances have been forthright and their staying power has been enormous. And both, oddly, discarding their family and given names, have produced their work under pseudonyms. [1967]

Louise Bogan. A Poet's Alphabet (N.Y.,
McGraw-Hill, 1970), pp. 290–91

Having read the whole of MacDiarmid's poetry as far as I was able to I have now come to the conclusion that MacDiarmid did take a wrong turning when he began on his poetry of ideas. At one time I did not believe this because I felt that cleverness and intelligence were very important. I still believe this but on the other hand I would not give them the high position that I once did. Now I believe there were a number of reasons for MacDiarmid to take this turning. The first reason was that he is naturally a very intelligent man. I do not mean by this that he is a great thinker for clearly this would be wrong, and he wouldn't claim this himself. I believe that a poet by definition cannot be a great thinker. However he clearly has a restless inquiring mind. He has also always been a great lover of books as he mentions in his autobiography. Therefore it was natural that he be led towards ideas and an investigation of them.

Secondly I believe that after the creation of his lyrics MacDiarmid, with that curious distrust that poets have about the value of something simply because of its smallness, felt that he ought to move on to more "serious" work. This I believe to have been a profound error, not the fact that he should have moved on, for perhaps he could not prevent himself from doing this, but the fact that he should think a poetry of ideas must necessarily be a more "serious" poetry. I believe that "The Watergaw" is in every way far more serious than anything he produced on the basis of ideas alone. These long poems may be intellectually exciting but they are not serious. They do not confront us with serious things. They do not, I think, react on us as whole human beings. Their explorations are not deep enough. This may seem a very odd thing to say when the present writer admits that there are great stretches of them that he cannot understand. Nevertheless MacDiarmid was making the assumption that by injecting ideas into his work he would become serious. What poems could be more serious than Blake's lyrics . . . and yet are they full of ideas in any detachable sense? [1967]

Iain Crichton Smith. In Duncan Glen, ed.,
Hugh MacDiarmid: A Critical Survey
(Edinburgh, Scottish Academic Press, 1972),
p. 129

Hugh MacDiarmid's work has always been rooted in locality; it is as local as the poetry of Wordsworth or Basil Bunting, both in language and in its sense of place, and, because of this, the intelligence that informs it is international in the best sense. While fighting the stupidity of parochialism throughout his life, he has always realized that true internationalism grows out of, and is indissolubly part of nationalism. It is consequently essential that his work is seen in a native, and European setting and not as an appendage to English poetry whose tradition is at least partially alien to that Scotland. . . .

Doubts are still expressed from time to time, South of the Border, about the value of MacDiarmid's restoration of Scots as a language for poetry, despite the fact that most of his finest work is written in it. I believe that T. S. Eliot effectively answered these criticisms from the point of view both of the English and the Scottish traditions when he wrote: "While I must admit that Lallans is a language which I read with difficulty and the subtleties of which I will never master, I can nevertheless enjoy it, and I am convinced that many things can be said, in poetry, in that language that cannot be expressed at all in English. I think that Scots poetry is, like that of other Western European languages, a potentially fertilising influence upon English poetry, and that it is in the interests of English poetry that Scots poetry should flourish. It is uncontested and now everywhere recognised that Hugh MacDiarmid's refusal to become merely another successful English poet, and his pursuing a course which at first some of his admirers deplored and some of his detractors derided, has had important consequences and has justified itself. It will eventually be admitted that he has done also more for English poetry by committing some of his finest verse to Scots, than if he had elected to write exclusively in the Southern dialect."

William Cookson. Agenda. Autumn–Winter,
1967–68, p. 35

A recent critic was only echoing earlier cries of not a few predecessors when he suggested that "there are few things in modern verse more dismal than MacDiarmid's furious frequent flogging of the dead Scottish Pegasus" and there is no doubt that Hugh MacDiarmid has written some very bad poetry under the flag of his nationalism, although I doubt if there was much of it in the *Collected Poems* and *A Lap of Honour* that were under review. Generally, however, MacDiarmid's commitments have been beneficial to his poetry. Indeed, what Mac-Diarmid has, among other things, been doing here is providing himself with intellectual poetic equipment to support his imagination. This is, of course, a device common to many poets, although some may feel less need than MacDiarmid to turn their systems of thought into public campaigns. Much of his campaigning, no doubt, is a reflection of Mac-Diarmid's fighting personality, but the subliminal ego of the poet may have known what it was about here in that, in the fractured and isolated cultural situation which existed in Scotland, this public campaign was probably as essential to the poet's survival as was a personal belief in his cultural theories.

MacDiarmid was building much further back than a poet fortunate enough to be born in a time and in a culture which could give the sort of supporting environment MacDiarmid made for himself through his nationalistic and other theories. Of course, the public battles which his theories produced would have killed most poets quicker than any sense of isolation.

Some of MacDiarmid's theories strike me as plain daft, although I find others very convincing and all of them stimulating and, in themselves, a fascinating monument to the most fertile mind Scotland has produced in centuries.

Duncan Glen. Agenda. Autumn–Winter,
1967–68, p. 53

Scots, or Scotch, the speech of Scotland's country people and proletariat, has often been declared dying, but is still alive. I spoke it when I was a boy in the Forties, believing it would soon be gone. Writing in his *Journal* a hundred years earlier, in 1844, Lord Cockburn thought the same thing. . . . If Scotch is lost, warned Cockburn, then "we lose *ourselves*. Instead of being what we are, we become a poor part of England."

Hugh MacDiarmid has treated Scots as a living language, and was determined that Scotland should not be a poor part, or any part, of England. He dreamt of a time when the Lowlands and Gaelic-speaking areas would be the one place, detached from England: the truth is that they are two places, and that Gaelic Irredentism, where it exists among artists and writers, should steer them in a different direction— toward union with Ireland. Hugh MacDiarmid is a *nom de guerre*—his real name is Christopher Grieve. He is now seventy-nine. He has been a communist, one who rejoined the Party, after a falling-out, at the time of the Russian invasion of Hungary, and he has also been a Scottish Nationalist and England-baiter. Between the world wars he took an interest in ideas of a fascistic character (such as Hitler's *Blutsgefühl*— the principle that "like mates with like," the principle of apartheid). Like Pound, he was attracted to Major Douglas's doctrine of Social Credit, with its phobia about usury. So it would appear that he has been the sort of communist who isn't shy about expressing views that are incompatible with communism.

When MacDiarmid began to publish poems in the Twenties, the fear that Scots might not survive was attended by a second fear that, even if it did, it could no longer support a literature worth the name. He disproved this with his volumes *Sangschaw* and *Penny Wheep*, where he devised a literary Scots which came to be known as Lallans. Lallans owed something to certain lonely predecessors such as Charles Doughty and incorporated attitudes to language that place MacDiarmid with Joyce and with the other innovators and renovators of the modern movement. It was both an attempt to say in his own words and ways what a Scotsman might feel, and a poetic diction in which the rhythms of the modern vernacular were fed with a vocabulary of "queer words" drawn from the past: the dictionary of Cockburn's contemporary Dr. Jamieson was its chief source.

Lallans was highly artificial: the spoken Scots of his own time was, as MacDiarmid put it, "aggrandized" by the presence of these queer words, just as Pope's verse was made majestic by the poeticisms that denoted a classical decorum. MacDiarmid's, of course, was a very different decorum, marked by surprise and surmise on the reader's part. Lallans was an exercise of pride; it worked because it was impossible; it involved a self-inflicted attempt to bring forgotten words to life, to coax up Lazarus from the depths of the dictionary. I think MacDiarmid was aware that, here as elsewhere in Scotland, a miracle was needed: at the outset of his career he liked to write about resurrections.

Karl Miller. *NYR*. Dec. 2, 1971, p. 13

MACINNES, COLIN (1914–   )

To issue these three very disparate books as *The London Novels* of
Colin MacInnes is, by virtue of the act itself, a brave thing to do and,
by virtue of the actual title, a remarkably accurate focus upon the
essence of MacInnes's talent as a novelist. The bravery consists in publishing, for an American audience, something as obsessively *local*, and
hence untranslatable, as, say, Henry Roth's *Call It Sleep* or Daniel
Fuch's three Brooklyn novels. Not that MacInnes's books are Jewish,
although he has an intuitive understanding of, and sympathy for, Jews.
Yet, although these three books were published separately and deal
with, chiefly, Negroes (*City of Spades*), teenagers (*Absolute Beginners*), and policemen and pimps (*Mr. Love and Justice*), the one factor that unites them is the almost tangible feeling for London which
causes, as much as his empathy with his protagonists, a close sense of
identification in his English readers that must necessarily be lacking in
an American audience.

   City of Spades is MacInnes's third novel, but his first good one.
His *To the Victors the Spoils* was about the European war and, unfortunately, contrived to communicate the boredom of war in a way that
the author did not perhaps intend. His next, *June in Her Spring*, a touching, but slight, account of young love blighted in philistine Australia,
reads, although it was published second, like the classic first novel of
adolescent agony. Consequently, when *City of Spades* appeared, one
greeted it with a double pleasure; that of reading a good book and
that of seeing a talent one had previously believed in, without adequate
evidence, come to fruition.

T. G. Rosenthal. NR. Feb. 15, 1969, p. 23

Most modern writers who borrow character types and situations from
18th-century novels find the episodic looseness of plot, the rootless
hero, the constant sense of incongruity peculiarly adaptable to contemporary experience. Certain forms may be borrowed, but the psychology and the scenery are meant to be new. In his three London
novels Colin MacInnes showed picaresque tendencies, but his homeless
blacks and juvenile delinquents were modern outcasts. In *Westward to
Laughter*, MacInnes has done a rash and remarkable thing; he has
written an 18th-century adventure novel for a contemporary audience.

On its own merits, the book is morally provocative and entertaining; as a literary imitation, it is quite extraordinary. MacInnes has done his homework in Defoe and Smollett and, very likely, in those 19th-century writers like Scott, Thackeray and Stevenson who tried to write novels in an 18th-century manner. But what is more to MacInnes's credit is that the consequence of labor, not the labor itself, is what shows. His "18th-century" style is neither a dull, pedantic copy nor a barbarous and artificial mixing of thous and thines. It is the invention of a disciplined mind and a sensitive ear, an imitation not so much of the detailed habits of one or two writers but rather of the rhythm, tone and usage common to a number of British writers in the first half of the 18th century.

Robert Kiely. *NYT*. Jan. 18, 1970, p. 1

In many ways Mr. Colin MacInnes's area has always been something one might call the romance of manners. Whether he is exploring London's coloured world, investigating teen-age sub-cultures, venturing into Stevenson country or—as he is doing here [in *Three Years to Play*]—re-creating the Elizabethan underworld, the method has been fundamentally the same. Each time an entire section of society, unfamiliar or misunderstood, is given us in authentic and exuberant detail, all its bizarre customs gaily re-enacted. And into this setting he introduces a requisite range of odd, lively, essentially sketchy characters whose unlikely escapades graft fantasy on to historical or sociological fact. Frequently, his shrewd and zestful observation and engaging, farcical humour succeed in passing off the whole thing as truth and insight. Such an impression is surely a mistake. This virtuoso display of unknown worlds is sheer romantic fiction. The weight of minutely bizarre particulars, conjured up in *Three Years to Play* as racily as before, should strain the credulity of the reader who thinks twice. Mr. MacInnes has also extended elaborate but insubstantial plots at no inconsiderable length, and when something very like boredom intervenes, as in his new novel, the doubts begin to assemble menacingly. . . .

His people are a faithful gallery of rogues and sweet cheats. But the energetic contrivance leads him on, and on, to a point where one asks whether all this invention was worth it after all. Violence is never lacking, but tenderness and understanding are, and the outcome is a novel where intelligence is strangely squandered on pointless ingenuity.

TLS. April 23, 1970, p. 456

MACNEICE, LOUIS (1907–1963)

Louis MacNeice, like most poets, was a good critic, and his criticism seems to me to have been unjustly neglected. His early book *Modern Poetry: A Personal Essay* is unobtainable, while many far more dated and trivial books are re-issued in paperback; his *The Poetry of W. B. Yeats* (1941) is also unreprinted at a time when inert academic books on that poet are distributed by the hundredweight. And when his *Varieties of Parable* appeared last autumn, reviewers—the ones I saw, at any rate—seemed curiously unwilling to take it seriously, as the considered and wide-ranging utterance of an important English poet. It came out at the same time as the posthumous autobiography, *The Strings Are False*, and the reviews concentrated on the autobiography and bundled *Varieties of Parable* into a perfunctory last paragraph. I have even heard it dismissed as "just reprinted lectures," as if some of the most important English criticism, from Coleridge through Arnold to Eliot, were not reprinted lectures.

Perhaps MacNeice's modesty of tone is against him; many reviewers think that a critic who hasn't a portentous tone must have nothing to say, and Cambridge, where *Varieties of Parable* was given as the Clark Lectures, is the home of a certain critical cant, a tone at once bullying and pious, from which again MacNeice is entirely free. . . .

Tolerance, decency, acuteness, the honest facing of difficulties: these are the marks of MacNeice's criticism, and when they are added to his initial advantages—a good education (particularly a first-hand acquaintance with Greek and Latin) and the imagination of a practitioner—the result is criticism which has few equals in our time. One other quality should be added: the courage to tackle a large general subject. The theme of *Varieties of Parable* is nothing less than the basic question, "How does literature make its statements? Why are they not the same as the statements of science or history?" By discussing a line of writers who either ignore surface realism or, as in Bunyan, employ surface realism but wed it to a subject-matter avowedly emblematic, MacNeice was evidently concerned to open the reader's mind to the great things that are possible to a literary art which has cast off "realism" in the old hampering sense. Indeed, a recurring fault in the book is that "realism" is used too exclusively as a term of disapprobation. . . .

The Strings Are False, though beautifully written, is minor MacNeice; most of it is anticipated either in the poems or in the interesting "Case-Book" chapters of *Modern Poetry*. It is *Varieties of Parable* we should read carefully; for all its modesty it makes many important observations, some of which had waited twenty years to get on to paper, and good criticism is not so common that we can leave it to gather dust.

John Wain. Enc. Nov., 1966, pp. 49, 54, 55

Louis MacNeice's last volume of poems, *The Burning Perch*, went to press in January 1963; he died suddenly in September of the same year at the age of 56. Critics since have generally acknowledged that he was a poet of genius, and that much of his finest work was produced in the three years immediately preceding his death. While granting him his place in the front rank among the poets who came to prominence in the thirties—W. H. Auden, Stephen Spender, Cecil Day-Lewis— they have had considerable difficulty in assessing the nature of his achievement. On his death, T. S. Eliot commented that he "had the Irishman's unfailing ear for the music of verse." During his lifetime, however, many readers felt that his ear did indeed fail him, that his rhythms were frequently too easy, and his parodies and imitations of jazz lyrics too flat and mechanical in nature to hold one's interest for long. While he had much in common with his contemporaries, he was, in many ways, totally unlike them. His poems are easy to understand on the surface (seemingly far less complicated than those of Auden or Dylan Thomas), but they present deeper, less obvious, difficulties. They appear to be the open, easy expression of an engaging and intelligent personality, but basically that personality, and the poems through which it manifests itself, is not easy to grasp. . . .

There is in everything that Louis MacNeice wrote a surface brilliance, an extraordinary verbal dexterity, a poise that shows itself in a command of complicated verse forms. There is a distance maintained, even when he is being most personal, that gives his poetry, at best, a cold classical power, and, at its worst, the casualness of an uncommitted poetic journalist. MacNeice during his career engaged in many literary pursuits which took him away from the writing of poetry. But he was never deceived, no matter how well he succeeded in journalism, criticism, translation or radio work, that these were anything but diversions from his main course. . . .

William Jay Smith. HC. April, 1967, pp. 1–3

The collected poems of Louis MacNeice form a thick volume of 575 pages, running from a section of "Juvenilia, 1925–29" to poems written shortly before his death in 1963 at the age of fifty-six. His poems thus span the central creative era of twentieth-century poetry, the great age that emerges emphatically with Eliot's *Waste Land* in 1922 and closes with Eliot's own death in 1965. Whether it comes to be called the Age of Eliot or the Age of Pound, it is an era that surely achieved the beginning of the Renaissance that Pound prophesied in 1914. Mac-Neice's work shows everywhere the liberating influence of those early masters who made it possible for the poets of MacNeice's generation to break with the Victorians and the Georgians, to bring into their poetry the modern colloquial idiom and the imagery of the daily world, urban and industrial. . . .

Pound and Eliot could write in the eclectic manner of exiles; they could override the English tradition with French and Italian and Chinese examples. But a poet like MacNeice had the idiom of Wordsworth and Hardy indelibly in his mind. We can see the situation more clearly in MacNeice than in Auden, for Auden's technical brilliance and his removal to America, Ischia, and Austria have veiled and in the end, I think, have broken his allegiance to the English scene. But with Mac-Neice (though he was born in Belfast) the English tradition moves on into the modern age with unbroken power. . . .

MacNeice seems to be outlasting the vogue of Auden, and we can now read him for what he always offered: an acute sense of the changes that England has been reluctantly enduring under the impact of the various forces that, both in war and in peace, have undermined the sovereignty of her ancient ways.

Louis L. Martz. YR. Summer, 1967,
pp. 593–95

For this apparent falling off in [MacNeice's] powers it was fashionable to blame his long years of work as a feature-writer at the B.B.C. Well, he had his living to earn, and he found the work and the company congenial, more congenial, I am pretty sure, than the obvious alternative, which was university teaching. And the work he wrote for the B.B.C. was a completely legitimate extension of the function of poetry as he understood it. He took to writing for radio and to production too—he was a very brilliant producer—like a duck to water. One looks back to perhaps the first half of his years in radio as to the high peak of sound broadcasting, when the radio feature became an art, an ephemeral art admittedly but still an art. MacNeice, of course, was not alone in making radio an art; he was one among many; but he did give it an elegance, a sense of style, a vividness, and a verbal distinction that was his own and essentially that of his poems.

In any event, it is a rash act to write off any poet, or novelist for that matter, so long as he is still alive; and in MacNeice's case there was in the last years of his life a new outburst of creative energy that produced poems certainly as fine as any he had written before. This is particularly true of the poems in the collection <i>The Burning Perch,</i>

which appeared within a matter of weeks after his unexpected death in September 1963. Posthumous volumes, especially when they appear so quickly after a poet's death, are an open invitation to sentimentality: it is almost impossible not to read them differently from the way in which we read the work of the man while alive; and it would be easy to read into the poems of *The Burning Perch* premonitions of the poet's death. MacNeice himself said that he had been "taken aback," while preparing the volume for the press, "by the high proportion of sombre pieces, ranging from bleak observations to thumbnail nightmares." He had, of course, always been aware of the dark underside of things, of the terror of life, and mortality; they are there in his work from the beginning. He was, I think, an unillusioned, stoic humanist very much in the tradition of E. M. Forster; and like Forster's Mrs. Moore, he had heard the "oum-boum" of the echo in the Marabar Caves. And certainly *The Burning Perch* is the most sombre of his collections: "bleak observations," "thumbnail nightmares"—the descriptions are accurate. All the same, the sombreness is lit up by the energy of the wit and a grim, sardonic, almost contemptuous gaiety. They are the poems, I feel, of a man who knows the worst and is not intimidated, the poetic equivalents of the smile, almost the snarl of derision, one had sometimes seen on Louis's face in life.

Walter Allen. In *Essays by Divers Hands*,
Vol. 35 (Oxford Univ. Pr., 1969), pp. 15–16

There can be no question that MacNeice cast himself in the part of Everyman in his "modern morality" play, *One for the Grave*, so loaded is it with autobiographical items, with attitudes and props that appear repeatedly in the poems. There is a prevailing tone of tragic despair, uncertainty and resentment in Everyman's attitude. . . .

Does the best poetry of MacNeice carry any "implications of bulk, depth and width"? In the terms of our present study, we might venture the explicit claim that his poetry *has* depth, and that the depth derives from his belief in the existence of ultimates that will reveal their real presence in the face of disciplined and persistent questioning—which belief underlies his best poems. As for the width of his poetry, it surely derives from the degree to which he succeeded in resolving his personal paradoxes (while the paradoxes themselves remain stubbornly present) and, in so doing, achieved the status of Everyman—a very rare and particular Everyman.

William T. McKinnon. *Apollo's Blended
Dream: A Study of the Poetry of Louis
MacNeice* (Oxford Univ. Pr., 1971),
pp. 211, 217–18

MacNeice remained the prisoner of his childhood. He could never escape the nostalgic chains this placed upon him either as lover or thinker. That his love for his mother rested, not unusually, on so profound a sexual base that her early death was permanently crippling emotionally, he half realized, as we see from the story of the twig that he tells in *The Strings Are False.* . . .

In *Experiences with Images* he comments in a note:

> Almost the most disastrous experience of my childhood is for ever associated in my mind with a doubled-up poplar twig—but I have never yet used this image as a symbol of evil. Were I to do so, I should certainly elucidate the reference.

The importance of this lies in the last phrase. He never brought himself to "elucidate the reference." His ambivalent attitude to this story, so that he must tell it, shows that he realized that it contained a significance which it was difficult to face. His inability to use it in his poetry constituted in a major degree a moral failure in one for whom self was a major source of interest and inspiration. A parallel and not dissociated failure lay in his inability to make the intellectual effort either to achieve faith, to deny all belief, or to systematize his agnosticism.

This ethical and intellectual weakness led to a certain sentimentality in his approach to social criticism and equally made any firm political attitude impossible. So MacNeice could find neither spiritual faith, political belief, or personal love and understanding to form the basis of his poetry, but relied instead on the conflicts of indecision. In so far as it lacks a passionate attempt to cope with the conflicts that arise from doubt and indecision, the poetry of MacNeice sometimes falls short of greatness. The tragedy is that he could not escape from within himself to wider exploration.

D. B. Moore. *The Poetry of Louis MacNeice*
(Leicester, Leicester Univ. Pr., 1972),
pp. 248–49

MANNING, OLIVIA (? –   )

Olivia Manning has an exceptional capacity for wriggling into the skin of a character unlike herself and staying there with a minimum of obvious effort. This capacity is all the more impressive for being—I have to admit it—rarer in women novelists than in men. One does not have the feeling with her, as one does with most of our other distinguished women novelists, that each novel is one more disguised instalment of the author's personal life. If Miss Manning identifies herself with any of the characters in *The Play Room*, she has dissembled so adequately that it becomes irrelevant. The artifice is perfect, the consistency flawless.

Not that this is entirely to the book's advantage. While admiring its pristine, economic style, vivid yet cool, I find myself wondering a little what, of value or originality, Miss Manning is trying to say? Briefly (and the novel is brief, though not simple) it views events through the eyes of a teenage girl, Laura, bored and ill-at-ease in a drearily genteel home, seeking excitement and also a meaning to life with Vicky, an adored school-mate. Laura watches uneasily as Vicky takes up with a psychopathic baddy, half foreseeing—yet, with the ignorance of adolescence never really fearing—the terrible real-life fate that overtakes Vicky on the lonely wastelands beyond the factory estate.

This climax, powerfully and even movingly described, convinces: these things *do* happen. But other things about Vicky tend to make her seem a synthetic character, a symbol, perhaps, or a slightly obvious "example" of her generation and class. She is beautiful, which is unfortunately not an effective attribute for a character in a novel; she rides the motor-bike on which her only brother was killed; charmingly amoral, she has a passionate lesbian relationship with another schoolgirl: there are moments at which one wants to say "Come off it!" Laura may well see her as a kind of devil-angel, but must we? The suggestion of symbolism is reinforced by an odd incident in Laura's life which prefigures Vicky's end; on holiday with her young brother, Laura comes across a bizarre man-woman figure who makes suggestive remarks and shows them a room full of pornographic dolls. Again, this incident is brilliantly written in its way, but there is, too, something contrived about it. One is not convinced that the dolls really cropped up naturally in Laura's formless experience. I felt they were put there, just a shade too neatly, by Miss Manning.

Gillian Tindall. *NS*. April 11, 1969, p. 522

A solid, monolithic theme projects from Olivia Manning's *Balkan Trilogy* and that is "uncertainty." The series concerns itself neither with abstract or metaphysical theories of time, refashioned or shifting ideologies, nor various plays for power or status; but with the often bare, ironically conditioned facts of living in uncertainty—uncertainty not as an accident, but as a constant of life—in a world over which hangs the certainty of ruin.

[Of contemporary British novel sequences], Miss Manning's is the least self-conscious, the least arty, in a sense the easiest, but one of the most knowledgeable about common experience. It strives not for effects but for a single effect: to show a society teetering on, about to plunge into, an abyss, and to show people caught up in the making of history at a time when the mere debacle of the First World War was about to yield to the holocaust of the Second. Yet to show all this with something rivaling an antiepic, antiromantic sweep, to show how in this extraordinary decade the everyday world, through uncertainty, runs down.

For most of the trilogy Miss Manning's extraordinary world is Bucharest during the early years of the war, a city crammed with its complement of adventurers, expatriates, emigrés, opportunists, money barons, civil servants, and princes who suddenly find themselves on the threshold of history. Part comic-opera Ruritania in its feudality, its gilt and gaudiness; part political nightmare in its ferment of royalist, liberal, and fascist factions, Bucharest reflects the pretensions and tensions of a Rumania as heterogeneous as Durrell's Alexandria or Burgess's Malaya. It is a presence, a force of some magnificence before it squanders "the great fortune" (the title of the first volume in the sequence) to become "the spoilt city" (the title of the second). Pressured from within and without, part of a country neutered by its fence-sitting neutrality, ransacked of its dignity, culture, wealth, and civilization, Bucharest becomes the battleground for a kind of primal survival, and, as Miss Manning makes symbolically apparent, a Troy fallen anew.

Robert K. Morris. *Continuance and Change:*
The Contemporary British Novel Sequence
(Carbondale, Southern Illinois Univ. Pr.,
1972), pp. 29–30

MANSFIELD, KATHERINE (1888–1923)

Once upon a time a sensitive soul was born in New Zealand, took the name Katherine Mansfield and came to Europe, where she wrote evocative fragments, loved delicately, and died young—technically of pulmonary tuberculosis but really because life was too gross for her.

Fortunately, this banal person never existed. Katherine Mansfield was in the habit of running up spare personalities for herself: one evening she would wear the decadent sophisticate, the next the unfathomable Russian. The fragile stray from elfland was the least pleasing of her creations but the longest-lasting—because it had the backing of her second husband, John Middleton Murry; and not only did Murry represent her after her death, but throughout their life together she was trying—to the point of falsifying her true personality—to capture his approval or even attention.

Her true personality, which includes the polymorphous poseuse, is at once more attractive, more cogent, and more bitingly tragic. This did not become wholly accessible to the public until the 'fifties, when Murry published the uncut text of her journal and of her letters to him and when the biography by Antony Alpers told the full facts of her picaresque life: the inconsequential, almost surrealistic first marriage; the two extramarital pregnancies, ending in a miscarriage and an abortion; the dash almost to the Front in 1915 for a few days' love affair with a literary French conscript. The life of the "free woman," which is now being imposed on us as a postwar phenomenon—post *our* war—was being lived by Katherine Mansfield, and with incomparably more style, before women were properly out of long skirts.

Brigid Brophy. MQR. Spring, 1966, p. 89

In the annals of literature, [Katherine Mansfield] will be remembered if not as a great short story writer, at least as an experimenter, innovator and inspirer of the great art. She will be remembered with fondness, with affection, and with admiration not only by Englishmen and New Zealanders, but by all who love literature. In the centuries to come, when greater geniuses than herself will carry torches and blaze trails in literature, her small lamp will continue to shed light in the dark, unexplored corridors of life and letters and guide those who follow. It is an irony of fate that she died a premature death; inevitably all her ambitions of reorienting art collapsed; all her hopes returned with the return of the spring, but the spring of 1923 never returned for her.

With what regrets she died, we shall never know. She did not find complete satisfaction in her love life or in her married life. Perhaps she wanted to become for Murry the whole of his life; she could not give him the whole of her life which he demanded; nor was he capable of understanding her complex emotional nature. Consequently, he could not give her what she most wanted—companionship.

Nariman Hormasji. Katherine Mansfield:
An Appraisal (Collins, 1967), p. 153

Katherine Mansfield is not a great writer, though in a very few stories she approaches artistry of the first rank. Her significance to the contemporary critic is as an authentic and original talent in fiction. Like

Virginia Woolf in the novel, Mansfield felt the need to break windows. Her emulation of her Russian predecessors in her inimitable English prose helped alter the reading tastes of an English public surrounded by insipidity and pretension in short fiction available at the time of the First World War.

Like Joseph Conrad and James Joyce, she wrote at a time when a breakthrough in the representation of reality was not only desirable but also possible in the English short story: when the tools of psychology might be employed to construct meaningful symbolic structures in fiction; and when literary characters might be examined from the inside as well as from the outside, whole or fragmented into aspects of themselves. She wrote at a time when the furniture of fiction was largely being scrapped in favor of concentration on essences: the spirit that moved human beings rather than the scene in which they moved. Her recognition of these new directions came early. Her determination to follow them, not as a member of a coterie but because she understood that they were the only paths open to her kind of talent, has assured her a small but secure place in literary history. Much more than the influence of her literary criticism, her short stories have played a large part in shaping the contemporary short story in our language.

But Mansfield does not belong entirely to history. There is a vitality in "The Daughters of the Late Colonel" and "The Garden Party" and (with due respect to Virginia Woolf's strictures) "Bliss" that will outlast their historical importance. "At the Bay," "Prelude," and "The Stranger" will be read with approval by those who delight in an artistically controlled and verbally harmonious vision of reality. The same desire to get beneath the apparent ugliness of life to the hidden beauty that Mansfield gives voice to in her letters is occasionally satisfied in this short story or that. When it happens, the result more than justifies her hope that her stories may truly matter.

> Marvin Magalaner. *The Fiction of Katherine Mansfield* (Carbondale, Southern Illinois Univ. Pr., 1971), pp. 131–32

MASEFIELD, JOHN (1878–1967)

Another man's nostalgia can become tiresome because we are left out of it. Masefield [in *Grace before Ploughing*] took me along and I saw with wide-eyed wonder the sights of his childhood and felt something of the terror planted in his young mind by protective, well-meaning adults

—the fear of bulls which could "gore a little boy so that his own mother couldn't know him," of gypsies whom he was not entirely persuaded to fear, whom in fact he greatly admired for their waistcoats, their gold buttons, "their choice of vans as homes and the breadth of England for their doorsteps." He would not believe the popular accusation of child-stealing made against these kindred spirits. His wanderlust was later to draw him physically and imaginatively to even wider expanses, with "the lonely sea and the sky" for *his* doorstep.

Masefield's art astonished by the simplicity of its line. I think it comes from a rare gift of sight that reveals to those who possess it "the unutterable worth of humble thing." We feel the boy's wonder at the passage of a strange cloud formation; his sorrow at the death of the stag he had seen "leap the stile with unspeakable, matchless grace." . . .

In his last chapter, in which the adult Masefield allows himself a say, it is to counterbalance his personal happiness as a child and darken the picture a little. It was beautiful for him, he says, but he also saw children in rags and barefooted in frost; "men unable to read or write; men marked with smallpox and many young men getting out of England to begin elsewhere at all costs." But in his lifetime he also saw these things change beyond the expectation of even the most generous heart, which gives him great hope for what's to come.

Masefield's spirit of optimism is remarkable for a man who witnessed the disappearance of so much that he had enjoyed as a child. He achieves this spirit because, I think, he sees life as a continuing adventure in which what's to come has always been unsure. . . .

Chinua Achebe. NS. June 17, 1966, p. 886

Masefield's place among the Poets Laureate is that of a poet well qualified, by practice and by temperament, for his post. His celebration of England, as has been shown above, began long before his appointment to an official post. He fulfilled the obligations of the Laureateship as conscientiously as Tennyson, more ably than Austin, and more generously than Bridges. Masefield's activities in behalf of the theater, the speaking of verse, and other arts were many; in his person the Poet Laureate changed from the incumbent of a nominal office to "a living symbol of the power and authority" of poetry.

It is not the task of this study, however, to attempt judgment of Masefield's comparative success in these individual fields; it is, rather, to consider his overall significance as the interpreter of many varied phases of English character and English landscape and life.

The Englishness of Masefield's work is the heart of it. If the prose and poetry that are characteristically and openly English are separated from the rest of his work, little of major importance remains. The greater body of Masefield's work, and the finest part of it, is that in which he dedicates himself to the portrayal and the interpretation of English landscape and life. In this England of Masefield, John Bull sometimes makes an appearance, but always he is countered by St. George. And the spirit of St. George shines brightest in those longer poems and tales which are most likely to live – *The Everlasting Mercy, Dauber,* "August, 1914," *Gallipoli, Reynard the Fox, King Cole,* and the *Midsummer Night* stories.

There is no inconsistency in Masefield's apparent shift from a consecration to the common man to a consecration to England. His England is the England of the common man; and the beauties of that England of the future for which he calls repeatedly in his later work are dedicated to the refreshment and the recreation of the common man in England and throughout the world.

Fraser Drew. John Masefield's England
(Rutherford, N.J., Fairleigh Dickinson Univ.
Pr., 1973), p. 230

M/●'GHAM, W. SOMERSET (1874–1965)

At the heart of the literary career of Somerset Maugham lies a baffling enigma: Here was a writer equipped at most points—a born storyteller, a shrewd observer of men and manners, and an able technician; blessed with a long and not uneventful life enriched by wide travel and experience; the author of about one hundred literary contributions which have won popular acclaim—and yet what did he leave, ultimately, by way of lasting creative achievement? Nothing except a "slender baggage," as he himself admitted with his characteristically ruthless honesty—"two or three plays and a dozen short stories," to which may be added a couple of novels for fair measure. How did this happen? The usual explanation, "Just for a handful of silver he left us," is too facile to be completely satisfying.

At the center of the Maugham-enigma lies a deep-seated conflict, a conflict between cynicism and humanitarianism, which is discernible in his early work, and the growth and influence of which can be traced through his career to his final achievement.

M. K. Naik. W. Somerset Maugham (Norman,
Univ. of Oklahoma Pr., 1966), p. 3

In a few years time, inevitably, Maugham's reputation will undergo a slump. He has been so long supreme, and those who enthrone a new deity will find it necessary to increase the praise of the new god by decrying the qualities of the old. But I cannot believe that the reaction will last for long. Several of his books may go out of print for ever, but there are so few great story-tellers, and few have equalled Maugham's capacity to carry your interest on from one page to the next. You cannot put him down, not only because of the excellence of the plot but for the manner of its telling. It is not chance that led him to put an Arab charm against the evil eye upon the covers of his books. He has a deep affinity with those story-tellers of the market-place who hold their audience with the power of their eye, the intonation of their voice, the movements of their hands. He lays his individual spell upon you, so that in retrospect you remember not only the tale itself, but the teller of it.

The story is a medium, a means to the end, and future generations will, I am very sure, be as fascinated as we ourselves have been by this enigmatic man, the object of so much conjecture, a man who at the same time so thwarted and so rewarded, a man who has been offered the sampling of every dish the banquet of life has for offering, yet has been denied on his own admission the very consolations that alone make life tolerable for the vast majority of human beings; a man so disillusioned, so unself-deceived, so ruthless towards himself yet to others so invariably helpful; a man who in the last analysis has always been upon the side of what was true and simple, of what the Greeks called "the beautiful and good."

Alec Waugh. *My Brother Evelyn and Other
Portraits* (N.Y., Farrar, Straus and Giroux,
1967), pp. 293–94

Maugham declared that he had no illusions about his status as a writer. He said that only two important critics in his own country had troubled to take him seriously and that the bright young men who wrote essays on contemporary fiction never considered him at all. I noticed with surprise that J. B. Priestley in his massive, internationally comprehensive, and in many ways most valuable book on *Literature and Western Man* (1962) mentioned Maugham only in a single line about the Ashenden stories while Galsworthy and E. M. Forster were each given a full page, despite the latter's tiny output in a quiet, retired life lasting over eighty years.

Maugham suggested that the neglect of his work was due to the fact that he had never been a propagandist. There was, in his opinion, a prevailing taste for novels "in which the characters delivered their views on the burning topics of the day" and that "a bit of love-making thrown in here and there made the information they were given sufficiently palatable." There is a thrust in that at Wells and Priestley; both made their personal opinions about the state of the world apparent when they told a story. Both have been first-rate journalists. Maugham could be called a purist in his attitude to fiction. As a novelist he would not be a publicist.

Ivor Brown. *W. Somerset Maugham*
(Cranbury, N.J., Barnes, 1970), p. 23

The real inadequacy of Maugham's writing—his lack of true warmth and intimacy—is a natural extension of his own life. Reacting to the unhappiness of his childhood, to what he felt were physical handicaps, and to unfortunate experiences with others as a young man, he sought protection in freedom and detachment. The wall which he created between his essential self and those he met could not help influencing the tone of his writings, and as a result most of his writings lack the willingness to expose the soul which is in some form the mark of all great writers. In *Of Human Bondage* Maugham unashamedly bared his innermost obsessions and fears for the scrutiny of all readers, and thus it has a sincerity and credibility which appears infrequently in his other writing.

Of Human Bondage was an act of catharsis, however, and afterwards Maugham retreated to the position of the tolerant detached observer, and he revealed little of himself, even indirectly, through his fiction. This is somewhat surprising since in other respects he is one of the least pretentious and devious of writers. His sincerity in recognising his limitations and in professing few illusions about the role of the writer in society is not simply a professional stance. Nevertheless, this refreshing honesty and humility should not deceive readers into believing that Maugham very often ever completely exposed himself. After *Of Human Bondage*, he revealed only what he wished, and this was a carefully edited version of W. Somerset Maugham. His homosexual tendencies, for example, are never even hinted at in the millions of words he wrote. In 1900 the young author had written in his notebook: "Am I a minor poet that I should expose my bleeding vitals to the vulgar crowd?" The answer should surely be: yes. The truly great writers have always bared their souls, albeit in devious and conventionalised ways, to the gaze of their readers. This true intimacy between the reader and the author is a quality which one unmistakably senses in the greatest literature, and it is not an element which can be artificially created.

Maugham's own concern for detachment and reluctance to expose himself is largely responsible for his failure to create many well-developed characters. His belief, developed from his medical studies, that there is no such thing as the normal, that each person is a mixture of warped and noble elements, makes it difficult for him to draw characters with a universal quality. His conviction that each person is essentially unable ever to understand fully or communicate with his fellows leads to his treating his characters as unfathomable mysteries. . . . Unlike the protagonists of the greatest writers, these figures never remain in one's memory as people one has actually known and understood.

Robert Lorin Calder. *W. Somerset Maugham and the Quest for Freedom* (Garden City, N.Y., Doubleday, 1973), pp. 258–59

● MCGAHERN, JOHN (1934–   )

Mr. McGahern [in *The Barracks*] is . . . concerned with characters in an institutional setting who fear that life is slipping away from them, its joys untasted. Reegan is a sergeant in the Irish police, stationed in the West, a volunteer in the early days of the Irish Free State whose hopes and ambitions have been dissipated by the mediocrity of modern Ireland, and whose energies are increasingly drained by a bitter feud with his superintendent. His wife Elizabeth, whose thoughts occupy most of the book, balances the small satisfactions of her provincial life against the keener joys and sorrows of her past in London, and the uncertainty of death forced upon her by the knowledge that she has cancer.

These themes are elaborated against the rhythms of domestic and barrack life, the details of which are evoked with a scrupulous yet enchancing accuracy that reminds one of the young Joyce. Where Joyce would have concentrated the experience of *The Barracks* into a short story, Mr. McGahern has extended it over the length of a novel whose structure is too frail to support the weight of detail. But for a young man of twenty-seven, he is astonishingly successful in penetrating the mind of a mature woman confronted with pain and death. Mr. McGahern is the real thing, and his development will be well worth watching.

David Lodge. *Spec.* March 8, 1963, p. 300

When I was in Ireland in the summer of 1965 for the first time in twenty years, I was loaned John McGahern's *The Dark*, together with a farmyard of criticism, comment and gossip concerning the man and his work.

I had not read McGahern's first work, *The Barracks*. It was, apparently, very well received in England *and* in Eire, winning a number of lucrative awards. Unfortunately, as things are in Eire, the gaining of official plaudits could be much the same thing as consenting to wear a strait jacket. . . .

Eire refused McGahern's second book, *The Dark*, and has more or less disowned the man with, I suppose, after the gratis recognition of *The Barracks*, the implication that he has also spurned the feeding hand. This circumstance is a small but interesting facet of the entire relationship of the Irish artist with his own society, and which is in turn an active part of the world contest between art and power politics. I can well imagine that many an apparently democratic politician might secretly wish for the authority to gag his working artists who are always prone to describe the clay feet of his otherwise expensive idols. As regards McGahern, it seems that *The Dark* has also cost the man his teaching job: the subtle operation of the immortal sanction, I suppose —a kind of material excommunication. Recently, the whole affair was aired on a television program.

The Dark attempts to describe certain series of unadorned existences as they are today. It seems to be the author's basic working conception to tell the story in a hard, stark, sparse and unexploited way, from the outset setting his mind against any inherent and related softening: after all, he is post-Beckett and may well have been influenced by the latter's strictly exiguous technique.

Nature, even Irish nature, hardly enters the book. Nor is anything mentioned about the vast mythological background, although the book is placed near Rath Cruachan, the royal mystical capital of the ancient province that goes back to De Danann days. I don't even know how many children there are in the family. The household is presented as a kind of lone bush without a tap root, a kind of island. (Maybe the household *is* Ireland?) With the exception of Father Gerald, there are really only two main measurable characters, the boy and his father. McGahern has omitted details, I think, with the intention of presenting a picture of spiritual barrenness—a wilderness that can only be lived in by clinging to cold and detached noninvolvement; by growing an exoskeleton and keeping the soft parts inside.

Anthony C. West. *Nation*. Nov. 7, 1966,
p. 488–89

A short but penetrating comment by Michael Foley on the novels of John McGahern (in the September, 1968 issue of *The Honest Ulsterman*) is, clearly, the response of one who has warmed to this writer's sterling qualities of tenderness and compassion. Mr. Foley has sympathetically indicated the sombre nature of the writer's vision, the dark conditions of his fictional universe. He prompts me to take the matter a little further and to enquire into the degree of the writer's success, in novelistic terms, in the realization of that vision. It seems to me that McGahern's first novel, *The Barracks*, a remarkable *tour de force* for a young writer, perfectly achieved his purpose but that *The Dark*, which attempts to present a similar universe in confessional form is, though often interesting and compelling, ultimately much less successful. I do not suggest that Elizabeth Reegan's view of the nature of life is argued more convincingly than young Mahoney's, rather that McGahern makes her predicament vividly credible but fails to repeat this effect in the second novel. The success and the failure depend, I think, on form.

The form of *The Barracks* perfectly suits the writer's purpose. Elizabeth Reegan is thirty-nine years old and soon to die. This life has been lived and its imaginative reality is vividly created for us in a series of capably controlled flashbacks. The boy in *The Dark* is embarking on life—flashbacks are impossible here, the experience must be created chronologically. The second book is, thus, denied one of the earlier work's most powerful ingredients, the moving current of nostalgic regret which rolls through the novel like a dark tide. The middle-aged woman, dying of cancer, trapped in a marriage which has tenderness but no real sympathy in it, is the perfect vehicle for McGahern's purposeful pessimism. Elizabeth Reegan's life is made up of long periods of gallant, dogged silence and occasional moments of visionary joy which blaze like meteors in the darkness of her ordinary existence.

John Cronin. *Studies*. Winter, 1969, p. 427

[*Nightlines*] is an extremely good book of short stories, and one which quite plainly reveals a talent in the process of striding development. The stories in the earlier part, though true and spare, don't always free themselves from the two conventional categories into which short stories are apt to fall: the inexplicit slice-of-novel category and the moment-of-revelation category, often of childhood or adolescence. Apart from some occasional (and successful) oddnesses of syntax, Mr. McGahern is a traditional writer: he employs no gimmicks to relieve him from the grave obligation of giving us a fresh view of human beings and human relations, of landscapes, thoughts and dialogues. . . . One must add, too, that even at his most conventional Mr. McGahern rarely fails to present us with the moral questions whose presence is the hallmark of a considerable writer, and though he is helped in this by the Irish society that forms the basis of most of the stories, the thing is also carried into the long piece with a Spanish setting, "Peaches," which is one of the most remarkable in the book.

In "Peaches" Mr. McGahern moves into dangerous fictional seas —the creative artist "abroad," with a writer's block and a matrimonial problem—but comes through them triumphantly unbattered. There is a rather poker-faced emotionalism, a committed concern with food and other apparatus of day-to-day life, and even a political delineation harking back to the Spanish Civil War. These Hemingwayesque properties, however, the author makes entirely his own: and we don't feel, as so often with Hemingway himself, any sentimentality beneath the mask, or mere literary contrivance in the described sensuous aspects of existence, or oversimplification in the questions raised of courage, the ability to love, and so forth. Possibly we may judge that Mr. McGahern is in safer waters when he returns in the fine last story to the Ireland of primitive schools and religious bigotry that is also the setting of his two novels, but we are grateful for the indisputable evidence of ambition and the continuing absorption of experience (also shown in another strong story about a London building site).

Reviewers confronted suddenly by an author of this quality are apt to make wild and perhaps unhelpful comparisons, but it is worth saying that for me the present book constantly recalled *Dubliners*. Joyce's collection, in the publishing convention of its time, was bulkier and therefore constituted somewhat more solid grounds for optimism about the author's future; but *Nightlines*, too, has an exciting blend of penetrating realism and sad lyricism, and a sympathy with and understanding of great stretches of human life extraordinary in a young writer.

Roy Fuller. *List*. Nov. 26, 1970, pp. 752, 755

● MIDDLETON, CHRISTOPHER (1926–   )

After nearly ten years of the "consolidation" practised by the supporters of the Movement, there are signs that the avant-garde is again pricking its ears. Christopher Middleton's *Torse 3* is the best book of poetry since the war which is demonstrably in the tradition of Eliot and Pound. No other poet writing in English has come so near in attitude to the recent work of a French poet like Dupin or a German one like Enzensberger. Even the titles of some of Mr. Middleton's poems recall that rather twenty-ish fascination with the teasingly contemporary which we all thought had gone out of fashion in England for ever; "Rhododendron Estranged in Twilight" must surely be the title of an early poem by Wallace Stevens, and "Cadgwith: 6 p.m." looks like an aide-memoire scribbled by Burbank in the margin of his famous Baedeker. "Matutinal Adventures of a Third Person Illustrating the Untold Agony of Habit" has the flamboyant disrespect for simplicity which we've associated with the titles of paintings by some of the Surrealists, like Duchamp. All these influences have certainly gone to mould Mr. Middleton's highly individual and eccentric style: what gives his work its unique importance is the originality with which he's combined them to break through almost all the accepted conventions of English poetry in the early 1960s. . . .

Mr. Middleton is primarily concerned, at any rate as a technician, with avoiding both of the cramping fallacies that poetry must never be paraphrasable and that poetry must always be paraphrasable. For him, as for a graphic artist like Steinberg, the world can only be represented by violent transitions of manner, and consistency would be a kind of insincerity as well as a curb on the creative impulses.

The second and major challenge to the current English poetic conventions which Mr. Middleton's work launches lies in his implicit acceptance of Eliot's doctrine that "poetry can communicate before it is understood." In reading the best work of Ted Hughes or Philip Larkin, my own experience has been that understanding and communication tend to go hand in hand, and I think this is broadly true for all the best English poetry of the last ten years. If the poem hasn't seemed clear, it usually hasn't seemed good. In Mr. Middleton's case this rule doesn't work. I'm quite convinced the "Five Psalms For Common Man," which ends *Torse 3*, is an important and moving poem, which I've enjoyed reading; but I know that I couldn't pass an examination on what exactly it's about. The authority of the poem lies in the ever-present evidence of control in the choice and arrangement of words—in the sensuousness of the descriptions and the musical quality of the sound. . . .

George MacBeth. *L*. April, 1962, pp. 83–84

Christopher Middleton's first book, *Torse 3*, was something of a gift for reviewers jaded by Movements and Groups; it seemed to be out on some mannered, well-read limb of its own, inviting us to be teased and European again, to be cunningly misled and yet its heart—where it could be seen to have one—seemed more or less in the right place. It risked pastiche as bravely as it teetered now and then on the edge of the wispily religiose (a "calm of visions") and though it did not finally settle for any single or original direction, it seemed full of usable, neglected possibilities. And these were vaguely welcome; it was good, at any rate, to have a poet ready to look beyond the diary, the daily news, the gloomy paradoxes of the marriage bed and whose eye could play so dashingly across a universe more full of mysteries than ironies. Maybe it was not so good to have a poet who a lot of the time was impenetrably difficult to understand but there were decent precedents. The book was widely praised.

Just as it is hard, though, in *Torse 3* to pin down Middleton to any one poetic manner, to say—for instance—that surrealistic flights of fancy were better for what he had to say than Dylanesque labyrinths of rhetoric, or the optical exercises of Wallace Stevens, so in his new book *Nonsequences* it is enormously difficult—and in spite of the sub- or joint-title, *Selfpoems*—to discover *him*. The style is more consistent, a chaste, neutral, rather laborious diction that can tighten up where it needs to but is mostly low-pressure and very humbly painstaking; he toys a bit with pregnant line-breaks and odd layouts but never takes the full experimentalist plunge—he is most easy, in fact, with longer lines and fairly formal stanzas. What mostly worries, though, throughout the book is this absence of any unifying personal pressure, an absence which one suspects to be deliberate. This is not to ask for autobiography or straight confession—there is in fact plenty of personal data in the poems—but somehow to miss the sense that all the words come naturally or necessarily from the one mouth, or are even weighed by the same imaginative measure.

Ian Hamilton. L. Feb., 1966, p. 81

[Middleton's] poems strike one at once as the expression of a sophisticatedly elusive personality. He too responds actively and sensuously to the impact of literal scenes, but the source of his art is usually something else, a dance of the mind among perceptions and eccentric associations.

He *can* be as much a localist as the other poets, as . . . his first book, *Torse 3* (1962), shows. . . . But most of the poems in the same book take their pitch and movement from the lyrical key and the level of fantasy established at the beginning, and then from a process of rapidly shifting association along the way. . . .

Lightness of movement, sureness of ear, a serious intelligence, unpredictability of form and association—a most unusual combination in British poetry—mark Middleton as the most varied and original of the younger English poets, if not the most powerful.

M. L. Rosenthal. The New Poets (N.Y.,
Oxford Univ. Pr., 1967), pp. 257, 260

Apart from fear and ideas of order and chaos, and despite acknowledgment of the subjective conditions of knowing, few men escape the conviction that reality endures according to its own laws quite apart from our will or perception. Several poems in *Torse 3* are precise, detailed descriptions of scenes, people, or events. Delightful in and of themselves, inexhaustibly resourceful in their language, they occasionally include an arresting image or curious turn of phrase that a more conventional poet would exclude because it violates the tonal or thematic unity of the poem. We are often told that literature is an ordering of reality; whether true or false, the statement calls attention to the disorder of reality itself. The descriptive poems in *Torse 3* are realistic *because* they include incongruent details. On the other hand, one poem in the volume, "Climbing a Pebble," is completely imaginary and perfectly logical. The consequences of this antithesis are revealed in Middleton's second collection, *Nonsequences/Selfpoems* (1965).

In discussing one theme in *Torse 3*, the relationship between the self and the world, I have not attempted to give a representative picture of the volume as a whole. Every poem is different; the stylistic variety is unparalleled in contemporary poetry, ranging from casual narration to elliptical precision, from portentous rhetoric ("Metropolitan Oratory," which echoes Eliot's "Animula") to transparent lyricism. Because style and tone shift so quickly, complete empathy is precluded in all but a few of the shorter poems. The reader becomes conscious of a deliberately chosen attitude intervening between the poet and his materials. Brecht's argument that the audience must be separated emotionally from dramatic action in order to understand it could provide an explanation of Middleton's disinterestedness. What the reader must often share if he is to appreciate the poems is an intellectual and aesthetic vigilance detached from the emotions represented. While such vigilance is assumed in comedy (and many of Middleton's poems are comic), its presence elsewhere inhibits immediate response in the interests of endowing the poem with meanings that become apparent only through contemplation.

The variegated personae of *Torse 3* are replaced in *Nonsequences* by a single speaker whose attention is fixed on the world, leading to a structural shift from a dialectic of awareness to a dialectic of reality. It is difficult to generalize about the meaning of the poems in *Nonsequences* because their occasions are varied and their implications ambiguous. What does emerge from the volume as a whole is a "syntax" of meaning—a structure of conceptual relationships indicating how elements of experience interact.

Wallace D. Martin. CL. Autumn, 1971,
pp. 426–27

● MOORE, BRIAN (1921–   )

Modern "tragedy" has moved far from the majesty of Oedipus and King Lear. Its most somber dramas are played out in essentially mediocre spirits: in the death of a salesman we feel our own death and, recently, we queued up in New York to join two tramps in a hopeless wait for Godot. *The Lonely Passion of Judith Hearne*, too, is the tragedy of a third-rate soul, and in its pathetic history we are moved to pity and fear.

In this, his first novel, Brian Moore has done his native Belfast somewhat the same service James Joyce did his native Dublin: he has taken an Irish city and laid bare its most secret soul through a character who could not have been born elsewhere. Stephen Dedalus, at the end of *A Portrait of the Artist as a Young Man*, goes forth from Dublin to seek freedom, but we know that Dublin's mark will be forever upon him. At the end of Mr. Moore's novel, Judith Hearne has lost everything—her pride, her friends, her faith—but she has lost them on Belfast's terms and we know that it is on Belfast's terms alone she will continue, however wretchedly, to live. The city is not a place; it is a colossus that creates, shapes, and then devours its children. . . .

In resume, Mr. Moore's novel may seem merely maudlin. But it is not. In its relentless pursuit of this woman's sorrow, in its refusal to sentimentalize or easily alleviate her plight, the book achieves a kind of vision, and it is a tragic vision. As she accepts, finally, the end of all her hopes, Judith Hearne attains, as the publishers claim, a certain grandeur. There is something awful in the death of even the meanest thing, and Judith Hearne, for all her delusions and mediocrity, had dreamed of those minimal things that all of us feel we have some right to expect from life—love, kindness, truth. Her defeat is the defeat, in a way, of all mankind, so relentless, final, and universal has Brian Moore made it. . . .

William Clancy. *Com.* Aug. 3, 1956, p. 448

Can talent travel? Of course there have been such writers as Turgenev and Conrad who have needed richer, foreign soils before their imaginations could take root and flower. But can a talent full-grown in one culture ever successfully transplant to another? Brian Moore, who by all accounts showed himself in *Judith Hearne* and *The Feast of Lupercal* a very full-grown talent indeed, should make one of the most interesting test cases. His first two novels were ripe, crabbed fruit of the environment where he was bred: those northern Irish counties where the sombre conscience of Calvinism takes on a mad, particular Celtic darkness. But in fact since 1948 he has lived in Canada, and in *The Luck of Ginger Coffey* he has tried not merely to work against a Canadian setting, but to write a North American novel.

Its theme is the one which takes the place there of tragedy, the form in which fate works for Dreiser, O'Neill, Saul Bellow and Arthur Miller: failure. Ginger Coffey is a harmless enough blusterer. At home in Dublin, his little Alpine hat and big, silly moustache would mark him as nothing worse than a pub-Micawber. But in the strange, snowy air of Montreal—more like a Russian city than an American one, with its domed churches and booted, muffled crowds—failure settles on him like a disease with a smell. His jobs have run out, the return fares are spent, the one friend he has made in the city, it transpires, tolerates him guiltily for love of his wife. While she—long-suffering, fortyish, much-lied-to—is determined to seize the chance, if Ginger cannot, of the luxury of the New World for herself and their daughter. It is the classic North American nightmare of *Death of a Salesman*; except that in booming post-war Canada one does not die like Willy Loman, one simply learns to settle for disillusion.

It is an impressive try, thick, comic and frightening. If it doesn't wholly come off (the wife is a cipher, her lover a satiric stook of Canadian banalities, the ending is spread out a trifle flatly), its short-comings aren't so much falsities as holes in the experience of Mr. Moore's new environment. What he has mastered, he has mastered brilliantly: the odd, drifting Canadian underworld of winoes and lonely men in YMCAs, taking mail-order muscle-building courses, rambling on about fabulous jobs up North; the bleak, neon-lined sprawl of the sub-Arctic city, with its tough French police and anonymous apartment-blocks. It's a panoramic picture which also extends in depth; deep enough to raise the hope that he has not merely transplanted a talent, but found soil to grow into the novelist who will speak at last for the huge, cryptic country he has chosen.

Ronald Bryden. *Spec.* Aug. 26, 1960, p. 316

The singular strength of Brian Moore's novels is manifest in their abolishing brow-distinction. Their way of doing so is not by what is essentially a highbrow strategy: the offering of different "levels," with its implicit condescensions (they read it for the story, we read it for the symbols and themes). Mr. Moore's new novel [*The Emperor of Ice-Cream*], like its predecessors, makes itself accessible to everyone, not by offering different things to different men, but by concentrating simply, directly and bravely on the primary sufferings and passions that everybody feels. Of all our present novelists he is for me ("for me," not because of any hesitation, but because of the nature of the praise) the one whose books most immediately evoke and touch my private feelings and fears, memories of what it was, when one was like that in the past—dismay at what it will be, when one is like that in the future. Kingsley Amis, not a lachrymose man, once paid R. S. Thomas's poems a tribute such as few reviewers feel it quite proper to pay: "It is enough to say he often moves to tears." The best moments in these novels have such a power—you have to pull yourself together. Agreed, it is a power that can often be felt strongly enough in bad films, but few good novels can do any such thing.

Sentimentality, some will say. But a novel such as Mr. Moore's first, *The Lonely Passion of Judith Hearne*, does not move us by any kind of illicit manipulation. Humphry House spoke of sentimentality as "the imposition of feeling as an afterthought upon literalness." But that wouldn't apply to *Judith Hearne*, where the emotion is intrinsic to the description, itself a matter of sharp delineation. It is natural that it should have been a literary critic of the Victorians who found so good a definition, and Mr. Moore's novels belong without any embarrassment in the tradition that the Victorians magnificently established. He is, if you like, a "conventional" novelist, quite without experimentalisms and gimmicks. In none of the novels is anything concealed except the art by which they transmute "an ordinary sorrow of man's life" into something we care about.

Christopher Ricks. *NS.* Feb. 18, 1966, p. 227

The style of *I Am Mary Dunne* is at first puzzling and disappointing, for it suggests the slick women's magazines with their chic female protagonist's quest for fulfillment and happiness in the first-person point of view, and even in the precious nicknames of several of the male characters—Bat, Tee, Hat. Moore again makes the risky decision (as in all his novels) to explore that territory dangerously close to melodrama, a decision that has opened his works to the criticism of sentimentality. But it is Moore's conviction that the serious writer must skirt the melodramatic on his way to an honest resolution of events, that he must take chances; and if he fails, his work may lapse into melodrama. Moore has not failed yet: he has succeeded remarkably well in *The Lonely Passion of Judith Hearne, The Luck of Ginger Coffey* and *An Answer from Limbo*. For the final terrain which Moore reaches with his protagonist Mary Dunne is not country for the young women of the slick magazines.

The shock of the novel has its legitimate basis, I think, in this stylistic and thematic approach: what appears to be superficial and leading to easy answers moves instead into the horror void that underlies the daily activities of the "successful" American. The irony of the search for identity is that it may end successfully. The deception of the style only adds force to that revelation when it comes. Moore has shown before, in *An Answer from Limbo*, that his view of the abyss need not be limited to failures in Ireland; he has demonstrated again in *I Am Mary Dunne* that hell is here as well.

Richard B. Sale. Nation. June 24, 1968, p. 832

Moore's third novel [*The Luck of Ginger Coffey*], published in 1960, represents a breakthrough for him on a number of counts: it is his first work with a North American setting, it is the first one in which the central character achieves at least a partial triumph, and it is the first one which departs from the predominant naturalism of his earlier work. These three factors are clearly related, and taken together, they represent a movement on Moore's part towards an essentially comic mode in his fiction; it is in this respect that *Ginger Coffey* differs sharply from both *Judith Hearne* and *Lupercal*, and sets a tone which is to prevail throughout his subsequent fiction. . . .

In *The Emperor of Ice-Cream*, as in his four previous novels, Moore is concerned with the insignificant member of society. Perhaps it is this concern for the hero of non-heroic stature that makes his fiction convincing; Gavin Burke is not an imposing figure, but he is a believable one, even though his triumph in a sense is accidental in that he capitalizes on a situation not of his own making—the disintegration of his society. In some ways he is as weak as his Belfast predecessors, Judith and Devine, who failed to make the breakthrough because the forces against them were stronger than their individual wills. Nevertheless, Moore seems to be saying that when there is a chance for fulfilment, one must be ready to act meaningfully; this is the burden of *Emperor*, and the reader is convinced that for Gavin there will be no turning back, regardless of what happens to his society.

With Gavin Burke and *The Emperor of Ice-Cream*, Moore modifies his vision of the world to the point where the reader can share the fulfilment of the seized moment, and though this is not his strongest novel, it is, along with *Mary Dunne*, his most optimistic work. This altered perspective is also, as Moore has pointed out, a product of changes in his personal affairs, and it seems clear from his comments that *Emperor* marks a significant modification of the spirit which informs his work. "I don't know whether this great change will make me a better or a worse writer," he has admitted, "but I'll be a different writer."

Hallvard Dahlie. Brian Moore (Toronto, Copp
Clark, 1969), pp. 48, 102–3

The characteristic shape of Brian Moore's novels, like that of Proust's great masterpiece and Lowry's *Under the Volcano,* is the circle, the clockface of cyclical existence, in which the end of a novel coincides with the beginning. In Moore's first and last novels the pattern is obvious. *The Lonely Passion of Judith Hearne* begins with Judith arranging her aunt's photograph and a print of the Sacred Heart in a new Belfast lodging; it ends with Judith performing the same ritual in the hospital to which her alcoholism has led her, and, now as then, she reflects—the same words end the last chapter as terminate the first chapter—"When they're with me, watching over me, a new place becomes home."

In his sixth and most recent book, *I Am Mary Dunne,* published thirteen years later, the same obvious circle exists. The novel, which strictly preserves the classical unities by confining its action to a single day in a single city, though its memories plunge back over twenty years, begins with a recollection of Mary Dunne in a convent school arguing that *memento ergo sum* was a more valid philosophical statement that the *cogito ergo sum* of Descartes, and ends, at the nightfall of this day when a series of coincidences has astonishingly stirred up the depths of the past, in the same maxim re-stated, and supported by the heroine's dogged assertion: "I say it over and over and over, I am Mary Dunne, I am Mary Dunne, I am Mary Dunne," in spite of the fact that since she used that childhood name she has run through three husbands and has been Mary Phelan and Mary Bell and is currently Mary Lavery.

In Brian Moore's other novels, the cyclical pattern is not quite so neatly achieved that the end verbally repeats the beginning. But the pattern nevertheless persists. In *The Feast of Lupercal,* the prim and routine-ridden schoolmaster Diarmuid Devine has his season of rebellion when Una Clarke comes to Belfast from Dublin, but the adventure ends with nothing won, and Old Dev returns to his familiar life, diminished by the knowledge that he can never change. *The Luck of Ginger Coffey* ends with the Coffey family re-established after what had seemed an irrevocable parting; Ginger, his ambitions crushed, returns to the role of glorified secretary which had been his in the past, and all that he is promised is the ever-lasting repetition of Sisyphus and his rock.

George Woodcock. *Odysseus Ever Returning*
(Toronto, McClelland and Stewart, 1970),
pp. 41–42

Moore's fiction strikes me as interesting and refreshing precisely because it does not focus upon an essentially twentieth-century predicament. The dilemma faced by Moore's important characters—with few exceptions—is in fact a primitive rather than modern dilemma. It is created by the characters' exclusion from the community and their subsequent occupation of a ritual limbo through which they seek to pass as quickly and as successfully as possible. Though Moore occasionally diverges from this theme—most notably in *An Answer from Limbo*—each of his novels remains to greater or lesser degree a variation of it, but a variation that contributes to the pattern of the total canon. . . .

Moore's two early Belfast novels explore ritual failure and the punishment and exclusion attendant upon such failure in a rigidly structured and provincial community. Ritual failure I define as the inability to perform the rites of passage on the way to self-fulfillment within one's own group. This theme extends with variation into the North American novels, but later gives way to the cognate theme of ritual displacement which Moore exploits most fully in *I Am Mary Dunne*. Ritual displacement occurs when the individual is unwilling or unable to perform the rites of incorporation into a new society and thereby find happiness and fulfillment. Since Moore is a novelist and not a sociologist, I want to make it clear that I use the term "ritual" not in reference to specific rites and ceremonies, but rather to the rhythms of separation, initiation, and incorporation common to all societies and communities.

John Wilson Foster. Critique. Vol. 13, No. 1,
1971, pp. 5–6

Brian Moore's novels focus on the breakdown which occurs when an individual alters or represses his deepest desires for the sake of social recognition. His characters, whether they be drab Belfastian spinsters or promising Irish artists, are victimized by desire and guilt. They want warmth, recognition and understanding, but they are tyrannized by an inner sense of inadequacy and failure. Driven by shame and loathing for what they might be, they seek an alternate image of self in the distorted mirror of socially accepted norms of behavior and appearances. Moore recognizes the petty forms of tyranny practiced on a personal level by one's family and friends, on a broader social level by one's colleagues at work, on a spiritual level by the priestly arbiters of moral values and on a purely impersonal level by bellhops, storekeepers, policemen, and judges. Ironically, the values which support this chain of intimidation are upheld by the very people who suffer the guilts and inadequacies it generates. The most pathetic aspect of Moore's characters is not the humiliation they suffer because they fear rejection;

it is the necessity they feel to vindicate their abusers by rejecting themselves.

The secular city and the spiritual temple are shaped by the same desires and fears which divide the individual. In novels reflecting Moore's earliest experiences, he uses Belfast and the Catholic Church as social constructs which reenforce repression and provincialism. But his purposes are equally served by the sophisticated urban societies of New York or Montreal. The Catholic Church and the cultural centers of the world are intimately connected with the contradictory impulses and motives which dominate human behavior. What appears to be a character's inability to reconcile his needs to what society demands is founded on his inability to reconcile disparate elements in himself. Social institutions are hostile and remote when they reflect this inner failure. When Moore's characters reach a critical juncture where they can no longer sustain their illusions, their despair is compounded by a brief vision of the inadequacy and fragility of the entire social fabric. This vision, in turn, creates an unbearable emotional strain. Consequently, they desperately cling to a fabricated memory of a past undefiled or an identity unbetrayed.

The structure of Moore's novels is based on this general pattern of response. . . .

Murray Prosky. Éire-Ireland. Fall, 1971,
pp. 106–7

Brian Moore is too modest, both about Belfast and himself. First of all, no one could distract Joyceans from reassembling the stones of ancient Dublin; secondly, Brian Moore's work deserves critical attention for its own unique virtues and not as part of a scholarly layoff at the Joycean distillery. Last of all, "distressful" Belfast in its time of troubles has more urgent things to do than stand still for literary scholars. . . .

The Belfast of Moore's first novels is not a place where you want to go. As the rainclouds move endlessly up the Lough, landladies peer through from parlor curtains alert for signs of sin in the air. Over the thick walls of colleges the swish of magisterial canes stirs the unlearned air. In these novels, everyone one knows is Catholic, but somewhere out there a Protestant majority holds power across a gulf of prejudice. One marvels how Moore could write so much about Belfast and so little about Protestants, but perhaps that may be the point he is trying to make. From that tight narrow world, the only other well-known city is Dublin, and even Dublin Catholics are regarded with suspicion. England, never mind America, is culturally on another planet.

The major characters of this fictional world—perhaps not representative, but at least typical—are in their thirties or forties, and unmarried. The women miss marriage, but not for sexual reasons (at least as far as they are aware), and they tend to go on secret benders. The males content themselves with "impure thoughts"—proof of their normality, and practice the rite of Onan. These people are marooned on plateaus of gentility and bestir themselves at their peril, for to rise is unlikely and to fall is without recourse. When you sin, your landlady knows it, and out you go.

Such is the damp moral atmosphere of Moore's Belfast. . . .

John P. Fraye. In Raymond J. Porter and
James D. Brophy, eds., *Modern Irish
Literature* (N.Y., Iona College Pr., Twayne,
1972), pp. 215–17

To anyone who has lived through and cared about the recent convulsions of the Roman Catholic Church, the basic situation of *Catholics* is full of interest and promise, and Mr. Moore handles it with the skill and poise that one expects of him. The physical setting of the rain-swept island, "riding the sea like an overturned fishing boat" and the homely routine of the monastic life there, are vividly evoked. Suspense about the outcome of Kinsella's mission is well maintained. Yet *Catholics* is, in the end, a disappointment.

The ending turns upon a reversal by which the Abbot, who appears for most of the action to be cannily directing the resistance of the monks to Kinsella's mission, is revealed as a man who has lost his faith some years before, and who regards his vocation as a secular, managerial task. Pragmatically accepting the orders from Rome, he sees his main problem as how to maintain the solidarity and efficiency of the community—scandalised and demoralised as it is by the attack on its antiquated faith. The story ends with the Abbot leading the monks in prayer, a prayer in which he does not believe, forcing himself into the terror of *nada*, the metaphysical vacancy which he knows will result from this hypocrisy, sacrificing his own peace of mind for the sake of his community.

It's a neat resolution, but it leaves one feeling a little cheated because it shifts the focus of the story from public to private experience. If you set a story in the future you almost inevitably engage the reader's interest on the level of ideas. Mr. Moore, having mounted an interesting conflict between traditionalist and progressive parties in the Church, seems to evade the issue by the revelation about the Abbot's scepticism. Perhaps he is telling us that both the traditionalist and progressive arguments miss the point—that there is a void at the heart of modern man's spiritual experience against which Rosary-and-

Benediction Catholicism and Marxist-Ecumenical Catholicism seem equally shallow and irrelevant. A valid point of view—but one that gains nothing from being worked out in an imagined future. The void that waits upon the disillusioned Catholic is nowhere more powerfully evoked than in Mr. Moore's own fine novel *The Lonely Passion of Judith Hearne*, that scrupulously realistic portrait of petit-bourgeois life in post-war Belfast. *Catholics* is too short and too schematic to achieve that kind of intensity, but it doesn't fully satisfy either as a novel of religious ideas.

David Lodge. NS. Nov. 3, 1972, p. 647

● MOSLEY, NICHOLAS (1923–   )

The corruption of Mr. Nicholas Mosley's title [*Corruption*] is something which his hero, Robert, who tells the story, sees in the world around him, very vividly, but cannot diagnose, until it is almost too late, as it grows up in himself. Robert, in fact, discovers that there is something to be despised in himself and something to feel humble about in people he has despised. He grows, through pain, into greater self-knowledge. It is this theme which gives a considerable moral interest to a novel which, on the surface, looks like a rather too preciously written comic, and here and there slightly sentimental, melodrama about trivially self-indulgent people.

Mr. Mosley's people, except for a beautifully drawn rather Salingerish schoolboy, Julius, who represents assailed innocence, are certainly not, either by ideal or conventional standards, particularly nice. The heroine, Kate, is an arrogant, handsome creature who sleeps around a great deal just because the experience (with everyone except the hero) has always dissatisfied her. The hero has a great capacity for sulky self-pity and when he has made and lost Kate for the second time in his life—she first seduced him when he was a boy of sixteen—he goes slumming in the bohemian bottle-party world, picking up women there whom he regards with contemptuous condescension.

G. S. Fraser. NS. April 20, 1957, pp. 521–22

I note with shame that *Impossible Object* is Nicholas Mosley's seventh novel. With shame, because he is so good and this is the first of his books I have read, though I saw the Pinterized film version of his *Accident*. And I wonder, has he always been this good, hidden among the unappreciative English? Or has he developed from book to book the mastery he exhibits in *Impossible Object*? All I know is that he now has under full control four of the novelist's priceless gifts. He knows how to exploit the metaphoric possibilities of language. He has a shrewd grasp of the dynamics of emotional and sexual relationships. He has a developed sense of the philosophical, which lends resonance to the situations and people he presents. And he knows how to handle the storyteller's fundamental tools: suspense and revelation. . . .

Mr. Mosley's book is an impossible object in that it is constructed of eight separate stories, all fairly straightforward and realistic in presentation, which cannot be brought into three-dimensional congruity. The same characters—or characters with many of the same attributes—reappear frequently, but it is hard to sort their lives into any single story. The central characters seem to be a woman with a daughter and a man with three sons, who love one another and labor furiously to keep their love and their lives from becoming ordinary. For the man in particular this is a major goal in life, almost an obsession. He knows that "love flourishes in time of war" and that life dwindles unless we "make impossibilities." Love itself, conceivable as an idea, is impossible as an object. It exists in two or four dimensions and cannot be brought into three; it cannot be realized and made permanent. And neither can life. The essence of life is that it is transitory yet repetitive. If we seek by an act of will to freeze certain recurring moments into the permanence of art, we engage in a heroic but doomed struggle. That is what Mr. Mosley's book is about. . . .

Interpolated among the eight stories, and standing as prologue and epilogue to the larger sequence, are nine little fables or parables on related themes. These are brilliant prose constructions, combining images and perspectives with a vigor and control reminiscent of the later work of Picasso. The scenes they present are grotesque and bizarre, but always rooted in life and returning to life. These little pieces frame the "real" action, but the work "frame" is too inactive to convey how they really operate. Mosley uses his perspectivist parables as a way of generating an emotionally charged field of ideas and attitudes which then cluster around the situations in the "real" stories, illuminating them with a fabulous phosphorescence.

After John Fowles's *The Magus* (a very different kind of novel), this is the best book by a young Englishman that I have read in recent years.

Robert Scholes. *Sat.* Jan. 25, 1969, p. 31

Who is Nicholas Mosley? In the end this is a fairly difficult question, but a crude beginning is easy enough; he's upper-class (alias Lord Ravensdale), has a private income, a notorious father (Sir Oswald), a wife and four children in Hampstead; and his eighth novel is beautifully named, *Natalie Natalia.*

Is he perhaps a white elephant? In the old days these rare creatures were sacred in Siam, cosseted in the royal paddock, both magical and useless. The emperor used to bestow them upon troublesome courtiers, who were often duly beggared by their upkeep. As a rich English aristocrat with a very considerable intelligence, Mosley is certainly rare. And as one of the last high priests of European romanticism, many would call him useless. The difficult question is whether he's got any magic, and if so how much should we pay for its upkeep.

The motto of the Symbolists was "as for living our servants will do that for us." Although there are no French maids in Mosley's books, none of his characters remembers much of hard labor or economic necessity. They would agree with Henry James that the moral life begins with a private income and an empty engagement book. And yet they know that book is more difficult to fill nowadays, house parties not being what they were; so the narrator of *Natalie* says, "We were the generation of children blessed with nowhere to go."

Not unlike Mosley's previous novel, *Impossible Object, Natalie Natalia* is a dark comedy of the sexual life as practiced amongst the rich and intelligent in the West End of London. . . .

Natalie Natalia is a book full of gaps, syntactic gaps composed to register the fragmentary nature of contemporary experience, and above all, the absence of God from all the centers he used to inhabit. The highbrow London papers were not impressed by *Natalie*, and one can hardly predict a large sale. Nor is it obvious where Mosley goes from here. But then white elephants in an age like ours have a difficult time; people tend to laugh at their magic and sell them to the circus. And indeed Mosley seems to be submitting to this declension in *Natalie*, as for example when he says, "I frighten the wolves away with my magician's rod, my bangs and crackers." From "frighten" to "crackers" is quite a long way. . . .

Dudley Young. *NYT*. Oct. 24, 1971, pp. 5, 28

MUIR, EDWIN (1887–1959)

Edwin Muir will remain among the poets who have added glory to the English language. He is also one of the poets of whom Scotland should always be proud. But there is, furthermore, it seems to me, something essential which is neither English nor Scottish, but Orcadian. There is the sensibility of the remote islander, the boy from a simple primitive offshore community who then was plunged into the sordid horror of industrialism in Glasgow, who struggled to understand the modern world of the metropolis in London and finally the realities of central Europe in Prague where he and his wife—to whom together we owe our knowledge of Kafka—saw the iron curtain fall and where they saw their friends gradually finding it safer to avoid their company. And all this experience is somehow concentrated into that great, that terrifying poem of the "atomic age"—*The Horses*.

T. S. Eliot. Preface to Edwin Muir, *Collected
Poems* (N.Y., Oxford Univ. Pr., 1965),
unfolioed

As a poet who seeks his truths in "dreams and fantasies" Edwin Muir summons the phantoms of his own unconscious life with the certainty that these are not merely the tormented or triumphant imaginings of one particular man, but take their forms and reveal their meanings as part of the inheritance of the race. In his *Autobiography* Muir has much to say about his dreams and their sources in childhood memories stirred up by later conflicts. It is quite clear that the images of animals, of struggles, of journeys, of recurrent visitations in certain landscapes attained to by great effort and endured with a sense of inevitability— all these materials are akin to those patterns of memory which Jung has proposed as the archetypes, residing not in exterior experience but inherently in the human mind. It is clear, too, that a workable correlation exists between such a theory of psychology and the Platonic conception of reality, a conception particularly attractive to a poet who inherits the intellectual attitudes of late Romanticism. . . .

In Muir's thought both the Matter of Scotland and the Matter of Troy are subordinate to his most insistent theme, the Matter of the Fable, which indeed the lesser themes exemplify. In poems in which he tried to discover the fable independently of the concrete situations these lesser themes provided, however, Muir often wrote gropingly or abstractly. He felt early the compulsion toward an intuitive understanding of destiny, but what full course of action the fable required was not revealed to him until the end of his life.

Daniel Hoffman. *Barbarous Knowledge: Myth
in the Poetry of Yeats, Graves and Muir*
(N.Y., Oxford Univ. Pr., 1967),
pp. 227–28, 251

How essentially serious Muir's poetry has always been, the themes he consistently made his own sufficiently prove. They are the traditional themes of the great poets, from Homer's time to the present: the struggle between good and evil in the individual, in society, in the universe; the loss of innocence and the quest for its recovery; the nature of human destiny; the destructiveness of time; the enduring joy and power of love. At the same time, Muir has had the strength to handle this traditional material in his own way, on his own terms. Whether he borrows the figures and myths in which he dramatizes his themes from Homer and Sophocles, the Bible and Milton, or finds them in contemporary events and in his own dreams, he always recasts both borrowings and findings to fit his particular vision, to carry his particular signature.

And he has had the still greater strength to bear the consequences of his vision. When it reveals, as so often in his earlier volumes, nothing but futility and frustration, madness and despair, he never looks for a simple escape, nor evades the reality which his own experience so painfully proved, that life is ruled by an "iron law," that cruelty and betrayal undermine all hope of safety and negate all faith. He simply grapples with this undeniable reality until, like Lawrence, he "comes through," and on the "far side of despair" finds the possibility of rebirth.

Elizabeth Huberman. *The Poetry of Edwin Muir: The Field of Good and Ill* (N.Y., Oxford Univ. Pr., 1971), pp. 4–5

MURDOCH, IRIS (1919–   )

All Miss Murdoch's novels can in an important sense be seen as studies of the "degrees of freedom" available to individuals. . . . The kinds of freedom studied vary, and the style and matter of the novels also vary greatly, but there is, I would maintain, a surprisingly constant unity of theme underlying the ideas of all the seven novels we have so far. Between the first two novels, *Under the Net* and *The Flight from the Enchanter*, and the third, *The Sandcastle*, there is a break—not only a stylistic attempt to move from fantasy-myth to depiction of character, but a break in subject-matter. The first two books have a social dimension, an emphasis on the possibilities of man's freedom in society at large and mechanized, an interest in work, in the sense of jobs, which is not importantly present in the later novels, which are more concerned with freedom within personal relationships, with Jamesian studies of one person's power over, or modification of another person—although both ideas are of course present in most of the novels.

The Flight from the Enchanter is certainly concerned with one individual's power over another within relationships as well as socially, and the problem of freedom in work, or how work limits freedom, recurs both in the organization of the community in *The Bell*, and in Mor's struggles with his job and the Labour party, or even Rain Carter's painting, in *The Sandcastle*. And the problem which Jake Donaghue encounters from time to time in *Under the Net*, the problem of economic freedom, of whether he can accept large sums of dishonourably earned money in order to live free of economic necessity, also, in a different form, besets Randall in *An Unofficial Rose*, who buys a kind of freedom with the money obtained from the sale of his father's Tintoretto.

But the general idea with which I want to begin the study of the freedom of the characters in the novels is that this freedom is worked out, very broadly speaking, in terms of a constant—and, in the nature of things, incomplete and unresolved—interaction of their own attempts to act, or to order their experience (a process which constantly degenerates into "deforming" reality by fantasy) with the transcendent "reality."

> A. S. Byatt. *Degrees of Freedom: The Novels of Iris Murdoch* (N.Y., Barnes & Noble, 1965), pp. 11–12

Iris Murdoch appears to be on the verge of achieving a major reputation in contemporary English fiction, and, as is so often the case today, hers is an achievement that does not depend upon any single work. It is rather the totality of her work which we are asked to examine, and it is that totality with which we are meant to be impressed. Miss Murdoch is prolific enough. Since 1952, she has published eight novels, her short and incisive volume on Sartre, and a number of philosophic and literary essays. One continues to expect a distinctly major work from her, and one is continually disappointed. . . . She leaves us . . . essentially unsatisfied, expecting something more, some synthesis of myth and contemporaneity that will do what great art alone can do, fuse past and present and future in a vital crystallization of our world. And it is in just this, that quest for reality toward which the novelist must bend his efforts, that her novels seem curiously lacking. Her novels contain the language of ideas, but what they lack is the reality of flesh touching flesh (and this despite the great deal of sexual busyness in her books, almost all of it sex without salt and gesture without touch).

To her credit, Miss Murdoch has brought the free play of intelligence to the task of the novelist; she has taken the chances a novelist must take with language and she has emerged with a clear, incisive, determined prose; she possesses a sense of craft and an obvious dedication to the demands that novel writing make upon one; and she has accepted a world complex enough to make even the absence of tragedy endurable. She possesses humor and broad human sympathies, but for all of its turbulence and violence her world is surprisingly calm. What she lacks is rage . . . and her novels impress one as containing order at the expense of rage. The world she creates is permeated with too much Victorian insularity; it is not our world.

Leonard Kriegel. In Charles Shapiro, ed.,
Contemporary British Novelists (Carbondale,
Southern Illinois Univ. Pr., 1965), pp. 62–63

I feel obliged to clarify further my use of the term *philosophical novelist* as it applies to Iris Murdoch. Unlike L. H. Myers or Thomas Mann in *The Magic Mountain*, she does not openly discuss philosophical ideas in her fiction. When her characters consider problems in ethics and morals, the problems are never presented as abstract doctrine. Her philosophical interest is always social morality rather than a moral code or set of principles that the reader is invited to apply to action and plot. Blending moral action and narrative structure, her novels convey a great urgency. The theme of prose fiction since the eighteenth century has been man's life in society, and the prevailing narrative method has been empirical. By refusing to sacrifice the individual to a principle or a universal, Iris Murdoch has contributed to and possibly enlarged the great tradition. Her philosophical essays make clear that without theory there can be no morality; with Socrates, Buber, and Marcel, she believes that the clarification of thought must precede man's redemption. This theoretical bias gains expression in the novels in the form of closely observed character interaction. The portrayals of Michael Meade in *The Bell*, Emma Sands in *An Unofficial Rose*, and Otto Narraway in *The Italian Girl* reveal that ethical systems matter far less than personal conduct. The final test of any professed morality is direct social experience. Life is not a thought system, and any attempt to reduce it to one involves a falsification. But by dramatizing concrete situations, the novelist shows personal conduct fortifying and even creating moral value.

The priority of distinct, incarnate beings and the attendant belief that man is his own measure also rule out a political reading of the novels: Iris Murdoch's primary emphasis as a moralist is the free discovery of self and of other selves within the living tissue of human imperfection. Although she has stated an academic preference for Guild Socialism in one of her essays, I do not find the criticism of political institutions a major accent in her novels, with the possible exception of *The Flight from the Enchanter*. Like Amis, Wain, and Sillitoe in this aspect, she never uses such terms as *the proletariat* and *dialectical materialism*. But, unlike these writers, she studies the individual as a conscious entity responsible for making decisions that acknowledge the same degree of consciousness and reality in others. In this respect her awareness of social life may be called philosophical, for she sees the concrete presence of other people as something to be thought as well as perceived through the senses. The emphasis in her work on immediate experience suggests the term *novels of social education* rather than *novels of ideas*, per se. And her philosophical attitude is permeated by her artistic method, which combines objectivity and closely observed social relations; in our contingent world, dynamic interpersonal relations furnish the only escape from materialism and abstraction and the only likely approach to transcendent values.

Peter Wolfe. *The Disciplined Heart: Iris
Murdoch and Her Novels* (Columbia, Univ.
of Missouri Pr., 1966), pp. 23–24

A lot of dirty water has fallen since Miss Murdoch first caught Jake under the net of merciful exposure [in *Under the Net*]. Eight novels have followed that first one published in 1954, and within the last five, the course of the stream Miss Murdoch is pursuing is clear and very treacherous. Miss Murdoch has turned from investigating the sane to propagating the grotesque as a high religion of behavior. She has gone from situations in which people are troubled by empty-of-center idiosyncrasies to situations in which characters justify their aberrations as superior ways of attacking life. . . .

The good news about Miss Murdoch's newest novel [*The Red and the Green*] is that she has dropped some of her tricks. The detailed fantasies and the spiral comic twists of her plot furniture she now reveals in a manner that no longer overwhelms the reader. In this sense, Miss Murdoch has "prepared" the reader for her characters' devious behavior and consistent inconstancies. . . .

Miss Murdoch has moved forward in this work, for which all of her readers will be grateful. Perhaps it is more accurate to say she has moved backward—back to the deeper feeling displayed in *The Bell*, without recourse to intellectual comedy or wit to hide the pain of her feelings; and backward to the simplicity of style of *The Sandcastle*. Certainly she is still dealing with deviant behavior, but she has dropped much of her devious and gimmick-ridden manner. Her interest in character has grown closer to acceptance of it for its own value.

Martin Tucker. *NR*. Feb. 5, 1966, p. 26

With a living writer one must remind oneself to resist the progressivist or growth-rate fallacy. *The Time of the Angels* is an absorbingly interesting novel by the most seriously and, I think, consequentially entertaining of contemporary English novelists. Is it Iris Murdoch's best novel? I think not. Returning to the Gothic mannerisms of *The Unicorn* and *The Italian Girl*, it is also flawed in rather the same way; plot-rigging is flagrant, and main narrative resolutions are blatantly forced (though by now a certain kind of boisterous melodrama might as well be recognized as one of this author's stable and generally effective defenses "against dryness"). Being her latest book *should* this be her best, glibbest, most perfect? Certainly not. It is enough to say that *Angels* is as serious and vivacious, as secure in its diversely compassionate characterizations, as touching and forgiving in its pictures of the spiritual ordeal of human life, as the most admired of its predecessors. What more at present can one say than that a season without its new Murdoch would seem a dry season indeed?

Of course the possibility remains—this book renews it—of thinking that Iris Murdoch is mistaken in her calling and is no novelist. . . . But . . . if Iris Murdoch does not touch our consciousness of real life and move us with her projections of familiar experience, who in our literature does? Who *has* avoided her lapses into abstraction, contrivance, sensationalist over-management? Who *can* write—or see—like Tolstoy, or who work the Jamesian apparatus? Or is it equally possible that new uses and mutations of the still open form of the novel remain to be created and secured, and that the clear facts in the case of Iris Murdoch—her executive energy, the self-amplification and assurance of her fictional world, the promptness and persistence of her reception—are as good evidence as can be had for thinking that some part of major literary history (at once a history of forms and a history of consciousness and sensibility) is moving through the channel of her performance? On whom, in this case, is the critical *onus probandi*?

Warner Berthoff. *MR*. Summer, 1967, p. 581

More than any other novelist around, [Iris Murdoch] brings to the surface the question . . . Can people who think as we have come to think write good novels? For she maintains a potentially reductive double reality—representative figures, revolving perspectives that bring the writer near to being a central character. She invites, and investigates, the question, Is it perceived order or performance? She responds naturally to the mind as force, but has to look for what it can apply itself to and wonder how it can maintain its humanity against its destructive tendency. So action and scene inevitably overshadow identification with character.

Unquestionably, defense by reduction hurts an expansive form like the novel. The unevenness of Miss Murdoch's work suggests how unsure anyone is what will help it. For Miss Murdoch is, in Waugh's phrase, a "good trier." (She would please some readers more if she were not always writing the novel she does not yet know how to write.) . . .

Miss Murdoch has by now progressed enough with her fictional world for it to have its own fable, told with increasing awareness and willingness to face new difficulties created by old solutions. The fable in its developed form goes like this. People of above-average competence, with no resources outside themselves, begin as egoists doing what comes naturally, and in the process injure and get injured. This first impulse exhausts itself in unsatisfying activism, which finally seems pointless. In this injury-inflicting world, eros is overmatched against aggressiveness. At some stage the individual naturally—not on existentialist principle—begins to think of regrouping, gathering his scattered forces and centering on his best possibilities. The effort, because it is a counterattack, becomes a private attempt at rebirth, vulnerable because unsupported in the confusing social fabric.

At this point Miss Murdoch's most original insight appears. G. S. Fraser has noted her skill at giving solidity to the normal. But normalcy is more than solid: it is the ultimate test of the unsupported will. Yet this norm, for which the personality is willing to fight so hard, seems in itself unattractive—amounts at bottom to an active, resentful, self-distrusting directionlessness. The characters who invoke this impulse against unconventional efforts to deal with defeat see in the attempted rebirths at best absurdity and worst danger to sanity. The skill Miss Murdoch has developed in giving life to the struggle between these two claims is her own greatest claim to significance.

> James Hall. *The Lunatic Giant in the Drawing*
> *Room: The British and American Novel since*
> *1930* (Bloomington, Indiana Univ. Pr., 1968),
> pp. 181–83

In Iris Murdoch's new novel, *The Black Prince*, the . . . broad theme [of the conspiracy theory of reality] wears, at first glance, a familiar shop-soiled air. Here are editorial prefaces and appendices, a middle-aged man in pursuit of a girl-child who hardly exists outside of his writing about her, a sprinkling of chess-symbolism, numerous diversions and dissertations upon aesthetics and the morality of literary creation, some dusty scholarship, and a catch-as-catch-can title (Edward II, Hamlet, the Prince of Darkness, perhaps an extra piece for the chess-board . . . Bradley Pearson takes a shine from all of these). A great deal of the book including the fussy pedantry of the narrator, all squeam and arch quotation marks and italicisations, looks as if it has been ransacked piecemeal from the Nabokov shelf. Yet this novel, despite its trail of still-bloody umbilical cords, is Miss Murdoch's best for a very long time; an uneven haphazard book which never seems to be quite sure about where it is going, but which is so ambitious in its—rather too many—directions that it can afford its failures. It has a reassuringly old-fashioned lumpish density, resonant with atmospheric detail, strong on incident, and marvellously satirically observant of the society it embodies. . . .

As a book about evil, a devil's monologue, *The Black Prince* is superb. In Bradley Pearson, Miss Murdoch has found a persona in which she can satisfactorily sink the awkwardness of her own prose; in him that curious alternation between the tone of a tart philosophy seminar and that of a purple passage in Ouida sounds perfectly convincing. He is, one suspects, the writer whom Miss Murdoch fears herself to be, and by exposing him she has written a very fine, very black book. I have hardly mentioned the tricksy apparatus which surrounds it; it is just scaffolding—necessary, perhaps, for the novel's construction, but unsightly and distracting now it's finished. *The Black Prince* does not need to advertise its modernity so modishly; it is too good for that.

Jonathan Raban. *Enc.* May, 1973, pp. 84–85

● MURPHY, RICHARD (1927–   )

After a long eclipse there are signs that the narrative poem is on the way back in. The recent taste for verse autobiography (well-exemplified by Edward Lucie-Smith's *A Tropical Childhood*) has helped to restore faith in the old-fashioned virtues of honesty, concrete detail and story-line; and the experiment of John Wain with an open-ended long poem which may go on for thirty years is refreshing evidence of rebellion against the tyranny of the symbolist lyric. Richard Murphy's *Sailing to an Island* develops this rebellion further, expanding the autobiographical formula to include the history of a family and a landscape as well as a person. His book depends on a clear narrative outline and a severe purity of style which has deceived reviewers into underrating its originality and its excellence.

Richard Murphy's poetry depends on the classical art which Hemingway described in (I think) *Death in the Afternoon* as "turning the gas as low as possible without letting the flame go out." . . .

Richard Murphy will develop into an important force in the poetry of the sixties. Already his Spartan style (and, let's face it, rather Spartan view of the world) mark him out as an individual voice in an age of moral conformism. I should be tempted (were he not an Irishman) to rank him with Gunn, Hughes, Middleton and Porter as one of the half dozen most distinctive English poets under forty.

George MacBeth. *L.* July, 1963, pp. 87–89

Of the significant Irish poets to emerge since the last war, Richard Murphy is the least introspective or tempted toward confessional writing. He shows exceptional narrative and elegiac powers, and his poems are highly local, sentimentally so when they are not rescued by his talent for loading every rift with objective details—and quite deliberately not with Romantic ore, especially of the psychomined variety. Fundamentally, he is an old-fashioned, rather conventional poet. Reading his "The Cleggan Disaster" and "Sailing to an Island," both poems about stormy sailing off the Connemara coast, one wants to check back to poems like Masefield's neglected *Dauber* or even to the relevant passages in Hopkins's "The Wreck of the *Deutschland*" for comparison. Mr. Murphy knows sailing—it has almost become his trade—and these accounts are sparklingly concrete and exciting. They serve a timeless artistic purpose in the way they repossess a particular kind of experience and life-style. Nostalgia for a lost and (sayeth the poet) a nobler past, as seen from the viewpoint of the Ascendancy, is heavy in these pieces. . . .

M. L. Rosenthal. *The New Poets* (N.Y.,
Oxford Univ. Pr., 1967), pp. 306–7

The theme of [*The Battle of Aughrim*] is land, rent-paying land. Protestants wanted more land in Ireland and they could get it by expropriating the gentry who had taken the side of James II. This down-to-earth involvement gives *The Battle of Aughrim* its tone. The excremental epithet that the Irish soldiers gave James II after he ran away from the battle of the Boyne is used again and again. . . .

The dirty atrocities that go with battles are recorded, and dirty names are given to them. Richard Murphy allows only one gleam of glory to appear in that sunset—the emergence of the general who was to leave a legend to Ireland, Patrick Sarsfield. . . . (Sarsfield survived the battle of Aughrim to lead 10,000 troops—known as the Wild Geese—to France, where he died in the service of the French King.)

The Battle of Aughrim is about people. And when I write that I have to acknowledge some disappointment. For a poem dealing with a significant historical situation the poem lacks volume. That could not be said if it had more dramatis personae, more people than those Murphy has done so well—St. Ruth, Sarsfield, the defector Colonel Luttrell. The Dutch general Ginkel is an interesting man, a professional European soldier who was above the bigotry and greed that disgraced the conquerors. But there will probably be other editions of *The Battle of Aughrim*, and Richard Murphy may find it in his mind to enlarge the cast. . . .

An original and vigorous poem. The book also contains another poem, "The God Who Eats Corn," about the life of the poet's father as a farmer and schoolmaster in Southern Rhodesia, that exhibits what I think is Richard Murphy's best quality—a strong sense of the external world.

Padraic Colum. NYT. March 2, 1969,
pp. 10, 12

Some may hold that a poem should contain its own clarifications, but Mr. Murphy [in *The Battle of Aughrim*], speaking in the present (in his opening section) can justly say, "The past is happening today." The Matter of Aughrim is remote only in its particulars. In the week in which I write this, the Ulster government of Captain O'Neil has barely survived riots and a bitter election brought on by the most recent exacerbation of the very issues left, alas, unsettled by Aughrim or by any subsequent battle: these painful divisions of English vs. Irish, Catholic vs. Protestant interests survive, the unhealed wounds of a country tragically divided.

Mr. Murphy is a proven adept of the long narrative poem, but he has eschewed the straightforward telling of "The Cleggan Disaster" in *Sailing to an Island* (1963). A modern poet writing of history cannot help but have in mind the example of *The Cantos*, and an Irish poet must, besides, come out of the long shadow cast by Yeats. Mr. Murphy sounds a different note, his own, by adopting strategies consonant with his rather Augustan sensibility. An inheritor of traditions of the Ascendancy, he takes an objective view of history. His crucial event is chosen from a period not preempted by Yeats— neither the mythopoesis of Bronze Age demigods, nor the Easter Rising. To be sure, there are some intentional Yeatsian echoes. . . .

The first of the poem's four sections is "Now," a series of lyrics, some personal, which clarify the legacy of the battle—the despair and hatreds it bequeathed—before we participate in the ironical design of the event. The three succeeding sections are set "Before," "During," and "After" the battle. Each contains from five to ten brief poems, some lyric, some dramatic, some narrative, in various forms and meters. One—St. Ruth's sanctimonious address to his troops—is in prose; another, a versified quotation from a contemporaneous English history. Thus the texture is continually varied, juxtaposing effectively to the foreign commander's hauteur, his distrust of the lowly people he was commissioned to defend; juxtaposing to the righteous rhetoric of apologists for either side, the barbarity of both armies toward civilians and to each other; juxtaposing, too, the self-serving treachery of Luttrell and lesser turncoats to the butchery of their defeated countrymen. As Murphy says of Sarsfield, "Nothing he will do, or has done/ Can stop this happening."

The directness of diction reinforces the dramatic objectivity of vision, isolating significant action with the economy of an ancient ballad. Though the texture of the lines is simple, the movement of history in the poem is complex. *The Battle of Aughrim* is surely one of the most deeply felt and successfully rendered interpretations of history in modern Irish verse, and in poetry in English in our generation. Seeking an American analogue, only Lowell's *Benito Cereno* seems comparable in intention, scope, and achievement.

Daniel Hoffman. *Poetry*. Aug., 1969,
pp. 342–44

NEWBY, P. H. (1918–)

Newby's novels, dealing with . . . questions of personal problems and personal vision, are most often worked out on a level of abstraction that could not well be represented in realistic terms of normal behavior: a characteristic often encountered in the novels of Iris Murdoch and William Golding as well as in those of Newby. His plots thus transcend the realistic; the reader accepts the action for its significance, not for its verisimilitude, in much the way that he accepts, for instance, the literal action of the last plays of Shakespeare. A passage in *A Journey to the Interior* aptly describes this method of presentation: "The words that were uttered were like beads that a woman will finger as she talks—the real conversation was carried on at a higher level, without words." External action, in other words, is metaphorical and is relevant to the novelist's purpose only in so far as it reflects the inner states of the characters. Consequently, one critic [Anthony Burgess] can speak of *The Barbary Light* as seeming "to suggest occasionally the unreality of delirium," and one reviewer of the novel [Maurice Richardson] notes the "equivocal, semi-fantastic atmosphere" that surrounds the hero.

Not the literal words, then, but their symbolic implications and suggestions are the key to the meaning of Newby's novels of quest; and he structures them with an originality that approaches innovation of form. The first chapter of *The Barbary Light* serves as an excellent illustration of his technique. Owen is in bed with his mistress, Alex, and she is exploring his body with her hands, his past life with questions. This device serves to foreshadow, at the same time that it initiates, the thematic exploration of Owen that is made throughout the novel not only by the characters themselves but by the reader as well. In this chapter, Alex moves back and forth from the waking to the sleeping state and, in doing so, she intermingles the real with the illusory—that is, she intermingles on the literal level the thematic subject-matter of the whole novel, appearance and reality. But Alex also weaves contrapuntally her own memories with Owen's reported memories of his boyhood; and with this technical polyphony Newby stresses, by ironic contrast, the elements of isolation and solitude that constitute the major aspect of Owen's predicament. Here, as Owen says, only "memory was identity." That the reader is in this opening chapter slightly confused on a first reading is evidently Newby's precise intention; the rest of the novel will, like the Barbary light in Carthage to which both hero and reader progress, clarify this particular situation and define the relationship of Owen to the other characters (and himself). Thus technique, looking forward while gazing backward, formulates the hero's problem, structures the complex design of narrative, and involves the reader himself as quester in an amazingly original manner. Form and meaning seldom blend more effectively into a unified whole.

E. C. Bufkin. *Critique*. Vol. 8, No. 1, 1965,
pp. 61–62

Instinct in ascendancy over reason is in part the theme of P. H. Newby's fine novel, *Something to Answer For*, written at times in a highly textured poetic prose that never interferes with action often carried on at white heat. The protagonist, Jack Townrow, while hardly monstrous, is nevertheless something of a pariah, an incredibly inept, rootless, but sympathetic Artful Dodger who returns to Egypt shortly before the Suez crisis both to help and defraud the widow of an old friend, and ends as a man instead. Like other Newby settings, Port Said in 1956 is less realistic than mythic, at times reminiscent of Conrad's inscrutable sea- and landscapes or the even stranger fissures of Graham Greeneland. . . .

As [Townrow's] "grip on reality" grows more and more tenuous, reason and caution are thrown to the winds, and he is left to shift as best he can by instinct alone. He realizes that you "can't answer for anything outside your own personal experience," but that "[remembering] experiences wrong you didn't count at all. You weren't human." Part scapegoat, part pawn in the movement of history, and part mover, Townrow is all too human. His quest for stability in a mad world, for identity and individuality—is he ex-Sergeant Townrow, or his aliases, Captain Ferris and Major Bray? or is he the imperfect anagram of one of his names: wornout?—is in a way everyone's search for self-knowledge, for an end to illusion and innocence, and finally for responsibility to oneself before (to reiterate Walter Allen's phrase) "inescapable involvement in society."

Indeed, if the societal code is wrong, why become involved at all. Townrow apparently doesn't. Alone, he takes to sea in a small boat, having "no option but [to] hang on and hope the dreaming would stop," protecting his "light," struck with a "damp match," against the wind. What Townrow learns, and what is learned through different means by Appleyard, Jenkins and Eliot, is nearly the same in the end.

That a man must "decide, absolutely, to answer for himself" is not merely something, but perhaps the hardest thing.

Robert K. Morris. *Nation*. April 28, 1969,
p. 547

Like Newby's last novel, *Something to Answer For*, this [*A Lot to Ask*] is one of those slightly too consciously concocted enigmas in which the reader is discouraged from supposing (as nature would have him do) that the hero is prey to some fairly ordinary fit of madness. *Something to Answer For* got off to a brisk and felicitous start: Town-row, another stout extrovert who "liked nice things: food, clothes, drink, women," gets hit hard over the head in Port Said. Novels of this kind, touching on questions of identity, a disorientation of the individual's relations with the external world, need to be very good, and preferably funny, on incidentals if they are not to melt into some ghastly psychopoeticality. When "something odd is going on behind the scenes," the scenes themselves must be sharp and rich and (the only word) gripping. The new novel is saved by firm, stabilising moments, such as Poumphrey's attempt to interview a Syrian colonel while the latter is being coached for TV; the Foreign Office man who "was nearly seven feet tall and, properly greased, could have been slid through quite a small-bore drainpipe"; and Poumphrey's recognition as he looks at himself across the table that he has "the face of a minor Roman emperor who, when checked up on, did something noble like not poisoning his mother." But *Something to Answer For* had the distinct advantage of Egypt (Newby's great fertilising influence), Israel (a reality, not a telephoned threat), the invasion of Suez and gun-running to Cyprus. Like Townrow, Poumphrey is born again, or reckons he is somehow a better man, but the East Dene Conservative Association and the board of Murex Oil make rather too dim a backdrop to these melodramas of the soul.

A Lot to Ask reads like a relatively austere replay of the earlier novel in which the troubled hero is to be taken further, or be seen to be taken further, or at all events not left floating in the Mediterranean in a small waterlogged boat thinking about honour. It could be said of *Something to Ask For* that the whole was rather less than the sum of the parts. *A Lot to Ask* may be more of a whole, but I think its parts add up to a smaller sum.

D. J. Enright. *List*. May 3, 1973, p. 591

● **NICHOLS, PETER (1927–   )**

[*A Day in the Death of Joe Egg*] is exceedingly cunning, allowing the characters to come in and out of its realistic box set and address the audience in a manner which is never forced. There are some dazzling bits of theatre, and a set of characters instantly identifiable in the world of pop art and comprehensives. Mums mourning their lost promiscuity and Dads mourning their missed opportunities, potted ivy and Drama groups and Dr. Spock and booming middle-aged Socialists who sound and behave for all the world exactly like booming middle-aged Young Conservatives. The clarity of all this provides the cool and disarming style with which the play approaches its central problem, the cruel practical joke the universe has played on a couple, no braver than us, by presenting them with a spastic daughter; a senseless vegetable with a beautiful face whose nappies must be changed at the age of 10, and whose life is a frightening succession of small fits. . . .

If this sounds sick, it is, in fact, extremely healthy. Peter Nichols has approached the play's problem, which was also his own, with all the courage of the absurd man aware of, and accepting, his limitations. If it sounds depressing it is for a great deal of the evening hilariously funny. You leave the theatre feeling in every way better for having shared the author's experience, and for having, as he also had, the sensibility to laugh.

John Mortimer. NS. July 28, 1967, p. 125

There are plenty of aesthetic reasons for standing up and cheering this play [*The National Health*]: but, as in the case of *A Day in the Death of Joe Egg*, it makes you feel ashamed to talk about art. We are not short of good playwrights in Britain, but I know of none with Peter Nichols's power to put modern Britain on the stage and send the spectators away feeling more like members of the human race.

The National Health can only be described as a portrait of six male inmates in a hospital ward. It also amounts to a study of organization versus the individual, and to a microcosm of our society; but such themes only arise from his detailed concern for the people themselves and their response to seeing each other die.

As in *Joe Egg*, the writing combines scrupulous naturalism with music-hall turns. This is thoroughly appropriate for the macabre normality of the situation, and it allows Mr. Nichols to turn the relationships around so that the balance of sympathies is constantly changing. . . .

Irving Wardle. *TL*. Oct. 17, 1969, p. 15

As well as being a devastatingly acute dissection of the family situation (any family situation), [*Forget-me-not-Lane*] is, for a start, a riotously funny theatrical entertainment. Of course it is not "just" funny; as we know already from *A Day in the Death of Joe Egg* and *The National Health*, Nichols is most serious when he is most funny, he has a unique gift of finding the laughter in pain without diminishing its painfulness. If you think about his plays, you don't know whether to laugh or to cry; but in the theatre, for the moment at least, you laugh. And in *Forget-me-not Lane* the laughter comes loud and long. The character of the father is quintessentially the sort of parent who is fine in someone else's family but agonising in one's own, especially amid the manifold built-in embarrassments of adolescence. We laugh, as an outsider would, at his catch-phrases (beautifully graded, incidentally, to indicate the passage of time and shifts of relationship) and his little jokes, but at the same time we cringe along with his son at the sheer social horror of it all.

And above and beyond all that, the play is a hymn to the Forties, to the generations whose monument was the Festival Hall. . . . If [Frank] ends by turning into his father (his lecture on his own now-teenage son on noise and motor-bikes is a masterly transposition of his father's thought-patterns into his own generation's liberal vocabulary) it is not only the genetic trap which has done this to him; it is the times he has lived through, and his understandable but misplaced nostalgia for them.

From almost every point of view *Forget-me-not Lane* looks like a summary of Nichols's work to date, gathering together its various threads and presenting them to us in a satisfactorily rounded whole with even more dazzling skill than *A Day in the Death of Joe Egg* or *The National Health*. And yet it is a real play; it gives completely the illusion (if it is an illusion) of organic growth; it resolutely shows us everything, tells us nothing. That is why we understand so much from it. And indeed the success of Nichols's campaign to broaden our dramatic responses probably derives first and foremost from the fact that he never set out to mount such a campaign, never had any intention except to write single plays mirroring an aspect of the world as he sees it.

John Russell Taylor. *The Second Wave* (N.Y.,
Hill and Wang, 1971), pp. 34–35

It's easy to see why [*Chez Nous*] has divided Nichols' fans at this moment in British history. To admit you like it is to admit, more or less, that you accept that liberal attitudes are largely a matter of self-flattering adolescent fantasy. To those who refuse this confession, it's a mocking accusation of bad faith, a challenge to come clean, act your age and give your vote to Edward Heath's brand of conservatism.

My own misgivings about the piece stem from a belief that this choice isn't what Nichols intended; that the play has to some extent slipped out of his control and wound up saying things that contradict itself internally.

The central situation seems under-imagined, under-written. Nothing in the character [Albert] Finney plays really explains how he came to tumble his best friend's child in the watercress—the only emotional line he can exploit with conviction in the part is Phil's undisguisable joy at discovering he has a son. Similarly, the relationship of the two wives . . . is so sketchy as to be almost nonexistent. It's hard to believe they were at school together, let alone friends—their conversations have the forced implausibility of most scenes between women imagined by men.

The only fully drawn figure is Dick. . . . As a result, the play's hinge-incident seems almost a figment of his overheated imagination, a sexy middle-aged nightmare sent to disturb a wine-induced siesta in the French sun and punish him for becoming wealthy enough to own a second home in the latest area of international Sunday-supplement chic. . . .

Personally, I suspect that the real division in audiences for *Chez Nous* is between those who respond to its first half and can't accept its ending and those who, accepting its ending, simply laugh at the first half. The bad faith isn't all in the people who feel got at by Nichols' comedy. Some of it is in the play.

Ronald Bryden. NYTts. March 17, 1974, p. 5

● O'BRIEN, EDNA (1932–   )

The Country Girls is a first novel of great charm by a natural writer. It is the story of two girls growing up in Ireland, first in a derelict village, then in a convent, then in Dublin. It is not a series of idylls nor a breathless account of hilarious adventures, though its tone is light and there are passages of comedy. In mood and manner Miss O'Brien's novel resembles *The Bachelor of Arts* by R. K. Narayan. Caithleen's mother dies shortly after the novel opens; her father is a drunkard who steadily impoverishes himself. Baba comes from a more ordered home, though her mother likes to spend the evenings on a high stool at the bar of the village hotel. Baba is adventurous and bullying, and where she leads Caithleen must follow. It is Baba who engineers their expulsion from the convent; and when they go to Dublin, it is Baba, innocently and pathetically rapacious, who takes Caithleen into hotel lounges to pick up elderly businessmen. Baba falls ill. Caithleen prepares to fly to Vienna with the elderly man with whom she is in love; but he does not turn up.

Neither of these events is explicitly tragic; both girls will recover. The true tragedy lies in the sense of time passing, of waste, decay, waiting, relationships that come to nothing. Yet Miss O'Brien never says so. She makes no comment, stages nothing. She simply offers her characters, and they come to us living. She does not appear to have to strive to establish anything; the novel, one feels, is so completely, so truly realised in the writer's mind that everything that comes out has a quality of life which no artifice could achieve. Miss O'Brien may write profounder books, but I doubt whether she will write another like *The Country Girls*, which is as fresh and lyrical and bursting with energy as only a first novel can be.

V. S. Naipaul. NS. July 16, 1960, p. 97

In 1960 Hutchinson of London published a novel, *The Country Girls*, by an unknown Irish writer called Edna O'Brien. The critical reception was considerable and Miss O'Brien was hailed as an important new Irish writer with a fresh, unselfconscious charm, an acute observation of life and a fine, ribald sense of humour. Her second book, *The Lonely Girl*, had the same kind of success and Miss O'Brien was regarded as having passed the difficult hurdle of the second novel. She had become an established literary figure and the third novel of the trilogy was awaited with considerable expectation. When this novel, *Girls in Their Married Bliss*, arrived, it proved to be so different from the first two books that readers were startled. The two girls, the heroines of these books, now married, had lost their girlish laughter. The book's title was seen to be bitterly ironic and the London life of Cáit and Baba was sordid. The writing tended to be slipshod in parts and a kind of humorous detachment that made the earlier adventures so enjoyable was missing. Miss O'Brien seemed in places to be writing a kind of neo-feminist propaganda. This committed writing was continued in *August Is a Wicked Month* and in *Casualties of Peace*. In this last novel there is perhaps evidence of further development, but it too is seriously clogged with a self-indulgent gloom. None of the later books has the deftness and tact of the Irish novels.

Miss O'Brien is still young and there is no reason to suppose that the present retardation is anything but temporary. Even these latest novels claim the same critical attention as those of her female contemporaries, Muriel Spark, Iris Murdoch, Brigid Brophy, Mary McCarthy and Doris Lessing. Though Iris Murdoch was born and educated in Ireland, and Brigid Brophy and Mary McCarthy can claim Irish descent, though Muriel Spark became a Catholic, Miss O'Brien is the only one of them all to be born, reared and educated Irish and Catholic. This may mean little or nothing at all in literary circles in London or New York but in Ireland there is considerable interest in such a writer. This interest is social rather than literary and Miss O'Brien shares with another Irish writer, Brendan Behan, the dubious fame of being better known than her works. It is peculiarly difficult to get past this public personality. All of her novels have been banned in Southern Ireland. . . .

Sean McMahon. Éire-Ireland. Spring, 1967, pp. 79–80

It is always hard to evaluate a literary work that provokes so many nonliterary judgments as this one by Edna O'Brien. But maybe literature only begins to matter when it carries us beyond the safe confines of literary criticism. D. H. Lawrence thought so, evidently Miss O'Brien does too.

Girls in Their Married Bliss is a sequel to *The Country Girls* and *The Lonely Girl* (filmed as *The Girl with Green Eyes*). Here again are those former convent schoolmates, Baba and Kate, less spirited now and more, to their horror, like their mothers. They are living in London, and have husbands, lovers, and plenty of trouble. Yet the novel is no bedroom or bedhopping farce. Each sexual skirmish in the girls' lives is both a calamity and a narrow escape from a worse one. Miss

O'Brien's portrayal of the psychology of adulterous love is brilliant. She describes how lovers are more difficult than husbands; how, if marriage is boredom and compromise (but compromise with what?), then adultery is a cave of madness. The sensitive spot she probes is the knot of impulses that shape our basic needs and, therefore, our personalities.

The characters in *Girls in Their Married Bliss* are dreadfully alone. They are not interested in music, sports, or handicrafts; family, religion, and politics also exert small influence. Baba's and Kate's need to heal their broken, disconnected lives drives them to trade anything for a scrap of love. Here is where many readers will recoil. Do social institutions and ties matter as little as Miss O'Brien suggests? Are we so desperately detached from any living tradition or ideas? Conceding the difficulty of summoning moral principles in times of stress, do these stresses always take a sexual form?

If Miss O'Brien fails to answer these questions, she does examine them honestly and diligently. Her subject is sex, its dynamics and ethics, and she treats it as a many-sided problem. Where one character views a love affair as passionate, a second sees it as simply cheap, even boring. Either interpretation is as convincing as its opposite, and Miss O'Brien's narrative technique does not weight the scales.

This technique is the book's core. Miss O'Brien does not explain sex; she conveys its sensations—the excitements, the limits, the renewals. She wants us to react to her book as we would to a first-hand experience, and to achieve this purpose she alternates her narrative between voices, between dialogue and description, between epigram and summary. The suddenness of these changes jolts us; the off-key logic and rhythm communicate, probably better than conventional writing could do, the immediacy of the impact. . . . *Girls in Their Married Bliss* is a minor masterpiece. Though it lacks the range of major fiction, Miss O'Brien must be credited for inviting the comparison with it.

Peter Wolfe. *Sat.* Feb. 17, 1968, pp. 38–39

When Edna O'Brien ceased to be a country girl and turned her fancy to thoughts of sex, some people complained. The freshness and charm of her first two novels, we were told, had been routed by bitterness: all that was left were the unholy passions of flesh. In this first collection of her short stories [*The Love Object*] the two faces of Miss O'Brien are laid down side by side and it is at once apparent that between them the difference is slight. Solitude has always been her subject, and it remains so. The sex, in her later novels and in some of these stories, is a single aspect of it: her girls' final effort, often wrought of desperation, to belong and to communicate. . . .

Miss O'Brien's stories rattle with an honesty that is as compelling as the style that shapes her lively prose. Her girls are frankly presented, without romance. . . . If you read Miss O'Brien's first three novels, one after another as parts of a single whole, you will find a perfect balance of comedy and tragedy and a pattern that begins and ends with loneness. This brief collection, eight stories in all, more swiftly exposes that same breadth of talent. From the whiff of fair-day dung outside the Commercial Hotel to the rich after-dinner figs, symbol of sex in a London restaurant, there is a ring of reality in every movement. One or two of the pieces are slight, but none is false, and taken together they confirm my impression that rarely has an Irish woman protested as eloquently as Edna O'Brien. In sorrow and compassion she keens over the living. More obviously now, despair is her province.

William Trevor. *NS*. July 5, 1968, pp. 18–19

If a lesser author had written *Night*, one would never have bothered to read it through. But Miss O'Brien is a novelist of many gifts, including poetry and comedy and compassion: that is why the reader keeps the presumption of innocence alive by forced feeding to the very end, and why he then feels so frustrated and so cheated. The flash of poetry, of irony, of insight now and then is not enough to make a work of art out of a sentimental, predictably repetitious monologue of the kind that, at almost any hour, one can hardly escape in a certain category of Third Avenue bar. Even the pretentious malapropisms of those reduced sibyls are Mary's [the protagonist], too. But they serve no better than the lexicon of bed and bath to fashion drama or comedy.

The reasons for the book's failure may be indeed more interesting than the book. Is it conceivable that the vein has been mined out? Is it possible that virtually nothing new can be thought or said about the emptiness of lives that are just plain empty? Is it thinkable that there are really subjects that not even the finest writer can bring to life because there is simply nothing there? Apparently, yes.

In one of his essays on film and film criticism, René Clair has remarked on the fashionable fear of attacking vulgarity or tastelessness lest one be excommunicated as outmoded or prudish. The fact remains that much of *Night* is as gratuitous as those portentous examinations of nakedness, violence and real or simulated coupling that have become almost mandatory in films and novels—from the frankly commercial to the most solemnly "artistic."

Charles Lam Markmann. *Nation*.
May 14, 1973, p. 631

● O'BRIEN, FLANN (BRIAN O'NOLAN) (1911–1966)

This brilliant and wicked book [*At Swim-Two-Birds*] was first published in 1939, a bad year for originality and laughter. In spite of
praise from James Joyce—who was parodied in it—and Mr. Graham
Greene, and from the best critics, it reached only a small public. Let us
hope the prospects are brighter now, for Mr. O'Brien's is one of the
funniest "novels" to come out of Ireland. To describe it is difficult. One
could say that the author designed to reduce the total Irish literary
tradition to farce and to make hay of the modern novel, but his
irreverence is not journalistic. The book is not a skit. It is scholarly,
vigorous and creative. . . .

Mr. O'Brien's gifts are startling and heartless. He has the astounding Irish genius for describing the human animal, its shameless and
dilapidated body, its touching and proliferating fancy, its terrible
interest in useless conundrums. On top of this he has an extraordinary
freedom of the English language, perhaps because he is a Gaelic
scholar, perhaps because the Elizabethan tradition has survived in Ireland. His people are either seedy Dubliners or ludicrous giants, but
their wits are alight; they live in language, in comic image, rather than
in life. It looks as though his idea was to knock the regionalism out of
Irish literature by magnifying it. Since Joyce, the nose-picking, truculent porter-and-Guinness-swilling Dublin student has been an established figure in Irish literature, predating our own post-war Jimmies
and resembling, in their unemployable way, the over-educated rogues
of the Elizabethan universities and the picaros of Salamanca.

The sloth of Mr. O'Brien's sulky, superior narrator who, despite
his beatnik behaviour, triumphs with cynical ease in his examinations
at the end, is an enjoyable quality. I became tired of the joke only
when Mr. Trellis's characters started writing about him, simply because
of the excess. This kind of fantasy is apt to be self-destructive. But I
shall often return to Mr. O'Brien's diverting brainstorm and shall often
brood about one of his deluded characters who feared to sit down
because he imagined his bottom was made of glass.

V. S. Pritchett. NS. Aug. 20, 1960, pp. 250–51

Neither *The Hard Life* nor *The Dalkey Archive* has the authority and
inclusiveness of *At Swim-Two-Birds*, nor the deep, concentrated power
of *The Third Policeman*. Both the later books seem to toy with symbolic
overtones rather than genuinely incorporate them. They pick their way

round the edges of vitally important subjects rather than going hell-for-leather through the middle. And this realization gives us a vantage point to look back on *At Swim-Two-Birds*, noting clearly now its elegiac quality, its sense that the problems posed by time are not soluble; and also on the quietly agonized exploration of the damned state in *The Third Policeman*.

If, in his first book O'Nolan came close to Joyce, in his second he anticipated the best work of Beckett. In temperament, he stands somewhere between the two. He is more discouraged than Joyce, less of a Yea-sayer. Joyce's work is bleak, but it is not elegiac. It affirms the stature of man. The eighteen hours of Leopold Bloom's life which we follow in *Ulysses* are full of shabbiness, failure, and discouragement, but they are also Homeric. Joyce's purpose in elaborating his technique of literary *son et lumière* was to affirm that his wandering Jewish salesman was no less important than Odysseus. By contrast, O'Nolan's parallels between Trellis and Sweeney, between the bardic feast and the paralytic loquacity of the saloon bar, are parallels of hopelessness. On the other hand, he is not a connoisseur of hopelessness like Beckett, who seems to have cast himself in the role of a vulture, waiting on some dusty branch for the kicking human body to become a nice quiet corpse. The sense of doom, of the curse of meaninglessness laid on all that a man is and does, is brilliantly conveyed in *The Third Policeman*, but it is set within a religious framework and shown as the punishment for taking a man's life, cruelly, for gain. In Beckett's work, the capital crime is simply to be alive; *that* is the stupidity, the evil, the appalling metaphysical *gaffe* for which we are to be snubbed and punished for ever. O'Nolan does not talk in this strain; if he lacks the gigantic affirmative energy of Joyce, he nevertheless has some of Joyce's centrality and sanity.

When, early in 1966, the news came that O'Nolan had died, I felt both saddened and amazed. Saddened that a writer who so interested and engaged me would now write no more; amazed that he was only in his early fifties. He must have been so young when *At Swim-Two-Birds* came to him; it must have formed in his mind, shaking him with laughter and dismay, at a time when he was no older than the two of us who stared down at his book, knowing that a new chapter in our own history was beginning, that morning in the Eagle and Child. *Vale.* (1967)

John Wain. A House for the Truth
(Macmillan, 1972), pp. 103–4

I am not much taken with the "life is absurd" theory, because I'm tolerably sure life is, on the contrary, preposterous. This may well be an ancestral conviction on my part: for, now I think of it, some such proposition is the point of most Irish discourse and a good deal of Irish literature.

Certainly *The Dalkey Archive*, one of Irish literature's grand triumphs, asserts the preposterousness of life. In doing so, it redeploys much of the material of another Flann O'Brien novel, written earlier but only now—posthumously—published, *The Third Policeman*, which makes the same assertion about death. The book's "I," a murderer, learns in the last chapter that he's been dead for 16 years—since, to be exact, Chapter Two, where he is blown up by a mine planted by his co-criminal. His death and damnation consist of his trying to escape death—on, principally, the gallows of the local police. By the last page of the novel he's re-entering the police station and, unknowingly, starting the whole literally damned sequence again. That's death.

Of course, some of the minor characters in *The Dalkey Archive* are dead, too: Saint Augustine, for instance. But it's a great help to coherency that they *know* they are. It's also a help to credibility that the improbable events have to be swallowed or doubted by the two contrasted, third-person consciousnesses of Shaughnessy and Hackett, that pair of fine *ficelles* drawn out of Stephen Dedalus and Buck Mulligan. And the surrealisms themselves stand out hard-edged against the pebble dash and faded bathing towels of Dalkey.

The Third Policeman, by contrast, is confined by its very *donnée* to a single consciousness—and, unaware as it is of so cardinal a fact about itself, a befuddled one. The narrative goes into dream-like drifts; it's hard for the reader to feel enough suspense about the hero's suspension. If the Dalkey diction occasionally plunges into funny-column facetiousness, *The Third Policeman* shows less retrievable flaws in the imaginative material itself. Its unlocated, underpopulated Irish country-side is sometimes haunted as banally ("the light had some quality which was wrong, mysterious, alarming") as Versailles in those ladies' adventure.

For all that, the reader's attention is fiercely grappled to the book here and there along the line: by exquisite comic constructs, Nabokovian ingenuities and flights of Lodovico-Carolingian pseudo- or hyperlogic. Only the structure as a whole is less beautifully inventive than in *The Dalkey Archive*, whose trinitarian or leaf-of-shamrocks design is built of three interrelated yet cumulative preposterousnesses.

Brigid Brophy. *List*. Sept. 28, 1967, p. 403

Brian O'Nolan, alias Flann O'Brien (for novels), alias Myles na Gopaleen (in his newspaper column) died in Dublin on April Fools' Day last year. Universally mourned in the city he had delighted for so long, his death went almost unremarked in England or anywhere else. Like his life; few people outside Ireland have ever heard of his work. Astonishingly, *At Swim-Two-Birds*, the most purely comic book of this century, remained out of print for years. It gained itself only a very limited circulation when rescued in 1960; and its latest edition as a Penguin Modern Classic carries a biographical blurb that is full of errors. *At Swim-Two-Birds* has been one of those books doomed to an underground existence, with treasured copies lent only to trusted friends (much the same thing, apparently, happened to *Murphy*). It remains the property of isolated bunches of cognoscenti. They hold readings from it round kitchen tables. They huddle giggling, in the corners of bars. They—quite literally—know extensive passages by heart, and use it for hours of jesting. . . .

O'Brien's sense of humour is a sharp instrument; it penetrates the myth, its inexplicable and implacable violence and desolation, leaves it intact and makes it comic. His translations from Sweeny's lamenting poems are brilliant, transfixed. They are chill, pared, and with just that clipped quality that one immediately recognises as belonging to old British and Celtic epic poetry. . . .

A comparison with Beckett is not beside the point. For if *At Swim-Two-Birds* is O'Brien's *Murphy* (early, witty, convoluted, learned), *The Third Policeman* is his *Molloy*, moving with some of Beckett's gravity through a very similar landscape, and with its hero sharing blankness before justice and consequence.

Timothy Hilton. NS. Dec. 8, 1967, p. 815

The failure of Flann O'Brien to advance the potential of *At Swim-Two-Birds* parallels the failure of contemporary Ireland to fulfill the hopes engendered by political independence: Freedom from realism, like freedom from England, does not guarantee a superior product. The Ireland that spawned Flann O'Brien has never been content to see itself realistically depicted by its writers, and those who spurned the healthy paranoia that sent Joyce and O'Casey into self-exile have often had to avoid direct confrontation with native reality, lest they suffer the fate of John McGahern.

There is both mimetic appreciation and ironic deprecation in the treatment of Finn MacCool by Flann O'Brien, an envy of the heroic nature of the epic material of the past and a contemporary scorn for the outmoded. Joyce could translate the giant Finn into the hodcarrier Finnegan and pubkeeper Earwicker, into constables and postmen, savoring both the irony and the humanity of the transmigration, but O'Nolan could only reduce his Finn to literary depiction, keeping him safely unchallenged by a necessity to explain his human condition. In

At Swim-Two-Birds the author himself began the process of confusing himself with his literary creations; his admirers in Ireland have abetted this transformation by evolving a mythos about the Brian O'Nolan–Myles na Gopaleen–Flann O'Brien triumvirate. The suggestion seems to be that in this setting myth is greater than either life or literature: It is never as unseemly and makes far fewer demands.

Bernard Benstock. Éire-Ireland. Autumn,
1968, pp. 64–65

O'CASEY, SEAN (1884–1964)

After the plays, the most important of O'Casey's writings are the six autobiographical volumes that he published between 1939 and 1954. The reader who turns to them for a considered account of O'Casey's theory and practice as a dramatist will be disappointed, but he will find in them much of the source-material of *The Shadow of a Gunman, Nannie's Night Out, Juno and the Paycock, The Plough and the Stars, The End of the Beginning, Red Roses for Me, Hall of Healing, Oak Leaves and Lavender*, and *Time to Go*. He will also find in *Inishfallen, Fare Thee Well* an account of O'Casey's lost plays: *The Frost in the Flower, The Harvest Festival, The Crimson in the Tricolour*, and *The Robe of Rosheen*, and discover that O'Casey had only seen two performances of plays at the Abbey Theatre before he submitted a play to its directors, though he had seen many melodramas at the Queen's Theatre, Dublin. The same volume makes it clear that one of the saddest results of his break with the Abbey Theatre was the end of his association with Lady Gregory, who enjoyed more of his confidence and gave him better advice than any other writer that he met.

The literary reminiscences in O'Casey's autobiographies, however, are merely part of the pattern which gives unity to the six volumes, that pattern being an interrelated series of struggles: his fight for existence, his fight for an education, his fight for a vocation, his fight for recognition, his fight against criticism, and his fight for a better Ireland. This pattern reveals the child as father to the man; the blow he dealt a sadistic school teacher is paralleled by the blow he struck for Ireland when he unhorsed a mounted policeman with a flagpole during a demonstration against England during the Boer War. In this way, the first four autobiographies, *I Knock at the Door, Pictures in the Hallway, Drums Under the Windows*, and *Inishfallen, Fare Thee Well* acquire an epic breadth and depth as they unfold the story of

O'Casey's personal struggle against the background of Ireland's struggle for liberation.

William A. Armstrong. *Sean O'Casey*
(BC/Longmans, 1967), pp. 32–33

Cock-a-Doodle-Dandy is a song. "Enough, no more," one is compelled to add. " 'Tis not so sweet now as it was before." Still, an excess of melody is much better than too little, or none at all. The spirit and language of O'Casey's comedy are lovely. They voice a celebration of life, a lilting and laughing hymn, as well as its converse crow of mockery, rich curses at O'Casey s two *bêtes noires*, bigotry and money meanness. He harps to the point of shrillness against the enemy, but poetry, laughter and love finally triumph.

The weakness of the play is an insufficiency of dramatic content; there is almost no "story." O'Casey wrote it after he had left Ireland, injured and insulted by its hermetic religiosity, its unfrangible mythmaking. . . . As a result, plays of that period, though never without moments of beauty and scenes of both power and hilarity, are more more or less veiled preachments, with rumblings of rancor in the shadows. Therefore, the best work of O'Casey's last years is to be found in his multi-volumed autobiography, where his life struggle supplies a structure firm enough to sustain the rest.

What *Cock-a-Doodle-Dandy* does have, and what saves it, is a striking image and captivating speech. The image is that of the indomitably rebellious Cock, symbol of nature in its gloriously telluric force and in its capacity to demolish the constructions of reason. Nature is not all divine harmony; it is also demonic anarchy. O'Casey understands that this is part of its grandeur, to be embraced with a mighty whoop of brave affirmation.

Harold Clurman. *Nation*. Feb. 10, 1969, p. 187

In the twentieth century, as a reaction to the extreme transparency of natural activity, with its loss of theatrical excitement as well as generalized significance, playwrights and performers have experimented with a wide variety of techniques for achieving a viable "artificiality." . . . Sean O'Casey develops a mixed method of "naturalism" and "expressionism." These writers also utilize song and dance to considerable effect, but it is in O'Casey's work that one can see the growth of artifice most easily. In his early plays, O'Casey employed song as natural activity, but with his turn to expressionism, commencing with *The Silver Tassie*, O'Casey employs song, dance, and scenic display as a direct expression of the action he wishes to convey. His most ambitious effort is found in *Red Roses for Me*. . . .

O'Casey tries to establish a new convention, shifting from the photographic to the apocalyptic. He foreshadows the vision [of a society of beauty and spiritual exaltation] through the introduction of songs early in the play and through Ayamonn's yearning for joyful beauty. In Act III he makes that yearning palpable. The colors of the city and the sky change, ostensibly because of sunset, yet the changes go beyond sunset's changes. Ayamonn and the women sing and dance, yet the singing and dancing are more than natural joy. All changes partake of a symbolic celebration of the future. In these ways O'Casey endeavors to fashion a mode of action that, through its beauty and ebullience, can be simultaneously opaque and transparent.

Bernard Beckerman. *Dynamics of Drama*
(N.Y., Knopf, 1970), pp. 126–28

It is a commonplace assumption that the self-taught playwright underwent several distinct stages. [O Casey's] least friendly critics would classify these as first, that period of hit-and-miss dramaturgy which remained very close to traditional lines but somehow accidentally produced those early masterpieces; second, the attainment of an overenthusiastic bravado which allowed him to experiment with expressionistic techniques rather imitatively and clumsily; third, the time of his most naïve immersion in ideology which produced dull and wooden propaganda plays; and, fourth, a "sunset" stage in which he lost complete touch with the basic Irish sources for his material, but retained or regained his Irish sense of the wildly comic, adding an element of fantasy at times gay and at times obtrusive. No single critic actually rates O'Casey exactly in this way, but this is a composite of the general aspect of disapproval and the most frequent touches of begrudging praise.

The common denominator of all denigration of O'Casey's technique as a dramatist is the assumption that he never actually refined a fully conscious skill in *controlling* the important elements of his craft: that although he often created excellent pieces of drama and sketched some fine characterizations, O'Casey was never a play*wright*. Even those who insist upon O'Casey's "genius" use that term of exaggerated approbation to offset an insistence on his frequent gaffes. Yet these advocates perform an unnecessary disservice: Sean O'Casey is at his best precisely in what he had *wrought*.

Stagecraft at its most basic involves the necessity of setting a scene, and it is with this essential (often passed on instead to a designer) that O'Casey demonstrates his individual touch. The early naturalistic plays provided no difficulty for him; he was well versed in describing the basics of a tenement room, and if "photographic realism" means anything in regard to these plays, it is in such specific renderings as: "Between the window and the dresser is a picture of the Virgin; below the picture, on a bracket, is a crimson bowl in which a floating votive light is burning. Farther to the right is a small bed partly concealed by cretonne hangings strung on a twine." O'Casey would have been a poor choice indeed for an Abbey production had he not been able to pinpoint that facet of his known world, but it is in his later non-naturalistic works that his powers of evocative description are significant.

Bernard Benstock. Sean O'Casey (Lewisburg,
Pa., Bucknell Univ. Pr., 1970), pp. 89–90

O'CONNOR, FRANK (1903–1966)

In *The Mirror in the Roadway* (1956) the late Frank O'Connor described himself as a 19th-century realist. Many years earlier Yeats had said, "O'Connor is doing for Ireland what Chekhov did for Russia." Certainly the mythopoetic and symbolist strains in Irish writing of the Yeats-Synge generation do not survive in the fiction of O'Connor and his contemporary, Sean O'Faolain, and there is an equally sharp break between their work and that of expatriate figures like Joyce and Beckett. Yet O'Connor did write in this century, and his stories are as distant in feeling from Chekhov as Ireland is physically distant from Russia. It seems more adequate to say that O'Connor was of that small group of excellent writers whose task it became to register Irish realities, in city, town and countryside, as the nation emerged from rebellion and civil war to make its way quietly in the world under the cautious leadership of Eamon De Valera and other survivors of the Troubled Times. . . .

Brinsley Macnamara outstripped O'Connor in his depiction of the soul-killing aspects of Irish small-town life, but O'Connor has no rival as a historian of the submerged population's Woman and The Peasant. As with Lawrence, his deep insight into feminine psychology and unending curiosity about the minutiae of "domestic relations" stemmed from his earliest experiences as beloved son and oedipal rival in a hard-pressed, emotionally fraught, working-class household.

Stories like "The Holy Door," "The Mad Lomasneys," "The Masculine Principle" and "A Sense of Responsibility" represent Irish wives, daughters, mothers-in-law and sweethearts in all their strange and sometimes self-lacerating variety; on the one hand, slaves of religion and respectability, on the other, vivid, outspoken, proud and sensitive.

In their tendency to act against their own best interests, perhaps in some sort of final, wounded recoil against the entire puritanical conditioning to which they are exposed, these women may epitomize Ireland herself and disturb the memory in ways that Joyce's females, who tend toward the symbolic, the bovine and the archetypal, do not.

Julian Moynihan. *NYT*. May 28, 1967, p. 2

Frank O'Connor's kind of storytelling is not modish just now. He is recognized as a fine short story writer—anthologized under the aegis of Brooks and Warren—and until his recent death he undoubtedly occupied the position of being Ireland's foremost living short story writer. Yet his standing as a writer is uncertain, since critical commentators have either neglected or taken for granted his talents, as the dearth of O'Connor criticism shows. American short story writers of comparable parts at least enjoy critical notice, but like his Irish contemporaries, O'Connor is seldom courted, a situation partly due, one supposes to the fact that he writes stories in the manner of the nineteenth-century realists, stories in which plot and action interest him more than symbol, sensitivity, and experimentation.

Since an acquaintance with any short story writer is usually made through a few anthologized pieces, it is difficult to see the thematic unity and development of ideas that make the entirety of his work greater than the sum of its parts. Exposure to only "The Drunkard," "My Oedipus Complex," "Guests of the Nation," "Judas," or "Uprooted" obstructs a clear view of O'Connor's creative virtues. The selections often exploit the more specious aspects of his talent. Consequently he has become tagged as a humorist. And he is—a fine one. But unnoticed elements give him stature: his curious view of priestliness among the Irish laity; his probing into the themes of human loneliness and communication; his success at infusing new energy into stories about juveniles by creating not precociously passive sensibilities but active boys who get themselves into predicaments which incur both guilt and maturation; and his restoration of the storyteller's voice. But most important is his persistent sifting in the value of impulsive indiscretion and moral fecklessness in order to domesticate irrationality. And only by considering a larger sample of his work and the development of his canon can one see with some accuracy the value of this preoccupation.

Gerry Brenner. *TSLL*. Fall, 1968, p. 457

Though some people thought [O'Connor] flamboyant in his views, he did not so regard himself. He thought he was stating conclusions that nobody in his right mind could miss. The strength of *The Mirror in the*

Roadway and *The Lonely Voice* comes from this assumptive power. It begins in close observation, of course, but then, in an almost visionary way, renders writers, objects and themes malleable. Whoever the writer he discusses, O'Connor will not release him until he has yielded up the network of interconnecting passageways between behavior in society and talent at his desk. O'Connor's critical writing is hungry to judge, and unsatisfied unless it is deciphering a writer's mysteries, not necessarily mysteries of uneasy collaboration with another, as in Shakespeare's case, but mysteries of uneasy collaboration with an inner self. . . . He understood what James was doing, admired it somewhat, but did not follow. He saw that his own art must radiate out from a single nucleus, must not attempt detachment or alien centers-of-consciousness in the manner of James or Joyce.

He felt himself, nonetheless, to be in reaction against one nineteenth-century aspect, romantic color and extravagance. Often he humorously pretended to discount his own views as those of "a tough-skinned old realist" or of "an old-fashioned realist." Of one of his characters he says approvingly, "The real world was trouble enough for him." He encouraged Yeats to see him as more a realist than in fact he was, and for a time Yeats praised O'Connor for his sharp Corkman's eye, then, more knowledgeably, for his Chekhovian inspection of Irish life. The last romantic and the last realist found they had much in common. When they served together as directors of the Abbey Theatre, they surprised each other by a fairly steady agreement about plays or persons. Another bond became evident when O'Connor made his translations from Irish and Old Irish poetry. The gauntly expressed passions in them won Yeats over; he arranged for his sisters to publish them at the Cuala Press, and he graciously notified O'Connor that some of the good lines were making their way into his own poems. In exchange he proposed some revisions, to which O'Connor responded by dedicating the book to Yeats.

Richard Ellmann. In Maurice Sheehy, ed.,
Michael/Frank: Studies on Frank O'Connor
(N.Y., Knopf, 1969), pp. 25–26

Frank O'Connor's fame as a writer of short stories has somewhat overshadowed his achievement as a poet. It was as a poet, in fact, that he began his writing career, and he produced a number of original poems. Then he turned to the short story form and dedicated the greater part of his energy to that. But once a poet, always a poet, practising or otherwise, and while O'Connor created several masterpieces in his chosen form, he also continued his service to poetry, mainly by way of translation.

His *King, Lords & Commons* is a monumental work, containing excellent poems, the most impressive of which seems to me to be the translation of Brian Merryman's long poem, "The Midnight Court." . . . O'Connor's uncanny insight into the poetry of that time and that society enabled him to bring a remote eighteenth-century poet right into the heart of our times, portraying both the frustration and the ebullience with a vitality of language that Merryman himself would have loved.

> Brendan Kennelly. In Maurice Sheehy, ed.,
> *Michael/Frank: Studies on Frank O'Connor*
> (N.Y., Knopf, 1969), p. 103

When O'Connor writes of the short story, in *The Lonely Voice*, he is not so much doing what he professes to be doing—stating the nature of the form—as he is stating in general terms the characteristics of his own craft. His stories are plausible treatments of the plights of those he called "Little Men"—his capitalizations show he wasn't patronizing—written in an apt style, one both witty . . . and poetic. . . . His stories have no heroes, but memorialize "a submerged population group" as they group and regroup in variations of family patterns. His stories show "an intense awareness of human loneliness" and the tactics people use to relieve that loneliness. They follow no "essential form," but an "organic form"; this configurates aesthetic elements in infinitesimal variations which dictate vastly different implications (like the triangles and squares of color within a kaleidoscope).

Compared with Joyce, his craft might be narrow, but he sees more possibilities of fulfillment within the strictures and structure of the narrow world Joyce might too quickly reject in *Dubliners*. O'Connor's range might not be vast, but his eyes are clear, his ear is sharp, his heart is big and his craft is sufficient to his needs. The stories in *A Set of Variations* might be short and narrow, but they are more than small favors that he did for us in writing them before he died. We should be more than grateful.

> Shaun O'Connell. *MR*. Summer, 1969,
> pp. 612–13

O'FAOLAIN, SEAN (1900–   )

O'Faolain has been influenced in his novels, as in his short stories, by the Irish and European literary traditions. He emerges at a time in Irish literary history when the subjective, romantic attitudes of the Literary

Revival were being replaced by a more realistic and more analytical approach. In the Abbey Theater the work of the younger dramatists, such as Padraic Colum, T. C. Murray, and Lennox Robinson, had become more influential than the poetic plays of W. B. Yeats, the founder of the theater. Their interests lay in presenting Irish life, and particularly rural life, as they knew it from experience; their characters lacked the heroic mold that he sought for his plays on Irish mythological themes. Their work in the theater had been paralleled by the gradual emergence of a realistic prose tradition. George Moore and James Joyce laid the foundations of this movement in *The Untilled Field, The Lake*, and *Dubliners*. O'Faolain's generation of prose realists were, therefore, the inheritors of this prose realism.

But although they shared in that revolt against the romanticism of the Revival, their revolt was complicated by their youthful participation in the Revolution. All of them, and particularly the important ones, O'Flaherty, O'Connor, and O'Faolain, had been deeply affected by romantic nationalism, by the guerilla war against the Black and Tans, by the excitement of the founding of the Free State, and by the shock and humiliation of the Civil War. It was almost inevitable that their final disillusion should make them analytical and critical in their approach to life. So much had happened to them; they had moved so rapidly from youthful idealism to adult despair that they had to find reasons and answers. By necessity they became social commentators and questioners, searchers after personal and national identity.

They were not realists by nature or by choice. The conflict in *Midsummer Night Madness* between romance and realism is more than one man's problem; disillusion and bitterness run as an emotional undercurrent through all these writers. And it is this emotional conflict that separates O'Faolain from Moore or Joyce.

Maurice Harmon. *Sean O'Faolain: A Critical Introduction* (Notre Dame, Ind., Univ. of Notre Dame Pr., 1966), pp. 164–65

O'Faolain's perplexity over Realism and Romanticism in his own case appears . . . to be idle speculation. O'Faolain is essentially a Realist— in his objectivity, in his conscious intellectual handling of material, in his use of irony, in his grasp of truth, and in his portrayal of life as it is. Yet, at the same time, his work contains lyrical and atmospheric qualities that are usually labelled "Romantic." Like Chekhov, O'Faolain is a realist who can blend truth with mood and poetry so that his portrayal of existence is enhanced by nuances and subtleties which give a deeper meaning to the writing and a closer look into contradictions, deceptions, and mysteries. O'Faolain is more poetic and contemplative than Chekhov but less detached and less ironic.

Like Chekhov, O'Faolain is essentially an optimist. Despite man's follies and foolishness, O'Faolain still believes in humanity; he affirms man, although he is aware that man and man's problems are continually perplexing, that sadness and tragedy are common, and that existence is an enigma, which, nevertheless, must be probed and studied. The artist seeks answers even if there are no answers; and, above all, the writer uses all his intelligence and sensibility to ponder "the inscrutable mystery of human suffering." O'Faolain's best short stories must earn him the title of the Irish Chekhov. This statement redounds to the credit of both of these artists.

Paul A. Doyle. Sean O'Faolain (N.Y., Twayne, 1968), pp. 128–29

Sean O'Faolain has constructed another Daedalean maze [in The Talking Trees], and we must now decide whether that elusive Minotaur, the chaotic conscience of the Irish race, has been caught within the entanglements of his prose. O'Faolain describes an Ireland where some of the younger priests read Simone de Beauvoir, where the leap from feudalism into modern industrial society is finally becoming an actuality, and where sex is no longer the unspeakable area of life that it was in the pre-Leopold Bloom days. It's all the more striking, therefore, to find a mood of "spiritual paralysis" hovering over The Talking Trees—the same kind of paralysis that James Joyce discerned in the Dublin of seventy years ago. . . .

O'Faolain descends from a long line of Irish satirists, and when things get too sticky for his satire—when passion or death enters the picture—he regresses into the giddy provincialism that can be heard any evening in the pubs of Dublin or in the bars on Third Avenue. O'Faolain shows the true nature of this provincialism in "Thieves," where a cruel anti-Semitism intrudes upon a quiet Easter Sunday morning in the city of Cork. It is certainly brave of the author to mention this unsavory aspect of a society that is supposed to be founded on the Semitic idea of loving one's neighbor. But the reader may wonder why the glee of the little girls who witness it is allowed to divert our attention from the ugly underside of Irish Catholicism that has just been exposed. Or is this childish glee just another manifestation of those hidden forces?

Sean O'Faolain has brought courage and skill to the making of these stories, but the resolution of such problems is beyond his imaginative grasp. One is forced to conclude that the Irish Minotaur—the old sow who devours her farrow in more ways than one—has, in this case, escaped from the Daedalean labyrinth.

John W. Hughes. *Sat.* Feb. 6, 1971, pp. 30–31

O'FLAHERTY, LIAM (1896–   )

O'Flaherty's essential artistic vision derived from the intensity of his awareness of his own existence in a universe that gives no meaning for existence. His subject is man as he becomes aware of himself in a universe which his reason shows him is absurd. In this sense O'Flaherty can be considered an existentialist. His awareness of the absurdity of existence, however, was not a philosophical position but a condition of his being. It was a condition from which he constantly struggled to escape, not a way of seeing he wished to promulgate. O'Flaherty is an artist, not a thinker. Man's existential plight was the subject of art, not of truth. When O'Flaherty sought truth and became a positive thinker as the last novels indicate, he ceased being an artist.

O'Flaherty's subject is existence because he is a modern writer who sees man not as a manifestation of culture, tradition, or civilization, but as a naked soul alien to the culture, tradition, and civilization that offer only deceptions to obscure from men the true and awful nature of their being. His view of the artist is that which Lionel Trilling considers the characteristically modern belief: "the man who goes down into that hell which is the historical beginning of the human soul, a beginning not outgrown but established in humanity as we know it now, preferring the reality of this hell to the bland lies of the civilization that has overlaid it."

When O'Flaherty moved out from the isolated world of the Aran Islands into the world of Western culture, the image of reality that he bore from those elemental storm-lashed rocks was not shattered, but confirmed. The Aran Islands were reality in microcosm, for the Aran Islands were to earth as earth was to universe; and individual man on the islands, confronted with awesome nature, isolated, constantly aware of life because of his proximity to death, screaming out in horror at his inevitable fate, was true man, not overlaid by a complex culture that deceived. And because O'Flaherty was a modern writer he could not be an Irish writer in the sense of belonging to Ireland, speaking for Ireland, expressing Ireland and Irish dreams. What made Ireland significant for the Irish literary revival was a distinctive culture and tradition to which the Irish writers felt they belonged. It did not deceive them but sustained them.

O'Flaherty could only look at Ireland and envy, but he could not belong; for he had seen, felt to the marrow of his being, the awful truth of his own existence. He could cry out like Kurtz, "The horror! The horror!" but he could not deny that truth when, as an artist, he forced himself again and again to peer over the brink of chaos.

John Zneimer. *The Literary Vision of Liam O'Flaherty* (Syracuse, N.Y., Syracuse Univ. Pr., 1970), pp. 192–93

Some comment is required about the general neglect of O'Flaherty by literary critics. O'Flaherty is one of the significant Irish writers—Sean O'Faolain, Frank O'Connor, Mary Lavin, and Paul Vincent Carroll are some others—who have been pushed into the background because of the Irish Big Four syndrome that afflicts critics. Synge, Yeats, O'Casey, and Joyce have drawn so much attention that other important Anglo-Irish authors have either been neglected or unduly denigrated.

O'Flaherty must share much of the blame for his own critical neglect since he has taken every opportunity to censure, discourage, and mislead literary critics who might otherwise have given him a more complete hearing and might have been less inclined to judge him on the basis of his weakest books and his oral denunciations. Enraged that his first two novels did not receive the favorable critical reception he deemed them worthy of, O'Flaherty turned on the critics when they enthusiastically received *The Informer*. He then attempted to show how the critics had been easily deceived and erroneous about a book that he claimed to have written primarily as a prank.

O'Flaherty's overemphasis on the money motif for writers—some of this attitude being a pose and some of it again being a sneer at critics—also caused loss of critical prestige. Furthermore, O'Flaherty has too frequently with active belligerence met critical generosity or fair-minded attempts to analyze his work. Much evidence exists to support the theory that an ingrown sense of contrariness is forever active in O'Flaherty's makeup—some of the Samuel Johnson quality of taking the opposite side of an issue just for the sake of an argument also is present. O'Flaherty seems to enjoy a martyrdom complex. When he calls himself the "most unpopular man in Ireland," he takes a certain pleasure in this claim.

Paul A. Doyle. *Liam O'Flaherty* (N.Y., Twayne, 1971), p. 120

O'Flaherty records in his short stories vignettes of peasants, children, and animals; he fashions images of a life that seems timeless; men and nature function under laws that cannot be altered by legislatures or technology. In his novels, O'Flaherty examines peasant life not from a timeless perspective but in its historical setting, showing the peasant in transition to a society in which money, government, and Church play determining roles. In *Thy Neighbour's Wife, Skerrett*, and other novels he portrays people caught in changes that they cannot comprehend. Yet this historical study, valuable as it may be, provides a background for enlarged characters who wrestle with distorted dreams of perfection that are often obsessions that betray and destroy them. In several novels he portrays types of fanaticism that flourished in the new Free State as disillusionment captures the mind of men who had been unduly exhilarated from expectations of national freedom.

Like Lawrence and other modern writers, O'Flaherty tries to reconstruct images that recall man's instinctual life. He pursues his task energetically, as he must if he is to avoid the paralysis arising from passivity, violence, or sentimentality. As an artist, O'Flaherty is engaged, then, in the creation of cultural images, temporary though they may be, to supply what the civilization does not furnish—cultural images that lead to an integration of personality or, in Yeats's terms, to a unity of being. Beneath O'Flaherty's absorption in the physical, external world lies a belief in the evolutionary process, of men, especially artists, finding fulfillment in the struggle for perfection. This perfection may be elusive, even nonexistent, but nevertheless it is still the highest goal for man.

James O'Brien. Liam O'Flaherty (Lewisburg,
Pa., Bucknell Univ. Pr., 1973), pp. 116–17

● ORTON, JOE (1933–1967)

Joe Orton was the best farce writer of our time, and his last play, *What the Butler Saw*, underlines the loss to us all from his death. He had many good competitors. Ray Cooney and John Chapman, who wrote *Not Now, Darling* which is still running in London, are technically expert. They don't have, of course, Joe Orton's very individual wit, but neither are they lured into his pomposity, which often slowed down the story and gave some of his gags the crispness of cement. . . .

What marks out *Loot* and *What the Butler Saw* from rivals like *Not Now, Darling* is not Joe Orton's better technique, but the quality of his insight. He was in a casual, bland and curly-haired way, more daring. He was like the 14-year-old girl at a cocktail party who says, sipping her lemonade, "All of Daddy's business friends try to rape me.

It's not easy, you know, still being at school." He was quick to recognize the taboos, to pounce on them and send them up. All of his plays, with the exception of the disastrous double bill at the Royal Court, provoked accusations of bad taste.

Entertaining Mr. Sloane, his first major play, was immediately labelled a "bitter" comedy—because it was about a brother and sister, both middle-aged, who shielded the murderer of their father because he was an attractive young brute and they wanted to sleep with him. But the tone wasn't particularly bitter, far less so than Giles Cooper's *Happy Family:* he was simply stating a situation and making fun of it, and the play was called "bitter," because some critics felt that with such a theme, any reputable person *ought* to feel bitter. Joe Orton fortunately was not so defensive: he didn't feel compelled to justify himself morally.

Loot, more obviously farcical than *Entertaining Mr. Sloane*, was about a mother's corpse in a coffin, carefully guarded because the box also contained the proceeds from a robbery. When I first saw it, at Golders Green, some of the audience walked out, and the play was dropped for a year: then it was revived in a brilliant production at the Jeannetta Cochrane Theatre, and either tastes had changed, or Joe Orton suddenly discovered the right director and audience.

Some of the public also walked out on *What the Butler Saw* at the Cambridge Arts Theatre, and I spent the interval, wondering why. There were some "daring"-type lines: Dr. Prentice says to his wife, whom he has accused of nymphomania, "They'll carry you to your grave in a Y-shaped coffin." and later on, Mrs. Prentice protests that "My uterine contractions have been bogus for some time now!" but these remarks in context were so funny and inoffensive that one would have needed the hide of a butterfly to be hurt by them. The boundaries of good taste spread out more mysteriously as the permissive society supposedly advances.

John Elsom. *L.* April, 1969, pp. 92–93

It has nothing directly to do with the matter, but it struck me as I watched Joe Orton's two one-act plays collectively titled *Crimes of Passion . . .* that dramatists often foreshadow their own destinies in their writing. Marlowe's special ferocity presages his death by stabbing; Odets' *Golden Boy* points to his eventual creative collapse; Orton's violent end at the age of 34 complements the horror of his comedies.

He had an unmistakable talent. His pungently derisive dialogue captures the guying tone of contemporary London. There is something at once traditionally elegant and nasally obscene about his manner, as if Oxford had produced an irrepressible guttersnipe. If you open your mouth in laughter at an Orton play, a spoonful of acid is dashed into it. His jokes are a preamble to murder.

In *The Ruffian on the Stair*, the first of the two one-acters, something like a note of tenderness is introduced. But it is muffled either by technical deficiency in the plotting of the play or by some ambiguity of purpose. . . . If there is unity here, as on reflection there appears to be, it is in the inference that the world is full of foul folk whose only common trait is their aloneness and their shabby groping toward one another to insulate themselves against the chill of solitude. Yet one can hardly say that Orton finds any saving grace in this, because except for the "ruffian" and possibly the girl, he sprays everything with a shower of hate-filled mockery. We laugh because Orton writes sharply and can be funny, but the venom scalds. There is no pleasure in the fun.

When Orton turns to thoroughgoing farce, as in the second of his *Crimes, The Erpingham Camp* (it takes place in the sort of fun fair now popular in England's smaller towns), he becomes trigger happy, aiming a broadside of buckshot at the entire community, from officialdom and clergy down to the "little people" who frequent such resorts.

The play is too long. It provides moments of acrid entertainment especially through Orton's expert use of the common man's lingo cleverly patterned by his own sophistication—but it all ends by making humanity seem a sorry sell.

Harold Clurman. Nation. Nov. 17, 1969,
pp. 546–47

Orton gives a logic and an emotional truth to the perverse in experience. In his early plays—*The Ruffian on the Stair* (1964), *Entertaining Mr. Sloane* (1964)—the outrageous springs from an apparent realism. Society's mores are always butting heads with fatuous catastrophe. (As one prissy onlooker observes in the bedlam of Orton's *What the Butler Saw*: "Two young people—one mad and one sexually insatiable —both naked—are roaming this house. At all costs we must prevent a collision.") In Orton's plays, madness and reason inevitably collide. There is a humanity behind this, an attempt to make an audience learn from its outcasts and understand that every man is lost, bound together in communal madness. Orton tries to establish through theater the new channels of feeling R. D. Laing has postulated in psychology. . . .

Orton's plays offend in order to instruct and heal; they shatter the easy divisions of we and they, the good and the bad, the just and the unjust. . . .

Orton's farces make an audience confront the schizophrenic patterns of their lives, rather than evade them. By making a carnival of man's stupidity and superstition, by exposing the condition of social insanity, his plays hold out to an audience the possibility of humility and care. As a genre, farce has a power and insidious appeal which is becoming increasingly pertinent to our historical moment. Orton's plays, especially *What the Butler Saw*, pave a new way for playwrights to create dangerously with laughter in dangerous times. Orton's writing is a testament to what American society is just beginning to realize: reality is the ultimate outrage. [1970]

John Lahr. *Astonish Me* (N.Y., Viking, 1973), pp. 84, 101

In all the history of the New Drama in Britain there is no career more spectacular, and alas none briefer, than that of Joe Orton. Between his first play, *The Ruffian on the Stair*, produced on the Third Programme in 1964, and his sudden death in 1967, he wrote three full-length stage plays and three television plays, plus an original film script (which has not yet reached production) and various other oddments, including presumably the sketch about an incestuous county family which surfaced in the London version of *Oh! Calcutta!* (1970). But even within this brief period he had not only written two of the new dramatists' biggest commercial successes, *Entertaining Mr. Sloane* and *Loot*, but had developed his own unmistakable vision of the world and his own tone of voice as a dramatist—to such an extent that ever after one finds oneself reading actual news stories in terms of a Joe Orton script.

The key to Orton's dramatic world is to be found in the strange relationship between the happenings of his plays and the manner in which the characters speak of them. The happenings may be as outrageous as you like in terms of morality, accepted convention or whatever, but the primness and propriety of what is said hardly ever breaks down. And the gift of Orton's characters for intricate and inventive euphemism, so far from toning down the outrageousness of their actions and ideas, only places it in even stronger relief. Orton was, perhaps first and foremost, a master of verbal style—or of his own particular verbal style. And even during his short public career his mastery of that style may be observed increasing and refining itself.

John Russell Taylor. *The Second Wave* (N.Y., Hill and Wang, 1971), p. 125

Orton's skill in keeping his situations delicately balanced between real life and fantasy, daylight and dream can be seen developing steadily, it seems to me, between his first play, *Entertaining Mr. Sloane* and the posthumous *What the Butler Saw*. *Entertaining Mr. Sloane* is cast on more Pinteresque lines than the later plays: its terms are too human, the mechanism is too slow, to let us take the characters as figures of farce, and yet the central events, the brutal mishandling of the old man and the sexual blackmail that follows, are presented with a kind of unyielding comic aplomb that undercuts human responses and raises worrying doubts about the playwright's own sympathies. It's hard to avoid ordinary human uneasiness about Mr. Sloane's attack on Kemp: there's too strong a feeling of real pain and fear in it to allow the detachment Orton seems to invite with his tough jokes and his cool handling of the manslaughter (as it proves to be).

In *Loot* the cool convention is much more firmly established. "It's a theme which less skilfully handled could've given offence," Truscott says to Fay, complimenting her on the direct, simple style of her murder confession. Style does have this sort of vital function in the play, not to prevent offence exactly, but to keep feeling in its place. There is still a good deal of physical brutality: Truscott getting Hal on the floor and kicking him isn't a pleasant sight. But it's kept at a careful distance, partly by being taken so fast, partly by the jauntiness of the dialogue at the receiving end of the violence.

Katharine J. Worth. Revolutions in Modern
English Drama (Bell, 1972), p. 150

In light of the influences more obviously at work in following plays, I don't think it is claiming too much for Orton's conclusion [in *Entertaining Mr. Sloane*] to see it in the tradition of a Restoration comedy where, instead of the customary pairings-off, there is a bi-sexual triumvirate peculiar to a view of the decompartmentalised world which Orton poses. That this compromise flourishes while the only innocent character suffers—dies, in fact—suggests that as Orton perceives the modern world those clever enough to live by their wits are those in the end who inevitably prosper. And Orton doesn't appear to mind, so long as he is there to parody the manners which spring from an abyss between the characters' decorous language and their indecorous actions.

That brings me back to the earlier question of Orton's view of society, the motivation for his work. On the evidence of his aesthetic approach it would seem the discovery of society's stench delighted him much more than it ever incensed him. Maybe unsealing it assuaged the paranoia he suffered for persecution as a homosexual and an iconoclast. Anyway as this delight grew so his work became uniquely his own. *Loot* and *What the Butler Saw* . . . are "Ortonesque" in a way that *Sloane* is not. They take a step past mere parody of manners, and parody as well their own comic form. Farce, at least its ingredients, has attracted Orton as early as *The Ruffian on the Stair*. . . .

As a form, farce allowed Orton's imagination its most uninhibited panorama. If his pseudonymous letters to editors are proof of sheer fun at foxing society without reverence for a committed stance, they seem also a desire for an uncompartmentalised self-concept. (He claimed to be a puritan, and confirmation of his frugal living—even when he could afford less Spartan conditions—suggest his reactionary poses were as much a check to an over-indulgent view of himself, as they were meant to reinforce this own superiority.) Consistency of character appeared to interest him much less than tactical surprise. Thus farce permitted him to confront society with the sort of escapist entertainment it loved (much the same as with the mediocre books he made ridiculous by doctoring up), at the same time to parody the kind of established values which considered farce important enough to patronise.

Keath Fraser. *MD*. Feb., 1972, pp. 415–16

ORWELL, GEORGE (1903–1950)

Many people have argued that the man they know as George Orwell was more important as a personality than as a writer, for what he was than for what he said. I suspect that time will reveal this opinion to be a fallacy, as it did in the case of Samuel Johnson, who, even when we tire of Boswell, remains solidly there as one of the most peculiarly significant writers of his age. Even in his least perfect writings Orwell still stands out as different from his contemporaries, yet no one reflects more clearly or more poignantly the peculiar anxieties of the age in which he lived. . . .

[His] resemblance to Don Quixote was appropriate, for in many ways Orwell can only be understood as an essentially quixotic man. He regretted the fading of a past society which, for all its faults, seemed to him more generous and colorful than the present. He defended, passionately, and as a matter of principle, unpopular causes. Often without regard for reason, he would strike out against anything that offended his conceptions of right, justice of decency, yet, as many who crossed lances with him had reason to know, he could be a very chivalrous opponent, impelled by a sense of fair play that would lead him to the public recantation of accusations he had eventually decided were unfair. In his own way he was a man of the left, but he attacked its holy images as fervently as he did those of the right. And however much he might on occasion find himself in uneasy and temporary alliance with others, he was—in the end—as much a man in isolation as Don Quixote. His was the isolation of every man who seeks the truth diligently, no matter how unpleasant its implications may be to others or even to himself.

George Woodcock. *The Crystal Spirit: A Study of George Orwell* (Boston, Little, Brown, 1966), pp. v., 3–4

War made [Orwell] a political activist—like nearly all intellectuals of his generation he had always been politically conscious—and war made him a journalist, pamphleteer and polemicist. He went to the Spanish civil war with a strong but undefined feeling of "anti-Fascism." He came out of it a committed Socialist and a dedicated anti-Communist, knowing that he had witnessed an injustice which, if he could not right, he must use his ability as a writer to record so that justice should at least be done to the memory of his comrades and their vision of Revolution. It was only after his return from Spain that he became a journalist in any serious sense.

The outbreak of war in 1939 made it impossible for him to go on living in the country on about £5 a week, took away the quiet and peace of mind he needed to work out his projected Saga and forced him into journalism to earn his living since he was rejected as medically unfit for the army. But now he was also a journalist because he wanted to be effective, to raise his voice against the folly, stupidity and despair he saw and felt, and try to keep alive his belief in the free, equal and decent society he had briefly glimpsed in the early days of the Spanish civil war. From 1939 to his death the only writings which he thought of as serious literary productions were two more novels and some essays.

Until 1945 he made extremely little money and this, combined with natural inclination, made him a very economical writer in the sense that he published everything he wrote. He was not given to keeping notebooks, diaries, sketches or outlines of projected books or work-in-progress and threw away the drafts and manuscripts of his books when they were redundant. In fact he left very few of those "papers" which writers always seem to leave, providing such marvellous hunting-grounds for critics or biographers. He left no personal papers: there is nothing either concealed or spectacularly revealed in his letters. He was certainly reserved and undemonstrative, very "English" in the conventional use of the term although he was not secretive or inhibited. Throughout his life he wrote what he thought or felt and published it in one form or another.

> Sonia Orwell. Intro. to Sonia Orwell and
> Ian Angus, eds., *The Collected Essays,*
> *Journalism and Letters of George Orwell*
> (N.Y., Harcourt, Brace, 1968), Vol. I, p. xvi

Because Orwell believed it was natural for human beings to love each other rather than causes, he was the implacable enemy of ideologies which supplanted human loyalties. Paradoxically, the strongest political defense he devised against the monstrous totalitarian usurpers of "own-life" is an irrational, almost mystical belief—one he attributes to the English: "a respect for constitutionalism and legality, the belief in 'the law' as something above the State and above the individual," which however cruel or stupid its embodiment in particular laws at particular times, is held to be, in essence, *incorruptible.*

Orwell would seem to have in mind here a transcendent idea of right and wrong, which is bred in the bone like the "Christian moral code." But constitutionalism, unlike the ideological mystique which relies for interpretation upon mere expedience or the caprice of a Leader, establishes communal purposes and, in particular laws, defines areas in which the individual *shall not be eccentric* —the extent to which he is "*not* altogether an individual." These laws are neither unalterable nor impossible to keep. The area not so defined is the inviolable area of personal freedom and moral choice.

> Ruth Ann Lief. *Homage to Oceania*
> (Columbus, Ohio State Univ. Pr., 1969),
> pp. 144–45

The necessary element of perversity in Orwell's work was that he wrote best about the things he hated. When he tried to write lyrically it came out stilted and anonymous, and his poetry is flat and schoolboyish with a touch of E. M. Forster's "undeveloped heart" or at least undeveloped language of the heart. Like a great many writers (Graham Greene is a spectacular example), he could not use part of his character in his work, and we need other people's memoirs to fill him out.

Although he had found his material with the non-fiction of *Down and Out*, he did not abandon fiction itself, then or ever. In spite of all he had seen in Spain and Wigan, he praised Henry Miller in 1939 for his "irresponsibility" and his rejection of politics. He still wanted to write such novels himself, recording the actuality of middle- and lower-class life with absolute esthetic fidelity, using politics only in so far as they affect that consciousness and precisely as they affect that consciousness (i.e., if lads at pub think socialism means a fair shake, that's what it means and that's all it means).

He did not quite have the gifts to bring it off completely in fiction, but it would be a mistake to think he was trying something different in his non-fiction. *The Road to Wigan Pier* and *Homage to Catalonia* are superb expressions of this same esthetic, an attempt to render ideas as pure experience. Poverty and Communism are only what their victims think they are. Therefore it is the business of literature to dump conceptual baggage and find out, like Miller, Zola, Joyce (his heroes), what actually happens down there. Orwell's tantrums toward the pansy Left and his attempts to talk cockney are thus not affectations but a furious creative effort (well, perhaps that's what affectations are) to enter his subject.

Wilfrid Sheed. *NYT*. March 5, 1972, p. 2

Orwell's last book [*1984*] is in many ways a nightmare, but this particular nightmare could only have been dreamed by a writer of this century, circa 1947, post Russian revolution, post World War I, post Spanish civil war, post World War II. With all Shakespeare's knowledge of history and court intrigues, he could not have imagined this totalitarian world. Nor could Milton with all his knowledge of the classics, the Bible, and the cruelty of civil war.

When we realize that this novel could not have been written at any other time, we understand its relationship to us. The shadow of barbed wire, of the truncheon, of the boot, of unholy tortures in unholy settings, of thousands upon thousands executed for "deviational thinking," of sadism cloaked in political institutionalism, falls upon all of us. We are free not to like *1984*. We are free to reject it as extreme. We are not free to reject it from our political awareness. The question to ask about *1984* is not how precise its predictions are, but to what extent it approximates a direction, and how germane its vision of totalitarian power is to our century.

Roberta Kalechofsky. *George Orwell* (N.Y., Ungar, 1973), pp. 133–34

OSBORNE, JOHN (1929–   )

If anyone still doubts that art knows better than censorship, John Osborne's new play at the Royal Court should provide clinching evidence. With the excision of this scene for which it will clearly go down in theatrical history, the Lord Chamberlain apparently might have considered licensing *A Patriot for Me* for public performance. Apart from the fact that it is one of the best things Osborne has written, the deletion would have been ludicrously self-defeating—as well urge that, to raise its moral tone, Nabokov should have erased from his novel all physical contact between Humbert Humbert and Lolita. Without its climactic evocation of high Hapsburg queerdom at its annual drag ball, *A Patriot for Me* would be, more or less, a sentimental, high-flown piece of propaganda for the rights of a noble and oppressed minority. Osborne's ball scene is not only magnificently theatrical, the best thing in his play, but its centre, its validation, the image from which all else takes perspective and completeness. It is funny, compassionate, grotesque, humane and defiant. . . .

Ever since *Look Back in Anger*, people have been comparing him with Noel Coward; between personal statements he's been no more afraid than Coward of beguiling his audiences with bits of pure, picturesque theatre, big with ironic romanticism and slapstick spectacle—*Paul Slickey*, the *Plays for England*, his film-script for *Tom Jones*. They aren't his major work, but I'd rather have most of them than *Bitter Sweet, Conversation Piece* or *Operette*. Like *Luther, A Patriot for Me* comes from this side of his talent and then goes beyond it. Evidently he picked up the book about Alfred Redl which appeared two or three years ago, and seized on it simply as a marvellous story, crying for amplification into a full-blown Cinemascope spectacular-with-a-kink. Cooler reflection must have shown it to be too kinky for the commercial cinema but there's plenty of evidence still, in the play's huge cast, ambitious range and multiplicity of short, cross-cutting scenes, of fairly advanced early development as a film-scenario. Jocelyn Herbert has done wonders, with enormous back-projections and evocative bits of mobile decor, to give its 84 characters elbow-room on the little Court stage. But ideally it should have unfurled like *Cavalcade*, all gaslights, open carriages and chancellery staircases, over the stage-machines of Drury Lane.

Ronald Bryden. NS. July 9, 1965, p. 58

It is this innate ability of Osborne's to match language to character which marks his plays so indelibly as his own. This language is simple yet lyrical, contrived yet real. It is theatrically thrilling, and if the dialogue of the minor characters appears to be weak, might that not have been effected with the deliberate purpose of focusing our attention upon the central character. Had the "minor language" contained more substance, more argument, more invective, then our interest might have been diverted from the all-consuming heroes. What

Osborne needed was to create plots of reasonable verisimilitude, but which permitted the central character to legitimately express his view within the action of that plot. Whilst these heroes are unable to alter society, for the odds against them are too great, they dominate those around them, and this is only natural. They themselves prevent any substantial minor dialogue developing, for they are always interrupting, questioning, rebuking, and inexorably giving their own opinion. It is the strength of their feelings which charges the plays with "electricity" and gives them so much impact. Jimmy's incredulity at Alison's departure, Archie's breakdown during his nun's story, Bill's panic when legal contacts refuse to speak to him, Pamela's avoidance of an emotional scene with Murray and Constance; in each, the private fear becomes at the same time a public warning.

Osborne is not a didactic writer in the sense that he tries to turn his characters into socialist lecturers, although in fact one of them, Holyoake, is. He makes them believable human beings, and puts them in credible situations. If we choose to ignore the social or political implications of a play, we still have an effective drama. Osborne, knowing that his characters can never win their battle against society, spins a protective web around them, making a moral implicit rather than explicit, a hero human rather than symbolic. The heroes' failing is that they maintain idealistic purposes which are impossible to achieve, but their refusal to surrender to the social forces which threaten them is always plausible. Unless conditions are suitable (and they are not yet) ideals like theirs are meaningless in the practical sense. Such a high moral purpose endangers life, and ensures conflict and ultimate defeat. By witnessing the defeat of Osborne's heroes, we begin to question the means and ends of a society which ensures their failure. The playwright tries to impress his beliefs upon us within the action of his plays. If we recognised his principle as being substantially correct then he might well stir us to significant action; if on the other hand, we have rejected those principles, then he is more likely to arouse in us that hostility which his own characters seem to enjoy so much. In the sympathies and antipathies of a play we are able to make further refinements and definitions about ourselves, and about the playwright. We may feel ourselves into a play, or we may not. This accord will depend not only upon plot and character but upon thought and experience. The thought of a play will acquaint the spectator with what the playwright perceives as the forces which motivate men, and his view of the place of man in society and in the universe. Experience will condition whether we accept his view or reject it.

Alan Carter. <i>John Osborne</i> (Edinburgh,
Oliver & Boyd, 1969), pp. 172–73

Only in *The Hotel in Amsterdam*—and with unexpected abruptness after the archetypicality of *Time Present*—was Osborne able at last to render a balanced, mutually-adjusted group of characters. Simultaneously, he was also able to strip away most of the overlay of plot with which he had previously felt impelled to fill out—and sometimes to overburden—his plays. I think that *The Hotel in Amsterdam*, in these senses, marks the end of a phase in Osborne's creative development. His early preoccupation with the atrophying effects of rationalised nostalgia—with which Jimmy Porter and Archie Rice were both stricken —had persisted even in *Time Present*. But by this time Osborne's interest had already shifted to alienation of another sort—the existential alienation of the loss of one's sense of objective identity. This was Bill Maitland's estrangement, and the theme of *Inadmissible Evidence* —a theme expressed in a more appropriate *form* than in any of Osborne's previous plays. This same theme was latent, though buried beneath a debris of renaissance leftovers, in *A Bond Honoured*. And then, in *A Patriot for Me*, it was as if Osborne were trying to make out with a telescope what he had put beneath a microscope in *Inadmissible Evidence*: for instead of compressing a world into Bill Maitland's mind, he set Alfred Redl against a broader social tapestry than he had ever before tried to weave—reassembling its military, social and sexual patterns into all kinds of permutations, but permitting Redl himself to pick up threads in none. In that play, however, it was the society rather than the stranger lost in its midst which came to life: but in *Time Present* Osborne again chose to depict a solitary figure in an almost suspended environment, so that Pamela found herself alone against a hazily hostile background of family and friends, and of actors and affluent agents.

Simon Trussler. The Plays of John Osborne:
An Assessment (Gollancz, 1969), p. 221

I have always hoped that some day I would wholeheartedly like and admire a play by John Osborne and, during the opening scene of *West of Suez*, I thought the time had come at last. . . . The dialogue is sharp, elliptical and up-to-date; the outspokenness, which Mr. Osborne helped to introduce with *Look Back in Anger*, has been carried much further since then, so that he himself is now able to profit from the example of his successors. The scene also has a philosophical dimension, because the husband is a scientist, a pathologist, who is keen enough on his work but is aware that science is only something he has found to do to while away the time. . . .

Mr. Osborne has been credited by the reviewers with Chekhovian ambitions, and indeed this opening part of *West of Suez* has about it something of the expectant symbolic air of *The Cherry Orchard* or, to mention an early Chekhovian imitation, Shaw's *Heartbreak House.* There is the bringing together of a group of people under the same roof or in the same garden to express a collective mood at a given moment in time. There is the same feeling that the family microcosm is meant to convey a larger truth; just as Ranyevskaya and her cherry orchard represent the beautiful fecklessness of the doomed Russia, or Captain Shotover's ship-like house is the vessel of England about to face the storms and explosions of a European war, so these people assembled west of Suez are clearly intended to be saying something about the present state of English civilisation. Perhaps Mr. Osborne has written the representative play of his maturity, as *Look Back in Anger* was the representative play of his youth; perhaps he has progressed from individual resentment and emotional confusion to a more general and objective statement.

Well, in a sense he has, but the statement remains so muddled, and the play is so poorly constructed that, after the opening scene, I suffered a tremendous sense of let-down. If one did not know that this was the umpteenth play of a practised playwright, one might suspect that it was another promising piece by a relative beginner who had managed his first act but did not quite know how to go on from there. . . .

After a while it becomes clear that *West of Suez* is basically the usual Osborne piece, with a big self-loving, self-hating character rampaging at the centre, and still not quite sure what he is rampaging about.

John Weightman. Enc. Nov., 1971, p. 56

Looking over Osborne's sixteen plays and remembering that he probably has more playwriting years ahead of him than behind, what evaluation is useful? He has written no unflawed play and a cluster of bad ones—at least five. They are just *there*, and no amount of critical dodging ("if he hadn't gotten these out of his system, he wouldn't have had the inspiration for those") or authorial rationalization ("artists should have the right to relax . . . to indulge themselves") can disguise them. Nor would he rank high on the list of contemporary writers one would turn to for intellectual stimulation. Osborne is no playwright of ideas; his thought is easily compressible into a simple statement of experience-oriented humanist existentialism. All of his work, good or bad, is urgent, passionate, and deliberately anti-intellectual. Philosophy is embedded in behavior and affect usually organized into an action of increasing isolation of a main character. And he has had no lasting effect on dramatic form.

I must admit to frequent bafflement in trying to mobilize the tools of my trade—an exhaustive training in structural methodology—to deal with Osborne. He offers nearly none of the mythical density or intricate poetic patterning of a Beckett, Pinter, or Genet to test analytic ingenuity. His demands, rather, are almost solely on the store of our human sympathy. He always works in terms of immediate feeling and response, willing to risk a fall into sentimentality in order to gain a fierce truthfulness to "the burden of living" and "the texture of ordinary despair." This is another way of saying that he is essentially a man of the theater, particularly of an actor's theater. Undiminished is his amazing gift for creating magnificent roles that have been graced by some of the great performances of our time. And, although he has not written at the top of his talent for eight years, he remains the *exciting* dramatist he so brilliantly began as. Exciting because three times—in *Look Back in Anger, The Entertainer*, and *Inadmissible Evidence*—he has articulated as fully as any writer the central experience of his age. We look forward to his doing this again, anticipating that each next play might gather masses of the unclear feeling of these complicated times and help us to a harrowing revelation of the way we are living.

Harold Ferrar. John Osborne (N.Y., Columbia
Univ. Pr., 1973), pp. 46–47

OWEN, WILFRED (1893–1918)

Owen's influence on the postwar poets has been summarized by C. Day Lewis, who nominates Hopkins, Owen, and Eliot as the "immediate ancestors" of the Auden group. Owen's contribution, however, was less technical than inspirational. Auden, Day Lewis, and Louis MacNeice employed Owen's most notable innovation—half-rhyme—for a variety of effects, but with the exception of Day Lewis they did not seriously explore the musical possibilities of this device, which does not lend itself to every poetic purpose. It is rather as a prophet that Owen earns Day Lewis' designation as "a true revolutionary poet." Owen's protest against the evils of war has been rather unwarrantably extended to the social and economic evils of modern life; he "commends himself to post-war poets largely because they feel themselves to be in the same predicament; they feel the same lack of a stable background against which the dance of words may stand out plainly, the same distrust and horror of the unnatural forms into which life for the majority of people is being forced."

Owen is actually a symbol rather than a prophet; his youth, his small but eloquent body of verse, his intense dedication to the truth, his untimely and unnecessary death—all of these factors combined to make him an irresistible figure to the succeeding generation, whose "stable background" of traditional forms and values had, like Owen's, been destroyed by the war. He is a "revolutionary poet" not in the sense that he deliberately undertook any radical reformation of his art but in the sense that his work embodies, more dramatically than that of any other poet, the changing values of the time.

John H. Johnston. *English Poetry of the First
World War* (Princeton, N.J., Princeton
Univ. Pr., 1964), pp. 208–9

Owen's poems need to be read together: they mutually illuminate each other and have a cumulative power. In their totality . . . they have done more than any other work in English to form a sensibility that can grasp the nature of technological war. If Brooke and Binyon seem irrecoverably anachronistic, then that is largely because of what we have learnt from Owen. And he achieved this change in our perceptions by hammering hard at limited but intense areas of experience: for all his power, his emotional range is restricted. He wished it to be, as his "Preface" makes clear. (It also raises an odd problem: why should the officer-pacifist, the opponent of the war, say of his book: "if the spirit of it survives—survives Prussia"? Was Owen, after all, less single-minded than his poems suggest?) I find it hard to imagine how Owen might have developed had he survived: the war was his overwhelming subject, and the work of his great final year was, in more than one sense, a consummation. It seems to me that a total cessation of creative activity would have been as likely a result of the anti-climax of peace as the vein of Catullan love-poetry that Mr. Day Lewis tentatively suggests he might have gone on to produce.

Bernard Bergonzi. *Heroes' Twilight* (N.Y.,
Coward-McCann, 1965), pp. 134–35

It has become clearer and clearer in the years since Owen's death that both in talent and in achievement he was the greatest of the poets who wrote during and of World War I. Many of the poems he had time to write are, by any criterion, great; what he might have achieved, given more time, is impossible to predict—and also irrelevant in making a final judgment. . . .

If what Owen might have done cannot be known, we know what he did. Failing in his purpose of warning, he yet wrote poems which remain a living and a growing influence upon the minds of those who read them. His experiments in assonance and half-rhyme were soon assimilated and have long been used as a matter of course by contemporary poets. His diction played a part in revitalizing and refreshing the vocabulary of poetry and his experiments, together with those of Gerard Manley Hopkins, doubtless encouraged the free and uninhibited playing with language and syntax that has been a prominent feature of modern verse. F. W. Bateson has pronounced Owen "the one modern poet whom it is impossible not to hear," and compared his poetry in "its vigour, its freshness, and its tenacity, with that of such a forerunner of Augustan poetry as Rochester," though he warns also that it is too soon to be certain if the main body of modern poetry will follow in the same direction.

Gertrude M. White. *Wilfred Owen* (N.Y., Twayne, 1969), pp. 140–41

PINTER, HAROLD (1930–   )

Pinter's new play, *The Homecoming*, itself a welcome return of a gifted dramatist to his native habitats—the full-length play, the stage (in spite of his forays in film and television, his true *métier*), his major themes. It is a play which, in its complexity, its achieved style, its mastery over certain limited but characteristic linguistic rhythms, deserves to stand beside *The Caretaker*; though it may not in fact mark an advance into new territory. . . .

The Homecoming is a play about the family—or rather, a Pinter family, in this case "new" working class, and, as in *The Caretaker*, deprived of the sympathetic influences of Mum. This takes the sentimental prop from under the situation and provides, in effect, the pivot of the play. Mum is never defined retrospectively, except in the most ambiguous terms. . . . But she is a "felt absence" in so far as it is her withdrawal from the scene which has liberated the men and set them free to roam and prey upon one another. In this primitive male world, according to Pinter's rigid dialectic, some have been raised as winners and desperadoes—Max, the father, ex-butcher and bully-royal, and Lenny, the sharp Greek Street pimp and casual denizen of the house: while others are cast in the "feminine" role—Sam, Max's brother, unmarried, a car-hire chauffeur, whose domain in the household is the kitchen sink and the washing up; Teddy, the Camden Town scholarship boy, intellectual, whose "homecoming" (together with sleek wife) the play "celebrates," and Joey, the loutish would-be boxer, who winds up on his knees in Pinter's own very special version of "mother's boy.". . .

The brutally "present" quality of family life—if it can be called that—is established in the opening scene: first between Lenny and his father, and then between the father and Sam. Pinter sets this up with such enormous economy that it almost escapes our notice how it is done: but this is central to the whole play. Like all of Pinter's characters, the men—Max, Sam, Lenny, Joey—are all granted that extraordinary racy way with language, an idiom all Pinter's own, which has its roots in the rituals and repetitions of working class speech, but with an extra charge of articulateness and a high literalness, a grip on detail, behind it: a common idiom, which is specially *inflected* for each character.

Stuart Hall. Encore. July–Aug. 1965, pp. 30–31

I am not much interested in seeking the "meaning" of Pinter's plays. However, I do want to disagree with those who see in Pinter a protest against the dehumanization of contemporary man. They take the pursuer-victim pattern and the automatic (or "already said") quality of many Pinter dialogues as indications of this protest. What I see in Pinter is a fine contemporary example of the "disinterested" artist. His attention is turned inward on the mechanics of his art. He is meticulous in scenic structure and dialogue for their own sake. He seems to me further from social protest than Ionesco or Genet, both of whom negatively point a "better world." Nor do I see in Pinter's work an analogue to Beckett's, except from a purely technical point of view.

In his plays Pinter asks "what can the theatre do?" much in the way that contemporary painters ask "what can pigments and form do?" His plays are often riddles because the insoluble puzzle is paradigmatically theatrical. Only within an art form which exists in time and which creates "reality" can one pose real questions without suggesting real answers. The audience is led to believe in the reality of both characters and situations. But the theatre is, finally, an illusion. Once we bring realistic attention to focus on an illusionistic presentation, we have set the stage for insoluble riddles. It remains only for the playwright to pose the questions. But Pinter is different from that other great riddler, Pirandello. Pirandello built his plays around contradictions, Pinter around conceptual incompletion. We cannot know in Pirandello; we shall not know in Pinter.

If there is a "meaning" in Pinter, it seems to me closely related to both Henry James and Franz Kafka. James was most interested in probing the human psyche to its depths of confusion and fragmentary bases. Kafka was always telling stories in which his heroes had no sense of what was happening to them. Combine these two, and I think you have what Pinter seeks.

Richard Schechner. TDR. Winter, 1966,
pp. 183–84

[*The Homecoming*] parodies all those wet stories about sentimental homecomings. Like much postwar drama it will be—already has been —explained away as Absurdity, Anti-logic, The Impossibility of Communication, the Theaters of Cruelty, Menace and Metaphysical Mystery.

Since it is both farcical and melodramatic, a more rewarding guide is the chapters on melodrama and farce in Eric Bentley's *The Life of the Drama*. Bentley talks about the irrational fears that can be presented to us from a stage; we may thrill vicariously to the fears from a safe distance (melodrama), or laugh at them because they are somebody else's (farce). He writes, ". . . 'We have nothing to fear but fear itself' is not a cheering slogan because fear itself is the most indestructible of obstacles.'" . . .

Dreams articulated are the soul of Pinter's writing. Not dreams like Strindberg's *To Damascus, The Ghost Sonata* and *A Dream Play,* which are torn whole and quivering out of the unconscious, but portraits of fears that casually surface and take on an uncanny semblance of reality. In place of the commercial daydream-plays of affluence and ease, popularity and sexual go, Pinter (following Beckett, Adamov, Genet and Ionesco) dramatizes nightmares, the dread of death or of life in a dead world, a morgue in movement, the snatching away of somebody precious or of a characteristic (sanity, satisfaction, reputation) that is essential if one is really to live.

The playwright's dreads come forth to challenge his "hero," an incarnation of himself. The operative figures in the nightmare are relatives, supposed friends of relatives, rivals—takers all. They rob him; they humiliate him. But the injuries have no obvious motive. He may seek and find a motive, out of his torment: an accidental crossing of another person's wishes, an unmeant infraction of another's property. He may even bow to that motive and so justify in a fashion what is being done to him. But the motive is inadvertent, trivial, ridiculous.

Albert Bermel. *NL.* Jan. 30, 1967, p. 30

If, as it is sometimes suggested, the ambiguity and uncertainty of Pinter's plays really was no more than the outcome of a deliberate manipulation of his audience by a clever craftsman of theatrical trickery, his use of repetition and absurdly inconsequential conversation no more than mechanical mannerisms, his work would be highly ephemeral and have no chance of making an impact on future generations of playgoers who would no longer be taken in or shocked by such superficially effective devices. If, on the other hand, as I believe it to be the case, the uncertainties, ambivalences and ambiguities of plot and language in these plays are the expression of a genuine perplexity about the nature of our experience of the world, the distillation of a deeply felt, painfully sifted and conscientiously recorded creative process, then they will surely endure as works not only of brilliant craftmanship (which is already beyond doubt) but as considerable artistic achievements.

What speaks for the latter view is the undoubted evidence of a steady development in Pinter's style, his consistent refusal merely to reproduce the mannerisms and technical achievements of his early successes. *Landscape* and *Silence*, in particular, are so radically different from the formula of what is commonly regarded as Pinteresque, so uncompromisingly remote from cheap seeking after success, that the view of Pinter as a mere manipulator of mechanical formulae surely must break down. In these plays the *poet* following his own inner law and discipline is again to the fore. ". . . My last two plays," said Pinter in an interview before the first night of *Landscape* and *Silence*, "are really rather different. They had to be from my point of view: I felt that after *The Homecoming*, which was the last full-length play I wrote, I couldn't any longer stay in the room with this bunch of people who opened doors and came in and went out. . . ." . . .

Pinter's ability to transcend the merely autobiographical subject-matter puts him, in my opinion, into a different class from most of the other, social-realist, playwrights of his generation in Britain. Moreover, and surprisingly, since so much of his effect in his own country derives from his witty use of local speech patterns, Pinter's plays have been as successful in America and in Europe across the Channel as they were in England. . . .

The three longer plays have, in my opinion, proved themselves beyond a doubt: *The Birthday Party* and *The Caretaker* have stood the test of repeated survival; *The Homecoming* also seemed to me, after a considerable number of encounters with the play, fresher and more durable each time, and able to preserve its impact and essence even in bad translations and abominable performances. These three plays are classics of our time, even though only future generations will be able to judge whether they can become classics for all time.

Martin Esslin. *The Peopled Wound: The Plays of Harold Pinter* (Methuen, 1970), pp. 230–32, 234

Pinter's particular achievement has been to sustain linguistically the sort of tensions which seem to drive his characters from within. The fragmentary sentence, the phrase left hanging, the awkward pause, become outer manifestations of the inner anxiety, the deeper uncertainty. The discordant clash of language in, say, *The Caretaker*, is indicative of the discord that arises not only between character and character but within each of the characters. The fumbling efforts at conversation which ensue indicate the desperate need the characters have to make themselves known. Paraphrasing von Clausewitz's definition of "war," language becomes *a continuation of tension by other means*. On such occasions, Heidegger reminds us, language seems not so much a faculty that man possesses as that which possesses man.

But the "continuation of tension" may not always have the exchange of information as its goal. Many of Pinter's characters, on the contrary, go to some length to evade being known by others. The sounds these characters exchange are a holding action, a skirmish designed to avoid the larger confrontation. Pinter describes such a strategy, "communication itself between people is so frightening that rather than do that there is continual cross-talk, a continual talking about other things rather than what is at the root of their relationship." One source of this circumvention of communication may derive from opposing levels of knowledge or intelligence. In *The Birthday Party*, for example, Goldberg and McCann can badger Stanley to distraction because of their continued reference to unknown forces or significant but hidden events. Or, as in *The Caretaker*, Mick can keep ahead of Davies because of his superior intelligence and wit. But the more important source of evasion arises out of the character's fear that if he reveals himself, if he comes clean, he will be at the mercy of those who know him. Davies, for example, will never admit much about Sidcup and expose his illusion. Everything he says then, however insignificant it seems, remains a part of his larger attempt to learn vital details about others and keep his own secrets to himself.

James R. Hollis. *Harold Pinter: The Poetics*
of Silence (Carbondale, Southern Illinois
Univ. Pr., 1970), pp. 123–24

Ritual functions in Pinter's dramatic world much as Jane Ellen Harrison suggests it functions in religion to keep the individual fenced-in soul open—"to other souls, other separate lives, and to the apprehension of other forms of life." The daily rituals that protect man from such openness and awareness are constantly undermined in Pinter's dramas by those sacrificial rites that impinge upon them and force contact. Goldberg and McCann disturb the breakfast rituals of *The Birthday Party* to conduct their own ritual party at which Stanley is sacrificed; and Petey can no long hide behind his paper when the strips of it which McCann has torn during the party fall out to remind him of Stanley's victimization. In *The Room* Rose can no longer hide behind her ritual breakfasts with her husband when Riley appears from the basement and involves her in his fate as *pharmakos*. As much as his characters evade communication, Pinter involves them in an eventual confrontation. The structure is Aristotelian, the imitation of an action, and the impact of the characters upon one another, even in their silent exchanges, is as final and irrevocable as the impact of character on character in Greek tragedy.

The Golden Bough kings have served in this exploration of Pinter's dramatic world as a metaphorical clue to the ritual patterns that form the basis of it. The contests for dominance which are at the center of the dramatic action of each play invariably have been fought with the tenacity of those priests who defended the Golden Bough with their lives. The battles have also taken on the symbolic significance of seasonal change and renewal attached to the Golden Bough ritual by Frazer and the Cambridge school of anthropology. In the seasonal ritual the old king-priest-god invariably must suffer death or banishment (Davies, Teddy, Edward—all must be sacrificed), either to be reborn as the new spirit of spring and life (Edward becomes the match-seller, Stanley becomes the new creation of Monty and Co.) or to be replaced by a new god (Teddy is replaced by Lenny and Joey, Law is replaced by Stott, Davies loses the battle to the young gods already in possession, Mick and Aston). The role played by Pinter's women is also clearer if their place as fertility goddess in the ritual is understood: Flora's welcome of the match-seller as her new mate and Ruth's adoption of her new household both make ritual sense of what on the surface seem sluttish and irrational choices. The new god must receive a welcome and be joined with mother earth if life is to continue.

Katherine H. Burkman. *The Dramatic World of Harold Pinter: Its Basis in Ritual* (Columbus, Ohio State Univ. Pr., 1971), pp. 133–34

As a Romantic artist, Pinter has known as much as any modern playwright the appeal of the liberated self. He has sensed, and embodied in the plays, that impulse toward the unlimited expansion of the ego, toward dominance, luxury, action, possession, sensual gratification. But as a late and disillusioned Romantic, Pinter has also known from the first that such an impulse was not to be trusted, that such qualities were as destructive as gratifying. Davies of *The Caretaker* is as near as Pinter has come to drawing a portrait of archetypal man; and though we pity Davies because he is, like all of us, weak, ignorant, lost on an endless journey, subject to age and death, nevertheless, we know that the endless self-aggrandizement of so vain and dangerous a creature cannot go unchecked. Yet so pressed are Pinter's characters by the demands of the self that the only way they can escape them is through total retreat into some state of withdrawal—some room—where they will be sheltered. Persons such as Stanley, Aston, Teddy, and Kate are not hiding from the I.R.A., or the trauma of a mental home, or a coarse family, or a lesbian past but from the demands of the inner self.

Pinter has often spoken of his admiration for Samuel Beckett, and his stylistic debt to the great symbolist playwright is easily enough perceived. Yet, though he shares Beckett's recognition of human vanity and fallibility, Pinter lacks the Irish writer's sense of the metaphysical on the one hand and his humane whimsy on the other. Of all the major modern playwrights, Pinter seems in certain essentials most closely allied to one comparatively distant in time and very different in style, Henrik Ibsen. Pinter shares with Ibsen a kind of grim humor, but more significantly, an essentially ambiguous view of the human condition. Both have given us figures possessed by a desire for self-aggrandizement, dominance, fulfillment, yet forever held back in a state of psychic paralysis. If he were not still trailing some clouds of Faustian glory, the Master Builder might find a place in a Pinter play; Hilda Wangel, the embodiment of feminine power, would probably not object to making certain contractual arrangements with Lenny and his family in *The Homecoming*. For the creators of Solness and Davies, of Hilda and Ruth, are both attracted by the power of the vital inner self and repelled by its ruthlessness.

That there should be so marked a similarity between the first great modern playwright and the writer who has most recently assumed a place in the line of descent from him suggests not only a coincidence in personality but the extent to which the modern drama is a body of Romantic art. And as the Romantic writer has characteristically turned to the past as a source of fulfillment, so Pinter, *in Landscape, Silence,* and *Old Times*, has sought there for the resolution to the contradictions with which he has been concerned. If his search has not brought us answers, it has brought us his plays, which are significant records of his quest.

Arthur Ganz. In Arthur Ganz, ed., *Pinter: A Collection of Critical Essays* (Englewood Cliffs, N.J., Prentice-Hall, 1972), pp. 177–78

All attempts to explain [*Old Times*] involve an attempt to summarize something unsummarizable, and most of them enter too ingenuously into the game of finding different degrees of truthfulness in different speeches. "Yes I believed him when he said that but she wasn't telling the truth when she said that." No one in a play is telling the truth. None of the events happened in reality. But though we all know this very well, we still look for factual consistency in the fictional artifice that every play is, and Pinter is the first playwright fully to explore the theatrical potential of frustrating us.

The question of whether Anna really saw a man lying across Kate's lap is a meaningless question. What matters is the relationship between the words in which she speaks about it and the image we see at the end of the play when Deeley lies across Kate's lap. The question of whether Anna is alive or dead, an aspect of Kate, a separate person, or a set of memories in the minds of the other two is a question which deserves only a minimum of attention. It may not be wholly avoidable, but it does not need to be in the foreground of our minds; the criticism which sets out to bring it into the foreground is bad criticism. We go to the theater with our responses preconditioned by what we have heard and what we have read.

Old Times is not a puzzle to be solved; it is an elaborate construction of words, echoing silences and images which ought to be enjoyed as such. If it makes a statement—as every play, in some sense, must—it is a statement which could not have been made by Pinter in any other way, and which remains unparaphrasable. Murder plays are usually badly written and our interest in them exhausted as soon as the mystery is solved. *Old Times* is extremely well written, and the critic can best help us to relish the writing by weaning us away from trying to solve the mysteries.

Ronald Hayman. *Harold Pinter* (N.Y., Ungar,
1973), pp. 147–48

I am, in the last analysis, not quite so confident that Pinter's work will survive to "classic" status as Osborne's or Arden's—and he himself declares that "it's of no moment to me." For, so like yet so unlike his fellow Jewish writer Arnold Wesker, he is very much a man of his times, and writes for them—and for the actors who act in them. In another half a century there is the danger that performers may have lost the capacity to play Pinter as irrecoverably as we have today grown out of sympathy with the style of an Irving or a Tree, or even of a Wolfit.

Pinter is, then, an actor's playwright, with all the virtues and limitations that implies. He will, of course, continue to write—and, I suspect, continue to move disconcertingly from the master work of each period of his stylistic development to a formulaic *reductio ad absurdum* of the same manner. But he will remain, I think, a lyrical writer, choosing to ignore the possibilities of the narrative element in drama, continuing to write strong curtains—and continuing, above all, to write a play around a hard kernel of situation, enwrapping this in arbitrary layers of ambiguity at his worst, but at his best showing us the kaleidoscopic multiplicity of attitude, ambivalence, distortion and doubt that is the individual's attempt to bring reality within the bounds of personality, and so to make it bearable.

Simon Trussler. *The Play of Harold Pinter:
An Assessment* (Gollancz, 1973), pp. 187–88

PLOMER, WILLIAM (1903–1973)

When William Plomer sailed from Durban in 1926, his poetry soon ceased to speak of Africa with any frequency. Then he abandoned completely all reference to the country which had so deeply influenced him. During a thirty-year absence, he wrote many books, including a number of volumes of poetry. Often this work was light, witty, at times quite playful—characteristics not found in the poems about Africa. In 1956 he again visited the Transvaal, and suddenly there is a return of this exclusive seriousness. . . .

Nothing of the passionate quality of the South African poetry appears in the Japanese period. With little doubt, the poem which has the most to tell the reader about Japan does not appear in the section, said to be "Written in Japan," but is a portrait of Captain Maru, identified as "a Japanese nationalist between the two World Wars." . . .

Despite the fact that the immediate stimulus for Plomer's poems of Greece was temporary residence there, being present in the country was never more than one part. Wherever any Western educated poet might look in Greece, he would view it through his Classical background. Thus, when a reader turns to the first poem he meets Apollo, and there will be Corfu and Ulysses—and hints where there are not names and events. The Greek poems are pleasant, show skill, play upon memories, yet never undertake the penetration found in the South African and in at least one of the Japanese poems. . . .

When a reader opens Plomer's most recent volume of poems, *Taste and Remember* (1966), he discovers that the author is still doing some of his best work. One of the most subtle poems of his career is "Exit Lines," where "exit" means death and "lines" means one's last words. . . . It is the intention of the poem to be suggestive—as far as possible infinitely suggestive. A reader is made to understand clearly that these last earthly words are to be so stated that they will be especially for those present. . . . Self is rejected, and the thought of another is embraced—that is to say, "love." What is meant by love? Clearly love is *everything* an individual can give, always personal and individual, and what one has created one should never destroy.

John Robert Doyle, Jr. SwR. Autumn, 1967,
pp. 634, 646, 648, 659–61

William Plomer's latest poems [*Celebrations*] are couched in his characteristically lithe, unsensuous style, a language mostly low-keyed and always unobtrusive, but equipped with a sardonic cutting-edge which slices into social injustice and pretension. The lucid objectivity of the poems seems itself a kind of moral stance. . . . Objectivity means, not detachment, but cool confrontation—focusing an object or issue in the kind of even light which crops up more than once as an image within the poems, and so pruning away emotional excess, matching feeling and rationality in exact proportion. (Mr. Plomer is careful to tell us, in a poem about the death of a sparrow, that the pang he felt "was not excess of sentiment" but "proportionate . . . to what I saw.") Even on the rare occasion when imagery rises to more ambitiously fanciful heights (the sun as a "low-slung spotlight angled from emptiness"), the unelaborate precision of the language holds the impression firmly in place. The result is a spare, rational, clear-sighted poetry, an unlyrical verse yet one with complex, carefully regulated emotional undercurrents.

TLS. April 21, 1972, p. 441

● PORTER, PETER (1929–   )

Mr. Porter is a poet with one very desirable quality: enjoyability. Critics don't like admitting to enjoyment (it's a pleasure of the flesh). But of the postwar English practitioners he is perhaps the most outstanding for the originality and vitality of his thought and language. . . .

Porter has a freshness and concentration of thought that we have not known since the Master was writing all that trash in the Thirties. Indeed Spot the Auden is a game that can too easily be played with this book [*Poems, Ancient and Modern*]. . . . Porter has a lot in common with Auden: love of theories and ideas as such (even theology), love of unusual words . . . love—and knowledge—of music, interest in Germanic culture and the Ancient World. However, a certain Antipodean directness, tough and sexy, saves these poems from being simple applications of the Auden method. . . .

Poems, Ancient and Modern has, I think, more successful poems in it than *Once Bitten, Twice Bitten*, the first book. The props, historical, scenic and cultural, do not get in the way of the poetry. . . .

Another virtue of Porter's is his ability to write seriously without being solemn. . . . In fact, there are as many good poems here as anyone has a right to expect.

L. Feb., 1965, p. 100

If his new book [*The Last of England*] is not quite the overall success one would like to see for this poet, it has style and wit. The barbs catch, the burrs stick, the images register not because they are extreme but because they are exact. It is not a comfortable book; doubtless it was not meant to be and . . . I would occasionally have welcomed a little sheer old-fashioned poetic indulgence. With such a dazzling technique he could have afforded a few more poems as calmly effective as the title poem, and a few less of the men-of-the-world, don't-forget-the-poet-is-no-different-from-you, exercises in sardonic bonhomie. Porter has stature as a poet, and this book has stature as a book . . . but I wish there were a few poems I avidly wanted to return to.

John Smith. *PoetryR*. Winter, 1970–71, p. 364

It would be daft to say that Peter Porter [in *Preaching to the Converted*] is in any way similar to Auden, yet there is some evidence that Porter has learned about writing from him—something beyond a few cadences picked up here and there, or a shared fondness for German and Italian art and music. Porter's poems are as good as they are because his imagination is unusual and complex, and he has, from a dedication to craft, acquired a formidable technique.

Porter's imagination could be said to be energetically sub-Augustan. . . . It is no longer possible for an imagination, a way of conceiving, to be as unified or stable as "sub-Augustan" implies. If there is much of the dark underside of *The Dunciad* in Porter, there is a more Romantic regret and disappointment with the Age, and with himself, an elegiac, almost funerary obsession, that while penetrating Augustan concerns of Love, Truth, and Right Living, has less to do with Auden's "staid common-sense" than with mystery, intuition, and personality.

Porter's style is "impure"; it is, in the classical sense, "mixed," and wonderfully so, both as regards the writing itself—high style and low style—and thematic conjurations of past and present, as in "The Great Cow Journeys On," "Delphi," and in other poems when he assumes his role of historical caricaturist. His "low style" is probably the more striking; it springs on to the page as if from an overhearing of haywire metropolitan lunch-time conversations, but often in brilliantly conceived situations. In "An Affair of the Heart," for example, he can portray misgivings at the way his heart works in terms of sexual endeavour, and his invention here is exhaustive. "High style" is easier to write, and certainly what "poetry lovers" most like to read; in Porter's case it is often elegiac, as in "Fossil Gathering," or "Thomas Hardy at Westbourne Park Villas," which ends with "Ordinary gestures of time working on faces the watermarks of hell." Any more rhetorical, and the reader might have died of it.

For all the satirical appearance of many of his poems, only a few are attempts at precise satire . . . and even these have as much to do with conserving his own sanity as condemning the wastefulness of others. Instead of satire as such, the impression is that Porter's imagination has been infected by dislikes. He laments contemporary horrors as if he were the maestro of a famous Carnival shut down because of plague. . . . Porter is more than just a "social poet." He is a tragedian who can't stop laughing. At the same time, the feeling of the world we live in—the world of our art, the world of our lives—is gone over in these poems with a dire, disappointed gusto. There are few tunes, few melodies, very little praise, but a great deal of assurance.

Douglas Dunn. Enc. March, 1973, pp. 66–67

POWELL, ANTHONY (1905–   )

Unlike the hero of Kingsley Amis's recent novel, *I Want It Now*, Anthony Powell has always been content to have some of it now and plan for some of it to come later on. Thus far in his case the procedure has turned out a good one: five small gems of novels written before World War II, and now, with *The Military Philosophers*, nine volumes completed of the projected twelve which will make up his great work *The Music of Time*. And great work I am convinced it is, whatever happens in its composition from here on home; furthermore, a great work of comic realism.

Certain questions may be disposed of at the outset since they have often formed too much of the reviewer's concern as individual volumes appeared: (1) Can one read the book in question without having read the books previous to it? One can read it no doubt with some profit and delight, but there's no reason not to start where Powell starts (with *A Question of Upbringing*, 1951) and proceed leisurely through the next eight books. Then one can think about rereading, another essential act in the full appreciation of Powell's virtues. (2) Does one have to wait to make judgments until all the evidence is in, until the *roman fleuve* ceases to flow? Anthony Burgess, in reviewing the latest one, both argued in this way and rather ungraciously claimed he was tired of waiting for the end, that novels should be self-sufficient and dramatic in a way Powell's are not. In principle there's much to be said for speaking up against the *roman fleuve* as annoyingly evasive; but it makes all the difference who's doing the flowing: Powell, that is, not Lord Snow. (3) What is a particular novel in the sequence "about"? This question is no harder or easier or more useful to answer than it would be if put to one of the volumes in Proust's sequence: this one is "about" Nick Jenkins's experience in the army during the latter years of World War II as much as *Within a Budding Grove* is about Marcel's vacationing experience at Balbec. (4) Finally, do ordinary plain-readerish demands about how fiction should express life, say something meaningful and true about the human condition, do these demands have to be laid aside and replaced by much quirkier satisfactions in order for one to become an admirer of Powell's fiction? No, a thousand times no; he is not a delightful English eccentric to be enjoyed by those who like that sort of thing.

William H. Pritchard. *MR*. Autumn, 1969,
p. 812

Halfway through the 1960s, as readers are aware, Powell came to the point in *The Music of Time* of describing England at war. If I have seemed to rush toward reference to it, this has been because, by his own account, the war has been the fulcrum of his life and that of writers of his generation. "I suppose the fact is, one emerged from the war rather a different person." In his case the approach of war may have doubled in impendingness because of the fact that he was brought up an only child in a military family.

Following in the pattern of other sons of upper-middle-class and professional families, Powell went through the traditional educational stages of preparatory school, public school, and university. At Oxford especially, where he read history at Balliol, he became friends with artistically precocious young men who were on or beyond the verge of achievement while still undergraduates. Graham Greene, Evelyn Waugh, and Henry Green have been mentioned: other contemporaries were Cyril Connolly, Peter Quennell, Harold Acton, Robert Byron, John Betjeman, Alfred Duggan: all but the last two were to secure their literary reputations quickly—certainly before 1930. As Nick Jenkins, the narrator of *The Music of Time*, says of two acquaintances just down from the university: "I was almost startled by the ease with which both of them appeared able to write books in almost any quantity. . . ."

Ingenuously enough, Powell told a *New Yorker* interviewer that it was the very *ordinariness* of producing novels that was to send him in the same direction. "I was brought up to do ordinary things. My parents always insisted on that. . . . Everyone at Oxford was writing a novel. At Eton, my school, novel-writing was also an ordinary thing to do." It is safer to adhere more closely to the literal statement when assessing what Powell means than one might where another writer is concerned. Irony in the last quoted passage could occur only if one threw a bridge across the sentences and decided that Powell's parents told him to conform and get his novel started. Taking the statements sentence by sentence, there is no irony. They do tend to point to a temperamental difference between Powell's Eton and Oxford associates and himself, granting the independent spirit necessary for undertaking literary careers. As his memoir of Eton reveals, he was somewhat differently placed in being responsive to the social and aesthetic revolutions of the twenties without being weaned, as were so many, from a soldierly respect for subordination and duty.

John D. Russell. *Anthony Powell: A Quintet, Sextet, and War* (Bloomington, Indiana Univ. Press, 1970), pp. 4–5

Once we look beyond Doris Lessing and Anthony Powell, the 1960's were not a period of great distinction in English fiction. But Powell's work alone would suffice to mark the decade, and together they provide complementary views of considerable merit. It is, perhaps, not unusual that both writers have been engaged in writing a series, bringing a cumulative effect to work that in itself might not have been sufficiently solid. Unlike Mrs. Lessing, however, whose talents blossomed in two long novels in the sixties, Powell has worked at his same pace since 1951, publishing novels of almost congruent length, biding his time until his readers saw the mythical figure in the carpet.

The figure is now clearer, and the achievement after nine novels —with three more to appear—is that of the most elegant writer presently working in the English language. Powell has created nothing less than a chronicle of his times, what C. P. Snow, imitating Galsworthy, started out to do in his *Strangers and Brothers* series. It is instructive, surely, to try to ascertain why Powell's sequence, which starts with upper middle class assumptions, succeeds so generously when such assumptions no longer appear viable; while Snow's, with its strong views from beneath of a young man achieving success despite restricted opportunity, should have become both remote and cloying at a time when precisely such views appear the way of the world.

One of the personal disturbances a writer engaged in a series must confront involves the changes within himself as he spends fifteen to twenty years on his project. At some point, the series will call attention to him, and that in turn may bring about a different sensibility which is bound to run over to the rest of the series. Doris Lessing remained relatively unknown, almost a struggling author, throughout most of the *Children of Violence*. Until *The Golden Notebook*, in 1962—possibly the most ambitious British novel since *Ulysses*—she had not surfaced sufficiently so that her personal sense of achievement would enter into or distort her fictional values. On the contrary, C. P. Snow moved rapidly into the great world, a world whose normalizing values deny imaginative fiction, and his literary talents, modest to begin with, rarely had an opportunity to develop apart from his international activities. As Snow's journalistic voice became increasingly noticed in the early 1960's, his fiction was supererogatory, even self-serving.

Unlike Snow, Powell has chosen to speak solely through his novels. Since there is no competition between the public and private man—few interviews, only scattered journalism and reviews, no god-like pronouncements—his work has had the chance to develop and expand within its own terms. This condition is a constant in art, as Yeats so often reminded us: that is, the need to grow within one's personal values, so that public and private do not negate each other, so that art will ultimately synthesize. So much is clear, and obvious. None of this, of course, denies profound change in Powell; his sympathies have grown, his attitudes broadened. What began, in the pre-*Dance of Time* novels, as witty and somewhat superficial in the mode of early Waugh or Huxley, or even Firbank, has acquired darker hues, without losing wit or irony.

Frederick R. Karl. *Mosaic*. Vol. 4, No. 3,
1971, pp. 13–14

Enthusiasts for Anthony Powell wait for new volumes in *The Music of Time* much as in the early nineteenth century the people of Peebles waited for a man called Tam Fleck to call in the evening. Fleck is to be found in the memoirs of William Chambers, the Edinburgh publisher: he owned a copy of Josephus's history of the Jews, and went round from house to house in Peebles reading it as the current news. . . . So it is with Powell. It is news he seems to bring. . . .

The character of Nick, the narrator, becomes clearer than ever before, I think, in *Books Do Furnish a Room*, tenth and latest in the sequence. He never says much about himself, but he is far from being a negligible personality: what he has is an heroic curiosity at the same time as perfect good-breeding, a rare and continually exhilarating combination for his readers. He has also, of course, the indispensable knack of being around just when interesting things are happening—only so has he managed to fill ten books with accounts of his relatives and friends by the age of forty. . . .

The gravity of the incidents, for the participants, is never played down; yet they are displayed in their full entanglement in a thousand unrepeatable and hitherto unimaginable circumstances, in which the apt and the grating, the grotesque and the poignant, the poetic and the sordid tumble wildly over each other. . . . There is often gaiety, but never flippancy, in Nick's voice.

Derwent May. Enc. March, 1971, pp. 71–72

Making music out of words alone is a tricky business. Without the presence of notes to be played or tunes to be heard, the reader is put into a state of expectancy aroused by the *idea* of music that may alert him to notice subtleties of repetition and design he would otherwise have missed; on the other hand, he may also be led to demand more in the way of sensuous delight and lyric intensity than he ordinarily would. Taking music as poetic metaphor, he will strive to catch the unheard melody, the "deeper meaning," below the prose surface of something that offers itself as history, as chronicle.

In the series of twelve novels Anthony Powell is devoting to an epic scale treatment of his theme, the transformation of England during his lifetime, we are immediately struck by the author's skill in portraiture and his grasp of social reality. He understands those little telltale characteristics of look, of gesture, of voice, of manner that "place" a person irrevocably in a certain class or occupation or social situation. And a great deal of the interest of his work lies in seeing how, over a long period of years, the moral landscape changes, revealing surprising new perspectives on character that, on reflection, seem to have the inevitability of life itself. As we gradually get to know characters who appear, disappear, and reappear apparently at random, a sense of design emerges, though an equally strong sense of the impossibility of seeing the whole design comes through simultaneously. Mr. Powell refuses to pretend he is God. He is, in fact, prepared to risk a good deal to preserve the inconsequence of life: we are allowed brief snippets of information exchanged between characters who know a great deal more about the situation than we do, and we may have to wait hundreds of pages to have some puzzle cleared up, if it ever is. The reward of Mr. Powell's method is that, if we surrender ourselves attentively to sharing his narrator's viewpoint, we see a certain section of the world with uncommon vividness.

As for the music of time, it is unclear to me (at the end of ten volumes) how ironically we are to take this title. My guess is that Mr. Powell resolutely rejects any such mystic recovery of the past as Proust (to whom he is often compared) offers. English to the bone, he continually tests abstraction against experience, though he knows with the strength of a true artist's intuition the necessity of discerning a "music" somewhere in the jangle of sensation. And though he could hardly be considered an apologist for a "British" Ideology, or any other, he is very interested in ideas.

John Rees Moore. *HC*. Oct., 1971, pp. 1–2

The dance of Anthony Powell's characters to the Music of Time has now become grimly autumnal. In this eleventh novel [*Temporary Kings*] of the planned twelve, his fascination with the inexorable development of these people in the fulfilment of their life-roles has turned, of necessity, into a sad contemplation of the varying degrees of their decay. As always, the novel ultimately pivots on a concept of the profound comedy of all human postures and strivings. But the humour is indisputably darker; the wry, funny glances at everything from the vanity of the highest ambitions to the merest minutiae of individual behaviour are pervaded by a sense that soon, now, careers will be concluded, aspirations wither away, the places at the dinner tables be filled only by ghosts. . . .

It is customary, but even now not superfluous, to praise Mr. Powell's unobtrusively perceptive and dexterous handling of any kind of character. The scholarly, laconic, sexually mysterious Gwinnett is his finest new creation—pursuing his biographical data with a kind of diffident ruthlessness, an inscrutable catalyst. . . .

The fineness of Mr. Powell's art, the near-genius in his sense of design, consists in his ability to perceive and render believable in "fiction" the sheer multifariousness of real human experience in his age. Reputations founded on inventions less true and more feigning begin to wane almost irrecoverably in the light of his achievement. Obviousness, so often mistaken for originality and force, has always been the besetting sin of the inferior novelist. Which of the doubters will now still claim that Mr. Powell was wrong, in those unexpectedly solemn, measured cadences of *A Question of Upbringing* twenty-two years ago, to turn away from it and follow his own path?

TLS. June 22, 1973, p. 709

POWYS, JOHN COWPER (1872–1963)

Powys's poems, early narratives and lecturing correspond to Shakespeare's output before 1600; the famous sequence from *Wolf Solent* onwards to the dark tragedies; *Owen Glendower* and *Porius* to *Antony and Cleopatra* and *Coriolanus*; and both show final periods of myth and marvel, with a concentration on youth. Though Powys's technique is scarcely dramatic, his way of making each work a world of its own is Shakespearian, especially in his use of colourings: green for *Wolf Solent*, blue and purple for *A Glastonbury Romance*, white for *Jobber Skald*, red and gold for *Owen Glendower*, yellow for *Porius*, gold for *Atlantis*.

As always, certain strictures are possible. Powys can tire us by repetition; his vastly spatialised technique and massive deployments may intrude at the expense of narrative; and his mastery of the long sentence, like the wielding of a giant's club, tempts him, on occasion, too far. Nevertheless his choice of media has in the main been admirably attuned to his purposes. These are peculiarly his own; he is announcing a gospel, a *tao* or life-way, perhaps also a death-way, though when he likes, as in *The Meaning of Culture* (1930), he can write impersonally on a wide field.

To traditional religion he is deeply attuned while remaining sceptical. On Catholicism he comments with a peculiar sensitivity, especially in *The Meaning of Culture*; there and in both *The Pleasures of Literature* and *Mortal Strife* he writes profoundly of Christ; and for St. Paul his admiration is consistent. Theological disquisition is wonderfully handled on *Owen Glendower* and *The Brazen Head*. For some of us the Christian and bisexual idealisms, for the two involve each other, of *Owen Glendower* will remain the summit of his achievement. However, he is impelled to speak for our disturbed and sceptical age, distrusting bisexual unities in *Porius* and *Atlantis* in association with theology and science, though bisexuality still *fascinates* in *The Mountains of the Moon*; rigid systems lead to tyranny and torture; all easy solutions he refuses, never forgetting the horrors in nature and in man. His own choicest precepts he admits to be provisional and he is aware, despite theology, that Chance, honoured in book after book, and perhaps especially in *The Inmates*, is a determining power. But he also insists that from this ambiguous and indecipherable universe or multiverse, for he prefers the latter term, goodness, by which he means not zeal or "love" but rather tolerance, kindliness and humour, has somehow unaccountably arisen, to exert henceforward its own unavoidable compulsions. His gospel is not confined to generalities and probably his most important contribution to our religious tradition is his insistence that "no religion that doesn't deal with sex-longing in some kind of way is much use to us."

G. Wilson Knight. *The Saturnian Quest: A Chart of the Prose Works of John Cowper Powys* (N.Y., Barnes & Noble, 1964), pp. 122–23

It is not fantastic, despite John Cowper's absorption in post-Freudian psychology, to characterise him as an earth-man. What does rapidly prove fantastic, and then impossible, is to account for either his work or his limitations in any other way. His urban culture is the only urban thing about this supremely clever intellectual. His genius for being John Cowper has always been much more evident than his genius for any kind of writing. It is considering the oddness of the writings without relating it fully to the oddness of the man that has defeated his less sympathetic critics. But whatever we may feel about his natural aptitudes as a novelist, we can only get him into a proper perspective against the background of the novel, and of the "rural" novel at that. John Cowper has an inexhaustible and sometimes exhausting curiosity about many forms of human experience. But towards man's identification with the earth—and especially with his own . . . Wessex—he turns as the flower turns its face to the sun or the sparks fly upward. . . .

One cannot attempt an all-over summary of John Cowper or of his contribution and achievement without some consideration of his verse, although this may well seem the least essential part of him. His failure to become what he earliest desired is an indication of his nature: in effect it emphasizes the dangers of his fluid and chameleonish make-up. He had virtually abandoned verse composition before he found himself as a creative writer and there is little intellectual *progress*—less even than in his literary criticism—to lend any significance to the chronology of the poems. Of the enriched and deepening intimacy and nature that gave a greatness to the novels of his maturity there is hardly any foreshadowing in his verse: the verse comes out of books. *Lucifer*, sumptuously produced in 1956, being thus John Cowper's last serious challenge as a writer of verse, was in fact written just over half-a-century earlier. . . .

Certainly what strikes most formidably any one who makes a survey of John Cowper in all his variety of effect must be his vast scope and capacity. His power of absorbing and reproducing any sort of literature (in several languages) was enormous, and a novel like *Owen Glendower* shows a knowledge of its period so varied and intimate that one could suppose he had spent an academic lifetime in mastering it. His observations of the world, his sympathies, his interests have a range surely unsurpassed among English novelists. . . . While his persistent amateurishness of manner seems to defy current "sophistication," his intellectual resourcefulness, his readiness in allusion, his flair for precedents and parallels are almost breathtaking.

H. P. Collins. *John Cowper Powys: Old
Earth-man* (Barrie and Rockliff, 1966),
pp. 1, 193, 195–96

It seems probable that Powys came to be an anti-novelist not from any consideration of structure, or artistic form, but from his personal metaphysic, namely his faith in man's fictive power, as revolution, the perpetual creation of new life. In the *Autobiography*'s part-parody of *The Prelude* (and the schoolboy Powys's self-dedication to poetry between urinal and stars is in the same vein as Auden's comic rewriting, in *Letters from Iceland* (1936), of Wordsworth's "vows Were then made for me") Powys's discovery that he, self-created, self-analysed, self-mocked, was to be his poetry indicates his primary inspiration. (His amusing discovery here, and its accidental nature, contrasts with the young Yeats's earnest decision, revealed in his *Autobiographies*, to make his life into poetry, himself his own artefact.) His novels invite our conscious cooperation in making, because his concern is how we each make ourselves and our lives, and so what we all make of life.

Yet, before he first went to America, Powys began the ambition, still held at sixty, as he wrote the *Autobiography*, to write "a sort of mystic-humorous, Pantagruelian, Shandean, Quixotic Romance." Here his proposed masters are great eccentrics concerned with structural process that ridicules customary structure, and concerned to break down fossilised attitudes and to put their readers at unease. The prototypes of the anti-novel are to be found in literature long before "the rise of the novel" and Powys is a modern because of his sympathy with its grander ancestors. Although and because he writes as a prophet against the tyrannies and conformities of mechanised man of the twentieth century, he has masters like Homer (admiring Homer for the same reasons as Addison did, namely his representation of the permanent and natural in man) and Rabelais (whose exploration of the overlap in man of the excremental and the sacramental is imitated in *A Glastonbury Romance*). His novels are akin to earlier English works, of such different kinds as *The Faerie Queene* and *King Lear*, which move outside traditional literary forms, away from symmetry and exterior form in search of "unaccommodated man" and so push nature and experience to "the very verge of her confine."

> Belinda Humfrey. Intro. to *Essays on John Cowper Powys* (Cardiff, Univ. of Wales Pr., 1972), pp. 20–21

Is [John Cowper Powys] really as eccentric as he seems? Eccentricity is, of course, a relative term: perhaps it would be better to describe him as "individual." Powys's whole output, novels, criticism, philosophy, is a vast essay in self-exploration and analysis—so much can easily be established. What is more unusual and more remarkable is the fact that his work, far from being narrowly egoistic and inward-turning, is a projection of the self into an autonomous world of the imagination which is accessible to everyone. In this respect the novels are the natural centre and consummation of his achievement. This externalization of his own life-struggle and his own introspection makes of him a peculiarly liberating kind of confessional novelist. (One might compare his novels in this respect with the self-enclosed work of Malcolm Lowry.)

We have already noted the dual nature of his response to life: his withdrawal on the one hand into an emphasis upon and acceptance of solitariness, and his intense feeling for and contemplation of the inanimate. His two sources of strength are thus the cultivation of self-acceptance, and the cultivation of the widest possible physical sensitivity. Both movements are means of combating fear, fear of the self and fear of the external world; and the two movements may best be seen personified in his stoical egoists, such as Wolf Solent and Dud No-Man, and in his magician figures; but variations and combinations of both these attitudes are to be found in innumerable lesser characters.

What gives his work its particular energy and toughness is his complete self-sufficiency as an artist; his resolute adherence to his own inner light and vision; and his complete freedom from passing fashion. This singleness of mind, and this innocence of literary ambition in any worldly sense, while they have served to deny him the acclaim that is his due, are what is likely to ensure his acceptance in the future. In the vast output of contemporary novels his stand out for their sympathy with what it is to be alone. The word "sympathy" is exactly meant: loneliness as a condition has been dealt with exhaustively and usually with bitterness by contemporary novelists; but it is the condition of *being*, as distinct from feeling, alone that is John Cowper Powys's overriding concern. And far from protesting against the state he glories in it.

Glen Cavaliero. *John Cowper Powys: Novelist*
(Oxford, Clarendon, 1973), pp. 177–78

PRIESTLEY, J. B. (1894–   )

The work of J. B. Priestley spans five decades in time, and the novel, drama, criticism, essay, journalism and broadcasting in scope. His name has occupied a prominent place in the emotional and intellectual turbulence of twentieth-century social and political life. At one time, during the second world war, he seemed to be all reasonable men's epitome; at others, he has seemed to be the self-conscious conscience of society. He has been reviled, then admired; lauded, then ignored. Throughout, there has persisted the steadfast image (with its half-mocking studiedness) of the pipe-smoking realist. Like a chubby rock he has seemed capable both of withstanding the waves and, when it pleased him, of commanding them to stand off. Whenever there has been the need for the exertion of common sense, the image, and some-times the presence, of Priestley, has been called upon. Also, when society has seen the need for a whipping-block, the same has occa-sionally happened. He has been ubiquitous in his creative activity and in his influence, but the price he has had to pay, as an artist, for all his activities, is that of being known by many and really understood by few.

In an age of specialisation the man whose intellectual net is cast wide is often regarded with suspicion. But the merits of specialisa-tion, though no doubt admirable in the precise world of science and technology, do not necessarily have any potency for art. The evidence of literary history is against the Godhead of specialisation. Shake-speare, Johnson, Shelley, Arnold, Dickens and Eliot speak for the ubiquitous man of letters. But the modern academic critic, himself often a product of a constraining specialisation, sometimes mistakes dedication to a narrow field of activity for quality. The ceaseless and wide activity of Priestley has caused him to be judged by some as a Jack of all trades and a master of none. For others, his very ability to climb so regularly into the best-seller class is itself indicative of a partial talent. But, again, the evidence of history is against this notion of popularity as necessarily the stigma of the second-rate.

Gareth Lloyd Evans. J. B. Priestley—Dramatist
(Heinemann, 1964), pp. vii–viii

Musing about "the secret dream" in a selection from a book of musings called *Delight* (1949), J. B. Priestley writes: "All my adult life I have been more or less a Socialist Intellectual. I have tried to make myself —and other people—aware of the harsh economic and industrial realities of our time." A notable feature of Susan Cooper's splendid collection of essays covering five decades [*Essays of Five Decades*] is that the reader with no prior knowledge of Priestley will be taken by surprise by this confession of a commitment sufficiently strong to deserve the insignia of capitalization: Socialist Intellectual. Priestley's credentials for the title are authentic enough in a way; from the begin-ning of his literary career in the 1920s he has been a complete profes-sional, addressing an unusually wide audience in essay, fiction, drama and radio, and dedicated to responsible public performance. His career was nurtured by a sense of the value of "popularity" which has almost disappeared among writers (Mailer's hunger for a public relevance, often settling for publicity in default of more substantial fare, makes a revealing contrast). For an intransigent Yorkshireman in this period, deeply troubled by economic misery, "the deep cancer of injustice," and more recently the threat of nuclear warfare (Priestley was one of the originators of the Campaign for Nuclear Disarmament, CND), socialism, or the Labour Party version, was an inescapable commitment.

But in another sense, Priestley's self-proclaimed title needs considerable correction. If we expect the essays of a Socialist Intellectual to include some abstract thinking about society, let alone about socialism and its varieties, or "position papers" on burning issues, then Priestley will disappoint us. The term "socialism" points to one flank of the world of this remarkably versatile man of letters—the flank which regards rationality, organized politics, machinery, efficiency, cities, as at best necessary evils. After spelling out his acceptance of socialism as a way of rearranging social life on more equitable terms, Priestley continues in *Delight* to say, "But there was never anything here for my own secret delight. Nothing for the hunger of the heart." The inner life, which yearned for "a place with the dignity and style of a city, but reasonably small and clean, with genuine country only half an hour's walk from its centre," protested against the drabness and conformity of increasingly organized modern life, including the beneficent bureaucracies of socialism.

These simultaneous wishes, for social order and for personal anarchy, are the coordinates of Priestley's world, and their interplay might very well lay him down as a sentimentalist (a frequent accusation), or a bit of an old-fashioned grouch. One most definitely feels after a reading of this volume that to distill the ideas from the style—itself always charming and urbane, and a distinct "value" which needs to be addressed on its own—is to expose rather flimsy thinking about the world's problems.

But if Priestley does not recommend himself to us as a thinker, as a theorist, or indeed as a major literary talent with powers of synthesis (like Joyce), or passion (like Lawrence), his own special grounds of appeal are true and genuine enough. They rest almost entirely on the man's style.

Alan Trachtenberg. *Nation.* Nov. 18, 1968,
p. 534

For two years I had an office in Bradford scarcely ten minutes away from Mr. J. B. Priestley's home. The developer hasn't got round to that part of Bradford yet; the solid stone buildings which I saw around me were the same buildings which were part of the landscape of Mr. Priestley's youth. The novel I was working on then was giving me more than usual difficulty; I had at last to reveal something of myself and all my instincts argued against it. What kept me going, what enabled me to finish the novel, was the knowledge that a few hundred yards away another writer had begun his apprenticeship.

This is one of the reasons why I can never be entirely objective about Mr. Priestley. Even though I can't pretend that I always agree with him or that I've enjoyed absolutely everything that he's written, he's part of my life, one of the family, so to speak. Over and above all this, he's a magician; out of his hat for over fifty years now there have been produced other worlds, even glimpses of eternity. His great gift has always been a solid credibility; his rabbits may, so to speak, be cooked and eaten.

All this is relevant, since the subject of *London End*, the second section of *The Image Men* is, very specifically, illusion. Professor Cosmo Saltana and Dr. Owen Tuby, founders of the Institute of Social Imagistics, have now left the University of Brockshire and set up shop —if that's not too vulgar a phrase—in London. In one sense the Institute of Social Imagistics is a gigantic hoax. It has been created on the spur of the moment when in the first section, *Out of Town*, Saltana and Tuby, on their beam-ends in a London hotel, meet a rich widow, Mrs. Elfreda Drake. As they discover from a surreptitious glance at her papers, she's been left in charge of the Judson Drake Sociological Foundation. And very obviously she's not happy about it.

Instantly they decide that they are sociologists and over dinner— smoked salmon, saddle of lamb and claret chosen from "chateaux that up to now had been closed to them"—graciously consent to help Mrs. Drake to put the half-million-dollar Foundation into operation. . . .

The Image Men is a romp, an excursion into jollity, an unashamed piece of escapism. It's the kind of entertainment which I for one relish more and more, and I hope that Mr. Priestley wasn't serious when he said it would be his last novel. For I'm sure there are plenty more rabbits in the old magician's hat.

John Braine. NatR. June 3, 1969, pp. 544–45

Priestley and Eliot are about as dissimilar as it is possible for two writers to be, but perhaps in the end they arrive at very much the same point of focus. The difference lies in what they make of it. For Priestley, the hurrying white flame is numinous, but it is not God. "We might say it was moving to and from unimaginable creative Being, both away from and towards a blinding Absolute, possibly through the history of a thousand million planets. . . . We men on earth are probably on a very low level, but we have our task like other and higher orders of beings. As far as I can see—and I claim no prophetic insight —that task is to bring consciousness to the life of earth—or, as Jung wrote in his old age, 'to kindle a light in the darkness of mere being.' "

And as in the life of earth—in time One—Priestley has used the work of Gurdjieff and Ouspensky to expand his own consciousness, so he has always tried through all the different varieties of his own work to awaken and expand the consciousness of others. From this come the roars of rebellion against all totalitarian systems, the pleas for an end to Block Thinking and a resistance to the creeping anaesthesia of Admass; the humanitarian care for the condition of man and the urgent appeal to the latent brilliance of the Unicorn in his own nation; above all, perhaps, the echoing image of his ideal world, which may in the end turn out to have been the lost world of his youth translated into terms of time Two. "To bring consciousness to the life of earth": it is a fearsome undertaking. We shouldn't be disconcerted that Priestley has written so many books; we should marvel that he has been able, as few others have done, to encompass so much of this brave ideal without writing twice as much.

Susan Cooper. *J. B. Priestley* (N.Y., Harper & Row, 1970), pp. 228–29

PRITCHETT, V. S. (1900–   )

It is a great pleasure to read V. S. Pritchett's *A Cab at the Door*. The book is filled with charm, good nature, and intelligent wit—old-fashioned virtues—and, especially considering what one usually gets in memoirs these days, there is a curious absence of egotism and anxiety in the work. Mr. Pritchett has the grace and good sense not to assume the role of the *important* man writing an *important* book about the *important* people in his *important* past. Nothing is being advertised or peddled here—not an image of the self nor a theory of life. Readers will not learn how to succeed in journalism or how to overcome a difficult childhood. Mr. Pritchett relaxes into his past and presents the reader with the reflections of an intelligent and sympathetic mind at ease with itself. His very choice of the memoir as a form, rather than a strictly chronological autobiographical narrative, reflects his intention to wander rather freely where memory and inclination take him.

The unapologetic tendency to wander affects his style and tone as well as his subject matter. Whole sections of the book are constructed like episodes in a novel and are composed of quoted dialogue, physical details, and observations about gestures and attitudes which are not likely to have stayed in the mind of a child five minutes   nor to have remained in that form in the mind of a mature man. Mr. Pritchett alternates between re-creations of "how it must have been" and keen recollections of "how it was." The subject of the book is not his childhood and early youth but his *memory* of childhood and early youth. Since memory works in a variety of ways—retaining some things dramatically and verbally, others visually, and still others rather vaguely and emotionally—the book sometimes reads like fiction, sometimes like biography, and sometimes like undirected reminiscence. The writer tries to follow the contours of his own mind rather than those of a particular literary genre. . . .

Roberty Kiely. Cmty. Aug. 1968, pp. 73–74

In his engaging memoir, *A Cab at the Door*, V. S. Pritchett has told how, "caught by the passion for print as an alcoholic is by the bottle," he went through a period where he wanted to write verse: "To my usual nightly prayers that the house should not catch fire and that no burglar should break in, I added a line urging God to make me poet laureate 'before I am twenty-one.' " The prayer lasted until he was sixteen, and it was to prose that he remained devoted. "I had never really enjoyed poetry, for it was concerned with inner experience and I was very much an extrovert and I fancy I have remained so . . . in prose I found the common experience and the solid worlds where judgments were made and in which one could firmly tread." J. M. Barrie's *When A Man's Single*—a perfectly wretched Victorian novel, with chapter headings like Rob Angus Is Not A Free Man, Rob Becomes Free, and Rob Marches To His Fate—taught him that "there is copy in every man you meet," and "when you do meet him you feel inclined to tear it out of him and use it yourself." Stylistically, Barrie advised sureness of fact and avoidance of fine writing as much as dishonest writing. So Pritchett left trade and England to become a foreigner: "For myself that is what a writer is—a man living on the other side of a frontier."

These ten love stories [*Blind Love*], then concern more or less ordinary people, observed from without, and judged, albeit gently. I must confess to being baffled by their appeal. Pritchett the traveler is within my understanding. Pritchett the writer of fiction puzzles me. The stories are obviously professional, competent to the point of slickness. They feature well documented internal and external landscapes (there's that traveler again), well turned phrases, and vigorous dialogue underlined by asides from the narrator. The touch tends to be light, the flavor bittersweet, the "lasting taste for the wry and ironical" of which Pritchett has spoken surfaces frequently. There is also a disconcerting absence of flesh and blood guts, and a curious slyness—the characters take oblique pleasure in their own disasters; the unease is lovingly indulged and discussed. At the same time, the technique is mechanical and old-fashioned—basically it is that of the outdated character sketch, with a kind of Noel Coward cleverness superimposed. Psychology is rendered ABC explicit, and what Pritchett seems to be writing is contemporary comedy of humors. Each character is a stereotype, a one-characteristic one-dimensional person who works out his obsession in relation to other one-characteristic one-dimensional people.

Nora L. Magid. Com. May 15, 1970, p. 227

V. S. Pritchett insists on remaining a minor figure in the teeth of the evidence. "I have talent but no genius," he says on one page, and on another, sounding like the bluff salesmen he writes about so well, "I am no thinker or philosopher." And most poisonously modest of all: "I often wish I had had the guts to get into debt." The gamble in life that announces the high-roller in art.

Since his second volume of memoirs [*Midnight Oil*] reveals enough guts for all the regular bets—enough to strip himself of class, family, religion and country before he was 21, not to mention nearly starving to death—he must be talking about some other kind of guts, some aristocratic quality that Character can't buy—a death-wish "guts" much on the mind of the generation that just missed World War I. Or he may merely be seeing how he looks as a typical V. S. Pritchett character. "There is the supreme pleasure of putting oneself in by leaving oneself out," he says of his fiction; and what is good for a story may be good for a memoir. The Pritchett in this book could be a dummy, and the man behind the curtain may be the man to watch. As usual, beware the fictionist writing his own life. Even candor becomes a strategy.

Wilfrid Sheed. NYT. April 30, 1972, p. 3

RAINE, KATHLEEN (1908–   )

It is quite obvious from even a casual perusal of her poetry that Kathleen Raine has allied herself through the most fundamental spiritual and artistic inclination with the literary tradition and its practice of which she speaks. That tradition in English literature is the Romantic one, and Miss Raine has remarked that her "idea of what poetry was derived from the English Romantic poets"; but it also, in its emphasis on correspondences to be opened between earthly and spiritual reality by means of poetic images, and in its conception of the poet as medium as well as maker, has affinities with the line of French Symbolist poets from Baudelaire through Rimbaud and Mallarmé. Yet in choosing to work in the tradition she so strongly admires, Miss Raine has never overstepped the bounds of the most becoming modesty. While it would be inaccurate to rank her with the major poets of her tradition, such as Yeats or Shelley, the collected edition of her poetry (1956), with its careful pruning away of weak and, unfortunately, some good poems, and her new book, *The Hollow Hill* (1965), reserve a unique place for her in contemporary British poetry and in the small group of fine English women poets of our century, which includes Edith Sitwell, Ruth Pitter, Anne Ridler, and Elizabeth Jennings. The unrelenting manner in which she has committed herself to a vision of reality and the labor she has exacted of herself in shaping that vision poetically deserve closer attention and wider appreciation than they have usually received.

> Ralph J. Mills, Jr. *Kathleen Raine: A Critical Essay* (Grand Rapids, Mich., Eerdmans, 1967), p. 8

Kathleen Raine is not interested in charm, though she is indeed charming, by the way. She has a marvelous thing to say, and the saying is urgent. She is a Platonist by conviction, perhaps indeed a Christian Platonist, and she is a poet. . . . *Defending Ancient Springs* is a collection of essays on certain choice spirits in the Neoplatonic tradition, with three expository chapters on myth and symbol. The poets described are Blake, Shelley, Coleridge, Yeats, St. John Perse, David Gascoyne, Edwin Muir, and Vernon Watkins. These are the adepts, initiates. The essays are always appreciative, as one would speak of one's friends; appropriately and warmly. But it is an exclusive club. Here, indeed, is the weakness of the book. Miss Raine assumes that if you are not a Christian Platonist you must be a positivist. The argument will not hold. . . .

Miss Raine's heroes are all poets; she writes of their work, very often, in accents which we can hear in, say, Yeats's essay on Shelley. She does not number the novelists or the dramatists among her friends. She tries to draw Shakespeare in, but the attempt is awkward. Novels and plays traffic with time, or they hardly live at all. History and fact constitute their element. Miss Raine writes of Vernon Watkins, but not of George Eliot or Henry James. She is free to choose; but a limitation of this kind casts a certain shadow upon the whole enterprise. It makes one wonder whether, in the nature of the case, her rhetoric has much to do with literature at all. *Defending Ancient Springs* may be read as chapters in Miss Raine's autobiography. Read in that way, the book is fascinating. But read as literary criticism, it is not convincing: it could not well convince, after all, since it argues that the world of imagination is outside history. Drama, fiction, and a thousand poems deny the claim.

Denis Donoghue. *SoR*. Autumn, 1969,
pp. 1245–49

● RAPHAEL, FREDERIC (1931–   )

If Mr. Angus Wilson had been a Jew he would probably have written a novel something like *The Limits of Love*. The wobbly construction would have gone and the uneven development would have been straightened out, but I don't see how he could have improved upon the suburban dialogue and the telly-tinged jargon, or better illustrated Anglo-Jewish attitudes in the post-war world. Mr. Raphael has not written a brilliant novel, but he has produced for us the ingredients of a brilliant novel.

We are in a suburban house on the Finchley side of Golders Green, with a green fish-scale roof, green tile lids over the dormer windows, potato crisps in the cocktail cabinet—and a *mezuza* on the doorpost. The newest arrival is Uncle Otto, back from Belsen, but it is the young ones we are most concerned with. This is their story, the story of young Jews who lack the old faith but have a faith of their own. They call Uncle Otto "the homespun philosopher who didn't pull the chain" and they do imitations of their orthodox parents who run a delicatessen business and talk standard music-hall Yiddisher. Among them—

selves the children (one of them a Communist) talk in jocular young speech that is almost embarrassing in its accuracy: "Bejasus, Benjamino, if one K. Marx esquire could hear you talking now"—and "Well, well, if it isn't the Napoleon of King Street, alias the Napoleon of King Street." But even away from the old traditions they are painfully conscious of their Jewishness, and one of the final episodes in the book is a long sequence where Paul, who marries into the family, runs into a savage campaign of schoolboy anti-Semitism.

Mr. Raphael is covering a long period in these young lives—from the end of the war up to the Suez crisis. In order to cram everything in he has to resort to flashbacks, and flashbacks within flashbacks, and long breaks in the continuity while a character is established. The result is that while we have one brilliant scene after another, the scenes do not quite jell together as a final, satisfactory narrative. There is also a sort of Writer's Statement at the end of the book that I could have done without, but Mr. Raphael is certainly more in a position to make statements than many writers I can think of, Jewish or Gentile.

Keith Waterhouse. NS. June 11, 1960, p. 869

The task of the writer, Philip Roth once observed, is to make credible the stupefying reality of our time. In <i>Lindmann</i>, Frederic Raphael, a young American-born Englishman, has harrowed the collective guilt to produce a novel of fury, humor, anguish and relevance. He cannot make credible the necessity for suffering, but he understands it to the last rictus. His laughter is that of a man through with screaming.

Who is the enigma, Jacob Lindmann? The records of the British Foreign Office say he is one of two survivors of the sinking of the S. S. Broda, an illegal derelict that went down off the Turkish coast in 1942 with more than 600 Jewish refugees aboard. To the people who know him in London after the war, he is a quiet man who lives in an eccentric rooming house, playing bridge and arranging his papers. Wise in the metaphysics of an insane social order, bent under the burden of survival, he stalks London in search of conscience, playing the Wandering Jew, dissociated, making spidery notes for letters he will never mail. . . .

Under the hot glare of Mr. Raphael's anger, surfaces shimmer and vanish like mirages. The conventions, which protect men from a sense of tragedy, shrivel. Art in the form of an American Negro painter talks hip and fornicates. Motherhood, in the form of a sweet young woman who sacrificed herself to an S. S. officer in the name of mercy, gives herself to the artist in the name of lust. The preacher raves; the Jews deny grief for a sunny Zion, and over mugs of whisky, intellect seeks formulae for a new television series.

Mr. Raphael's ear for the hyper-cadences of contemporary verbalizers is so acute it borders on pain. Everyone who talks to Lindmann says one thing and means another, or nothing at all. One wishes that Lindmann had gone on making people uneasy instead of turning out to be a mirage himself. His dysfunction saves the book from completeness, and what might have been an absolutely first-rate novel ends as a first-rate charade.

At the crucial moment, idea and character part company, but perhaps this is the flaw of prophecy. Stephen Spender, who in the Book Review recently mourned the lack of audacity in British fiction, should pay attention to Frederic Raphael. *Lindmann* is a most serious and courageous effort to set a mark and attempts what may be impossible, or intolerable—to answer major questions with ultimate ironies.

Conrad Knickerbocker. *NYT*. March 8, 1964,
p. 5

Because of the variety of his abilities and his use of techniques ranging from Wellsian naturalism in *The Limits of Love* to dissolving montage in *A Wild Surmise* to Joycean experimentalism in *Lindmann*, Raphael's books have not been unified in subject and approach. Instead he has written books that impress by their individual brilliance, rather than by what they have in common philosophically with each other. It is time, I think, to review the work of this distinguished writer and to define tentatively the sorts of experience he reflects in his novels and his qualities as an artist.

What his novels do possess in common are varied and authentic aesthetic excellences. Raphael reveals an inclusive and ranging imagination in his fiction with an ability, therefore, to flesh out a whole design with details at once appropriate and compelling. He has a sure sense of the structural importance of his materials, so that each subject receives appropriate aesthetic weight. He is sensitive, moreover, to the quirks of personality which make an individual different from his fellows. He is a novelist who is, accordingly, much preoccupied with the analysis of the motives and the internal states of his characters. He is likewise much interested in the development of his people under the stress both of inner compulsions and outward pressures. He knows not only the distinctive features of personality, but how to embody them in the words of his characters. Of all novelists now writing in England, Raphael seems to me to have the sharpest ear for all the varieties of speech and the greatest ability to reproduce them with effectiveness in his fiction. He is able to do many things well in the novel. He does with aplomb the powerful dramatic scene; he recreates with equal authority the ordinarily overlooked parts of experience and elicits their true significance; and he inhabits comprehendingly an individual's mind and analyzes with precision his conscious and unconscious states.

Although a powerful, sometimes idiosyncratic, mind shapes the novels, Mr. Raphael has achieved, at least beginning with *The Limits of Love*, an appropriate distance between himself and his creations. Upon occasion he shows command of an ironic sense as he records the intricate contrast between illusion and reality, between expectation and meager fruition, and between a man's ideals and his actions. Raphael also relates his characters in subtle and necessary ways to their backgrounds. He understands, furthermore, the inescapable connections between past, present, and future, and conveys with entire credibility the illusion of passing time. Raphael's style, moreover, is flexible, and he uses it to secure a multiplicity of effects. If anything, his verbal resourcefulness is so great that it occasionally registers as a stridency in descriptive passages or as a greater exuberance than his art requires in books like *The Limits of Love* and *Lindmann*.

Frederick P. W. McDowell. *Critique.*
Vol. 8, No. 1, 1965, pp. 21–23

[*Like Men Betrayed*] is a novel of luxurious talent desperately in need of pruning. It is sensitive, poetic, witty, and ironic. Here and there its words come tumbling like flowers into a perfume factory, a whirl of blossoms, a confusion of scents.

Reading, however, requires us to take one petal at a time; and some of these flowers are wormy. All the wit in the world, and all the sensitivity, will not give life to death nor fragrance to corruption. *Like Men Betrayed* is an immensely gifted work, but parts of it should be excised. Their daring will not turn the world upside down; it is more likely to have that effect on the stomach. They are not strong meat; they just smell strong.

Set in Greece about 30 years ago, the plot is woven of talk and history, talk and lust, talk and war, talk and symbol, talk and brief action. Talk and talk.

And narrative in enormous paragraphs. That's a kind of talk also, paradoxical, perceptive, and ultimately neutral. This is a book of many colors, all darker than gray.

The many subtleties of thought and plot, often self-mocking, are somewhat bloodless. The hero's sexual activities, normal or otherwise, are portrayed with unfailing ugliness. Perhaps Mr. Raphael is youthful and old-fashioned enough to want to shock the middle class—a very middle class desire. Or perhaps he believes that a writer should "Tell All."

Telling all is impossible, of course, and to attempt it is to abdicate the artist's responsibility for discovering a work of art. Art is a selection of the essential and rejection of everything else. Too much of this novel consists of unhappy flecks of everything else.

Neil Millar. *CSM*. March 18, 1971, p. 11

● RAVEN, SIMON (1927–   )

Simon Raven's *The Feathers of Death* is a clever and impressive novel; composed in a pattern of tragic necessity, it assumes values that make that tragic pattern a romantic assertion. The milieu of the novel is a British regiment called Martock's Foot; by an accident of history it is a regiment of mounted infantry, free of the usual drudgery of foot soldiers, ready to be swept into battle for the last gallant engagement that may snatch an impossible victory. . . . The ends for which these men fight are never apparent; they are professional soldiers resisting the pressures of the politicians at home, of the careerist sticklers in the field, of "middle-class prejudices" and patriotic zeal. They are concerned with the decorum of ritual so long as it is not invested with moral signifi-cance; they profess to value good food and wine, witty conversation, skeptical humor. Their relationship with the non-commissioned officers and soldiers is one of informal authority which rests on the easy assur-ance of caste. They are, as the narrator puts it, "reactionary," and there are just enough officers among them with "dowdier" views to establish more firmly the cohesiveness of the group. . . .

Such a society is obviously the stuff of romantic tragedy. The catalyst in Mr. Raven's novel is a graceful young man, Alastair Lynch. When his father refuses to send him to Oxford, he joins the regiment rather than the family business. Lynch is charming, able, but uncon-trolled. The action of the novel is the growth and catastrophic end of his sexual attachment to a young soldier in his company. The last part of the book deals with Lynch's trial for the murder of the soldier; and it is there that the final weakness of his nature becomes apparent. It is not simply the arrogance of his self-assertion, for this has its own boldness and style. "By being an open pederast," his commanding officer re-marks, "a man is *openly* arrogant, openly rich, openly skeptical. And hence the offense openly given to Mrs. Smith of Birmingham, to our 'young and lovely queen' in Buckingham Palace, to trades-union leaders, to good-form conservative politicians—to everything and everybody in the Mediocrity State." But the arrogance becomes a threadbare assertion of style at the point when moral claims are overwhelming: the reality of the dead soldier, however stupid, and of his vengeful "mate" asserts itself and dims Lynch's rhetoric. And finally we see Lynch's desertion of his own standards, his failure of the truthfulness which gave him dignity. Mr. Raven has the skill to make the grossness a more telling disclosure than the evil.

Martin Price. *YR*. Spring, 1960, pp. 445–46

It is an intriguing problem as to why a novelist as breezily confident and sharp as Simon Raven has never really made it with the switched-on set. A social renegade with a nice turn of wit, he would seem a dead ringer for their applause. Yet he remains comparatively neglected. Why? Is Mr. Raven not considered frank enough about sex or sufficiently scurrilous in his assault on our sacred cows? Hardly. His worst enemy could scarcely deny that much of Mr. Raven's work suggests nothing more than that he has written it erect, beyond the pale and hungover. What more could be asked of a writer? On the other hand it could be that Raven is a trifle too uninhibited for a game in which, even under a revised code, dirty play should be confined to making old maids faint and apoplectic colonels turn purple with rage. This seems a safer bet. Mr. Raven has yet to learn that inflammatory novelists are expected to outrage the fuddy-duddies of our society without offering offence to the po-faced intelligentsia. God knows the task is simple enough if one is only prepared to follow the slick routines devised by professional heretics to make the whole business of shocking people as respectably innocuous as Harold Wilson's image. But Raven doesn't seem to give a damn about whose toes he is treading on or how far he goes. And there *are* limits. I mean to say, one enjoyed [Waugh's] *The Loved One* because it was satire, an unpleasant but purposeful comment on how Americans are even prepared to cash in on death. But simply to dwell on a man's graveside erection as Raven does in *Close of Play*, well, that's neither mindful of human dignity nor funny. It's just plain *distasteful*.

Friends in Low Places* is the second novel of his monster project *Alms for Oblivion* but gives no firmer indication of what the whole thing will add up to than the first.

Frank McGuinness. *L*. Jan., 1966, pp. 85–86

Since 1959, when his first book was published, Simon Raven's literary output has been prolific. To date he has published ten novels—the last six of which form part of the as yet uncompleted *Alms for Oblivion* sequence; *The English Gentleman*, a volume of social analysis; *Boys Will Be Boys*, a miscellany of occasional pieces; *Royal Foundation, and Other Plays*, a collection of radio and television dramas; and a book of translations of Greek poetry. There has also been a steady stream of book reviews, travel sketches, short essays, and the like. The very bulk of Raven's writing might suggest what a reading of his novels confirms: they are uneven in quality, occasionally repetitious and forced, and sometimes no more than entertaining. Only a few of them exhibit all of Raven's appreciable gifts as a novelist working together in harmony. These flaws should not, however, be allowed to obscure the fact that Raven is a serious and interesting novelist, whose works have yet to receive, at least in North America, the attention they deserve. . . .

The action of Raven's novels all takes place within a world of privilege, leisure, and power, and it is his principal intention in them to describe, scrutinize, and judge the men who inhabit this world. The settings of major scenes are often described by Raven in careful and loving detail. They include gambling casinos and an opulent masked ball in Venice, regimental messes and courts-martial, London clubs and country houses, cricket matches and horse races, senior common rooms and college feasts. Raven is very good at rendering these settings and the activities they encompass. There is nothing in them of the vulgarity of Ian Fleming, the merely sociological interest of John O'Hara, or the supernal glow of Scott Fitzgerald. Sometimes the function of these descriptions is purely decorative, but more often they are linked to the central themes and conflicts of the novels in such a way as to deepen and enrich them. When setting and theme are fully united the former become images of order, tradition, and seemliness (a favorite word of Raven's), or of their perversion.

The privileged people who inhabit this world are the *dramatis personae* of Raven's novels. What Raven anachronistically calls the "lower orders" seldom appear in his fiction except as private soldiers or servants. Another substantial portion of the human race who do not figure prominently in the fiction are women, for the enclaves of privilege about which Raven writes are almost exclusively male. In several of the novels virtually no female characters appear, and in the others their role tends to be unimportant and their characterization rudimentary. Most of them—from peeresses to prostitutes—tend to be unbelievably oversexed and dispassionately promiscuous, and either absurd or titillating, depending solely on their looks and sexual expertise. The inadequacy of his portrayal of women is one of the more serious shortcomings of Raven's fiction.

Kerry McSweeney. *QQ*. Spring, 1971,
pp. 106–7

There are certain problems which this reviewer—and, I dare say, many like him—must overcome before settling down to enjoy a Simon Raven novel. The first may be described as sociological, or pedantic or even as snobbish. The people he chooses to describe as gentlemen are simply not recognisable as such. . . .

Captain Raven's other fatal flaw, it has often seemed to me, concerns the vexed question of sex. He writes of other people's sexual behaviour with a quivering distaste which would only be acceptable if he offered his readers any alternative. What, we ask, is the Raven way? Or should we all retreat into monastic meditation? If the latter, I can only say that his methods of persuasion are extremely unpleasant, like the cruel habit of making an alcoholic vomit every time he sniffs a glass of sherry, or showing a homosexual photographs of Grenadier Guardsmen and then giving him a violent electric shock.

However, when one has overcome the sociological and sexual horrors of a Raven novel, one must admit that the Captain's plots are better constructed than those of almost any other regular English novelist of the moment, and that in between some rather bad jokes there are other extremely good ones.

Auberon Waugh. *Spec.* Oct. 28, 1972, p. 676

READ, HERBERT (1893–1968)

We must all respect Sir Herbert Read's total achievement. He served with great bravery and distinction as an infantry officer in the first world war; at the Victoria and Albert Museum he became an authority on English stained glass and English ceramics; he edited the *Burlington Magazine* from 1933 to 1939; he is a publisher, a literary critic, a writer on aesthetics, education, modern art, politics and sociology and he has written a considerable amount of poetry. He has consistently kept up with the latest manifestations of the arts and can always name the Poet of the Week or the Painter of the Month. His enthusiasm has led to the discovery of many poets, sculptors and painters, in particular Henry Moore, who would, without his public and private encouragement, have had to wait much longer for the recognition that they merited. He has done more than anyone else to bring contemporary British art to the notice of the rest of the world.

It is sometimes stated that Sir Herbert Read is primarily a poet and that his multiple activities are not only different aspects of a single mind, but are all related to his "basic impulse as a poet." This does not appear to me to be correct. As I see it, his multifarious interests have led him to will himself to be a poet, the most universal of human beings. This is emphasised by the vast gulf between his theory and his practice. His fondness for categories has prompted him to divide poetry into "organic form" and "abstract form." In the first the imagination creates the shape of the art form, gives it its own inherent laws and fuses "in one vital unity both structure and content." In contrast "abstract form" occurs when the structure is stabilised and repeated as a pattern. The description of "organic form" is an admirable definition of what is loosely called lyric poetry and Sir Herbert Read has further elaborated it in "What Is a Poem?" which appears at the end of the *Collected Poems.* "True poetry," he writes, "was never speech, but always song. . . . A poem is therefore to be defined as a structure of words whose sound constitutes a rhythmical unity, complete in itself." He goes on, "It may be that some poems are enhanced by a meaning, but I have never been able to discover what difference the inclusion of a verifiable meaning made to any person."

Sir Herbert Read's poetry is, curiously enough, deficient in just those qualities which his theories insist are essential. His rhythms are monotonous and dry, his image-content thin, in spite of his acute powers of observation, and there is much more speech than song in most of his work.

Ronald Bottrall. PoetryR. Autumn, 1966,
p. 185

The great confrontation for Herbert Read was with tradition. "Without contraries there is no progress"; Herbert had seen a truth, and his affirmation of a vital imaginative principle throughout a protean sequence of changes of theoretical ground, was his great contribution to his time and the future. In reading his early criticism we often feel that Herbert is talking to T. S. Eliot; and especially so on the issue of tradition. On Eliot's *Tradition and the Individual Talent* he wrote, in *The Poetic Experience*, "there is not one literary tradition but many traditions; there is certainly a romantic tradition as well as a classical tradition, and, if anything, the romantic tradition has the longer history" and he quotes a famous passage from the *Ion* on poetic inspiration. His temperamental affinity with Wordsworth notwithstanding he was continually drawn back to Coleridge; and in this too his afterthoughts were best. In his lecture on *Coleridge as Critic* (Johns Hopkins University, 1949) he reverses his earlier adherence to Locke and Hartley and (by implication) Behaviourism: "There are in our world currents of thought that are central and others that are merely contributaries and wander off into the bogs and deserts of philosophy: that stream which first became defined in Kant's philosophy and continued to flow however irregularly through the minds of Schelling, Coleridge, Kierkegaard, Hegel, Nietzsche, Husserl, Heidegger, divided by a watershed from the contrary stream to which we can attach the names of Locke, Condillac, Hartley, Bentham, Marx and Lenin—that first stream to which we give the fashionable name of Existentialism but which is really the main tradition of philosophy itself—in that stream Wordsworth is confidently carried."

Kathleen Raine. *MalahatR*. Jan., 1969,
pp. 151–52

Herbert Read's writings about poetry have overshadowed his actual compositions. The authority with which he wrote about the poetry of others and about the creative process makes it difficult for us to approach his poems with an open mind. We expect the poems to support the critical theories, and to evince the same wayward brilliance as the essays. We search for examples of Imagism, of Vers Libre, and Organic Form. We suppose that the philosophical and radical temper of the essays will appear with even more intensity in the poetry, and we are frequently disappointed.

It would be a sad disservice to the memory of so great a man to adopt a merely pietistic attitude to his work, and to praise that which deserves to be put aside. Herbert Read himself, though the kindliest of critics, was not the least rigorous, and in writing of his poetry I feel compelled to attempt standards of honesty which he himself set, and obliged to look at the poems themselves without attempting to justify their failures or magnify their achievements by relating them to their author's critical theories. What matters is the quality of the poetry as poetry, and not its relationship to other writings.

Robin Skelton. *MalahatR*. Jan., 1969, p. 161

Read died believing that his philosophy of life—the aesthetic philosophy—was valid, and that some day, if the world was not destroyed by technicians, mankind would come to live by it, through true education and a life in which work and art would become indistinguishable. He never denied his anarchist convictions, and though he became reconciled to thinking of the free society as a point on a distant horizon, he refused, in republishing his early libertarian writings, "to give an air of caution to the impetuous voice of youth. Indeed, I now envy those generous feelings." He believed in the great art of his time, and he continued to write poetry as he felt it should be written, in spite of his lack of popularity as a poet. He realized the hollowness of much of the popularity he did enjoy in his later years, and he recognized that his works most likely to survive were precisely those least noticed in his time—the poems, the autobiographies, *The Green Child*.

In a historical sense, I believe that Read will also retain a unique place as an interpreter of his time, for few writers have probed so deeply and so intelligently into the nature of our culture, and none has brought together so suggestively the insights of modern philosophers and critics, poets and artists, psychologists and social scientists, as Read did in the varied corpus of his work. In the visual arts his criticism was illuminated by a peculiar intensity of empathic understanding and an unrivalled breadth of curiosity. In literature, his criticism was limited by the personal intensity of his interests, but he remains one of the best writers on romanticism in English poetry. He was an able popularizer, and not ashamed of the role, but he also contributed profound philosophic insights into the problems of aesthetics, and if he left no system of thought the omission was as deliberate as the lack of elaborate structure in his writings. The word *deliberate*, indeed, can be applied to him in more than one sense, for it is in the studied nature of his casualness in writing, in the unsought perfection of phrase and image, that one sees his classicism and his romanticism coming together. In his writing, spontaneity was controlled by a discipline that had become unconscious, and here lay the secret of Read's charm and clarity as a writer, which alone will ensure that, like Bagehot whom he so much admired, he is likely to be read long after the immediate occasions of his writing have passed away.

I have no inclination to rank Read among the writers of his time; the last thing he would have desired would be such evaluation, for a poet, to him, was a poet true to himself, true to his vision. In this sense Read stands among his peers and contemporaries, a poet true also to his time and hence one of its authentic seers.

George Woodcock. *Herbert Read: The Stream
and the Source* (Faber and Faber, 1972),
pp. 291–92

● RENAULT, MARY (1905–   )

As a story of high-keyed passion, *Promise of Love* is both complex and intense, yet it never loses touch with the solider kind of reality. The world—in this case the world of a great hospital—presses very closely upon Miss Renault's two lovers, conditions their moods, their problems, the ways in which they fail one another. A nurse, and a humble research worker, they are at the mercy of hard, driving, severely disciplined forces which do much to thwart and dissipate their love. They are governed, in short, as most of us are, by financial stress and the kind of job they hold. Therefore their predicament is acute and human. Even if Miss Renault's novel were not an extraordinarily moving love story, it still would be notable as a picture of hospital life. . . .

On a double count . . . *Promise of Love* strikes me as an unusually excellent first novel. There is a fusion here between background and personal drama, between inner and outer reality, which enriches and dignifies both. The story of Mic and Vivian would not be nearly so arresting as it is if one were not so sharply aware of the pressure of their environment. One sees them at work as well as in love—an important dualism which too many novelists neglect. When one adds to this that Mary Renault's style has a sure, fluid quality, that she possesses humor as well as sensitiveness, that even her minor characters are shrewdly drawn—the sum total is quite impressive. *Promise of Love* is a good novel. It deserves success and very probably may have it.

Edith Walton. NYT. March 12, 1939, p. 24

In *The Friendly Young Ladies*, Miss Renault . . . uses the technique of the "point of view," and gives us that of the adults as well. When the point of view is that of the girl, Elsie, she is wholly and admirably successful. The opening chapters in Cornwall are amusing, sensitive and well written; the ridiculous middle-class parents and the atmosphere of the middle-class home are perfect. In Elsie's family there is a skeleton, tightly cupboarded: years earlier Elsie's sister, Leonora, has run away. Liberally over-interpreting the advice of a young doctor acting as a *locum tenens* in the neighbourhood, Elsie runs away and joins her sister. As soon as Elsie gets into the world of the friendly young ladies, Miss Renault's troubles begin. Thenceforward, whenever things are seen from Elsie's angle, the book is lovely and real; her misunderstanding of the personal relationships around her is well done, and so are the few later actions to which her author commits her, including the final one. Unfortunately, a fog descends whenever Miss Renault tries to get inside her grown-ups, and a most promising book gets lost.

The book aims at depths which are impenetrable because Miss Renault has ignored the preliminary necessities of organisation on the surface. It is a real lack of invention that makes Leonora and Joe seem so unreal and so nebulously conceived: both have pasts which are left too much to conjecture for their pressure on the present to be comprehensible to the reader; and the love scenes between these and other characters which mark the progress of such story as there is do not bring the characters any more clearly before us. One cannot even tell precisely *how* friendly the young ladies have been to each other. Miss

Renault is at the difficult stage of being able to express subtle thoughts and truths about personality without being able always to attach them to personalities whom they fit; but she is a very able writer, and her younger heroine alone makes her book worth reading.

Henry Reed. *NSN*. Oct. 14, 1944, p. 256

The basic line of *The King Must Die* is uncomplicated and horizontal —one exploit after another, with each of which the hero's strength and self-knowledge increase. It ends, thus, with a round, full picture of the real beginning of King Theseus' manhood soon after a climactic, shuddery version of the story of Ariadne on Naxos, a scene of Dionysian celebrations, obliquely rendered and awful. . . .

Miss Renault has a vigorous sense of the life and variety of the cities and personalities of the era, and renders them without a trace of effort or monotony. The language in which she has Theseus tell his story is not elaborate, but it has elegance and pace; consistently clear, this story does not have such complicated passages on politics and philosophies as sometimes blur *The Last of the Wine*, her very interesting novel of a later Greece. Theseus is a bold and shrewd young man, much attracted to women and much endowed with a quickness of decision and dramatic sense of gesture that enable him to lead men successfully. Miss Renault, from her modern vantage point of psychological sophistication, gives him a simple but sure insight into human behavior.

At Knossus, having volunteered to go along with the other youths and maidens demanded as a tribute from Athens by King Minos, Theseus becomes part of the band of prisoners dedicated as "sacrifices" to the Bull God. Instead of their being killed and offered, the practice is that they become teams who perform dangerous acrobatic feats with bulls in an arena for the mere amusement of the spectators. Miss Renault's reconstruction, through her narrator, of the psychology of the teams, each member depending for his life on the skill and courage of the others, is a remarkable blend of research, style, and imagination— as, indeed, is the entire story.

Edwin Kennebeck. *Com*. Aug. 1, 1958, p. 454

The Last of the Wine, The King Must Die, and *The Bull from the Sea* are set in eras far different from our own, yet even in the legendary world of Theseus, we recognize men who, like ourselves, are only men. As men they cannot escape the condition to which all men are born— the hardship and perplexity of a world which all too often is alien and evil. Alexias and Theseus, however, because they come to know themselves, are "ready" to do battle in that world for the values of truth, freedom, justice, and love which they hold dear. The battle has always been, and will always be, unequal; grief and loss are inevitable. But these men accept their *moira*, and by the end of their respective lives consent to give themselves completely in meeting that appointed end.

These three novels by Mary Renault will not begin a great movement back to the writing of historical fiction. The temper of our time seems to demand novels of social conscience in the world of atom bombs, labor unions, and committee meetings. Moreover, good as they are, Miss Renault's books have flaws. *The Bull from the Sea* is too episodic, partly because Miss Renault has been less skillful in reshaping the plot than she was in *The King Must Die*. In both of these books, the presentation of Theseus as a tragic figure suffers at the expense of action (interesting as that action may be for its own sake). Despite the surface restraint of *The Last of the Wine*, there are sections which appeal to the prurient.

But these are relatively minor faults to find in novels which have so many obvious virtues. The reconstruction of the historical era is achieved with such vitality and authenticity that setting and atmosphere play a major part in the shaping of character and theme. The prose style is flexible and at times capable of great force and poetic intensity. The structure of the books is carefully molded to define and reinforce theme. Thus, Miss Renault's novels are not merely good historical novels, they are good novels. And they should do much to alleviate the anomalous plight into which historical fiction has fallen.

Landon D. Burns, Jr. Critique. Vol. 6, No. 3,
1963, pp. 120–21

Although her classical novels bristle with excitement and adventure, the action is carefully monitored by technique. The first-person narrative in the four classical novels creates a critical perspective, deepened by time, from which to view the action, and it does so without any corresponding loss in dramatic impact. Stylistically, too, Mary Renault's classical fiction overtakes the conventional romantic legend or adventure story.

The sonorous cadences of the two Theseus novels match the heroic exploits described in the books. But *The Mask of Apollo* . . . succeeds best in aligning style and subject matter. While less flowing and colorful than the language of *The King Must Die* and *The Bull from the Sea*, the novel's harsh, angular style stands closer to the events it reports. This genius for clinching language to theme allows Mary Renault to use historical fiction as a comment on her own times. If her reputation rests on the five novels published since 1956, justice will be served; for they both enlarge and dignify the tradition of historical fiction. Worth noting in the context of this achievement is the fact that few artists, indeed, can boast of having revolutionized the mode in which they did their best work. . . .

Judging from her last five novels, once again, posterity will praise her for her brilliantly documented Classical settings and her ability to infuse modern themes into ancient history. How long it will take literary scholars to awaken to her art is another matter. The prevailing critical animus against homosexual fiction and historical fiction has already delayed the recognition she deserves. . . .

> Peter Wolfe. *Mary Renault* (N.Y., Twayne,
> 1969), pp. 187–88

Fire from Heaven covers only the first two-thirds of Alexander's life, from his fifth to his twentieth year. It is the perfection of a technique that appeared inchoatively in *The Middle Mist* and has been the author's trademark since *The Charioteer*—tracing an adult's failure or success to his childhood environment. That Mary Renault should make Alexander's boyhood the key to his personality is not surprising, since she has been approaching characterization in this way since 1944. That she has succeeded in spite of odds that were almost self-defeating is another tribute to her talent for "wringing lilies from the acorn."

Alexander made a brief appearance at the end of *The Mask of Apollo*. Niko gazed at his piercing blue eyes and knew instinctively, as only an actor could, that he was destined for glory and suffering. Mary Renault has isolated that suffering in a childhood where a son was forced to choose between a bisexual father whose ambition he admired and a possessive mother whose affection he craved. The critic who might feel the novelist is repeating what is now a typical Renault boyhood would be correct; Alexander's youth could easily constitute a case history of parental polarization, but with one essential difference: most children facing the dilemma of divided allegiance would acquire a lasting neurosis; Alexander was a world conqueror when he died at thirty-three.

Mary Renault did not invent the facts of Alexander's scarred boyhood; history provided them, however obliquely, and the author interpreted them according to the canons of fiction. *Fire from Heaven* is her most Plutarchan novel. . . .

> Bernard F. Dick. *The Hellenism of Mary
> Renault* (Carbondale, Southern Illinois Univ.
> Pr., 1972), pp. 101–2

I am particularly puzzled (and pleased) by the success of Mary Renault. Americans have always disliked history (of some fifty subjects offered in high school the students recently listed history fiftieth and least popular) and know nothing at all of the classical world. Yet in a dozen popular books Mary Renault has made the classical era alive, forcing even the dullest of bookchat writers to recognize that bisexuality was once our culture's norm and that Christianity's perversion of this human fact is the aberration and not the other way around. I cannot think how Miss Renault has managed to do what she has done, but the culture is the better for her work. . . .

In *The Persian Boy* Miss Renault presents us with Alexander at the height of his glory as seen through the eyes of the young eunuch Bagoas. Miss Renault is good at projecting herself and us into strange cultures. With ease she becomes her narrator Bagoas; the book is told in the first person. . . .

The device of observing the conqueror entirely through the eyes of an Oriental is excellent and rather novel. We are able to see the Macedonian troops as they appeared to the Persians; crude gangsters smashing to bits an old and subtle culture they cannot understand, rather like Americans in Asia. But, finally, hubris is the theme; and the fire returns to heaven. I am not at all certain that what we have here is the "right" Alexander but right or not, Miss Renault has drawn the portrait of someone who seems real yet unlike anyone else, and that divinity the commercialites are forever trying for in their leaden works really does gleam from time to time in the pages of this nice invention.

Gore Vidal. *NYR.* May 31, 1973, p. 15

● **RHYS, JEAN (1894–   )**

Setting aside for a moment the matter of [Miss Rhys's] very remarkable technical gifts, I should like to call attention to her profound knowledge of the life of the Left Bank—of many of the Left Banks of the world. For something mournful—and certainly hard-up!—attaches to almost all uses of the word *left*. The left hand has not the cunning of the right: and every great city has its left bank. London has, round Bloomsbury, New York has, about Greenwich Village, so has Vienna—but Vienna is a little ruined everywhere since the glory of Austria, to the discredit of European civilization, has departed! Miss Rhys does not, I believe, know Greenwich Village, but so many of its products are to be found on the Left Bank of Paris that she may be said to know its products. And coming from the Antilles, with a terrifying insight and a terrific—and almost lurid!—passion for stating the case of the underdog, she has let her pen loose on the Left Banks of the

Old World—on its gaols, its studios, its salons, its cafés, its criminals, its midinettes—with a bias of admiration for its midinettes and of sympathy for its law-breakers. It is a note, a sympathy of which we do not have too much in Occidental literature with its perennial bias towards satisfaction with things as they are. But it is a note that needs sounding—that badly needs sounding, since the real activities of the world are seldom carried much forward by the accepted, or even by the Hautes Bourgeoisies!

When I, lately, edited a periodical, Miss Rhys sent in several communications with which I was immensely struck, and of which I published as many as I could. What struck me on the technical side—which does not much interest the Anglo-Saxon reader, but which is almost the only thing that interests me—was the singular instinct for form possessed by this young lady, an instinct for form being possessed by singularly few writers of English and by almost no English women writers. I say "instinct," for that is what it appears to me to be: these sketches begin exactly where they should and end exactly when their job is done. No doubt the almost exclusive reading of French writers of a recent, but not most recent, date has helped.

Ford Madox Ford. Preface to Jean Rhys,
The Left Bank (N.Y., Harper, 1927),
pp. 23–25

After *Good Morning, Midnight*, Jean Rhys disappeared and her five books went out of print. Although these had enjoyed a critical success, their true quality had never been appreciated. The reason for this is simple: they were ahead of their age, both in spirit and in style. One has only to compare Miss Rhys's early books written during the 1920s, with contemporary work by Katherine Mansfield, Aldous Huxley, Jean Cocteau, and other celebrated writers of the period, to be struck by how little the actual text has "dated": the style belongs to today. More important, the novels of the 1930s are much closer in *feeling* to life as it is lived and understood in the 1960s than to the accepted attitudes of their time. The elegant surface and the paranoid content, the brutal honesty of the feminine psychology and the muted nostalgia for lost beauty, all create an effect which is peculiarly modern.

The few people who remembered their admiration for these books, and those even fewer who (like myself) were introduced to them later and with great difficulty managed to obtain second-hand copies, for a while formed a small but passionate band. But nobody could find her; and nobody would reprint the novels. Then, as the result of a dramatized version of *Good Morning, Midnight* broadcast on the Third Programme in 1958, she was finally traced to an address in Cornwall. She had a collection of unpublished stories, written during and immediately after the Second World War, and she was at work on a novel.

Francis Wyndham. Intro. to Jean Rhys,
Wide Sargasso Sea (Deutsch, 1966), pp. 10–11

Readers of Charlotte Brontë will recall Jane Eyre's first glimpse of the mysterious prisoner in the garret of Thornfield. . . . It is the Creole Bertha Mason, of course, the first Mrs. Rochester, the announcement of whose existence, just as the wedding ceremony is about to be performed, prevents Mr. Rochester's marriage to Jane. It is Bertha Mason who is the heroine and, for the greater part of the novel, the narrator of *Wide Sargasso Sea*; and she is indeed a plausible re-creation and interpretation of the one character in *Jane Eyre* that Charlotte Brontë tells us next to nothing about, presumably because she knew next to nothing about her. Jean Rhys, who herself comes from the Caribbean, convinces us that she does, and she does so because of her extraordinarily vivid rendering of life in Jamaica in the early 19th century, immediately after the emancipation of the slaves.

The novel is a triumph of atmosphere—of what one is tempted to call Caribbean Gothic atmosphere—brooding, sinister, compounded of heat and rain and intensely colored flowers, of racial antagonisms and all-pervasive superstition. It has an almost hallucinatory quality—and this is Bertha Mason's contribution, for it is through her mind, from childhood to her incarceration at Thornfield and her dreams of firing the house, that we view the action.

From the beginning she reveals herself as beautiful, pathetic and doomed, doomed both by heredity and environment. She is the child of generations of slave-owners who have suddenly been plunged in poverty by the emancipation and become objects of contempt for the freed Negroes, who call them "white niggers," and of the English alike. Her younger brother is dumb and bed-ridden, her mother distraught by circumstances to the point finally of madness.

What I find especially interesting in *Wide Sargasso Sea*, apart from the relationship with *Jane Eyre*, is that Bertha Mason seems to sum up in herself, more closely than ever before, the nature of the heroine who appears under various names throughout Jean Rhys's fiction. She is a young woman, generally Creole in origin and artistic in leanings, who is hopelessly and helplessly at sea in her relations with men, a passive victim, doomed to destruction. It is remarkable that after so many years Miss Rhys should have pinned her down in a character, however sketchily presented, from another novelist.

It is here that the critical problem arises. Francis Wyndham rightly says that Miss Rhys's book is in no sense a pastiche of Charlotte Brontë. But does it exist in its own right? I think not, for the reason that her Mr. Rochester is almost as shadowy a figure as Charlotte Brontë's Bertha Mason. One still, in other words, needs *Jane Eyre* to complement it, to supply its full meaning.

Walter Allen. *NYT*. June 18, 1967, p. 5

It is perhaps too soon to assign Jean Rhys a definite place in literary history, although we can notice her relationship to her contemporaries. The story of her life inevitably makes us compare her to Katherine Mansfield. Both women were ex-colonials who never forgot the islands where they were born. Both of them—like many another colonial newly come to London or Paris—discovered a madder music in a bohemian life morally more lax than that which the natives of Swiss Cottage or the Boul' Mich ever enjoy. And although both Mansfield and Rhys frequently wrote about the helpless woman who needs the love and protection of a man, they were themselves solitary artists who knew their true life best when they were seated at the lonely writing desk.

Yet the differences in their personal attitudes make their writings quite different. Katherine Mansfield, in spite of her labors to master the Continental tradition of writing *contes* and her desire to be like a Chekhov or a de Maupassant who could fleetingly turn the brilliance of his genius upon prosaic events, illuminating and fixing them forever as he saw them, never departs from the traditional moral stance of the British novelist, except, from time to time, to slip from it into sentimentality. Jean Rhys, in contrast, employed not only the *mise en scène* of the Continent, but also the European *Zeitgeist*—its new ideas in psychology, its aesthetic application of certain philosophical ideas, and, most of all, its between-the-wars appreciation of the plight of the individual, the isolation of existentialism. Caught up in such ideas, she quickly leaves behind her the traditions of realism as practiced by earlier British novelists and, neither commenting upon nor manipulating her characters according to any moral pattern, allows them (or more accurately, the single character) to express what is. Relentlessly she develops her single vision of a world in which free will is a myth and the individual has no power to control his destiny. She pays little or no heed to the reader's resulting depression or occasional mystification and never, like Mansfield, utilizes an irony to exalt the reader. Katherine Mansfield often puts him on the side of the gods where he can feel superior to the self-deluding Miss Brills who flounder before him; Jean Rhys does not salve our pride, but aims through her various technical devices to make us experience the degradation and humiliation

of her characters. In the Rhys world there is no superior vantage point
for anyone.

Elgin W. Mellown. *CL*. Autumn, 1972,
pp. 473–74

To my mind, [Jean Rhys] is, quite simply, the best living English
novelist. Although her range is narrow, sometimes to the point of obsession, there is no one else now writing who combines such emotional
penetration and formal artistry or approaches her unemphatic, unblinking truthfulness. Even the narrowness works to her advantage. She
knows every detail of the shabby world she creates, knows precisely
how much to leave out—surprisingly much—and precisely how to
modulate the utterly personal speaking voice which controls it all, at
once casual and poignant, the voice of the loser who refuses, though
neither she nor God knows why, to go down. Because of this voice, the
first four novels read as a single, continuing work. They have the same
heroine—although she goes by different names—the same background
of seedy hotels and bedsitters for transients in Montparnasse and
Bloomsbury, and they recount the single, persistent, disconnected disaster of a life in which only three things can be relied on: fear, loneliness
and the lack of money. . . .

   The purity of Miss Rhys's style and her ability to be at once
deadly serious and offhand make her books peculiarly timeless. Novels
she wrote more than 40 years ago still seem contemporary, unlike those
of many more popular authors. More important, her voice itself remains
young. She was about 30 before she began to write—apparently having
other things on her mind before that—yet the voice she created then,
and still uses, is oddly youthful: light, clear, alert, casual and disabused,
and uniquely concerned in simply telling the truth.

A. Alvarez. *NYT*. March 17, 1974, pp. 6–7

RICHARDS, I. A. (1893–   )

Anyone acquainted with *The Meaning of Meaning* or *Science and
Poetry* would think that *Speculative Instruments* had been written by a
different author. The brash, cocksure tone of the earlier works has
given way to a hesitant and timid one; assertions have been replaced
by questions. Moreover, the change is not merely one of tone. Obvious
demons of the early works, including Plato, have become idols of the
later works. Richards even seems to have supplied a transitional work,

Coleridge on Imagination, in which he investigates the work of the extreme idealist from the standpoint of a materialist. . . .

I find both change and continuity in Richards' work. While I would agree with Richards that there has been a change in his mode of presenting similar ideas, I would add that the modes of presentation adopted in the earlier and later works have had crucial effects of their own. His use of the impulse theory to present his ideas in the early works had the effect of forcing him to certain conclusions not in keeping with the general trend of his thought; this accounts, in large part, for the inconsistencies and ambiguities of the early writings. On the other hand, the fluctuating, free, almost poetic style of the later works has hidden many of his most important points from his readers. I agree that *Coleridge on Imagination* is a transitional work—not, however, one in which his ideas change, but one in which he is forsaking the misleading framework of the earlier books and adopting the obscure style of the later.

The peculiarities of Richards' writings determine the approach needed to uncover his theory of literature. It is easy, but fruitless, to criticize Richards for his oversimplified scientism or for his obscurity. One must, instead, use the inconsistencies and ambiguities implicit in the scientistic scheme to indicate the proper interpretation of the difficult later writings.

Jerome P. Schiller. *I. A. Richards' Theory of Literature* (New Haven, Conn., Yale Univ. Pr., 1969), pp. 15–16

Richards' career has shown a steady concern for "critical balance," a drive to control the often conflicting forces at work in any full, lively act of reading and understanding. This emphasis on checks and balances may help to explain a recent development in his own literary life —his turn to poetry—since Richards the poet at once extends and holds in balance the dynamically opposed energies of the analytic and the visionary intelligence. His work has always been articulated through questions and question-marks, so that, for example, while he promises "space-ship" adventure in his "Goodbye Earth," the poem also proclaims a painful "comprehending," which "knows not what it knows/ Nor what its knowing is—and knows thereby." Richards, questioning, forces the reader into a Platonic exercise of dramatized "internal colloquy." He follows the star of Plato's *Dialogues* and continues the tradition of late Elizabethan and seventeenth-century metaphysical verse, whose forming principle was also that of internal colloquy. Like the Metaphysicals, also, he subjects a Golden Age technique of song to the taut strain of a supervening intellectual struggle. He has come to poetry through a personal history of analytic, pragmatic response to the poetry of others. Further, he has built theories to sustain his practical criticism. How striking, then, that his poetry now should remove the methodical armor of discursive thought, to expose the more frail, human body of intuition.

To be or to become a poet, having formed major critical theory, is a dangerous game. Yet for a theorist in the Coleridgean line it is a natural shift. By turning to poetry, the philosopher modulates from the explicit to the implicit. Coleridge, perhaps first among English critics, looked for the principles of an intrinsic criticism of poetry, and one tenet of his method was a refusal to separate criticism from its object, poetry. Richards has followed this tenet, both knowing and enjoying its attendant risk, whose limits he has sought to define. A speculative poetry, the *Internal Colloquies* are a natural culmination of the Coleridgean intermarriage (Richards would call it a "troth") between the poetic and the critical acts. The critical balance of poetry finally meets the poetry of critical balance.

Angus Fletcher. In Reuben Brower, Helen
Vendler, and John Hollander, eds., *I. A.*
Richards: Essays in His Honor (N.Y., Oxford
Univ. Pr., 1973), pp. 85–86

RICHARDSON, DOROTHY (1873–1957)

Truly enough, Dorothy Richardson's propaganda reflects the period through which she wrote, and readers today are not likely to be stirred by *Pilgrimage* because they agree or disagree with her views on "the woman question." They will look for other values in her journey. One of these—and this has something to do with her subterranean influence on modern English writing—was her candid approach in dealing with the careers of women. *Pilgrimage*, then, was a long step toward Virginia Woolf's famous essay, "A Room of One's Own"—and that influence was even deeper than Mrs. Woolf's adaptations of the "stream of consciousness" technique to her own uses. Dorothy Richardson's example inspired self-confidence in other women writers and permitted them to assert their independence (in print) with far more ease than their predecessors had. *Pilgrimage* created an atmosphere in and from which other journeys could make their start. We must remember that its beginnings were actually gas-lit glimmerings out of Victorian darkness.

But the more enduring interest of *Pilgrimage* is very closely allied to the kind of journey taken by its heroine. We know at once that the journey has something to do with education, and from the predominant imagery of its first section, "Pointed Roofs," the journey moves from darkness toward light, toward hoped-for illuminations in the future. Miriam Henderson's journey, however realistic it may have been, had transcendental elements and associations. Her education included ardent readings in the essays of the American, Ralph Waldo Emerson, seemingly a strange choice for one so stoutly English in her likes and dislikes. But the choice is less strange if one assumes that she adopted him as a shining figure of Unitarianism—and of Protestant dissent.

> Horace Gregory. *Dorothy Richardson: An*
> *Adventure in Self-Discovery* (N.Y., Holt,
> Rinehart and Winston, 1967), pp. 108–9

The technique invented by Dorothy Richardson has become familiar to us through all those later writers who knowingly or not have derived something from her. It is hard for us today to grasp how difficult and strange her way of writing first appeared. Those early reactions of readers and critics, with their inevitable misunderstandings of her work, have dimmed her reputation to this day.

Some of her seeming limitations—occasional prosiness or blurred characterization, lack of compression or selection, or too much—these are part of her method, and therefore part of the cumulative effect of *Pilgrimage*.

The method was evolved to express her vision in the new world of the twentieth century with its changing ways and attitudes. A new kind of voice was needed: not specifically a woman's voice, but one expressing all the awareness and self-doubt of modern people in a world where traditional beliefs had been called into question.

She created, therefore, through her narrator Miriam just such a voice and viewpoint, taking nothing for granted, expressing nothing in the conventional or accepted way. It was a method belonging to the new age but stemming from the nineteenth-century analytical approach. It was closely equivalent to Impressionism in painting.

Pilgrimage might be called the first full-scale Impressionist novel. As never before in a novel, Dorothy Richardson attempted to show us what we really perceive, not what we accept as reality according to certain conventions. In her descriptions and also in depicting emotion and thought, her novel portrays reality as continual movement and fluctuation. To let this reality filter through as lucidly as possible, the novelist must keep his own voice from obtruding—from commenting, summarizing, drawing hard lines of demarcation of character or incident—just as the Impressionist painters had rejected the convention of firm outline. Similarly there could be no arbitrary "plot" imposed on the material, distorting the truth. If a novel were made alive enough by capturing the flow of reality, then its immediacy should be more exciting than any contrived plot.

Pilgrimage is literally a "motion picture," in its view of the ceaseless fluctuation of people's lives, minds and hearts, and in its prismatic analysis of perceptions into their elements. But its author was searching as well for something constant and essential underlying the continual movement in beings or objects. "There was something in matter that had not yet been found out." The search for reality, in this new writing, was also an attempt to rediscover meanings and truths that the twentieth-century mind could no longer take on trust. This is the search that gives the novel its title *Pilgrimage* and its central theme.

John Rosenberg. *Dorothy Richardson* (N.Y., Knopf, 1973), pp. 161–62

ROLFE, FREDERICK (BARON CORVO) (1860–1913)

With his fascinating "experiment in biography," *The Quest for Corvo,* A. J. A. Symons opened in 1934 the case of Frederick Rolfe—prototype and emblem of the eccentric and alienated artist, of the *poète maudit*. Rolfe had died in Venice in 1913, in complete poverty and having finally surrendered to his sexual aberrations. Under the pseudonym of Baron Corvo, he had published in 1904 a remarkable book, *Hadrian VII*, which was to prove a fictional transposition of his life of penury and destitution, and a projection of the unfulfilled dream of his life—as is the case with the protagonist of the book, entering priesthood, and being summoned to the Holy See.

Working on these two polarities, Symons emphasized the human figure of Rolfe, a mysterious, abnormal and baffling character, half genius and half charlatan, full of whims and resentments, who had devoted himself to "the noble art of making enemies" after being expelled from two seminaries. Born in 1860 of a Protestant family, Rolfe had become a Catholic in 1886: the wreck of his ecclesiastical dream was to become the trauma, and the dividing point, of his life. In constant peregrination, afflicted by debts, often living from day to day and from hand to mouth, trying without success a variety of activities—teacher, private secretary, photographer, painter and eventually writer—obsessively looking for "divine friends" who invariably turned into "despoilers," Rolfe created with objective facts leavened by an enormous amount of resentment the mythology of the outcast. Violently attacked by the Catholic press, at war with everything and with everyone and above all with himself, at the turn of the century Rolfe courted literary, as well as human, martyrdom.

Applying on a personal level a typical aspect of the Decadent Movement, he sublimated frustration into the dream of literary excellence. Claiming for the artist the right to be supported by others, he sees enemies wherever someone gives him a hand; breaks with society, but seeks its comforts; turns private resentments into metaphysical hatreds; and strikes back in retaliation. Exceptional in every sense of the word, he is, as Graham Greene has remarked, on the devil's side, while showing that he can write like an angel—even if a fallen one.

Using these contradictions as guiding lines, Symons traced the parable that led Rolfe from religious yearnings to sexual aberration and, in the process, turned Corvo into an object of reprobation and/or worship. Now that his works are available, one has to reconsider the relation between the man and the writer, his biography and his fiction, his fiction and his times. Rolfe is often very much present in his fiction, writing about his story of deprivations and humiliations, yearnings and retaliations. But it is exactly here that one has to distinguish what refers to the man from what refers to the writer, what is mere expression of personal obsessions from what acquires specific artistic and historical significance through literary transposition.

Two facts must be kept in mind. If Rolfe's autobiographical fiction is often a direct expression of the defenseless and alienated self, it shows on the other hand revealing links and coincidences with the historical experience of the Decadent Movement. Secondly, the main characteristics of his historical, or pseudo-historical fiction, can often be related to the ideals and the forms of Decadent literature and reveal striking experimental aspects which foreshadow some important trends of twentieth century fiction.

Sergio Perosa. Mosaic. Vol. 4, No. 3, 1971,
pp. 111–12

Corvo's trials and tribulations took many forms. He was a frustrated writer, with interest in his books limited to a small public of erudite esthetes; he was hated, even after 20 years, by his former comrades at the seminary (whom he regarded as vulgar and ignorant); and he was looked upon with spite by the number of women whose advances he had spurned in true misogynist fashion. All of this could well account for the fragile sensitivity which drove him to write alternately letters of petition (with undertones of blackmail) and insults to those who had helped him most. Few ingrates have as readily bitten the hand that fed them. Yet he was hungry. Contempt in Corvo always won over gratitude. . . .

Literature helped Baron Corvo bear his horrible solitude. His pen, with vaguely Gothic handwriting, was handmaiden to his delusions: His Excellency accepting hand-kisses from small Romans, a courtier of the Borgias and, ultimately, the Sovereign Pontiff. Never have day-dreams been more logically pursued than in his writings.

Corvo took himself for a Renaissance man, as far removed as possible from the mediocrities surrounding him. His characters, like the Borgias, were free to satisfy their instincts, or, like his fictional Hadrian VII, to remake the world in their own image. . . .

As Mario Praz has written, "Baron Corvo does not truly belong to the world of men, but that of fallen angels: that is to say, the world of demons."

Philippe Jordan. *NYT*. Jan. 28, 1973, p. 32

SANSOM, WILLIAM (1912–   )

Sansom does borrow technique from Kafka—specifically the technique of meticulous and unornamented delineation of the object described. And Sansom's landscapes do symbolize (or echo) states of mind, as do Kafka's (and as may be said do those of Edmund Spenser and Thomas Hardy, too). And from Sansom's sharply outlined objects, a dark shadow of suggestion seems to extend and to cast over the most trivial items and fleeting moments a burden of import, and often of menace, far greater than the mere empirical existence of the objects would seem to necessitate. And, finally, in his earlier stories Sansom shared Kafka's preoccupation with the lost and anchorless condition of man in a world without landmarks, in which the waves are so enormous as to overwhelm the most resolute of the puny efforts of a mortal.

But always Sansom's unease seems to have been a less compulsive one, as is shown by his frequent persona, the bemused bystander. Moreover, we should note that Sansom has said (and even a cursory glance at his writings will show the statement to be true) that his work *now* is not much influenced by Kafka. That, too, is understandable, for though Kafka (and Brecht), who asked strangely final questions, and who postulated absurd non-answers, were the two German writers who had a considerable English following in the mid-nineteen forties, their influence began to wane by the nineteen fifties. Perhaps some of their non-answers became less absurd. Or perhaps even their questions became absurd.

Peter F. Neumeyer. *WSCL*. Winter–Spring,
1966, p. 84

Ever since he began writing, around the beginning of the last war, Sansom has been very much his own man. It is true that his first stories were written under the influence of Kafka, but that choice of influence by a young English writer at that time was itself an individual and almost eccentric act of abasement. It did not prove, in the event, to be a particularly significant one; for Sansom soon moved away from the allegorizing fantasies of his early stories to a sort of wayward and highly personal realism. He has chosen, ever since, to look at the familiar but to look at it with such a raking and transforming eye that the familiar, in Sansom's books, has taken on qualities and aspects which it had never displayed before.

Another thing that needs to be said is that this very independent writer has always seemed to be more concerned with how to write than with what to write about. That may be the wrong way of putting it. It might be truer to say that he has always had a natural talent for vigorous and original expression, and that his material has really exercised his attention *more* than his manner, simply, because there was no material which he felt to be naturally his own. If this is so, it is important to recognize that it makes Sansom a very rare bird indeed among the various and noisy flocks of the last twenty-five years. At a time when a new novelist could make a name for himself, not for any new quality in his writing, not for any freshness of vision or originality of language, but simply because he had written the first novel ever about life in a dental supply factory on the Trent, William Sansom has always been remarkable for the quality of his writing, rather than the terrain of his investigation.

Philip Toynbee. *L.* March, 1966, pp. 80–81

SASSOON, SIEGFRIED (1886–1967)

The quality of Sassoon's war poetry is remarkable, not when it is compared stylistically with the work of his more original contemporaries, but when its content is viewed in relation to the cramping Edwardian social and literary context in which Sassoon himself was reared. Looking back, one must wonder at how, by sheer truth and force of feeling, he broke out of the constricting mould of dead poeticism which, at nearly thirty years old, had almost stifled him. If he was no prophet, his famous war poetry makes him a portent. In his raw and heated satires the emasculated versifying of an outworn society is betrayed from within—his contributions to the 1918–1919 volume of *Georgian Poetry* give the lie to its heart. They are symptomatic of a new vitality which was to undermine the irresponsible rule of Marshianism. Sassoon's revival of the Byronic protest vigorously renewed the involvement of the poet with society *at the centre of society*. The excellence of his war satire was, like that of much Byron wrote, one less of form than of "sincerity and strength."

Yet his example had to wait another decade for effective followers —who were not, however, to take their leadership from him or to earn his sympathy. After the First World War, he rapidly lost his hold upon his time. He could not sustain the indignant protestant's role in the peace-time world. The Pacifist Muse is a noble one, but she is apt to repeat herself: though she was briefly revived in *The Road to Ruin*, it was to speak with baffled feeling rather than force. Social issues were many and blurred: humanitarian feeling could distinguish no plain target. His satire in the 'Twenties, like that of Osbert Sitwell and the embittered prose of Richard Aldington, was primarily an emotional outlet. So far as it can be traced to identifiable causes, it arose from the frustrating denial of the old positives: unquestioned peace, an apparently assured future, and, when garnished with Socialism, the war's solitary fruit—the uplifting experience of men's capacity for kinship—had a bitter taste. It was marginal satire, directed upon social and political aberrations: beside the slick surgery of Auden, the leader of an unwearied later generation, it seems exhausted and querulous.

Michael Thorpe. Siegfried Sassoon (Leiden,
Universitaire Pers Leiden; Oxford Univ. Pr.,
1966), p. 254

In 1939, Siegfried Sassoon looked back over the preceding 15 years and lamented that "the writing of straightforward and whole-hearted verse has been increasingly out of fashion and indirect utterance has been indulged in to an unprecedented degree." His own straightforward and wholehearted moment had, of course, been brief and spectacular. Although in 1919 "everybody suddenly burst out singing" (everybody, Robert Graves was careful to point out, did not include Graves) Sassoon never managed to adjust his army issue liveliness to peace time. "Aftermath," for instance, is an embarrassing poem not just because of its rotund clichés and faked-up sonorities but because it is saturated with nostalgia for precisely the dreadful situations which it insists must never "happen again." There is more than a little wistful retrospection in these pious pieces left over from the late thirties that talk of the body as "only shrivelling grass" and the soul as "a starlit sentry." . . .

Sassoon could legitimately claim a humane virtue for most of his poetic vices. That he should have run to a religiose and feeble middle-age is not so surprising when it is recognised that the shallow vulgarity which makes it easy for us to dismiss volumes like Vigils and The Heart's Journey is what permitted him to plaster his early poems with corpses and thrust his barbed tongue at the brass hats. To have paused, as Owen did, over an individual agony; to have worried that there was something too perfunctorily glamorised, too heavily mock-tough in his breezy accumulation of maimed witnesses, would have struck him as self-indulgent and beside the point. No poet since has been quite as sure what the point really is. Sassoon certainly hasn't, and if he is valuable it must be for what he did then, rather than for what those same poems are likely to do now.

Ian Hamilton. NS. Feb. 3, 1967, p. 160

SAYERS, DOROTHY (1893–1957)

An interesting clue (and when writing about Miss Sayers, it is tempting to use the detective-story terms she herself employs so interestingly as critical tools) to the "problem" of a writer who is perhaps equally famous as a detective novelist, theologian, and scholar (and peripherally, as a writer of children's books) is furnished by a tantalizing statement in *The Mind of the Maker*. . . . The key phrase is "a hymn to the Master Maker," and the "youthful set of stanzas" contain the essential theme: man's striving to praise God, the "Master Maker," through his own earthly creations and the inevitable frustrations and disappointments which stem from his inability to reach perfection. And, as Miss Sayers states, this great theme runs, in a number of keys and modes, through all of her works, from the detective novels of the 1930's through the religious plays and Dante papers of the 1940's and 50's.

Miss Sayers quite rightly points to *Gaudy Night* and *The Zeal of Thy House* as focal points of the fictional presentation of this theme, which is most fully and explicitly developed in *The Mind of the Maker*. *Gaudy Night* is perhaps the most complex of Miss Sayers' novels; indeed, as in a number of her other works, particularly *The Nine Tailors*, the "detective" element plays so minor a role in *Gaudy Night* that it demands the title "novel" rather than "detective story." *Gaudy Night* also marks the climax not only, as Miss Sayers says, of "a long development in detective fiction," but also of the courtship of Lord Peter Wimsey, Miss Sayers' detective-hero, and Miss Harriet Vane, whom Lord Peter had saved from the gallows in *Strong Poison*. And the courtship of Lord Peter is of great importance here, since it is by means of this "second" plot ("subplot" would here be too strong a term) that Miss Sayers introduces a series of variations upon the Creator theme and its implications in human affairs.

Charles Moorman. *The Precincts of Felicity:*
The Augustinian City of the Oxford Christians
(Gainesville, Univ. of Florida Pr., 1966),
pp. 113–15

Dorothy L. Sayers, the creator of Lord Peter Wimsey, has been dead eleven years, and there is many a detective story reader, including some who never read any detective stories but hers, who would, if they could, offer her resurrection on condition that she produce more

Lord Peter novels. Over thirty years ago, alas, Lord Peter (having married, solved a most cunning and intricate crime, and wept out his horror at the murderer's execution in the arms of his new-wed wife), departed forever from the world of the detective novel.

True, he made one or two casual, short appearances—in the course of one of which his first baby was born—but with the coming of the war his creator finally succeeded in her earlier determination to marry Peter off and get rid of him. It is forty-five years since Lord Peter's first appearance, and all of the books about him are still in print in hard cover. Lord Peter's admirers continue to turn to his adventures more than three decades after his creator abandoned detective fiction to take up the mysteries of theology.

Dorothy Sayers was no fly-by-night writer of thrillers. Not only did she write superbly constructed detective plots, played out in witty comedies of manners; she was also a scholar of great erudition who had taken first honors in medieval literature at Oxford, and who was to become, after the disappearance of Lord Peter, one of the outstanding translators and interpreters of Dante, as well as a formidable Christian apologist. She has written what is widely accepted as the best history of the detective story and has managed, in addition, to draw the fire of such notable critics as Edmund Wilson, Q. D. Leavis and W. H. Auden, and the attention of everyone who has ever written about detective fiction. In Howard Haycraft's *The Art of the Mystery Story*, a collection of every notable essay on the detective story written prior to 1948, her name is mentioned more frequently than any save that of the fictional Sherlock Holmes. Indeed, Q. D. Leavis, with that lack of courtesy as marked in the Leavises as their astuteness, railed at her in *Scrutiny* with such vehemence as positively to affirm Miss Sayers's importance as a literary figure. Can Agatha Christie or Erle Stanley Gardner match that? Eleven years dead, Dorothy Sayers is yet a literary and social phenomenon to be grappled with.

So is Lord Peter. It is certainly arguable that no marriage in literary history has caused as much interest as Lord Peter's. If female readers complained that Peter was throwing himself away on Harriet Vane, there was a strong male faction who insisted, according to his creator, that Harriet was thrown away on Peter. As these two fell into each other's arms at the end of *Gaudy Night* and spent the subsequent hours, before Lord Peter rushed off on one of his assignments for the Foreign Office, kissing each other madly in a punt, Dorothy Sayers found herself with a best seller on her hands. Hers was a success that the years, as is not their usual fashion in the matter of detective novels, have steadily increased.

Carolyn G. Heilbrun. AmS. Spring, 1968, p. 324

● SHAFFER, PETER (1926–   )

Mr. Shaffer has many things on his mind in *Five Finger Exercise* besides the Oedipus theme, which is merely one strand in the cat's cradle of intertwined relationships that he sets before us. The five characters in his play are all in need of love. With fiendish skill Mr. Shaffer shows us how each of them seeks it in the very quarter from which it is least likely to be forthcoming. His purpose, implicitly moral, is to expose the pain and the rage that ensue when one human being ignores another's plea, however ill-timed or misguided, for sympathy. . . .

All the pieces of the puzzle interlock snugly and without strain, falling into place with a splendid, steely inevitability. Seeking comparisons, one's mind turns to Swiss watches or chess problems—especially the latter, since the contending forces in *Five Finger Exercise* take a long time to get to grips and the tension mounts very slowly. You will certainly be held, you may even be mesmerized, but you are not likely to be moved. The writing, expert though it is, has about it a curious bloodlessness, as you will see if you compare Mr. Shaffer's work with *A Month in the Country*, which also deals with the jealousy that overcomes a rural châtelaine when she fails to attract the affections of a hired tutor. Where Turgenev sprawls and smiles, Mr. Shaffer is tight-lipped and technical, constantly building up emotional climaxes that he lacks the verbal felicity to fulfil. The effect reminds one of a mountain range with all the peaks lopped off, or of a masterpiece of functional architecture from which the central heating has been inexplicably omitted. Despite these objections, *Five Finger Exercise* is the most accomplished new play Broadway has seen this wretched season. [1959]

Kenneth Tynan. *Curtains* (N.Y., Atheneum, 1961), pp. 335–37

Shaffer . . . can fashion handsome, civilized gadgets of entertainment which make intelligent pastimes without drawing blood—that is, without in any way arousing us from the comfort of convention, without changing us. Shaffer . . . probably aspires to be something more than a latter-day Pinero, but at present he reaches only as far as Terence Rattigan. His message is benevolence, a plea for tolerance, an exchange of sympathy among fellow men.

Shaffer is still a novice—albeit one of unmistakable assurance—
and no judgment about his evolution and future contribution should be
undertaken at this point. The sentiment which animates his work might
conceivably lead to creation. But up to now he has written as one
who demonstrates his thesis cleverly for stage purposes rather than as
one intimate with those for whom he begs our compassion.

There is an oblique confession of this in . . . *The Public Eye*. The
public eye is the author's. . . . The play is wittily written, a very agreeable confection . . . but it touches reality with its finger tips only. Its
connection with the truth of marital relations is largely conversational
—the wisdom of the glib acquaintance who drops in on a family quarrel
and gives apt yet irrelevant advice.

Where reality is approached somewhat more directly in *The
Private Ear*, the content is, oddly enough, closer to the trite. . . . Apart
from the ordinariness of the play's scheme, one finds the author manipulating his material for comedy gags on the one hand (malapropisms
and presumably hilarious variations on the types to be found in the
proletarian plays of the new British drama) and for tear-jerking pity for
the unfavored on the other. We are made to feel benign without the
least scratch of conscience.

Harold Clurman. Nation. June 2, 1962, p. 502

According to the "intellectual underground," *The Royal Hunt of the
Sun* is an overrated blunderbuss, portentous with "grand themes" and
let down by language. It's an insidious thing this "underground"
because its attitudes are frequently selected in relation to the verdicts
of the popular press . . . and are not arrived at naturally. This negative
groundswell exerted a real influence on me when I went to see Peter
Shaffer's play. . . . I felt that if I didn't register the proper attitude I
would be cast into some kind of intellectual slum and undoubtedly lose
the respect of my peers; those long-haired groundhogs that munch *New
Statesman* leaders and quaff *Observer* crits. . . .

Gauging my feeling as accurately as possible, I think they are the
following: (a) that I admired the play more than I expected to; (b)
that, quibbles notwithstanding, it is the best play Peter Shaffer has ever
written. . . .

It is puerile to shoot the play down on intellectual grounds
because, essentially, it is an adventure story; one of the greatest. . . . It
is not the sort of story that has to be intellectually assembled like a
Dürrenmatt magnum opus. Merely to tell the tale is to plunge the
spectator into an interlocking network of powerful themes. On one
level, the corrupting influence of commercial Christianity; on another,
the extremes of imperialist greed; on a third, the unkillable, primitive

urges in so-called civilised men that respond to cult, ritual and the power of deities, even when false. It is not Shaffer who is saying all this; it is history, and by reporting it accurately, it just gets said.

The chief trouble with the language is that it is asked to do too much. There is a point (and Shaffer reaches it about the middle of the second act) beyond which words, no matter how evocative, simply do not operate. After high spectacle and bold physical actions, we can no longer abide the clang of language. It becomes emotionally redundant to listen to verbal elaborations of what most of us are already feeling. . . .

What I think I am saying, ultimately, is that the achievement is too real, the story too good, and the entire effort too praiseworthy to convert one's reservations about the play (and its overrated success) into an involuntary negative reaction.

Charles Marowitz. Encore. March–April,
1965, pp. 44–45

The Royal Hunt of the Sun has arrived from London with the same director, scenic designer, costumer, movement coordinator, and composer; every effort has been made to reproduce the effects of the brilliant National Theatre production; but because of the new cast and a more restricted stage, a good deal of its atmospheric pageantry has been lost. This is a shame because without spectacular theatricality, the play amounts to very little; it may be total theatre but it is strictly fractional drama; and being exposed to Peter Shaffer's meditations on religion, love, life, and death for three solid hours is rather like being trapped in a particularly active wind tunnel with no hope of egress. In the London production, there were always choreographed massacres, treks through the Andes, harvest dances, ritual gestures, and an extraordinary performance by Robert Stephens as the sovereign Inca, Atahuallpa, to distract one from the pretentiousness of Mr. Shaffer's theme, the conventionality of his characters, and the poetastrical quality of his dialogue ("Look into him," says one character of the hero, "you'll see a kind of death"). But in New York, with a more limited physical production and a more insecure cast, such distractions no longer work, and one finds escape from the play only in reflections on how the author has muffed his opportunities.

For the conquest of Peru by the Spanish invaders is a natural subject for the theatre; it is the kind of dark myth that fascinated Antonin Artaud as an alternative to the decaying subject matter of the Occidental stage. The idea for the play, as a matter of fact, was probably suggested to Mr. Shaffer by Artaud's first scenario for his projected Theatre of Cruelty, a tableau sequence called *The Conquest of Mexico*. In this unproduced spectacle, Artaud hoped to "contrast Christianity with much older religions" and correct "the false conceptions the Occident has somehow formed concerning paganism and certain natural religions," while dramatizing, in burning images, the destruction of Montezuma and his Aztecs by the armies of Cortez: "Space is stuffed with whirling gestures, horrible faces, dying eyes, clenched fists, manes, breastplates, and from all levels of the scene fall limbs, breastplates, heads, stomachs like a hailstorm bombarding the earth with supernatural explosions." Mr. Shaffer treats the annihilation of the Incas in a similar manner, and (having done his history homework carefully) occasionally engages in some speculative comparative anthropology. But at the same time that he is fashioning cruel Artaudian myths, he is mentalizing, psychologizing, and sentimentalizing these myths. Underneath the tumult and the swirl lie a very conventional set of liberal notions about the noble savage, the ignoble Catholic, and the way brotherly love can bridge the gulf that separates cultures. By the end of the play, in fact, the whole brutal struggle has degenerated into a fraternal romance between a lissome young redskin and an aging lonely paleface—a relationship which is illuminated less by Artaud than by Leslie Fiedler in his essay "Come Back to the Raft Again, Huck Honey." [1965]

Robert Brustein. *The Third Theatre*
(N.Y., Knopf, 1969), pp. 114–15

Peter Shaffer is a working playwright who uses a modest but very wisely directed talent to fashion a wide variety of theater exercises. Because he is neither cryptic nor fiery, we tend to place him in the same category with Robert Bolt, somewhere slightly beneath Arden, Osborne, Pinter, and Wesker. He is further contaminated because he has enjoyed greater success in London's West End than any of the others, and in another era might well have become a Terence Rattigan rather than the author of *The Royal Hunt of the Sun*, which the distinguished intellectual critic, Bernard Levin, called the "greatest play of our generation."

To define Shaffer's position is not to minimize his achievements. His special assets are an undoctrinaire sense of what can be created in the special world of the stage, an extreme objectivity about his own work that somehow stops short of becoming inhibitory, and a realization that the world's conventional institutions can be effectively assaulted with trivial comedy, naturalistic suspense drama, and common-man explorations of complex cosmic issues.

His newest effort is a shamelessly farcical concoction facetiously titled *Black Comedy* that sets out to squeeze every last drop of theatrical fun from a simple comic situation. When the curtain rises the stage is black, but we hear a young artist conversing with the sex-hungry debutante with whom he is having a love affair. They are preparing the apartment for a visit from both a wealthy art patron who may buy the artist's works and her ultra-conservative father who may reluctantly approve his daughter's engagement to the young Bohemian. To impress the visitors, they have, without permission, borrowed some elegant furniture and valuable antique objects from a neighbor who is away. Although the stage remains black for several minutes, it does not take us long to realize that what is black to us is light to the characters. . . .

Is there an implied criticism of social hypocrisy in all this, a suggestion that truer behavior ensues when we are relieved of the burden of appearances? Perhaps. But it is certainly not essential to the popular enjoyment of this season's most risible romp.

Henry Hewes. *Sat.* Feb. 25, 1967, p. 59

Mr. Shaffer's play [*Equus*] does an unusual thing. It asks why? Most plays tell us how. *Equus* is a psychological inquiry into a crime, a journey into someone's mind. It is a kind of highbrow suspense story, a psychic and mythic thriller, but also an essay in character and motive. It is the documentation of a crime. . . .

The play . . . is richly rewarding on a number of levels. It is by no means a clinical documentary, though it does have elements of this about it. Yet its nub is to be found in the doctor's relationship with the boy, and his growing realization that the boy has a fantasy love for horses. For it is a love; he actually finds in horses the spirit that Mr. Shaffer calls Equus, a deification of the horse as a life force, and the boy has entered realms of passions and, in a sense, reality, that his own humdrum existence has never known. He has an unkissed wife, an antiquarian interest in Greek relics and a whole tally of little, medium boredoms. He lives, as he recognizes, to a small if safe scale. . . .

The play is quite different from anything Mr. Shaffer has written before, and has, to my mind, a quite new sense of seriousness to it. It has all of Mr. Shaffer's masterly command of the theater. He has his theater set up here as a kind of bullring with a section of the audience actually sitting on stage, like confident graduate students watching a class. And most adroitly, he runs through many of the patterns of clinical psychiatry, from elementary hypnotism to the abreaction, whereby the patient re-enacts circumstances of his trauma.

Mr. Shaffer was always a great juggler of the theater, whether it was in making his well-made play, such as *Five Finger Exercise*, or constructing a musicless Verdi spectacular in *The Royal Hunt of the*

Sun. But in *Equus* he has found a different métier. It is still a popularly intended play—it is essentially a Broadway vehicle for star actors—but it as a most refreshing and mind-opening intellectualism. It has the power of thought to it. Take one: "A child is born into a world of phenomena, all equal in their power to enslave." This, just as sample, has a quality of thoughtfulness to it that is rare in the contemporary theater.

Clive Barnes. NYTd. Oct. 25, 1974, p. 26

SHAW, GEORGE BERNARD (1856–1950)

The "significant action," in a dramatic sense, of Shaw's playwright career can be given brief statement: he converted a rhetorical drama of the passions into a rhetorical drama of impassioned ideas, using as his vehicle the most popular and "theatrical" modes of the nineteenth-century theater. Such a synopsis leaves much to be inferred. But Shaw's exploitation of stock-company stereotypes; his deliberate attempts to embarrass, if not destroy, certain romantic conventions and genres; his exploitation of the rhetorical aspects of opera and music; his campaigns as a critic for and against certain kinds of drama and action; even his use of "comedic paradox," and of the wit and irony, the flirtation with logic and illogic, which are the weapons of intellect however impassioned, are all implicit in the central, governing action of Shaw's playwriting career. . . .

In a study of Shaw's relations with the nineteenth-century theater, it becomes notably apparent that stage conventions, critical debates, and indeed whole genres which went into the shaping and the substance of Shaw's drama of ideas have altogether dropped out of view without damaging his vitality. Revivals of Shaw are frequent, and they are not yet made in an antiquarian spirit. However, where a theater is literarily self-conscious, plays survive their initial productions by virtue of qualities which, after they charm in the theater, can capture an audience outside it. Consequently, however much Shaw was indebted to the dead conventions and genres, they are much more indebted to him. The nineteenth-century theater had a most awesome vitality which rose from other than literary greatness. Therefore, in its proper self, it was a perishable theater, and its literary remains, which were then most warm, are now most cold. Nevertheless, Shaw brought it into our time in his own plays, in a form not only literary, but theatrically viable and theatrically fertile. He saves the uses and the energies of the mortal nineteenth-century popular theater for a future classical repertory and for the living tradition.

Martin Meisel. *Shaw and the Nineteenth-Century Theater* (Princeton, N.J., Princeton Univ. Pr., 1963), pp. 446–47

What essentially distinguishes *Candida* and the great plays that follow it from these four [*Plays Pleasant and Unpleasant*] is not simply the perfecting of technique or the clarification of themes. It is that in the earlier plays the socialism, anti-romanticism, Ibsenism, and so on exist for themselves alone, are disparate and in a sense constricting. In *Candida* and after, these themes have come under the control of a vision that is large enough to contain them, and can see them from without even when it is presenting them from within. That vision is Shaw's intuition of reality, felt by him as co-extensive with his experience, fully coherent within the framework of a hypothesis by which he is entirely resolved to stand or fall. In *Candida*, in short, we have entered the world of the mature artist, as distinctive and coherent as the artist's self, with a degree of communicability, that is commensurate with his mastery of the medium.

What then are the characteristics of this Shavian world? I suggest that the most important fact about it is that it is a world not of being but of becoming. Its people are not called into existence for the sake of what they are and what they do, but for what they may and ought to be and do. Their actions raise questions of morality, but those actions are not contained within an unchanging moral order that commends the poisoned chalice to the poisoner's own lips and causes rebellion ever to find rebuke. . . . They are often creatures of laughter, but what makes them comical is not their extravagant departure from some conventional norm, as in the plays of Molière or Johnson. Shaw's comic figures themselves contain the criteria by which we judge them; indeed, they judge themselves. His world is not permeated by divine unalterable order to which all must return, but by living change in which all must participate.

He is thus, surely, one of the first writers to exemplify fully the plight of modern man, for whom every fact turns out to be a question, and especially of the modern artist, facing the problem of imposing a meaningful permanence on what is constantly shifting.

J. Percy Smith. *The Unrepentant Pilgrim* (Boston, Houghton Mifflin, 1965), pp. 253–55

"Learn everything," Shaw once advised novelists in a lecture on fiction, "and when you know it, stick to naturalism, and write every word as if you were on your oath in a witness box." It is not generally realized how seriously Shaw took his own advice as far as naturalism was concerned. Most training in literary tradition is in fact a positive impediment in understanding Shaw. When Shaw introduces literary conventions into his plays, it is most often to demonstrate how absurdly they misrepresent human behavior, or how silly the moral assumptions behind them are. The effect of boldly introducing what he had observed in life onto the stage fell so far short of theatrical expectations that audiences frequently mistook Shaw's realism for perverse farce.

Sometimes the character types Shaw copied were common everywhere but in the playhouse. Sometimes his characters were the highly individualistic men and women who formed part of the same radical circles Shaw moved in at the turn of the century. To free Shaw from the charge of arbitrarily fantasticating, I have regularly related the characters in the plays to their real-life prototypes where they were identified by Shaw himself or where I felt I could make a reasonably safe guess at Shaw's models. If this leaves me open to the charge of counting Lady Macbeth's children, I can only reply that, in the long run, such efforts are less debilitating to literature than making it an autonomous activity sealed off from the rest of our existence.

Is Shaw dated? The answer is yes, as every classic is dated. The specific personalities and political crises that moved him to write are now part of history, as Plato's and Aristophanes' debaters and statesmen are. The images of his plays belong to an eternal world, as his ideas on government, economics, sex, psychology, logic, and art, now seen apart from the novel and amusing expression he gave them, form part of a perennial philosophy which we can call "Shavian." But there is still a third aspect of the question. One might perhaps hope that the particular social outrages Shaw wrote about in his "problem" plays might by now be things of the past. Nothing could be more gratifying than to pronounce Shaw hopelessly out of date in such matters. Unfortunately, I cannot see that this is so. To take two clear-cut examples: the demoralization of men by poverty is still the world's first problem, and our national system of criminology is still outrageously perverse in its intentions and pernicious in its results.

Louis Crompton. *Shaw the Dramatist*
(Lincoln, Univ. of Nebraksa Pr., 1969),
pp. vi–vii

Although Bernard Shaw called his *Heartbreak House* (written in 1916–17) a fantasia in the Russian manner upon English themes, and echoes of *The Cherry Orchard* unquestionably reverberate through it, the play might be profitably viewed as a fantasia in the Shakespearean manner upon Shavian themes. Whether or not Shaw recalled Swinburne's curious remark that *King Lear* was the work of Shakespeare the socialist, *Heartbreak House* seems clearly to have been designed, at least in part, as Shaw's *Lear*. Earlier he had tauntingly titled part of a preface to his *Caesar and Cleopatra* (1898) "Better than Shakespeare?"—suggesting a parallel with the Bard's *Antony and Cleopatra*; yet by presenting a kittenish young queen and an aging Caesar, rather than an aging but still sultry Cleopatra and a younger admirer, he had evaded any direct comparison. Like his Cleopatra play, Shaw's Lear was offered not in competition but as commentary.

G. B. S. waited until his nineties to point publicly to *Heartbreak House* as his *Lear*. Even then he did so guardedly through the disarming medium of a puppet play, perhaps to prevent the comparison from being taken as seriously as he inwardly still meant it to be, for in his lifetime the play's now very considerable reputation had never measured up to his expectation for it. "If the critics had the brains of a mad Tom," he grumbled, using a suggestive association with *Lear*, "they would realize it is my greatest play. But they don't. They all go following after the Maid of Orleans." Privately Shaw had hinted at the *Lear* connection almost as soon as he had completed the play. In 1917 actress Lillah McCarthy had asked him for details of the work, hoping to convince him to let her produce it or at least acquire a starring part in it. Shaw put her off. It was wartime, he pointed out, and the play was unpleasant, unsuitable fare for war conditions. The hero was an old man of eighty-eight, and there were no young males in the cast at all (its implicit recognition of the wartime dearth of leading men). The women were either too young or too old—an ingenue and two sisters in their middle forties. The sisters, Shaw confided—"I don't find them much more popular than Goneril or Regan"—were the old man's daughters. Disgusted with the dragged-out war and its effect on theatre as well as much else, he confessed that his heart was not in a London production of a new play. And Miss McCarthy—creator of some of Shaw's greatest roles, beginning with her Ann Whitefield in *Man and Superman*—appeared neither then nor afterward in a performance of *Heartbreak House*.

Stanley Weintraub. *Journey to Heartbreak:*
The Crucible Years of Bernard Shaw
1914–1918 (N.Y., Weybright and Talley,
1971), pp. 333–34

The difficulty in finally assessing Shaw's relationship to the aesthetes is that he took pains to dissociate himself from the "art for art's sake faction" but was closer to it than he admitted, perhaps closer than he realized. Like Whistler, who also denounced aestheticism, Shaw has many of the characteristics of the fin-de-siècle aesthetes; he consciously employs masks as a manner of coping with the world; he feels alienated from the world; he is aesthetically sensitive, at times hypersensitive; he defends immorality and the value of shocking conventional people; and he respects artifice, the craft of art.

His theory of art is the result of a curious ambivalence; he denounced art for art's sake but argued, as an aesthete would, that a work of art exists independent of conventional morality and expresses the artist's individual vision. Art for art's sake he associates with academicism and a decorative impulse arising from following rules of art instead of the writer's inner convictions. The passage repudiating art for art's sake in the Epistle Dedicatory to *Man and Superman* is really an attack on academic art which arises out of a knowledge of art rather than a vision of man; Shaw denies that style is possible without opinions, but he recognizes the fact that, long after the ideas are dated, "the style remains." His defense of didacticism is really on aesthetic grounds: the artist's convictions produce art; without them, art is impossible; hence he has "contempt for *belles lettres*, and for amateurs who become the heroes of the fanciers of literary virtuosity" because, having no convictions, they cannot produce great art. . . .

Though his final faith in the power of thought to transcend all sensory appeals, including the sensory appeal of art, keeps him from aestheticism, no aesthete could have placed more emphasis on the place of art in man's life than Shaw did. He believed that the artist's role is "to catch a glint of the unrisen sun," to "shew it to you as a vision in the magic glass of his artwork," or, as the She-Ancient who was once an artist says in *Back to Methuselah*, to provide a "magic mirror . . . to reflect your invisible dreams in visible pictures." Shaw saw himself in this role, and his plays are a testament to the poet-prophet who created them.

Elsie B. Adams. *Bernard Shaw and the Aesthetes* (Columbus, Ohio State Univ. Pr., 1971), pp. 157–58

Shaw has been more underestimated since his death than he was overestimated in his lifetime. His long-continuing artistic fertility and the variety and inventiveness still evident in the plays of his last period are impressive in themselves and contribute to the character of his eminence in the European theatre. If we are looking for signs of decline in his last plays, it may be granted that they are more simply and directly conceived and constructed, that the powerful control is less impressive as the vision is less complex, and fewer interrelated conflicts are held suspended in the artistic pattern than in some of the plays of twenty years before.

Yet, *The Millionairess* is enough to challenge any generalization that dynamism has been lost, as clarity and poise prevail. And none of his plays is stronger testimony to his penetration of the nature of his own genius. The bright light it sheds retrospectively on his whole career as a political dramatist may serve in guiding the present study to its conclusions. Epifania Orgisanti di Parerga is the Shavian muse unveiled and magnificently named. The power in Eppy has burnt up the ambiguousness that clung to Ann Whitefield, or to Candida, as a vessel of the Life Force. In the line of Shaw's women characters, she is the ultimate successor to Julia Craven of *The Philanderer*, not now condemned and rejected, but purified and apotheosized. The unhappy passion of Mrs. Jenny Patterson was not wasted after all: the young man she seduced and pursued grew to be an old man whose art acknowledged the glamour and potency of the life he had feared and fled. An essentially poetic manifestation took place in a context of economic thinking.

Margery Morgan. *The Shavian Playground*
(Methuen, 1972), p. 326

Dramatic art consists, according to Shaw, in the truthful representation of reality and results in a picture of ourselves as we really are. This is not a very useful definition, but, in the light of his plays, it serves to indicate what Shaw meant in calling himself a realist.

Aristotle seems to have thought that the chief concern of the dramatist is drama. Shaw considered that the principal business of the dramatist is truth. The dramatist, in his opinion, is a philosopher. He does not create illusions; he dispels them. He is an observer and a thinker, concerned primarily with reality, and reality is what is perceived when the essential design of things becomes visible. A work of art based on such premises will be, above all, meaningful, and result in an aesthetic experience founded on comprehension. His pleasure of the theater is the pleasure of understanding.

But, in spite of Shaw's convictions and his manifest intent, what we miss in his comedies is precisely that sense of reality on which he prided himself. His characters are memorable, but they are partial, they cast no shadow. In his plays there are no bad people. There are stupid people, mistaken people, romantic people comically contrasted with the enlightened, the skeptical, and the wise. Shaw's characters, even the least admirable, are rational beings. They are moved, it is true, by varying degrees of intelligence, but they are all explicable and subject to analysis, motivated by their own ideas of self-interest toward goals which they consider desirable. The remedy against their shortsightedness, when they are shortsighted, is enlightenment, and enlightenment is the result of education. Thus, all Shaw's comedies are in some sort pedagogical exercises.

The dark side of human nature, which has increasingly absorbed the attention of the dramatists of our time, did not interest Shaw. What impressed him was not the madness of mankind, but its stupidity. Shaw's plays exhibit, accordingly, a view of life which is so far from reality that one thinks of them as fables. It is evident that in presenting them as authentic "natural history," Shaw was thinking of the underlying motives rather than the realism of the demonstration. These motives are rooted in a purely philosophic conception, for Shaw made no effort to sound the depths of the soul below the rational threshold. His comedies therefore go only a little way beyond common sense; but on this level, they have their truth; and in comparison with what ordinarily passes for truth in the theater, it is at first sight dazzling.

Maurice Valency. *The Cart and the Trumpet*
(N.Y., Oxford Univ. Pr., 1973), pp. 396–97

Bernard Shaw's sole aim in life was to make the world a better dwelling place for his fellow human beings. From *Widowers' Houses* to *Far-fetched Fables* a genuine desire for the eventual perfection of the human race transcends all of his bitterness and devastating criticism of institutions which, to his way of thinking, were deterring mankind from achieving so lofty a goal. Even his last unfinished play, *Why She Would Not*, written three months before he died, shows evidence of his life-long purpose. Although it is far too fragmentary to suggest a clear-cut theme, there is a suggestion that the harnessing of atomic energy and rapid advances in American technical improvements may eventually offer man the needed leisure to cooperate fully with the Life Force in evolving a perfect state. Perhaps, had he lived, this method would have replaced his always reluctant acceptance of revolution as the most efficient means of achieving a society wherein such leisure could be realized.

Be that as it may, it is hoped that this study will help to perpetuate an image of one of the greatest humanists of all time and that its readers will regard his Marxian romance successfully culminated in the reconciliation of Fabianism with Marxism, as further evidence of Shaw's intense search for a better world. Perhaps it was inevitable that the graphs and formulas of one of the most influential economic and political theorists of the nineteenth century should help to unleash and direct the comic genius of one of the most influential English dramatists whose life bridged the nineteenth and twentieth centuries.

Paul A. Hummert. *Bernard Shaw's Marxian Romance* (Lincoln, Univ. of Nebraska Pr., 1973), pp. 216–17

SILKIN, JON (1930–   )

Jon Silkin is an excellent young English poet who has published four volumes over there, and now Wesleyan has brought out his first volume in this country [*Poems, New and Selected*]. Since the American book contains selections from his entire corpus, including some new poems that have not appeared in book form before, it is not surprising that Mr. Silkin should appear not merely a skilled poet, but one of considerable range of tone and command of material.

I had come across what I took to be representative poems of his in anthologies, but his book, for its breadth and variety, is enormously impressive. It prevents us from labelling him a "nature poet," though many of his most beautiful successes (and I would want to place a new poem, "Brought Up With Grass," among them) stem from a deep concern with and for plants and animals and birds. Some of his themes are familar to the pastoral tradition: the unsettling fact that man is both a part of nature but painfully cut off from it. And some of his work has that radical vegetal passion that reminds us a bit of Theodore Roethke, though Mr. Silkin has a diction which is quite different, and his own. Again like Roethke, but again in a manner all his own, he is not above being funny. . . .

Anthony Hecht. *HdR*. Summer, 1966, p. 335

It is beyond the scope of this discussion to do more than point to the ubiquity, in *Amana Grass*, of such references to a webbed, veined, filamented, interlinked world—though here these images are deeply infected. I do not believe the poem to be successful. It attempts to carry more weight than its mode permits, and the poet has not solved the problems raised by his introduction of dialogue. But this is a growing-point: a long narrative poem on which Silkin has recently been engaged tackles the problems of dialogue and of social scope much more convincingly. My point is, simply, that the matrix is still, in this latest book, a viable basis for further development.

It would be wrong to follow such a short discussion with any overall judgment. Silkin is a genuine artist: an explorer, never a reproducer of his own or of other writers' acquisitions. He is often felicitous, and often clumsy or archaic; at times crystalline (in the fullest sense), at others difficult, even matted. He has, indeed, the faults of his qualities. It is as easy to point to awkwardness in such a writer as it is foolish to stop at it. His work embodies vital impulses and these are bound not to be self-protectingly tidy: they are about other business. The "open" overall form of the best poems, together with the complex internal controls that operate on syntax, word-choice and imagery, convey on a stylistic level a dominant onward thematic process, together with a minute hold on the "perpetual combinations and permutations" which that process must not sacrifice or brutalise. There is, I think, something of crucial value for the 'seventies in a poet who can conceive, utterly without mere fancifulness, of a world of "mind and matter" whose various elements conflict and yet enter into (generally symbiotic) relationships that effect both personal and social realities.

> Anne Cluysenaar. In Michael Schmidt and
> Grevel Lindop, eds., *British Poetry since 1960:*
> *A Critical Survey* (Oxford,
> Carcanet, 1972), p. 171

Out of Battle is a series of essays on poetry of war, beginning with a chapter on the romantic poets, and moving on to Hardy and Kipling, and then to the principal soldier poets of 1914–18. Mr. Silkin takes for granted that the war poets' preoccupations are also ours, and that their poems are therefore "relevant" (that dreadful, misused word). A critical consequence of this assumption is that Mr. Silkin falls into a kind of critical Whiggery, analysing poets of a now rather remote past in terms of a contemporary view of nationalism, international socialism, and war. . . .

This is one serious flaw in the book, but there are others. Perhaps most obviously, Mr. Silkin has simply taken his examples too seriously, has assumed too much complexity in relatively simple, often awkward, poems, and has brought up his critical heavy artillery where it is not appropriate.

> *TLS.* Sept. 29, 1972, p. 1131

SILLITOE, ALAN (1928–   )

That Alan Sillitoe should have had so immediate and resounding an impact upon the contemporary British novel is as much a sociological as a literary phenomenon. In fact, he is a writer of limited resources—stylistically and imaginatively—and of limited thematic and dramatic range, so that his work, though it includes three novels and two volumes of short stories . . . seems composed of episodes in a single immense fiction that gains in intensity and comprehensiveness what it lacks in scope and variety. Save for *The General*, which in superficial ways appears to deviate from the pattern of his work, Sillitoe has been, from the outset of his career, the chronicler of working-class life in industrial Nottingham—the "permanent" working class on the edges of society.

The edges of society—that metaphor for the literature of alienation—has another significance in Sillitoe's work; and it is this difference which defines his interest for us—his distinctness from other writers of his generation—and accounts in some large measure for the attention he has attracted. Sillitoe is a throwback, an old-fashioned realist—in fact, a regionalist. He has attempted to make viable as art what was called, without embarrassment or sneering, the "proletarian novel" in the 1930's. His protagonists are profoundly rooted in their class, and draw such strengths as they possess—or come finally to possess—from that identification. This is, strikingly, not the case with the typical protagonist of the contemporary "picaresque" novel: whatever the picaro's origins, whatever his relation to society, he rejects affiliation, including class affiliation. He has opted out of the system entirely. In this central respect, Sillitoe is almost a solitary figure among the writers of the post-war generation.

Saul Maloff. In Charles Shapiro, ed.,
Contemporary British Novelists (Carbondale,
Southern Illinois Univ. Pr., 1965), p. 95

[*The Death of William Posters*] is certainly, by any standards the author would accept, a failure. The first—the Country—section has excellent passages registering the cold, the hero's adaptation to country ways, the fantasy of life in the cottage of the primitive painter (his masterpiece is "Christ the Lincolnshire Poacher"). The second section—London—has a not unsubtle contrast between Frank's integrity and the endangered gift of the painter when taken up by smooth metropolitan artmen; there is also some point in making the second girl's husband nice (he loves the country and goes on three-day drunks) so that Frank doesn't have to beat him up, as he did the adman husband of the nurse. But the final—Desert—section is the best-written; the style is released with the man.

The mythical figure of Bill Posters is certainly an agreeable invention. He is the figure who at all times and everywhere "will be prosecuted." He represents the indestructible cunning and evasiveness by which a man survives among the rammel [rubbish]; admirable in some ways, his is a way of life that has to be destroyed on the way to self-fulfillment. The myth is well, if predictably handled, and it will cause little surprise that Frank in a reverie associates him with his friend's picture of Christ. Breaking free from Bill Posters, Frank attunes himself first to a Mellors-like independence (sturdily antinomian, indifferent to work as the bosses understand it, educated) and then to the sort of anguish Bill Posters, preoccupied with his incessant tricks and escapes, has no time to feel. The conversation between him and the wild and wily painter on the subject of art and pessimism, and the rejection of art in favour of action, is beneficial to the novel; but mostly Frank preaches without resistance. His hatred of the telly, the ads, the London crowd scurrying for comfort into the tube at rush hour, have imaginative vivacity; but both he and Albert the painter sink into lay figures, flatly and feebly rendered from the outside. . . .

Frank Kermode. NS. May 14, 1965, p. 765

For Alan Sillitoe's heroes, to live at all is to fight, and this belligerence defines their existence in the English working-class world that they inhabit. Their struggles, while reflecting the difficulties of individual protagonists, are primarily class conflicts echoing the author's disillusion with contemporary English society. The early Seaton-family novels, *Saturday Night and Sunday Morning* and *Key to the Door*, along with the shorter works *The Loneliness of the Long-Distance Runner* and *The Decline and Fall of Frankie Buller*, offer a series of loud and angry protests which define Sillitoe's working-class perspective, while the later novels, *The Death of William Posters* and *A Tree on Fire*, move beyond this to a more positive approach to the problems of existence raised in the earlier work. The battles of his heroes, whether they are visceral or cerebral, internal or external, idealistic or pragmatic, are all fought to achieve Sillitoe's utopian dream of a better world.

The central campaigns in Sillitoe's war are aimed at toppling a social structure built on inequality and characterized by haves and have-nots. The early fiction makes it clear: the two groups are enemies. Smith, the Borstal boy in *The Loneliness of the Long-Distance Runner,* talks of "them" and "us" and reveals that "they don't see eye to eye with us and we don't see eye to eye with them." . . . The enemies, according to Smith, are generically called "bastard-faced In-Laws" (as opposed to Out-Laws) and the species includes "pig-faced snotty-nosed dukes and ladies," "cops, governors, posh whores, pen-pushers, army officers, Members of Parliament." Arthur Seaton, the protagonist of *Saturday Night and Sunday Morning*, includes "landlords and gaffers [bosses], coppers, army, government" in the list of enemies he plans to be "fighting every day until I die."

All these groups are targets for Sillitoe, for they are the bastions of an established order which he rejects. The army is particularly singled out for attack because it is a clearly visible instrument of reactionary government.

Stanley S. Atherton. The Dalhousie Review.
Autumn, 1968, p. 324

What Sillitoe's place in British literature will ultimately be is impossible to say. In several of his novels, in his collections of short stories, and in his most recent volume of poetry, he has made an important contribution to contemporary literature.

Saturday Night and Sunday Morning remains a unique and an authentic account of working-class culture, and it captures as well the particular sense of rebellion which has characterized the youth of both England and America during the past decade. Arthur Seaton's lack of identification with the relative affluence of his age is, in fact, a criticism of the mass culture which fills the stomach but offers the mind little more than the soporific programs of television. It is a criticism as well of the repetitious, mind-dulling work which is still performed—in the age of the computer—by those on the fringes of society. Perhaps even more important is the determined individuality and sense of self-worth which characterizes Seaton. In an age of increasing emphasis upon conformity in which the conception of "mass-man" predominates, Sillitoe has created a hero who refuses to believe that he is simply the sum of the statistical information which government officials, management, labor organizers, and educationists have compiled concerning him. Arthur's milieu is not simply that of working-class man but of modern man in general— and therein lies the universal appeal of the novel.

Allen Richard Penner. Alan Sillitoe (N.Y.,
Twayne, 1972), p. 144

● **SIMPSON, N. F. (1919–   )**

If Pinter's plays transmute realism into poetic fantasy, the work of Norman Frederick Simpson is philosophical fantasy strongly based on reality. . . . Although Simpson's work is extravagant fantasy in the vein of Lewis Carroll, and is compared by the author himself to a regimental sergeant-major reciting "Jabberwocky" over and over again through a megaphone, it is nevertheless firmly based in the English class system. If Pinter's world is one of tramps and junior clerks, Simpson's is unmistakably suburban. . . .

One Way Pendulum owed its considerable success with the public to the sustained inventiveness of its nonsense and, in particular, to the brilliant parody of British legal procedure and language in the court scene, which occupies almost the whole of the second act. In fact, however, the play is far less amiable than it appears at first sight. What seems little more than a harmless essay in upside-down logic is essentially a ferocious comment on contemporary British life. . . . *One Way Pendulum* portrays a society that has become absurd because routine and tradition have turned human beings into Pavlovian automata. In that sense, Simpson is a more powerful social critic than any of the social realists. His work is proof that the Theatre of the Absurd is by no means unable to provide highly effective social comment.

Martin Esslin. *The Theatre of the Absurd*
(Garden City, N.Y., Doubleday, 1961),
pp. 217–18, 223–24

What N. F. Simpson seems to offer is an escape from problems of any sort into a dramatic world which exists in a different dimension. There is an Aristophanic quality in the absoluteness of Simpson's fantasy. In his best work he cuts all the cords connecting his characters with the mundane world, releasing them, and us, into a strangely exhilarating region of the mind, where the strictest logic operates upon the most fantastic premises.

Some of his admirers have denied him an English lineage, preferring to place him in the French tradition exemplified by Ionesco. But in Ionesco's world the fantasy is really of a different kind. Extravagant as it is, his symbolism has roots in reason. Far from escaping from intellectual judgements, we are constantly being required to exercise them. Sometimes, indeed, the moralising becomes tediously over-explicit; in *Rhinoceros* we are almost in the world of the medieval morality play.

Simpson does on occasion direct his fantasy satirically: in *The Hole*, for example, his crowd of imaginative by-standers studying a hole in the road provides him with material for a widely ranging satire on some contemporary forms of unreason. But this is not where his dramatic originality lies. Where he is unique, at least among living playwrights, is in his power to liberate us from the claims of reason. Farce, in his hands, effects what might be called a comic katharsis. We are freed for a time from all sorts of intellectual pressures, from the demands of logic, moral responsibility, and aesthetic judgement. At the same time, of course, the farce is relying on these very responses which it apparently ignores. To a person incapable of logic, Simpson's *non sequiturs* would hardly be funny, any more than his literal handling of metaphor would be fully appreciated by a literally minded person.

This is not to say that his appeal is limited to a coterie audience of intellectuals. His effects are not exclusively academic. They are, for the most part, as broadly based as radio programmes like Itma and the Goon Show which have many affinities with Simpson's plays and were immensely popular with bigger audiences than the theatre ever hopes to draw.

> Katharine J. Worth. In William A. Armstrong,
> ed., *Experimental Drama* (Bell, 1963),
> pp. 214–15

Simpson's drama is obviously a departure, a "new dimension," from other comic theatre, but his relation to other avant-garde authors is more difficult to determine. He is not a Beckett: Mr. Groomkirby stands at his five parking meters and has "got practically nothing to show for hours of waiting," yet disappointment is not Simpson's main concern. Nor is he an Ionesco; he seems to be more of an entertainer than a pioneer committed to the art of pure theatre and the projection of the inner man. Like other dramatists of the absurd, he adopts Brecht's idea of alienation, but with him it is the artificial alienation of the audience not from the action but from the characters, as all men are strangers to one another. Like these dramatists, too, he is consciously anti-philosophical. Before science challenged our concept of an objective world, men were preoccupied with formulating philosophies. . . . Since recourse to the objective world only leads to more philosophies and more paradoxes, our faith in a Meaning disintegrates. All concepts, in that they have no correspondence to the natural world, are nonsense. A concept is merely a prejudice which we have preserved by language. Yet without concepts, we cannot communicate a reality, we cannot formulate a philosophy. Conversely, without a philosophy, there is no "reality" to communicate—there is, in short, absurdity.

Simpson subtly follows these transitions throughout *One Way Pendulum*, dramatizing the absurdity of quantitatively verifiable reality and the banality of pseudo-metaphysical truth. If theatregoers more easily understood *Alice in Wonderland*, perhaps it was because Carroll was whimsically inverting reality, whereas Simpson is honestly presenting a comment upon it. In this sense, Simpson ranks among the major dramatists of the absurd, though he seems not to share much of their despair. He expects us to be entertained—but also to *miss* the poetic truths in the drama that we have missed in life as well. The "myth" of comedy has expired and the mystery of tragedy has evaporated in our hands. There is only a void left for Simpson to show us, a void which is inexplicable and ridiculous. But our laughter must not spring from the impersonal detachment or the sense of irrelevancy which we feel in farce, for the void of the absurd is not a fiction. The Groomkirbys watch us from our living-room mirrors.

Michele A. Swanson. DS. Winter, 1963,
pp. 330–31

Among the more remarkable results of the current so-called "renaissance" in the English drama has been the work of N. F. Simpson, a London schoolteacher. His four important plays are *A Resounding Tinkle, The Hole, One Way Pendulum*, and *The Cresta Run*. Like Alfred Jarry and his descendants, the 'Pataphysicians, Simpson has created a parallel reality that runs alongside our reality and clowns at it. Simpson's way of showing up what he considers the ridiculousness of the world is to create a special world in which reality is satirized by being placed in a new context. His plays, like 'Pataphysics, are a perversion of logic—the impossible carried out in accordance with the laws by which the possible exists. . . .

Simpson's first play, *A Resounding Tinkle*, seems to be an exercise in formlessness and free association which he uses as a vehicle for taking jabs at various aspects of social behavior. Like Ionesco, Simpson favors the average middle class home as a setting. He gets his humorous and satiric effects by turning the natural events of this setting topsy-turvy. . . . The only point in the play at which Simpson can be said to be really serious is in his satire on the ritual of religious services. Like Beckett, Simpson takes as the cardinal point of his *Weltanschauung* the paradox that human thought is useless. Man can know nothing, and his attempts to understand the universe and create a coherent place for himself in it, which have resulted in the elaborately and finely spun opacity of the mental network we call ritual, are consequently nothing but convoluted cerebrations continually twisting round on themselves.

This is the central theme which both Beckett and Simpson demonstrate in their plays. The difference between the two, apart from the obvious stylistic one, is in their attitude toward it. Beckett's despair is hidden under a sardonic objectivity and a deliberate choice of laconic and allusive speech patterns. Simpson's attitude, on the other hand, is one of hair-clutching hilarity. To him the world is not so much depressing as ridiculous—and therefore to be laughed at. The paradox renders the world so ridiculous to Simpson that he can express his feelings only in the "beyond realm" of nonsense. He becomes serious only infrequently, whereas Beckett does precisely the opposite: he lights the prevailing gloom with occasional flashes of ribald vaudeville humor.

When Simpson does get serious it is some time before the audience realizes it. The seriousness emerges slowly from the torrent of nonsense, most of which is extremely funny but hardly germane either to the philosophy or to the plot of the play. . . .

> George E. Wellwarth. *The Theatre of Protest
> and Paradox*, rev. ed. (N.Y., New York
> Univ. Pr., 1971), pp. 243–45

SITWELL, EDITH (1887–1964)

If ever a poet's personality affected the critical climate in which her work was considered, that poet was Edith Sitwell.

To anyone who had read her brother's autobiography, or who had heard Dame Edith talk about her upbringing, it was perfectly evident that the ornate flamboyance of her dress and appearance and the extraordinary manner of her public pronouncements were easily traceable to a very obvious inferiority complex. She was, in private, unsure of herself—and although we are all, I suppose, vulnerable to criticism where our work is concerned (and a poet *is* his work), she was more vulnerable than most, particularly to the personal criticism to which she was often subjected.

But critics very rarely consider poetry apart from personality where their contemporaries are concerned, and too many living critics have been blinded by "the enormous and gold-rayed rustling sun." It is true that Dame Edith's last years were made, all too often, sad by sometimes vicious attacks upon her. It was even suggested, in the month before her death, that she was incapable of being moved by the condition of others, which was to say that her poetry was insincere. She may indeed have been guilty of posturing in her public appearances and even in her writing on prosody; but poetry, as she said, was a kind of religion with her, and she was always and utterly true to her own conception of it. It is impossible to have too low an opinion of those ignorant critics whose lack of perception led them to think otherwise.

It is, however, true that it is difficult to disconnect the poet from her poetry: and for those who met her even occasionally, the difficulty is more subtle. When one's knowledge of her kindly patronage, her encouragement of numberless other writers, her practical support of the needy (often personally unknown to her), is joined to recollection of one of the most lovable and kindly human beings one has ever met, it is all too easy to overlook the faults in her work, and to take the will for the deed. . . .

One must I think dismiss her prose work as of far less value than the poems. She disliked writing prose, although some of her prose is good: there are passages in *Fanfare for Elizabeth*, particularly, which are (in a rather selfconscious manner) very finely wrought; *Pope*, although supplanted by later scholarship, contains some admirable complimentary passages; and there is some very witty occasional journalism. . . .

But her critical writing—both in *Aspects of Modern Poetry* and in the Forewords and Introductions and Notes on her own poetry—is frequently laboured and tiresome. It is again perfectly obvious that it was her basic lack of confidence in herself as a poet that forced her into those public explanations of her technique, her constant reiteration of her own value as a prosodist. Her long Introductions to the Penguin selection and to her *Collected Poems* were irrelevant to the poetry in them: the pages of explanation contributed nothing to one's enjoyment of her work, and convinced no-one of its value who was otherwise disposed. . . .

She was, however, a great anthologist—both of poetry and prose: her notes on Shakespeare, and on poetry in general, are, where they consist of a montage of apposite quotations, extremely valuable.

Derek Parker. *PoetryR*. Spring, 1965,
pp. 18–19

Taken Care Of, the autobiography of Edith Sitwell, would seem to be of clinical interest only (except to gossips) as a record of the largely paranoic ramblings of a poor old woman blighted by a most horrible childhood, if it did not contain a few pages that show the one peculiar good that managed to develop in this warped being.

Edith Sitwell appears to me to have been a monster, in a quite strict sense—"any plant or animal of abnormal shape or structure, as one greatly malformed or lacking some parts." But her ability to distinguish the affective properties of verbal sounds—the logic of melopoeia—was developed to a most extraordinary degree. This faculty is in itself a valuable phenomenon, and she was able to transmit its findings to her readers in some of her poems and in much of her critical writing, such as *A Poet's Notebook, A Notebook on William Shakespeare*, a book on Pope, some of her notes for *The Atlantic Book of British and American Poetry*, etc. But an autobiography asks the reader to look at the author as a human being; and it is hideous, shocking, painful, to witness the degree to which this one gift of hers was unaccompanied by any proportionate presence of other related properties. . . .

The human poverty self-revealed in all but a few pages of *Taken Care Of* does, after all, throw light on an aspect of her work. Her later poems, with their tragic themes, obsessive symbols and seemingly compassionate point of view, have never moved me, as did the light, crisp early work—which she herself describes precisely as showing in some poems, "a violent exhilaration, [in others] a veiled melancholy, a sadness masked by gaiety." I see now—reading her words of cheap contempt for anyone who has criticized her, of vulgar self-praise, her passages of heavy sarcasm (in the style of Mrs. Wilfer in *Our Mutual Friend*)—that though she also had, in her fierce and loyal affection for a few persons and for many books, moments when she did envision "the warmth of love that makes all men brothers" (she is alluding to her wartime poems), it must have remained largely a theoretical experience, which was not only constantly at variance with the spite and pettiness in her but was also a projection that helped prevent her from acknowledgment of that spite. All the world's evil comes from "them"; "they" are the crucifiers; Edith Sitwell identifies consistently with the poor, the long-suffering, the crucified. It is this that, quite naturally, makes the later poems seem false, lacking in the very depth they seem to claim so fervently for themselves. They are overextended, and any such overextension inevitably shows up in the language and rhythm, the very substance, of a poem.

Denise Levertov. Nation. June 7, 1965,
pp. 618–19

From the time [Edith Sitwell] wrote *Gold Coast Customs* there must have been a strong urge to take this step [conversion to Roman Catholicism]. In that poem she had for the first time fully and plainly realised a terrible range and depth of the truths she had been setting out in her earlier poems. She brought her intuitions sharply and fiercely down to earth; and thus for the first time a definitive statement of all that was implied by the alienating process of bourgeois society entered our poetry. A great deal of this realisation came through the workings of her own mind in the creation of her poems, and through her swift response to Swift and Blake and to the tradition of Baudelaire and Rimbaud. I do not think that any directly political writings had affected her. The 1844 Manuscripts of Marx had not yet appeared in Moscow in their difficult German text. She had however read a good deal of Hegel and the German Nature-Philosophers. She told me that the originating image of the *Gold Coast Customs* was the spectacle of some Hunger Marchers led by a blackened man who was jestingly acting the part of a skeleton or death figure; she felt that she was looking at a modern Dance of Death, and the fused image of London and the Gold Coast, expressing the final deprivation and dehumanisation of man, was born in her mind. . . .

Her thinking, as I have stressed, was emotional and intuitive rather than political and intellectual in the narrow sense. She was much taken up with the idea of revolutionary fires consuming a rotten society and clearing the earth for a better and cleaner growth; but always thought of the outbreak of fire as a sort of spontaneous combustion from below —something inevitable and finally necessary for the assertion of justice in the universe, but blindly violent and frightening. [1968]

Jack Lindsay. *Meetings with Poets* (N.Y.,
Ungar, 1969), pp. 79–80

Edith Sitwell's criticism . . . is not all splenetic expression of a highly eccentric taste. To those who associate only the outrageous with her and her poetry it will be a surprise to discover in her criticism a continual concern for form and a unified texture of language. An examination of her critical work reveals a duality of temperament: there is indeed the one that might be called her "way" of passionate individualism, but it is found to be joined with an abiding interest in the organic discipline of art.

Especially significant in the exposition of the disciplined esthetic that can be found in Sitwell's criticism is her frequent and unique usage of "shadow" as a term to explicate certain purposive relationships within a poem. This term is prominent in her explication of what she calls the "texture" of a poem: embodying for her the essence of interconnection, the term "shadow" clearly reveals her commitment to an organic theory of poetry, a commitment further confirmed by her many appreciative references to Coleridge. . . .

In discussing the meaning of Edith Sitwell's poetry no one has disputed the symbolist function of her work. Yet, while many symbols— Ape, Lion, Dust, Sun, Bone are prominent ones—have been adduced as evidence of her role as a symbolist, no comment has appeared on "shadow." It is, however, not only a term of Sitwell's critical vocabulary but (with its cognate "shade") even more importantly also a persistently recurring image from her earliest to her last poetry. The image of "shadow" holds a central position in the symbolist significance of her work because it embodies in its implications of interconnection all the order that her critical and poetic visions discover.

James Brophy. *Edith Sitwell: The Symbolist Order* (Carbondale, Southern Illinois Univ. Pr., 1968), pp. xiv–xvi

SITWELL, OSBERT (1892–1969)

It is, I think, a matter of fairly general agreement among Osbert Sitwell's admirers that they value him, and believe he has made his distinct contribution to the literature of his time, as a writer of prose; and that his prose *œuvre* reaches its culmination in the unique, five-volume masterpiece of his autobiography, *Left Hand, Right Hand!*

Nevertheless, he cannot be ignored as a poet. It was with poetry that he began his career . . . and this was not merely the characteristic start of an imaginative young man who was soon after to opt for fiction or biography or criticism. Osbert Sitwell's poetic production stretches from 1916 over nearly half a century, and the volume of *Selected Poems*, published in 1943 many years before he had finished writing verse, shows how varied his achievement had already been.

The corpus of original poetry (there are no translations or adaptations from the work of others) can, very roughly, be divided into three compartments or categories. There are, first of all, the satires, including the early anti-war poems, which may be viewed as an extension in verse of the pursuit of the "Golden Horde" and the various other quarry of his indignation and contempt which he hunted with such ruthless zeal (and obvious enjoyment) in his novels and stories. Then there are what one might describe as the general poems, some of them of great beauty, which include such linked series of lyrics as *Winter the Huntsman* and *Out of the Flame*, where the mood is now sombre and prophetic, now festive and full of imaginative colour, now elegiac and reflective. Finally, there are the "poetic portraits," which first made their appearance in *England Reclaimed* in 1926. . . . They are for the most part written in a relaxed recitative style, full of shrewd and humorous observations, with a descriptive vigour and a nostalgic music all their own.

They are perhaps not quite poetry in the strictest sense, but they are certainly more than light verse. It is difficult not to be captivated by them, and even to feel that they strike an entirely original and memorable note in the literature of our time.

John Lehmann. *A Nest of Tigers: Edith,*
Osbert and Sacheverell Sitwell in Their Times
(Boston, Little, Brown, 1968), pp. 155–56

SITWELL, SACHEVERELL (1897–   )

It is thirty years since Duckworth published the *Collected Poems* of Sacheverell Sitwell; but even in 1936 they formed a fat book of nearly six hundred pages of fairly small print. Since then the author has published only the occasional poem privately or in magazines—not more than half a dozen or so. That is not because he has stopped writing them; there exist in manuscript more than three hundred, and it is to be hoped that before long he will be persuaded to publish a selection in book form.

Of the three famous writing members of the Sitwell family, his name, and possibly his work, is much less well known than that of Osbert or Edith yet he is in many ways a more interesting writer than either. His range is enormous. . . .

There are none of the complexities that are to be found in the work of Eliot or Pound. He does not use so exacting a shorthand as these two poets; his style is more expansive, his manner more discursive. Where the knowledge intrudes is in the feeling the reader often has of the poet choosing the subject on which to write, rather than allowing the subject to impose itself on his imagination and force its utterance through an emotional necessity. This would have seemed less of a criticism in the nineteenth century, for the professional man of letters, in which the poet was allowed, was *supposed* to be engaged in the production of art as a working activity. Although it was required that the god should speak to him he was not allowed to sit back and wait hopefully for the miraculous voice. That Sacheverell Sitwell has worked is evident in the list of no less than seventy-seven books given at the front of the first volume (the second has not yet appeared) of *Journey to the Ends of Time*. The sheer professionalism is unnerving. But has the god spoken? Undoubtedly, yes.

John Smith. *PoetryR*. Summer, 1967, p. 121

Surveying the whole of Sacheverell Sitwell's poetic *œuvre* (though it is only partially possible today owing to the very large number of poems he has refused to publish), a hostile critic might say that his extraordinary facility for mellifluous verse-making has led him to a constant dilution of his inspiration, in which the intellectual muscles are too relaxed to produce that concentration of thought, wit and imaginative vision that is the especial province of poetry. . . .

Now I think I would find it difficult to refute this criticism in reference to the mass of short lyrical pieces which he has grouped together under the title of *Hortus Conclusus*. Their subjects are the flowers and fruits of garden and the wild countryside immediately surrounding a cultivated garden, with the figures of mythology introduced. Rarely does one feel the heart engaged. . . .

The greater part of Sacheverell Sitwell's poetry has been inspired, not by direct personal experience but by the emotions and reflections aroused by the contemplation of works of art. It is his peculiar idiosyncrasy and gift; where one poet might be impelled to write by deeply stirring experiences in his own life, or by the sympathetic hearing of the experiences of others—and I think most of English poetry lies in these two categories—Sacheverell's poetic temperament is responsive above all to great music, dancing, works of painting and sculpture, and literary masterpieces of the past. It is important to avoid prejudice here; whatever one's personal preference may be, it is possible to recognise legitimate inspiration in such themes.

John Lehmann. *A Nest of Tigers: Edith,*
Osbert and Sacheverell Sitwell in Their Times
(Boston, Little, Brown, 1968), pp. 164–66

In his precocious youth, at the age of twenty, Sacheverell Sitwell embarked on his first autobiography, *All Summer in a Day*. It was not the usual self-portrait in narrative terms though even then he felt that "without undue flattery to my twenty years of conscious experience . . . these have yielded tangible and personal memories enough for more than one volume did I chose to write the conventional autobiography." Instead he sub-titled the book "An Autobiographical Fantasia," and used it as a medium to "dangle in the light for a few minutes . . . one or two ghosts from my cupboard," figures like his tutor Colonel Fantock, or Miss Morgan, the diminutive creator of "Cloisonné" pottery, and other quaint characters from his early years in Scarborough.

Now, at the age of seventy-five, Sir Sacheverell has embarked on another self-portrait [*For Want of the Golden City*]. Or, at least, that is what his publisher calls it, for it is no more a straightforward narrative autobiography than the earlier work, in spite of the fact that in the intervening half-century he has visited almost every temperate and tropical country on the face of the earth except southern India and the South Seas, and has met almost all his contemporaries who were worth knowing. Indeed, in the opening sentence of the one avowedly personal section of the book, "Persona Perturbata," he declares that he would consider it ignoble to expose himself in any way by entering into details of personal sadnesses or disappointments, or even describing personal triumphs. The cure for the first two of these, he considers, is to be found in reading rather than writing about them. A refreshing viewpoint in an age which believes that Byronic overexposure is exactly the right treatment for a bleeding heart. Now, in what he calls "middle age or something more depressing," the time has arrived, he feels, "to offer thanks for having lived and been alive" rather than to dwell on such matters as the "terrible time in our family history" which has had such a cathartic effect on his brother and sister and himself. *For Want of the Golden City* therefore has little or nothing in common with his brother's highly successful five-volume autobiography.

To describe what the book is about, however, is less easy. Chiefly, it is a series of meditations on things which have interested the author, on places he has visited and sometimes about those rare ones he has never seen, on flowers and trees, and the past, the past of curious minor incidents rather than the past of the history books; though at one point he admits with shame that, as a boy, he was "frightened by anything that was old." There is a good deal, too, about the present, especially about the present as it differs from the past, and the appalling destruction of the environment due to the vast increase in population. Some of this is little more than "regretting the Bourbons," his one-time recreation in *Who's Who*. But there is very little about the author himself. "I am no longer interested in myself," he writes, belying the Sitwells' reputation for egocentricity.

TLS. Aug. 10, 1973, p. 920

SMITH, STEVIE (1902–1971)

It may be an indication of Stevie Smith's rapidly growing popularity as a poet and her ability to reach all sections of the public, at one level or another, that some of the younger poets, impressed by what she can achieve with her apparent facetiousness of manner, and emboldened, perhaps, by her success, are attempting to adopt her style—with somewhat disastrous results, let it be said. For of all the poets writing today Stevie Smith is one of the most original and certainly the most inimitable.

Her latest volume, *The Frog Prince*, consists of sixty-nine new poems and a selection from her previous volumes, supported by her typically zany drawings. Those who have acquired the taste for Stevie Smith will not be disappointed; they will find fresh specimens to add to their collections of extraordinary characters. . . .

Those who may not have had the complex experience of reading Stevie Smith are advised to start with *The Frog Prince*, for here they will find poetry of genuine merit quite unlike anything they can have seen or heard before. A childlike vision combined with maturity of outlook, a sense of compassion intermixed with a wry sense of humor, an acute feeling for humanity underlying the cold appraisal of the world in which we live, go to the making of these poems.

Howard Sergeant. *PoetryR*. Spring, 1967,
pp. 48–49

These adjectives, or some of them, could be applied to Stevie Smith's own poetry: severe, austere, simple, bracing, impersonal. If "this is truly Greek, and what the Greek is," then Stevie Smith is somewhat Greek. If to be classical is not to be (in a number of senses of that peculiar adjective) romantic, then she is in some senses classical. Like these adjectives, she is equivocal, not half so simple as she seems. . . .

If classicism is avoidance of the romantic, then one can adduce her best-known because most obvious attributes: the perverse, off-rhyming (she goes out of her way to rhyme impurely, but at other times thumps down on the most obvious if pure rhyme), the inevitably comic and deflatory effect of rhyming English words with French, and the bathos which W. McGonagall achieved effortlessly but she had to work for. . . .

In its essence Stevie Smith's poetry is uncluttered, and hence must leave out, for instance, the reservations and modifications and clarifications which a denser and slower-moving writing admits. But it leaves out what it could not accommodate and still be the kind of poetry it is: and that is all it leaves out.

D. J. Enright. *Enc*. June, 1971, pp. 53–54, 57

Florence Margaret Smith came by the more exotic name of Stevie as a side effect of her smallness. Her family is reported to have nicknamed her after the jockey Steve Donoghue, small even by the exacting standards of his profession. She was born in Hull in 1902, where her father was a shipping agent, who deserted the family for the sea. Her mother took Stevie and her sister to London three years later, and she was to live the rest of her life in the same house in Palmers Green. . . .

Stevie Smith's family context and private milieu are so important that it is necessary to get them straight from the beginning. Her poetry is continuously drawn from a setting of decaying gentility and a recognition of her own experience of Englishness. Personal loves and enmities expressed in her work issue starkly from her early experiences of domestic unhappiness; there is a feeling of unforgivingness. . . .

Stevie Smith is a problem poet to the critic. She encourages him to be too earnest, or too lax. Verse narratives no longer appeal to the critical or poetical imagination as they used to: the repeated poems of religious doubt, the to-die or not-to-die vacillations (not drowning but waving, it could be called), upper crust loneliness or malefaction, the despairs of the plain-faced, can be tedious at their worst. There is a great deal of moral captioning; many of her poems are as much "the higher doodling" as her drawings. But an interesting intelligence is engaged in her work—and it is a literary intelligence as much as the feeling that came from her despair: feminine, powerful, and far from inconsiderable. Too many people have read only the surface in which she disguised it. And if there are not true, plain love poems, no sonnets, no baroque cultural greetings sent out across the centuries, no masterful samples of orthodox iambic pentameter, it is because she was inscrutably loyal to her inner life and the styles she used to express it. Her career is a moving record of dedication, faithful to no fashion, astute and quirky perhaps, but unflinchingly honest.

TLS. July 14, 1972, p. 820

SNOW, C. P. (1905–   )

The characters in C. P. Snow's fiction operate according to a sensible plan or try to impose upon their world what they assume is a sensible plan. Unable to conceive of man's arrangements for himself as being so much confusion and chaos, Snow accepts what man has wrought as a form of order, not disorder, as pattern and scheme, not as accident or muddle. He sees the world as basically a projection of man's rationality, not as a manifestation of man's confusion and irrationality. He claims, further, that man's struggle with his self has been won—at least in part.

Neither Snow nor his characters would agree that man's arrangements are impermanent, a consequence of his fears, inadequate for happiness, and shot through with uncontrollable destructiveness. He eliminates soul-searching anxiety, or else submerges it deeply beneath his characters' public personality. . . .

Snow's view, acceptable as it may appear to those who accept it, is also very sad. For it is untrue and impossible, historically untrue and psychologically impossible. Men are not like this, have never been like this, and, short of being produced in test tubes, will never be like this. It's all a wishful dream—part of the illusions man holds about certain things so that he can continue to accommodate rather than lose hope in his kind. Such is the code of behavior that Snow's functionaries follow as they define England's role in the cosmos. The code is an illusion, just as it was in the nineteenth century. In the Victorian era, a "code" was derived to uphold a notion of progress and to disguise the fact that the Industrial Revolution might be plundering rather than aiding the English working class. The code, such as it is, is no more than a set of rules temporarily accepted, rules which exist to be broken as each man tries to fulfill personal ambitions and personal needs. Must we be reminded of this?

Frederick R. Karl. In Charles Shapiro, ed.,
Contemporary British Novelists (Carbondale,
Southern Illinois Univ. Pr., 1965), pp. 114–15

Not since Disraeli has a popular, political-minded novelist been so intimately involved with the actual exercise of power. Not since H. G. Wells has a popular, social-minded novelist known so much at first hand about science. For nearly twenty years before 1958, Snow had been in an ideal position to carry out in his fiction the program defined in "The Two Cultures." By bringing together two kinds of imagination which he had himself experienced, he could enable scientists and literary men to appreciate each other, and the lay public to appreciate both. He could dramatize for his readers the struggle toward those social goods which he condemned the major writers of his century for betraying.

But if we—by act of will—forget temporarily about "The Two Cultures" and read carefully through Snow's fiction to see what actually occurs there, we find it almost totally inconsistent with what we had been led to expect.

In all of C. P. Snow's novels taken together there is less concrete evidence of how the scientific mind works and how its methods and discoveries differ from those of the literary man or philosopher or theologian than we could find in almost any article in any issue of *Nature* or *Scientific American*. There is simply no comparison, in this respect, between his work and that of Aldous Huxley or of H. G. Wells himself.

Robert Gorham Davis. *C. P. Snow* (N.Y.,
Columbia Univ. Pr., 1965), p. 5

In opposing the experimental writers, Snow has frequently come out against "poetic" fiction and verbal innovation; his own fiction shows, perhaps, too little concern with individual words and concentrates more on the plot. Despite the fact that the use of a strong plot line had never fallen into disuse among popular writers of fiction, Snow was one of the first postexperimental writers to reassert the value of the plot, make his verbal texture subservient to the plot, and justify this shift of emphasis by actively opposing (rather than merely ignoring) those experimental writers who had deemphasized the value of the plot in their works.

Snow has succeeded, both with his criticism and with his fiction, in making the critical climate in England more receptive to his own type of realism. His novels represent a new phenomenon in that they deal with modern technical innovations, such as the development of the atomic bomb; but the language and style he uses in describing these phenomena are derived from the Victorian and Edwardian novelists. . . .

Snow's anti-existential, socially oriented point of view is as popular in communistic countries as it is in the West; he is one of the few contemporary writers who sells well both in the United States and in Russia. This is to be expected: Snow's hero is the bureaucratic man, and by romanticizing the roles of people in essentially mundane occupations Snow has endeared himself to readers in the countries with the largest bureaucracies, regardless of their political point of view. His heroes engage in no heroic quests; they seek good incomes, but not fortunes; instead of fame they are happy with a bit of official recognition; if they have any really great ambition, it is to be able to control their fellow men. People like to read about themselves: the professional, middle-class people Snow writes about are also his greatest readers. They, like Lewis Eliot, are happy in their professions, self-satisfied because of their incomes, and totally convinced of their value to the community. Their chief fault is similar to Lewis Eliot's: an unwillingness to fight against, or even to recognize, their own essential mediocrity.

Rubin Rabinovitz. *The Reaction against
Experiment in the English Novel,
1950–1960* (N.Y., Columbia Univ. Pr., 1967),
pp. 135–36, 165

The series [*Strangers and Brothers*] as a whole is not quite like any other work of fiction that I can think of. Snow has sometimes been criticized for using a Victorian technique: the heavy reliance on exposition, the flavorless chapter headings, the rather flat style. In his pamphlet on Snow in the Columbia Essays on Modern Novelists,

Robert Gorham Davis writes: "Stylistically, imaginatively, and mimetically, Snow's resources as a novelist are limited, but he husbands them carefully and employs them with conscious skill." Both parts of this statement are true, and the second part seems to me at least as important as the first. Snow has known better than most writers what he could do and what he couldn't, and the techniques he employs are right for both his materials and his gifts.

The pessimism Snow reveals in his Westminster address and in *The Sleep of Reason* is significant because he has seemed on the whole a cheery fellow. Although he has never denied, and has often shown, man's capacity for evil, he has been an optimist by temperament and has given the impression that in the long run good would triumph. He has granted that the human condition is tragic in essence, but he has concentrated on the remediable evils. Like any other post-Freudian, he has been compelled to recognize the limitations of reason, but he has believed that reason was our strongest weapon and in the long run perhaps a sufficient one.

As the title suggests, it is the problem of reason that most engages him in his tenth novel. The epigraph is from Goya's title for an etching: "The sleep of reason brings forth monsters." The ugliest monsters in the book are, of course, the two women who torture and kill a child for fun. Snow's response to these monstrosities is subtler than Lady Snow's response to the Moors murders. Whereas she calls for an end to permissiveness, an avowed war on iniquity, curbs on the circulation of books in praise of cruelty and perversion, and other such measures, he sadly reflects on what he has learned about the nature of man and his prospects for the future.

The somber note he strikes reminds us that he has never been so blithely cheerful as some of his critics have maintained. After all, the title he chose for the first novel in the series and for the series as a whole suggests that, if it is true that all men are brothers, it is equally true that all men are strangers. Whatever his shortcomings, his gifts are many, and never have they been displayed more effectively than in this novel. It will be a long time before we can judge the series as a whole even after it is finished, but there is no doubt that *The Sleep of Reason* is both an exciting and a thoughtful novel.

Granville Hicks. *Sat.* Jan. 11, 1969, p. 79

Capping as it does a fifty-year panorama of the crises of an individual, his country, and his world, *Last Things* remains healthily and hopefully open-ended, uncluttered with day-of-judgment visions. Snow, a perennial reconstructionist, fights shy of warnings of disintegrating values such as those in Hermann Broch's *Sleepwalkers* trilogy, and he is wary of the "after me the deluge" cry sounded by Zola in *La Débâcle*. Unlike Soames Forsyte of Galsworthy's *A Modern Comedy*, Eliot sings no swan song for an age that has turbulently rushed by, nor does he retreat, like Proust's Marcel, into esthetics because he cannot face realities. Snow writes about decay only as one part of change; growth is another, and both are part of the historic process.

To history, the final arbiter, C. P. Snow looks to supply the last word on "last things," and to his enlightened men of good will—men who, like himself, are thinkers before they are artists—to grapple and wrestle with the inevitable processes of change. One would like to feel, though it daily grows more difficult, that Snow is not too optimistic with too little cause. Should time prove his optimism justified, however, one may uncover between the lines of his dutifully marching prose more truths than in all the crackling rhetoric of handbooks by Che or Mao, and as many provocative insights as in the anti-utopian novels of Aldous Huxley, George Orwell, Anthony Burgess, or Yevgeny Zamyatin.

In any event, Snow will be remembered, I think, for giving us in the Lewis Eliots of our century possible models of privileged intellect worthy of emulation. He will also be remembered for nearly persuading us that every time is a "time of hope," but mainly for setting out those monolithic foundations of morality and conscience upon which men can build, not as strangers but as brothers.

Robert K. Morris. *Sat.* Aug. 22, 1970, p. 55

There is a strong sense, in C. P. Snow's novels, of circles overlapping, of year inextricably linking up with year, of old places trodden over with fresh footprints. The *Strangers and Brothers* sequence hovers back and forth in setting and time, so that even such a novel as *The Masters,* which covers events in only one year, casts its backward glances, and itself foreshadows its successors. What Anthony Powell does with a cool and almost disdainful use of coincidence in *The Music of Time,* Snow achieves more circuitously and, indeed, more crudely.

Strangers and Brothers is over. Yet *The Malcontents*, with a little juggling, can be seen as part of that familiar world. The place is recognizably the same nameless Midlands town (in fact Leicester) from which Lewis Eliot first emerges in 1914 in *Time of Hope*. The book opens in a topographical way that would not have surprised Trollope or Hardy, and it is a shock to find, after a few pages, that the year is 1970, so steady and leisurely is the comfortably ruminative Snow manner. . . .

As a fictional study of group motives, it leaves too many psychological questions unexplored, or even unasked. Snow is always serious, humane and concerned. What is missing, here as elsewhere in his novels, is an essential grip on so much that makes people various, complex and mysterious, and any real imaginative apprehension of anything beyond the decencies and the conventions.

Anthony Thwaite. *NYT*. May 7, 1972, p. 5

C. P. Snow is one of those novelists whom one feels one can't do without; and yet there are times when, disturbed again before his books, one wonders why. The critics have not, on the whole, been very kind to him, and it is not hard to see why he should come in for a good deal of critical assault. He has made his peculiar mixture of the reasonable, neo-scientific, positivistic literary imagination into a kind of test case, a radical opposite to literary despair; and precisely because he has done that his weaknesses have a kind of emblematic significance.

One weakness in particular is disturbing, not only because it tends to get worse from book to book, but because it has importance for the metaphoric status he has acquired: it is the tendency imaginatively to let things slide, to leave unsaid and even worse unfelt, to gesture at the events of the book without dramatizing, shaping, feeling into, making human. It is matched by a want of imagination of another kind, by a deliberate narrowing of the human scale—as if life has all its order in relation to the particular worlds one happens to live in now, and to no other life, and can be summed up on that evidence; as if the world ages as one ages, significantly sympathizes with oneself, can be amended by oneself, and as if all the important places of human action and feeling are the places one frequents, the places within a convenient taxi ride or train journey; as if, finally, the liberal reasonableness represented by the author and his fictional surrogate, Lewis Eliot, can cope with the bulk of human experience, and faces only one imponderable obstacle, that of death.

But against that impression of Snow there is much to set, though setting it requires something like personal testimony. For there are few contemporary writers who have managed, as Snow has, to give us the dense feel of contemporary social experience, and in so doing to make it a matter of history, few who have identified our basic realities, recognitions, moral dilemmas and landscapes, and then drawn these into the order of time, of changing national and local event, of shifting temper and feel. His work recreates recognizable experience almost as an act of memory, not the significant, vividly recreative yet aesthetic Proustian memory to which he has himself drawn a comparison, but a much more public, communal, shared type of memory. He appeals, not as Proust does, to the surprise of psychological truth, but to the more muted shock of having set before one the detail of a known or very knowable world.

Malcolm Bradbury. *Possibilities* (Oxford
Univ. Pr., 1973), pp. 201–2

SPARK, MURIEL (1918–   )

There are . . . as I see it, two high points to date in the output of [Spark,] this brilliant and unconventional writer. Each stands out from among works related to it but lesser in overall quality and effectiveness. *Memento Mori* is the more objective of the two, a Swiftian vision of the world which overshadows even such ingenious works as its predecessors *Robinson* and *The Comforters. The Prime of Miss Jean Brodie* restates the problems of these earlier books in somewhat more subjective terms. Here the Spark persona finds herself the absolute center of the novel.

There is no indication, however, that these two books, fine as they are, have succeeded in resolving what I believe to be the conflict that called them into being: the fundamental duality of Muriel Spark's worldview. There is in fact every reason to believe that Mrs. Spark's private war continues in unabated violence, and may shortly necessitate from her another gesture of dazzling virtuosity, perhaps this time a novel with an American setting. For unlike her great spiritual ancestor, she does not intend to stick pretty much to London, the British country-side, or to Bath. We are fortunate in this: if our time has brought forth new confusions, it has give us the writers to deal with them: new Jane Austens for new realities.

Charles Alva Hoyt. In Charles Shapiro, ed.,
Contemporary British Novelists (Carbondale,
Southern Illinois Univ. Pr., 1965), p. 143

Perhaps because I first read Muriel Spark merely for the sake of reading, perhaps because I read her books in odd foreign parts where they had been untimely ripped from their dust-covers and hence bore no biographical data, I did not realise that she was a Catholic Novelist. The one thing that everybody knew about this author lay unknown to me. But this deficiency is now supplied, and I can see that the novels could be held to bear out the dust-cover's directions: they have Catholics in them, and a good deal of reference to Catholic doctrine. Mrs. Spark's new novel, *The Mandelbaum Gate*, would itself suggest quite strongly, by its detailed and sometimes "loving" descriptions of the Holy Land, that its author could well be a practising Christian, or else a practising archaeologist, or (though less likely) a botanist with a particular interest in wild-flower seed-dispersion. And its characters might seem to indicate that their author is a Christian, or else a Moslem, an Israeli, or an Arab, a diplomat, or a spy—or even, come to that, possibly a novelist.

Not that I wish to take Mrs. Spark's faith—that "beautiful and dangerous gift"—away from her. On the contrary. But there is a difference between a Catholic who writes novels and a Catholic Novelist. This latter term evokes, even if it shouldn't, an unholy mixture of the Claudelic, the Mauriacesque and the Greenean, a browbeating either direct or indirect, a stifling odour of incense or of fallen sweat or of both. Mrs. Spark's writing seems to me altogether dissimilar: even a lapsed Wesleyan can approach her without too painful a sense of intimidation or exclusion. Yet most discussion in print of Mrs. Spark's work centres on her Catholicism—and rarely gets far away from it. In an otherwise subtle article appearing in this journal on the publication of *The Girls of Slender Means*, Frank Kermode described her as "an unremittingly Catholic novelist"—unremitting? Mrs. Spark?—while Granville Hicks has faintly deplored her as "a gloomy Catholic, like Graham Greene and Flannery O'Connor, more concerned with the evil of man than with the goodness of God." Far from gloomy, I would even have thought her positively funny, and—though admittedly this new novel lends one more conviction on the point than might otherwise have been felt—concerned with the evil of man no more than is to be expected in a fair-minded though shrewd observer of humanity.

D. J. Enright. *NS.* Oct. 15, 1965, p. 563

The Transfiguration of the Commonplace. That is the title of pig-eyed Sister Helena's famous treatise in *The Prime of Miss Jean Brodie*; it is also an appropriate description of the fictive method of Muriel Spark.

Approaching the novel with all the suspicions of a poet accosting an alien, and perhaps inferior, medium, Miss Spark uses a dazzling assortment of techniques to accomplish in prose what she had first attempted in verse: to create by cutting through the barriers of over-used language and situation a sense of reality true to experience, an imaginative extension of the world, a lie that shows us things as they are —a supreme fiction.

But although it admits of endless variation, her apparently complex method is simple. She uses a momentous, sometimes supernatural event violently to shift perspective and reveal the bizarre underpinnings of the superficially conventional. The agent of transfiguration differs from novel to novel; a character's involvement in the process of writing the novel of which she is part; an airplane crash on a lonely island; a series of phone calls reminding the elderly recipients that they soon must die; a diabolical intruder descending upon a working-class community; the trial of a medium for fraudulent conversion; the betrayal of a charismatic schoolteacher by her most trusted disciple; a catastrophic fire at a boardinghouse for single girls; a forbidden pilgrimage to the Holy Land. Each time, the cataclysmic event has the same effect. It forces the reexamination of circumstances long since taken for granted; it forces the protagonists to confront the terms of their existence.

Muriel Spark was born in Edinburgh in 1918. Her father Jewish, her mother Presbyterian, she was educated in the latter faith, an unlikely beginning for one of England's more important contemporary Catholic writers. Like Joyce's feelings for dear, dirty Dublin, Miss Spark's feelings for the city of her birth are ambivalent. . . .

The long title poem [in *The Fanfarlo, and Other Verse*] is a "symbolist ballad" based on some lines in Baudelaire's short story "La Fanfarlo." Narrative and allegorical, the poem anticipates the modes with which Miss Spark will ultimately be most comfortable. It also develops one of her novels' most persistent themes: the inadequacy of a self-indulgent approach to experience. The romantic, Samuel Cramer, in No-Man's Sanitarium, had in life projected his self upon the world; with Dantesque appropriateness, Death offers him neither Heaven nor Hell, either of which would be acceptable, but Limbo, the nonbeing he thoroughly fears. For Miss Spark, as for Hulme and Eliot, it is form, both in art and in life, that brings out what is decent in man. Without strict controls based outside the individual, art disintegrates, life becomes meaningless in the face of death.

Ultimately, the poems of this volume are of limited success, demonstrating that without concentrated, richly suggestive language, even sharp wit and a fine ear for rhythms may not be sufficient. For Miss Spark, the communication of experience is largely dependent on an intricate use of structure and pattern more appropriate to the novel.

Karl Malkoff. *Muriel Spark* (N.Y., Columbia
Univ. Pr., 1968), pp. 3–5

Muriel Spark has always been an interesting, and a very amusing, novelist; but observers of her recent work will have noticed that something fresh has been happening with her—she is turning into a very high stylist indeed. A new authority has come into her work, in the form of great tactical precision and a growingly high-handed manner both with her readers and her characters; and from *The Public Image* (1968) on she has given herself over to works in the novella form, very tight, very clear, works in which every compositional decision and every compositional device is traded at the same high economy as in Hemingway's better stories, though for very different reasons.

The result is in some ways a limiting of the pleasures—especially the comic ones—of the earlier books; but Mrs. Spark has not ceased, in the process of self-purification, to be a comic writer, a Catholic comic writer. She remains as macabre as ever; the tactics of indifference which make her aesthetic manner so poised are also part of an appalling *moral* manner, a splendid impudence; as with a number of our Catholic writers (who have contributed more than their proportionate share to aesthetic speculation in the English novel), an ingrained casuistry has always touched her dealings with the form, and these recent books have been open celebrations of it. As to the kind of Catholic aesthetics, it is not the tradition of humanism in the Catholic novel that lies behind her—Mauriac's "the heroes of our novels must be free in the sense that the theologian says man is free. The novelist must not intervene arbitrarily in their destinies" is hardly for her a conviction but a matter of witty speculation. She is much closer to the Catholic novelists of detachment, to Joyce's God-like writer, paring his fingernails, or to Waugh at the height of his comic powers—who, despairing of God's sensible presence in modern history, feels free to represent the contemporary world as chaos, and his characters as bereft of significant moral action.

This makes for an absurd and macabre universe, but at the same time for a sense of what is absent, a knowledge of true things and last things. Like Waugh, in fact, Muriel Spark is very much a *memento mori* writer, and indeed her novel of that title is a central testament—a farce which shows the comic unreality of human and historical concerns in its senile cast, and also evokes for the human lot a cool, instructive pathos. Unlike Waugh, though, she is decidedly an aesthetician, not only because she is a poet and one of our most intelligent novelists, but also because she senses a necessity for wholeness and coherence. Indeed that seems at present her main preoccupation; and it is the relation between the chaotic or contingent and the teleological that seems now to direct both her artistic and her moral interests and to make her recent books into very exact, very formal, and very duplicitous objects. [1972]

Malcolm Bradbury. Possibilities (Oxford Univ.
Pr., 1973), pp. 247–48

Since *The Public Image*, [Spark] has been putting her writing through a sieve, working towards a light, transparent, musical prose which is capable of supporting a heavy burden of meaning on the frailest of details. In *The Driver's Seat* and *Not to Disturb,* I felt that she was like a conjuror whose technique is so perfect that he loses the rabbit altogether and the point of his act disappears with the animal. Both novels were so scrupulous, so drained of the superfluous ordinary world, that they were hardly more than gossamer webs of theology and literary theory. In *The Hothouse by the East River,* the sleight of hand is brilliantly timed; the rabbit goes, then comes back again . . . and Miss Spark pitches her troubling parable exactly midway between pure metaphysical illusion and the solid landscape of bourgeois fact and society.

Her literary models now are professedly Robbe-Grillet and the nouveaux romanciers. She despises the novel as a form of mere social mimesis and writes a kind of polyphonic prose (the term is Amy Lowell's) which is closer to allegorical verse than to the loose fustian of conventional fiction. Every sentence *sounds*; each one poses what Miss Brodie would call Poise—its syntax is painfully simple, its stresses fall regularly, it has a contrived delicious clarity. One can almost scan a page of Miss Spark's writing, and its predominant rhythms are those of a nursery-rhyme of pure statement. . . .

Jonathan Raban. Enc. May, 1973, p. 83

SPENDER, STEPHEN (1909–   )

Stephen Spender's reputation, his editorial prowess, his personal qualities are finally, and sadly, beside the point. The Muses are stern autocrats, and those without a birthright do not get in. The birthright is a gift for language, and Spender does not adequately qualify. He has facility, some rhythmic grace, some lyric moments, and a feeling of excited possession of the ideas alive in an age, but that does not remain enough.

The ideas have some potency and some truth; he shares them with mighty poets. . . . Why then do Spender's ideas in the poems that gave him repute seem insufficient now? Is it just that he, of his generation, fails, as is common, to speak a language that reaches us who are of the subsequent generation, caught by a fashion momentarily changed and, as fashions can be, partially blind? It may be; but I fear not. His ideas in the pre-World War II poems look somewhat dated and more than somewhat ironic now because they were too simple then, and because they entered too little into the nerves and rhythm of his poems. . . .

There are a few beautiful moments in his poems. . . . They are for this reader too few.

Paul Ramsey. *SwR*. Autumn, 1966, pp. 940–41

Since the 1930s, the poetry of Stephen Spender has been in relative obscurity, partly, no doubt, on account of other poetry which has successfully competed for general attention and partly for certain of its intrinsic qualities. Many of the poems are pure: they do not come to us immediately; they are detached from the everyday things of the world and cannot be approached in the workaday frame of mind in which one comes in from the street to read the headlines and throw away the bulk mail. Their neglect is due also, perhaps, to the quality of uncertainty, which results in embarrassment to the reader when his expectations in a poem are suddenly defeated by a word or phrase which injures the tone that had been established. For often there seem to be two impulses at work, which do not blend but remain awkwardly at odds. . . .

In the well-known poem "Not palaces, an era's crown," number XXXIII of *Poems* (1933), Spender reveals more clearly than anywhere else a conflict that determines the features of many of his poems. This particular poem has a political message, and the conflict here has a political coloration incidental to one's immediate interests; but it presents in more or less fundamental terms the two poles between the influences of which the poetry is largely composed. . . . The conflict is between the will, on the one hand, which is to work in the outside world, and the senses, on the other, that work in their own leisure to spell out the lyrical poetry. If, as I suggest, these lines reveal a principle that works throughout the poetry of Stephen Spender, they remind one also to remark that this talent, one of the purest lyrical talents of the century in English, has never been entirely liberated from the conscience, the call of duty, the structural needs of the poem, and the world itself to issue its own spontaneous utterances.

These then are the poles exerting the influences of which the conflict can be felt in the large parts of a long poem or even the small elements of a line. With the will is associated the outer world and the poet as a person in that world and in its light; also associated with the will is the descriptive poem (or the descriptive elements in a poem), of which there are only a few in Spender, and the structure, the form of the poem. Associated with the other pole is the spontaneous lyric impulse, the nondescriptive or "literal" poem or images that do not primarily reflect the world, the poet's withdrawn self—his self at the "still centre," to use his own term, or what in a political discussion, in defiance of the Marxist theory of the economic control of the intellect, he calls that margin of freedom which no system can deny where there is room always for "pure states of being," and, finally, associated with this pole is what seems to be a species of negative capability that in one important poem the poet designates his weakness. If in Milton or Dante the colossal informing will is the chief agent of the poetry, it is not so in the lyrical poetry of Spender, for whom the will opposes the poetry.

A. K. Weatherhead. *CL*. Autumn, 1971.
pp. 451–53

● STEINER, GEORGE (1929–   )

The main argument of the book [*Tolstoy or Dostoevsky*] is convincing. But a heavy apparatus of allusion and of philosophical phraseology is scarcely needed to make these and similar points, which are more directly demonstrable. Mr. Steiner is sometimes portentous, particularly in his opening chapter, with its repeated drum-roll of great names and great works which produces only a vague, diffused sense of grandeur and no kind of precise statement. "This confrontation [between Tolstoy and Dostoevsky] touches on some of the prevailing dualities in western thought as they reach back to the Platonic dialogues. It is also tragically germane to the ideological warfare of our time." To use Mr. Steiner's word, the "tonality" of such sentences is inadequate to their topic, being too near to *Time Magazine* and too remote from critical interest. Or "the nineteenth century had come a long way since the 'dawn' in which Wordsworth proclaimed that it was bliss to be alive." This is true, but not helpful.

After this first chapter, with the inevitable allusions to Mario Praz's *The Romantic Agony* and its rough survey of modern man, serious criticism begins. On Tolstoy's hatred of Shakespearean drama, and his obsession with Lear; on Tolstoy's reflections on death and survival: on some of his literary ancestors: and, above all, on his only alleged weakness as a novelist—that he writes too easily and too directly of the movements of the soul; on all these points, Mr. Steiner is interesting. He is interesting also when he discusses Dostoevsky's realism, his use of the symbolism of the Orthodox Church and of other recurrent images, and of indirection and ambiguity in Dostoevsky's dialogue. Much of this is criticism at the level of the common reader's exchange of impressions, supported by an unusually wide range of comparison; and, as such, it will often draw attention to something unnoticed, to an implication missed. But in our present situation it is no substitute for a close examination of the original texts, of the order and method of their composition, of Tolstoy's own statements of his aims, and of the background of the intellectual and social movements in Russia, from which the works emerged.

Sartre's dictum, which Mr. Steiner quotes, that differences of technique in the novel reflect philosophical differences, is a demand for precision, for an observation of idiom and detail. "To have carved the figures in the Medici Chapel, to have imagined Hamlet and Falstaff, to have heard the Missa Solemnis out of deafness is to have said, in some mortal but irreducible manner: 'Let there be light.'" Perhaps "close reading" can be exaggerated: but this is surely not close enough. The vacuum, the great critical blank, that surrounds Tolstoy for the Anglo-Saxons is still undisturbed.

Stuart Hampshire. NS. March 12, 1960, p. 370

Near the end of this long essay on the decline of tragic drama (*The Death of Tragedy*) George Steiner expresses a credo that might more serviceably have appeared at the beginning. "I believe that literary criticism has about it neither rigour nor proof," he writes. "Where it is honest, it is passionate, private experience seeking to persuade." You can't ask for anything fairer than that, but it might, as I say, have better been told to us earlier, criticism of this kind not being to everyone's taste.

It is, with slight reservations, very much to my own taste, I had better say before I go further; without at all gainsaying the achievements of the textualists, I believe we need more of this kind of "old criticism," as Steiner has elsewhere described it, provided it's understood that something quite different from Van Wyck Brooks or J. Donald Adams is meant by the term. Mr. Steiner is no literary sociologist or patriot, nor is he a Houseman poised at his mirror ready to slice his throat at the memory of some devastating line. You will find here almost as close a reading of texts as is being performed at Chicago or Gambier, Ohio.

You will also find as brilliant, thorough and concerned a contemplation of the nature of dramatic art as has appeared in many years. Steiner doesn't have a profoundly original thesis, which along with the self-imposed limitation on his subject—there is scarcely any discussion of comedy—keeps me from placing his book in the company of such ur-works of recent drama criticism as Eric Bentley's *Playwright as Thinker*, Francis Fergusson's *Idea of a Theater* and H. D. F. Kitto's *Form and Meaning in Drama*, but *The Death of Tragedy* seems to me to rank not far below.

Richard Gilman. Com. May 12, 1961, p. 180

George Steiner's *Language and Silence* is a collection of essays and reviews culled from work written over the past nine years. The fashion, it seems, is for critics to present, like painters and writers, one-man shows of their work. Since our age is dominated by the magazine and the paperback, both of which encourage composing for the moment or the occasion, such exhibitions are inevitable, for what man could resist the opportunity to collect his own footprints from a vanished terrain? Happily, in some cases, such collections, when they emerge in book form, disprove the myth that literary journalism cannot be serious and rewarding. On the other hand the writer runs the risk—if he is neither an Edmund Wilson nor a V. S. Pritchett, or if he is not prudent enough to realize the special burdens of a book, and revise and rethink accordingly—of displaying a certain glib shrewdness in place of considered judgment. Partly because Steiner is not an especially accomplished essayist, and partly because the burdens of a book have not been generally accepted, Steiner rises only at times above the former category, and only rarely manages the latter.

These thirty-one essays, whch range from Kafka to McLuhan, from Shakespeare to Schoenberg, from Marxism to pornography, are of a much more autobiographical and personal nature than, say, Steiner's study on Tolstoy and Dostoevsky. In their abiding concern with the fate of Humanity and the Humanities, these essays quite clearly set out the author's own personal history. Thus to an unusual extent we are invited to judge the man as separate from the critic. Indeed, the book is at its best when the voice is purely autobiographical, as in the essay, "A Kind of Survivor." *Language and Silence* also contains the author's premises for his general approach to literature, as well as many samples of specific analyses of works. (It is unfortunate in this respect that Steiner the critic is so often a professor in his writings, that the strain of didacticism runs so deeply throughout the work.)

Alan Lelchuk. *PR*. Fall, 1968, p. 624

A phalanx of crucial topics, a tone of high-church gravity, a light sprinkle of multilingual erudition, a genteel stab at prophecy (Mr. Steiner will be remembered as the critic who reminds us not to forget the Holocaust)—it's easy to imagine the strong impression these lectures must have made when first delivered for the T. S. Eliot Memorial Foundation at the University of Kent. And now, when we read his first sentence announcing that this book [*In Bluebeard's Castle*] is written "in memoration" of T. S. Eliot, we are immediately prepared for some very high-class prose.

Western culture, Mr. Steiner says, is irremediably shattered, all our certainties destroyed and axioms bent; yet not for a moment does this cause him to strain his syntax, lose his cool, or breathe an ill-mannered rasp. His style, in all its mincing equanimity, can assimilate equally a few paragraphs on Milton's verse and a few on the slaughter of six million Jews. His prose remains creamy and mellifluous, a high Mandarin patter that reads at times as if it were a parody by Lucky Jim. . . .

In *Bluebeard's Castle* is divided into four chapters, of which the second and third form a unit. . . . Each is marked by an overriding strategy: the author announces urgent themes, names burning problems, dances around them a little, and then avoids every difficulty they raise. . . .

Irving Howe. *Cmty.* Feb., 1972, pp. 96–97

These books by George Steiner are surprisingly different in character and quality. *Extraterritorial* is a loose collection of essays reprinted from various journals; the literary personality they express is often insufferable. *In Bluebeard's Castle* consists of four admirable lectures on the theme proposed by T. S. Eliot in 1948—admirable not because they compel assent but because they raise serious questions in a fitting manner. The first book is too clever by half, the second is intelligent.

Can it be that Mr. Steiner is not really at home in dealing—as it were, on the molecular level—with matters of language as they affect literature? I think that is the case, and what we must value in his criticism is something quite different, the kind of moral imagination that enables a critic to arrive at an adequate estimate of the significance of a literary work and of the literary enterprise in general. I should regard that as being the higher faculty, but the tone of the essays of *Extraterritorial* suggests that Mr. Steiner prizes disproportionately the ability to make a skillful analysis of literary means. Now, the moral vision suffereth long, it is not puffed up, while the "papers on literature and the language revolution" are bursting with pride. Mistaken pride. They certainly make a great display of stylistic and cultural instrumentation, but how are we to put our trust in an author who writes "language revolution" with no sense of having wounded not only the language of literature but the decent speech of educated men?

Emile Capouya. *ModOc.* Spring, 1972, p. 195

STEPHENS, JAMES (1882–1950)

It is easy to expatiate on Stephens's qualities as a writer, on his attractive personality, the individualism and the whimsy; the love of exaggeration and the fantastic stories; the tendency to treat serious matters with apparent levity; the ability to talk for hours on any subject. But when judging him in the general context of English Literature one cannot deny that his output was small for a writer of eminence—half a dozen "novels," two books of short stories and a volume of his collected poems. It is rather unfortunate that he matured early as a writer, for, having adopted an ideal philosophy at the beginning of his career, his work had little chance to develop. There is no history of an internal struggle and resultant triumph.

Nevertheless, he has proved himself worthy of a permanent place in English literature. In a world grown pessimistic after the downfall of established customs he offered ultimate values where human ones were fast becoming standard. He exalted the spirit of literature rather than the letter, preaching that the author has a spiritual duty as well as an artistic one. "Success depends on the variety of one's inner life" was his dictum; and he reminded the critic, in "An Essay in Cubes," that he "is not celebrating a man, but a soul." His career as a writer is the story of the development of this inner life. His religious sensitivity was fortunately combined with a talent for artistic expression, and he had a distinct advantage in his large and aptly chosen vocabulary, the result of omnivorous reading, so that he could range from a leisurely narrative to an incantatory prose in *The Crock of Gold*; and the impersonal tones of *Here Are Ladies*, where he preoccupied himself with the rambling of the individual's thoughts, and the dramatic opening paragraphs of *The Demi-Gods* were equally his own. His poetic insight displayed itself in the gift of remembering what happened in the flush of a moment and recreating the full richness of an experience directly instead of by intimation.

His limitation was that as a writer he stood alone; he founded no school of writing and the threads of tradition which he picked up were absorbed into a style that was his and inimitable.

Hilary Pyle. *James Stephens: His Work and an Account of His Life* (Routledge & Kegan Paul, 1965), pp. 174–75

● STOPPARD, TOM (1937–   )

Tom Stoppard's *Rosencrantz and Guildenstern Are Dead* is obviously giving considerable pleasure to large numbers of people, so I advance my own reservations feeling like a spoilsport and a churl: the play strikes me as a noble conception which has not been endowed with any real weight or texture. The author is clearly an intelligent man with a good instinct for the stage, and his premise is one that should suggest an endless series of possibilities. But he manipulates this premise instead of exploring it, and what results is merely an immensely shrewd exercise enlivened more by cunning than by conviction.

As is now generally known, *Rosencrantz and Guildenstern Are Dead* is a theatrical parasite, feeding off *Hamlet, Waiting for Godot*, and *Six Characters in Search of an Author*—Shakespeare provides the characters, Pirandello the technique, and Beckett the tone with which the Stoppard play proceeds. Like Pirandello, Stoppard tries to give extradramatic life to a group of already written characters, introducing elements of chance and spontaneity into a scene previously determined by an author. His object is to discover what happens to people whose lives are completely fixed and formalized when they are allowed to meditate, self-consciously, upon their own predestination. . . .

It is, in fact, the characters of Rosencrantz and Guildenstern that account for a good deal of my queasiness about the play. In Shakespeare, these characters are time servers—cold, calculating opportunists who betray a friendship for the sake of a preferment—whose deaths, therefore, leave Hamlet without a pang of remorse. In Stoppard, they are garrulous, child-like, ingratiating simpletons, bewildered by the parts they must play—indeed, by the very notion of an evil action. It is for this reason, I think, that Stoppard omits their most crucial scene —the famous recorder scene where they are exposed as spies for Claudius—for it is here that their characterological inconsistency would be most quickly revealed. Since the author is presumably anxious to demonstrate the awful inevitability of a literary destiny ("We follow directions—there is no *choice* involved. The bad end unhappily, the good unluckily. That is what tragedy means"), it hardly serves his purpose to violate the integrity of Shakespeare's original conception. But I suspect the author has another purpose here—that of amusing the audience with winning heroes—and the necessity to be charming is not always easily reconciled with the demands of art. [1967]

Robert Brustein. The Third Theatre (N.Y.,
Knopf, 1969), pp. 149, 151–52

Tom Stoppard's *Rosencrantz and Guildenstern Are Dead* . . . is *Waiting for Godot* rewritten by a university wit. Based on a nice conceit, it is epigrammatically literate, intelligent, theatrically clever. It marks a scintillating debut for its author.

An English drama critic was skeptical of its success in America because to appreciate it one had to be familiar with *Hamlet!* We may now reassure that critic as to our familiarity with *Hamlet* since Stoppard's play is a Broadway hit and our reviewers, to judge by the ads, have called it "a superb play," "very brilliant, very chilling," etc., etc.

Rosencrantz and Guildenstern are two ordinary youths called to the court of Elsinore to detect what it is that troubles the young Prince. They haven't the faintest idea of the tragedy into the midst of which they have been thrust. They do as they are bid and for their pains meet with sudden death.

This is a parable of little Everyman. We are thrown into a world in which events of great moment apparently take place, have only an inkling of our role in them and in one way or another we are their victims.

As bits of *Hamlet* are enacted in swift and dim outline, the dilemma of poor Rosencrantz and Guildenstern—confused even as to their own names or identities, though one is supposed to be smarter than the other—is immediately clear, and the intellectual pattern of the play is firmly set. . . .

There are jokes about the theatre and amusing cracks about Hamlet himself, who is described as being "stark raving sane." The best of these occurs when Rosencrantz decides what he ought to say to Hamlet. "To sum up: your father whom you love dies, you are his heir, you come back to find that hardly was the corpse cold before his young brother popped on to his throne and under his sheets. . . . Now why are you behaving in this extraordinary manner?"

All this entertaining stuff leads on to the play's profounder purpose, which is to declare that with life, "Wheels have been set in motion, and they have their own pace to which we are condemned." There is no true answer. "Uncertainty is the normal state." "But what are we supposed to *do*?" The answer is "Relax. Respond. We only know what we're told. And for all we know it isn't even true." The only certainty is death. "The bad end unhappily, the good unluckily."

The quips sparkle, the portentous reflections are neatly phrased.

The play is civilized pastime, which is certainly as unusual as it is agreeable, and we are duly grateful. But we need not take the play's "deeper significance" too seriously; it is not thought but student chatter on a brightly dignified level.

Harold Clurman. *Nation*. Nov. 6, 1967, p. 476

Stoppard loves to sport with conventions. Old-fashioned melodrama, drawing-room comedy, ladies' magazine fiction, westerns, vaudeville, cinema, but especially absurdist literature (the conventions of which he, in part, takes seriously) are grist to his parodic mill. Though generally sophomoric, his novel [*Lord Malquist and Mr. Moon*] is often droll, clever, and able to tickle the imagination.

Stoppard's two heroes represent alternative responses to the chaos of modern life. Malquist believes in style: "since we cannot hope for order, let us withdraw with style from the chaos." Moon believes in substance, in "getting things down." He is the bewildered little man (a virgin though married) who wants things to make ordinary sense. He would like to write history but is frustrated by the difficulty of stating any truth absolutely and of discovering any historical cause without going back to the beginning of the world. Stoppard places Moon in a situation of seeming incoherence, and Moon is increasingly distressed. Since others (like Malquist who has hired Moon to be his Boswell) seem to accept the absurd as commonplace, Moon wonders why he alone should bear the burden of craving order, and he decides to release a homemade time bomb as a way of shocking them into a recognition of disorder. . . .

The novel, when pressed, does not really seem to be taking the experience of discontinuity seriously, for Moon, through whose eyes we see most of the action, is gradually allowed to make the necessary connections. . . . Moon in fact is finally shown to be not so much the farcical victim of Stoppard's contrived nonsense as a pathetic victim of his contrived sense. After he releases the timer of his bomb, events are allowed to gain coherence, but this new coherence invalidates the solution he has chosen and seems to him a "conspiracy." Even his bomb mocks him by exploding like a balloon. . . .

In a crucial exchange Moon asks, "But if it's all random then what's the point?" And the clinching answer is, "What's the point if it's all inevitable?" There is confusion here (and in other absurdist documents) between the ideas of cause and inevitability. To trace causes as science does, is not to say that a result is inevitable, and does not require us to postulate a universe of accident in a pitiful defense of human freedom. Cause is an hypothesis, not an empirical generalization. Science deals in probabilities, whereas the arts and religion are interested in (the experience of) certainties. Stoppard as artist is entitled to render the experience of total randomness or total inevitability, but then whence the special pathos? Why is one man more a victim than another?

David J. Gordon. *YR*. Autumn, 1968,
pp. 123–25

Critical jargon—highbrow and philistine—is one of the things parodied in Tom Stoppard's new one-act comedy, *The Real Inspector Hound*, and it would require some courage to parrot, even approximately, Moon, the second-string critic, who makes this pronouncement about the Agatha Christie-type thriller he has just been watching (from the far side of the stage where another "audience" confronts the audience):

> If we examine this more closely, and I think close examination is the best tribute that the play deserves, I think we will find that within the austere framework of what is seen to be on one level a country-house weekend, and what a useful symbol it is, the author has given us—yes, I will go so far—he has given us the human condition.

We need not then go so far as to see in the two-level action of the play "the human condition." On the contrary, the play's interest may well lie in the cheerful and seemingly amoral way in which it makes the theatre feed on the theatre without urging us to perceive the old analogies between the world and the stage. When, towards the end of the play, the two parodied critics one after another step on the stage, get sucked into the mad logic of a theatrical thriller and assume parts that lead to a quick death by revolver shot, nobody is likely to experience the "felt life" that is always there in Pirandello's theatricality; nor is one invited to recognize some social nightmare as in the somewhat over-obvious metamorphosis of logical-political man into Ionesco's rhinoceros.

No-one, not even a critic, needs to feel involved beyond the level of a fine cerebral farce. It is comfortingly classical, as though Sheridan's *The Critic* were performed in Alice's Looking Glass; and the element of absurdity in the play rests in the comfortingly witty dream where everything is topsy-turvy—the Inspector turns critic, the Critic inspector, and so on—and the words of a card-game are jumbled up into the familiar stage rhubarb. The point is that Stoppard is not only using absurd elements that pre-date the so-called theatre of the absurd, but he plays with the latter—parodistically.

Andrew K. Kennedy. *MD*. Feb., 1969, p. 437

Tom Stoppard's world is like Camus's telephone booth, except that there are many occupants and none has the proper change. And Camus can conceive of heroes flourishing inside: Don Juans, adventurers, actors pounding the walls in healthy revolt. But Stoppard's characters suffer. Most of those who survive become desensitized and unquestioning; the rest are overcome by madness or death.

Despite these distinctions, the world views of the two writers are basically alike. Both belong to what Camus terms the "tradition of . . . humiliated thought," born of the struggle to make reasonable and human a universe which is neither. Both are concerned with the nature and effects of absurdity. It is the expression of their concern and of their questions that differs. Almost immediately, Stoppard's plays and fiction abandon the conventional rhetoric that characterizes the work of Camus, Sartre, and many others who explore the absurd through art. Logical arguments and the devices they demand are replaced by features peculiar to the Theatre of the Absurd as Martin Esslin has described it. Stoppard's characters are rarely three-dimensional, his plots rarely linear. Though his settings generally are localized, the random action and dialogue they compass dramatize a confusion that has no bounds.

Stoppard's debt to the Theatre of the Absurd, particularly to Beckett, is often acknowledged without being analyzed. The connection with Beckett is especially important, a means of refuting the general notion that Stoppard is a clever prodigy whose productions do little more than glitter at the surface. For correspondences exist that are far more profound than casual parallels in situation and technique. They have to do primarily with characterization.

Jill Levenson. QQ. Autumn, 1971, p. 431

[Jumpers is] a delightfully Absurdist play, more successful in some respects than Rosencrantz and Guildenstern, although still a bit too scrappy and incoherent for my taste. I laughed almost continually and came out of the theatre feeling cheered up; but quite a bit of the action did not seem necessary and I have failed to understand a number of points, even after reading the text. Why, for instance, has Dorothy gone off sex with her husband, after the shock of the de-poeticisation of the moon? She is still fond of him, and she is not totally traumatised since she is having some sort of affair with the Vice-Chancellor. I suspect that it is simply because Mr. Stoppard wants to make a pun about a consummate artist refusing consummation. And why is the play weighted down at the end with the rather tedious coda? It could have stopped five minutes before it does. Is it because Mr. Stoppard cannot quite control his flow of language and gimmicks?

To judge by the extremely silly programme interview, it is almost as if he were afraid to think commonsensically, in case his demon should be castrated. In my opinion, this is an error which has weakened the work of some other Absurdists, such as Ionesco. But then my contention is that the conquests of the irrational should always be explicable eventually in terms of the rational, and that one should feel them to be rational even before one can discover why they are so. According to my antennae, quite a few bits of this play have not been brought fully into intellectual or aesthetic focus.

John Weightman. Enc. April, 1972, p. 45

In spite of all its merits, the first act of *Jumpers* left me unsatisfied. Mr. Stoppard's basic joke is the old one about the absent-minded professor: George's preposterous lecture is really a set of variations on this joke, and as George bombinates on and on, the joke begins to wear thin. (This parody-lecture, by the way, owes a good deal to a Jonathan Miller sketch from *Beyond the Fringe*, in which the Cambridge philosopher G. E. Moore figured very prominently. Mr. Stoppard's George, of course, is also a G. Moore. And while we're at it, Inspector Bones of the Yard bears a distinct resemblance to Inspector Truscott in Joe Orton's play *Loot*.) The bickerings between George and Dorothy verge at times on the tiresome. Worse, the play seems to be about nothing in particular at all; it appears to be a self-indulgent, wayward excuse for Mr. Stoppard to be too clever by at least three-quarters.

But in the second act, the various threads begin to weave together. Slowly it becomes clear that George, fatuous as he is, is the last of the civilized humanists (like that other George in *Who's Afraid of Virginia Woolf?*), doomed to go down before the soulless, crass "rationality" of the future that is represented by Sir Archibald Jumper. . . . The moon's violation by astronauts—Dorothy's obsession—is another symbol of the inexorable pollution of old purities by the Faustian mechanistic juggernaut that arrogantly proclaims, "No problem is insoluble given a big enough plastic bag."

George has two beloved pets, a tortoise and a hare that have been specially trained to refute Zeno's paradox. Their unhappy fate makes George keenly aware of his own weakness, caught between the egregious Archie and his jumper on the one hand, and the malevolence of chance on the other. . . . This second act, for me, tips the balance in the play's favor. Just in time, it becomes clear that Mr. Stoppard's cleverness is not just cleverness in a vacuum. My point is not that pathos is more satisfying than comedy, but that coherence is more satisfying than sprawl; coherence is what *Jumpers* attains, just in time.

Julius Novick. VV. May 2, 1974, pp. 83–84

● STOREY, DAVID (1933–   )

The miners' sons are keeping busy these days, beavering away there in the chunky substratum and sending up one slice of life after another. The latest faceworker on the craggier seams of literature is David Storey, son of a Yorkshire pit deputy, who gives us [in *This Sporting Life*] an account of life in a North of England industrial town. This is by now a familiar locale to American readers, but the background—the world of professional football—probably isn't. Rugby football, that is; not the Tom Brown's school days version (although God knows that was rough enough) but the tougher, bitchier, backbiting game that is played in the West Riding on frost-hard clearing between the mills and the cooling towers.

Arthur Machin, working on a lathe, decides that he is meant for better things. . . . Yet he is a kind of Midas in reverse; everything he touches turns to dross. He cannot catch the elusive beams of love or tenderness or whatever it is that makes little heroes happy. His tepid affair whimpers to a stop and he goes back to his football.

Love considered as a gray waste, a length of shoddy; this is something that Mr. Storey brilliantly evokes. But he is not so confident when it comes to filling in the rest of the picture. His portrait of the local idol is not complete. . . . I have a feeling—because the book has so many jagged edges to it—that Mr. Storey has pared his novel down from a much longer manuscript, and I wouldn't be surprised if he has cut some of the best bits out. On the other hand, there are a few *Room at the Top* touches that could have gone, and a surprising *Lucky Jim* relic—a scene in which Arthur dines in a posh restaurant in his football boots—that I wish he had omitted. But Mr. Storey's working-class dialogue is superb, and his picture of a small-town society is just right. In fact, as one of those slices of life that keep coming to the surface it's good.

Mr. Storey has a real live talent, which he seems to be chasing through these uneven pages. In his next novel he will probably catch it, pin it down, and with it produce something that is memorable.

Keith Waterhouse. Sat. Dec. 17, 1960, p. 21

David Storey (like David Mercer and David H. Lawrence before him) is concerned with the beast beneath the skin of civilised man. Sometimes his beasts rampage, terrorising the neighbourhood, as in *This Sporting Life*. At others they lurk neglected until such time as they can no longer be evaded, then rise up and tear a man to pieces—as in *The Restoration of Arnold Middleton*. . . .

Arnold himself is a schoolmaster, in a classical schizophrenic family situation. Being somewhat mother-obsessed, and having married his wife for maternal qualities which she refuses to display, he finds everything he needs in his mother-in-law, who is young enough to be still sexually viable, but old enought to be, as it were, his mother. As the three of them live together in one small house, the structure of Interpersonal Perceptions (and deceptions) becomes complex and frightening. He refuses to allow his wife to send her mother away (on grounds of human kindness—oh charity, your depths are murky!) until, at the climax of the piece, in chagrin at his own mother not turning up to see him, goaded on by the inanities of the schoolmasterly world around him, he gets moody, drunk, and sleeps with his mother-in-law. From this point onwards, temporary insanity sets in to express his inability to cope: it is only when the whole situation is destroyed by the removal of mother-in-law to a flatlet, that normality beckons and his wife takes him back to her bed.

It is unfortunate that the last part of this story is such a schematic affair, because in principle it explores a resolution—a restoration—comparatively new to the theatre: I suspect that if it had been handled at the same pace (in the writing) as the first two acts—had, in fact, been two acts instead of one, David Storey would have had time to tease it out, give it that air of truth and humour which makes the first part of this play so memorable. Perhaps it is over-schematic because it owes too much to psychological theory: intellectual abstracts, however truthful, play havoc when allowed to creep in and dominate first-hand perception in a personal play. O'Neill often found a fourth act useful, and there is indeed something of his genius in the grandeur of Storey's transmogrification of ordinary mortals, with less poetry, but more psychological awareness than O'Neill; less passion, but more wit. One can't help regretting that in the 10 years since he wrote this play, David Storey has not written 10 more. . . .

All in all, *The Restoration of Arnold Middleton* is worth seeing and worth following up by those concerned. The beasts that lurk in Arnold are ashamed to show their heads for the same reasons that the British bulldog is ashamed to bite: guilt, and lack of direction. The results in Arnold's life: bad faith, ignoble gestures, deceit, rash acts of aggression followed by temporary insanity, have their parallels in our public life. Arnold's constant reference to Robin Hood, heraldry and the many other myths of the late great Britain indicate that Storey is not altogether unaware of the connections. Arnold Middleton has meaning on several levels, and remains a brilliant portrayal of a person: a considerable creation in a considerable play.

John McGrath. *NS*. Sept. 8, 1967, pp. 298–99

The automobile is the most commonplace example of a consistent "hard" image employed from the book's [*This Sporting Life*] opening page to keep the reader aware that Arthur's powerful body and iron will are subject to the even more inanimate world, which he cannot alter no matter how much the town worships him. We begin with an action scene, told in the present tense, in which Arthur's teeth are knocked into his mouth somehow through the error of one of his mates. It is a brilliant device. The loss of the teeth becomes a controlling metaphor, used at various stages in the novel to keep Arthur and the reader aware of his inevitable emasculation. They are hard, white, material and thus relate not only to his virility but to the outside world of things, as when Arthur, trapped on the roof of Weaver's house (itself a symbol of impossible achievement), begins tearing away the tiles to find a way in, or down. The falling tiles, their hardness, their shape, remind the reader of Arthur's teeth, recently removed.

The connection is closer than the mere fact that tiles and teeth bear a chance resemblance: immediately after the accident someone remarks that Arthur looks ancient; he has began to resemble the "wrecks" (Johnson, his father) whose lives, ambitions, he fears as having something to do with his own future. Tearing away the tiles from the roof of Weaver's house, therefore, is a complicated kind of defeatist action; it reminds me of Kenneth Burke's discussion of symbolic action in his *Philosophy of Literary Form*, his mention of the traditional lover who breaks the window of his would-be mistress's house. Burke calls this "symbolic rape," taking the window as membrane, I gather. Arthur's action is made to seem aggressive and uncontrolled. He is still slightly doped from the operation at the dentist's office.

We should keep in mind, too, that within the house—close enough to have just viewed Arthur "swinging" along the drain to the corner of the house and the tiles—are the power people of the novel, Weaver, his wife, whose body by this time Arthur has regretfully rejected, and the cripple Slomer. These three have no idea that the "ape" who swung past the window is in fact the star of their rugby team, but they speak caustically of his performance when later in the evening Arthur is shown into the bedroom where the three are drinking. We know even as Arthur regretfully eyes the delectableness of Mrs. Weaver's form (wondering if lying with her were, after all, the one sure way to success) and Slomer in his strange, misshapen suit ("Some kind of tailor that") that for him there is no way to the room at the top. You can claw at the castle and hover around the mistress, play the padded clown for the lord of the team, even suck up to Merlin (Slomer is a catholic), but as long as people in power cast you as "ape," an ape you will remain. The ape metaphor is a good one. Arthur is quite aware of it; he uses it to criticize himself and goes by the nickname, Tarzan.

Thomas Churchill. Critique. Vol. 10, No. 3,
1968, pp. 79–80

Now that David Storey has taken on shape and substance for me, I would like to take another look at *This Sporting Life*. When I saw Lindsay Anderson's 1963 film, for which Storey did the screenplay based on his own novel, it came as just another of those English movies about sad, grimy life in provincial industrial towns—*Saturday Night and Sunday Morning, The Loneliness of the Long-Distance Runner*— in which the toughness and realism were tinged with sentimentality and soap opera. Since the film was made, Storey, the novelist, has become a playwright, the most impressive one to turn up in the English theater since those early angry days when John Osborne, John Arden and Harold Pinter emerged. When I was in England in May, I saw two of his plays—*The Contractor*, in the best production I saw in London, and *In Celebration*, in a less happy production in Salisbury. The potential for sentimentality is still there, but these two plays, again in provincial settings, do not cluck over their characters as *This Sporting Life* seemed to do. What Storey has done in both instances is to establish a revelatory occasion, gather the characters and set them talking, uncovering in the course of the play the emptiness and pain in the characters and, at the same time, positing their solidarity, the force that sustains them. The means to these two ends are the words the characters speak, apparently random, often funny talk which establishes a stage reality that gives the plays their strength.

Storey is now making his American debut with *Home*, his most recent play. For the press, it is an occasion not so much for Storey's sake but because those two redoubtable English knights, John Gielgud and Ralph Richardson, are back on the American stage together for the first time since that lamentable *The School for Scandal* they brought over in 1962. This time they are superb, but since I like to think of the arrival of *Home* as the Storey hour, I want to look first at the play. On the face of it, *Home* appears to be a departure for Storey, for in this play he is very much in the Beckett-Pinter tradition. Yet, the jump from the working-class living room of *In Celebration* to the almost bare stage of *Home* is not so great as it seems. The action is minimal in the earlier plays—in *In Celebration*, an offstage anniversary dinner, in

The Contractor, the raising and striking of a tent for a wedding that takes place between the acts—and the drama lives in the lines. The occasional rhetoric of the earlier plays gives way in *Home* to simple sentences—more often fragments—but there is still a family resemblance between this play and the ones that preceded it.

Gerald Weales. *Com.* Jan. 15, 1971, p. 373

Pasmore is a simple story, though not always simply told. A London college lecturer, the son of a coal-miner, suddenly suffers from unaccountable fits of depression. His historical work seems meaningless, and he cannot bear to touch or be touched by his wife. He stumbles, or sleepwalks, into an affair with another woman. In spite of her quite superhuman blankness, his joy in life is briefly restored. (So is his feeling for his wife: a syndrome for which there should be some regular paramedical title, like Zeno's Complaint.) But things cannot last. He tells his wife, moves out, gets done over by a strong-arm man sent by a jealous husband. It seems time for the ritual journey North, for explanations to indignant parents and uncomprehending sisters. Pasmore is always polite, taciturn, apt to agree with those who find his behaviour impossible either to understand or to excuse. But he never budges from the notion that his passions are both above and beyond his control. . . .

Pasmore is far from a silly book, and its ravenous demands cannot merely be met with a few pieties about the importance of developing moral relationships based on tender feelings for the sovereignty of others. It is a fine piece of masculine subjectivism, a bawl from the heart well worth setting opposite *The Pumpkin Eater* or *The Love Object*. Its settings and trappings are conventional: Mr. Storey is interested in inner life, not interior decoration. If he sometimes abuses his talent, it can stand the strain; and the overworked adjective "powerful," in his case, does not merely mean writing in a loud voice.

TLS. Oct. 6, 1972, p. 1184

I am not really sure what makes David Storey's *The Changing Room* so fascinating to me as a woman. It has no plot, no clearly individualized characters, no real dramatic conflict. It is about a group of working-class men in the north of England who play a game I am totally unfamiliar with, except that I know (mainly from the film *The Sporting Life*, based on a novel by Storey) that it is horribly brutal. If the play were about Tibetan monks it could not be more foreign to me. Even the language is half incomprehensible to me: Rugby jargon spoken in a Yorkshire accent. It is as though I had been allowed to see the exotic activities of a men's room for the first time in my life, and perhaps that is one reason the play held me, good or bad as that reason may be. . . .

The play calls for meticulously directed ensemble acting and gets it from an American cast who handle their North country accents deftly. Equally believable are the actors who play the club owner and the club secretary, and if there is any direct social comment, it comes from the appearance of these two, for the players are very deferential to their titled owner; class barriers hold sway to a certain extent even under the stadium. Sir Frederic, the owner, loves his lads, but he also loves the brutality, vicarious as it may be for him. Perhaps what this play is really about is that love among males that flourishes especially in the world of sports, a love embarrassed at tenderness, which finds its outlet instead in the communion of organized violent contact and its bitter-sweet aftermath.

It is not really a homosexual love (Storey has wisely avoided this obvious and faddish possibility) but rather a comradeship that enables male athletes to retain, or recapture, the irresponsibility of boy-hood, to touch one another physically with impunity and without arousing suspicion. In a world dominated by the cult of machismo, competitive team sports would seem to satisfy distinctly opposite urges. Male ego is bolstered by the toughness of play and the drive to win. On the other hand, nothing is more sentimental than the male sports world; and the locker room scene, the part the public, and especially women, do not get to see, is a place where conventionally "masculine" men can be less masculine, truer in themselves, perhaps, than their super-male image demands. It is this revelation that is at the center of *The Changing Room*.

Rita Stein. ETJ. Oct., 1973, pp. 370–71

"No nothing!" is the point of what Mr. Storey is doing [in *The Contractor*]. Heartened, evidently, by the example set by Samuel Beckett as to how little conventional "action" need be put in a play, Mr. Storey has carried theatrical naturalism farther than the canonical naturalists ever dared. The old naturalists took care to cut their slices of life at some point of crisis. . . . But Mr. Storey shows us days on which nobody's life is destroyed.

His aim, if I understand him, is to see whether the process of work itself, and the ordinary relationships that develop among workers, are enough to hold an audience. He makes theatre by counterpointing the broad, impersonal, cyclical rhythms of work with the irregular, erratic personal rhythms of the individual workers.

Did I "like" *The Contractor*? Did I "enjoy" it? I'm not sure. The work processes in it are less interesting than those in *The Changing*

Room: tent-raising imposes much less pressure on the people who do it than rugby, and is thus intrinsically less dramatic. Furthermore, it offers the playwright less of a chance to make theatrically effective contrasts between fast and slow, noisy and quiet. On the other hand, in *The Contractor*, Mr. Storey has permitted himself the luxury of assembling a rather peculiar cast of characters. . . .

I found *The Contractor* tantalizing. Enough happens to the characters so that I wanted more to happen to them. The two Irish workers are wantonly cruel in their joking, and in the third act conflicts come to a flash-point—and stop before very much comes of them. We learn enough about the characters so that I wanted to know more about them. Why is there such a bitter undertone to the Irishman's constant joking? (The jokes, incidentally, are pungent enough, and quite believable in context, but only occasionally funny.) The workers are counterpointed against the contractor and his family, who have scenes and troubles of their own—but this middle-class family, again, is never probed quite deeply enough. Symbolic patterns, too, always seem on the point of emerging, and never quite emerge. . . .

I hope it is clear that I was impressed and interested by many things in *The Contractor*: by the naturalness and ease of the dialogue and the acting, by the interplay among the characters, and by the rise and fall of the play's central character, the tent. I was tantalized not because I was given nothing, but because I was given enough to make me want more.

Julius Novick. *VV*. Oct. 25, 1973, p. 76

SYNGE, JOHN MILLINGTON (1871–1909)

John Millington Synge, poet and playwright, the youngest son of a conventional, middle-class Protestant family living in the Dublin suburbs, a rationalist, anticlerical descendant of Anglican bishops, was a writer who gave up Paris for the hills of Wicklow and the bogs of Mayo, preferring the conversation and friendship of tramps and tinkers to the company on the Left Bank.

Although Yeats and Lady Gregory are rightly regarded as the centerpieces of the Irish theatrical renaissance, it was Synge far more than either of these who gave the movement its national quality, and left to the world the type of play that has since become the prototype of Irish folk drama. Yet he managed to get the entire Abbey Theatre Company arrested in Philadelphia, and is still viciously denounced as anti-Irish by most of the grimmer Gaelic enthusiasts.

There are other paradoxical aspects to this strange, sociable hermit —this glum-faced humorist—the associate of a generation of intellectuals, who nevertheless was neither an intellectual nor a nationalist himself. He was a storm-tossed genius, but not a frustrated one. Whether he realized the extent of the international fame that was to be his is something that it is impossible to say: but he certainly gave no signs of caring about it. He was a writer of love passages of enormous lyrical beauty who was never much of a hit with the women he wanted to marry. He was a celebrity about whom the general public, until recently, knew very little—thanks to the disapproving attitude of his family toward its principal claim to distinction.

> Denis Johnston. *John Millington Synge* (N.Y., Columbia Univ. Pr., 1966), p. 3

When we turn from the quarrels they have evoked to [Synge's] works themselves, we find that they are essentially personal rather than social. Synge's plays are, in fact, more expressive than has been generally supposed of certain questions concerning the nature and function of art prevalent both in Synge's day and in ours. Yeats told Synge to go Aran to "express a life that has never found expression," but in reality Synge expressed not so much the life of the Irish peasant as his own feelings about the relationship of art to existence and of the artist to the society around him. . . .

The ending of his preface to *The Playboy of the Western World* suggests Synge's attitude towards his material. . . . Synge has here let slip the truth, that Irish life is material for "those of us who wish to write." That wish is Synge's central impulse. More than anything else, he desired to create an image of beauty that would stand against the sense of the absoluteness of death that rarely seems to have been far from his mind. Just as the "springtime of local life" is threatened by the encroachments of a vulgar urban civilization, so in Synge's plays, the beauty that he longs for is subject to destruction by the forces of life and time unless it is metamorphosed into the eternal beauty of art. It is one of the minor ironies of literary history that despite Yeats' injunction to Synge to express the life of Aran, Synge in actuality expressed through his concern for art as a response to the pain and transience of life something much closer than perhaps either of them consciously realized to the central concerns of Yeats himself.

> Arthur Ganz. *MD*. May, 1967, pp. 57–58

An innovator in the theatre, [Synge] based his innovations upon a strong belief in the significance of traditional elements in Irish culture, and upon his observation of the richness that came into being when old and new ways of life existed alongside each other. He was a highly conscious and deliberate writer, who took everything he wrote through numerous drafts, paying attention to every smallest detail. He was thrifty in that he threw very little away that might conceivably serve for future use; notes made in his twenties were pressed into service for works written in his middle thirties. Though he developed considerably over the years, the obsessions of his youth still operated during his maturity, and his earliest and latest writings have much in common; his vision is a unity from first to last. His influence upon later Irish and other writers has been immeasurable. The work of Sean O'Casey, George Fitzmaurice, Jack Yeats, Samuel Beckett and a host of lesser writers owes an inestimable debt to Synge's discoveries. Perhaps one of his greatest debtors, however, was W. B. Yeats, to whom he himself owed so much, for it was Synge's poetry that taught Yeats to move ahead to his greatest work as a lyric poet, and was directly responsible for the shift in Yeats' style that occurred in the years 1908–10.

Synge does not fit easily into any of the pigeon-holes allotted him by his critics. Long regarded with Lady Gregory as the originator of a school of naturalistic peasant drama, he was, in fact, less concerned with naturalism than almost all his followers. Believed to be a simple, though eloquent, recorder of peasant life, he was, in truth, intent upon the creation of universal myth from particular experience. Dismissed for years as a poet of no importance, he wrote poems of an originality and strength far greater than those of many more lauded writers. His true qualities have been obscured from us by many accidents of history. Too many critics have, like Daniel Corkery, viewed his work only in relation to the nationalist movement of his time and to the theatrical revival of the Irish Renaissance. When these limitations upon one's vision are removed, it becomes clear that, while J. M. Synge was indeed passionately concerned with what was essentially Irish, and emotionally involved in working for the cultural renaissance of his country, his work is, in any serious sense of the word, international, for he tackled fundamental crises of the human spirit, and, in his shanachie plays especially, did not limit but extended the territory of twentieth-century drama.

Robin Skelton. The Writings of J. M. Synge
(Indianapolis, Bobbs-Merrill, 1971),
pp. 172–73

The position of Synge . . . within the Irish Tradition is a special one; he cannot be simply accommodated within the early Abbey Theatre and left there. From one point of view he accepted the idea of the early movement and exhausted its possibilities. From another point of view be brought to that ideal a complex sensibility which modified radically the implied romanticism of a drama "of the noble and the beggarman." And I believe this sensibility can be understood by way of reference to that first rejected play, which Synge, incidentally, continued to nurse with a personal attachment even after its rejection. He exhausts the early ideal in several ways. Firstly, his plays unite, often within the one theatrical image, the aristocratic and the humble, imposing an heroic mould on common life, as in "Riders to the Sea" and a peasant mould on heroic myth, as in "Deirdre of the Sorrows." Above all, perhaps, he solved more successfully than anyone else in the early days the stated ambition to revive poetry in the theatre. His theatrical language is a highly stylised, artificial medium, combining the poetic and demotic, some of the properties of formal poetry with a particular kind of relationship to a rooted, vernacular, spoken speech. And lastly, the truth of Synge's dramatic action, the truth of his dramatic language is a poetic truth, not a social truth as in Ibsen or Shaw. The important thing, which his critics at all times have failed to appreciate, is not the way in which his plays imitate life in the West of Ireland as he observed it. The important thing is the way in which the plays conform to a shaping imagination, the way in which they serve a personal, poetic idea of what a work of art should be.

But a great deal of energy has already been expended down the years analysing the way in which Synge the playwright was conditioned by his part in the Irish Dramatic Movement and by his immersion in the rich folk culture of Ireland. It is time that we began to assess what Synge himself brought to the drama from outside. I have already tried to suggest the source of Synge's radical, subversive spirit and its kinship to the modernist drama outside Ireland. . . .

Where . . . does Synge get his models in stage-craft? Not, I believe, from Lady Gregory or Yeats whose dramatic skills at this point are rudimentary. Nor indeed from contemporary European models, although I think the influence of modernist drama on Synge, while oblique, is important. Synge looks back into the past for his models, to sixteenth- and seventeenth-century drama. As an artist he is technically conservative while one of the very distinctions of modernism in the theatre has been its progressive search for new forms to match the radical social programme of the dramatists themselves. This, it seems to me, is the important distinction between Synge and his contemporaries of equal stature in the theatre outside Ireland.

Thomas Kilroy. *Mosaic*. Vol. 5, No. 1, 1971,
pp. 14–15

The usual theory among historians of the Irish dramatic movement is that Synge was viewed by his contemporaries as a realist and that his influence impelled the dramatic movement away from the direction Yeats had charted for it towards realism. Thus it was Synge and not Yeats who was responsible for Lennox Robinson, Brinsley Mac-Namara, Sean O'Casey, Paul Vincent Carroll and Brendan Behan. Yeats and Lady Gregory talked about the folk, and yet the Abbey Theatre produced only one folk dramatist—George Fitzmaurice—whom it then proceeded to ignore. Earlier critics claimed that Fitzmaurice was a disciple of Synge, but it would have been more accurate to have described him as a casualty of Synge's influence. After Synge, it seemed, realism counted.

Synge, of course, wrote one play—*In the Shadow of the Glen*—which romanticized an authentic folktale. But the audience were unable to recognise the fact that the play *was* based on a folktale and insisted upon seeing it as a realistic treatment of loveless marriage among the country people. No wonder Synge was puzzled by the violent reaction his work received. His unfortunate statement in the preface to *The Playboy* about lying with his ear to a crack in the floor listening to the servant girls talking in the kitchen of a County Wicklow house and his defense of the authenticity of the language of that play not only made things worse but diverted attention from his real purpose.

Synge, as we know now, was not a realist. His vision was unique, personal, poetic, romantic. His view of Irish rural life was, in its own way, just as romantic as Yeats's. Yeats wrote nonsense about the peasant being the key to the collective unconscious of the race. Synge indulged in no such fantasies, but he nevertheless tended to idealize Irish rural life. He could, for example, convince himself that tramps were all artists or that when he listened to Pat Dirane reciting an ancient Gaelic poem he could hear the intonation of the original voice of the ancient poet. These are of course more acceptable myths, but myths nevertheless.

David H. Greene. In Maurice Harmon, ed.,
J. M. Synge: Centenary Papers 1971
(Dublin, Dolmen, 1972), pp. 194–95

THOMAS, DYLAN (1914–1953)

In his attempt to fashion a comprehensive view of existence, Thomas was one with all the major poets of the century, and his efforts are comparable to theirs in kind, although admittedly not in degree. Hart Crane with his "Bridge"; Pound with myth, history, and economics; Eliot with Frazer, philosophy, and Christianity; Yeats with occultism and Byzantium—all were seeking symbols whereby they might present a total and unified perception of human life. In the sense that Thomas attempts much the same ends with his adaptation of a Biblical *Weltansicht*, he makes larger demands upon history than would an author of a handful of exquisite lyrics. He is, then, to be viewed finally not simply as a writer of particular poems but as a poet of comprehensive vision.

It is perhaps possible—though it does not seem likely—that the longer view of history will discover qualities of visionary excellence where the contemporary critic has been unable to discover them. If we are to judge by the examples of Blake, Smart, and Whitman, it would seem prudent to conclude that what are for us the most obscure poems may be the most interesting to subsequent generations. It may be, for example, that such opaque poems as "I Dreamed My Genesis" and the "Altarwise" sequence will be regarded as wells of richness.

The limitations of Thomas, however, for our own age, remain those poems which seem like gibberish to the occasional reader and remain a quagmire to the persistent explicator. Because Thomas's most obscure poems were written before he was twenty-five, and because his most generally acclaimed poems were written after that time, one is tempted to see Thomas as a maturing poet whose career was cut short by death. The truth would seem otherwise. Thomas matured early, and by thirty-eight he was anxious to turn from lyric poetry to other forms of art. The poems Thomas was working on at the time of his death seem to me noticeably inferior to most of his other work. The "Elegy" Vernon Watkins reworked, for example, despite suggestions of new metrical interests by Thomas, cannot be compared to the earlier poem to his father, "Do Not Go Gentle."

William T. Moynihan. *The Craft and Art of
Dylan Thomas* (Ithaca, N.Y., Cornell Univ.
Pr., 1966), pp. 292–93

I have stressed Dylan's fear and dislike of intellectualism. His effort to start poetry off from the simplest organic basis of experience, the birth-movement, implied a rejection of all imposed ideas or guiding lines. Not that Dylan of all people was so naïve as not to recognise that in any concatenation of words there must necessarily cohere meanings applicable at all levels, social as well as personal, political as well as aesthetic. But this fact did not make the effort of reduction seem any the less significant or worthwhile in his eyes. It merely meant that the expanded meanings and complex associations should emerge from, and find their verification in, the organic image at its highest point of concentration—not from any intellectual line of argument or any external wish to be on the side of the angels. Thus Dylan was constantly aware of the wider relations of his images. Only the slightest oscillations of their particular point of balance was indeed needed to bring out a plain social application, as occurs, for instance, in an early poem *Our Eunuch Dreams*. Here his reaction to the world of the cinema, which meant so much to him, is so sharp that he is caught at the moment of the direct blow, a moment that he usually let pass before he mustered his poetic energies. He demands that the existing situation be reversed and that its false art, the anti-art of alienation, give way to the positive art of truth in which the liberated powers of men may be realised. . . .

At the outset (in *New Verse* in 1934) Dylan had defined his creed: "I take my stand with any revolutionary body that asserts it to be the right of all men to share, equally and impartially, every production of man from man and from the sources of production at man's disposal, for only through such an essentially revolutionary body can there be the possibility of a communal art." Treese has stated, "By 1938, when I was discussing this statement with him, Thomas felt that he should withdraw it, and that it no longer applied." I should like to know in more detail how that conversation with Dylan went. Certainly by 1938 he would have felt that the wording was too naïve and absolute, too little related to actual politics; and perhaps at that moment he was at the height of his struggle to concentrate on the birth-death image. In any event the 1934 announcement remained in all essentials his creed, though in later years he understood something of the complexity of the issues that it raised. What had changed and developed were both his ideas of poetry and his ideas of revolution. Or, rather, what had changed was the perspective in which he viewed his original ideas, the range of possibilities that he now intuited. [1968]

Jack Lindsay. *Meetings with Poets* (N.Y.,
Ungar, 1969), pp. 27–29

It was . . . into a literary London temporarily steeped in surrealism that Dylan Thomas plunged during his earliest visits—a London of psychedelic parties that would not be unfamiliar to the inhabitants of Haight-Ashbury and the East Village of the sixties. On December 9, 1935, nonetheless, he wrote in response to Richard Church's letter concerning the surrealist elements in his poetry that "I am not, never have been, never will be, or could be for that matter, a surrealist. . . . I have very little idea what surrealism is; until quite recently I had never heard of it; I have never, to my knowledge, read even a paragraph of surrealist literature." By 1936, however, he had attended the surrealist exhibition with Vernon Watkins (where Thomas offered around tea brewed of string) and was invited to give a reading with Eluard and others at a surrealist poetry gathering in July of the same year. It was at this same time that he was preparing "The Mouse and the Woman" for publication in the fall issue of *transition*. . . .

We know from his "Answers to an Enquiry" that appeared in the October 1934 issue of *New Verse* that Dylan Thomas was sufficiently aware of the central contribution of Freudian psychology to criticize it intelligently. It is also probable that he perused Jung's essay on "Psychology and Poetry" in the June 1930 issue of *transition*; his feminine characters spring from within the heroes, closely resembling the mother-sister-wife figures described by Jung as preexistent archetypes accompanied by symbolism of water and submersion. Although one should not be tempted to apply Jung's psychological apparatus systematically to Thomas' work, there is no doubt that in his early prose he was trying to combine sexual and mythological patterns in a unique literary form. Eugene Jolas' editorship of *transition* was probably influential in Thomas' decision to construct personal myths: "We want myths and more myths!" Jolas declared in a flier to the June 1930 issue. It seems hardly coincidental that Thomas, who had already created a number of successful quasi-mythological tales, should have presented the psychologically complex dream story "The Mouse and the Woman" for publication in the 1936 issue.

Annis Pratt. *Dylan Thomas' Early Prose*
(Pittsburgh, Univ. of Pittsburgh Pr., 1970),
pp. 17–18

A great deal of Dylan Thomas's poetry, though it is fascinating, eludes us and is not meaningful by itself. In some way it is not complete: and the critic's task is to complete it, so that the meaning can be found. This involves us in attempting to decode the "code of night," and I believe an understanding of the problems of symbolising found in schizoid patients can help us. But we first have to decide *what kind of meaning this poetry could possibly have*. Here we need to introduce various possible patterns of human experience like Cinderella's slipper, to see if they fit. Many have applied the patterns of Christian symbolism to Dylan Thomas, and they have found that in the light of them his poetry makes a kind of sense. I have seldom found such explanations convincing. After studying object-relations psychology I came to believe that the feelings of identification with Christ, of wanting to be born again, and of arrested birth in Thomas's work are symbols to which a better key is the deeper pattern of the schizoid predicament, and the dynamics of the schizoid individual wanting to become a person and find meaning in his life. Insofar as these are Christian they are symbols belonging to elements in Christian mythology itself which express man's universal need to overcome despair and find a meaning in his existence.

David Holbrook. Dylan Thomas: The Code of Night (Athlone, 1972), p. 22

Thomas's religious position has been the topic of much discussion and various formulations have been offered, from Empson's "pessimistic pantheism" to FitzGibbon's suggestion of something like a reluctant agnosticism. One thing which seems certain is that we ought not to place the poet inside any orthodoxy. That the poems are often full of a wide range of quite orthodox allusions has only a limited significance. The received Christian framework is often an imagistic means whereby we provide ourselves, in conversation or creative work, with a structure for thought—and without which, in certain imaginative contexts, we cannot think at all.

In the absence of a Christian persuasion, a poet like Yeats created his own intellectual frameworks for his poems, occult and often freakish. Dylan Thomas, with a resistance to any kind of dogmatic conclusiveness, nevertheless accepted a tradition whose images, and indeed some of whose insights he felt to be congenial as poet and man. Reared in a society whose local version of that tradition must have struck him as having more to do with negative control of secular activity than with any penetration of the numinous, and deeply affected throughout his life by the independent pessimism of his father, he had had a leeway to make up which was not spanned by any firm theological development. His career was the refinement, not of belief, but of the emotions.

Walford Davies. Dylan Thomas (Cardiff, Univ. of Wales Pr., 1972), pp. 79–80

THOMAS, EDWARD (1878–1917)

To read and re-read the *Collected Poems* of Edward Thomas is to become aware of two principal themes, which are, indeed, as I have suggested, not so much themes as mental and emotional experiences that have coloured the poet's mind so thoroughly that they dye almost all his utterances. First, one realizes that these poems, written in the shadow of an annihilating war, have some of the darkness of that shadow in them. In a few reference to the war is explicit, but in many the shadow is palpable (visible, but also felt by us as a physical sensation—the shadow's coldness—deriving from a potent mental influence upon the poet. Its cold touch makes more urgent the poet's self-consciousness to the self-awareness which is also, inevitably, his awareness of others, and leads him to express with increasing directness his fears, his loves, and his failures in love and the achievement of wholeness. One feels, too, that the death this war has made him foresee, not as dream but as dung, has thrust upon him the desperation to write, thus acknowledging himself to be the poet he has always been too modest, too proud and too afraid to acknowledge before.

To the influence of Robert Frost in making Thomas know himself a poet must be added the war's influence in actualizing the ever-present sense of death that is, too often in his prose, more literary than real. As if to acknowledge the debt, as Keats does in his Odes, death is the most prominent hero in these poems. . . . Secondly, and . . . by no means divorced from the companionship of death, we are made aware of Thomas's solitude—call it, less poetically, his loneliness—which is much more than the sense of solitude common to most lyrical poems and demanded by the medium. In part this is because, although he writes three poems called "Home," he has no real home—and we must take the force of the word's metaphorical sense. He is homeless literally; in a way, I believe, because of his Welsh ancestry and his consequent pain at exile from a tradition which, though he loves it, he cannot be absorbed by wholeheartedly; and he is also homeless for other reasons . . . in the broadest but most pressing sense he feels himself to have no place in human society.

Jeremy Hooker. AWR. Autumn, 1970,
pp. 66–67

Throughout his twenty years as an active writer, Edward Thomas's work reveals a remarkable degree of uniformity in subject matter and content. Unsure of himself in pursuing practical day-by-day aims and purposes, he contrived to preserve intact the inner core of his creed and practice as a writer. Frequently assailed by periods of depression from early manhood until his final pre-embarkation training in firing camp, and strongly imprisoned within an inherited Victorian compulsion to make adequate middle class financial provision for his family, Thomas attempted at various times to enlarge the basis of his natural gifts as a writer in order to earn enough to pay his way and yet to preserve large tracts of free time in which he could write as he chose. He often accepted unworthy commissions. He engaged in multiple reviewing and the rapid production of many books, with the result that a few journalistic-critics, some of whom have never read much of his vast journalistic output, now label him thoughtlessly with the phrase "hack-writer."

The evidence of his letters, articles, books, and reviews points towards quite a different interpretation of his compulsive attention to bread-and-butter work. They suggest a somewhat different approach to the unity of Thomas's writing. There is a clear connection between his bouts of depression and his desire to impose a severe work pattern on himself. The acute sense of failure and the accompanying wandering that marks the year 1913 were undoubtedly the result of his exhausting personal fight against this condition, combined with the apparent inability of doctors to help him. His sense of inadequacy was coloured by a real change in popular taste which forced him to seek new markets for his writing which, according to Thomas Seccombe, was "apt to be too costly for the modern market; and the result was often Love and Literature, with its precarious rewards, literally in a cottage." Along with the usual ascription of tiredness, over-production, and listless drifting that is usually offered as evidence of Thomas's failure as a popular writer between 1912 and 1914, one is expected to swallow the miraculous emergence of a fully-blown poet in the winter of 1914/15, aided by the magic inspiration and example of the American poet Robert Frost. The sudden growth and ripening of their friendship is indisputable, as is Thomas's acknowledgment of his debt to Frost's personal inspiration, but the legend is a shade too like a fairytale. The facts are less dramatic.

R. George Thomas. *Edward Thomas* (Cardiff,
Univ. of Wales Pr., 1972), pp. 23–24

THOMAS, R. S. (1913–   )

For the last twenty years R. S. Thomas has added a new colour to the broad spectrum of contemporary English verse and, since 1952, his verse has reached a wide audience through its regular appearance in periodicals. Its formal qualities are unmistakable and are remarkably consistent. A strong visual sense is conveyed to the reader in hard taut rhythms which are dominated by monosyllables and riveted together by short, alliterative phrases, e.g., *day's dirt, tall tree, huge hunger, dead day, race root*. Each subject is presented with a fierce honesty of inward vision—a truly innocent eye—which refuses to blink at the crudities and violence of rural and natural life. . . .

Herein lies the secret of R. S. Thomas's best poetry. The mind is always in control of the verse, yet, underneath the control, are warring emotions: fierce hatred, deep compassion, and a priest's daily exercise in rigorous self-examinations. But the poet's hard-won understanding of the human lot is clarified and interpreted for the modern reader in terms of the husbandman's age-old love-hate relationship with the soil —the source of toil, sorrow, desire, and spiritual anguish. The conversation between the poet and the creatures of his imaginative world is offered clearly and starkly to the reader for his own consideration, reflection, and participation. The poet's initial, myopic concern with his own parishioners is gradually extended to include a wider community. The experience which began as an exercise in observation and contemplation and which developed into a ruthless act of national dissection, gradually became a variation on the theme of the ivory tower of the poet in a twentieth century community and, finally, a series of conversations about deadly sins and the need for forgiveness.

The poet's path towards vital issues has been circuitous but progressive. He began, one must conclude, in conscious imitation of Scottish and Irish writers who were in stated opposition to "the English urban and mechanized civilization." His rhetorical cry: "Why lament Troy fallen, when Mathrafal lies in ruin?" suggests the emergence of a national poet, writing on national themes for a nation that needed a stern awakening. His achievement to date is something quite different: the chronicler of a distant Welsh parish now points his sharp finger at the poetic conscience of a wide English reading public and invites it to re-examine the accepted premises of its over-intellectualized way of life. Yet the poet's call to contemplate and examine a dying way of life is not an act of nostalgia: this poetry abounds in thinly-disguised comments on our urban and industrial civilization. . . . The chronicler of a parish has become a significant mid-century English poet.

R. G. Thomas. R. S. Thomas (BC/Longmans,
1964), pp. 39–41

I remember reading in an early review of *Pietà* in *The Listener* that it was more "ideological" than R. S. Thomas's previous volumes and therefore disappointing. By "ideological" the writer apparently meant "settled in life-attitude": he implied that the painful questioning was at an end, and that which had settled was a sediment of gloom. . . .

I may be wrong about this, but I am not wrong in finding the poems as a whole less "settled," less addicted to the rut, more diversified in subject and gentler in tone. There is more ideology of a Christian sort, less of a nationalist. The echoes of nationalist despair in *Rhodri* and *Gifts* bear feeble comparison with the bitterness of say, "A Country," in *The Bread of Truth* and many another poem in the earlier volumes. The accusatory finger wags less and here only against those who leave Wales and care nothing for it, poor or rich, thereafter. There is, indeed, a more positive patriotism of an attractive kind in "A Welshman at St. James Park." . . .

There are perhaps too many nostrils in this book. And the air *crumbles* more than once. But I do not expect to read for a long time poems that so shake the inoculated, unfeeling spirit as "In Church" and "The Face." At times in the past R. S. Thomas has seemed tired, his verse free-wheeling from a long-past impulse. But this book marks a new, sharp turn of the wheel.

Roland Mathias. AWR. Spring, 1967,
pp. 158–59

Symbolically equating country with the physical world, and the city with spirit, Thomas sees the Nativity story as an emblem of integration. It is this wholeness of body and soul together, sensitive to beauty and the things of the spirit, and yet instinctually in touch with the dark power of trees and flowers to endure through the seasons, that emerges as Thomas' vision of the ideal. Often the affirmation is a negative one, as he describes the tragedy of men who are merely brutalized by the soil they work, but always there is the vision of a better way, an awakening of the "shy soil," which would permit not only the full realization of man's potential in individual cases, but the rebirth of an entire Welsh nation.

The reawakening will not happen of itself, however, but only if those men who still remember the old greatness can find a way to

communicate their vision, and it is here that the poet must acknowledge his responsibility. Throughout his verse Thomas is working to
define and reveal his vision of Wales's shame and its potential salvation—he moves through history and myth and through the brutal
ugliness of the present, and his role is nowhere better defined than in a
poem called "Taliesin 1952." Taliesin was an ancient Welsh bard, and
for Thomas he becomes a symbol of the poet's long struggle to learn the
truth, and finally to communicate that truth to men who continue to
suffer in darkness, to heal them, if he can, by showing them what he has
seen. . . .

As Taliesin, poet and seer, R. S. Thomas would seek a new myth
for his people. And he knows well that "a new world, risen" will be
found nowhere but "out of the heart's need." Focusing relentlessly in on
his peasants, on their gaunt faces and vacant eyes, and on the green,
living world all unseen around them, he writes of people who are out of
touch with their world, and with themselves. The power of myth in
Thomas' poetry derives from just this insight into the deep levels of
man's need, and from his capacity to convince us that in those barren
hearts there is a new world waiting, "stubborn with beauty."

James F. Knapp. *TCL.* Jan., 1971, pp. 8–9

R. S. Thomas glories in the Midas touch—and to some degree suffers
from it, as the case may be. There are very few poets to whom one
could point confidently, helping out some stranger to the earth and its
great forms, and say, of almost any one of his pieces, *that* is poetry,
and not fear that one had failed to show the thing in its purity. R. S.
Thomas is happily such a poet. Though he lacks the big, dredging gift
of his countryman Dylan Thomas, though his poetry cannot stir us in
our very bones, like new marrow, as "Fern Hill," "The Force that
Through the Green Fuse," and a few other of Dylan Thomas's poems do,
it is yet, unlike his, never lost in the rhythm and the words. It stands
out clear, lighter in weight because of its very clarity, but with a flame
as intense and fine.

R. S. Thomas's poems have an almost visible brilliance, an unremitting sensual poignancy. Never, perhaps, has firmness seemed so
ready a conductor for emotion. "Concrete" is too heavy a word for the
texture of Thomas's poems. For all their particularization, they are air-
borne, penetrated with light. . . .

The great quality of Thomas's work is . . . a passionate naturalness. Thomas makes most other poets seem stale, stuck away in rooms,
or carrying *The Oxford Book of English Poetry*, if not Webster's *Third,*
across a desert. His feeling, his movement, his diction, are light and
unlabored. He seems to enter each of his conceptions as if into a

stream that has just sprung out of the ground before him, that takes him abruptly and resistlessly on, and banks him in sight of the sea, the far silence, where all poems end. Though he rides his inspiration, it yet runs away beneath him. He is the current as well as the poised canoe. Of studied progress, of painful trial-and-error adding on, there is never a note. For all one knows, of course, Thomas may labour every one of his unfinicky lines, and he has said of being a poet that from forty on you recognize that the Muse's smile is not for you. Yet the poem on the printed page, his gift to us, affords the joy of a passionate and effortless openness before experience.

Calvin Bedient. *CQ*. Autumn, 1972, pp. 253–54

TOLKIEN, J. R. R. (1892–1973)

A vast compendium of elves, dwarves, and men; history, saga, and poetry; philosophy, adventure, and sentiment, *The Lord of the Rings* is unique in modern fiction. No contemporary novel, perhaps no work of prose fiction, in any way rivals its scope and diversity. For while *The Lord of the Rings* has much in common with and derives a great deal of its technique from the tradition of the English novel, its ultimate fore-bears must be sought elsewhere, in the forests and mountains of the Nordic lands and in the sagas, lays, eddas, and fairy tales which the inhabitants of those lands sang and passed on to their progeny.

The Lord of the Rings is essentially a Nordic myth and its distinc-tive qualities become clear only when it is approached as a myth rather than as a novel or as a children's book or even as a fantasy. In a sense, it defines its own genre, just as *Moby Dick* does, and like *Moby Dick*, it is as bewildering in its variety as it is convincing in its unity. The great difficulty, in fact, in discussing in any organized fashion either of these two created myths, however different their problems may appear to be on the surface, lies in losing one's way among the many diverting side-tracks which intersect the highway. It is altogether too easy to become diverted by the lore of whaling or by the geography of Gondor, by the symbolism of the Pequod's gams or by the significance of the twenty Elven rings of Middle-earth.

The reader of the "genreless" work is thus left without the con-venient key to itself with which genre usually provides him. Once he has established that a given work is an elegy, or a novel, or a play (or for that matter a sonata or a still life), he can begin to apply principle to particular with at least some good hope of constructing a fair analysis of the book's central issue. With *The Lord of the Rings* this particular device (happily perhaps) is denied the reader and another key must be sought. Here *Moby Dick* again provides a useful comparison. For as both books are myths, both revolve about a journey, and it is by following the progress of the journey, the quest of the mythical hero, whether Ishmael the New Englander or Frodo the Hobbit, that we can see the central pattern of the work emerge, the plain way from which all other paths are merely diversions.

Charles Moorman. *The Precincts of Felicity:*
The Augustinian City of the Oxford Christians
(Gainesville, Univ. of Florida Pr., 1966),
pp. 86–87

As we grow older in the Primary World, we realise more and more how much an individual's notion of good and evil and his power to resist temptation depend, not upon his reason and will, but upon the kind of family and society into which he happens to have been born and by which he has been educated. At any given time in history, some families and some societies are in a better state of moral health than others. In *The Lord of the Rings*, full justice is done to this fact. It is indeed "providential" that it should have been a hobbit, Bilbo, who founded the Ring, and a hobbit, Frodo, who has the task of taking it to Mount Doom. . . .

The Lord of the Rings ends, as a fairy tale should, with what Tolkien calls a *eucatastrophe* (when a fairy tale ends unhappily, like the French version of *Rapunzel*, the reader feels that the story has been broken off in the middle) but we are spared the pious fiction of the conventional concluding formula: *And so they lived happily ever after*. . . .

Good has triumphed over Evil so far as the Third Age of Middle-Earth is concerned, but there is no certainty that this triumph is final. . . . Victory does not mean either the restoration of the Earthly Paradise or the advent of the New Jerusalem. . . .

If, as I believe, a good story is one which can persuade us to face life neither with despair nor with false hopes, then *The Lord of the Rings* is a very good story indeed.

W. H. Auden. In C. B. Cox and A. E. Dyson,
eds., *Word in the Desert* (Oxford Univ. Pr.,
1968), pp. 139, 142

In any study of modern heroism, if J. R. R. Tolkien's *The Lord of the Rings* did not exist it would have to be invented. For at one place or another in this massive trilogy all the heroic issues of the western world, from *Beowulf* to D. H. Lawrence, are enacted, and the matter of these many heroisms is also the matter of the work's worth and ability to out-last its cults. Just why Tolkien has established himself so strongly among the eager young is not yet clear, and his popularity there is probably much more significant than his gradual acceptance into those academic realms that are loyal to the likes of C. S. Lewis and Chesterton. For the young show no signs of admiring Anglo-Oxford as such and generally have no positive response to the Old and the old heroic ways. What they see, then, in *The Lord of the Rings* may be a good part of what is really there, but because the enthusiasts as yet are more excited than articulate they have not really been able to say what makes Tolkien such an exciting author for them. As a result, literary assessment of the achievement is in its infancy and liable to remain so as long as elvish runes and details discussed in the appendices are still lively issues. . . .

Tolkien's biographer will someday be able to say just when the myth of the Ring and the idea of heroism attendant upon it came into being. For an outsider only a few things are clear. *The Lord of the Rings* was published as separate volumes in the middle fifties—*The Fellowship of the Ring* (1954), *The Two Towers* (1955), *The Return of the King* (1956)—but the work had been in the making for more than fifteen years. Tolkien had published *The Hobbit* in 1938, and the end of that book clearly foreshadows the later trilogy; he may have had the work in mind before then. It looks, strictly on the basis of internal literary evidence, as though Tolkien had been musing about Middle-earth for a long time but did not discover until he was finishing *The Hobbit* just how his vastly inventive genius could be used to make a story. For most of its length *The Hobbit* is the sort of book—*The Wind in the Willows* and the Pooh books are other examples—that appeals to a particular sort of reader, be he child or adult, whose sense of wit is near his sense of fun and whose willingness to pretend is akin to his ability to remember. The hobbits are not strictly human, but, like Mole and Toad in Kenneth Grahame or Pooh and Rabbit in Milne, they are based on recognizable English types. Hobbits are smaller and longer-lived than men, fond of living in houses without windows, fond of beer and good conversation, always in need of tobacco and able to live without the usual restraints of police or unfriendly women—indeed, C. S. Lewis' reminiscences of life at Oxford with Tolkien and others are often descriptive of hobbit life.

Roger Sale. In Neil D. Isaacs and Rose A.
Zimbardo, eds., *Tolkien and the Critics* (Notre
Dame, Ind., Univ. of Notre Dame Pr., 1968),
pp. 247–49

The Tolkien style in creating secondary worlds did not spring full-blown but developed out of his experience in writing *The Hobbit*, his first attempt at narrative. In that story Bilbo travels from Shire to Rivendell, as Frodo does, and meets Gandalf, Elrond, Gollum, and other characters who appear also in the epic. But the world of *The Hobbit* is not called Middle-earth, its vegetation and creatures are not visualized in patient detail, and it has no larger geographical or historical context whatever. Nor are the characters the same, although they bear the same names. Gandalf is merely a funny old wizard, for instance. And in a mistaken attempt to please an audience of children Tolkien trivializes and ridicules his elves and dwarves in precisely the manner he later comes to deplore. To call *The Lord of the Rings* a sequel to this childhood tale, as Tolkien does for the sake of continuity in the Ring plot, is to disguise the immense progress in technique evident in his epic fantasy.

Having once found his characteristic combination of the familiar with the unfamiliar, Tolkien never departed from it in any of the short verse and prose fiction he wrote after finishing the epic. "The Homecoming of Beorhtnoth" is an imagined sequel to the battle of Maldon between Vikings and Saxons in Essex in A.D. 991. "Farmer Giles of Ham" is set in the valley of the Thames in pre-Arthurian Britain. "Smith of Wootton Major" takes place in an essentially medieval English village, slightly hobbitized, which is a point of departure and return for excursions into a country called Faery. "Imram" tells of St. Brendan's sea voyage into the West in the sixth century. It starts and ends in Ireland. "The Lay of Aotrou and Itroun" is a Breton lay centering on the south coast of Britain in the chivalric age. "Leaf by Niggle" shows us a modern English village complete with neighbors, bicycles, housing regulations, a town council, and the rest, before taking off into a rather minutely pictured landscape where the soul after death goes through purgation.

In his unfinished *The Silmarillion* Tolkien faces the same problem in naturalizing the potentially fabulous happenings of Middle-earth's First Age.

> Paul H. Kocher. *Master of Middle-earth: The Fiction of J. R. R. Tolkien* (Boston, Houghton Mifflin, 1972), pp. 17–18

TOMLINSON, CHARLES (1927–   )

While Hughes and Larkin are the best-known of the relatively younger British poets in England, Charles Tomlinson is probably better known than either of them in the United States. He is well enough respected in England, but Americans have recognized more sharply just what, formally, he was up to. Tomlinson is one of the few British poets to go to school with the French symbolists and with the American masters of the generation of Pound, Stevens, Eliot, Williams, and Marianne Moore. His first book to be published in the United States, *Seeing Is Believing* (1958), gave clear evidence of this study. . . .

Another side of Tomlinson revealed in *Seeing Is Believing* is his strong feeling for the English past. He shares this feeling with many other English writers, including Larkin. However, poems like "On the Hall at Stowey" and "The Ruin" are not wry in the Larkin manner. Rather, they subordinate the speaker's personality to the search for empathy with their subjects. . . .

Tomlinson's two more recent volumes, *A Peopled Landscape* (1963) and *American Scenes* (1966), reflect a continuing relationship with the formal discoveries of American poetry and also with literal American experience. Since the appearance of *Seeing Is Believing*, he has taught at the University of New Mexico for a year and made other American visits. Although many other British poets have had similar American sojourns, Tomlinson is almost unique in the way these experiences have taken with him. Without surrendering either his British consciousness or the special characteristics of his earlier style—the restraint, precision, fine "sculptural" eye, and feeling for the literal realities of place and atmosphere—he has come rather strongly under the influence of Williams and of the Black Mountain poets.

M. L. Rosenthal. *The New Poets* (N.Y.,
Oxford Univ. Pr., 1967), pp. 244, 246, 248–49

The recognition accorded to Charles Tomlinson's experiments with poetic form ought not to obscure his more traditional critical and philosophical position. In a genteel, restrained, but resolute voice he defies our program-obsessed and manipulative age. Pointing to inflexible natural laws and to processes beyond our control, he argues against the premise that the natural world is the plaything of man and concludes that we are shaped by our surroundings. If we wish to know ourselves, then, we must permit the world unobstructed entry to our senses, seek to determine its "facts." As Tomlinson says of the landscape painter Constable, "what he saw/Discovered what he was."

Through his verse this poet brings many such facts to the attention of his readers. In the process he finds it necessary to entertain several fundamental questions concerning apprehension itself. Particularly in his first two volumes, *The Necklace* (1955) and *Seeing Is Believing* (1960), he is preoccupied with such issues as relative perspective, light and darkness, space, and motion. As he resolves these issues through his own poetic practice, he turns increasingly in his next three volumes to the assignment of human meaning to the "plenitude of fact" revealed in his verse.

Julian Gitzen. CQ. Winter, 1971, p. 355

With the exception of Donald Davie—who, however, turns out more verse than poetry—no other English poet of Tomlinson's generation so strongly gives the impression of being an artist modestly but seriously at work—a poet equally intense about his message and his craft. Tomlinson's dedication is deep and unmistakable; and joined with his rare if quiet talent, it has created not only poetry of the highest quality, but success after success, in a period when the successes of more striking and seductive poets—Ted Hughes, R. S. Thomas, Philip Larkin —have seemed haphazard. Of all these gifted poets it is Tomlinson who best survives the rub and wear of repeated readings; indeed, only Tomlinson's poetry improves under such treatment, like a fine wood under polish.

Part of the reason that Tomlinson tells slowly is that he has gone farther than any of his contemporaries—though Ted Hughes and Thomas Kinsella follow close—in outstaring and outmanoeuvring facility. He waits in advance, as it were, of his readers, who, burdened with ageing notions of what makes up poetic appeal, must labour to come abreast. In consequence, until Tomlinson is admired, he must be tolerated. His meticulous descriptions, so often hard to seize with the eye, his laconic meditations, his uncertain, demanding rhythms, his frustrations of expectations of various kinds—these one must struggle through as if through scrub, until one emerges, pleased and surprised, into the clearings that, in reality, the poems usually are. Because of both an increased dynamic clarity and a more definite music, Tomlinson's latest poems are probably his most readily accessible; they still, however, constitute a language to be learned, a flavour to be found, and to care about Tomlinson is to approve of this difficulty. Just as the later Yeats makes the early Yeats seem somewhat facile and obvious, so Tomlinson, asceticising poetry as he has, gives one a new sense of what the art can be. His is the sort of modification of poetry that ultimately makes it incumbent on other poets to change, to make it new, to work passionately at their craft.

As for the sensibility that Tomlinson's poetry expresses, its value, I think, should be self-evident. The truth it has seized upon, indeed the truth that seems native to it, is the lesson implicit in art itself—that contemplation is the fulfilment of being. Of course we have always to know what needs to be changed; but we also do well to praise and reverence what is sufficient for the day and the vast design that, though it impinges on us, ultimately lies beyond our human agency. For without this reverence we can scarcely be committed to the value of being; it is the secret of what Pasternak called "the talent for life." Tomlinson is certainly out of season to recall us to the life of the moment conceived as an end in itself; and yet it is just this unseasonableness that puts him in harmony with what is lasting in our relations with the world.

Calvin Bedient. In Michael Schmidt and Grevel
Lindop, eds., British Poetry since 1960: A
Critical Survey (Oxford, Carcanet, 1972),
p. 189

● TREVOR, WILLIAM (1928–   )

From Alec Waugh's *Loom of Youth* to David Benedictus's *The Fourth of June*, there have been many devastating, funny, or clever exposés of "what really goes on" at an English public school. But in his first [sic] novel, *The Old Boys*—which is certainly clever, in places very funny, and in a quiet way quite devastating—William Trevor has chosen to show us the anti-life force of the public school as it bears upon the existences of eight "boys," all of whom are now over seventy.

These eight old boys are members of the committee of the Old Boys' Association of an unnamed public school at which, long ago, they were contemporaries. The main thread of the story concerns the efforts of Jaraby to make certain that he will be elected the next chairman of the committee. In fact his election is opposed only by Nox, who bears an ancient schoolboy spite against Jaraby.

The principles of the Old School are personified by Dowse, the long-dead housemaster, who believed that "you must apply to the world the laws that apply to this school." In faithful obedience to these laws, Jaraby has bullied his wife, rejected his ineffectual son, periodically released his sex in a brothel (recommended by Dowse), and lavished his only affection on Monmouth, a huge, one-eyed, and loathsome cat. . . .

Mr. Trevor's deliberately stylized dialogue beautifully conveys a peculiar quality of unreality; for, although all of *The Old Boys* are close to the grave, this is not a book about death, but about unlived life. It is an original novel and a very good one.

Julian Gloag. *Sat.* May 2, 1964, p. 37

William Trevor is in the happy position of having scored a thumping success with his first novel. *The Old Boys* was described by no less a figure than Evelyn Waugh himself as "uncommonly well-written, gruesome, funny and original." Praise like this from such an exalted quarter is almost akin to beatification but it was richly deserved. In his account of the Machiavellian skulduggery surrounding the election of the President of the Old Boys' Association, Trevor demonstrated a remarkable flair for dry, elegant comedy, and his book somehow contrived to be both extremely funny and very sad. A dazzling triumph, all that remained to be seen was whether or not he could follow it up with something as good.

We now know. *The Boarding-House* is an accomplished and highly entertaining novel which established beyond any doubt that Mr. Trevor is a writer to be reckoned with. His touch here is as confident as ever as he weaves a complicated web of plot, counterplot, deception, misunderstanding and plain, downright dottiness round his central theme. As in *The Old Boys*, his story combines an acute appreciation of human psychology with a sparkling wit and inventiveness that make it a delight to read.

Frank McGuinness. *L.* Aug., 1965, pp. 104–5

Muriel Spark's brilliant novels have been admired. It now seems that they are emulated. She has, like Miss Brodie, her pupils, and if William Trevor is in his prime, it must be said that he owes much to her example. The very notion of being in your prime, on which she has established a kind of copyright, appears recurrently in his new novel [*The Love Department*]: the novel also has pyromaniac imaginings which might be thought to correspond to the conflagration in *The Girls of Slender Means*—sparks off the old block with a vengeance. His first novel, *The Old Boys*, offered many reminiscences of *Memento Mori*, while the new one resembles, in particular, *The Ballad of Peckham Rye*. Mrs. Spark has a tendency to be arch: Mr. Trevor is very arch. A fey atmosphere is common to both. A faintly prissy, school-mistressly, old-fashioned formality of speech, as of Miss Brodie, is favoured by both, together with a calculated quaintness and unsmiling humor: as originally mediated by Mrs. Spark, these things could possibly be regarded as Edinburgh's gift to the world. Fine old expressions like "be your age" are conjugated like Latin verbs by Mr. Trevor, in the manner of Mrs. Spark: "in your prime" could, I suppose, be considered the future tense of "be your age." Mrs. Spark's is not the only influence, however: she is supplanted at times by Ivy Compton-Burnett. *The Old Boys*, for example, has a vein of stoical dialogue: "It is only right that the past should be forgotten and the prodigal receive a welcome. It is the human thing." . . .

Mr. Trevor's sparkling prose does indeed sparkle. He is deft and felicitous, and carries off his litany-like conversations with never a wrong word. None of the characters stays in the mind but the farcical ensembles are often funny, as on the night when the evil Mrs. Hoop gets her deserts from a fractious monkey. Mr. Trevor performs well. But I doubt whether he performs well enough to take away the tedium of its having been done before, and by a novelist of distinguished talent. The interest is, to a fair extent, that of discovering how such a writer can feed another writer. The novel teaches a lesson in the diffusion of culture. . . .

Karl Miller. *NS*. Sept. 23, 1966, p. 441

William Trevor, an immensely gifted short story writer, is known as a writer of television plays, though all the plays he has written have been adaptations of his short stories. But you can hardly blame him. His new collection, *The Ballroom of Romance*—two or three of the stories have appeared on television—confirms the reputation he gained on the publication of his previous collection, *The Day We Got Drunk on Cake* (best since *The Wrong Set*, best since the war, critics said). . . .

Though the characters in Mr. Trevor's novels are quite different from his short story characters (the former are several degrees more perverse than the latter, as well as—usually—from a different social class), Mr. Trevor's achievement has been to create, by means of the clearest and most original prose in this generation and a compassionate balance of fascination and sympathy, real people of flesh and blood out of characters another writer would dismiss as goons or drudges.

It is for the women in this collection that one feels most deeply. Indeed, the thread that runs through all the stories is of brittle or urgent femininity thwarted by rather boorish maleness. Mr. Trevor's men are feckless, or else malicious snobs, or drunkards, or comradely and exclusive old boys; his women are victims of, at once, their own strength and the men's weakness, isolated by their longings or by the perversity of their husbands or lovers. . . .

Some of the stories are heartrending, but Mr. Trevor writes with a light touch, without sentimentality and always with humour. There is a crotchety precision about his narration; what other writer would be able to get away with the sentence, "No alcoholic liquor was ever served in the Ballroom of Romance, the premises not being licensed for this added stimulant"? He is the master of exasperation, of the person speaking at length in tones of formal annoyance; and he is at his best when dealing with a condition of lucidity one has always thought of as madness. His real skill lies in his ability to portray this behaviour as a heightened condition of life; in his work there is no madness, but there is much suffering.

Paul Theroux. Enc. Sept., 1972, pp. 69–70

WAIN, JOHN (1925–   )

While he is no Homer—and who is?—John Wain smites his lyre with accomplished versatility as an astute, lively critic, a fine poet (too little known over here), and a fiction writer whose highly lauded first novel, the picaresque *Hurry On Down*, is still a re-readable delight. Following that notable debut, however, his indubitable gifts have been applied to curiously uneven material so that his irony and pointed social comedy are diminished, in some of his work, by his subject-matter, instead of the subject-matter remaining under the control of his dispassionate viewpoint.

This fluctuation is more evident in his short stories, it seems to me, because the form literally cramps his reach. However, as always, in the present collection [*Death of the Hind Legs*] he moves easily in diverse social directions, probing human pretensions and self-deceptions, though with less of the devastating comic put-down that so enlivens his novels. The situations, too, have the variousness characteristic of Wain.

In "King Caliban" a gentle hulk of a man is forced into professional wrestling against his will, with brutalizing consequences; while in "Further Education" a cynically urbane tycoon renews acquaintance with a couple he knew during his Oxford undergraduate years, only to cuckold the idealistic husband, as he had done twenty years before. "Down Our Way" exposes another kind of ruthlessness, that propelled by the shibboleths of self-righteous "respectability." Most movingly, in "A Visit at Teatime," the reality of a child's imagination vanquishes the unreality of nostalgia in a man revisiting his boyhood home. But in the title story nostalgia drenches the scene: a tacky pantomime troupe, playing a last round in a condemned theater, includes a valiant old pro who, fallen on dark days, is now the hindquarters of a make-believe-horse routine, and it is while he is in this guise that death overtakes him. Even John Wain's skilled manner barely saves the matter of the tale from the abyss of bathos.

It's bemusing, the fuzzing-off that Wain is prone to from time to time, bemusing because, at its best, his talent for limning the more sardonic foibles of the human caper just doesn't fit with the disparities you'd accept in a lesser writer.

Patricia MacManus. *Sat.* Dec. 3, 1966, p. 60

Wain is a "serious" novelist who, being quite competent to satirize, to exhort, even to retreat, too often does these things all at the same time; and his confusion of purpose results in artistic failure.

Our appreciation of Wain's novels comes then to the question of artistry and its composition. Technical skill with the storyteller's tools? or an understanding of life that illuminates the work and the beholder? or—the obvious answer—that fusion of the two which can rightfully be called *vision*. Wain has the requisite technical skills, and often his understanding is significant; but only occasionally have these two come together to form an indestructible work of art. In "The Conflict of Forms in Contemporary English Literature" (*Essays on Literature and Ideas*, 1963), Wain wrote that if the writer "needs elbow-room he will tend to go for a large, capacious form such as the novel," and almost immediately afterward the confession that for himself "the problems of form have always seemed very difficult to solve." Here is an essential problem in John Wain's novels to date: only in parts do they convince one that they should be novels rather than stories, or poems, or even essays.

The short stories in *Death of the Hind Legs* (1966) seem to prove this point. They were originally published in various slick magazines; and their content and form, skill and attitude are so perfectly balanced that they reach an artistic level which Wain just misses in his novels. This problem of form relates to the length at which Wain spins out his material, for too often in his novels the subject is not big enough for the extended treatment; yet it may also be that Wain's actual understanding of his subject is not adequate. Whatever his problem is, however, these novels are the most impressive output of any of the postwar British writers; and they show that when Wain at last finds that understanding, or perhaps that special subject, which he has approached so often but never quite reached, then we can expect from him some of the most important novels of the second half of this century.

Elgin W. Mellown. *SAQ*. Summer, 1969,
pp. 341–42

WARNER, SYLVIA TOWNSEND (1893–   )

Ordinarily, our sensible parent, *The New Yorker*, doles out Sylvia Townsend Warner's stories one at a time. But her collected stories, like her favorite sweets, *marrons glacés*, make way for immoderate consumption and some indigestion.

The unfaltering texture and taste of the latest in *Swans on an Autumn River* are admirable, but disconcerting too. Small talents seem properly more restless in the United States than in England. Truman Capote feels new literary forms thrust upon him; both he and we envisage the writing career as an infinite beanstalk to climb, an ascent which Miss Warner would snub as otiose, also ungainly. She herself minds her neat, confined talent like a shop for gourmets; her products aim at the choice modesty of kumquats and button mushrooms. . . .

A collection of such stories is like an annual surprise party: within the total predictability of the gathering, each story calls out, in its well-bred accent, "Surprise! Surprise!" And we experience, against our will, the same small ridiculous sensation of pleasure we felt the year before. In the past, Miss Warner's interest in the preternatural was more distinct, but it is sensed still in the titivations of her new stories. Across the placid surfaces of her characters run inexplicable tremors. Minute unseen forces play minute tricks, equivalents of curdling milk and dropping stitches and hiding best umbrellas. Each story is allotted its moment of witchery: a sudden, often mischievous, seldom malign, and never prolonged interruption of the habitual state.

And how it is told fits like hook and eye what is told. Each sentence too executes its tweak of the mind. A shock, slightly more emphatic than others to come, sets the story in motion. Miss Warner likes to make the start startling and seemingly disconnected, a shopping list, a notice posted in a French dining car. (Eventually, of course, these things will be unremittingly connected.) A short, level plain ensues, time to cross our legs and wind our watches. Then come the dips and turns of observation ("Dissatisfaction is a mildew, and creeps"), the near crises ("An instant later, deftly and deliberately, she knocked over her coffee-cup"), a dark tunnel with small shrieks, moments of birdlike suspension above beechwoods and bungalow roofs. The pace quickens, to outdistance ennui, and then we absorb the sharp, conclusive jolt, the laconic solution of a telegram: MOTHER DIED CLIMBING BOX HILL.

Mary Ellmann. *Nation*. April 11, 1966, p. 431

● WATERHOUSE, KEITH (1929–   )

This pungent, shapely and instructive novel [*Billy Liar*] begins, and for the first half continues, comically. Billy Fisher, an ambitious and mendacious teenager in the Yorkshire town of Stradhoughton, describes his progress through one critical Saturday. As he tells it, his family is a pack of harping drudges, his employers (undertakers) are a pair of futile fools, and his town is a dismal muddle of moldering churchyards and modernist record shops, of despairing institutions and desperate Americanisms.

Along these drab streets Billy trundles a complicated apparatus of fantasy worlds. . . . The friction of all these revolving spheres strikes a wonderful number of comic sparks. And it all seems true. The author gives us adolescence full-bodied, in its raucous ferocity. The well-known "sensitive" youth, so pitiably oppressed in American fiction, is here shown wounding, with his callousness and derision, society in turn; "Stradhoughton was littered with objects for our derision," Billy says.

In the second half of the book the demands of that wearisome old fellow Plot, or perhaps the inherent seriousness of the material itself, press hard upon the humor. Apparently Billy must, if he cannot unravel, at least confront the tangle he has made. His bad checks roll in. His ebullience weakens, and with it the mainspring of the comedy. Mr. Waterhouse rushes new, more somber resources to the fore. He creates several harrowing and touching scenes. But he is handicapped, I think, by the determinedly comic tone of the beginning. . . .

It comes down to the doubtful compatibility, over the length of a book, of comedy and realism. Even novels as funny as Joyce Cary's *Herself Surprised* and Henry Green's *Nothing* do not strike us as purposely comic, but, rather, accidentally so, like reality itself. The publicized Anger of England's younger writers may seem to lead easily into satire and hence into the also publicized Renascence of the Comic Novel. But, in Mr. Waterhouse's case, there is much more at stake than a view, indignant or amused, of the contemporary scene; and, while I would not really want this excellent book (except for a phrase about "the eyes that laughed aloud") any different, I hope that the author in his future work does not confine himself to a genre possibly too small for his experiences and his feelings about them.

John Updike. NYT. Jan. 3, 1960, pp. 4, 22

Billy Liar is a harrowing and very funny funeral ode on the English provinces. Everything has turned to stone: behind everybody's rubber mask of a jolly-old-England face, provincial-dialect face, coy-maiden face, sexy-waitress face, angry-dad face, weary-forgiving-ma face, surly-old-Gran face, rests the insensate petrifaction of cliché: the skull of dead glories. Billy wanders like the last Earthman among these touchy humanoids and the slagheaps of their homes, shops, squares, milkbars, dancehalls, cinemas. He lies as easily as he breathes, to exhaust the vital energy that makes him a pariah among them, to conjure up jokes out of nightmares, to hear the echo of his solitary voice, to propitiate these monsters of his beleaguered imagination. The book's only mistake—a big one—is the abruptly upbeat ending, wherein the author, as well as Billy, seems to lose his nerve.

Jubb, on the other hand, is all nerve. . . . [It] takes the cadaver of English propriety for a ride, this time to the end of the road. . . . This . . . time round, Waterhouse has written a not so funny funeral ode on the English middle class; a true allegory, not tosh about a lot of rain and stowaways; a Passion according to the daily papers, our newest testament.

Marvin Mudrick. *NYR*. March 19, 1964,
pp. 16–17

Waterhouse's third novel, *Jubb* (the first is called *There Is a Happy Land*), gives more weight to my reading of Billy Liar—that Waterhouse's heroes, though perverse, are supposed to command more than our interest. I hesitate to say "respect," although at times that is my inclination. They are both basically moral human beings who are turning or have turned "queer," because their particular environments will such a change. At one point during this century they might have been picaresque heroes, gifted with what critics call unselfconsciousness; Waterhouse calls it fantasy—everyone has such a gift—and notes what happens to the man, who, without reservation, "follows his thoughts."

I am not trying to make Cyril Jubb respectable. The point is elusive. Jubb is a minority group spokesman: Mussolini, too, "followed his thoughts" and Jubb envies him not only his "twenty mistresses" but his black-booted virility and power. I am not impressed, either, by the argument that Jubb's desires are "no different from those of the average middle class citizen" of the crowded world. That may be so but such reading misses the inevitability of Jubb's compulsion, his exasperating but thoroughly sympathetic struggle to make the world into his own image. (Snapping Mrs. Rosen with the empty camera—you just know that acts of that kind in front of women of her mentality will lead him into trouble.) We see him losing his mask step by step; at the same time he is unable to keep from becoming a part of things. Why, for a start, is he compelled to peep? Perhaps to make up somehow for the fact that his wife is so inordinately square, but beyond that—and this is perhaps as literal an "interpretation" as one can offer—to be there, inside the room towards which he longs. "There is a happy land" that is not in the future for Billy or for Jubb, but in the past, some frozen moment when the world held out its arms to them, or seemed to.

Thomas Churchill. *Critique*. Vol. 10, No. 3,
1968, p. 76

As in *Jubb*, Keith Waterhouse continues in *Everything Must Go* his dissection of the introspective personality begun in *Billy Liar*. The first two novels utilized provincial and urban settings, the new one invades the London theatrical fringe, a background appropriate to Waterhouse's gifts for caricature and the grotesque. Bitterly humorous, *Everything Must Go* demonstrates again the author's wit and moral detachment, a detachment reminiscent in many ways of Evelyn Waugh. . . .

Billy Liar dealt brilliantly with prolonged adolescence, *Jubb* with the psychotic-introspective personality. *Everything Must Go*, while still concerned with the relationship of guilt and responsibility, the individual and the social order, indicates that Waterhouse is expanding his scope. If several of the scenes appear forced, if coincidence plays a strong part in the action, if at times the irony seems all too convenient, rich comic invention and precise characterization do much to offset these minor negative aspects.

A. A. DeVitis. *Sat.* March 1, 1969, p. 50

WATKINS, VERNON (1906-1967)

Friendship with Dylan Thomas, and certain affinities of theme with the younger poet, helped to link the late Vernon Watkins decisively with the Forties neo-Romantics. When the Forties mode lost favour, his reputation lost ground with the rest. He was Welsh, he tended to get excited and rhapsodic about nature, and he admired some of the mystics and sages adopted by the New Apocalypse—what more was needed to place him? And his uncompromising pursuit of poetry as a sacred and honourable vocation didn't exactly impress Fifties poets busy being sceptical, robust and ironic. As a result, one looks almost in vain for any fair and considered assessment of Watkins's verse in critical writings published since 1955. Yet his was, by any standards, a major talent; and the publication of *Fidelities*, his last and perhaps his best book, should help to correct a persistent underestimation.

For Watkins, poetry was a continual celebration of the forces of nature, a deeply honest aspiration to truth through sea, wind, sky and stone. Despite the ambitiousness of his themes, the power in his poetry is of a quiet kind. The splendour of his effects is hardly ever sudden: the very deliberate diction does lack a final grandeur or resolving excitement, his shots at sturdy Yeatsian sonorities didn't work, and he too often wrote lengthily in strict forms which encouraged a sort of high-flown, orderly vagueness. But his best work has a grave purity and measured impressiveness that stands firmly based on exact and brilliant observation.

Alan Brownjohn. *NS*. Dec. 13, 1968, p. 843

Much could be said of Vernon Watkins's verse, of his skill in the use of many forms both English and Classical. Perfectionism of verse has been the heritage of Welsh-born poets down to Vernon Watkins's generation, perhaps the last inheritors. English poets, whose ears are attuned to blank verse, sonnet and couplet, may envy poets of the Celtic tradition the intricate rhymes and assonances of the *cynghanedd*. Vernon Watkins was not a Welsh speaker, though his parents were; but he remained within earshot, so to say, of the language. We can already see in retrospect that the innovations of modern poetry have not been those much-publicised rejections of traditional forms, the "free" verse introduced by Pound and Eliot, French prose-poetry, or the succeeding chaos, but (in these islands, for America is another matter) the skilful, careful and gifted prosody of poets within the Celtic tradition of Wales and Ireland, and perhaps of the "makars" of Scotland. Hopkins, an Englishman, studied Welsh verse. In his use of verse Vernon Watkins comes perhaps nearest to his early friend Dylan Thomas, with whom he shared the years of learning the poet's craft. Yet it is not in these poems in which he most resembles Dylan Thomas that Vernon Watkins is at his best—rather the reverse—and the same is true of the influence upon him of Yeats, whom he already had taken as a model while his Cambridge contemporaries were concerned only with Pound and the Imagist theories of T. E. Hulme. His note is his own; yet at the same time a voice more of the race than that of Dylan Thomas.

Like Dylan Thomas he was a perfectionist, never allowing any poem short of attainable perfection to appear in print; he left unpublished as many poems as he ever passed for publication. Like David Jones it was his habit to keep poems and to work over them at long intervals until he was satisfied that they were right. He was cut off in the prime of a talent slowly and continuously developed.

So much of his best work is so recent that it is hard to realise his death. Yet in another sense death has set a seal of perfection on Watkins's work in a sense beyond the universal finality of death. Because the wholeness of life and death within immortality was the theme of his work, the poet seems now to have been writing from his own experience no less of death than of life; which was not nor could have been so while he was working on the pattern from the side of life. To say his poetry "foresaw" his own death is too personal a way of expressing the integrity of what was a universal vision of the human condition, comparable with that of Henry Vaughan or Thomas Traherne. Like these, Vernon Watkins had discovered that mysterious light or life of which the visible world is woven; the ultimate alchemical mystery whose realization brings to those who achieve it a supreme joy, and the all but lost sense of "the holy" which illuminates the work of Vernon Watkins, as it does the finest work of Dylan Thomas.

Kathleen Raine. In Leslie Norris, ed., *Vernon Watkins 1906–1967* (Faber and Faber, 1970), pp. 42–43

WAUGH, EVELYN (1903–1966)

Though passionately and patriotically English, [Waugh's] Catholicism saved him from insularity and I regarded his tilting at my cosmopolitanism as a sort of family joke. Each of us tended to exaggerate his foibles for the other's benefits. Thus he was apt to play the crusty colonel in later years in a vain attempt to set the unrepentant aesthete a good example. He had earned other beside literary laurels for he had been heroic during the war, throwing himself heart and soul into hazardous operations rather too strenuous for his age, and the strain of these buffetings must have affected his health. The semi-autobiographical *Ordeal of Gilbert Pinfold*, to me a painful document, was one of the consequences. He forced himself to be more robust than his physique. The epicurean wore the mask of a stoic until he became one.

Art benefited by an effort more sublime than Flaubert's on account of the physical sacrifice it entailed. Waugh on war rose to the highest peak of his narrative creation. *Sword of Honour*, his masterpiece, will be studied and remembered long after most chronicles of the Second World War as it was seen, endured and fought by characteristic as well as uncharacteristic Englishmen.

He thought of himself as uncharacteristic, but in my opinion he possessed the most typical English virtues, great courage, deep faith, romantic idealism and a strong sense of duty.

Harold Acton. *Adam*. Nos. 301–2–3, 1966, p. 11

If Waugh is to be remembered as a comic novelist, that implies no relegation to a secondary status, as though it were a meaner achievement to make people laugh than to make them cry. He recognized his kinship with P. G. Wodehouse, but comedy with him was not merely entertainment, summer-holiday stuff: it was a medium for the expression of ultimate truths, some of them very bitter. Apthorpe, like young Lord Tangent, has to die. The appalling "nonsense" which Cedric Line makes of the embarkation in *Put Out More Flags* is desperately funny, but it also encapsulates the real nonsense of the pre-Churchillian days, when England had still not learned what war was about. And even at its most light-hearted, the comedy finds an exact gravity of locution: Waugh's comic underworld—smugglers, deserters, burglars, night-club courtesans—are accorded the dignity of language appropriate to personages who have, in their various bizarre ways, arrived at acceptable modes of order. The humour is, in the best sense, aristocratic.

Critics may now go to work on Waugh's place in the hierarchy of British writers (equal to Greene? to Forster?) and list his literary creditors (Firbank? Ford Madox Ford?), but mere authors will continue to despair of their ability to approach that prose perfection, though the mere existence of the challenge must make them better writers. Readers will regret that the *Autobiography*, which promised so brilliantly, can now never take the shelf as an expository masterpiece, and that the crass patterns of modern life—on both sides of the Atlantic —will never again find so detached and elegant and devastating a castigator. But, to use Evelyn Waugh's favourite phrase, we must not repine. We have what we have, which is a great deal, and—as the author would wish, if he could have brought himself to accept that we should be thankful at all—we thank God for it.

Anthony Burgess. *Spec.* April 15, 1966, p. 462

Waugh apparently realized the shortcomings of *Brideshead Revisited* for in several "interludes," pieces immediately following this novel, he returns to the techniques and themes of the early novels. It is not until *Men at Arms* that he confidently resumes the development of the expanding thematic concerns and the maturing artistry of the novels preceding *Brideshead Revisited*. In this first of the war trilogy, and in *Officers and Gentlemen* and *Unconditional Surrender*, Waugh demonstrates an assured handling of the exigencies of the ironic mode, particularly the personae technique, toward the formulation of a serious and plausible moral statement; the result is a trilogy which in sheer artistry surpasses all of the previous fiction and which in thematic impact identifies Waugh as an outstanding moralist of the age. . . .

Irony is not compromised; it is rather disciplined into a "hardness of mind" which can realistically accept the fact that the hero's quest is predoomed and at the same time ungrudgingly extend sympathy to less chivalric but no less noble segments of the society. This is but a culmination of the growing realism of the previous novels. Although the quest is characterized by a note of high romance (Captain Truslove style) at the outset of *Men at Arms*, and although the original vision of knightly duty to church and state is never destroyed, it eventually finds its fulfillment not in the Arcadian splendor of Brideshead nor in the chivalric world of Roger of Waybroke, nor even in the Royal Corps of Halberdiers, but in the physical suffering and spiritual chaos of war, within the individual human spirit. In fact this pervasive "ironic realism" ultimately comes to sustain a whole philosophy of life—not the harsh repudiation of *Decline and Fall* or *Vile Bodies*, not the mere seriousness of *Put Out More Flags*, nor the optimism of *Brideshead Revisited*, but a resigned and compassionate wisdom.

It is Waugh's uniquely contrived personae technique—working through all the various novels, simultaneously and purposefully developing narrative, controlling tone, and discovering and extending theme —which proves that the author is both a master craftsman and a sincere moralist whose works, viewed collectively and in context, are a single earnest attempt to identify and to reconcile within the artistic medium of the novel a moral dilemma of universal proportions. The attempt is a tribute to the man; the astounding degree of success is testimony to the greatness of his art and to his status as a major novelist of the twentieth century.

William J. Cook, Jr. *Masks, Modes, and Morals: The Art of Evelyn Waugh* (Rutherford, N.J., Fairleigh Dickinson Univ. Pr., 1971), pp. 342–44

WELLS, H. G. (1866–1946)

Wells turned naturally and easily to the writing of science fiction because he possessed what demands to be called "the Wellsian imagination." This Wellsian imagination is the key to his science fiction as well as to the nature of its impact, and I shall attempt to describe it briefly.

Wells is, of course, closely identified with a particular vision of a utopian World State, a vision which is important in explaining his relationship to the anti-utopians. . . . As [Van Wyck] Brooks remarked about Wells's fiction in general, and as we would say particularly about his scientific romances, future histories, and utopias, Wells saw men chemically and anatomically, the world astronomically. Brooks also put it another way: it is the distinction between the intellectual, who views life in terms of ideas, and the artist, who views life in terms of experience. Generally speaking, the intellectual dominated Wells's writings, though sometimes—most continuously in *Tono-Bungay*, *Kipps*, and *Mr. Polly*—the artist took over. But it must be emphasized that this distinction between "intellectual" and "artistic" refers to the angle at which reality is viewed, not to the quality of writing. Even at his most "intellectual," as in, say, *The Time Machine*, Wells was capable of vividness in both conception and expression. *The Time Machine*, though it differs greatly from ordinary fiction, has some right to the title "art."

Surely the single most spectacular manifestation of this detached quality of the Wellsian imagination is its preoccupation with the future. . . .

Along with the detached imagination and its preoccupation with the future go certain clearly defined and inevitable values and interests. Wells—not surprisingly for a former student and admirer of T. H. Huxley—was a supreme rationalist and believer in science and the scientific method, a Francis Bacon reborn. And so for Wells, as for one of his Utopians in *Men Like Gods*, there was no way out of the cages of life but by knowledge—knowledge of man himself and of man in relation to the things about him. Naturally the Wellsian imagination is drawn to certain characteristic subjects. It is fascinated by the revelations of man's place in time and space given to us by science, fascinated by the vistas of astronomy, particularly the death of the world and the vastness of interstellar space, fascinated by the vision of geological epochs, the evolution of life, and the early history of man vouchsafed by geology, paleontology, and archaeology.

The first, brilliant fruit of this Wellsian imagination were the scientific romances and stories written in the 1890's which led, in their turn, by a complicated process which also involved reaction against the Wellsian utopias, to the major anti-utopias of the twentieth century.

Mark R. Hillegas. *The Future as Nightmare:
H. G. Wells and the Anti-Utopians* (N.Y.,
Oxford Univ. Pr., 1967), pp. 13–15

Wells's world outlook was constrained and made acceptable by his impressive commitment to the facts of scientific discovery and the faculty of rational analysis. His recourse to the irresponsible magic of the fictional persona was not altogether consistent with this. As the science was superseded and the flaws of the reasoning became exposed, the currency of the late novels naturally ceased. But there is another way of imposing yourself on your readers which is more lasting in its effects. Every artist expresses his own "adventure," but he must somehow use the constraints of his chosen form to make good the deficiencies of merely personal experience. Wells did so in the scientific romances, through the alternation of imaginative worlds, and in the comedies, through the interplay between interpreting narrator and created hero.

In this universe of plasticity and surprise, of images and types, the modes of scientific investigation and human response are combined. Microscopy is paired with the sense of wonder, taxonomy with the sense of fun. It is in these joint exercises of the scientific and literary imagination that his creative energy continues to renew itself.

Patrick Parrinder. *H. G. Wells* (Edinburgh,
Oliver & Boyd, 1970), p. 102

Wells came at a stifling period in England's history when an age, the Victorian, had long outlived those vital forces which moved men to think and act for the good of their species. He came at a period which was growing more and more content with the lifeless formulas of society and growing more and more impervious to needed changes in those formulas. He came at a period when the masses were growing more and more conscious of the power which was in their numbers. He came when a new age, the Edwardian, and a new century, the twentieth, were waiting expectantly to take their places at the center of the stage. He came when science and technology were beginning to make the first great advances into the ignorance which had clouded humanity for so many centuries. He came when these advances were effecting rapid changes in all aspects of man's life save one, seemingly, the novel.

Paradoxically, these effects which were altering life so radically were ignored by an art which prided itself on its close relationship to that life. Wells was one of the first to sense the great need to probe in the realm of the novel the growing social and moral unrest occasioned by the applications of the discoveries of this new science and technology to the long unchanged conditions of man's daily life. In doing so he discovered and discussed many of the major social, psychological, and moral questions which plague us today and are as yet unanswered satisfactorily.

His greatest fault, however, was his fundamental inability to develop his suspicions that these problems are not solely the province of contemporary man, nor solely attributable to scientific and technological advances, nor to a deadening social system, but have plagued man throughout his existence. He failed to understand that these problems rise up out of man's nature. In his failure to come directly to grip with the root cause of humanity's difficulties, he supplied answers that were and are too simple to believe and too idealistic to be completely achieved. As a result, he committed the unpardonable aesthetic sin of misreading human nature and translating this misreading into characters who became merely puppets for their creator to move as he willed. . . .

In loving mankind so much, he lost, ironically, a love for man. Like Swift, whom he somewhat resembles, he failed to discern the glory of man which lies behind man's stupidities, his inconsistencies, cantankerousness, and the evil he does. Consequently, Wells failed in the first immutable requirement of the novel—that its creator love his creatures. Wells paid the full price for his failure—despair in his later years and oblivion for much of his work.

Alfred Borrello. *H. G. Wells: Author in Agony*
(Carbondale, Southern Illinois Univ. Pr.,
1972), pp. 119–20

WESKER, ARNOLD (1932–   )

The enormous time-span and the frequent time-changes [in *Their Very Own and Golden City*] (whether seen as forward or back) inevitably make for a sequence of loosely-linked episodes. The last quarter of the play is described by the author as a "continuous scene," which in fact means only that the scenes become even shorter and the advance into the future more rapid. This possibly is intended to suggest that time appears to pass more quickly as a man grows older, but more likely Wesker gave so much space to Andy's early days that the building of the City had to be compressed. The pattern of the decline of a man morally paralleling the rise of his tangible achievements is a good one, but this contrast enters only in the second half, leaving the first part on Andy's youth awkwardly detached.

Nevertheless, Wesker has attempted a highly ambitious work, in content and form. The man who moved from the accomplished use of three conventional acts in *Chicken Soup* to the four balanced phases of *The Four Seasons*, with its subtle changes in pace and tension, could no doubt have repeated mastery of structures like these. Instead he adventurously tries something different, and in the London production, Trussler reported, "the potentially bitty action fell together into a final shape that can only be described as epic."

The mention of "epic" suggests Brecht, and *Golden City* and *Chips* are probably influenced by the form of plays like *Galileo* and *Mother Courage*. Some scenes in *Chips*—bayonet-drill, stealing coke, the party—are amongst Wesker's finest theatrical effects, but the uncertainty of style and multiplicity of themes limit the total achievement.

The strengths of the trilogy included a strong social conscience, concern with the nature of life in England in his lifetime, and effective studies of ordinary people (including Wesker himself and several members of his family). In these three later plays he no longer needs to draw on relatives for characters, and his own experiences come into wider perspective. *Chips* examines how his air force years helped form Wesker, especially the public man, while *The Four Seasons* examines an important aspect of Wesker the private man. His own experiences and idealism, and a scrutiny of public events that have affected his generation, are all in *Golden City*. In *Golden City*, in addition, he is for the first time analysing, albeit clumsily, one of his present problems rather than a past one. The seriousness and the choice of big issues is admirable; perhaps all these pieces are preparatory to political plays about Britain in the sixties and seventies. Though I judge only *The Four Seasons* to be successful of these three plays, they show Wesker striving to extend his range, moving through structural experiments to greater self-knowledge and new linguistic attainment.

Malcolm Page. *MD*. Dec., 1968, pp. 324–25

The most pervasive and unifying concern that runs through all Wesker's plays and draws in most of the other themes could hardly be more basic —the search for systematic sense in life, for an interpretation that is at least workably inclusive yet also life-affirming. The lack of this, though scarcely articulated, bewilders the cooks in *The Kitchen*, caught in their enervating routine and groping in unresponsive isolation for an alternative. Ronnie's search for it, as embodied in his political philosophy, is, it seems, close to being abandoned by the end of the Trilogy: for him, it is irreconcilable socially with what he experiences as an individual—whilst for Dave and Ada it fails to offer even the personal salvation it maybe promises Beatie Bryant. And Beatie's problem has been precisely a rootlessness that denies her not so much her rural inheritance as a means of grasping, ingesting, co-ordinating and communicating *all* experience. A fallen, sterile substitute of a system subjugates the airmen of *Chips* in their faith-sustained, hierarchical world; and in *The Four Seasons* Adam and Beatrice fail to live with and for each other because they have failed to live with and for anybody else. Finally, and most fully, the search for a unifying order infuses the patchwork and fragmentation themes of *Golden City* and *The Friends*.

What does seem to have changed is the emphasis: in the earlier plays the central characters are baffled and dismayed by the inordinate muddle of society, so meekly accepted by its members, whilst, after the transitional *Chips*, the protagonists are aware not only of the confusion that surrounds them in their sense of community, but of the dislocation and unpredictability within themselves. To have sought to cope with such a theme as this within even so tentatively naturalistic a framework as *The Friends* was to invite ridicule and rebuke—just as the Trilogy, once its polemical appeal begins to wane, may seem only overweeningly ambitious, and presumptive in its ambition, alike to the enemies of its ideas and to friends who sincerely doubt the usefulness or the possibility of such a wide-ranging investigation as Wesker's work actually attempts. It is, of course, much more acceptable in the present theatrical climate to reduce a sense of anguish to formal, laughable or intractable absurdity, and it takes a brave mind to lay itself bare in a manner less allusively, more explicitly revealing. But because Wesker is seeking to reconcile individual anguish with social anger, the lonely lover with the golden city—and because, as *The Friends* confirms, he believes that such reconciliation is possible—he will probably continue to write plays which, self-consistent without being self-satisfied, continue his exploration from its original starting point, wherever that may lead, instead of distorting his talents into the latest modish mould.

> Glenda Leeming and Simon Trussler. *The Plays of Arnold Wesker: An Assessment* (Gollancz, 1971), pp. 191–93

The Journalists is both one of Wesker's most disciplined plays and one of his most relaxed. Certain points may be underlined too heavily; for example, towards the end we get too many repetitions of the point about the danger inherent in a newspaper's selective attention to detail. But there is a good deal of compensating comedy and vitality.

The organic movement of the play grows up around the newspaper's movement towards the moment when, at about six o'clock on Saturday evening, the printing presses start to roll. Toward the end of the week, there is an inevitable frenzy of last-minute activity as decisions are made about the allocation of front-page space. The physical bustle may be very different from that of cooks and waitresses in a busy restaurant, but more than in any other play since *The Kitchen*, Wesker cashes in on the theatrical possibilities of large-scale corporate activity reaching a climax of intensity; and he shows the same talent for dramatizing it.

Halfway through the final act he calls for a film projection of the turning presses, and as they start we hear the full blast of their noise. The volume of this has to be taken down for the dialogue which is to follow, but the hurried movements of the messengers, the speed with which decisions have to be taken, the changing rhythm of the characters' speech patterns, and the rhythm of the sequence of short scenes all contribute to the climacteric accelerando. As in *The Kitchen*, the full potential of the play can be realized only with the help of a director capable of disciplining his actors into an intricate choreography of physical actions; but *The Journalists* is much more complex than *The Kitchen*, more carefully structured, with a more calculated interdependence of dialogue and movement.

Since the over-ambitious *Their Very Own and Golden City*, each of Wesker's plays had been less ambitious than its predecessor, but with no compensating consolidation of technical *savoir faire*. Now, suddenly, he has bounded ahead to write an extremely ambitious play in which his technique matches up to the demands he makes on it.

Ronald Hayman. *Arnold Wesker* (N.Y.,
Ungar, 1973), pp. 122–23

WEST, REBECCA (1892–   )

[*The Birds Fall Down* is] a fascinating story, so contracted in time and focus as to resemble a thriller rather than a conventional novel, but a thriller infinitely superior in style and imaginative power to most of the breed. Miss West suggests in a foreword that the incidents recounted are more than symbolically true. Her allusions are appropriately sibylline, but they hint at real persons and real events. In any case, she proposes that the collapse of the liberal-idealist-terrorist groups, discredited by instances of police spying like that depicted in the story, opened the door to the professional revolutionaries like Lenin—presumably less romantic and less ambiguously "Russian" in their goals and methods.

As historiography, the hypothesis seems at least incomplete; the shape assumed by the Russian Revolution of 1917 cannot be explained on grounds of individual psychology alone. But Miss West's historical thesis is explicitly presented only in her brief foreword. In the novel itself, her psychological notations are perfectly convincing, the divided mind of the traitor—presented by indirection, but no less forcefully for that—provokes an answering anguish in the reader. It will be remembered that Miss West has examined the question of treachery on another occasion. I found *The New Meaning of Treason* objectionable for its cavalierly offered insights into the minds of convicted traitors. It seemed to me faintly indecent to clap a gloss upon the work of criminal tribunals, psychologizing the man in the dock with as much familiarity as if we had made him, when in fact we could only unmake him. But *The Birds Fall Down* is Miss West's own excellent invention, its characters are her creatures, and she may analyze and exhibit them as she pleases. That she has done and most happily.

Emile Capouya. *BW*. Oct. 2, 1966, p. 2

Rebecca West's literary career is outstanding both in scope and durability. She began writing reviews at age nineteen for *Freewoman*; the following year (1912) she joined *Clarion* as a political writer and has continued to write for British and American periodicals. Setting aside her hundred-odd early magazine pieces, the interval between her first and most recent book spans fifty years. Her output during this busy career is richly varied: political journalism, literary criticism, biography, history, travel sketches and fiction.

If this vast and varied output holds together, the unifying core must be the Augustinian doctrine of original sin. An effect, argued Augustine, cannot be greater than its cause. If we are nothing ourselves —not good or bad, but nothing—none of our strivings can have any reality. Although she has written an interpretive biography of St. Augustine (1933), she has never exorcised him. Her books continue to insist that there is more evil than good in our world and that the evil is more vivid. Man's depravity energizes the two myths symbolically designated in the title, *Black Lamb and Grey Falcon* (1941). It undergirds Rebecca West's distrust of the worldliness usually equated with the male principle. It saturates her reading of Shakespeare: the palace intrigues in the histories and tragedies show what happens when the will acts in a milieu where the will counts as nothing; *The Court and the Castle* (1953) claims that Calvin, who insures the salvation of a few, sparkles and glints sunshine next to Shakespeare, who damns all. Rebecca West's own characters seem determined by what they *are*, not by what they do. Their choices do not create new opportunities. Alice Pemberton, of "The Salt of the Earth" (1934), does evil things in order to punish herself for a nonspecifiable crime. This self-destructiveness, all the stronger for its involuntary nature, recurs in Rebecca West's criticism.

Peter Wolfe. *Rebecca West: Artist and Thinker*
(Carbondale, Southern Illinois Univ. Pr.,
1971), pp. 1–2

Rebecca West might be called a literary Paganini. She has written and published many words, most of them words of wisdom and wit, in almost every prose medium—journalism, history, literary criticism, short stories, novels. She is probably most famous as an interpreter of contemporary history, and *A Train of Powder* and *The New Meaning of Treason* justify this fame. Yet many consider her genius to lie essentially in literary criticism, and *The Strange Necessity, The Court and the Castle* bear this out. But what engages us here are the six serious novels, published over a period of almost fifty years from *The Return of the Soldier* in 1918 to *The Birds Fall Down* in 1966, novels which display an incredible eclecticism in style, structure, content, subject matter and technique.

What unifies her work is its brilliance of style and the wholeness and coherence of her world view. Whatever Miss West writes is distinguished by the tough elegance of her prose, by sentences as soundly conceived and executed as those of any living stylist. . . . The business of the artist, Miss West says in both *The Strange Necessity* and *The Court and the Castle*, is to analyze his experience and construct from his examination a synthesis for his readers which will clarify and focus, often correcting, their view of the universe. Miss West observes experience with an innocent and unclouded eye, accurate and farseeing. She constructs her syntheses out of a full understanding of what the eye has seen, coupled with a deep understanding of the culture and the literary tradition within which she works. And she contrives to perfect the form of the synthesis with grace and concentration.

These qualities account for much, but they do not explain her virtuosity. Nor is her rich eclecticism to be confused with experimentation. The six novels, in their startling and wide-ranging differences, give no evidence that the author has tried first one medium and then another, searching for the one which best suits her. On the contrary, she has been able to choose, out of limitless resources, whatever style and type of novel her analysis demands for its synthesis. To speculate *why* she has never needed to repeat herself is both impossible and absurd with so articulate an artist, who would share her motivations if she wished to.

Turner S. Kobler. Critique. Vol. 13, No. 2,
1971, pp. 30–31

● WHITING, JOHN (1915–1963)

The prurient would be well advised to stay away from *The Devils* should it ever be produced again in this country. For Whiting had no sensational purpose in mind, nor any desire to make theatrical capital of the infirmities, historical or otherwise, of priests and nuns. His drama is in the fullest sense a universal one: it is a complex, sometimes brutal and shocking but always beautifully passionate image of faculties and powers in collision with one another, of the body struggling against the spirit and becoming reconciled to it, of lust learning its own nature through sacrifice, and, on a different and more immediate level, of secular authority using religion for the consolidation of its control.

Grandier, the priest who stands at first as an incarnation of lust and pride, is brought to redemptive humility through the irony of being persecuted and tortured for a crime of which he is innocent, that of being the agent of the reputed possession. And it is precisely this irony, that the suffering the world inflicts may have no relation to men's true guilt, that Whiting builds upon in many subtle ways. "How can you be a man of God unless you are a man?," Grandier is asked. *The Devils*, with an impressive grandeur of conception and a fusion of sonorous poetry with crisp, colloquial speech, moves through the stages of discovery of what it means to be a man, what it means to face, with unblinking courage and unsentimental endurance, the truth of one's guilt.

John Whiting died last year at the age of forty-seven. *The Devils*, which was commissioned by the Stratford-on-Avon Company and first produced by the Royal Shakespeare Company in London two years ago, was his masterwork. For once the plaudits of the press were justified. If it is not a great breakthrough into new dramatic art, the play is as solid, brilliant and inspired a piece of traditional theater as we have had for many years, one point of comparison being Robert Bolt's *A Man for All Seasons*, to which it is measurably superior.

Richard Gilman. Com. Dec. 20, 1963, p. 371

[Whiting] was, or seemed to be, preoccupied with everything. In the main plays he explores an extraordinary wealth and variety of character, mood and relationship. But obsessions in Whiting's case are larger than any one person. He cannot contain any one obsession alone in one play and then and there finish with it. A main character like Paul Southman in *Saint's Day* is killed off at the end of the play, but phoenix-like his obsessions re-emerge in the next. Partly they have the feeling of wounds, for the cure of which he tries a different medicine each time, or a different poison. Partly there is a celebration of the obsession as a higher and ennobling feature of mankind: even a justification of man. The individual obsessions of his protagonists—that is to say Paul Southman in *Saint's Day*, Rupert Forster in *Marching Song* and Grandier in *The Devils*—are their own form of commitment. In the day-to-day existentialism of their lives, this is what steadies them, aims them, and jerks them up, putting them off target. Their obsessions are there by virtue of some egalitarian, antiseptic (for Whiting) principle of free choice operating. They have choice, yes, but their characters are their fate. . . .

Each is presented in a set of circumstances consequent to what they are, or have done. Egocentrically deployed in plots that have a hard, though abstracted precision, they are destroyed by a set of circumstances or people who don't allow their obsessions to come to fruition. They are all stopped short of complete achievement, yet ironically enough, they are all great because they have tried. . . .

John Whiting had begun work on another full-length play, *The Nomads*, and what little of it he managed to complete, together with his notes as to his intentions, promised a work as substantial as the three great plays. Above all, he was a dramatist of weight. The incisiveness of his style, the direct harshness of utterance, the technical skill of craft, musical and exact in balance, the ambiguities of thought and meaning which time will both harden and multiply, are but a few of the qualities which will increase the life and influence of *Saint's Day, Marching Song* and *The Devils*. . . . We are left the work of a writer who asserts the greatness of his individuality. For whom man made God in his image, and society in his image. Whiting's assertion of man aligns him to Shelley, to Byron, but it is a crystal-clear assertion— and tough.

Garry O'Connor. *Encore*. July–Aug., 1964,
pp. 27, 36

This lack of concern at [Whiting's] death, and what it might mean for the English-speaking drama, is hardly to be wondered at considering how little attention his work had received from critics in either country. Until the production of *The Devils* by the Royal Shakespeare Company at the Aldwych Theatre in 1961, reviewers had been unanimous in damning his plays; Harold Hobson's review of *Saint's Day* in *The Sunday Times* (London) for September 9, 1951, was matched for its hysterical savagery only by Ivor Brown's comments in *The Observer*. Until *The Devils*, none of his four plays enjoyed a long run. Yet *Saint's Day* received a £700 award in the Festival of Britain Drama Contest, and when it was attacked, Tyrone Guthrie and Peter Brook sprang to its defense in the correspondence columns of *The Times*. In fact, among British theater people Whiting has been something of a legend as a writer with a tremendous talent for providing theatrical impact—although the chief argument brought against him by the reviewers was his coldness, his literary obscurity, his failure to establish communication with audiences, and his excessive addiction to complex symbolism. In this country, he has remained almost entirely unknown. . . .

Probably the reason for this neglect is that although Whiting began writing for the theater at a time when England desperately

needed new playwrights, he remained outside the so-called "new movement" in either its Wesker-Osborne or its Pinter branches. He had no
allegiance to a social, political, or religious point of view, and he was
explicitly opposed to "committed" writing, on the grounds that art is
ineffectual as propaganda. The only engagement he recognized was a
personal and humanistic one: the commitment should be *by* art, not
through it. What this means, perhaps, is that he felt too strong a commitment to art as art to use it for ulterior purposes—though he was just
as adamant in condemning the idea of art for the sake of art alone. His
concern was simply that the artist should not be so involved with
nonartistic interests that he loses his artistic integrity and independence.
At least I assume that this is what he had in mind when in an interview with Tom Milne for the magazine *Encore* he cited approvingly
Aldous Huxley's statement "that the nearest he had ever been able to
define his own position as a writer was that of a gangster who lives
on society, but beyond it, on the edge of it."

John Dennis Hurrell. *MD*. Sept., 1965,
pp. 134–35

Only recently has the new drama begun to catch up with John Whiting, who if he were alive would now be almost fifty. He was out of
sympathy with the social commitment of the early days. Whiting was
not one of the cultural knight-errants who crusaded for working-class
culture and against the bomb; rather, he belonged instinctively to the
older tradition of the intellectual elite, writing difficult plays for a discriminating audience—an audience with which he never truly made
contact, and which perhaps had long ceased to exist.

Yet his lifelong preoccupations with the nature of violence and of
personal responsibility foreshadowed the concern of a younger generation of dramatists with issues more elemental than the kitchen sink.
Beyond defining these preoccupations, he did not regard his works as
needing explication; but a more objective critic might make a plausible
case for labelling him a closet dramatist, citing a structural and
thematic density—at least in the first three plays—too complex to be
disentangled in the immediacy of production. In this sense Whiting
was no precursor of the new wave, for its leading figures have been distinguished precisely by their ability to release drama from its academic
straitjacket. But by contrast with the formal tricksiness of the verse
dramatists, and with the well-made ephemera of the Rattigans and
the Hunters—in which uninspiring context his early work must be set—
his achievement was unique in combining intelligence and contemporaneity while remaining relevant for the predicaments of the sixties, and
in exerting, at least for a minority, a distinctively theatrical pull.

The range of his relatively small output, from delicately textured comedy to physically painful near-melodrama, was enormous. Each play was at once derivative and germinal, owing some debt to the mode of the theatrical moment, but contributing its significant share to recent developments. An aphorism summed up his own creative intention: the purpose of entertainment was to reassure, and the purpose of art to raise doubts. And it is probably by defining precisely *how* Whiting's works raise doubts that their structure, their ambiguity, and their essence can best be perceived. Fundamentally, the doubts he raises relate to the nature of reality itself: each of the four major plays has the sequential logic of dream, and each explores not merely man's responsibility for his actions, but the premises on which action itself depends. Where the absurdists, however, would explore these premises by a process of parodied and caricatured reality, Whiting ambiguities work within a sense of normality, and thus act more immediately and disturbingly upon an audience's assumptions. The heightened logic of *Saint's Day* is akin to the mad reasoning of [John Arden's] Serjeant Musgrave, but it is never arbitrary: and the fact that Whiting retains a relativistic hold on reality while rejecting its formal and logical restrictions probably explains the peculiar sense of bewilderment which seems to afflict his audience and his critics—who are prepared to go the whole hog to absurdity, or no hog at all, but don't like having to define a position somewhere in between.

Simon Trussler. *TDR*. Winter, 1966,
pp. 141–42

John Whiting's *Marching Song* (1954) is an interesting development of a familiar theatrical form: the house-party of representative characters, in which a phase of society and a crisis of conscience can be enacted. It is what Shaw made of Chekhov in *Heartbreak House*, and there are innumerable minor examples. Fry's *The Dark Is Light Enough*, which appeared in the same year, is a related example. What is unusual, about Whiting's play, is the tone: an understatement, in the direct terms of naturalist theatre and acting, in a form which is normally, by its whole stance, rhetorical. . . .

Marching Song is unusual in a special sense: in its concentration, into a single and restrained form and tone, of the representative themes and gestures of a late liberalism, a settled liberalism. It is not penetrating: not the savagely exposing, disturbed and distorted action of the post-liberal collapse. It is a late compression, internally honest and serious and restrained, of an achieved structure of feeling and its essential conventions. The tension, that is to say, has all gone inwards: into a stasis of mood and image; an unrhetorical heartbreak house, at the very end of a period. It is less showy, less crude, than the forms which succeeded it; its professional compression has that assurance that is possible in a stalemate of feeling and action, within which the words and movements and references are known. At the same time its anxious restraint shows clearly, if negatively, what would happen to this complex, if the controls were relaxed: a rush of feeling, and a loss of form.

Raymond Williams. *Drama from Ibsen to Brecht* (Chatto and Windus, 1968), pp. 316–18

At first sight one might suppose that the major plays of John Whiting were not written by the same man. *A Penny for a Song, Saint's Day, Marching Song*, and *The Devils* are bewildering not only for their occasional obscurities but also for the disparity in their content and execution. A brief summary will make the point.

A Penny for a Song (1951, revised 1962) is an ironic but gentle comedy which, as Whiting says in his introduction to *The Plays of John Whiting* (1957), pokes fun at "the finer lunacies of the English at war." Despite the many farcical misfortunes which befall its squire hero, Sir Timothy Bellboys, *A Penny for a Song* is a delicate, even nostalgic fantasy about the ideals and illusions which life destroys. *Saint's Day*, written immediately before *A Penny for a Song* but produced half a year after it in September, 1951 is a precursor of the absurdist plays. Its irrational nightmarish action is played out among obsessed self-destructive characters amid an atmosphere of mystery and doom. The play ends with the execution of the main characters at the hands of some absurd but apocalyptic force in the shape of three marauding trumpet-blowing soldiers. In contrast to *Saint's Day* Whiting's next play, *Marching Song* (1954), is clear and unemotional. But despite its coldness *Marching Song* is an intense play since Whiting focusses on the inevitable suicide of its hero, the defeated general. Again, *The Devils*, written in 1960 after a break with the theater of six years, differs from all of the previous plays. A diffuse historical drama based on Aldous Huxley's *The Devils of Loudun*, it is a clever, well-written but somewhat unsatisfactory play mainly because the characters are seen too much from the outside. In contrast to the straightforward story line of *Marching Song*, *The Devils* has an intricate network of plots and subplots, twenty-four characters and over sixty scene changes.

Yet there are elements common to all these plays; Whiting's sensitive and original language, his preoccupation with ideas rather than characters, and his predilection for rebel heroes who tend to be symbols rather than individuals, lacking as they do the emotions and concerns of ordinary mortals. But despite his concern for ideas Whiting never loses his sense of theater, which makes his plays immediately effective as visual and theatrical experiences.

Gabrielle Scott Robinson. *MD*. May, 1971,
pp. 23–24

● WILLIAMS, HEATHCOTE (1941–   )

"[Williams is] like Congreve," William Gaskill rather alarmingly volunteered during a broadcast discussion, and though the comparison seems far-fetched one can see what he means. The same obsessive regard for the exact placing of words, the same unreliability in calculating the overall dramatic effect of the words, the same tendency to let his characters' eloquence carry him beyond their words' dramatic value. The fault is less apparent in *The Local Stigmatic*, a one-act play of considerable verbal and physical violence, almost entirely unexplained. In fact the only assumption one can make, considering the play in even faintly realistic terms, is that all the characters are mad.

Probably that is right enough, if we look back from it to Williams's extraordinary book evoking the lunatic half-world of Speakers' Corner fanatics, *The Speakers* (1964) and then forward to his play *AC/DC*. In *The Speakers* Williams re-creates, with extraordinary powers of mimicry, the world—or rather the separate, self-defining, independently co-existing worlds—of a number of speakers at Speakers' Corner, all with some pretty weird bees in their respective bonnets. *AC/DC* is in some respects an extension of the technique, an exploration of some further aspects of the same theme. And here, as in the book, the miracle is how far the author has managed to write himself out of his work, to present us with a powerful picture of some very strange people with very strange ideas and leave it absolutely to speak for itself, without explaining, apologizing, hinting by the flicker of an eyelid at what sort of response we are expected to make. . . .

In any case, the play is a *tour de force*, whichever way one looks at it, and for all its frustrations and irritations a compelling piece of theatre, sometimes wildly funny, sometimes haunting. And in it, curiously, extremes meet: Williams is regarded in some respects as our most advanced dramatist, and yet in his meticulous concern for the written word, his almost painfully acute sense of style, he could also be seen as the most traditional of them all.

John Russell Taylor. *The Second Wave* (N.Y.,
Hill and Wang, 1971), pp. 219–20, 222

AC/DC is about the victims of historical velocity. Heathcote Williams' phenomenal play takes the television set as the central symbol of our technological age—an object in which our passion for speed and obsession with energy coalesce. Ours is the moment, as radio stations brag, of "all-information-all-the-time," and the medium of television feeds our craving the way Dr. Faustus's magic carpet served his insatiable appetite for knowledge and power. Flooded with imagery, modern man is isolated from events yet always conscious of them. He feels powerless in a universe that seems at his fingertips.

The new generation's desire to change shape is a survival tactic. No writer epitomizes and re-creates the anguish and visionary longing of this protean generation better than Williams, who admits to "feelings of extreme impotence and extreme inability to control one's environment." Although Williams is British, his plays speaks more accurately to the exaggerations of the American media. *AC/DC*—a title incorporating transformation and energy sources—synthesizes and clarifies deep areas of psychic dislocation in the culture. The play depicts the sensory overload. Its style is the same bombardment of information and ideas that makes Williams' claim that "the human animal is totally convertible" not only logical but necessary. *AC/DC* is a "brain-buzz," a bypass circuit for "media rash" which gives shape and definition to the behavioral effects of media static. [1972]

John Lahr. *Astonish Me* (N.Y., Viking, 1973),
pp. 157–58

While Pinter is undoubtedly the most influential and important craftsman in English theatre, Heathcote Williams, a writer Pinter has encouraged, has written perhaps the most theatrically inventive and prophetic work of the past decade, *AC/DC*. Nostalgia looks to the past for a future; but Williams diagnoses and faces the culture's sensory overload and works through all its fashionable intellectual bric-a-brac in an act of theatrical imagination which is astounding. He dramatizes the cultural isolation and argues, surprisingly, for an act of faith to heal the mind and raise it above the abrasions of daily life. . . .

Williams understands the life-death struggle of youth, and also finds a metaphor which incarnates the yearning for physical mutation —symbolized by drugs—to develop a higher, more profound and efficient consciousness.

The search is on for new symbols and new modes of survival. Other playwrights like Joe Orton and Edward Bond have sensed this and touched on the perimeter of the problem, but only Williams has had the manic strength and stage know-how to get to its core.

TLS. Dec. 29, 1972, p. 1570

Since the sixties, England has produced only one playwright whose inner resonance could compare with the front runners of the New Wave: Pinter, Osborne, Arden. That writer, on the strength of only one full-length play—*AC/DC*—and a single one-acter—*The Local Stigmatic*—is Heathcote Williams. . . .

There is an enormous amount of activity in England, but very few solid dramatic pieces; only a handful of plays are worth protecting or returning to. Among these plays, *AC/DC* rotates like that formidable missile out of *2001: A Space Odyssey*—not simply because it is a good play but because it is the *only* play yet written to capture the tremulously combustible nature of the 21st century, which, because our mortal lives always trail chronology, is the century in which we are actually living.

And *The Local Stigmatic*, which was created as a brilliant piece of effrontery to Pinter's *The Caretaker*, is to *AC/DC* what Chekhov's *The Wood Demon* is to his *Uncle Vanya*—a testament that the writer is thoroughly equipped to dole out the small change of the drama and that the full-scale investments are only a matter of time. . . .

I find Heathcote Williams one of the few people I have ever met whom I would call pure in heart. It is precisely this purity of heart that causes him to investigate the corrosion in the hearts of others. It is what fuels *AC/DC* with a power that is simultaneously satanic and deific. . . .

Charles Marowitz. *NYTts*. July 21, 1974,

pp. 3, 8

WILSON, ANGUS (1913–   )

It is evident in Wilson's work that he is a writer of the highest seriousness. His concern with that journey into the darkest recesses of the self is one which has inhabited all of literature. It is the passage of Oedipus, Gawain, Hamlet, Marlow, Raskolnikov. These comparisons are not meant to imply, however, that Wilson is of the stature of say Dostoevski or Conrad. It is easy to fall into the error of overpraising one's subject in order to justify it. Wilson has not yet made an achievement that would place him in the ranks of these great writers. Too much in his work violates the requisite set forth by James: that fiction must before all things be interesting. Too frequently the vacancy and drag, the deadly friction, of the failed lives which are his subject take command of his work. As in the case of James, however (and it would be sheer sentimentality to say that James always fulfills his own requisite), the very frictions against which he works are a measure of his ambition, of the task he has set for himself. More and more he has renounced the easy targets so vulnerable to heavy satire and concerned himself with the nuances and gradations of human fallibility, those accretions that grain by grain build not to the sudden and sensational shock but to that atmosphere of muted terror that is most pervasively true to human existence—the terror of felt hopelessness, the terror of that jungle of evasions which can finally trap a life inescapably in its senseless grip. Wilson has gone a long way toward accomplishing his task.

Arthur Edelstein. In Charles Shapiro, ed.,
Contemporary British Novelists (Carbondale,
Southern Illinois Univ. Pr., 1965), pp. 160–61

Late Call is the first novel to come from Angus Wilson since his highly controversial *The Old Men at the Zoo* set the English intelligentsia spitting at each other from the review sections of the various weeklies. Sadly for those of us who enjoy the splendidly diverting spectacle of the *literati* at loggerheads, its publication calls a halt to the venomous bickering in their ranks. The breach is healed. Warmly praised in both camps, the novel obviously establishes Mr. Wilson very much back in favour with even his harshest critics of three years ago. Indeed, many of the reviews read less like a critical appreciation of the book than a heartfelt vote of thanks that it avoids the tumescent morbidity so deplored in the earlier novel.

But there is more than this. Almost to a man, the critics have discovered a new element in Mr. Wilson's writing to be hailed as some outward sign of grace marking his redemption. For them, tenderness and a gentle concern for his creations—sentiments not hitherto markedly evident in his work—bathe each page in what one can only imagine to be the sort of earnest glow that illuminates political broadcasts on behalf of the Liberal Party. Not that one quarrels so much with the emphasis they lay on Wilson's changing attitudes as with their apparent conviction that it constitutes some kind of major breakthrough on his part. It is certainly true that *Late Call*, lacking both the satirical bite of the short stories and the melodramatic extravagance with which he depicted his vision of Fascist Britain, casts the author in a curiously mellow and compassionate light.

This much is commendable. Any novelist willing to abandon a successful literary formula in order to widen the area of his interest and sympathy deserves our praise. The trouble is that Wilson in his new image has not yet eliminated the penchant for excess that was wont to blemish the old. Where once satire and bold inventiveness occasionally blurred into spite and kinky flamboyance, sentiment now hovers on the brink of bathos and finally plunges into downright mawkishness. It is no less disappointing. Although the novel may well prove to be the new point of departure so widely predicted for its author, intermittent mush for occasional malice strikes me as no great step forward.

Frank McGuinness. L. Jan., 1965, pp. 100–101

Wilson may not be for the ages. His work has its obvious limitations of tone. The *raffiniert* note of Camp is never quite absent and sentimentalism is often just below the surface. It is too sophisticated for many people and too "nasty" for others. Wilson's admirable aloofness of depiction rules out his passionate emotional involvement with the fate of his characters and it leaves us a little lost too. To understand all is to forgive all but it is apt to leave us indifferent. His characters are fatiguingly self-analytic and see themselves, as Wilson does, rather too unsparingly. The action of his novels, notably in *Late Call*, is almost entirely psychological in ways that are convincing but not very likely, and Wilson's constant identification with the viewpoint of the old is not to everyone's taste.

Indeed Wilson's considerable popularity in this country is a little mystifying. Some of his material can only be baffling to Americans even of Anglophile tastes. The implications of a story such as "A Flat Country Christman" in *A Bit off the Map*, for example, can only mystify the average American reader, whose experience of social position and its importance will be so different. We may not in the United States have achieved a classless society but our experience of class is something far different. In England the old class order which is now breaking up was a horizontal one. In this country class distinctions have been much more on a vertical basis, with innumerable factors of wealth, education, national origin, color, individual talent, religion, and even geography playing a part such as they do not in England.

One has the feeling too that Wilson's preoccupations as a social historian have already become somewhat mysterious in England itself. He says as much himself in his books, where the difficulties of social change are spelled out precisely as that—no one knows his place in society any more. No one is willing any longer to be assigned the role of comic servant but no one will accept the role of benevolent master either. The Prime Minister's wife does her own cooking but no one is very happy about it, even in a Socialist state. We can suppose—perhaps hope—that the day will come when the egalitarian ironing-out will have banished all those decadent uncertainties of class, and human encounters will be on a truly man-to-man and not class-to-class basis. I expect

Wilson would rejoice to see it but I doubt that he does expect to see it and I doubt that he will.

Meantime, as a recorder of the scene as it passes, Wilson is doing a superb job. It is historical change as it is registered in the life of the individual remote from great events and often little conscious of the interlocking of forces and people that bring him to his decisions.

William Jay Smith. *Com.* March 26, 1965,
pp. 20–21

Angus Wilson is one of the most devoted exponents of traditionalism in fiction on the contemporary English scene. His knowledge of naturalism comes from one of naturalism's sources: his study of Zola appeared before his first novel. He has written many shorter pieces on the English Victorian novelists, especially on Dickens, who is his favorite. Though his subject matter is contemporary, his style is Victorian; in this way he seems similar to writers like C. P. Snow, who can write about the development of the atomic bomb using words and phrases which echo Trollope. Like Snow, Wilson has attacked the experimental writers, particularly Virginia Woolf, while attempting to reestablish the values of the great Victorian novelists. Like Snow again, he has often paid tribute to the novels of younger traditional writers, like Amis and Wain, who shared his aesthetic point of view.

The analogy to Snow, however, should not be drawn too far; though Wilson has supported writers with outlooks similar to his own, he has never been vehement in attacking contemporaries whose novels are not traditional. Wilson's attacks on the experimental novelists in the early fifties were usually moderate, and at times he followed these attacks with a qualification of his original position in the later fifties. Frequently, he asserts his belief in the value of the traditional novel, leaving a path open, however, for those who do not agree with him to go their own way. . . .

Like so many others in the thirties, Wilson assumed that Marx's thought would provide a panacea for social injustices, while Freud's ideas would bring an eventual end to inner disturbances. As Wilson says in *The Wild Garden*, this gave him a cosy sense of optimism that was finally destroyed by the impending Second World War. With this disillusionment came a lack of trust for any ideology which provided the foundation for Wilson's pessimism. He is sharp, for example, with some of the newer playwrights like Kops, Wesker, and Doris Lessing, whose plays contain a Marxist message. He is afraid that their messages may be as unsophisticated as the "naïvely Marxist" plays of the prewar years.

Wilson is less disturbed by naïve Marxism in the younger generation than he is by a growing wave of conservatism. A number of his
plots, and many of his subplots, deal with liberal-conservative conflicts;
very often these conflicts are between parents and children, or between
people of different generations. Characters with similar points of view
appear throughout Wilson's fiction.

Rubin Rabinovitz. *The Reaction against*
Experiment in the English Novel, 1950–1960
(N.Y., Columbia Univ. Pr., 1967),
pp. 64–65, 86–87

More than any other of his contemporaries, Angus Wilson seems deliberately concerned with the problem—in non-theological terms—of
good and evil in the English novel. We have his own word for this.
Writing in the *Kenyon Review* (March 1967), he has said: "As an
agnostic writer with apprehensions of evil over and above my ideas of
right and wrong, I have also been concerned to try to find ways of
introducing evil into my novels." This by way of concern over the
increasingly restrictive influence being exercised by the novel of manners upon English fiction (the problem, though Wilson does not say so,
is not, I think, applicable to the American novel). The question then
becomes one of finding ways in which the writer can preserve the
"packed, dense world of manners, while somehow finding a place for
transcendent values," for metaphysical ideas of good and evil as
opposed to merely ethical concepts of right and wrong. In all of his
novels, Wilson has shown this concern, but nowhere has he succeeded
in dealing with the issue so brilliantly as in his latest—and longest—
No Laughing Matter.

And size is, curiously enough, a real part of the measure of his
success. Heretofore, in *Anglo-Saxon Attitudes*, for example, Wilson
has had a "packed" world of manners, all right, but has hardly allowed
himself—for whatever reasons—a broad enough canvas to fill in sufficiently the implications of his material. Indeed, critics like myself have
tended to see that novel rather as a kind of sequel to his first one,
Hemlock and After. The Middle Age of Mrs. Eliot repeats the pattern of
the first two novels, but in order to concentrate upon the more profound
moral implications of their themes, it makes a compensating sacrifice
in breadth. *The Old Men at the Zoo*, a satirical novel set in the future,
recaptures some of the scope of *Anglo-Saxon Attitudes*, but its moral
configurations are perhaps not so well-developed. *Late Call* essentially
repeats the pattern of *Mrs. Eliot*, with the main difference that the
heroine is twenty years older and a much simpler sort of person. Now,
in *No Laughing Matter*, Wilson has drawn his themes to nearly epic

proportions and, as a testimony to his growth and skill as a novelist, his work suffers no dilution or diminution in force. Quite the contrary, this book is his masterpiece.

Jay L. Halio. MR. Spring, 1969, p. 394

The number of postwar English writers whom we can regard as major, as of long-term importance and representativeness, is clearly no more than a handful; still, Angus Wilson is obviously one. To many people he stands as the most developed and impressive novel-writer of his generation, the generation after Virginia Woolf, Evelyn Waugh, Graham Greene, Anthony Powell: a writer who carries an enormous substance in and behind his work, who has produced some of our bulkiest, socially most solid novels, who has expanded extraordinarily from the witty, economical brilliance of his malicious early stories into a fiction of extended historical and human scope—*Anglo-Saxon Attitudes* (1956), *Late Call* (1964), *No Laughing Matter* (1967).

He has brought alive the possibility of a substantial, compassionate fiction, a realistic writing of moral evolution and growth; he has humanistically reactivated the tradition of the past, so that to read him is to feel the force of what nineteenth-century novelists as various as Jane Austen and Dostoevsky might pass on to a contemporary author; he has lived a significant, central cultural life as an observer and a critic, existed seriously for us as, in the broadest sense, a modern man of letters. That said, we must add that his reputation, though very high in credit, is very mixed in basis; the admiration in which he is held is based on judgements remarkably varied. Moreover, nearly every critic who has written on him seriously has felt an ambiguity, of emphasis and perspective, in his writings. Wilson himself has encouraged them in doing so, pointing, for instance, to the "fierce sadism and a compensating gentleness" which leads to a simultaneous love and hate in his view of his characters, to his sense of the dual nature of all action, at once rational and self-satisfying, and his awareness of the strange autobiographical illusions and obsessions that are involved in all writing.

Malcolm Bradbury. Possibilities (Oxford
Univ. Pr., 1973), pp. 211–12

WILSON, COLIN (1931–   )

The novel [*The Mind Parasites*] is both Volume III of the *Cambridge History of the Nuclear Age* (2014) and the new gospel of Gilbert Austin, an archeologist who, in communion with a handful of colleagues, defeats the mind parasites and sets man on the next leg of his evolutionary journey, only to "vanish in such a way that the human race could never be certain of his death." The novel both parodies and develops the manner and situation of H. P. Lovecraft's *The Shadow Out of Time*, and uses the full panoply of science fiction devices—rockets and space travel, ESP, telekinesis and even a "neutron dater" lifted from John Taine's *Before the Dawn*. With good humor (one of the characters did "a term on Wilson and Husserl" at college) and real imaginative force, Wilson combines the familiar pieces of science fiction in a new way to form his own myth, a metaphor for his own vision of human destiny. His heroes commune to become a larger self; from the new perspective, they are able to view other men both as apes and as brothers; they form an evolutionary vanguard for the future and leave the account of their victory (the gospel according to Gilbert Austin) behind to guide their fellow men in taking the evolutionary leap. In some ways less emotionally powerful than *Necessary Doubt* or *The Glass Cage*, *The Mind Parasites* nevertheless is the fullest picture of the new hero as he can be and an apocalyptic parable of Wilson's insight into the nature of things. It and those other two most recent novels are meaningful examples of an imaginative and transforming art, an existential realism.

The novels of Colin Wilson are, then, a developing and growing artistic expression of the serpent's statement in Shaw's *Back to Methuselah* that "every dream could be willed into creation by those strong enough to believe in it." He has used literary forms as he has needed them to create love and life from the crude materials of sex, violence and death, and, as he says in the preface to *The Mind Parasites*, speaking of his use of detective and science fiction, "In every case, it has been my aim to raise the form to a level of intellectual seriousness not usually found in the *genre*, but never to lose sight of the need to entertain." He has succeeded in that purpose, and his novel in progress, *The Black Room*, a spy novel and therefore less cosmic than *The Mind Parasites*, will, as the excerpts published recently in *The Minnesota Review* indicate, also make effective and meaningful use of a popular form.

Wilson once said that "a good novel can't be faked," for it can only show "what it is actually like *to be* the writer." If doing and being are somehow one, his novels, with their developing manner and matter, their movement toward a viable existential realism of inner as well as outer truth, show Colin Wilson to be a young man of real vision who has never ceased to grow and whose promise, for that reason, outshadows even his present achievement.

R. H. W. Dillard. *HC*. Oct., 1967, p. 12

WODEHOUSE, P. G. (1881–1975)

[Wodehouse's] achievement is too formidable to be ignored, but his place in the literary history of the twentieth century is not easy to evaluate. The country in which his creation moves is not accurately charted in literary geography, and difficulty may be found in determining at what points it touches the frontiers of the known world, if it touches them at all. Literary appreciation for the most part takes the form of articles in which Wodehouse characters are treated without reference to their creator, as in the body of criticism which has grown up around Sherlock Holmes, which depends upon the convention that nobody ever mentions Conan Doyle.

The approach of reviewers usually has been to accept the Wodehouse books as products of pure fantasy. "I cannot criticise—I can only laugh," wrote a reviewer early in Wodehouse's maturity, and many readers will remember this, because his publishers for twenty years or more very properly continued to use it on the wrappers of the books. It was enough that Wodehouse was writing a long series of very funny books. To probe or dissect was neither necessary nor desirable, and reviewers might be satisfied if the new book maintained the standard of a recognisable but not easily defined lunacy. . . .

Whatever the local conditions in the Wodehouse country, it is not the realm of nonsense absolute. All comedy refines, selects, and exaggerates. It is possible to conclude too hastily that in Wodehouse the process is carried so far that contact is lost with the world of experience, its persons, its motives, its dilemmas, and its appetites. Motives in the books are real enough, and so are appetites. The characters will be found to exist well within the permissible limits of artistic presentation. They arouse laughter not because they are outside the human family but because they are so plainly within it. . . .

The test that the comedian must apply is the test of his own observation and knowledge of life. It is by applying it in his own way that he makes comedy an art and performs his function of correcting unworldly illusions and exposing what is pretentious and unreal; and so it is with Wodehouse.

R. B. D. French. *P. G. Wodehouse*
(Edinburgh, Oliver & Boyd, 1966), pp. 3–4

If asked whom I thought the most illustrious living novelist born in England, I would unhesitatingly say P. G. Wodehouse. To assert this, at one time, was to be named middle-brow, or an inverted snob. Can that "performing flea," as Sean O'Casey dubbed him (and as Wodehouse then titled his autobiography), be called *illustrious*? "Plum" Wodehouse, the comedian? Come, come!

Go, go, I would reply, as Hamlet did to Gertrude in a different context. I am saying "novelist" (and short story writer), for our finest writers today—as in our golden age from Chaucer to Milton—are dramatists and poets. But in prose fiction, I believe Wodehouse without peer.

First, the mere weight of his achievement. The title-page of his new novel, *A Girl in Blue*, lists two columns of books—without mentioning his scripts for musicals in the 1920's. Of course, Wodehouse (b. 1881) has been in business a long while; and of course, mass alone is no proof of quality; but coupled with sustained talent, it is impressive.

Then, his appeal is universal: the young like him as do the old— an amazing feat in our culture of warring generations. Nor is his lure only to the literate: a recent British television series of Jeeves and Bertie Wooster was a popular favorite. Nor, even, is he liked only in America and Britain, where his tales are always set. Blandings Castle and its many denizens delight the Japanese. I have tried Ukridge's villainies out on cynical West Indians—not intellectuals, but "saga boys"—and they split their Caribbean sides.

He has created an immediately recognizable world: "a Wodehouse situation," "Wodehouse people," "a P. G. Wodehouse kind of place"— anyone knows at once exactly what you mean. . . . Going deeper, we may see he is in the great line of artists who portrayed England to America, and vice versa. . . .

Comical! But can a humorous author be "illustrious"? Why not? Is not Mark Twain, with Melville, one of the two great seminal writers of America? What do we most remember of Voltaire, if not *Candide*? Is not the prime Spanish masterpiece (to which, by the way, Wodehouse owes much, with his Don Bertie and Sancho Jeeves) also a comedy? Ah, but Twain, Voltaire and Cervantes delved far deeper in the human soul. So they did, but so does Wodehouse operate on deeper levels than may at first appear.

Colin MacInnes. NYT. Feb. 28, 1971, p. 1

P. G. Wodehouse is the only living English author of whom one can say with confidence that his works are a classic. A minor classic maybe, but still a classic. If people doubt that, they should consider for a start just how many literary reputations have blossomed and died during his long lifetime whilst his has remained unfaded. There can be few cases of an author surviving the changes of literary fashion for so long a period; and the fact of his survival must be sufficient proof of his worth

It is particularly rare, I should imagine, for a funny writer to keep his readers for so many years. Nothing changes quicker than the fashion in humour and nothing dates more speedily than a joke. And yet Mr. Wodehouse continues to make us laugh. Why? Bearing in mind the thought that it is usually boring and almost always pointless to try to explain why jokes are funny, we might hazard a few suggestions.

To begin with, Wodehouse is definitely not a satirist. Savage indignation, of the type which lacerated the heart of Swift and others, is an emotion totally foreign to him. There has been some desultory discussion among critics as to what his attitude to the upper classes is and whether he intends to make fun of them. Such talk is completely wide of the mark. Wodehouse has no "attitude" in that sense at all. . . .

If there is any satire in Wodehouse at all it is of a basic and rather schoolboyish kind. It emerges in the discomfiture of primitive authority figures, usually aunts, creatures with whom he has something of an obsession, and characters like the brain surgeon Sir Roderick Glossop —"He had a pair of shaggy eyebrows which gave his eyes a piercing look which was not at all the sort of thing a fellow wanted to encounter on an empty stomach."

But the main humour of Wodehouse, so evident in this description of Sir Roderick, is in his style—a fact which helps to explain why his work has never been really successful when adapted for stage or TV. The plots are strong, as complicated as any detective story, and the reader must make sure in the early chapters that he has fully grasped which girl used to be engaged to Gussie Fink-Nottle and why that particular aunt has got it in for Lord So-and-So if he is going to keep abreast of things.

Richard Ingrams. In Thelma Cazalet-Keir, ed.,
Homage to P. G. Wodehouse (Barrie &
Jenkins, 1973), pp. 80–81

WOOLF, LEONARD (1880–1969)

One of the best-informed obituary articles about Leonard Woolf spoke of him as a many-sided man with a perfectly integrated personality. It also said that his autobiography was a masterpiece and the outstanding autobiography of our time. This opinion was presumably based on the first four volumes, because the fifth and last volume [*The Journey Not the Arrival Matters*] has only just appeared. Perhaps the greatest compliment that has been paid to the book came from E. M. Forster, who spoke of the "absolute honesty" of the first volume. It isn't often that an autobiography is praised for honesty, and I can't remember any previous one ever having been praised for absolute honesty.

Anybody intending to write about his own life might well pin up a list of things to be avoided—vanity, self-complacency, self-delusion, untruthfulness, boasting, vindictiveness, too much self-justification, and, perhaps above all, taking for granted that what interests himself is bound to interest other people. How well did Leonard Woolf avoid these things? So much better, surely, than most autobiographers that this alone puts his book in an uncrowded class. His own guiding principles are to be found in the second volume, called *Growing*: "The only point of an autobiography is to give, as far as one can, in the most simple, clear, truthful way, a picture, first of one's own personality and of the people whom one has known, and secondly of the society and age in which one has lived."

Like himself, his book has charm, dignity, a dry humour, and the absence of self-pity that goes with stoicism. I should think few women could read with indifference his account of the perpetual strain of his married life, during which he was always alert to guard his wife against the dangers of her mental instability. Anybody interested not only in Virginia Woolf but in the art of biography, or in the evolution of an independent man, who had close experience of colonial administration in the days of the British Empire, of socialist politics over the last 50 years, and of being a distinguished publisher for almost as long, is likely to find this, to a great extent, a most engaging book, and to feel that he is being taken into the confidence of the writer as if he were an equal.

William Plomer. *List.* Dec. 4, 1969, p. 789

Characteristically, as if he were deliberately keeping himself alive just long enough to finish his last work in the world, Leonard Woolf completed the fifth and final volume of his autobiography shortly before his death on August 14, 1969. *The Journey Not the Arrival Matters, 1939–1969* is the conclusion to both his life and his record of it in *Sowing, 1880–1904; Growing, 1904–1911; Beginning Again, 1911–1919;* and *Downhill All the Way, 1919–1939.* Together these volumes will stand out from all the memoirs associated with that difficult and amorphous group "Bloomsbury" as the most important, illuminating and humane account of British intellectual life in the first part of this century. . . .

This volume emphasizes the early forties, the years which, despite all of Woolf's efforts, brought the collapse of his public and private worlds. After all his work for peace, the world of savage imbecility created by Stalin, Mussolini, and Hitler broke out into war, Bloomsbury fell to ruins beneath fire bombs, and the Hogarth Press was buried under the rubble of Mecklenburgh Square. After his daily attempts to keep Virginia Woolf from insanity and death, she committed suicide. Everything that Leonard Woolf had worked to preserve was gone, everything he had worked to prevent had happened, and the whole man and his whole life were challenged by these failures.

Woolf's title, *The Journey Not the Arrival Matters*, from Montaigne, expresses Woolf's final attitude toward his failure to reach his goals. This volume describes "the most terrible and agonizing days" of Woolf's life; the restraint of his prose, which also recalls Montaigne, barely suggests the anguish of recounting them. . . .

His balanced view of life enabled him to continue working in the face of all the difficulties, all the insults, brutalities and defeats that face the committed man, without ever capitulating into either fanaticism or cynicism, responses to life which he abhorred. Woolf's vital and resilient ability to persevere in the cause of humanity without abusing it, giving up on it, or losing it himself is what constitutes his greatness as a man. His autobiography should remind us, especially in times of violence, that the civilized man represents the only genuine human victory over hatred, cruelty and chaos.

Edwin J. Kenney, Jr. Nation. April 20, 1970,
pp. 469–70

WOOLF, VIRGINIA (1882–1941)

Beneath the apparent variety of her writings, Virginia Woolf's work possesses remarkable unity. The fact that her novels represent less than half her production should not mislead us. Her reviews, her portrait sketches of literary figures, her general criticism, even her biographies, even *A Room of One's Own* betray a single preoccupation: the novel.

These writings are only a prolonged commentary in the margin of the various manifestations of that form of art to which she devoted her genius; thus she devoted her talent to it too, seeking, by setting her own experience against that of her predecessors, a definition, a formula for that literary genre which cannot be defined and knows no law. She acquired, in this field, a fame which none will dispute.

Her analyses are consulted by every critic. But we must not forget that such research was never for Virginia Woolf an end in itself; it was at once a preparation for her work as novelist and a residue of that work. However interesting, however highly esteemed these critical writings may be—and some attribute to them a surer and more enduring value than to her novels—they should be relegated to the secondary place and the accessory role that Virginia Woolf ascribed to them. By considering them from this point of view, moreover, we shall avoid the common error of believing that she took an interest in technique for its own sake, and that her perpetual experimenting with new forms was merely an aesthete's game, intended to compensate for or to disguise certain deficiencies in her creative genius. . . .

It is not because of her attack on the Holmeses and Bradshaws of the world, the Lord Mayors, the Church or the Army, commercialism, patriotism, or fascism, that Virginia Woolf will survive the test of time. I have stressed these examples of "commitment" to contemporary issues, not because they add any virtue to her work—I should be inclined to assert the contrary—but because they betoken a vitality, an awareness of the world, an infinitely richer kind of interest and contact than has commonly been ascribed to her. The figure of Antigone, which she evokes more than once with a sense of kinship, Antigone with her passion for truth, independence and integrity, holds undoubted fascination and wins our sympathy.

Jean Guiguet. *Virginia Woolf and Her Works*
(N.Y., Harcourt, Brace, 1965),
pp. 459–60, 464

The generation to which Virginia Woolf belonged was in revolt against Victorianism. Mrs. Woolf was extremely sensitive to the present, that is to say, to the spirit of modernism. She was also linked to the past by unusually strong bonds. Her father had believed in a certain kind of moral strenuousness, and although Virginia and her friends were serious young people, it was almost a point of honor with them to adopt an attitude as far removed as possible from that of their elders. . . .

Almost every writer on Virginia Woolf has commented on the fundamental dualism in her work. Unlike some of her contemporaries, she wished not only to criticize the tradition which she had inherited, but in a sense to renew it. Her goal was to write in such a way as to satisfy the utilitarian philosophy of her father, while remaining true to the artistic mood of her own generation. The former demanded that her books contribute something to the welfare of mankind, the latter taught her that every work of art is autonomous, a purely aesthetic skirmish in the struggle to achieve "significant form." The moralist in Virginia

Woolf is most in evidence in her feminist writings, and the aesthete in her novels; neither is entirely lacking in anything she wrote.

> Herbert Marder. *Feminism and Art: A Study of Virginia Woolf* (Chicago, Univ. of Chicago Pr., 1968), pp. 16–17

An understanding of Mrs. Woolf's concept of the creative reader brings to light more sharply the contemporary nature of her work. She died in 1941. Nearly thirty years later, ideas and trends whose shape could be glimpsed in her novels have become visible, not only in fiction—as in the *nouveau roman* of Nathalie Sarraute or Alain Robbe-Grillet, which carries subjectivity to its outermost limits—but also in music and especially in the theatre of the absurd. The participating audience, the random act; the emphasis on the global rather than the linear, on the kinetic instead of the static; experiments with mass, rhythm, and space —all suggest a creative and innovating intellect whose ideas fit intuitively into emerging patterns of artistic thought.

Her approach to certain philosophical and psychological problems was also far ahead of her time. One may be reminded of Bergson, William James, and Freud in reading her novels. But contemporaries like Edmund Husserl's disciple Merleau-Ponty, the Swiss psychologist Jean Piaget (whose studies of the child mind bear out many of Mrs. Woolf's own observations), the school of Cassirer, Whitehead, and Susanne K. Langer, seem just as pertinent. Indeed—and every generation approaches a great writer from its own perspective—Virginia Woolf belongs to the moment of now. On her work, as in her concept of the moment, the future already lay "like a piece of glass, making it tremble and quiver"—by which she meant that the immanence of the future in the present brings it vitally alive.

This is not to imply, however, that Mrs. Woolf conforms to this or that current mode of thought. One does not draw a particular philosophy or discipline from her work. One can only conclude that her examination of her own encounter with lived experience was transmuted into the novel's form: modes of life became modes of fiction. And since a writer's apprehension of his methods, as Virginia Woolf was only too ready to admit, is apt to be mainly unconscious, so is the reader's participation in them.

> Harvena Richter. *Virginia Woolf: The Inward Voyage* (Princeton, N.J., Princeton Univ. Pr., 1970), pp. 244–46

We may come to see Virginia Woolf as less frail in her life and in her art than we have heretofore. Her productivity was, for example, striking. She did not match the torrential outpourings of her father, Sir Leslie Stephen, and other Victorians, but she did write 17 books in 21 years (too much perhaps by current standards). Her illness cannot make us ignore this fact. She appears to have been in life an example of the contrary states she explored in her novels: solid and shifting, male and female, a creature made up of fact and vision, subject to terror and ecstasy. The oppositions she lived and wrote about may, in the words of one critic, be identical, "insofar as one logically 'implies' the other," or contains the other—whether we speak of isolation and connection, uniqueness and anonymity or of any of the other pairings we have used. What Virginia Woolf called the "amphibious" periods of her life ("I'm amphibious still, in bed and out of it.") seem to have been a necessary part of her creative life. She is capable of a detached, even implicitly arrogant, appraisal of her amphibious self: "this state, my depressed state, is the state in which most people usually are."

Two years before her death she thought how interesting it would be to treat the "tremendous experience" of aging, one "not as unconscious . . . as birth is." This may or may not have been the subject she had in mind at the time of her death. But she was already thinking about her next novel while she was revising *Between the Acts*. "It will be a supported-on-fact book" she had decided. That unwritten work was likely to have been another voyage out.

Claire Sprague. Intro. to Claire Sprague, ed.,
Virginia Woolf: A Collection of Critical Essays
(Englewood Cliffs, N.J., Prentice-Hall, 1971),
pp. 12–13

[*A Room of One's Own*] is, I think, the easiest of Virginia's books, by which I mean that it puts no great burden on the sensibilities. The whole work is held together, not as in her other works by a thread of feeling, but by a thread of argument—a simple well-stated argument: the disabilities of women are social and economic; the woman writer can only survive despite great difficulties, and despite the prejudice and the economic selfishness of men; and the key to emancipation is to be found in the door of a room which a woman may call her own and which she can inhabit with the same freedom and independence as her brothers. The lack of this economic freedom breeds resentment, the noisy assertive resentment of the male, who insists on claiming his superiority, and the shrill nagging resentment of the female who clamours for her rights. Both produce bad literature, for literature—fiction, that is—demands a comprehensive sympathy which transcends and comprehends the feelings of both sexes. The great artist is Androgynous.

This argument is developed easily and conversationally, striking home in some memorable passages but always lightly and amusingly expressed. It is that rare thing—a lively but good-tempered polemic, and a book which, like *Orlando*, is of particular interest to the student of her life. For in *A Room of One's Own* one hears Virginia speaking. In her novels she is thinking. In her critical works one can sometimes hear her voice, but it is always a little formal, a little editorial. In *A Room of One's Own*, she gets very close to her conversational style.

Quentin Bell. *Virginia Woolf*, Vol. II: *Mrs. Woolf 1912–1941* (Hogarth, 1972), p. 144

Throughout Mrs. Woolf's work, the chief problem for her and her characters is to overcome the space between things, to attain an absolute unity with the world, as if everything in the environment were turned into water. This desire for absolute union can be expressed in both physical and spiritual terms, and in Mrs. Woolf it nearly always has sexual connotations. . . .

The generally erotic nature of her art has never received proper emphasis from critics, though many have pointed to lighthouses, pocket-knives, bodies of water, and windows as evidence of sexual symbolism. She has been portrayed as a prudish lady, a "peeper," as Wyndham Lewis once called her. It is true that her novels are often reticent about sex (Lytton Strachey's chief criticism of *To the Lighthouse* was that it avoided reference to copulation—a remark that tells as much about Strachey as it does about Mrs. Woolf), and sometimes she is manifestly prudish, as in *The Voyage Out*.

This does not mean, however, that her work is sexless. On the contrary, her prose is full of erotic impulses, and sexual themes are major elements in all her books. Again and again she either hints at or explicitly portrays homoeroticism: consider, for example, St. John Hurst, Clarissa Dalloway, Lily Briscoe, Neville, Orlando, and William Dodge. Mrs. Woolf's indirection in some of these cases may reflect her concern for decorum, or Bloomsbury's proclivity to a love that even in the twenties was careful not to speak its name. On the other hand, when she does portray sexual emotions, she often injects an element of fear. Her nervous, barely concealed eroticism is . . . related to the wish to find some permanent, all-embracing union: in effect, to the death-wish.

James Naremore. *The World without a Self: Virginia Woolf and the Novel* (New Haven, Conn., Yale Univ. Pr., 1973), pp. 242–43

Virginia Woolf would have agreed with D. H. Lawrence that human beings have two ways of knowing, "knowing in terms of apartness, which is mental, rational, scientific, and knowing in terms of together-ness, which is religious and poetic." . . . Virginia Woolf associated these two ways with the two sexes. In *A Room of One's Own* she suggests that every mind is potentially bisexual. But she finds that among writers, and particularly among her contemporaries, most men tend to develop only the analytic, "masculine" approach, what Law-rence calls "knowing in terms of apartness," and most women only the synthetic, "feminine," that is, "knowing in terms of togetherness." In her opinion, however, to be truly creative one must use the "whole" mind.

In keeping with this, the greatest writers are "androgynous": they use and harmonize the masculine and feminine approaches to truth. They do not suffer from what T. S. Eliot calls the "dissociation of sensibility" or what Carl Jung calls the "split consciousness" of modern man; for in Jungian terms, they have discovered the "self," "a point midway between the conscious and the unconscious," in which there is a reconciliation of opposites. Like Jung, Virginia Woolf felt that neither an individual nor an age can find its point of equilibrium without frankly confronting and understanding the exact nature of the oppos-ing forces. Thus, her interest in what it means to be a male or female was related to her quest for the self or the point of balance that would stabilize her personality and give her the sense of wholeness and unconsciousness which characterizes the androgynous writer.

Nancy Bazin Topping. *Virginia Woolf and the*
Androgynous Vision (New Brunswick, N.J.,
Rutgers Univ. Pr., 1973), pp. 3–4

[Virginia Woolf] was not political—or, perhaps, just political enough, as when Chekhov notes that "writers should engage themselves in politics only enough to protect themselves from politics." Though one of her themes was women in history (several of her themes, rather; she took her women one by one, not as a race, species, or nation), presumably she would have mocked at the invention of a "history of women"—what she cared for, as *A Room of One's Own* both lucidly and passionately lays out, was access to a unitary culture. Indeed, *Orlando* is the metaphorical expression of this idea.

History as a record of division or exclusion was precisely what she set herself against: the Cambridge of her youth kept women out, and all her life she preserved her resentment by pronouncing herself under-educated. She studied at home, Greek with Janet Case, the sister of Wal-ter Pater, literature and mathematics with her father, and as a result was left to count on her fingers forever—but for people who grow up counting on their fingers, even a Cambridge education cannot do much.

Nevertheless she despised what nowadays is termed "affirmative action," granting places in institutions as a kind of group-reparation; she thought it offensive to her own earned prestige, and once took revenge on the notion.

In 1935 Forster, a member of the Committee of the London Library, informed her that a debate was underway concerning the admission of women members. No women were admitted. Six years later Virginia Woolf was invited to serve; she said she would not be a "sop"—she ought to have been invited years earlier, on the same terms as Forster, as a writer; not in 1941, when she was already fifty-nine, as a woman.

Nor will she do as martyr. Although Cambridge was closed to her, literary journalism was not; although she complains of being chased off an Oxbridge lawn forbidden to the feet of women, no one ever chased her off a page. Almost immediately she began to write for the *Times Literary Supplement* and for the *Cornhill*; she was then twenty-two. She was, of course, Leslie Stephen's daughter, and it is doubtful whether any other young writer, male or female, could have started off so auspiciously: still, we speak here not of "connections" but of experience. . . .

Virginia Woolf was a practitioner of her profession from an early age; she was not deprived of an education, rather of a particular college; she grew rich and distinguished; she developed her art on her own line, according to her own sensibilities, and was acclaimed for it; though insane, she was never incarcerated. She was an elitist, and must be understood as such. What she suffered from, aside from the abysses of depression which characterized her disease, was not anything like the condition of martyrdom—unless language has become so flaccid that being on occasion patronized begins to equal death for the sake of an ideal. What she suffered from really was only the minor inflammations of the literary temperament.

Cynthia Ozick. Cmty. Aug., 1973, p. 43

YEATS, WILLIAM BUTLER (1865–1939)

Responsibilities is remarkable for the appearance in it of poems concerned with public issues such as the *Playboy* crisis and the controversy over Sir Hugh Lane's offer to give a collection of pictures to Dublin if a suitable gallery were supplied for them. Through the rest of his life Yeats continued to write poems on men and events; taken together they are a splendid achievement and one almost unique in our time, since few other great poets of the twentieth century have commented so directly on our tragic history as it was being made.

One could hardly deduce this history from the corpus of Wallace Stevens' poetry, and Eliot has largely confined himself to one aspect of it, the loss of traditional faith and his own efforts to regain it. Pound is occasional in his special way: he becomes occasional to denounce, with the result that he often seems to beat a dead horse. Yeats's stance is different from any of these. He addresses himself in work after work to the moral question how modern man is to act in typical situations, in the process powerfully asserting custom and ceremony and extracting from the traditions of western man all that is most viable. The poems in which he does this are the cause, I think, of the continuing popularity of Yeats. Whereas for the special student Yeats's art may well seem to culminate in such cryptic poems as "Supernatural Songs," the general reader will continue to prefer "Nineteen Hundred and Nineteen."

Curtis B. Bradford. *Yeats at Work*
(Carbondale, Southern Illinois Univ. Pr.,
1965), p. 47

The Yeats whom I now met as a man of the theatre was getting on to his fortieth year. He had written *The Wind amongst the Reeds*, and it was known that he was eager to pass from such tremulous kind of poetry to the more public kind that he would have to grapple with in the theatre. Therefore, it was at a developing period in his life that I was fortunate enough to meet the great poet. He was preparing himself for a new career—indeed I might say for a new sort of being. He was reading all the dramatists, including the dramatists of the day, Ibsen and Maeterlinck. I remember I spoke of these two dramatists with fervour. Yeats spoke a word of warning in that voice of his that had something oracular in it. "We are obsessed with the translation. . . ." He meant that the personal style that all great writers have was blurred in translation and that we mustn't give a complete adherence to the text. . . .

At this time, Yeats was still the youngish man of the velvet jacket and the flowing tie. To the Catholic intelligentsia who had a few years before, picketted his play, *The Countess Cathleen*, he was subversive. But that did not recommend him to the other side, the Ascendency side, the side of his father's friend, Professor Dowden. They had seen him from the site of the projected Wolfe Tone monument make a speech that was not at all in the spirit of Queen Victoria's Jubilee and denouncing that eminent lady in letters to the press. . . . But the fact that two sides of the Irish public were hostile to him made this thirty-year-old man interesting, and to be interesting, Yeats would probably have said, was the first duty of a public man. And Yeats wanted to be a public man. I fancy that if, at this stage, someone had said to him, "But you are a poet. Why want to be a public man?" Yeats would have told him that the entry into public life would give what he thought the entry into the theatre would give a poet, "more manful energy." [1965]

Padraic Colum. In Francis MacManus, ed.,
The Yeats We Knew (Dublin, Mercier, 1969),
pp. 13–15

It is a fact of literary history that the Anglo-Irish literary tradition since the seventeenth century, up to and including Synge, had scored all its most brilliant successes in comedy, even in stage-comedy; whereas Yeats, from the days of his youthful campaigning for the National Literary Society, had hoped and worked for an Irish literature that should be, on the contrary, heroic. That hope he had abandoned in 1912. The events of 1916, which proved that Irishmen were capable of a tragic gesture, seemed to show Yeats that he had abandoned hope too soon, and in the poem ["Michael Robartes and the Dancer"] he seems to reproach himself for this.

Yet does he, in fact, reproach himself? Certainly there is no evidence from elsewhere that the Rising made Yeats embrace with renewed enthusiasm the hopes he had entertained for Irish national culture in his youth. The truth is that the poem is an expression of self-reproach only so far as "Hearts with one purpose alone." At that point Yeats's reflections on the Rising move beyond Maud Gonne's, and only at that point does Yeats ask himself if the Rising makes him revise all his scheme of values. He decides that it does not; or rather, since the pity of the subject rules out any decisions being taken, he does not decide that it does. And this is perhaps the most impressive thing about the whole poem, with the impressiveness of a human utterance rather than a fashioned artifact—that the 1916 leaders are mourned most poignantly, and the sublimity of their gesture is celebrated most memorably, not when the poet is abasing himself before them, but when he implies that, all things considered, they were, not just in politic but in human terms, probably wrong.

Donald Davie. In Denis Donoghue and J. R.
Mulryne, eds., <i>An Honoured Guest</i> (N.Y.,
St. Martin's, 1966), p. 87

Yeats was a poet very much in the line of vision; his ancestors in English poetic tradition were primarily Blake and Shelley, and his achievement will at least be judged against theirs. . . .

Yeats, Hardy, and Wallace Stevens seem to me the poets writing in English in our century whose work most merits sustained comparison with the major poets of the nineteenth century. I am aware that such an opinion will seem extreme to scholars and admirers of Eliot, Pound, Williams, Frost, Graves, Auden, and others, but the phenomenon of high contemporary reputations dying away permanently has occurred before, and will again. Donne and Shelley vanish for generations and are then revived, but Eliot and Pound may prove to be the Cowley and Cleveland of this age, and a puzzle therefore to future historians of our sensibilities.

Though this book sets itself against the prevalent critical idolatry of Yeats, I do not believe that Yeats (or Stevens) will vanish as Eliot and Pound will, and I do not desire to deny the undoubted stature of Yeats's achievement. But I do want to set that achievement in a historical perspective, and to examine its quite genuine limitations more fully than I have seen them examined. It may be that Yeats is as good a poet as a bad time for the imagination could produce, but we will hardly learn the imaginative limitations of our own age if we inflate Yeats's value beyond all reasonable measure. One distinguished modern critic, R. P. Blackmur, asserted that Yeats was the most considerable lyric poet in the language since the seventeenth century, a judgment that is astonishing, but which has gone uncontroverted except by the equally distinguished critic Yvor Winters, who sensibly condemned Yeats as a talented but confused Romantic poet. I say "sensibly" because Yeats, as Winters accurately observed, was a Romantic poet, who grew only more Romantic despite all his attempts to modify his tradition, and if you are as massively anti-Romantic a critic as Winters was, then you are as sensible to condemn Yeats as you are to discard Blake, Wordsworth or the later Wallace Stevens. What is not very sensible, but is still prevalent, is to praise Yeats for being what he was not, a poet of the Metaphysical kind.

Harold Bloom. <i>Yeats</i> (N.Y., Oxford Univ. Pr.,
1970), pp. v–vi

The peculiar virtue of Yeats's attitude toward myth lies precisely in his ability to use it as a way of *seeing* his contemporary world. This would not have been possible if he had merely retreated into a more congenial land of dreams. What he did was to conduct a life-long search for a connection between the powerful fantasies that plagued and delighted him in childhood and youth and their source in that greater imagination out of which every man and every civilization has been created. From earliest childhood his outlook was specifically *poetic*, if we think of the poet as being obsessed with the act of creating not only poems but the whole universe that gives them context and meaning. Mythology *was* that universe for Yeats, for in myths peoples and nations had embodied their vision of themselves, and poets had been the custodians of the myths.

In trying to construct a system which would provide a place for everything in man's history, Yeats was primarily concerned to account for the way man's desires interact with circumstance to transform his own life, to make and unmake nations, even to bring about the rise and fall of entire historical epochs. The brute weight of the physical world, untouched by imagination, was an objective fact—the kind of fact he mistakenly regarded as belonging to the province of science. When touched by imagination, this inert mass came to life, poetically speaking. . . .

This ability to focus the world's meanings on himself did not signify, however, that the "subjective" man could make the world according to his liking; it only meant that he might, if will and understanding and desire were strong enough, achieve a completeness of character undreamt of by lesser men, though the very reach of his imagination would make him painfully aware how far he fell short of the perfection his mind conceived.

For such a man, the world was bound to be a theater of conflict. Circumstance was recalcitrant; not only the shortcomings of his own character but the inability of other men to see the world with his imaginative intensity stood in the way. At one end of the spectrum was the image of a perfectly realized, self-sufficient beauty; at the other, the mindless existence of mere things, passively waiting to be acted upon by something outside. And all men and times were somewhere in between, more or less blindly moving toward their opposites. Only the heroes could hope, perhaps, to escape from the endlessly turning wheel which brought things around to their beginnings again according to a regular schedule. For oddly enough, despite the imaginative ingenuity of its details, Yeats's system is quite mechanical in its workings. It seems as little dependent on the presence of God as any deist could ask for. Yet the motive that compelled Yeats to create it was far from mechanical, nor does it actually "contain" his mythology. For that we must go to the poems and plays.

John Rees Moore. *Masks of Love and Death:
Yeats as Dramatist* (Ithaca, N.Y., Cornell
Univ. Pr., 1971), pp. 43–44

Yeats was born in an unfortunate time for poets and took unfortunate models and spent the rest of his life learning his mistake. His good work is achieved in spite of this, and we are doing him no service by ignoring the difference. Even worse, we are doing our students a disservice, for it isn't a dead poet's reputation that is at stake, it is the quality of life now.

What is it that makes eminently practical scholars put aside their common sense in approaching this poet? As one did recently, sidestepping the whole issue of political violence implied by Yeats's unreal cult of heroic violence by saying, "We all need a bit of heroism," and another endorsing Cuchulain's Fight with the Sea by saying, "It will inspire new generations of Irish youth to heroic valour." They both know better than I do with what horror the mature Yeats examined the chain of responsibility that led to the Easter Rising, wondering if any link was from his workshop. He may have temporized at first and allowed beauty to the terror; but when he faced the reality in 1919 and wrote "Meditations in Time of Civil War" the terror was unrelieved, as it is now in Belfast and Derry.

James Simmons. *Confrontation*. Spring, 1973,
pp. 84–85

BIBLIOGRAPHY

These bibliographies are not intended to be complete. Their primary purpose is to indicate the availability of important new material published since the original three volumes of *Modern British Literature* were issued. Consequently, the following guidelines have been followed:

INCLUSIONS

—For authors from the original volumes updated in this supplement, only works published since 1965, except when earlier works were inadvertently omitted in the original volumes.
—For authors new in this supplement, all published works, with the exceptions noted below.
—Only significant reissues, such as new scholarly editions.
—Only translations of particular importance.

EXCLUSIONS

—Limited editions, privately printed material, and pamphlets, except where noted.
—Children's books, except those of particular significance, or if the author is especially known as a writer of juvenile literature. These works are marked with a (j).
—Produced but unpublished plays, and filmed but unpublished screenplays.
—Works edited or compiled by the author, except where noted.
—Contributions to anthologies.

Bibliographies of individual authors published since 1965, when available, are listed after the author's works. In the absence of a bibliography, a biography or a critical work, in that order of preference, is noted; this work usually contains a bibliography.

GENRE ABBREVIATIONS

a	autobiography	j	juvenile literature
ac	art or architecture criticism	m	memoirs or reminiscences
		misc	miscellany
b	biography	n	novel
c	criticism	p	poetry
d	drama	pd	poetic drama (verse play)
e	essays	rd	radio drama
g	general (nonfiction not covered by other categories)	s	short stories
		t	travel or topography
		tr	translation
h	history		

SOURCES

The following sources have been consulted in compiling these bibliographies:
British Books in Print
British Museum General Catalogue of Printed Books
British National Bibliography
Card catalogues of the Columbia University Library and the New York
    Public Library
Contemporary Authors
Contemporary Dramatists
Contemporary Novelists
Contemporary Poets
Cumulative Book Index
The National Union Catalogue
TLS
Who's Who

● **DANNIE ABSE**
   1923–

After Every Green Thing, 1949 (p); *Walking under Water*, 1952 (p); *Ash on a Young Man's Sleeve*, 1954 (n); *Fire in Heaven*, 1956 (p); *Some Corner of an English Field*, 1956 (n); *Tenants of the House*, 1957 (p); *The Eccentric*, 1961 (d); *Poems, Golders Green*, 1962 (p); *Dannie Abse: A Selection*, 1963 (p); *Three Questor Plays* (*House of Cowards*; *Gone*; *In the Cage*), 1967 (d); *Medicine on Trial*, 1967 (g); *A Small Desperation*, 1968 (p); *O. Jones, O. Jones*, 1970 (n); *Selected Poems*, 1970 (p); *Funland, and Other Poems*, 1973 (p); *The Dogs of Pavlov*, 1973 (d); *A Poet in the Family*, 1974 (a)

● **A. ALVAREZ**
   1929–

Poems, 1953 (p); *The Shaping Spirit* (Amer. ed. *Stewards of Excellence*), 1958 (c); *The School of Donne*, 1961 (c); *Under Pressure: The Writer in Society: Eastern Europe and the U.S.A.*, 1965 (c); *Beyond All This Fiddle: Essays 1955–1967*, 1968 (c); *Lost*, 1968 (p); *The Savage God: A Study of Suicide*, 1971 (g, c); *Apparition*, 1972 (p); *Beckett*, 1973 (c); *Hers*, 1974 (n)

KINGSLEY AMIS
   1922–

The James Bond Dossier, 1965 (c); (with Robert Conquest) *The Egyptologists*, 1965 (n); *The Anti-Death League*, 1966 (n); *A Look Round the Estate*, 1967 (p); *I Want It Now*, 1968 (n); (as Robert Markham) *Colonel Sun: A James Bond Adventure*, 1968 (n); *Lucky Jim's Politics*, 1968 (e); *The Green Man*, 1969 (n); *What Became of Jane Austen? and Other Questions*, 1970 (c); *Girl, 20*, 1971 (n); *Dear Illusion*, 1972 (n); *The Riverside Villas Murder*, 1973 (n); *On Drink*, 1973 (g); *Ending Up*, 1974 (n); *Kipling and His World*, 1974 (b)

● JOHN ARDEN
1930–

Serjeant Musgrave's Dance, 1960 (d); *The Business of Good Government*, 1963 (d); *The Workhouse Donkey*, 1964 (d); *Three Plays* (*The Waters of Babylon*; *Live Like Pigs*; *The Happy Haven*), 1964 (d); *Armstrong's Last Goodnight*, 1965 (d); *Left-Handed Liberty*, 1965 (d); (with Margaretta D'Arcy) *Ars Longa, Vita Brevis*, 1965 (d); *Ironhand* (after Goethe's *Götz von Berlichingen*), 1965 (d); *Soldier, Soldier, and Other Plays* (with *Wet Fish*; *When Is a Door Not a Door?*; *Friday's Hiding* [with M. D'Arcy]), 1967 (d); (with M. D'Arcy) *The Royal Pardon; or, The Soldier Who Became an Actor*, 1967 (d); (with M. D'Arcy) *The Hero Rises Up*, 1969 (d); *Two Autobiographical Plays* (*The True History of Squire Jonathan and His Unfortunate Treasure*; *The Bagman; or, The Impromptu of Moswell Hill*), 1971 (d); (with M. D'Arcy) *The Ballygombeen Bequest* (in *Scripts 9*), 1972 (d); (with M. D'Arcy) *The Island of the Mighty*, 1973 (d)

Albert Hunt, *Arden: A Study of His Plays*, 1974

W. H. AUDEN
1907–1973

Selected Essays, 1964 (e); *About the House*, 1966 (p); *Collected Shorter Poems 1927–1957*, 1966 (p); *The Orators*, 3rd ed., 1966 (p); (with Chester Kallman) *The Bassarids* (libretto for opera by Hans Werner Henze), 1967; (with others) *Antiworlds* (poems by Andrei Voznesenskii), 1967 (tr); *Collected Longer Poems*, 1968 (p); *Selected Poems*, 1968 (p); *Secondary Worlds* (The T. S. Eliot Memorial Lectures, 1967), 1968 (c); *City without Walls*, 1969 (p); *The Elder Edda*, 1969 (tr); *A Certain World: A Commonplace Book*, 1970 (misc); *Academic*

Graffiti, 1971 (p); *Epistle to a Godson*, 1972 (p); *Forewords and Afterwords*, 1973 (c, e); (with Leif Sjöberg) Pär Lagerkvist, *Evening Land*, 1974 (tr); *Thank You Fog: Last Poems*, 1974 (p)

B. C. Bloomfield and Edward Mendelson, *W. H. Auden: A Bibliography 1924–1969*, 1972

GEORGE BARKER
1913–

Collected Poems 1930–1965, 1965 (p); *The True Confession of George Barker*, 1965 (p); *Dreams of a Summer Night*, 1966 (p); *The Golden Chains*, 1968 (p); *Runes and Rhymes and Tunes and Chimes*, 1969 (p); *Essays*, 1970 (c); *To Alysham Fair*, 1970 (p for children); *At Thurgarton Church*, 1971 (p); *Poems of Places and People*, 1971 (p); *The Alphabetical Zoo*, 1972 (p); *In Memory of David Archer*, 1973 (p)

John Heath-Stubbs and Martin Green, eds., *Homage to George Barker*, 1973

● STAN BARSTOW
1928–

A Kind of Loving, 1960 (n); *The Desperadoes*, 1961 (s); *Ask Me Tomorrow*, 1962 (n); *Joby*, 1964 (n); *The Watchers on the Shore*, 1966 (n); (with Alfred Bradley) *Ask Me Tomorrow*, 1966 (dramatization of novel); *A Raging Calm* (Amer. ed. *The Hidden Part*), 1968 (n); *The Human Element*, 1970 (s); (with A. Bradley) *A Kind of Loving*, 1970 (dramatization of novel); *A Season with Eros*, 1971 (s); (with A. Bradley) *Stringer's Last Stand*, 1973 (d)

SAMUEL BECKETT
1906–

Robert Pinget, *The Old Tune* (English adaptation by Beckett), 1963 (also in *Three Plays* by Pinget, 1966); *Play, and Two Short Pieces for Radio*, 1964

BECKETT (cont'd)

(d, rd); *Proust, and Three Dialogues* by Beckett and Georges Duthuit (*Proust* orig. pub. 1931, *Three Dialogues* orig. pub. in *Transition* 149, no. 5), 1965 (c); *Imagination Dead Imagine* (tr. of *Imagination morte imaginez*, 1958, from French by the author), 1966 (e); *Come and Go*, 1967 (d); *Eh, Joe, and Other Writings* (with *Act Without Words II*; *Film*), 1967 (d); *No's Knife: Collected Shorter Prose, 1945–1966*, 1967 (s, e); *A Samuel Beckett Reader*, ed. John Calder, 1967; *Cascando, and Other Short Dramatic Pieces* (with *Words and Music*; *Eh, Joe*; *Play*; *Come and Go*; *Film*), 1968 (d); *Film: Complete Scenario, Illustrations, Production Shots*, 1969; *Lessness* (tr. of *Sans*, 1969, from French by the author), 1970 (misc); (with others) *Jack B. Yeats: A Centenary Gathering*, 1972 (ac); *The Lost Ones* (tr. of *Le dépeupleur*, 1971, from the French by the author), 1972 (n); Guillaume Apollinaire, *Zone* (orig. pub. in *Transition*, 1950), 1972 (tr); *The North*, 1972 (misc); *Breath, and Other Shorts*, 1972 (d); *Not I*, 1973 (d); *First Love* (tr. of *Premier amour*, 1970, from French by the author), 1973 (n); *Mercier and Camier* (tr. of *Mercier et Camier*, 1970, from French by the author), 1974 (n)

Raymond Federman and John Fletcher, *Samuel Beckett: His Works and His Critics: An Essay in Bibliography*, 1970

MAX BEERBOHM
1872–1956

Seven Men, and Two Others (orig. pub. 1950), 1966 (s); *More Theatres 1898–1903*, comp. Rupert Hart-Davis, 1969 (c); *Last Theatres 1904–1910*, comp. Rupert Hart-Davis, 1970 (c); *The Bodley Head Max Beerbohm*, ed. David Cecil (Amer. ed. *Selected Prose*), 1970 (e, c); *A Peep into the Past, and Other Prose Pieces*, coll. by Rupert Hart-Davis, 1972 (e)

BRENDAN BEHAN
1923–1964

With Breast Expanded, 1964 (a); *Confessions of an Irish Rebel*, 1965 (a); *Moving Out, and A Garden Party*, 1967 (d); *The Wit of Brendan Behan*, comp. Sean McCann, 1968 (misc); *Richard's Cork Leg*, 1973 (d)

Ulick O'Connor, *Brendan Behan*, 1970

HILAIRE BELLOC
1870–1953

Belloc: A Biographical Anthology, ed. Herbert Van Thal and Jane Soames Nickerson, 1970 (selections); *Complete Verse*, new ed. rev. and reset, 1970 (p); *Hilaire Belloc's Prefaces Written for Fellow Authors*, sel. J. A. De Chantigny, 1971 (c)

ARNOLD BENNETT
1867–1931

Letters of Arnold Bennett, ed. James Hepburn: Vol. 1: *Letters to J. B. Pinker*, 1966; Vol. 2: *1889–1915*, 1968; Vol. 3: *1916–1931*, 1970; *The Author's Craft, and Other Critical Writings*, ed. Samuel Hynes, 1968 (c); *The Journal of Arnold Bennett, with the Addition of Journal Vol. 6 Newly Discovered*, ed. Frank Swinnerton, 1971; *Arnold Bennett in Love: Arnold Bennett and His Wife Marguerite Soulié: A Correspondence*, ed. George Beardmore, 1972; *The Evening Standard Years: Books and Persons 1926–1931*, ed. Andrew Mylett, 1974 (c)

Norman Emery, *Arnold Bennett (1867–1931): A Bibliography*, 1967; Margaret Drabble, *Arnold Bennett*, 1974

● JOHN BERGER
1926–

A Painter of Our Time, 1958 (n); *Permanent Red: Essays in Seeing* (Amer. ed. *Toward Reality*), 1960 (ac);

The Foot of Clive, 1962 (n); *Corker's Freedom*, 1964 (n); *The Success and Failure of Picasso*, 1965 (ac); (with Jean Mohr) *A Fortunate Man: The Story of a Country Doctor*, 1967 (g); *Art and Revolution*, 1969 (ac); *The Moment of Cubism*, 1969 (ac); *Selected Essays and Articles: The Look of Things*, 1972 (ac); *G.: A Novel*, 1972 (n)

JOHN BETJEMAN
1906–

The City of London Churches, 1965 (ac); *High and Low*, 1966 (p); *Victorian and Edwardian London*, 1969 (g); *Ghastly Good Taste; or, A Depressing Story of the Rise and Fall of English Architecture*, new ed., 1970 (ac); *Collected Poems*, 3rd ed., 1970 (p); *Victorian and Edwardian Oxford from Old Photographs*, 1971 (g); *London's Historic Railway Stations*, 1972 (ac); *A Pictorial History of English Architecture*, 1972 (ac); *Victorian and Edwardian Brighton from Old Photographs*, 1972 (g); *West Country Churches*, 1973 (ac); *A Nip in the Air*, 1974 (p)

EDMUND BLUNDEN
1896–1974

Undertones of War, new ed., 1965 (m); *Eleven Poems*, 1966 (p); *A Few Not Quite Forgotten Writers*, 1967 (c); *John Keats*, rev. ed., 1967 (c); *The Midnight Skaters: Poems for Young Readers*, chosen and introduced by C. Day Lewis, 1968 (p); *John Clare: Beginner's Luck*, 1971 (c)

● ROBERT BOLT
1925–

Flowering Cherry, 1958 (d); *A Man for All Seasons*, 1961 (d); *The Tiger and the Horse*, 1961 (d); *Gentle Jack*, 1964 (d); *Doctor Zhivago*, 1966 (screenplay); *The Thwarting of Baron Bolligrew*, 1966 (d); *Vivat! Vivat Regina!*, 1971 (d)

● EDWARD BOND
1934–

Saved, 1966 (d); *Narrow Road to the Deep North*, 1968 (d); *Early Morning*, 1968 (d); *The Pope's Wedding, and Other Plays* (with *Mr. Dog*; *The King with Golden Eyes*; *Sharpville Sequence*), 1971 (d); *Lear*, 1972 (d); *The Sea*, 1973 (d); *Bingo*, 1974 (d)

ELIZABETH BOWEN
1899–1973

Bowen's Court, 2nd ed., 1965 (a); *A Day in the Dark*, 1965 (s); (with others) *These Simple Things: Some Appreciations of the Small Joys in Daily Life, from "House and Garden,"* 1965 (e); *Eva Trout; or, Changing Scenes*, 1969 (n); *Pictures and Conversations*, 1975 (misc)

J'Nan Sellery, "Elizabeth Bowen: A Check List," *Bulletin of the New York Public Library*, 74 (April, 1970), 219–74; Allan E. Austin, *Elizabeth Bowen*, 1971

MALCOLM BRADBURY
1932–

Evelyn Waugh, 1964 (c); *Stepping Westward*, 1965 (n); *What Is a Novel?* (textbook), 1969 (c); *The Social Context of Modern English Literature*, 1971 (c); *Possibilities*, 1973 (c)

JOHN BRAINE
1922–

The Crying Game, 1968 (n); *Stay with Me till Morning* (Amer. ed. *The View from Tower Hill*), 1970 (n); *The Queen of a Distant Country*, 1972 (n); *Writing a Novel*, 1974 (g)

James V. Lee, *John Braine*, 1968

RUPERT BROOKE
1887–1915

The Letters of Rupert Brooke, ed. Geoffrey Keynes, 1968; *The Poetical Works*, 2nd ed., 1970 (p); *Rupert Brooke: A Reappraisal and Selection from His Writings, Some Hitherto Unpublished*, ed. Timothy Rogers, 1971

Michael Hastings, *The Handsomest Young Man in England: Rupert Brooke*, 1967; John Schroder, comp., *Catalogue of Books and Manuscripts by Rupert Brooke, Edward Marsh, and Christopher Hassall*, 1970

CHRISTINE BROOKE-ROSE
1923–

Such, 1966 (n); Alain Robbe-Grillet, *In the Labyrinth*, 1968 (tr); *Between*, 1968 (n); *Go When You See the Green Man Walking*, 1970 (s); *A ZBC of Ezra Pound*, 1971 (c)

BRIGID BROPHY
1929–

Don't Never Forget: Collected Views and Reviews, 1966 (c, e); *Religious Education in State Schools*, 1967 (g); (with others) *Fifty Works of English and American Literature We Could Do Without*, 1967 (c); *Black and White: A Portrait of Aubrey Beardsley*, 1968 (b, c); *The Burglar*, 1968 (d); *In Transit: An Heroi-cyclic Novel*, 1969 (n); *The Rights of Animals*, 1970 (g); *The Waste Disposal Unit* (in *Best Short Plays of the World Theatre 1958–67*), 1968 (d); *Prancing Novelist: A Defence of Fiction in the Form of a Critical Biography in Praise of Ronald Firbank*, 1973 (b, c); *The Adventures of God in His Search for the Black Girl*, 1973 (s)

● BASIL BUNTING
1900–

Redimiculum Matellarum, 1930 (p); *Poems: 1950*, 1950 (p); *The First Book of Odes*, 1965 (p); *Loquitur*, 1965 (p); *The Spoils*, 1965 (p); *Briggflatts*, 1966 (p); *Two Poems*, 1967 (p); *What the Chairman Told Tom*, 1967 (p); *Collected Poems*, 1968 (p); *Descant on Rawley's Madrigal (Conversations with Jonathan Williams)*, 1968 (p)

ANTHONY BURGESS
1917–

The Eve of Saint Venus, 1964 (n); *The Long Day Wanes: A Malayan Trilogy* (previously published separately as *Time for a Tiger*; *The Enemy in the Blanket*; *Beds in the East*), 1964 (n); *Here Comes Everybody* (Amer. ed. *ReJoyce*), 1965 (c); *A Vision of Battlements*, 1965 (n); *Tremor of Intent*, 1966 (n); *Coaching Days of England* (historical commentary), 1966 (h); *The Novel Now*, 1967 (c); *The Age of the Grand Tour*, 1968 (h); *Enderby Outside* (Amer. ed. *Enderby* [with *Inside Mr. Enderby*]), 1968 (n); *Urgent Copy*, 1968 (c); *Shakespeare*, 1970 (b); *MF*, 1971 (n); *The Worm and the Ring*, rev. ed., 1971 (n); Edmond Rostand, *Cyrano de Bergerac*, 1971 (tr); *Joysprick: An Introduction to the Language of James Joyce*, 1972 (c); Sophocles, *Oedipus the King*, 1973 (tr); *Napoleon Symphony*, 1974 (n); *The Clockwork Testament*, 1974 (n)

A. A. De Vitis, *Anthony Burgess*, 1972; Beverly R. David, "Anthony Burgess: A Checklist (1956–1971)," *Twentieth Century Literature*, 19, 3 (July, 1973), 181–88

ROY CAMPBELL
1902–1957

Selected Poetry, ed. J. M. Lalley, 1968 (p)

Rowland Smith, *Lyric and Polemic: The Literary Personality of Roy Campbell*, 1972

PAUL VINCENT CARROLL
1900–1968

Farewell to Greatness, 1966 (d); *Goodbye to the Summer,* 1970 (d)

Paul A. Doyle, *Paul Vincent Carroll,* 1972

JOYCE CARY
1888–1957

Cock Jarvis (resurrected ms.), ed. A. G. Bishop, 1974 (n)

Malcolm Foster, *Joyce Cary, a Biography,* 1968; Barbara Fisher, "Joyce Cary's Published Writings," *Bodleian Library Record,* 8, 4 (April, 1970), 213–28

G. K. CHESTERTON
1874–1936

Chesterton Continued: A Bibliographical Supplement Together with Some Uncollected Prose and Verse, 1968 (e, p); *G. K. Chesterton: A Selection from His Non-fictional Prose,* sel. W. H. Auden, 1970 (e); *Chesterton on Shakespeare,* 1972 (c); *Selected Stories,* ed. Kingsley Amis, 1972 (s); *Greybeards at Play, and Other Comic Verse,* ed. John Sullivan, 1974 (p)

John Sullivan, *G. K. Chesterton: A Bibliography,* 1958; John Sullivan, *Chesterton Continued: A Bibliographical Supplement,* 1968; Dudley Barker, *G. K. Chesterton: A Biography,* 1973

AUSTIN CLARKE
1896–1974

Mnemosyne Lay in Dust, 1966 (p); *Old-fashioned Pilgrimage,* 1967 (p); *Echo at Coole,* 1968 (p); *A Penny in the Clouds: More Memories of Ireland and England* (orig. pub. 1937), 1968 (m); *Two Interludes, Adapted from Cervantes (The Student from Salamanca* and *The Silent Lover),*

1968 (pd); *The Celtic Twilight and the Nineties,* 1969 (c); *Collected Poems,* ed. Liam Miller, 1974 (p)

PADRAIC COLUM
1881–1972

Images of Departure, 1970 (p)

Zack Bowen, *Padraic Colum: A Biographical-Critical Introduction,* 1970; Alan Denson, "Padraic Colum: An Appreciation with a Check-list of His Publications," *The Dublin Magazine,* 6, 1 (Spring, 1967), 50–67

IVY COMPTON-BURNETT
1892–1969

A God and His Gifts, 1963 (n); *Ivy and Stevie: Ivy Compton-Burnett and Stevie Smith: Conversations and Reflections,* by Kay Dick (record of conversation with I. C.-B. and S. S.), 1971; *The Last and the First,* 1971 (n)

Elizabeth Sprigge, *The Life of Ivy Compton-Burnett,* 1973

JOSEPH CONRAD
1857–1924

Joseph Conrad's Letters to R. B. Cunninghame-Graham, ed. C. T. Watts, 1969

T. G. Ehrsam, *A Bibliography of Joseph Conrad,* 1969

NOEL COWARD
1899–1973

The Lyrics of Noel Coward, 1965; *Pretty Polly Barlow,* 1965 (s); *Suite in Three Keys: A Song at Twilight, Shadows of the Evening, Come into the Garden Maud,* 1966 (d); *Bon Voyage,* 1967 (s); *Not Yet the Dodo,* 1967 (p); *The Wit of Noel Coward,* comp. Dick Richards, 1968 (misc); *The Collected Short Stories,* new ed., 1969 (s); *A*

COWARD (*cont'd*)
Song at Twilight (authorized shorter version), 1973 (d); *Sir Noel Coward: His Words and Music*, 1973

Milton Levin, *Noel Coward*, 1968; Sheridan Morley, *A Talent to Amuse: A Biography of Noel Coward*, 1969

DONALD DAVIE
1922–

Russian Literature and Modern English Fiction, 1965 (c); *Ezra Pound: Poet as Sculptor*, 1965 (c); *Purity of Diction in English Verse*, new ed., 1967 (c); *Essex Poems 1963–67*, 1969 (p); *Poems*, 1970 (p); *Six Epistles to Eva Hesse*, 1970 (p); (with others) *The Survival of Poetry: A Contemporary Survey*, ed. Martin Dodsworth, 1970 (c); *Thomas Hardy and British Poetry*, 1972 (c); *Collected Poems 1950–1970*, 1972 (p); *The Shires*, 1974 (p); *The Augustan Lyric*, 1974 (c)

C. DAY LEWIS
1904–1972

The Lyric Impulse, 1965 (c), *The Room*, 1965 (p); (with R. A. Scott-James) *Thomas Hardy*, reprinted with the addition of a new chapter by C. Day Lewis, 1965 (c); *Selections from His Poetry*, 1967 (p); *A Need for Poetry?*, 1968 (c); *The Whispering Roots*, 1970 (p). Also, under pseudonym Nicholas Blake: *The Morning after Death*, 1966 (n); *The Nicholas Blake Omnibus*, 1966; *The Private Wound*, 1968 (n)

Geoffrey Handley-Taylor, *C. Day Lewis, the Poet Laureate: A Bibliography*, 1968

NIGEL DENNIS
1912–

Jonathan Swift, 1964 (b); *A House in Order*, 1966 (n); *August for the People* (in *Novelists' Theatre*), 1966 (d); *Exotics*, 1970 (p)

● DENIS DEVLIN
1908–1959

(with Brian Coffey) *Poems*, 1930 (p); *Intercessions*, 1937 (p); Saint-John Perse, *Rains* (*Pluies*), 1945 (tr); *Lough Derg, and Other Poems*, 1946 (p); Saint-John Perse, *Exiles*, 1949 (tr); *The Heavenly Foreigner*, ed. Brian Coffey, 1950 (p); René Char, *Poems*, 1952 (tr); *Selected Poems*, preface by Allen Tate and Robert Penn Warren, 1963 (p); *Collected Poems*, ed. Brian Coffey, 1964 (p)

● KEITH DOUGLAS
1920–1944

Alamein to Zem Zem, 1946 (m); *Collected Poems*, ed. John Waller and G. S. Fraser, 1951 (p); *Selected Poems*, ed. Ted Hughes, 1964 (p); *Collected Poems*, ed. John Waller, G. S. Fraser, and J. C. Hall, 1966 (p)

Desmond Graham, *Keith Douglas 1920–1944: A Biography*, 1974

● MARGARET DRABBLE
1939–

A Summer Bird-Cage, 1963 (n); *The Garrick Year*, 1964 (n); *The Millstone*, 1965 (n); *Wordsworth*, 1966 (c); *Jerusalem the Golden*, 1967 (n); *The Waterfall*, 1969 (n); *The Needle's Eye*, 1972 (n); (with B. S. Johnson and others) *London Consequences: A Novel*, 1972 (n); *Arnold Bennett*, 1974 (b)

LAWRENCE DURRELL
1912–

Acte, 1965 (d); *The Ikons*, 1966 (p); *Sauve Qui Peut*, 1966 (s); *Sappho*, new ed., 1967 (pd); *Collected Poems*, new and rev. ed., 1968 (p); *Tunc*, 1968 (n); *Spirit of Place*, ed. Alan G. Thomas, 1969 (t); *Nunquam*, 1970 (n); *The Red Limbo Lingo: A Poetry Notebook*,

1971 (p); *Vega*, 1973 (p); *Monsieur; or, the Prince of Darkness*, 1974 (n)

G. S. Fraser, *Lawrence Durrell: A Study*; with a bibliography by Alan G. Thomas, 1968; rev. ed., 1973

T. S. ELIOT
1888–1965

To Criticize the Critic, and Other Writings, 1965 (c); *Dante* (orig. pub. 1929), 1965 (c); *Poems Written in Early Youth* (orig. pub. Stockholm, 1950), 1967 (p); *The Complete Poems and Plays*, 1969 (p, pd); *The Waste Land: A Facsimile and Transcript of the Original Drafts Including the Annotations of Ezra Pound*, ed. Valerie Eliot, 1971 (p)

David Gallup, *T. S. Eliot: A Bibliography*, new ed., 1969

D. J. ENRIGHT
1920–

Figures of Speech, 1965 (n); *The Old Adam*, 1965 (p); *Conspirators and Poets*, 1966 (c); *Unlawful Assembly*, 1968 (p); *Selected Poems*, 1968 (p); *Memoirs of a Mendicant Professor*, 1969 (m); *Shakespeare and the Students*, 1970 (c); *The Typewriter Revolution*, 1971 (p); *Daughters of Earth*, 1972 (p); *Man Is an Onion: Reviews and Essays*, 1972 (c); *The Terrible Shears*, 1973 (p); *Rhyme Times Rhyme*, 1974 (p-j)

William Walsh, *D. J. Enright: Poet of Humanism*, 1974

GABRIEL FIELDING
1916–

The Birthday King, 1962 (n); *Gentlemen in Their Season*, 1966 (n); *Collected Short Stories*, 1971 (s); *New Queens for Old*, 1972 (s)

RONALD FIRBANK
1886–1926

The New Rythum [sic], *and Other Pieces*, 1962 (s)

Miriam J. Benkovitz, *Ronald Firbank: A Biography*, 1969

FORD MADOX FORD
1873–1939

Buckshee (Poems from *Collected Poems*), 1966 (p); *Memories and Impressions* (Vol. 5 of *The Bodley Head Ford Madox Ford*), sel. Michael Killigrew (Amer. ed. *Your Mirror to My Times: The Selected Autobiographies and Impressions of Ford Madox Ford*), 1971 (m)

Arthur Mizener, *The Saddest Story: A Biography of Ford Madox Ford*, 1971

E. M. FORSTER
1879–1970

Selected Writings, ed. G. B. Parker, 1968 (c, e); *Albergo Empedocle, and Other Early Writings*, 1971 (s, e); *Maurice*, 1971 (n); *The Life to Come*, 1972 (s); *Goldsworthy Lowes Dickinson, and Related Writings*, ed. Oliver Stallybrass (*Dickinson* orig. pub. 1934), 1973 (b); *The Manuscripts of "Howards End" Correlated with Forster's Final Version*, ed. Oliver Stallybrass, 1973; also other reprints in the Abinger Edition of the works of E. M. Forster

Brownlee Jean Kirkpatrick, *A Bibliography of E. M. Forster*, 1965; 2nd rev. ed., 1968

● JOHN FOWLES
1926–

The Collector, 1963 (n); *The Aristos: A Self-Portrait in Ideas*, 1965 (e); *The Magus*, 1966 (n); *The French Lieutenant's Woman*, 1969 (n); *The Ebony Tower: Collected Novellas*, 1974 (s)

FOWLES (cont'd)
Prescott Evarts, Jr., "John Fowles: A Checklist," *Critique*, 13, 3 (1972), pp. 105–7

● **MICHAEL FRAYN**
   1933–

The Day of the Dog, 1962 (e); *The Book of Fub*, 1963 (e); *On the Outskirts*, 1964 (e); *The Tin Men*, 1965 (n); *The Russian Interpreter*, 1966 (n); *At Bay in Gear Street*, 1967 (e); *Towards the End of the Morning* (Amer. ed. *Against Entropy*), 1967 (n); *A Very Private Life*, 1968 (n); *The Two of Us: Four One-Act Plays for Two Players*, 1970 (d); *Sweet Dreams*, 1973 (n); *Constructions*, 1974 (e)

● **BRIAN FRIEL**
   1929–

The Saucer of Larks, 1962 (s); *Philadelphia, Here I Come!*, 1965 (d); *The Gold in the Sea*, 1966 (s); *The Loves of Cass McGuire*, 1967 (d); *Lovers: Part 1: Winners; Part 2: Losers*, 1968 (d); *A Saucer of Larks: Stories of Ireland*, 1969 (s); *Two Plays: Crystal and Fox, and The Mundy Scheme*, 1970 (d); *The Gentle Island*, 1974 (d); *The Freedom of the City*, 1974 (d)

D. E. S. Maxwell, *Brian Friel*, 1973

CHRISTOPHER FRY
   1907–

A Yard of Sun, 1970 (pd)

Emil Roy, *Christopher Fry*, 1968

ROY FULLER
   1912–

Buff, 1965 (p); *My Child, My Sister*, 1965 (n); *Catspaw*, 1966 (n-j); *New Poems*, 1968 (p); *Off Course*, 1969 (p); *The Carnal Island*, 1970 (n); *Owls and Artificers: Oxford Lectures of Poetry*, 1971 (c); *Seen Grandpa Lately?*, 1972 (p-j); *Tiny Tears*, 1973 (p)

JOHN GALSWORTHY
   1867–1933

(No new publication except reprints)

WILLIAM GOLDING
   1911–

The Hot Gates, and Other Occasional Pieces, 1965 (e); *The Pyramid*, 1967 (n); *The Scorpion God: Three Short Novels*, 1971 (n)

Jack I. Biles, "A William Golding Checklist," *Twentieth Century Literature*, 17, 3 (April, 1971), 107–21

ROBERT GRAVES
   1895–

Love Respelt, 1965 (p); *Collected Poems, 1965*, 1965 (p); *Collected Short Stories*, 1965 (s); *Majorca Observed*, 1965 (t); *Mammon and the Black Goddess*, 1965 (g); *Two Wise Children*, 1967 (j); *Poetic Craft and Principle*, 1967 (c); *The Rubaiyyat of Omar Khayyam*, 1967 (tr); *Spiritual Quixote*, 1967 (e); *Poems 1965–1968*, 1968 (p); *Poems About Love*, 1969 (p); *The Poor Boy Who Followed His Star, and Children's Poems*, 1968 (j); *The Crane Bag, and Other Disputed Subjects*, 1969 (e); *On Poetry: Collected Talks and Essays*, 1969 (c, e); *Love Respelt Again*, 1969 (p); *Poems 1968–1970*, 1970 (p); *Poems: Abridged for Dolls and Princes*, 1971 (j); *Poems 1970–1972*, 1973 (p); *Difficult Questions, Easy Answers*, 1973 (misc)

Fred H. Higginson, *A Bibliography of the Works of Robert Graves*, 1966

HENRY GREEN
   1905–

(No new publication)

GRAHAM GREENE
1904–

The Comedians, 1966 (n); *May We Borrow Your Husband?*, 1967 (s); *Collected Essays*, 1969 (e); (with Carol Reed) *The Third Man: A Film*, 1969 (film script); *Travels with My Aunt*, 1969 (n); *A Sort of Life*, 1971 (a); *The Pleasure Dome: Collected Film Criticism 1935–40* (Amer. ed. *Graham Greene on Film*), 1972 (c); *Collected Stories*, 1972 (s); *The Honorary Consul*, 1973 (n); *Lord Rochester's Monkey* [written in the 1930s], 1974 (b)

Peter Wolfe, *Graham Greene the Entertainer*, 1972

LADY [AUGUSTA] GREGORY
1852–1932

Coole, ed. Colin Smythe, 1971 (e, t); *Poets and Dreamers: Studies and Translations from the Irish*, 1974 (c, tr); also numerous reprints in the Coole Edition of Lady Gregory's Works

Hazard Adams, *Lady Gregory*, 1973

GEOFFREY GRIGSON
1905–

The Shell Book of Roads, 1964 (t); *The Shell Country Alphabet*, 1966 (t); *A Skull in Salop*, 1967 (p); (with Jane Grigson) *Shapes and Adventures*, 1967 (ac-j); *Ingestion of Ice Cream*, 1969 (p); *Poems & Poets*, 1969 (c); *Looking and Finding and Collecting and Reading and Investigating and Much Else*, rev. and enl. ed., 1970 (prev. ed. 1958) (archeology); *Notes from an Odd Country*, 1970 (e); *Shapes and People*, 1970 (ac-j); *Discoveries of Bones and Stones*, 1971 (p); *Shapes and Creatures: A Book about Pictures*, 1973 (ac-j); *Sad Grave of an Imperial Mongoose*, 1973 (p); *Angles and Circles*, 1974 (p)

THOM GUNN
1929–

A Geography, 1966 (p); *Positives*, 1966 (p); *Touch*, 1967 (p); *Poems 1950–1966*, 1969 (p); *Moly*, 1971 (p); *To the Air*, 1974 (p)

JAMES HANLEY
1901–

The Inner Journey, 1965 (d); *Plays One* (*The Inner Journey* and *A Stone Flower*), 1968 (d); *John Cowper Powys: A Man in the Corner*, 1970 (b); *Herman Melville*, 1971 (b); *Another World*, 1972 (n); *A Woman in the Sky*, 1974 (n)

THOMAS HARDY
1850–1928

The Architectural Notebook of Thomas Hardy (facsimile reproduction), 1966; *Some Romano-British Relics Found at Max Gate, Dorchester* (8 pages), 1966 (g); *Personal Writings*, ed. Harold Orel, 1967 (e)

L. P. HARTLEY
1895–1972

The Betrayal, 1966 (n); *The Novelist's Responsibility: Lectures and Essays*, 1967 (c); *The Collected Short Stories*, 1968 (s); *Poor Clare*, 1968 (n); *The Love-Adept*, 1969 (n); *My Sisters' Keeper*, 1970 (n); *The Harness Room*, 1971 (n); *Mrs. Carteret Receives*, 1971 (s); *The Collections*, 1972 (n); *The Will and the Way*, 1973 (n); *The Complete Stories*, 1973 (s)

Paul Bloomfield, *L. P. Hartley*, rev. and enl. ed., 1970

● SEAMUS HEANEY
1939–

Eleven Poems, 1965 (p); *Death of a Naturalist*, 1966 (p); *Door into the Dark*, 1969 (p); *A Boy Driving His Father to Confession*, 1971 (p); *Wintering Out*, 1972 (p)

RAYNER HEPPENSTALL
1911–

Raymond Roussel: A Critical Guide, 1966 (c); *A Little Pattern of French Crime,* 1969 (g); *Portrait of the Artist as a Professional Man,* 1969 (m); *The Shearers,* 1969 (n); *French Crime in the Romantic Age,* 1970 (g); *Bluebeard and After: Three Decades of Murder in France,* 1972 (g); *The Sex War and Others,* 1973 (g)

● AIDAN HIGGINS
1927–

Felo de Se (Amer. ed. *Killachter Meadow*), 1960 (s); *Langrishe, Go Down,* 1966 (n); *Images of Africa: Diary (1956–60),* 1971 (t); *Balcony of Europe,* 1972 (n)

● GEOFFREY HILL
1932–

Poems, 1952 (p); *For the Unfallen: Poems 1952–1958,* 1959 (p); *Preghiere,* 1964 (p); *King Log,* 1968 (p); *Mercian Hymns,* 1971 (p)

● THOMAS HINDE
1926–

Mr. Nicholas, 1952 (n); *Happy as Larry,* 1957 (n); *For the Good of the Company,* 1961 (n); *A Place Like Home,* 1962 (n); *The Cage,* 1962 (n); *Ninety Double Martinis,* 1963 (n); *The Day the Call Came,* 1964 (n); *Games of Chance: The Interviewer, and The Investigator,* 1965 (n); *The Village,* 1966 (n); *High,* 1968 (n); *Bird,* 1970 (n); *Generally a Virgin,* 1972 (n); *Agent,* 1974 (n)

GERARD MANLEY HOPKINS
1844–1889

The Poems of Gerard Manley Hopkins, 4th ed., rev. and enl., ed. W. H. Gardner and N. H. Mackenzie, 1967

Edward H. Cohen, *Works and Criticism of Gerard Manley Hopkins: A Comprehensive Bibliography,* 1969

A. E. HOUSMAN
1859–1936

The Making of "A Shropshire Lad": A Manuscript Variorum, ed. T. B. Haber, 1966 (p); *The Collected Poems,* new ed., 1967 (p); *The Confines of Criticism: The Cambridge Inaugural, 1911,* 1969 (c); *The Letters of A. E. Housman,* ed. Henry Maas, 1971; *The Classical Papers of A. E. Housman,* 3 vols., ed. F. R. D. Goodyear and J. Diggle, 1973 (c, e)

ELIZABETH JANE HOWARD
1923–

After Julius, 1965 (n); *Something in Disguise,* 1969 (n); *Odd Girl Out,* 1972 (n)

RICHARD HUGHES
1901–

Gertrude's Child, 1967 (j); *The Wooden Shepherdess* (Vol. II of *The Human Predicament*), 1973 (n)

TED HUGHES
1930–

Wodwo, 1967 (p); *Scapegoats and Rabies,* 1967 (p); *The Iron Man,* 1968 (j); *Oedipus,* 1969 (d); *Crow, From the Life and Songs of the Crow,* 1970 (p); *A Crow Hymn,* 1970 (p); *Five Autumn Songs for Children's Voices,* 1970 (p); *Martyrdom of Bishop Farrar,* 1970 (p); *Selected Poems, 1957–1967,* 1972 (p); A. C. H. Smith, *"Orghast" at Persepolis: An Account of the Experiment in Theatre Directed by Peter Brook and Written by Ted Hughes,* 1972; *The Tiger's Bones, and Other Plays for Children,* 1974 (d)

ALDOUS HUXLEY
1894–1963

The Crows of Pearblossom, 1967 (j); *Letters of Aldous Huxley,* ed. Grover Smith, 1969; *The Collected Poetry,* 1971 (p); also reprints in *The Collected Works,* 1970–

Sybille Bedford, *Aldous Huxley: A Biography,* 1974

CHRISTOPHER ISHERWOOD
1904–

Ramakrishna and His Disciples, 1965 (b); *Exhumations: Stories, Articles, Verses,* 1966; *A Meeting by the River,* 1967 (n); *Essentials of Vedanta,* 1969 (g); *Kathleen and Frank,* 1971 (b)

Selmer Westby and Clayton M. Brown, *Christopher Isherwood: A Bibliography 1923–1967,* 1968

● DAN JACOBSON
1929–

The Trap, 1955 (n); *A Dance in the Sun,* 1956 (n); *The Price of Diamonds,* 1957 (n); *A Long Way from London,* 1958 (s); *The Zulu and the Zeide,* 1959 (s); *No Further West: California Visited,* 1959 (t); *The Evidence of Love,* 1960 (n); *Time of Arrival,* 1963 (e); *Beggar My Neighbour,* 1964 (s); *The Beginners,* 1966 (n); *The Rape of Tamar,* 1970 (n); *A Way of Life,* 1971 (s-j); *Through the Wilderness,* 1968 (s); *Inklings,* 1973 (s); *The Wonder-Worker,* 1973 (n)

Myra Yudelman, *Dan Jacobson: A Bibliography,* 1967

HENRY JAMES
1843–1916

Reprints of the novels in *The Bodley Head Henry James,* 1967–

● ANN JELLICOE
1927–

The Rising Generation (in *Ark* 25), 1960 (d); (adaptor) Ibsen, *Rosmersholm,* 1960 (d); *The Knack,* 1962 (d); *The Sport of My Mad Mother,* 1964 (d); *Shelley; or, The Idealist,* 1966 (d); *Some Unconscious Influences in the Theatre,* 1967 (c); *The Giveaway,* 1970 (d)

ELIZABETH JENNINGS
1926–

Robert Frost, 1964 (c); *Christianity and Poetry,* 1965 (c); *The Mind Has Mountains,* 1966 (p); *The Secret Brother,* 1966 (p-j); *Collected Poems,* 1967 (p); *The Animals' Arrival,* 1969 (p); *Lucidities,* 1970 (p); *Relationships,* 1972 (p); *Reaching into Silence: A Study of Eight Twentieth–Century Visionaries,* 1974 (c)

● B. S. JOHNSON
1933–1973

Travelling People, 1963 (n); (with Julia T. Oman) *Street Children,* 1964 (g); *Poems,* 1964 (p); (with Zulfikar Ghose) *Statement against Corpses,* 1964 (s); *Albert Angelo,* 1964 (n); *Trawl,* 1966 (n); *The Unfortunates,* 1969 (n); *You're Human Like the Rest of Them* (in *New English Dramatists 14*), 1970 (screenplay); *House Mother Normal,* 1971 (n); (with Margaret Drabble and others) *London Consequences: A Novel,* 1972 (n); *All Bull: The National Servicemen,* 1973 (g); *Christie Malry's Own Double Entry,* 1973 (n)

PAMELA HANSFORD JOHNSON
1912–

Cork Street, Next to the Hatter's, 1965 (n); *On Iniquity: Some Personal Reflections Arising Out of the Moors Murder Trial,* 1967 (e); *The Survival of the Fittest,* 1968 (n); (with C. P. Snow)

JOHNSON, P. H. (cont'd)

The Public Prosecutor (adaptation of a play by Georgi Dzagarov, tr. by Marguerite Alexieva), 1969 (d); The Honours Board, 1970 (n); The Holiday Friend, 1972 (n); Important to Me, 1974 (a)

DENIS JOHNSTON
1901–

John Millington Synge, 1965 (c)

DAVID JONES
1895–1974

The Tribune's Visitation, 1969 (p); The Sleeping Lord, and Other Fragments, 1974 (p)

David Blamires, David Jones: Artist and Writer, 1972

JAMES JOYCE
1882–1941

The Cat and the Devil, 1964 (j); Letters of James Joyce, ed. Richard Ellmann, 1966; Giacomo Joyce, 1968 (prose poem)

● PATRICK KAVANAGH
1904–1967

Songs, 1930 (p); Ploughman, 1936 (p); The Green Fool, 1938 (a); The Great Hunger, 1942 (p); A Soul for Sale, 1947 (p); Tarry Flynn, 1948 (n); Skinyou's Beauty Parlor, 1951 (d); Come Dance with Kitty Stobling, 1960 (p); Collected Poems, 1964 (p); Self-Portrait, 1964 (a); Collected Pruse [sic], 1967 (e)

● THOMAS KINSELLA
1928–

The Starlit Eye, 1952 (p); Poems, 1956 (p); Another September, 1958 (p); Moralities, 1960 (p); Poems and Translations, 1961 (p, tr); Downstream, 1962 (p); Wormwood, 1966 (p); Nightwalker, 1968 (p); Davis, Mangan,

Ferguson? Tradition and the Irish Writer: Writings by W. B. Yeats and by Thomas Kinsella, 1970 (c); The Táin, 1970 (tr); Notes from the Land of the Dead, 1972 (p); Butcher's Dozen, 1972 (p); New Poems 1973, 1973 (p); Selected Poems 1956–1968, 1974 (p)

Hensley C. Woodbridge, "Thomas Kinsella: A Bibliography," Éire-Ireland, 2, 2 (Summer, 1967), pp. 122–33

RUDYARD KIPLING
1865–1936

Rudyard Kipling to Rider Haggard: The Record of a Friendship (letters), ed. Morton Cohen, 1965

● BERNARD KOPS
1928–

Poems, 1955 (p); Poems and Songs, 1958 (p); Awake for Mourning, 1958 (n); An Anemone for Antigone, 1959 (p); The Hamlet of Stepney Green, 1959 (d); The Dream of Peter Mann, 1960 (d); Motorbike, 1962 (n); The World Is a Wedding, 1963 (a); Four Plays (The Hamlet of Stepney Green; Enter Solly Gold; Home Sweet Honeycomb; The Lemmings), 1964 (d); Yes from No-Man's Land, 1965 (n); The Boy Who Wouldn't Play Jesus, 1965 (d-j); The Dissent of Dominick Shapiro, 1966 (n); Erica I Want to Read You Something, 1967 (p); By the Waters of Whitechapel, 1969 (n); David It Is Getting Dark, 1969 (d); For the Record, 1971 (p); The Passionate Past of Gloria Gaye, 1971 (n); Settle Down Simon Katz, 1973 (n)

PHILIP LARKIN
1922–

All What Jazz? A Record Diary 1961–68, 1970 (c); (editor) The Oxford Book of Twentieth-Century English Verse, 1973; High Windows, 1974 (p)

David Timms, Philip Larkin, 1973

● **MARY LAVIN**
1912–

Tales from Bective Bridge, 1942 (s); *The Long Ago*, 1944 (s); *The House in Clewe Street*, 1945 (n); *The Becker Wives* (Amer. ed. *At Sallygap*), 1946 (s); *Mary O'Grady*, 1950 (n); *A Single Lady*, 1951 (s); *The Patriot Son*, 1956 (s); *A Likely Story*, 1957 (s); *Selected Stories*, 1959 (s); *The Great Wave*, 1961 (s); *The Stories of Mary Lavin*, Vol. 1, 1964 (s); *In the Middle of the Fields*, 1967 (s); *Happiness*, 1969 (s); *Collected Stories*, 1971 (s); *The Second Best Children in the World*, 1972 (j); *A Memory*, 1972 (s); *The Stories of Mary Lavin*, Vol. 2, 1973 (s)

Paul Doyle, "Checklist of Mary Lavin," *Papers of the Bibliographical Society of America*, 63, 4 (1969), 317–21

D. H. LAWRENCE
1885–1930

The Complete Plays, 1965 (d); *Selected Literary Criticism*, 1967 (c); *Phoenix II: Uncollected, Unpublished and Other Prose Works*, ed. Warren Roberts and Harry T. Moore, 1968 (misc); *The Quest for Rananim: D. H. Lawrence's Letters to S. S. Koteliansky, 1914–1930*, ed. George J. Zytaruk, 1970; *John Thomas and Lady Jane* (2nd version of *Lady Chatterley's Lover*), 1972 (n); *Lawrence on Hardy and Painting*, ed. J. V. Davies (orig. pub. in *Phoenix*, 1936), 1973 (c)

F. R. LEAVIS
1895–

Anna Karenina, and Other Essays, 1967 (c); (as compiler) *A Selection from "Scrutiny,"* Vols. 1 and 2, 1968; (with Q. D. Leavis) *Lectures in America*, 1969 (c); (with Q. D. Leavis) *Dickens: The Novelist*, 1970 (c); *English Literature in Our Time and the University*, 1970 (c); *Nor Shall My Sword: Discourses on Pluralism, Compassion and Social Hopes*, 1972 (lectures); *Letters in Criticism*, ed. John Tasker, 1974 (c)

D. F. McKenzie and M. Allum, *F. R. Leavis: A Check List, 1924–1964*, 1966

DORIS LESSING
1919–

Landlocked (Vol. IV of *Children of Violence*), 1965 (n); *Winter in July* (orig. pub. in *African Stories*), 1966 (s); *The Black Madonna* (orig. pub. in *African Stories*), 1966 (s); *Particularly Cats*, 1967 (g); *Nine African Stories*, 1968 (s); *The Four-Gated City* (Vol. V of *Children of Violence*), 1969 (n); *Briefing for a Descent into Hell*, 1971 (n); *The Story of a Non-Marrying Man* (Amer. ed. *The Temptation of Jack Orkney*), 1972 (s); *Collected African Stories*, 2 vols., Vol. I: *This Was the Old Chief's Country*, 1973 (s), Vol. II: *The Sun between Their Feet*, 1973 (s); *The Summer before the Dark*, 1973 (n); *A Small Personal Voice: Essays, Reviews, Interviews*, ed. Paul Schlueter, 1974; *The Memoirs of a Survivor*, 1974 (n)

Selma R. Burkom with Margaret Williams, *Doris Lessing: A Checklist of Primary and Secondary Sources*, 1973; Agate Nesaule Krouse, "A Doris Lessing Checklist," *Contemporary Literature*, 14, 4 (Autumn, 1973), 590–97

C. S. LEWIS
1898–1963

A Grief Observed (orig. pub. 1961 as by N. W. Clerk), 1964 (e); *Letters to Malcolm: Chiefly on Prayer*, 1964; *Letters*, ed. W. H. Lewis, 1966; *Of Other Worlds*, ed. Walter Hooper, 1966 (e, s); *Christian Reflections*, ed. Walter Hooper, 1967 (e); *Spenser's Images of Life*, ed. Alastair Fowler, 1967 (c); *A Mind Awake: An Anthology*, ed. Clyde S. Kilby, 1968 (misc); *Letters to an*

LEWIS, C. S. (*cont'd*)
American Lady, ed. Clyde S. Kilby, 1969; *Narrative Poems*, ed. Walter Hooper, 1969 (p); *Selected Literary Essays*, ed. Walter Hooper, 1969 (c); *God in the Dock: Essays on Theology and Ethics* (Brit. ed. *Undeceptions*), ed. Walter Hooper, 1970 (e)

Walter Hooper, "A Bibliography of the Writings of C. S. Lewis," in *Light on C. S. Lewis*, ed. Jocelyn Gibb, 1965

[PERCY] WYNDHAM LEWIS
1886–1957

Wyndham Lewis: An Anthology of His Prose, ed. E. W. F. Tomlin, 1969 (e); *Wyndham Lewis on Art: Collected Writing 1913–1956*, 1971 (ac); *Unlucky for Pringle: Unpublished and Other Stories*, ed. C. J. Fox and Robert T. Chapman, 1973 (s); *The Roaring Queen* (written 1936?), 1973 (n)

Robert T. Chapman, *Wyndham Lewis: Fictions and Satires*, 1973

● HENRY LIVINGS
1929–

Stop It, Whoever You Are (in *New English Dramatists 5*), 1962 (d); *Nil Carborundum* (in *New English Dramatists 6*), 1963 (d); *Kelly's Eye, and Other Plays* (with *Big Soft Nellie* and *There's No Room for You Here for a Start*), 1964 (d); *Eh?*, 1965 (d); *The Day Dumbfounded Got His Pylon* (in *Worth a Hearing*), 1967 (rd); *Good Grief!* (contains *After the Last Lamp*; *You're Free*; *Variable Lengths*; *Pie-Eating Contest*; *Does It Make Your Cheeks Ache?*; *The Reasons for Flying*), 1968 (d); *The Little Mrs. Foster Show*, 1968 (d); *Honour and Offer*, 1969 (d); *Pongo Plays 1–6*, 1971 (d); *This Jockey Drives Late Nights: A Play from "The Power of Darkness" by Leo Tolstoy*, 1972 (d); *Brainscrew* (in *Second Playbill 3*), 1973 (d); *The Ffinest Ffamily in the Land*, 1973 (d)

MALCOLM LOWRY
1909–1957

Selected Letters, ed. Harvey Breit and Margerie Bonner Lowry, 1965; *Lunar Caustic*, 1968 (novella reprinted from *Paris Review*, No. 29, 1963); *Dark as the Grave wherein My Friend Is Laid*, 1969 (n); *October Ferry to Gabriola*, 1971 (n)

J. Howard Woolmer, *A Malcolm Lowry Catalogue*, 1969; Douglas Day, *Malcolm Lowry: A Biography*, 1973

GEORGE MACBETH
1932–

A Form of Words, 1954 (p); *Lecture to the Trainees*, 1962 (p); *The Broken Places*, 1963 (p); *A Doomsday Book: Poems and Poem-Games*, 1965 (p); *Noah's Journey*, 1966 (p-j); *The Colour of Blood*, 1967 (p); *The Night of Stones*, 1968 (p); *A War Quartet*, 1969 (p); *Jonah and the Lord*, 1969 (p-j); *The Burning Cone*, 1970 (p); *Collected Poems, 1958–1970*, 1971 (p); *The Orlando Poems*, 1971 (p); *Lusus: A Verse Lecture*, 1972 (p); *Shrapnel*, 1973 (p); *My Scotland: Fragments of a State of Mind*, 1973 (e); *A Poet's Year*, 1973 (p)

NORMAN MACCAIG
1910–

Measures, 1965 (p); *Surroundings*, 1966 (p); *Rings on a Tree*, 1968 (p); *A Man in My Position*, 1969 (p); *Selected Poems*, 1971 (p); *The White Bird*, 1973 (p)

HUGH MACDIARMID
1892–

The Company I've Kept, 1966 (m); *Collected Poems*, rev. ed., 1967 (p); *A Lap of Honour*, 1967 (p); *Early Lyrics by Hugh MacDiarmid, Recently Discovered among Letters to His Schoolmaster and Friend George Ogilvie*, ed.

J. K. Annand, 1968 (p); *The Uncanny Scot: A Selection of Prose*, ed. Kenneth Buthlay, 1968 (misc); *A Clyack-Sheaf*, 1969 (p); *Selected Essays*, ed. Duncan Glen, 1969 (e); *More Collected Poems*, 1970 (p); *Selected Poems*, 1970 (p); *The Hugh MacDiarmid Anthology: Poems in Scots and English*, 1972 (p)

W. R. Aitken, "A Hugh MacDiarmid Bibliography," in *Hugh MacDiarmid: A Critical Survey*, ed. Duncan Glen, 1972

COLIN MACINNES
1914–

All Day Saturday, 1966 (n); *Sweet Saturday Night* (about popular songs, 1840–1920), 1967 (g); *Visions of London* (contains *City of Spades, Absolute Beginners*, and *Mr. Love and Justice*; Amer. ed. *The London Novels*), 1969 (3n); *Westward to Laughter*, 1969 (n); *Three Years to Play*, 1970 (n); *Loving Them Both*, 1973 (g)

LOUIS MACNEICE
1907–1963

The Strings Are False: An Unfinished Autobiography, 1965 (a); *Varieties of Parable* (Clark Lectures, 1963), 1965 (c); *Collected Poems*, ed. E. R. Dodds, 1967 (p); *One for the Grave: A Modern Morality Play*, 1968 (pd); *Persons from Porlock, and Other Plays for Radio*, 1969 (rd)

C. M. Armitage and Neil Clark, *A Bibliography of the Works of Louis MacNeice*, 1973

OLIVIA MANNING
?–

Friends and Heroes (Vol. 3 of *The Balkan Trilogy*), 1965 (n); *A Romantic Hero*, 1967 (s); *Extraordinary Cats*, 1967 (g); *The Play Room* (Amer. ed. *The Camperlea Girls*, 1969 (n); *The Rain Forest*, 1974 (n)

MANSFIELD, KATHERINE
1888–1923

Undiscovered Country: The New Zealand Stories of Katherine Mansfield, ed. Ian A. Gordon, 1974 (s)

Marvin Magalaner, *The Fiction of Katherine Mansfield*, 1971

JOHN MASEFIELD
1878–1967

Grace before Ploughing: Fragments of Autobiography, 1966 (a); *In Glad Thanksgiving*, 1967 (p); *The Twenty-Five Days* (about evacuation from Dunkirk; first time in print), 1972 (h)

W. SOMERSET MAUGHAM
1874–1965

Seventeen Lost Stories, ed. Craig V. Showalter, 1969 (s); *Plays*, 3 vols., 1970 (d)

Raymond Toole Stott, *A Bibliography of the Works of W. Somerset Maugham*, 1973

● JOHN MCGAHERN
1934–

The Barracks, 1963 (n); *The Dark*, 1965 (n); *Nightlines*, 1970 (s); *Sinclair*, 1972 (d)

● CHRISTOPHER MIDDLETON
1926–

Torse 3: Poems 1949–61, 1962 (p); *The Metropolitans*, 1964 (opera libretto); *Nonsequences/Selfpoems*, 1965 (p); *Our Flowers and Nice Bones*, 1969 (p); *The Fossil Fish*, 1970 (p); also numerous translations from the German

● BRIAN MOORE
1921–

Judith Hearne (Amer. ed. *The Lonely Passion of Judith Hearne*), 1956 (n);

MOORE (*cont'd*)
The Feast of Lupercal, 1958 (n) (re-pub. 1966 as *A Moment of Love*); *The Luck of Ginger Coffey*, 1960 (n); *An Answer from Limbo*, 1962 (n); *The Emperor of Ice-Cream*, 1965 (n); *I Am Mary Dunne*, 1968 (n); *Fergus*, 1970 (n); *The Revolution Script*, 1971 (n); *Catholics*, 1972 (n)

Hallvard Dahlie, *Brian Moore*, 1969

● **NICHOLAS MOSLEY**
   1923–

Spaces of the Dark, 1951 (n); *The Rainbearers*, 1955 (n); *Corruption*, 1957 (n); *African Switchback*, 1958 (t); *The Life of Raymond Raynes*, 1961 (b); *Meeting Place*, 1962 (n); *Accident*, 1965 (n); *Experience and Religion: A Lay Essay in Theology*, 1965 (e); *Assassins*, 1966 (n); *Impossible Object*, 1968 (n); *Natalie Natalia*, 1971 (n); *The Assassination of Trotsky*, 1972 (h)

EDWIN MUIR
1887–1959

Essays on Literature and Society, rev. and enl. ed., 1965 (e); *Collected Poems*, ed. with a preface by T. S. Eliot, 1965 (p); *Selected Letters*, ed. P. H. Butter, 1974

Elgin W. Mellown, *Bibliography of the Writings of Edwin Muir*, 2nd ed., 1966

IRIS MURDOCH
1919–

The Red and the Green, 1965 (n); *The Time of the Angels*, 1966 (n); *The Sovereignty of Good over Other Concepts*, 1967 (e); *The Nice and the Good*, 1968 (n); *Bruno's Dream*, 1969 (n); (with James Saunders) *The Italian Girl*, 1969 (d); *A Fairly Honourable Defeat*, 1970 (n); *An Accidental Man*, 1971 (n); *The Black Prince*, 1973 (n); *The Three Arrows, and The Servants and the Snow*, 1973 (2d); *The Sacred and Profane Love Machine*, 1974 (n)

Laraine Civin, *Iris Murdoch: A Bibliography*, 1968

● **RICHARD MURPHY**
   1927–

The Archaeology of Love, 1955 (p); *Sailing to an Island*, 1963 (p); *The Battle of Aughrim*, 1968 (p)

P. H. NEWBY
1918–

One of the Founders, 1965 (n); *The Spirit of Jem* (reprint), 1967 (n-j); *Something to Answer For*, 1968 (n); *A Lot to Ask*, 1973 (n)

● **PETER NICHOLS**
   1927–

Promenade (in *Six Granada Plays*), 1960 (d); *Ben Spray* (in *New Granada Plays*), 1961 (d); *A Day in the Death of Joe Egg* (Amer. ed. *Joe Egg*), 1967 (d); *The National Health; or, Nurse Norton's Affair*, 1970 (d); *Forget-me-not Lane: Humorous, Serious and Dramatic Selections*, 1971 (d); *The Gorge* (in *The Television Dramatists*), 1973 (d); *Chez Nous*, 1974 (d); *The Freeway*, 1974 (d); *Italia, Italia*, 1974 (t, g)

● **EDNA O'BRIEN**
   1932–

The Country Girls, 1960 (n); *The Lonely Girl*, 1962 (n); *The Girl with Green Eyes*, 1962 (screenplay); *A Nice Bunch of Cheap Flowers*, 1963 (d); *Girls in Their Married Bliss*, 1964 (n); *August Is a Wicked Month*, 1965 (n); *Casualties of Peace*, 1966 (n); *The Love Object*, 1968 (s); *A Pagan Place*, 1970 (n); *Zee & Co.*, 1971 (screenplay); *Night*, 1972 (n); *A Pagan Place* (play based on the novel), 1973 (d); *A Scandalous Woman*, 1974 (s)

● FLANN O'BRIEN
(BRIAN O'NOLAN)
1911–1966

At Swim-Two-Birds, 1939 (repr. 1960) (n); pseud. Myles na gCopaleen, *An Beal Bocht*; *no, An Milleanach* (in Irish), 1941 (as *The Poor Mouth: A Bad Story About the Hard Life*, tr. by Patrick C. Power, 1974) (n); pseud. Myles na gCopaleen, *Faustus Kelly*, 1943 (d); *The Hard Life: An Exegesis of Squalor*, 1961 (n); *The Dalkey Archive*, 1964 (n); *The Third Policeman* (written 1940), 1967 (n); *The Best of Myles: A Selection from "Cruiskeen Lawn,"* 1968 (e, humorous prose); *Stories and Plays*, 1973 (s, d)

Timothy O'Keefe, ed., *Myles: Portraits of Brian O'Nolan*, 1973

SEAN O'CASEY
1884–1964

Blasts and Benedictions, comp. Ronald Ayling, 1967 (e, s); *The Sean O'Casey Reader*, ed. Brooks Atkinson, 1968 (d, misc); *The Sting and the Twinkle: Conversations with Sean O'Casey*, ed. E. H. Mikhail and John O'Riordan, 1974; *The Letters of Sean O'Casey 1910–1941*, Vol. I, ed. David Krause, 1975

Bernard Benstock, *Sean O'Casey*, 1970

FRANK O'CONNOR
1903–1966

The Big Fellow, rev. ed., 1966 (b); *The Backward Look: A Survey of Irish Literature*, 1967 (c); *My Father's Son*, 1968 (a); *Collection Three*, 1969 (s); *A Set of Variations*, 1969 (s); also numerous reprints in the Cuala Reprint Series

Maurice Sheehy, ed., *Michael/Frank: Studies on Frank O'Connor*, 1969

SEAN O'FAOLAIN
1900–

The Heat of the Sun, 1966 (s); *Constance Markevicz*, rev. ed., 1968 (b); *The Talking Trees*, 1971 (s)

Maurice Harmon, *Sean O'Faolain: A Critical Introduction*, 1966

LIAM O'FLAHERTY
1896–

Irish Portraits: 14 Short Stories, 1970 (s)

Paul A. Doyle, *Liam O'Flaherty: An Annotated Bibliography*, 1972

● JOE ORTON
1933–1967

Entertaining Mr. Sloane, 1964 (d); *Crimes of Passion (The Erpingham Camp* and *The Ruffian on the Stair)*, 1967 (d); *Loot*, 1967 (d); *What the Butler Saw*, 1969 (d); *Funeral Games, and The Good and Faithful Servant*, 1970 (d); *Head to Toe*, 1971 (n)

GEORGE ORWELL
1903–1950

Decline of the English Murder, and Other Essays, 1965 (e); *The Collected Essays, Journalism and Letters of George Orwell*, ed. Sonia Orwell and Ian Angus, Vol. 1: *An Age Like This, 1920–1940*; Vol. 2: *My Country Right or Left, 1940–1943*; Vol. 3: *As I Please, 1943–1945*; Vol. 4: *In Front of Your Nose, 1945–1950*, 1968 (e)

JOHN OSBORNE
1929–

Inadmissible Evidence, 1965 (d); *A Patriot for Me*, 1966 (d); *A Bond Honoured* (from Lope de Vega), 1966 (d); *Time Present, and The Hotel in Amsterdam*, 1968 (d); *The Right Prospectus*, 1970 (d); *Very Like a*

OSBORNE (*cont'd*)

Whale, 1971 (d); *West of Suez*, 1971 (d); adaptation of Ibsen's *Hedda Gabler*, 1972 (d); *The Gifts of Friendship: A Play for Television*, 1972 (d); *A Sense of Detachment*, 1973 (d); *A Place Calling Itself Rome* (based on *Coriolanus*), 1973 (d); *The Picture of Dorian Gray: A Moral Entertainment* (adapted from the novel by Oscar Wilde), 1973 (d)

Alan Carter, *John Osborne*, 2nd ed., 1973

WILFRED OWEN
1893–1918

Collected Letters, ed. Harold Owen and John Bell, 1967; *War Poems and Others*, ed. Dominic Hibberd, 1973 (p)

William White, *Wilfred Owen (1893–1918): A Bibliography*, 1967; Jon Stallworthy, *Wilfred Owen: A Biography*, 1974

HAROLD PINTER
1930–

The Dwarfs, and Eight Review Sketches, 1965 (d); *The Homecoming*, 1965 (d); *Tea Party, and Other Plays* (with *The Basement* and *Night School*), 1967 (d); *Poems*, sel. by Alan Clodd, 1968 (p); *Landscape, and Silence* (with *Night*), 1969 (d); *Old Times*, 1971 (d); *Five Screenplays* (*The Servant*; *The Pumpkin Eater*; *The Quiller Memorandum*; *Accident*; *The Go-Between*), 1971; *Monologue*, 1973 (d)

Martin Esslin, *Pinter: A Study of His Plays*, 1973 (2nd ed. of *The Peopled Wound*)

WILLIAM PLOMER
1903–1973

Taste and Remember, 1966 (p); *The Burning Fiery Furnace*, 1966 (libretto, music by Benjamin Britten); *The Prodigal Son* (set to music by Benjamin Britten), 1968 (d); *The Diamond of Janina: Ali Pasha 1744–1822* (reprint of *Ali the Lion*, 1936), 1970 (b); *Continental Coloured Glass*, 1971 (ac); *Meissen*, 1971 (ac); *Objects of Vertu*, 1971 (ac); *Tyneside Pottery*, 1971 (ac); *Celebrations*, 1972 (p); *Collected Poems*, 1973 (p)

John R. Doyle, *William Plomer*, 1969

● PETER PORTER
1929–

Once Bitten, Twice Bitten, 1961 (p); *Poems, Ancient and Modern*, 1964 (p); *A Porter Folio*, 1969 (p); *The Last of England*, 1970 (p); *New Poems 1971–1972*, 1972 (p); *Preaching to the Converted*, 1972 (p); *After Martial*, 1972 (p)

ANTHONY POWELL
1905–

Continuation of *A Dance to the Music of Time*, consisting of the following novels: *The Soldier's Art*, 1966; *The Military Philosophers*, 1968; *Books Do Furnish a Room*, 1971; *Temporary Kings*, 1973; also *Two Plays* (*The Garden God* and *The Rest I'll Whistle*), 1971 (d)

John D. Russell, *Anthony Powell: A Quintet, Sextet, and War*, 1970

JOHN COWPER POWYS
1872–1963

Letters from John Cowper Powys to Glyn Hughes, ed. Bernard Jones, 1971; *Letters to Nicholas Ross*, ed. Arthur Puhill, 1971

Derek Langridge, *John Cowper Powys: A Record of Achievement*, 1966; Arthur J. Anderson, "John Cowper Powys: A Bibliography," *Bulletin of Bibliography*, 25, 4 (Sept.–Dec., 1967), 73–78, 94

J. B. PRIESTLEY
1894–

Lost Empires, 1965 (n); *Moments, and Other Pieces*, 1966 (e); *Salt Is Leaving*, 1966 (n); *It's an Old Country*, 1967 (n); *The World of J. B. Priestley*, comp. Donald G. MacRae, 1967 (misc); *The Image Men*, Vol. 1: *Out of Town*, 1968 (n); Vol. 2: *London End*, 1968 (n); *Essays of Five Decades*, 1968 (e); *All England Listened: J. B. Priestley's Wartime Broadcasts*, 1968; *Trumpets over the Sea*, 1968 (g); *The Prince of Pleasure and His Regency, 1811–20*, 1969 (b); *The Wonderful World of Theatre*, 1969 (g); *Charles Dickens and His World*, 1970 (b); *The Edwardians*, 1970 (h); *Snoggle: A Story for Anybody between 9 and 90*, 1971 (j); *Over the Long High Wall*, 1972 (e); *Victoria's Heyday*, 1972 (h); *The English*, 1973 (g); *A Visit to New Zealand*, 1974 (t); *Outcries and Asides*, 1974 (e)

Alan E. Day, "J. B. Priestley: A Checklist," *Bulletin of Bibliography*, 28, 2 (April–June, 1971), 42–48

V. S. PRITCHETT
1900–

New York Proclaimed, 1965 (t); *The Working Novelist*, 1965 (c); *Dublin: A Portrait*, 1967 (t); *A Cab at the Door*, 1968 (a); *Blind Love*, 1969 (s); *George Meredith and English Comedy*, 1970 (c); *Midnight Oil*, 1971 (a); *By My Own Hand*, 1971 (e); *Balzac*, 1973 (b); *The Camberwell Beauty*, 1974 (s); *London Perceived*, new. ed., 1974 (t)

KATHLEEN RAINE
1908–

The Hollow Hill, and Other Poems 1960–1964, 1965 (p); *Defending Ancient Springs*, 1967 (c); *Ninfa Revisited*, 1968 (p); *Blake and Tradition* (Amer. ed. *William Blake and Traditional Mythology*), 1969 (c); *Six Dreams*, 1969 (p); *William Blake*, rev. ed., 1971 (c); *The Lost Country*, 1972 (p); *Faces of Day and Night*, 1972 (e); *Yeats, the Tarot and the Golden Dawn*, 1973 (c); *Farewell Happy Fields*, 1973 (a); *On a Deserted Shore*, 1973 (p)

Ralph J. Mills, Jr., *Kathleen Raine: A Critical Essay*, 1967

● FREDERIC RAPHAEL
1931–

Obbligato, 1956 (n); *The Earlsdon Way*, 1958 (n); *The Limits of Love*, 1960 (n); *A Wild Surmise*, 1961 (n); *The Graduate Wife*, 1962 (n); *The Trouble with England*, 1962 (n); *Lindmann*, 1963 (n); *Darling*, 1965 ("novelization" of screenplay); *Orchestra and Beginners*, 1967 (n); *Two for the Road*, 1967 (screenplay); *Like Men Betrayed*, 1970 (n); *Who Were You with Last Night?*, 1971 (n); *April, June and November*, 1972 (n); *Richard's Things*, 1973 (n)

● SIMON RAVEN
1927–

The Feathers of Death, 1959 (n); *Brother Cain*, 1959 (n); *Doctors Wear Scarlet*, 1960 (n); *The English Gentleman* (Amer. ed. *The Decline of the English Gentleman*), 1961 (g); *Close of Play*, 1963 (n); *Boys Will Be Boys*, 1963 (e); *The Sconcing Stoup*, 1964 (rd); *Alms for Oblivion*, consisting of the following novels: *The Rich Pay Late*, 1964; *Friends in Low Places*, 1965; *The Sabre Squadron*, 1966; *Fielding Gray*, 1967; *The Judas Boy*, 1968; *Places Where They Sing*, 1970; *Sound the Retreat*, 1971; *Come Like Shadows*, 1972; *Bring Forth the Body*, 1974; also *Royal Foundation, and Other Plays*, 1966 (d)

HERBERT READ
1893–1968

Contemporary British Art, rev. ed., 1965 (ac); *Henry Moore: A Study of His Life and Work*, 1965 (ac); *The Origins of Form in Art*, 1965 (ac); *Collected Poems*, 1966 (p); *The Redemption of the Robot*, 1966 (e); *Art and Alienation: The Role of the Artist in Society*, 1967 (ac); *Poetry and Experience*, 1967 (c); *Art Now*, 5th ed. rev. and enl., 1968 (ac); *A Concise History of Modern Painting*, rev. and enl. ed., 1968 (ac); *Arp*, 1968 (ac); *The Cult of Sincerity*, 1969 (e)

Julia Richardson, *Sir Herbert Read: Bibliography Research*, 1970; George Woodcock, *Herbert Read: The Stream and the Source*, 1972

● MARY RENAULT
1905–

Purposes of Love (Amer. ed. *Promise of Love*), 1939 (n); *Kind Are His Answers*, 1940 (n); *The Friendly Young Ladies* (Amer. ed. *The Middle Mist*), 1944 (n); *Return to Night*, 1947 (n); *North Face*, 1948 (n); *The Charioteer*, 1953 (n); *The Last of the Wine*, 1956 (n); *The King Must Die*, 1958 (n); *The Bull from the Sea*, 1962 (n); *The Mask of Apollo*, 1966 (n); *Fire from Heaven*, 1969 (n); *The Persian Boy*, 1972

Bernard F. Dick, *The Hellenism of Mary Renault*, 1972

● JEAN RHYS
1894–

The Left Bank, 1927 (s); *Postures* (Amer. ed. *Quartet*), 1928 (n); *After Leaving Mr. Mackenzie*, 1930 (n); *Voyage in the Dark*, 1934 (n); *Good Morning, Midnight*, 1939 (n); *Wide Sargasso Sea*, 1966 (n); *Tigers Are Better-Looking*, 1968 (s)

I. A. RICHARDS
1893–

Why So, Socrates?, 1964 (pd); (as comp.) *So Much Nearer: Essays toward a World English*, 1968 (g); *Design for Escape: World Education through Modern Media*, 1968 (g); *Poetries and Sciences* (rev. ed. of *Science and Poetry*, 1935), 1971 (c); *Internal Colloquies: Poems and Plays*, 1972 (d, p); *Beyond*, 1974 (e)

Jerome P. Schiller, *I. A. Richards' Theory of Literature*, 1969; Reuben Brower, Helen Vendler, and John Hollander, eds., *I. A. Richards: Essays in His Honor*, 1973

DOROTHY RICHARDSON
1873–1957

Pilgrimage: Collected Edition, 4 vols. (contains *March Moonlight*, not previously included), 1967

John Rosenberg, *Dorothy Richardson*, 1973

FREDERICK ROLFE (BARON CORVO)
1860–1913

Stories Toto Told Me, pref. by Christopher Sykes, 1971 (s); *Letters to James Walsh*, ed. Donald Weeks, limited ed., 1972

Cecil Woolf, *A Bibliography of Frederick Rolfe, Baron Corvo*, 2nd impression, revised and greatly expanded, 1972

WILLIAM SANSOM
1912–

Goodbye, 1966 (n); *The Ulcerated Milkman*, 1966 (s); *Christmas* (Amer. ed. *A Book of Christmas*), 1968 (e); *Grand Tour Today*, 1968 (t); *The Vertical Ladder*, 1969 (s); *Hans Feet in Love*, 1971 (n); *The Birth of a Story*, 1972 (c); *Marcel Proust and His*

World, 1972 (b); *The Marmalade Bird*, 1973 (s); *A Young Wife's Tale*, 1974 (n)

SIEGFRIED SASSOON
1886–1967

Something about Myself, by Siegfried Sassoon, Aged Eleven, 1966 (n); *Siegfried Sassoon: Poet's Pilgrimage: Unpublished Journals, Letters, Poems*, assembled and introduced by Felicitas Corrigan, 1973 (misc)

Michael Thorpe, *Siegfried Sassoon: A Critical Study*, 1966

DOROTHY SAYERS
1893–1957

Striding Folly, Including Three Final Lord Peter Wimsey Stories, 1973 (s); collected edition of the detective stories of Dorothy L. Sayers in process of publication

● PETER SHAFFER
1926–

(with Anthony Shaffer, as Peter Anthony) *How Doth the Little Crocodile?*, 1951 (n); (with Anthony Shaffer, as Peter Anthony) *Woman in the Wardrobe*, 1952 (n); *Withered Murder*, 1955 (n); *Five Finger Exercise*, 1958 (d); *The Private Ear, and The Public Eye*, 1962 (d); *The Royal Hunt of the Sun*, 1965 (d); *Black Comedy, Including White Lies* [i.e., *The White Liars*], 1967 (d); *Equus, and Shrivings: Two Plays*, 1974 (d)

GEORGE BERNARD SHAW
1856–1950

Collected Letters 1874–1897, ed. Dan H. Laurence, 1965; *Complete Plays*, 1965 (d); *Complete Prefaces*, 1965 (e); *The Bodley Head Bernard Shaw: Collected Plays with Their Prefaces*, 7 vols., 1970–1973; *Shaw: An Autobiography*, selected from his writings by Stanley Weintraub, 2 vols., 1969–1970; *Collected Letters 1898–1910*, ed. Dan H. Laurence, 1972; *Bernard Shaw's Nondramatic Literary Criticism*, ed. Stanley Weintraub, 1972 (c)

JON SILKIN
1930–

Nature with Man, 1965 (p); *Poems, New and Selected*, 1966 (p); *Amana Grass*, 1971 (p); *Kilhope Wheel*, 1971 (p); *Out of Battle: The Poetry of the Great War*, 1972 (c); *The Principle of Water*, 1974 (p)

ALAN SILLITOE
1928–

The Death of William Posters, 1965 (n); *A Tree on Fire*, 1967 (n); *Guzman Go Home*, 1968 (s); *Love in the Environs of Voronezh*, 1968 (p); *A Sillitoe Selection*, 1968 (s); *A Start in Life*, 1970 (n); *Travels in Nihilon*, 1971 (n); *Raw Material*, 1972 (n); *Men, Women and Children*, 1973 (s); *Barbarians*, 1973 (p); *The Flame of Life*, 1974 (n); *Storm: New Poems*, 1974 (p)

Allen R. Penner, *Alan Sillitoe*, 1972

● N. F. SIMPSON
1919–

A Resounding Tinkle (in *The Observer Plays*), 1958 (d); *The Hole*, 1958 (d); *One Way Pendulum*, 1960 (d); *The Form*, 1961 (d); *The Hole, and Other Plays and Sketches*, 1964 (d); *The Cresta Run*, 1966 (d); *Some Tall Tinkles: Television Plays* (*We're Due in Eastbourne in Ten Minutes*; *The Best I Can Do By Way of a Gate-Leg Table Is a Hundredweight of Coal*; *At Least It's a Precaution against Fire*), 1968 (d); *Was He Anyone?*, 1973 (d)

EDITH SITWELL
1887–1964

Taken Care Of, 1965 (a); *The Collected Poems*, 1968 (p); *Selected Letters, 1919–1964*, ed. John Lehmann and Derek Parker, 1970

Richard Fifoot: *A Bibliography of Edith, Osbert, and Sacheverell Sitwell*, 2nd ed., rev., 1971

OSBERT SITWELL
1892–1969

Poems about People; or, England Reclaimed, 1965 (p); *Queen Mary and Others*, 1974 (e); *Collected Stories*, 1974 (s)

Richard Fifoot, *A Bibliography of Edith, Osbert, and Sacheverell Sitwell*, 2nd ed., rev., 1971

SACHEVERELL SITWELL
1897–

Monks, Nuns and Monasteries, 1965 (ac); *Southern Baroque Revisited*, 1967 (ac); *Baroque and Rococo*, 1967 (ac); *Conversation Pieces: A Survey of English Domestic Portraits and Their Painters*, 1969 (ac); *Gothic Europe*, 1969 (ac); *Narrative Pictures*, 1969 (ac); *Great Houses of Europe*, 1971 (ac); *For Want of the Golden City*, 1973, (a, ac)

Richard Fifoot, *A Bibliography of Edith, Osbert, and Sacheverell Sitwell*, 2nd ed., rev., 1971

STEVIE SMITH
1902–1971

The Frog Prince, 1966 (p); *The Best Beast*, 1969 (p); *Two in One: Selected Poems, and The Frog Prince*, 1971 (p); *Ivy and Stevie: Ivy Compton-Burnett and Stevie Smith: Conversations and Reflections*, by Kay Dick (record of conversation with I. C.-B. and S. S.), 1971; *Scorpion*, 1972 (p)

C. P. SNOW
1905–

The Two Cultures, and A Second Look: An Expanded Version of "The Two Cultures and the Scientific Revolution," 1964 (e); *Variety of Men*, 1967 (b); Continuation of *Strangers and Brothers*, sequence of novels: *The Sleep of Reason*, 1968, *Last Things*, 1970; (with Pamela Hansford Johnson) *The Public Prosecutor* (adaptation of a play by Georgi Dzagarov, tr. by Marguerite Alexieva, 1969 (d); *Public Affairs*, 1971 (e); *The Malcontents*, 1972 (n); *In Their Wisdom*, 1974 (n)

MURIEL SPARK
1918–

The Mandelbaum Gate, 1965 (n); *Doctors of Philosophy* (in *Novelists' Theatre*), 1965 (d); *Collected Poems, I*, 1967 (p); *Collected Stories, I*, 1967 (s); *The Public Image*, 1968 (n); *The Driver's Seat*, 1970 (n); *Not to Disturb*, 1971 (n); *The Hothouse by the East River*, 1973 (n); *The Abbess of Crewe: A Modern Morality Tale*, 1974 (n)

Karl Malkoff, *Muriel Spark*, 1968

STEPHEN SPENDER
1909–

The Year of the Young Rebels, 1969 (e); *The Generous Days*, 1971 (p); *Love-Hate Relations: English and American Sensibilities*, 1974 (c)

● **GEORGE STEINER**
1929–

Tolstoy or Dostoevsky, 1960 (c); *The Death of Tragedy*, 1961 (c); *Anno Domini*, 1964 (s); *Language and Silence*, 1967 (c); *In Bluebeard's Castle: Notes Towards the Re-definition of Culture*, 1971 (e); *Extraterritorial: Papers on Literature and the Language of Revolution*, 1971 (c); *The Sporting*

Scene: White Knights of Reykjavik (Amer. ed. Fields of Force: Fischer and Spassky at Reykjavik), 1973 (g); After Babel: Aspects of Language and Translation, 1974 (c)

JAMES STEPHENS
1882–1950

James, Seamus & Jacques: Unpublished Writings, ed. Lloyd Frankenberg, 1964 (misc)

Hilary Pyle, James Stephens: His Work and an Account of His Life, 1965

● TOM STOPPARD
1937–

Lord Malquist and Mr. Moon, 1966 (n); Rosencrantz and Guildenstern Are Dead, 1967 (d); The Real Inspector Hound, 1968 (d); (adaptor) Slawomir Mrozek, Tango, 1968 (d); Enter a Free Man, 1968 (d); A Separate Peace (in Playbill 2), 1969 (d); Albert's Bridge, and If You're Glad I'll Be Frank, 1969 (rd); After Magritte, 1971 (d); Jumpers, 1972 (d); Artist Descending a Staircase, and Where Are They Now?, 1973 (rd); Travesties, 1974 (d)

● DAVID STOREY
1933–

This Sporting Life, 1960 (n); Flight into Camden, 1960 (n); Radcliffe, 1963 (n); The Restoration of Arnold Middleton, 1967 (d); In Celebration, 1969 (d); The Contractor, 1970 (d); Home, 1970 (d); The Changing Room, 1972 (d); Pasmore, 1972 (n); The Farm, 1973 (d); Cromwell, 1973 (d); A Temporary Life, 1973 (n); Life Class, 1974 (d)

JOHN MILLINGTON SYNGE
1871–1909

The Autobiography of J. M. Synge, constructed from the manuscripts by Alan Price, 1965 (a); Collected Works, Vol. 2: Prose, ed. Alan Price, 1966 (e); Collected Works, Vols. 3 and 4: Plays, ed. Ann Saddlemyer, 1968 (d); Some Letters of J. M. Synge to Lady Gregory and W. B. Yeats, sel. Ann Saddlemyer, 1971 (limited ed.); Letters to Molly: J. M. Synge to Maire O'Neill, 1906–1909, ed. Ann Saddlemyer, 1972

Robin Skelton, The Writings of J. M. Synge, 1971

DYLAN THOMAS
1914–1953

Miscellany: Poems, Stories, Broadcasts, 1964 (misc); Twenty Years A-Growing: A Film Script from the Story by Maurice O'Sullivan, 1964 (film script); Me and My Bike, 1965 (film script); Rebecca's Daughters, 1965 (n); Collected Poems 1934–1952, 1966 (p); Selected Letters, ed. Constantine Fitz-Gibbon, 1966; Miscellany, Two: A Visit to Grandpa's, and Other Stories and Poems, 1966 (misc); The Notebooks of Dylan Thomas (Brit. title, Poet in the Making), ed. Ralph Maud, 1967; Twelve More Letters, 1970; The Poems of Dylan Thomas, ed. Daniel Jones, 1971 (p); Early Prose Writings, ed. Welford Davies, 1971 (misc); Living and Writing, ed. Christopher Copeman, 1972 (misc)

Ralph Maud, Dylan Thomas in Print: A Bibliographical History, 1970; Constantine FitzGibbon, The Life of Dylan Thomas, 1966

EDWARD THOMAS
1878–1917

The Green Roads, comp. Eleanor Farjeon, 1965 (p); Letters from Edward Thomas to Gordon Bottomley, ed. R. George Thomas, 1968; Edward Thomas (selections), 1970 (p)

William Cooke, Edward Thomas: A Critical Biography 1878–1917, 1970

R. S. THOMAS
1913–

Pietà, 1966 (p); *Not That He Brought Flowers*, 1968 (p); *R. S. Thomas* (selections), 1970 (p); *Young and Old*, 1972 (p) *H'm: Poems*, 1972 (p)

J. R. R. TOLKIEN
1892–1973

The Tolkien Reader, 1966 (misc); *Smith of Wootton Major*, 1967 (j); *The Road Goes Ever On* (music by Donald Swann), 1938 (p)

Bonniejean McGuire Christensen, "J. R. R. Tolkien: A Bibliography," *Bulletin of Bibliography*, 27, 3 (July–Sept., 1970), 61–67

CHARLES TOMLINSON
1927–

Poems: A Selection, 1964 (p); *American Scenes*, 1966 (p); *The Necklace*, 1966 (p); *The Way of a World*, 1969 (p); *America West Southwest*, 1969 (p); *To Be Engraved on the Skull of a Cormorant*, 1969 (limited ed.) (p); *Written on Water*, 1972 (p); *The Way In*, 1974 (p)

● WILLIAM TREVOR
1928–

A Standard of Behaviour, 1958 (n); *The Old Boys*, 1964 (n); *The Boarding House*, 1965 (n); *The Love Department*, 1966 (n); *The Day We Got Drunk on Cake*, 1967 (s); *The Girl*, 1968 (d); *Mrs. Eckdorff in O'Neill's Hotel*, 1969 (n); *Miss Gomez and the Brethren*, 1971 (n); *The Old Boys* (dramatization of novel), 1972 (d); *The Ballroom of Romance*, 1972 (s); *Going Home*, 1972 (d); *A Night with Mrs. da Tanka*, 1972 (d); *Elizabeth Alone*, 1973 (n); *Marriages*, 1973 (d)

JOHN WAIN
1925–

Wildtrack: A Poem, 1965 (p); *The Young Visitors*, 1965 (n); *Death of the Hind Legs*, 1966 (s); *Arnold Bennett*, 1967 (c); *The Smaller Sky*, 1967 (n); *Letters to Five Artists*, 1969 (p); *A Winter in the Hills*, 1970 (n); *The Life Guard*, 1971 (s); *Interpretations: Essays on Twelve English Poems*, 2nd ed., 1972 (c); *The Shape of Feng*, 1972 (limited ed.) (p); *A House for the Truth*, 1972 (c); *Samuel Johnson*, 1974 (b)

SYLVIA TOWNSEND WARNER
1893–

A Stranger with a Bag (Amer. ed. *Swans on an Autumn River*), 1966 (s); *T. H. White*, 1967 (b); *The Innocent and the Guilty*, 1972 (s)

● KEITH WATERHOUSE
1929–

(with Guy Deghy) *The Café Royal: Ninety Years of Bohemia*, 1955 (g); (with G. Deghy) *How to Avoid Matrimony*, 1957 (g); (with Paul Cave) *Britain's Voice Abroad*, 1957 (g); *There Is a Happy Land*, 1957 (n); *The Future of Television*, 1958 (g); (pseudonym Lee Gibb, with G. Deghy) *The Joneses: How to Keep Up with Them*, 1959 (g); *Billy Liar*, 1959 (n); (with Willis Hall) *Billy Liar: A Play*, 1960 (d); (pseudonym Lee Gibb, with G. Deghy) *The Higher Jones*, 1961 (g); (with W. Hall) *Celebration*, 1961 (d); (with W. Hall) *All Things Bright and Beautiful*, 1963 (d); (with W. Hall) *The Sponge Room, and Squat Betty*, 1963 (d); *Jubb*, 1963 (n); (with W. Hall) *England, Our England*, 1964 (d); (with W. Hall) *Come Laughing Home*, 1965 (d); (with W. Hall) *Say Who You Are* (produced and published in New York, 1966, as *Help Stamp Out Marriage*), 1967 (d); *The Bucket Shop* (Amer. ed. *Everything Must Go*), 1968 (n); (with W. Hall) *Who's Who?*, 1974 (d); *The Passing of the Third-Floor Buck*, 1974 (n)

VERNON WATKINS
1906–1967

Selected Poems 1930–1960, 1967 (p); *Fidelities*, 1968 (p)

Jane L. McCormick, "Vernon Watkins: A Bibliography," *West Coast Review*, 4, 1 (Spring, 1969), 42–48

EVELYN WAUGH
1903–1966

Robert Murray Davis (and others), *Evelyn Waugh: A Checklist of Primary and Secondary Material*, 1972

H. G. WELLS
1866–1946

Journalism and Prophecy 1893–1943, ed. W. Warren Wagar, 1964 (misc); *A Short History of the World*, rev. ed. brought up to date by Raymond Postgate and G. P. Wells, 1965 (h)

H. G. Wells Society, *H. G. Wells: A Comprehensive Bibliography*, 2nd ed. rev., 1968; Norman and Jeanne Mackenzie, *The Time Traveller: The Life of H. G. Wells* (Amer. ed. *H. G. Wells: A Biography*), 1973

ARNOLD WESKER
1932–

The Four Seasons, 1966 (d); *Their Very Own and Golden City*, 1966 (d); *The Friends*, 1970 (d); *Fears of Fragmentation*, 1970 (e); *Six Sundays in January*, 1971 (misc); *The Old Ones*, 1973 (d); *The Journalist*, 1973 (d); *Love Letters on Blue Paper*, 1974 (n)

Glenda Leeming and Simon Trussler, *The Plays of Arnold Wesker: An Assessment*, 1971

REBECCA WEST
1892–

The New Meaning of Treason, 1965 (g); *The Birds Fall Down*, 1966 (n); *McLuhan and the Future of Literature*, 1969 (c)

Peter Wolfe, *Rebecca West: Artist and Thinker*, 1971

● **JOHN WHITING**
1915–1963

Marching Song, 1954 (d); *The Plays of John Whiting* (*Saint's Day*; *A Penny for a Song*; *Marching Song*), 1958 (d); *The Devils*, 1961 (d); *On Theatre*, 1966 (e); *The Collected Plays*, ed. Ronald Hayman, 2 vols. (Vol. 1: *Conditions of Agreement*; *Saint's Day*; *A Penny for a Song*; *Marching Song*; Vol. 2: *The Gates of Summer*; *No Why*; *A Walk in the Desert*; *The Devils*; *Noman*; *The Nomads*), 1968 (d); *The Art of the Dramatist*, ed. Ronald Hayman, 1970 (c)

Simon Trussler, *The Plays of John Whiting: An Assessment*, 1972

● **HEATHCOTE WILLIAMS**
1941–

The Speakers, 1964 (g); *The Local Stigmatic* (in *Traverse Plays*), 1965 (d); *AC/DC*, 1972 (d)

ANGUS WILSON
1913–

Tempo: The Impact of Television on the Arts, 1964 (c); *Emile Zola*, rev. ed., 1965 (c); *No Laughing Matter*, 1967 (n); *Death Dance: 25 Stories*, 1969 (s); *The World of Charles Dickens*, 1970 (b); *As If By Magic*, 1973 (n)

COLIN WILSON
1931–

Beyond the Outsider: The Philosophy of the Future, 1965 (e); *Eagle and*

WILSON, C. (cont'd)
Earwig, 1965 (c); The Glass Cage: An Unconventional Detective Story, 1966 (n); Introduction to the New Existentialism, 1966 (g); Sex and the Intelligent Teenager, 1966 (g); The Mind Parasites, 1967 (n); Colin Wilson on Music (rev. ed. of Brandy of the Damned; Amer. ed. Chords and Discords), 1967 (c); The Philosopher's Stone, 1969 (n); Bernard Shaw: A Reassessment, 1969 (c); A Casebook of Murder, 1969 (g); Voyage to a Beginning, 1969 (a); Strindberg, 1970 (d); The Killer (Amer. ed. Lingard), 1970 (n); Poetry and Mysticism, 1970 (c); The God of the Labyrinth (Amer. ed. The Hedonists), 1970 (n); The Black Room, 1971 (n); The Occult: A History, 1971 (g); New Pathways in Psychology: Maslow and the Post-Freudian Revolution, 1972 (g); Order of Assassins: The Psychology of Murder, 1972 (g); The Schoolgirl Murder Case, 1974 (n)

P. G. WODEHOUSE
1881–1975

Galahad at Blandings (Amer. ed. The Brinkmanship of Galahad Threepwood), 1965 (n); Plum Pie, 1966 (s); The World of Jeeves, 1967 (s); Company for Henry (Amer. ed. The Purloined Paperweight), 1967 (n); Do Butlers Burgle Banks?, 1968 (n); A Pelican at Blandings (Amer. ed. No Nudes Is Good Nudes), 1969 (n); The Girl in Blue, 1970 (n); Much Obliged, Jeeves (Amer. ed. Jeeves and the Tie That Binds), 1971 (n); The World of Mr. Mulliner, new and enl. ed. (previous ed. pub. as Mulliner Omnibus, 1935), 1972 (s); Pearls, Girls and Monty Bodkin, 1972 (n); The Golf Omnibus, 1973 (s); The Plot That Thickened, 1973 (n); Bachelors Anonymous, 1973 (n); Aunts Aren't Gentlemen (Amer. ed. The Cat-Nappers), 1974 (n)

David A. Jasen, A Bibliography and Reader's Guide to the First Editions of P. G. Wodehouse, 1970

LEONARD WOOLF
1880–1969

Downhill All the Way, 1967 (a); Empire and Commerce in Africa, 1968 (h); The Journey Not the Arrival Matters, 1969 (a)

Leila M. J. Luedeking, "Bibliography of Works by Leonard Sidney Woolf (1880–1969)," Virginia Woolf Quarterly, 1, 1 (Fall, 1972), 120–40

VIRGINIA WOOLF
1882–1941

Contemporary Writers, 1965 (c); Collected Essays, Vols. 1 and 2, 1966 (c, e); Collected Essays, Vols. 3 and 4, 1967 (c, e); Mrs. Dalloway's Party, ed. Stella McNichol, 1973 (s)

Brownlee Jean Kirkpatrick, A Bibliography of Virginia Woolf, rev. ed., 1967

WILLIAM BUTLER YEATS
1865–1939

The Variorum Edition of the Plays of W. B. Yeats, ed. Russell K. Alspach, 1966 (d); Ah, Sweet Dancer: W. B. Yeats, Margot Ruddock: A Correspondence, ed. Roger McHugh, 1970; Uncollected Prose, ed. John P. Frayne, Vol. 1: First Reviews and Articles, 1886–1896, 1970 (c); Druid Craft: The Writing of "The Shadowy Waters," manuscripts of W. B. Yeats transcribed, edited and with a commentary by Michael J. Sidnell, George P. Mayhew, David R. Clark, 1971 (pd); A Tower of Polished Black Stones: Early Versions of "The Shadowy Waters," arranged and ed. by David Ridgley Clark and George Mayhew, with five illustrations by Leonard Baskin and drawings by the poet, 1972 (pd); *Memoirs: Auto-biography—First Draft Journal*, transcribed and ed. Denis Donoghue, 1973 (a); (editor) *Fairy and Folk Tales of Ireland* (repr. of *Fairy and Folk Tales of the Irish Peasantry*, 1888, and *Irish Tales*, 1892), 1973; *The Writing of "The Player Queen,"* ed. Curtis Bradford, 1974 (pd); also reprints in the Cuala Reprint Series

Allen Wade, *A Bibliography of the Writings of W. B. Yeats*, 3rd ed. rev., 1969

COPYRIGHT ACKNOWLEDGMENTS

The editors and publisher are grateful to individuals, literary agencies, periodicals, newspapers, and publishers for permission to include copyrighted material. Every effort has been made to trace and acknowledge all copyright owners. If any acknowledgment has been inadvertently omitted, the necessary correction will be made in the next printing.

CYRILLY ABELS. For excerpt from Frank O'Connor, *The Lonely Voice* (Lavin).

ADAM. For excerpt from article by Harold Acton on Waugh.

AGENDA EDITIONS. For excerpts from articles by William Cookson on MacDiarmid; Duncan Glen on MacDiarmid; Peter Levi on Jones; Julian Symons on W. Lewis; Charles Tomlinson on Bunting in *Agenda*.

EDWARD ALBEE. For excerpt from Introduction to *Three Plays by Noel Coward*.

WALTER ALLEN. For excerpt from *Essays by Divers Hands* (MacNeice).

AMERICA. For excerpt from Francis Canavan's "Brian Friel." Copyright © 1966 America Press, Inc. Reprinted with permission from *America*. All Rights Reserved.

THE AMERICAN SCHOLAR. For excerpt from Carolyn G. Heilbrun's "Sayers, Lord Peter and God" (*Reappraisals*). Reprinted from *The American Scholar*, Volume 37, No. 2, Spring 1968. Copyright © 1968 by the United Chapters of Phi Beta Kappa. By permission of the publishers.

ANGLO-WELSH REVIEW. For excerpts from articles by Jeremy Hooker on E. Thomas; Roland Mathias on Abse, on R. S. Thomas.

ARIEL. For excerpt from article by Brendan Kennelly on Kavanagh.

WILLIAM A. ARMSTRONG. For excerpt from *Sean O'Casey*.

EDWARD ARNOLD LTD. For excerpts from Elizabeth Bowen's essay in *Aspects of E. M. Forster*, Oliver Stallybrass, ed.; Donald Davie's essay in *An Honoured Guest*, Denis Donoghue and J. R. Mulryne, eds. (Yeats).

ASSOCIATED UNIVERSITY PRESSES. For excerpts from Hazard Adams, *Lady Gregory*; Bernard Benstock, *Sean O'Casey*; Laurence Brander, *Aldous Huxley: A Critical Study*; Paul A. Doyle, *Paul Vincent Carroll*; D. E. S. Maxwell, *Brian Friel*; James O'Brien, *Liam O'Flaherty*, published by Bucknell University Press. From William J. Cook, Jr., *Masks, Modes, and Morals: The*

Art of Evelyn Waugh; Fraser Drew, *John Masefield's England*, published by Fairleigh Dickinson University Press.

ATHENEUM PUBLISHERS, INC. For excerpt from *Curtains* by Kenneth Tynan. Copyright © 1959, 1960 by The New Yorker Magazine, Inc. Copyright © 1961 by Kenneth Tynan. Reprinted by permission of Atheneum Publishers, N.Y. (Shaffer).

THE ATHLONE PRESS. For excerpts from David Holbrook, *Dylan Thomas: The Code of Night*; Michael Kirkham, *The Poetry of Robert Graves*; Kenneth Marsden, *The Poems of Thomas Hardy*.

A. S. BARNES & CO., INC. For excerpt from Ivor Brown, *W. Somerset Maugham*.

BARNES & NOBLE BOOKS. For excerpts from John Fletcher, *The Novels of Samuel Beckett*; Jerome Meckier, *Aldous Huxley: Satire and Structure*.

BARRIE & JENKINS. For excerpt from Frederick Lumley, *New Trends in 20th Century Drama* (Arden).

CALVIN BEDIENT. For excerpts from articles on T. Hughes, on R. S. Thomas in *The Critical Quarterly* and reprinted in *Eight Contemporary Poets*.

G. BELL & SONS, LTD. For excerpts from Katharine J. Worth, *Revolutions in Modern English Drama* (Orton); Katharine J. Worth's essay in *Experimental Drama*, William A. Armstrong, ed. (Simpson).

MICHAEL BILLINGTON. For excerpt from article on Coward in *Plays and Players*.

PAUL BLOOMFIELD. For excerpt from *L. P. Hartley*.

THE BOBBS-MERRILL COMPANY, INC. For excerpt from Robin Skelton, *The Writings of J. M. Synge*.

THE BODLEY HEAD, LTD. For excerpt from Michael Killigrew's Introduction to Ford Madox Ford, *Memories and Impressions*; Michael Millgate, *Thomas Hardy: His Career as a Novelist*.

FREDERICK BOWERS. For excerpt from article on Fielding in *Queen's Quarterly*.

BRANDT & BRANDT. For excerpt from Sonia Orwell's Introduction to *The Collected Essays, Journalism and Letters of George Orwell*, Vol. I, edited by Sonia Orwell and Ian Angus.

GEORGE BRAZILLER, INC. For excerpt from Elizabeth Sprigge, *The Life of Ivy Compton-Burnett*. Copyright © 1973 by Elizabeth Sprigge. Reprinted with the permission of the publisher.

THE BRITISH COUNCIL. For excerpts from William A. Armstrong, *Sean O'Casey*; Paul Bloomfield, *L. P. Hartley*; Isabel Quigly, *Pamela Hansford Johnson*; R. G. Thomas, *R. S. Thomas* in "Writers and Their Work" series.

BRIGID BROPHY. For excerpts from articles on Mansfield in *The Michigan Quarterly Review*, reprinted in *Don't Never Forget*; on F. O'Brien in *The Listener*.

CURTIS BROWN LTD. (London). For excerpts from Jerry Allen, *The Sea Years of Joseph Conrad*; Lawrence Durrell's Introduction to Keith Douglas, *Alamein to Zem Zem*; John Wain, *A House for the Truth*. (F. O'Brien).

CURTIS BROWN, LTD. (NEW YORK). For excerpt from Sean O'Faolain's article on Mary Lavin's *The House on Clewe Street* in *The Bell*.

CAMBRIDGE UNIVERSITY PRESS. For excerpts from M. C. Bradbrook, *Malcolm Lowry*; Keith Sagar, *The Art of D. H. Lawrence*; Norman Sherry, *Conrad's Western World*; William Walsh, *D. J. Enright*.

JONATHAN CAPE LTD. For excerpts from Brigid Brophy *Don't Never Forget* (Mansfield); Robert Brustein, *The Third Theatre* (Shaffer, Stoppard); Anthony Burgess, *Urgent Copy* (Greene).

EMILE CAPOUYA. For excerpts from articles on Steiner in *Modern Occasions*, on West in *Book Week*.

CHATTO AND WINDUS LTD. For excerpts from Peter Bien, *L. P. Hartley*; A. S. Byatt, *Degrees of Freedom: The Novels of Iris Murdoch*; John Fletcher, *The Novels of Samuel Beckett*; Jerome Meckier, *Aldous Huxley: Satire and Structure*; Raymond Williams, *Drama from Ibsen to Brecht* (Whiting).

CHILMARK PRESS. For excerpts from Edmund Blunden's Introduction to Keith Douglas, *Collected Poems*; Ted Hughes's Introduction to Keith Douglas, *Selected Poems*.

THE CHRISTIAN SCIENCE MONITOR. For excerpt from Neil Millar's article on Frederic Raphael's *Like Men Betrayed*. Reprinted by permission from *The Christian Science Monitor*. Copyright © 1971 The Christian Science Publishing Society. All rights reserved.

THE CLARENDON PRESS. For excerpts from Glen Cavaliero, *John Cowper Powys: Novelist*. Copyright © 1973, Oxford University Press. Reprinted by permission of The Clarendon Press, Oxford; Terry Eagleton's article on Malcolm Bradbury's *The Social Context of Modern English Literature* in *Review of English Studies* Vol. XXIII © 1972 Oxford University Press. Reprinted by permission of The Clarendon Press, Oxford.

H. P. COLLINS. For excerpt from *John Cowper Powys*.

COLLINS PUBLISHERS. For excerpts from Stella Gibbons's article in *Light on C. S. Lewis*, Jocelyn Gibb, ed.; Nariman Hormasji, *Katherine Mansfield: An Appraisal*.

COLUMBIA UNIVERSITY PRESS. For excerpts from Robert Gorham Davis, *C. P. Snow*; Harold Ferrar, *John Osborne*; Carolyn G. Heilbrun, *Christopher Isherwood*; Samuel Hynes, *William Golding*; Denis Johnston, *John Millington Synge*; David Lodge, *Graham Greene*; Karl Malkoff, *Muriel Spark*; William Van O'Connor, *Joyce Cary*; Edward M. Potoker, *Ronald Firbank*; Rubin Rabinovitz, *The Reaction against Experimentation in the English Novel 1950–1960* (Snow, A. Wilson); Robert S. Ryf, *Henry Green*; George Stade, *Robert Graves*; Simon Trussler, *John Arden*; John Unterecker, *Lawrence Durrell*; John Wain, *Arnold Bennett*.

DALE EDMONDS. For excerpt from article on Lowry in *Tulane Studies in English*.

EDUCATIONAL THEATRE JOURNAL. For excerpts from article by John Gassner on Livings; Rita Stein, "The Changing Room" (Storey); Gordon M. Wickstrom, "The Heroic Dimension in Brendan Behan's 'The Hostage.'"

WM. B. EERDMANS PUBLISHING CO. For excerpts from Peter Kreeft, *C. S. Lewis*; Ralph J. Mills, Jr., *Kathleen Raine: A Critical Essay*. Used by permission.

ÉIRE-IRELAND. For excerpts from articles by Bernard Benstock on F. O'Brien; Gratan Freyer on Kavanagh; Milton Levin on Friel; Sean McMahon on E. O'Brien; Murray Prosky on Moore; Robin Skelton on Kinsella. Reprinted by permission of The Irish American Cultural Institute.

RICHARD ELLMANN. For excerpt from essay in *Michael/Frank: Studies on Frank O'Connor*, Maurice Sheehy, ed.

ENCOUNTER. For excerpts from articles by Douglas Dunn on Porter; D. J. Enright on Smith; Robert Lowell on Larkin; Derwent May on Jacobson, on Powell; Jonathan Raban on B. S. Johnson, on Murdoch, on Spark; Paul Theroux on Trevor; John Wain on MacNeice; John Weightman on Bond, on Osborne, on Stoppard.

D. J. ENRIGHT. For excerpt from article on Newby in *The Listener*.

EYRE & SPOTTISWOODE (PUBLISHERS) LTD. For excerpt from Martin Esslin, *The Theatre of the Absurd* (Simpson).

EYRE METHUEN LTD. For excerpts from John Fletcher and John Spurling, *Beckett: A Study of His Plays*; G. Wilson Knight, *The Saturnian Quest: A Chart of the Prose Work of John Cowper Powys*.

FABER AND FABER LTD. For excerpts from W. H. Auden's Foreword to *G. K. Chesterton: A Selection of His Non-fictional Prose*; Edmund Blunden's Introduction to Keith Douglas, *Collected Poems*; H. M. Daleski, *The Forked Flame: A Study of D. H. Lawrence*; Martin Dodsworth's essay in *The Survival of Poetry*, Martin Dodsworth, ed. (Gunn); Lawrence Durrell's Introduction to Keith Douglas, *Alamein to Zem Zem*; T. S. Eliot's Preface to Edwin Muir, *Collected Poems*; G. S. Fraser, *Lawrence Durrell: A Study*; Geoffrey Keynes's Preface to *Letters of Rupert Brooke*, Geoffrey Keynes, ed.; Mark Kinkead-Weekes and Ian Gregor, *William Golding: A Critical Study*; Ted Hughes's Introduction to Keith Douglas, *Selected Poems*; Kathleen Raine's essay in *Vernon Watkins 1906–1967*, Leslie Norris, ed.; George Woodcock, *Dawn and the Darkest Hour: A Study of Aldous Huxley* and *Herbert Read: The Stream and the Source*.

FARRAR, STRAUS & GIROUX, INC. For excerpts from *Beckett: A Study of His Plays* by John Fletcher and John Spurling. Copyright © 1972 by John Spurling; *The Angry Theatre: New British Drama*, revised and expanded edition by John Russell Taylor. Copyright © 1962, 1969 by John Russell Taylor (Arden, Jellicoe, Kops, Livings); *The Second Wave: British Drama for the Seventies* by John Russell Taylor. Copyright © 1971 by John Russell Taylor (Nichols, Orton, Williams); *My Brother Evelyn and Other Portraits* by Alec Waugh. Copyright © 1955, 1956, 1957, 1963, 1967 by Alec Waugh (Maugham). Reprinted with the permission of Farrar, Straus & Giroux, Inc.

Hugh Kenner. For excerpt from article on Bunting in *Poetry*.

Robert Kiely. For excerpt from article on V. S. Pritchett's *A Cab at the Door* in *Commentary*.

Paul Kirschner. For excerpt from *Conrad: The Psychologist as Artist*.

Robert Langbaum. For excerpt from *The Modern Spirit: Essays on the Continuity of Nineteenth- and Twentieth-Century Literature* originally published in *The Southern Review* (Forster).

Mary Lavin. For excerpt from Lord Dunsany's Preface to Mary Lavin, *Tales from Bective Bridge*.

Naomi Lebowitz. For excerpt from *The Imagination of Loving* (James).

Leicester University Press. For excerpt from D. B. Moore, *The Poetry of Louis MacNeice*.

Alan Lelchuk. For excerpt from article on Steiner in *Partisan Review*.

Jill Levenson. For excerpt from article on Stoppard in *Queen's Quarterly*.

David Lewis, Inc. For excerpt from Hélène Cixous, *The Exile of James Joyce*.

Jack Lindsay. For excerpts from *Meeting with Poets* (E. Sitwell, D. Thomas).

Little, Brown and Company. For excerpts from Martin Gottfried, *A Theater Divided* (Jellicoe); John Lehmann, *A Nest of Tigers*. Copyright © 1968 by John Lehmann (O. Sitwell, S. Sitwell); Lord Dunsany's Preface to Mary Lavin, *Tales from Bective Bridge*; George Woodcock, *The Crystal Spirit: A Study of George Orwell*.

Liveright. For excerpt from Walter Allen's Introduction to Wyndham Lewis, *The Roaring Queen*.

David Lodge. For excerpt from article on B. S. Johnson in *The Critical Quarterly*.

London Magazine. For generous permission to reprint excerpts from numerous articles.

Robert Lowell. For excerpt from Introduction to Ford Madox Ford, *Buckshee*.

Loyola University Press. For excerpt from Christopher Hollis's Foreword to *Hillaire Belloc's Prefaces*.

Macmillan Administration. For excerpts from articles by F. W. Bateson and Terry Eagleton in *Eliot in Perspective*, Graham Martin, ed.; Brendan Kennelly's essay in *Michael/Frank: Studies on Frank O'Connor*, Maurice Sheehy, ed. Reprinted by permission of Macmillan, London and Basingstoke.

Macmillan Publishing Co., Inc. (New York). For excerpt from Irving Howe, *Thomas Hardy*.

Manchester University Press. For excerpt from David Blamires, *David Jones: Artist and Writer*.

HERBERT MARDER. For excerpt from *Feminism in Art: A Study of Virginia Woolf.*

DAVID MARKSON. For excerpt from article on Malcolm Lowry's *Dark as the Grave* in *Book World.*

CHARLES MAROWITZ. For excerpt from article on Shaffer in *Encore.*

THE MASSACHUSETTS REVIEW. For excerpts from articles by Warner Berthoff on Murdoch; Lee R. Edwards on Fowles; Jay L. Halio on A. Wilson; F. R. Leavis on Eliot; Shaun O'Connell on O'Connor; William H. Pritchard on Burgess, on Powell; Richard Weber on Clarke.

DERWENT MAY. For excerpts from articles on Frayn in *The Listener*; on T. Hughes in *The Survival of Poetry*, Martin Dodsworth, ed.

MCCLELLAND AND STEWART LIMITED. For excerpt from George Woodcock, *Odysseus Ever Returning.* Reprinted by permission of The Canadian Publishers, McClelland and Stewart Limited, Toronto (Moore).

MCGILL-QUEEN'S UNIVERSITY PRESS. For excerpt from Rowland Smith, *Lyric and Polemic: The Literary Personality of Roy Campbell.*

MCGRAW-HILL BOOK COMPANY. For excerpts from Louise Bogan, *A Poet's Alphabet.* Copyright © 1970. Used by permission of McGraw-Hill Book Company. Originally published in *The New Yorker* (Kavanagh, MacDiarmid).

DAVID MCKAY COMPANY, INC. For excerpt from Stanley Weintraub, *Journey to Heartbreak: The Crucible Years of Bernard Shaw 1914–18.* Copyright © 1971 by Stanley Weintraub, published by Weybright and Talley. Reprinted with permission of the publisher.

KERRY MCSWEENEY. For excerpt from article on Raven in *Queen's Quarterly.*

THE MERCIER PRESS LIMITED. For excerpt from Padraic Colum's essay in *The Yeats We Knew*, Francis McManus, ed.

METHUEN & CO. LTD. For excerpts from John Russell Taylor, *Anger and After* (Arden, Jellicoe, Kops, Livings); Martin Esslin, *Pinter: A Study of His Plays*; Margery Morgan, *The Shavian Playground.*

THE MICHIGAN QUARTERLY REVIEW. For excerpt from article by Brigid Brophy on Mansfield.

MICHIGAN STATE UNIVERSITY PRESS. For excerpt from Norman Leer, *The Limited Hero in the Novels of Ford Madox Ford.*

MODERN DRAMA. For excerpts from articles by Anselm Atkins on Bolt; Joan Tindale Blindheim on Arden; Keath Fraser on Orton; Arthur Ganz on Synge; Louis D. Giannetti on Livings; John Dennis Hurrell on Whiting; Andrew K. Kennedy on Stoppard; Malcolm Page on Wesker; Martin Price on Jellicoe; Gabrielle Scott Robinson on Whiting.

SYLVÈRE MONOD. For excerpt from essay in *Imagined Worlds* (Heppenstall).

WILLIAM MORRIS AGENCY. For excerpt from Martin Gottfried, *A Theater Divided* (Jellicoe).

PETER OWEN LTD. For excerpt from Kenneth Allsop, *The Angry Decade* (Hinde).

OXFORD UNIVERSITY PRESS (LONDON). For excerpts from Malcolm Bradbury, *Possibilities: Essays on the State of the Novel* (Fowles, Snow, Spark, A. Wilson); Donald Davie's and A. Walton Litz's essays in *Eliot in His Time*, edited by A. Walton Litz; Douglas Day, *Malcolm Lowry: A Biography*; Bonamy Dobrée, *Rudyard Kipling: Realist and Fabulist*; W. H. Gardner, *Gerard Manley Hopkins*; William T. McKinnon, *Apollo's Blended Dream: A Study of the Poetry of Louis MacNeice*. All published by Oxford University Press and reprinted by permission of the publisher.

OXFORD UNIVERSITY PRESS, INC., NEW YORK. For excerpts from *Eight Contemporary Poets* by Calvin Bedient. Copyright © 1974 by Oxford University Press (T. Hughes, R. S. Thomas, Tomlinson); *Yeats* by Harold Bloom. Copyright © 1970 by Oxford University Press, Inc.; *D. H. Lawrence and the New World* by David Cavitch. Copyright © 1969 by David Cavitch; *Thomas Hardy and British Poetry* by Donald Davie. Copyright © 1972 by Donald Davie (Betjeman, Hardy); *Malcolm Lowry: A Biography* by Douglas Day. Copyright © 1973 by Douglas Day; Angus Fletcher's essay in *I. A. Richards: Essays in His Honor*, edited by Reuben Brower, Helen Vendler, and John Hollander. Copyright © 1973 by Oxford University Press, Inc.; *The Future as Nightmare: H. G. Wells and the Anti-Utopians* by Mark R. Hillegas. Copyright © 1967 by Mark R. Hillegas; *Barbarous Knowledge: Myth in the Poetry of Yeats, Graves, and Muir* by Daniel Hoffman. Copyright © 1967 by Daniel Hoffman (Graves, Muir); *The Poetry of Edwin Muir: The Field of Good and Ill* by Elizabeth Huberman. Copyright © 1971 by Elizabeth Huberman; *The Modern Spirit: Essays on the Continuity of Nineteenth- and Twentieth-Century Literature* by Robert Langbaum. Copyright © 1970 by Robert Langbaum (Forster); *New Trends in 20th Century Drama: A Survey since Ibsen and Shaw* by Frederick Lumley. Copyright © 1967 by Frederick Lumley (Arden); T. S. Eliot's Preface to *Collected Poems* by Edwin Muir. Copyright © 1960 by Willa Muir; *The New Poets: American and British Poetry since World War II* by M. L. Rosenthal. Copyright © 1967 by M. L. Rosenthal (Clarke, Davie, Enright, MacBeth, Middleton, Murphy, Tomlinson); *The Cart and the Trumpet: The Plays of George Bernard Shaw* by Maurice Valency. Copyright © 1973 by Maurice Valency; *Drama from Ibsen to Brecht* by Raymond Williams. Copyright © 1952 and 1968 by Raymond Williams (Whiting). All reprinted by permission of Oxford University Press, Inc.

CYNTHIA OZICK. For excerpt from article on V. Woolf in *Commentary*.

PATRICK PARRINDER. For excerpt from *H. G. Wells*.

PARTISAN REVIEW. For excerpt from Alan Lelchuk, "The Sound of Silence." Copyright © 1968 by *Partisan Review* (Steiner).

PENGUIN BOOKS LTD. For excerpt from Mervyn Jones's Introduction to *The Dream of Peter Mann* by Bernard Kops, Introduction copyright © 1960 by Penguin Books Ltd.

A. D. PETERS AND COMPANY. For excerpts from Kingsley Amis's Introduction to G. K. Chesterton, *Selected Stories*; Ivor Brown, *W. Somerset Maugham*; Gareth Lloyd Evans, *J. B. Priestley: Dramatist*; Frank O'Connor, *The Lonely Voice* (Lavin); V. S. Pritchett, *The Working Novelist* (Galsworthy); John Russell Taylor, *The Second Wave* (Orton, Nichols, Williams); Alec Waugh,

S. Sitwell, Smith, Storey, Williams in *TLS*. Reproduced from the Times Literary Supplement by permission. For excerpts from articles by Irving Wardle on Bolt, on Livings, on Nichols in *The Times* (London).

CHARLES TOMLINSON. For excerpt from article on Alvarez in *Poetry*.

TULANE STUDIES IN ENGLISH. For excerpt from article by Dale Edmonds on Lowry.

TWAYNE PUBLISHERS, INC. For excerpts from Ted E. Boyle, *Brendan Behan*; A. A. DeVitis, *Anthony Burgess*; Paul A. Doyle, *Sean O'Faolain* and *Liam O'Flaherty*; Martha Fodaski, *George Barker*; John P. Fraye's essay on Moore in *Modern Irish Literature*, Raymond J. Porter and James D. Brophy, eds.; Tom Burns Haber, *A. E. Housman*; Bruce R. McElderry, Jr., *Max Beerbohm*; James D. Merritt, *Ronald Firbank*; Allen Richard Penner, *Alan Sillitoe*; William Pritchard, *Wyndham Lewis*; Joseph N. Riddell, *Cecil Day Lewis*; Gertrude M. White, *Wilfred Owen*; Peter Wolfe, *Mary Renault*.

TWENTIETH CENTURY LITERATURE. For excerpt from article by James F. Knapp on R. S. Thomas.

ESTATE OF PARKER TYLER. For excerpt from article by Parker Tyler on Firbank in *Prose*.

KENNETH TYNAN. For excerpt from *Curtains* (Shaffer).

UNIVERSITAIRE PERS LEIDEN. For excerpt from Michael Thorpe, *Siegfried Sassoon*.

UNIVERSITY OF CALIFORNIA PRESS. For excerpts from H. Porter Abbott, *The Fiction of Samuel Beckett*; Gerald Nelson, *Changes of Heart: A Study of the Poetry of W. H. Auden*. Originally published by the University of California Press; reprinted by permission of the Regents of the University of California.

UNIVERSITY OF CHICAGO PRESS. For excerpt from Germaine Brée's essay in *Samuel Beckett Now*, Melvin J. Friedman, ed. Copyright © 1970 by the University of Chicago. Herbert Marder, *Feminism and Art: A Study of Virginia Woolf*. Copyright © 1968 by the University of Chicago.

THE UNIVERSITY OF MINNESOTA PRESS. For excerpts from Robert Hogan, *After the Irish Revolution*. Copyright © 1967 by the University of Minnesota (Carroll, Johnston).

UNIVERSITY OF MISSOURI PRESS. For excerpt from Peter Wolfe, *The Disciplined Heart: Iris Murdoch and Her Novels*. Reprinted by permission of the University of Missouri Press. Copyright © 1966 by the Curators of the University of Missouri.

UNIVERSITY OF NEBRASKA PRESS. For excerpts from Louis Crompton, *Shaw the Dramatist*, copyright © 1969 by the University of Nebraska Press; Paul A. Hummert, *Bernard Shaw's Marxian Romance*, copyright © 1973 by the University of Nebraska Press; Samuel Hynes's Introduction to *The Author's Craft, and Other Critical Writings of Arnold Bennett*, copyright © 1968 by the University of Nebraska Press; Walter F. Wright, *Arnold Bennett: Romantic Realist*, copyright © 1971 by the University of Nebraska Press. Reprinted by permission of University of Nebraska Press.

CROSS-REFERENCE INDEX TO AUTHORS

Authors from all four volumes are included.

INDEX TO CRITICS

Names of critics are cited on the pages given.